# The Interpersonal Communication Book

**11th Edition**

# The Interpersonal Communication Book

**Joseph A. Devito**

Hunter College of the City University of New York

PEARSON

Boston    New York    San Francisco
Mexico City    Montreal    Toronto    London    Madrid    Munich    Paris
Hong Kong    Singapore    Tokyo    Cape Town    Sydney

Editor-in-Chief, Communication: Karon Bowers
Senior Series Editor/Series Editor: Brian Wheel
Series Editorial Assistant: Heather Hawkins
Editorial Production Service: Nesbitt Graphics, Inc.
Composition Buyer: Linda Cox
Manufacturing Buyer: Andrew Turso
Electronic Composition: Nesbitt Graphics, Inc.
Interior Design: Nesbitt Graphics, Inc.
Photo Researcher: PoYee Oster
Cover Designer: Joel Gendron

For related titles and support materials, visit our online catalog at www.ablongman.com.

Between the time Website information is gathered and then published, it is not unusual for some sites to have closed. Also, the transcription of URLs can result in typographical errors. The publisher would appreciate notification where these errors occur so that they may be corrected in subsequent editions.

Library of Congress Cataloging-in-Publication Data
DeVito, Joseph A.
    The interpersonal communication book / Joseph A. DeVito.—11th ed.
        p.     cm.
    Includes bibliographical references and index.
    ISBN 0-205-47288-5
    1. Interpersonal communication.    I. Title.
BF637.C45D49 2007
302.2—dc22          2005048196

Printed in the United States of America
10  9  8  7  6  5  4  3  2  1    VHP    09  08  07  06  05

# Brief Contents

# Contents

## 12 Interpersonal Relationships: Friendship, Love, Family, and Workplace  *259*

## 13 Conflict in Interpersonal Relationships  *285*

## 14 Power in Interpersonal Relationships  *308*

# Specialized Table of Contents

## Understanding Interpersonal Theory and Research

## Understanding Interpersonal Skills

# Welcome to

# The Interpersonal Communication Book

It's a wonderful privilege to present this eleventh edition of *The Interpersonal Communication Book*. With each revision I've been able to improve the presentation of interpersonal communication so that it accurately reflects what we currently know about the subject and is as up-to-date, as clear, as interesting, and as involving as it can possibly be.

This eleventh edition continues to provide in-depth coverage of interpersonal communication, blending theory and research on the one hand and practical skills on the other. The book's philosophical foundation continues to be the notion of choice. Choice is central to interpersonal communication; as speaker, listener, and communication analyst, you are constantly confronted with choice points at every stage of the communication process—and these choices will influence the effectiveness of your message and your relationships. This text provides you with worthwhile options for a vast array of interpersonal situations and discusses the theory and research evidence bearing on your communication choices. After completing this text, you should thus be better equipped to make more reasoned, more reasonable, and more effective communication choices.

##  THE TEXT

When the first edition of this book was written, the field of interpersonal communication had no clear and agreed-upon focus, and courses varied widely in what they covered. Consequently, a text of numerous short units (the first edition contained 42 units) from which instructors could select those they wanted to cover and arrange them into patterns that made sense for their unique courses seemed the logical way to present the area of interpersonal communication. Gradually, however, the field of interpersonal communication became more focused; as a result, the basic course became more standardized and came to be built largely around the topics considered here. Thus, the book's 42 units were winnowed down with each edition, and in the previous edition the units were consolidated into 14 focused chapters. This eleventh edition maintains that well-received structure.

Part One, "Interpersonal Communication Preliminaries," covers the foundation concepts, concepts that are basic to all forms of interpersonal communication and relationships.

- Chapter 1, "Universals of Interpersonal Communication," discusses the importance of interpersonal communication and its fundamental concepts and principles.
- Chapter 2, "Culture in Interpersonal Communication," presents the central role of culture in all aspects of interpersonal communication, explains how cultures differ, and introduces the nature and principles of intercultural communication.

- Chapter 3, "The Self in Interpersonal Communication," discusses the basic dimensions of the self (self-concept, self-awareness, and self-esteem), self-disclosure, and communication apprehension.
- Chapter 4, "Perception in Interpersonal Communication," covers the principles and processes of perception and examines ways to make your perceptions more accurate.
- Chapter 5, "Listening in Interpersonal Communication," considers the stages in the listening process, styles of effective listening, and the role of culture and gender in listening.

Part Two, "Messages: Verbal and Nonverbal," covers the varied aspects of verbal and nonverbal messages and brings them all together in a discussion of conversation.

- Chapter 6, "Universals of Verbal and Nonverbal Messages," covers the interaction of verbal and nonverbal messages and the principles of meaning and messages.
- Chapter 7, "Verbal Messages," focuses on the verbal message system and identifies the principles for making your language more accurate, more logical, and more effective.
- Chapter 8, "Nonverbal Messages," covers the research on nonverbal communication functions, reviews the major nonverbal channels, and examines the influence of culture on all aspects of nonverbal communication.
- Chapter 9, "Messages and Conversation," brings the material on verbal and nonverbal messages together in an examination of the conversation process, considers how conversations can be managed and how conversational problems can be prevented and repaired, and looks briefly at gossip and the grapevine.

Part Three, "Interpersonal Relationships," covers the nature and stages of interpersonal relationships, the major types of relationships, and the central concepts of conflict and power.

- Chapter 10, "Universals of Interpersonal Relationships," introduces the characteristics of interpersonal relationships, the stages relationships may pass through, and the influence of culture and technology on relationships.
- Chapter 11, "Interpersonal Relationships: Growth and Deterioration," traces the stages of relationships: development, maintenance, deterioration, repair, and dissolution.
- Chapter 12, "Interpersonal Relationships: Friendship, Love, Family, and Workplace," discusses the major types of interpersonal relationships.
- Chapter 13, "Conflict in Interpersonal Relationships," covers the principles of interpersonal conflict, the stages you'd go through in resolving or managing conflict, and the strategies you can use for effective conflict management.
- Chapter 14, "Power in Interpersonal Relationships," covers the principles of power, the major types of power, and how you can communicate power.

This text is a complete learning package that will provide you with the opportunity to learn about the research and theory in interpersonal communication and to practice and acquire the skills necessary for effective interpersonal interaction.

Each chapter opens with a photo from a film that visually introduces the topic of the chapter. A connecting paragraph then points out the relationship between the film and the contents of the chapter. In addition, the chapter opener contains a list of the major topics covered in the chapter.

Each chapter has a three-part ending: (1) **Reviewing,** a summary in full-sentence outline form; (2) **Applying,** a series of questions to provide opportunities to apply the material from the chapter; and (3) **Experiencing,** a guide to 95 experiential vehicles that are especially useful in enabling you to work with the chapter contents and that are easily accessible on the text's website.

New to this edition are two **Glossaries** included at the end of this text: a glossary of interpersonal concepts and a glossary of interpersonal skills.

# FEATURES OF *THE INTERPERSONAL COMMUNICATION BOOK*

You'll get maximum benefit out of this text if you understand the way the book was written and some of the logic underlying the book's features. Instructors who used the previous edition will find identified here some of the major new and revised features.

## Speaking Interpersonal-E

Because of the importance of computer-mediated communication (CMC)—any form of communication between people that takes place through computers—a new feature has been added to this edition. In each chapter several marginal items called **Speaking Interpersonal-E** discuss aspects of CMC and ask you to examine the similarities and differences between CMC and face-to-face interpersonal communication.

## Ask Yourself

Also new to this edition are **Ask Yourself** marginal items that present you with interpersonal communication choice points and ask what you would do in each situation. These items are designed to encourage you to participate actively in the presentation of text material. Instead of simply reading the material, you're asked to involve yourself, to examine possible choices, to assess potential consequences, and ultimately to make your own interpersonal choices.

## Ask the Researcher

A feature introduced in the ninth edition, **Ask the Researcher**, is continued in this edition and emphasizes the close connection between theory and research on the one hand and practical skills on the other. In these Ask the Researcher items—all of which are new to this edition—nationally and internationally known theorists and researchers respond to questions typical of those students ask about interpersonal communication. You'll find their responses—one in each chapter—both provocative and practical. A complete list of these Ask the Researcher items and their distinguished authors is provided in the Specialized Table of Contents on page xiii.

## Ethics in Interpersonal Communication

Each chapter contains an **Ethics in Interpersonal Communication** box presenting a brief discussion of an ethical issue related to the content of the chapter. These ethics discussions cover issues such as ethical listening, keeping secrets, lying, interpersonal silence, your obligation to reveal yourself, workplace ethics, and communicating in cyberspace. Ethics boxes new to this edition include information ethics, relationship ethics, and the ethics of compliance-gaining strategies. In addition to discussing these specific ethical issues, each box presents a related scenario and asks you to consider how you would respond. A complete list of these Ethics in Interpersonal Communication boxes is provided in the Specialized Table of Contents on page xiii.

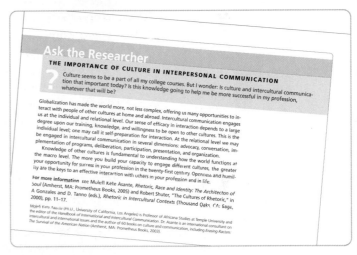

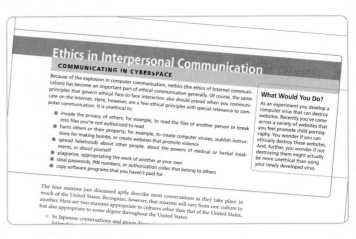

## Workplace Communication and Relationships

As in the previous edition, this edition integrates coverage of workplace communication into the various chapters, once again incorporating new examples, new research, and new applications. This integrated approach reflects the increasing importance of interpersonal communication in the workplace and responds to students' growing desire for insights into the ways in which interpersonal communication functions in the business world. For example, different chapters cover romantic relationships in the workplace, mentoring, the grapevine, and networking.

## Culture and Interpersonal Communication

As our knowledge of culture and its relevance to interpersonal communication grows, so must culture's presence in an interpersonal communication textbook and course. An entire chapter devoted to culture (Chapter 2, "Culture in Interpersonal Communication") is presented early in the text as one of the foundation concepts for understanding interpersonal communication. This chapter covers the relationship of culture and interpersonal communication, the ways in which cultures differ, and ways in which you can make intercultural communication more effective. In addition to this separate chapter, the entire text stresses the importance of culture to all aspects of interpersonal communication. Here are some of the more important discussions:

- The cultural dimension of context; culture in complementary and symmetrical relationships, in the principle of adjustment, and in ethical questions (Chapter 1)
- The role of culture in the development of self-concept, culture as an influencing factor in self-disclosure, and culture's importance in communication apprehension (Chapter 3)
- Culture and schemata, implicit personality theory, the self-serving bias, uncertainty, and developing cultural sensitivity (Chapter 4)
- Listening, culture, and gender (Chapter 5)
- Cultural and gender differences in politeness, directness, and assertiveness (Chapter 6)
- Cultural identifiers, ethnocentrism, sexism, heterosexism, racism, and ageism in language and in listening (Chapter 7)
- Culture and body gestures, attractiveness and culture, the influence of culture on facial and eye communication, gender and cultural differences in touch, silence in culture and in a sociopolitical world, space expectations and culture, color and culture, gifts and culture, time and intercultural communication, and culture and immediacy (Chapter 8)
- Conversational maxims, culture, and gender; culture and expressiveness (Chapter 9)
- Relationships in cultural context; positiveness and culture (Chapter 10)
- Attitude similarity and culture; equity, culture, and gender (Chapter 11)
- Cultural differences in friendship, cultural differences in loving, culture and the family (Chapter 12)
- Conflict, culture, and gender; culture and face-saving; culture and equality (Chapter 13)
- The cultural dimension of power (Chapter 14)

People with disabilities may also be viewed from a cultural perspective, and in this edition four special tables offer suggestions for communication between people with and people without disabilities. These tables provide tips for communication between blind and sighted people (Chapter 1); between people with disabilities—such as people who have cerebral palsy or who use wheelchairs—and people without disabilities (Chapter 2); between deaf and hearing people (Chapter 5), and between people with and people without speech and language disorders (Chapter 9). All four of these tables have been extensively revised for this edition.

## Technology

New to this edition, as already noted, are brief marginal items on computer-mediated communication. These Speaking Interpersonal-E items stress the growing importance of CMC and integrate it with the concepts and principles of face-to-face interpersonal communication.

In addition, technology is integrated in the form of discussions of the Internet, e-mail, instant messaging, cell phones, and the like—all of which have had a major impact on all aspects of interpersonal communication and interpersonal relationships—throughout the text. Examples of these technological discussions include e-mail, listservs, and chat groups as forms of interpersonal communication, the uses of the Internet, cautions to observe in e-mail communication, and an extensive table comparing face-to-face and computer-mediated communication (Chapter 1); lurking as a means for uncertainty reduction (Chapter 4); ethical guidelines for Internet communication (Chapter 6); politeness guidelines for Internet communication (Chapter 6); conversational maxims and e-mail (Chapter 9); opening and closing e-mail conversations (Chapter 9); online relationships (Chapter 10); the Internet and relationship maintenance (Chapter 11); and online conflicts (Chapter 13).

A third way in which technology is integrated is through the use of an extensive package of electronic supplements that is updated regularly. A listing of available ancillaries may be found at the end of this preface. Frequent updates may be found at www.ablongman.com/communication.

A fourth way in which technology is integrated—perhaps for the first time in a communication (or any) text—is **The Communication Blog** available at http://tcbdevito.blogspot.com or through the text website (www.ablongman.com/devito). Come visit.

## Self-Tests

Seventeen **Test Yourself** self-tests help personalize the material and are presented throughout the text. These quizzes cover such topics as your cultural beliefs and values, how ethnocentric you are, your degree of communication apprehension, your verbal aggressiveness and argumentativeness, and your interpersonal power. Approximately half of these self-tests are used regularly in interpersonal communication research; the other half were developed to highlight and preview some part of the text material. Each self-test concludes with a two-part discussion: "How Did You Do?" contains the scoring instructions, and "What Will You Do?" asks what steps you might consider taking as a result of the insights provided by the self-assessment. A complete list of self-tests appears in the Specialized Table of Contents on page xiii.

In addition, brief items (called "I See," for "Integrated Self-Exploration Experiences," in the previous edition) are presented throughout the text to encourage you to examine your own experiences with interpersonal communication in light of the theory, research, and skills presented in the text. These are signaled by a change in typeface.

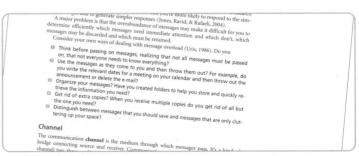

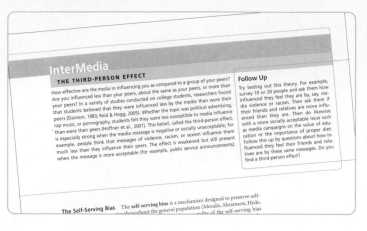

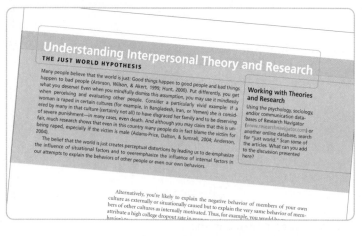

## InterMedia

Because of the importance and pervasiveness of the mass media and the interdependence of the media and interpersonal communication, an **InterMedia** box appears in every chapter. These boxes identify areas where interpersonal communication and mass media intersect. Among issues addressed are cultural imperialism, the third-person effect, gatekeeping, hate speech, the spiral of silence, parasocial relationships, and media violence. The title for these features is taken from Gary Gumpert and Robert Cathcart, who introduced the term to the field in their *Inter/Media: Interpersonal Communication in a Media World,* and who advocated looking at interpersonal communication and the mass media as closely related and interdependent. A complete list of InterMedia boxes appears in the Specialized Table of Contents on page xiii.

## Theory/Research and Skills

Coordinate boxes covering some of the essential theories and research and some of the essential skills in interpersonal communication are presented in each chapter. New to this edition, each chapter now contains an **Understanding Interpersonal Theory and Research** box highlighting a particular area of theory and research in interpersonal communication. Although theories and research are integrated throughout the text, these boxes highlight specific theories and ask you to work with them and apply them to your own experiences. Coordinated with these are boxes that highlight the essential skills of effective interpersonal communication. Each of these **Understanding Interpersonal Skills** boxes contains a discussion of an important aspect of effectiveness and points up ways in which you can better communicate using these qualities of effectiveness. Complete lists of these Understanding Interpersonal Theory and Research and Understanding Interpersonal Skills boxes appear in the Specialized Table of Contents on page xiii.

## ViewPoint

As in previous editions, the photo captions here contain substantive material rather than the typical brief descriptions of the photos that appear in many texts. These captions, called **ViewPoints,** present issues to be discussed and should provide useful stimuli for class discussion.

## Interactivity

Of course, a printed text cannot be truly interactive; but this edition of *The Interpersonal Communication Book* offers an expanded and improved array of features that invite you to involve yourself, that encourage you to participate actively with the material, and that provide you with lots of material for classroom dialogue. For example:

- *Speaking Interpersonal-E* marginal items ask you to examine your own computer-mediated communication and to compare it with your face-to-face interactions.
- *Ask Yourself* marginal items present interpersonal dilemmas and invite you to consider how you would respond.

- *Self-tests* in the text provide opportunities for you to examine your own communication behaviors on a wide variety of issues discussed in the text.
- *Ethics in Interpersonal Communication, InterMedia,* and *Understanding Interpersonal Theory and Research* boxes all contain questions to help you personalize the concepts.
- *Integrated interactives*—highlighted by a different type face—appear throughout the text and provide pause points for you to think about your own interpersonal communication and perhaps consider what you might change.
- *ViewPoint* photo captions also ask for your active involvement in examining selected issues discussed in the text.

##  CHAPTER-BY-CHAPTER CHANGES

In addition to new material in many self-tests, Ask the Researcher items, Ethics in Interpersonal Communication boxes, and InterMedia boxes as well as the new features on Understanding Interpersonal Theory and Research and the new marginal items (Speaking Interpersonal-E and Ask Yourself), the text of this edition incorporates a variety of new concepts and principles, new examples, and new illustrations. Perhaps most important: Findings from more than 250 new research studies—most from the last few years—have been integrated into this new edition.

All chapters have improved orienting paragraphs that clearly spell out the topics to be covered in the chapter or section, and all chapters include additional and recent research findings. Most of the tables have been streamlined and updated.

Other material has been added, expanded, substantially revised, and updated. And, as already mentioned, lots of new references reflect the enormous output of research in the field of communication. By chapter, the most notable of these changes are:

- Chapter 1, "Universals of Interpersonal Communication": New to the chapter are an expanded and updated discussion of the importance of interpersonal communication to effective relationships and to the workplace, an extensive table comparing computer-mediated communication with face-to-face communication, a table on the uses of the Internet, an expanded discussion of the purposes of interpersonal communication, a new diagram comparing the transactional views of face-to-face and computer-mediated communication, and an expanded discussion of communication and relationship ambiguity.
- Chapter 2, "Culture in Interpersonal Communication": Updated discussions of the role of culture in contemporary life, new headings to clarify and highlight the most important concepts, and a table on Internet use by country have been added. Time orientation has been moved to the chapter on nonverbal communication; and a section on stereotypes, formerly in the perception chapter, has been integrated into the principles for intercultural communication.
- Chapter 3, "The Self in Interpersonal Communication": The discussion of self-destructive beliefs has been expanded somewhat, and the discussions of self-disclosure and communication apprehension have been streamlined for a better balance with the other topics in the chapter. A variety of studies on the influence of culture, gender, and technology on these processes have been integrated.
- Chapter 4, "Perception in Interpersonal Communication": The discussion of stereotypes has been moved to the chapter on culture, and the self-test on perception has been shortened.
- Chapter 5, "Listening in Interpersonal Communication": Implications of the model of listening, a reworked discussion of the benefits of listening, a clarification of inappropriate active listening tendencies, and a more focused presentation of the situational nature of listening are new to this revision.

- Chapter 6, "Universals of Verbal and Nonverbal Messages": Meaning and message characteristics are now presented as principles, additional research and insight into politeness have been added, and the assertiveness self-test has been rewritten to focus more clearly and more succinctly on the major concerns of assertive messages.
- Chapter 7, "Verbal Messages": The self-test on confirmation has been deleted (but is available on the text's companion website), additional suggestions for criticizing have been added, and a thorough discussion of ageist language has been added along with a discussion of ageism as part of listening effectiveness.
- Chapter 8, "Nonverbal Messages": A new section on current research on the functions of nonverbal communication now introduces the chapter; the sections on culture have been pulled together into a new section, "Nonverbal Communication and Culture"; and time orientations, formerly in the culture chapter, now appear in this chapter along with the discussion of time communication.
- Chapter 9, "Messages and Conversation": A new section discussing gossip and the workplace grapevine has been added to this chapter.
- Chapter 10, "Universals of Interpersonal Relationships": The discussion of what relationships do for you has been shortened and focused more clearly on the essential advantages and disadvantages; two additional relationship models have been added as tables to further clarify the progression of relationships.
- Chapter 11, "Interpersonal Relationships: Growth and Deterioration": The sections on attraction theory and romantic rules have been expanded somewhat. The section on relationship deterioration has been rewritten to focus on causes and effects, the long list of stages of relationship deterioration has been deleted, and the self-test on commitment has been recast as a theory and research box.
- Chapter 12, "Interpersonal Relationships: Friendship, Love, Family, and Workplace": The romanticism and the relationship preference self-tests have been moved to the website to improve the flow of topics. Comparisons of face-to-face and online relationships have been added, and the table on the changing American family has been redone based on the most recent data available.
- Chapter 13, "Conflict in Interpersonal Relationships": The basic concepts of conflict have been recast as principles; discussions of the inevitability of conflict, styles of conflict, and the factors that influence conflict management strategies have been added.
- Chapter 14, "Power in Interpersonal Relationships": The feature on Machiavellianism has been moved to the companion website, and a self-test on the types of power has been added to introduce the discussion of power types.

##  ANCILLARIES/SUPPLEMENTARY MATERIALS

### Instructor Supplements
### Print Supplements

- **Instructor's Manual/Test Bank** by Rebecca E. Bailey, Valparaiso University.
  This Instructor's Manual/Test Bank includes sample syllabi, chapter outlines, classroom activities, discussion questions, and video suggestions. The Test Bank contains more than 1,000 items, including challenging multiple-choice, true/false, and short-answer essay questions along with an answer key that ranks the difficulty level of each item.

- **The Blockbuster Approach: Teaching Interpersonal Communication with Video, Third Edition** by Thomas E. Jewell, Marymount College.
  This guide provides lists and descriptions of commercial videos that can be used in the classroom to illustrate interpersonal concepts and complex interpersonal relationships. Sample activities are also included.

## Electronic Supplements

■ **TestGen EQ: Computerized Test Bank**

This user-friendly interface enables instructors to view, edit, and add questions, transfer questions to tests, and print tests in a variety of fonts. Search and sort features allow instructors to locate questions quickly and arrange them in a preferred order.

■ **PowerPoint Presentation Package** by Dan Cavanaugh.

This text-specific package consists of a collection of lecture outlines and graphic images keyed to every chapter in the text.

■ **Allyn & Bacon Digital Media Archive for Communication, Version 4.0**

This CD-ROM contains electronic images of charts, graphs, maps, tables, and figures, along with media elements such as video, audio clips, and related Web links. These media assets are fully customizable to use with our preformatted PowerPoint outlines or to import into instructor's own lectures. (For Windows and Mac.)

■ **VideoWorkshop for Interpersonal Communication—Instructor's Teaching Guide**

VideoWorkshop for Interpersonal Communication is a new way to bring video into your course for maximized learning! This total teaching and learning system includes quality video footage on an easy-to-use CD-ROM plus a Student Learning Guide and an Instructor's Teaching Guide—both with Textbook-specific Correlation Grids. The result? A program that brings textbook concepts to life with ease and that helps your students understand, analyze, and apply the objectives of the course. VideoWorkshop is available for your students as a value-pack option with this textbook. Go to www.ablongman.com/videoworkshop for more details.

■ **The Allyn & Bacon Interpersonal Communication Videos**

Allyn & Bacon offers three Interpersonal Videos ranging from 30 to 50 minutes that contain scenarios illustrating key concepts in interpersonal communication. Accompanying user guides feature transcripts, teaching activities, and class discussion questions for each episode. Contact your Allyn & Bacon sales representative for ordering information. Some restrictions apply.

■ **The Allyn & Bacon Communication Video Library**

A collection of communication videos produced by Films for the Humanities and Social Sciences. Topics include, but are not limited to: *Business Presentations, Great American Speeches,* and *Conflict Resolution.* Contact your Allyn & Bacon sales representative for ordering information. Some restrictions apply.

■ **Interpersonal Movie Library**

This collection is available to adopters and contains popular feature films dealing with a range of interpersonal topics. Contact your Allyn & Bacon sales representative for ordering information. Some restrictions apply.

■ **CourseCompass**

Powered by Blackboard and hosted nationally, this is the most flexible online course management system on the market today. By using this powerful suite of online tools in conjunction with Allyn & Bacon's preloaded textbook and testing content, you can create an online presence for your course in less than 30 minutes. The communication course features preloaded content such as quiz questions, video clips, instructor's manuals, PowerPoint presentations, still images, course preparation and instruction materials, VideoWorkshop for Interpersonal Communication, Web links, and much more! Log on www.coursecompass.com to access this dynamic teaching resource. The content is also compatible with Blackboard and WebCT.

■ **The Communication Blog** (http://tcbdevito.blogspot.com)

Maintained by the author, this site offers a forum for people teaching basic courses in interpersonal communication as well as the hybrid and public speaking courses. Regular posts by the author update the text material and share ideas for teaching.

## Student Supplements

### Print Supplements

■ *Research Navigator Guide for Speech Communication* by Terrence Doyle, Northern Virginia Community College.
This resource guide is designed to teach students how to conduct high-quality online research and to document it properly. The guide provides access to Research Navigator (www.researchnavigator.com), which contains exclusive databases of credible and reliable source material, including EBSCO's ContentSelect Academic Journal Database and the *New York Times* Search by Subject Archive.

### Electronic Supplements

■ **Companion Website with online practice tests** by Joseph A. DeVito and Judy Nelson, Itasca Community College.
This site includes skill-building exercises and extensions and elaborations on the text. The website (http://www.ablongman.com/devito) also includes an online study guide with practice tests and weblinks.

■ **VideoWorkshop for Interpersonal Communication Student Learning Guide**
VideoWorkshop for Interpersonal Communication is a new way to bring video into your course for maximized learning! This total teaching and learning system includes quality video footage on an easy-to-use CD-ROM plus a Student Learning Guide and an Instructor's Teaching Guide—both with textbook-specific Correlation Grids. The result? A program that brings textbook concepts to life with ease and that helps you understand, analyze, and apply the objectives of the course. VideoWorkshop is available as a value-pack option with this textbook.

■ *Allyn & Bacon Communication Studies Website* by Terrence Doyle, Northern Virginia Community College, and Tim Borchers, Minnesota State University at Moorhead.
This site includes modules on interpersonal and small group communication and public speaking and includes Web links, enrichment materials, and interactive activities to enhance your understanding of key concepts. Access this site at www.ablongman.com/commstudies.

■ **Tutor Center** (Access Code Required) www.aw.com/tutorcenter
The Tutor Center provides free, one-on-one interactive tutoring from qualified public speaking instructors on all material in the text. The Tutor Center offers students help with understanding major communication principles as well as methods for study. In addition, students have the option of submitting self-taped speeches for review and critique by Tutor Center instructors to help prepare for and improve their speech assignments. Tutoring assistance is offered by phone, fax, Internet, and e-mail during Tutor Center hours. For more details and ordering information, contact your Allyn & Bacon representative.

 ## ACKNOWLEDGMENTS

I owe a great debt to the many researchers who responded to my call for responses to a variety of questions and whose answers appear in the Ask the Researcher features throughout the text. Without your cooperation, goodwill, and support, this feature obviously could not have been done. I thank you all (in order of appearance):

Sherwyn P. Morreale (National Communication Association)
Molefi Kete Asante (Temple University)
Linda C. Lederman (Arizona State University)

Elizabeth M. Perse (University of Delaware)
Deborah Borisoff (New York University)
Teresa L. Thompson (University of Dayton)
Lance Strate (Fordham University)
Kelly A. Rocca (St. John's University)
Susan B. Barnes (Rochester Institute of Technology)
Barbara Montgomery (University of Southern Colorado)
Shirlee A. Levin (College of Southern Maryland)
Anita L. Vangelisti (University of Texas)
Carolyn M. Anderson (University of Akron)
John Daly (University of Texas)

I want also to express my appreciation to the many specialists who carefully reviewed the previous edition. Your comments resulted in a large number of changes; I'm extremely grateful. Thank you:

Josephine Benavidez, University of Colorado
Diane Blomberg, Metropolitan State College of Denver
Marguerite Cantu, University of Colorado
Judy Nelson, Itasca Community College
Rebecca Bailey, University of Valparaiso
Natalie Sydorenko, University of Akron

In addition, I wish to express my appreciation to the people at Allyn & Bacon who contributed so heavily to this text, especially editor Brian Wheel and editorial assistant Heather Hawkins. I also wish to thank photo researcher PoYee Oster, project editor Tom Conville, and copy editor Jay Howland. All did excellent work for which I'm deeply appreciative.

*Joseph A. DeVito*
jadevito@earthlink.net

Elizabeth M. Perse (University of Delaware)
Deborah Borisoff (New York University)
Teresa L. Thompson (University of Dayton)
Lance Strate (Fordham University)
Kelly A. Rocca (St. John's University)
Susan B. Barnes (Rochester Institute of Technology)
Barbara Montgomery (University of Southern Colorado)
Shirlee A. Levin (College of Southern Maryland)
Anita L. Vangelisti (University of Texas)
Carolyn M. Anderson (University of Akron)
John Daly (University of Texas)

I want also to express my appreciation to the many specialists who carefully reviewed the previous edition. Your comments resulted in a large number of changes; I'm extremely grateful. Thank you:

Josephine Benavidez, University of Colorado
Diane Blomberg, Metropolitan State College of Denver
Marguerite Cantu, University of Colorado
Judy Nelson, Itasca Community College
Rebecca Bailey, University of Valparaiso
Natalie Sydorenko, University of Akron

In addition, I wish to express my appreciation to the people at Allyn & Bacon who contributed so heavily to this text, especially editor Brian Wheel and editorial assistant Heather Hawkins. I also wish to thank photo researcher PoYee Oster, project editor Tom Conville, and copy editor Jay Howland. All did excellent work for which I'm deeply appreciative.

*Joseph A. DeVito*
jadevito@earthlink.net

# The Interpersonal
# Communication Book

CHAPTER

# 1

# Universals of Interpersonal Communication

🔺 *The Aviator* (2004)

The life of Howard Hughes, one of the most interesting and eccentric people of all time, and his relationships with very different people are the subjects of the film *The Aviator*. In many ways *The Aviator* covers just about all the topics discussed in this text—the importance of the self, verbal and nonverbal messages, interpersonal relationships, and perhaps especially conflict and power.

> "If your lips would keep from slips
> Five things observe with care;
> To whom you speak, of whom you speak,
> And how, and when, and where."
>
> —W.E. Norris

**Interpersonal communication** is something you do every day:

- talking with coworkers
- giving or responding to a compliment
- making new friends
- asking for a date
- communicating through instant messaging
- maintaining and repairing relationships
- breaking off relationships
- applying for a job
- giving directions
- persuading a supervisor

Understanding these interactions is an essential part of your education. Much as an educated person must know geography, history, science, and mathematics, you need to know the how, why, and what of interpersonal communication. It's a significant part of the world in which you live, and it's becoming more significant daily.

##  THE IMPORTANCE OF INTERPERSONAL COMMUNICATION

Interpersonal communication is an extremely practical art, and your effectiveness as a friend, relationship partner, coworker, or manager will depend largely on your interpersonal skills. For example, in a survey of 1,001 people over 18 years of age, 53 percent felt that a lack of effective communication was the major cause of marriage failure, significantly greater than money (38 percent) and in-law interference (14 percent) (How Americans Communicate, 1999). The relevance of interpersonal communication skills to relationships is, of course, a major theme of this text and will be returned to repeatedly.

In a similar way, interpersonal skills are crucial to professional success, a relationship that has been widely documented. Not long ago the *Wall Street Journal* published an article titled "How to get hired: We asked recruiters what M.B.A. graduates are doing wrong. Ignore their advice at your peril" (Alsop, 2004). The article reported that among the 23 attributes ranked as "very important" in hiring decisions, "communication and interpersonal skills" was at the top of the list, noted by 89 percent of the recruiters. This was a far higher percentage than noted "faculty expertise" (25 percent of the recruiters), "content of the core curriculum" (34 percent), or "overall value for the money invested in the recruiting effort" (33 percent). And in a survey of employers, it was the "soft skills" that distinguished successful from unsuccessful employees (Coplin, 2004). Employers identified "work ethic, communications, information gathering, and people skills at the top of the list, followed by analytical and problem-solving skills. These capabilities apply across all fields," the researchers reported. These findings, although interesting, reveal nothing new. For example, more than 10 years ago the Collegiate Employment Research Institute of Michigan State University studied more than 500 employers and found that "good oral, written, and interpersonal communication skills were reported among the most notable deficiencies observed in new college graduates" (Scheetz, 1995). And in the same year, in a study of the qualities that college recruiters seek, students, faculty, and recruiters themselves all identified communication skills as the most important (Bauer, 1995).

Interpersonal skills have long been recognized as critical to professional success in hundreds of studies (Morreale, Osborn, & Pearson, 2000). In fact, interpersonal skills are regarded as so important that the U.S. Department of Labor, in its report "What Work Requires of Schools"—a report based on interviews with managers, employers, and workers who described the skills needed to function effectively at their jobs—identified interpersonal skills as one of five sets of skills essential for a nation and an individual to be economically competitive in the world marketplace (*New York Times,* July 3, 1991, p. A17). Interpersonal skills are considered to be "key in [the] office of the future" (*TMA Journal,* 1999, p. 53), to offer a "key career advantage for finance professionals in the next century" (Messmer, 1999), and to play an important role in preventing workplace violence (Parker, 2004). In studies in the health care industry, communication skills figure prominently in enabling nurses to rise in the corporate hierarchy, in building patient trust (Nordhaus-Bike, 1999; Titlow, Rackoff, & Emanuel, 1999), and in reducing medical mishaps and in improving doctor–patient communication (Sutcliffe, Lewton, & Rosenthal, 2004; Smith, 2004). Interpersonal skills are also identified as one of six areas that define the professional competence of physicians and trainees (Epstein & Hundert, 2002). Research focusing on the education of hotel and restaurant administrators concluded that the realm of "communication and interpersonal skills" was one of the three vitally important subjects that need to be emphasized (Dittman, 1997); and a study of IT professionals identified these skills as an essential part of business competence (Bassellier & Benbasat, 2004). The importance of interpersonal communication skills, then, seems to extend over the entire spectrum of professions.

Clearly, then, interpersonal skills are relevant to your relationship and professional success: They will help you become a more effective relationship partner and a more successful professional, regardless of your specific professional goal.

Understanding the theory and research in interpersonal communication and mastering its skills go hand in hand. The more you know about interpersonal communication, the more insight and knowledge you'll gain about what works and what doesn't work. The more skills you have within your arsenal of communication strategies, the greater will be your options for communicating in any situation. In a nutshell, the greater your knowledge and the greater the number of communication options at your disposal, the greater the likelihood that you'll be successful in achieving your interpersonal goals.

This book emphasizes your understanding of interpersonal communication: its theories and research and its practical skills. Theory/research and skills are considered together as we progress through the elements of interpersonal communication, the ways verbal and nonverbal messages operate in interpersonal encounters, and the ways relationships are developed and maintained, repaired, and even dissolved. As a preface to an area of study that will be enlightening, exciting, and extremely practical, examine your assumptions about interpersonal communication by taking the accompanying self-test.

# TEST YOURSELF

## WHAT DO YOU BELIEVE ABOUT INTERPERSONAL COMMUNICATION?

Respond to each of the following statements with T if you believe the statement is usually true or F if you believe the statement is usually false.

_____ 1. Good communicators are born, not made.

_____ 2. The more you communicate, the better at it you will be.

_____ 3. In your interpersonal communications, a good guide to follow is to be as open, empathic, and supportive as you can be.

_____ 4. The best guide to follow when communicating with people from other cultures is to ignore the differences and treat the other person just as you'd treat members of your own culture.

_____ 5. Fear of public speaking is detrimental and must be eliminated.

_____ 6. When there is conflict, your relationship is in trouble.

**HOW DID YOU DO?** As you probably figured out, all six statements are generally false. As you read this text, you'll discover not only why these beliefs are false but also the trouble you can get into when you assume they're true. For now, and in brief, here are some of the reasons each of the statements is generally false: (1) Effective communication is a learned skill; although some people are born brighter or more extroverted, all can improve their abilities and become more effective communicators. (2) It's not the amount of communication people engage in but the quality that matters; if you practice bad habits, you're more likely to grow less effective than more effective, so it's important to learn and follow the principles of effectiveness (J. O. Greene, 2003; Greene & Burleson, 2003). (3) Each interpersonal situation is unique, and therefore the type of communication appropriate in one situation may not be appropriate in another. (4) This assumption will probably get you into considerable trouble, because people from different cultures will often attribute different meanings to a message; members of different cultures also follow different rules for what is and is not appropriate in interpersonal communication. (5) Most speakers are nervous; managing, not eliminating, the fear will enable you to become effective regardless of your current level of fear. (6) All meaningful relationships experience conflict; relationships are not in trouble when there is conflict, though dealing with conflict ineffectively can often damage the relationship.

**WHAT WILL YOU DO?** This is perhaps, then, a good place to start practicing the critical thinking skill of questioning commonly held assumptions about interpersonal communication and about yourself as an interpersonal communicator. Consider, for example, what other beliefs you have about communication and about yourself as a communicator. How do these beliefs influence your communication?

#  THE NATURE OF INTERPERSONAL COMMUNICATION

We can best understand interpersonal communication by looking at its major characteristics, forms, and purposes.

## Characteristics of Interpersonal Communication

**Interpersonal communication** is the communication that takes place between two persons who have an established relationship; the people are in some way "connected." Interpersonal communication would thus include what takes place between a son and his father, an employer and an employee, two sisters, a teacher and a student, two lovers, two friends, and so on.

You could argue that it's impossible to have dyadic (two-person) communication that isn't interpersonal. Invariably, there is some relationship between two people who are interacting. Even the stranger who asks directions of a neighborhood resident has an identifiable relationship with the resident as soon as the first message is sent. This interpersonal (but nonintimate) relationship will then influence how the two individuals interact with each other.

**Dyadic Primacy**   Even when you have triads (groups of three people), dyads (two-person relationships) are still primary; dyads are always central to interpersonal relationships, a principle referred to as **dyadic primacy** (Wilmot, 1999). Consider, for example, the following situation: Al and Bob (a dyad) have been roommates for their first two years of college. Expenses have increased, so they ask Carl to join them and become a third roommate. Now a triad exists. But the original dyad has not gone away; in fact, now there are three dyads: Al and Bob, Al and Carl, and Bob and Carl. Al and Bob are ballplayers and talk a lot about sports. Al and Carl are both studying communication and talk about their classes. Bob and Carl belong to the same religious club and frequently discuss the club's activities. At times, of course, all three interact, but even here the topic of conversation will determine who talks primarily to whom. If the topic is sports, Al and Bob will primarily address each other; Carl will be a kind of outsider. When the topic is classes, Bob is the outsider.

If you examine families, workers in a factory, neighbors in an apartment house, or students in class, you'll find that each large group breaks down at times into a series of dyads. The specific dyad formed naturally depends on the situation, and dyads will probably change over time. As in the case of Al, Bob, and Carl, different dyads will form, depending on the nature of the interaction.

**Dyadic Coalitions**   A **dyadic coalition** is a two-person relationship formed by members of a larger group for achieving a mutually desired benefit or goal (Wilmot, 1999). Coalitions—whether in the family, among friends, or at work—may be productive or unproductive. Two

**SPEAKING**
**Interpersonal-E**

**Computer-Mediated Communication.** Throughout this text you'll find marginal items labeled "Speaking Interpersonal-E," which draw to your attention the similarities and differences between computer-mediated and face-to-face communication. A definition from TheFreeDictionary.com will serve us well to begin: "Computer-mediated communication (CMC) is any form of communication between two or more individual people who interact and/or influence each other via separate computers"; CMC generally refers to "e-mail, video, audio or text conferencing, bulletin boards, listservs, instant messaging, and multiplayer video games."

workers may form a coalition to develop a program for improving worker morale. Two teachers may undertake research together. The result of these coalitions will benefit not only the individuals involved but also, eventually, all members of the group.

At other times, coalitions are unproductive. The grandparent who develops a coalition with a grandchild against the child's parent may cause all sorts of family difficulties; parental resentment and jealousy, as well as guilt for the child, are just a few possibilities. A parent experiencing marital difficulties may form a coalition with one of his or her children. This often results in alienating the left-out parent and preventing the child from benefiting from a close relationship with that parent.

**Dyadic Consciousness**   In addition to what you do and say, your interpersonal relationships depend on what you think about your relationship. As your relationship develops, a **dyadic consciousness** emerges; you begin to see yourself as part of a pair, a team, a couple. It's almost as if a third party enters the picture. No longer is it just you and the other person; it's now you, the other person, and the relationship. As the relationship becomes more involved, this third party takes on greater importance. Often individuals sacrifice their own desires or needs for the well-being of "the relationship."

## Forms of Interpersonal Communication

Often interpersonal communication takes place face-to-face: talking with other students before class, interacting with family or friends over dinner, trading secrets with intimates. This is the type of interaction that probably comes to mind when you think of conversation. Because of technological advances, however, much conversation now takes place online. Online communication is now a major part of people's experience throughout the world. Such communications are important personally, socially, and professionally. The four major online types of conversation—e-mail, the mailing list group, instant messaging, and the chat group—differ from one another and from face-to-face interaction in important ways (also see Table 1.5, pp. 19–20).

---

⊙ **TABLE 1.1**
### The Uses of the Internet

Here are the 10 most frequent activities Americans engaged in when they went online in the years 2000 and 2004. How many of these activities have you engaged in during, say, the last month?

| Activity | Number of Users 2000 | Number of Users 2004 |
|---|---|---|
| Use e-mail | 52,000,000 | 70,000,000 |
| Get news | 19,000,000 | 35,000,000 |
| Check the weather | 14,000,000 | 25,000,000 |
| Conduct job-related research | 14,000,000 | 24,000,000 |
| Research a product before buying | 12,000,000 | 19,000,000 |
| Search for political news or information | 9,000,000 | 24,000,000 |
| Send instant message | 10,000,000 | 15,000,000 |
| Conduct research for school | 9,000,000 | 14,000,000 |
| Get travel information | 6,000,000 | 10,000,000 |
| Get health or medical information | 6,000,000 | 7,000,000 |

*Source:* Data from the Pew Internet and American Life Project 4, The Mainstreaming of Online Life (http://www.pewinternet.org), accessed February 9, 2005.

---

*E-mail* is today the most common use of the Internet (see Table 1.1). In e-mail you type your letter in an e-mail program and send it (along with other documents you may wish to attach) from your computer via modem or cable to your server (the computer at your school or at some commercial organization like America OnLine), which relays your message through a series of computer hookups and eventually to the server of the person you're addressing. Unlike face-to-face communication, traditional e-mail does not take place in real time. You may send your message today, but the receiver may not read it for a week and may take another week to respond. Consequently, much of the spontaneity created by real-time communication is lost here. You may, for example, be very enthusiastic about a topic when you send your e-mail but practically forget it by the time someone responds. E-mail is more like a postcard than a letter and so can be read by others along the route. It's also virtually unerasable, a feature that has important consequences and that we discuss later in this chapter (p. 28).

The *listserv* or *mailing list group* consists of a group of people interested in a particular topic who communicate with each other through e-mail. Generally, you subscribe to a list and communicate with all other members by addressing your mail to the group e-mail address. Any message you send to this address will be sent to everyone who subscribes to the list. Your message is sent to all members at the same time; there are no asides to the person sitting next to you (as in face-to-face groups).

*Instant messaging* (often abbreviated IM) is an Internet text-based system that allows you to converse online with short messages in (essentially) real time. Through IM you can also play games, share files, listen to music, and send messages to cell phones. Approximately 42 percent of U.S. Internet users (more than 53 million Americans) use IM. Approximately 21 percent of IM users report that they use it at work; of these 40 percent use it to communicate with coworkers, 33 percent use it to communicate with friends and family, and 21 percent use it with both groups (Shiu & Lenhart, 2004). Among college students, as you probably know, the major purpose of IM seems to be to maintain "social connectedness" (Kindred & Roper, 2004).

*Chat groups* have proliferated across the Internet. These groups enable you to converse in real time. Unlike mailing lists, chat communication lets you see a member's message as it's being sent; there's virtually no delay, and recent innovations now enable you to communicate with voice as well as text. At any one time there are thousands of groups, so your chances of finding a topic you're interested in are high. As with e-mail and face-to-face conversation, the purposes of chat groups vary from communication that simply maintains connection with others (what many would call "idle chatter" or "phatic communication") to extremely significant discussions in science, education, health, politics, and just about any field you can name. Like mailing lists, chat groups have the great advantage that they enable you to communicate with people you would never meet or interact with otherwise. Because chat groups are international, they provide excellent exposure to other cultures, other ideas, and other ways of communicating.

## Purposes of Interpersonal Communication

People engage in interpersonal communication for a variety of purposes; for example, to learn, to relate, to influence, to play, and to help. Interpersonal communication enables you to *learn,* to better understand the external world—the world of objects, events, and other people. Although a great deal of information comes from the media, you probably discuss and ultimately learn or internalize information through interpersonal interactions. In fact, your beliefs, attitudes, and values are probably influenced more by interpersonal encounters than by the media or even by formal education.

Most important, however, interpersonal communication helps you learn about yourself. By talking about yourself with others, you gain valuable feedback on your feelings, thoughts, and behaviors. Through these communications, you also learn how you appear to others—who likes you, who dislikes you, and why.

**SPEAKING**
**Interpersonal-E**

**Gender Differences in E-Mail.** Studies of gender differences find that women's e-mails are more relational and expressive and that they focus more on domestic and personal topics than do men's e-mails (Colley, Todd, Bland, Holmes, Khanom, & Pike, 2004). Do you find this difference in your own e-mail experience?

Interpersonal communication helps you *relate*. One of the greatest needs people have is to establish and maintain close relationships. You want to feel loved and liked, and in turn you want to love and like others. Such relationships help to alleviate loneliness and depression, enable you to share and heighten your pleasures, and generally make you feel more positive about yourself.

Very likely, you *influence* the attitudes and behaviors of others in your interpersonal encounters. You may wish others to vote a particular way, try a new diet, buy a new book, listen to a record, see a movie, take a specific course, think in a particular way, believe that something is true or false, or value some idea—the list is endless. A good deal of your time is probably spent in interpersonal persuasion. Some researchers, in fact, would argue that all communication is persuasive and that all our communications seek some persuasive goal. Some examples (Canary, Cody, & Manusov, 2000):

- Self-presentation goals: You communicate to give others the image you want them to have of you.
- Relationship goals: You communicate to form the relationships that will meet your needs.
- Instrumental goals: You communicate to get others to do something for you.

# InterMedia

## THEORIES OF MEDIA INFLUENCE

Media messages—like all messages—have effects on readers, listeners, and viewers. Some of these messages influence in obvious ways; for example, advertisements on television, on the Internet, and in the print media as well as editorials in newspapers, magazines, and on television. Other media messages influence indirectly; for example the dramas and sitcoms that influence your ideas about family, about law-and-order agencies, or about friendship and love. Although not everyone is influenced at the same time or to the same degree, everyone seems to be influenced at least at some point and to some extent. So the question to consider is how the media exert their influence.

An early theory, call the one-step theory, argued that the influence of the media was direct and immediate; it occurred in one step—from the media to you. You read a newspaper or watched television and were persuaded by what was said. A variant of this theory, called the silver-bullet theory, held that the media worked like bullets aimed at a target. If the gun was loaded correctly and aimed accurately, the bullet would penetrate the target—the viewer or reader would be influenced as the media wished (Schramm & Porter, 1982). Both of these theories view the audience as relatively passive; the audience is a target that cannot resist being penetrated.

Another explanation visualizes media influence as a two-step process: First, the media influence opinion leaders (step 1); and second, these opinion leaders influence the rest of the people (step 2). A somewhat more complicated approach, the multistep theory, claims that media interact with interpersonal channels. So, for example, the media may influence certain people; these people interact with others, who then attend to the media themselves as well as interacting with other people, and on and on. This theory views the effects of media as products of all these influences from the media and from interpersonal interactions. A good example in support of this theory comes from a recent poll on what influences people's purchases. Survey respondents cited a mixture of interpersonal and media sources; word of mouth was mentioned by the largest number of respondents (26.7 percent). Among the media mentioned were "newspaper inserts" and "TV/broadcast" (*USAToday*, April 28, 2005, p. B1).

### Follow Up

Can you identify specific ways in which the media have influenced you? For example, have media messages influenced your buying habits, your view of relationships, or your attitudes toward other cultures? What theory seems to best explain how the media influence you?

In computer-mediated communication (CMC), a new study called captology has arisen. According to wikipedia.com, **captology** refers to "the study of computers as persuasive technologies" and focuses on the ways in which computers and computer-mediated communication generally can influence beliefs, attitudes, and behaviors. From a posting by Bj Fogg, the director of the Stanford Persuasive Technology Lab and the founder of captology, here are just a few examples of areas in which computers—from mobile phones to websites and blogs—can persuade (http://captology.stanford.edu/notebook/archives/000087.html, accessed February 11, 2005):

- politics—persuasion to vote for X or Y or to support this or that political position
- personal finance—guidance on managing your finances
- buying—encouragement to buy a particular product or service
- personal relationships—advice on establishing a romantic or friendship relationship
- occupational effectiveness—tips on how to increase your work productivity

And, as you probably have noticed from your own e-mail, social movement organizations are increasingly using the Internet to further their aims (Fisher, 1998; Banerjee, 2005).

Talking with friends about your weekend activities, discussing sports or dates, telling stories and jokes, and in general just passing the time are _play_ functions. Far from frivolous, this extremely important purpose gives your activities a necessary balance and your mind a needed break from all the seriousness around you. Perhaps the most obvious form of CMC play are the multiuser domains—MUDs and MOOs for example—where you interact with other participants in a virtual reality environment in real time. And even certain forms of cyberflirting may be viewed as play (Whitty, 2003b).

Therapists of various kinds serve a helping function professionally by offering guidance through interpersonal interaction. But everyone interacts to _help_ in everyday encounters: You console a friend who has broken off a love affair, counsel another student about courses to take, or offer advice to a colleague about work. And, not surprisingly, much support and counseling are currently taking place through e-mail and chat groups (Wright & Chung, 2001). Success in accomplishing this helping function, professionally or otherwise, depends on your knowledge and skill in interpersonal communication.

Popular belief and recent research both agree that men and women use communication for different purposes. Generally, men seem to communicate more for information, whereas women seem to communicate more for relationship purposes (Shaw & Grant, 2002; Colley, Todd, Bland, Holmes, Khanom, & Pike, 2004). Gender differences also occur in computer communication. For example, women ICQ (I seek you) users chat more for relationship reasons, while men chat more to play and to relax (Leung, 2001).

The purposes of interpersonal communication can also be viewed from two other perspectives (see Figure 1.1). First, purposes may be seen as motives for engaging in interpersonal communication. That is, you engage in interpersonal communication to satisfy your need for knowledge or to form relationships. Second, these purposes may be viewed in terms of the results you want to achieve. That is, you engage in interpersonal communication to increase your knowledge of yourself and others or to exert influence or power over others.

You can gain an additional perspective on interpersonal communication by looking at the major divisions or areas of the field as identified in Table 1.2.

Interpersonal communication is usually motivated by a combination of factors and has a combination of results or effects. Any interpersonal interaction, then, serves a unique combination of purposes, is motivated by a unique combination of factors, and can produce a unique combination of results.

## ELEMENTS OF INTERPERSONAL COMMUNICATION

The model presented in Figure 1.2 is designed to reflect the circular nature of interpersonal communication; both persons send messages simultaneously rather than as a linear

SPEAKING
>> Interpersonal-E

**Cyberflirting.** One of the differences research finds between face-to-face and online flirting is that in the online situation reality and fantasy become somewhat blurred (Whitty, 2003a). What other differences do you find between flirting in face-to-face and computer-mediated situations?

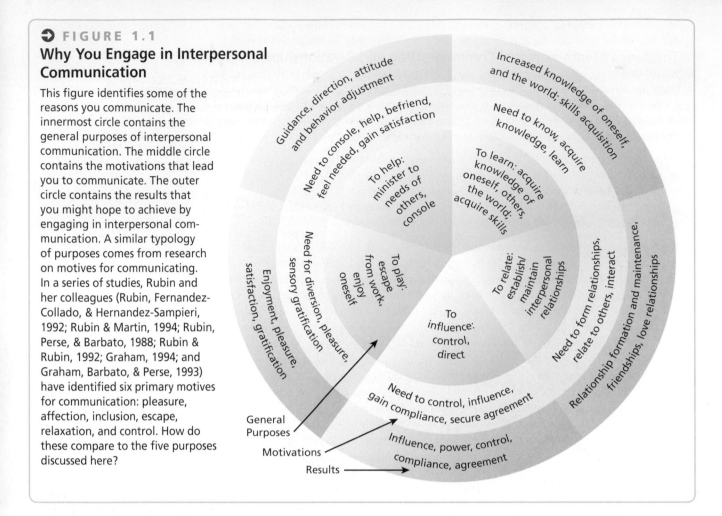

**FIGURE 1.1**

**Why You Engage in Interpersonal Communication**

This figure identifies some of the reasons you communicate. The innermost circle contains the general purposes of interpersonal communication. The middle circle contains the motivations that lead you to communicate. The outer circle contains the results that you might hope to achieve by engaging in interpersonal communication. A similar typology of purposes comes from research on motives for communicating. In a series of studies, Rubin and her colleagues (Rubin, Fernandez-Collado, & Hernandez-Sampieri, 1992; Rubin & Martin, 1994; Rubin, Perse, & Barbato, 1988; Rubin & Rubin, 1992; Graham, 1994; and Graham, Barbato, & Perse, 1993) have identified six primary motives for communication: pleasure, affection, inclusion, escape, relaxation, and control. How do these compare to the five purposes discussed here?

sequence where communication goes from person 1 to person 2 to person 1 to person 2 and on and on. Each of the concepts identified in the model and discussed here may be thought of as a **universal of interpersonal communication,** in that it's present in all interpersonal interactions: (1) source–receiver, (2) encoding–decoding, (3) messages, (4) channels, (5) noise, (6) contexts, (7) ethics, and (8) competence.

## Source–Receiver

Interpersonal communication involves at least two persons. Each person performs **source** functions (formulates and sends messages) and also performs **receiver** functions (perceives and comprehends messages). The term *source–receiver* emphasizes that both functions are performed by each individual in interpersonal communication.

Who you are, what you know, what you believe, what you value, what you want, what you have been told, and what your attitudes are all influence what you say, how you say it, what messages you receive, and how you receive them. Likewise, the person you're speaking to and the knowledge that you think that person has will greatly influence your interpersonal messages (Lau, Chiu, & Hong, 2001). Each person is unique; each person's communications are unique.

**⊙ TABLE 1.2**

## The Areas of Interpersonal Communication and Relationships

This table is intended as a guide for identifying some of the important areas in the general topic of "interpersonal communication and relationships" and not as a formal outline of the field. The six areas of interpersonal communication interact and overlap; they're not independent. For example, interpersonal interaction is a part of all the other areas; similarly, intercultural communication can exist in any of the other areas. The related academic areas illustrate the close ties among fields of study and the centrality of communication to all academic areas.

| General and Related Areas | Selected Topics |
|---|---|
| **Interpersonal interaction**<br>Communication between two people<br>*Related areas:* Psychology, education, linguistics, counseling | Characteristics of effectiveness, conversational processes, self-disclosure, active listening, verbal and nonverbal messages in conversation, e-mail, chat room talk, instant messaging |
| **Health communication**<br>Communication between health professional and patient and between the health profession and the public<br>*Related areas:* Medicine, psychology, counseling, health care | Increasing doctor–patient effectiveness, talking about AIDS, communication and aging, therapeutic communication, counseling, communication safe-sex guidelines |
| **Family communication**<br>Communication within the nuclear or extended family system<br>*Related areas:* Sociology, psychology, family studies, social work | Couple communication, power in the family, dysfunctional families, family conflict, heterosexual and homosexual families, parent–child communication |
| **Intercultural communication**<br>Communication between members of different races, nationalities, religions, genders, and generations<br>*Related areas:* Anthropology, sociology, cultural studies, business | Cross-generational communication; male–female communication; black–Hispanic–Asian–Caucasian communication; prejudice and stereotypes; barriers to intercultural communication; the Internet and cultural diversity; sexism, racism, heterosexism, and ageism |
| **Business and organizational communication**<br>Communication among workers in an organizational environment<br>*Related areas:* Business, management, public relations, computer science | Interviewing strategies, sexual harassment, upward and downward communication, increasing managerial effectiveness, increasing worker productivity and morale, leadership in business, mentoring and networking |
| **Social and personal relationships**<br>Communication in close relationships such as friendship and love<br>*Related areas:* Psychology, sociology, anthropology, family studies | Relationship development, maintenance, deterioration, and repair; gender and cultural differences in relationships; increasing intimacy; dealing with relationship breakdowns; verbal abuse |

## Encoding–Decoding

*Encoding* refers to the act of producing messages—for example, speaking or writing. *Decoding* is the reverse and refers to the act of understanding messages—for example, listening or reading. By sending your ideas via sound waves (in the case of speech) or light waves (in the case of writing), you're putting these ideas into a **code,** hence *en*coding. By translating sound or light waves into ideas, you're taking them out of a code, hence *de*coding. Thus, speakers and writers are called **encoders,** and listeners and readers are called **decoders.** The term *encoding–decoding* is used to emphasize that the two activities are performed in combination by each participant. For interpersonal communication to occur, messages must be encoded and decoded. For example, when a parent talks to a child whose eyes are closed and whose ears are covered by stereo headphones, interpersonal communication does not occur because the messages sent are not being received.

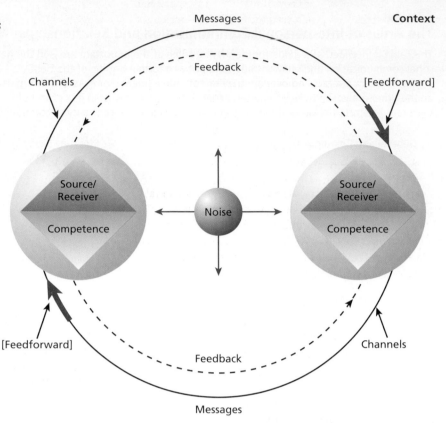

→ FIGURE 1.2
## A Model of Some Universals of Interpersonal Communication

After you read the section on the elements of interpersonal communication, you may wish to construct your own model of the process. In constructing this model, be careful that you don't fall into the trap of visualizing interpersonal communication as a linear or simple left-to-right, static process. Remember that all elements are interrelated and interdependent. After completing your model, consider, for example: (1) Could your model also serve as a model of *intrapersonal* communication? A model of small group, public, or mass communication? (2) What elements or concepts other than those noted here might be added to the model?

## Messages

**Messages**—signals that serve as **stimuli** for a receiver—may be auditory (hearing), visual (seeing), tactile (touching), olfactory (smelling), gustatory (tasting), or any combination. You communicate interpersonally by gesture and touch as well as by words and sentences. The clothes you wear communicate to others and, in fact, to yourself as well. The way you walk communicates, as does the way you shake hands, tilt your head, comb your hair, sit, smile, or frown. These signals are your interpersonal communication messages. Similarly, the colors and types of cell phones, the wallpaper and screen savers on your computer, and even the type and power of your computer communicate messages about you. Interpersonal communication can take place by telephone, through prison cell walls, through web-cams, or face-to-face. Increasingly, it's taking place through computers.

Messages may be intentional or unintentional. They may result from the most carefully planned strategy as well as from the unintentional slip of the tongue, lingering body odor, or nervous twitch.

Messages may refer to the world, people, and events as well as to other messages (DeVito, 2003a). Messages that are about other messages are called **metamessages** and represent many of your everyday communications; they include, for example, "Do you understand?" "Did I say that right?" "What did you say?" "Is it fair to say that . . .?" "I want to be honest," "That's not logical." Two particularly important types of metamessages are feedback and feedforward.

**Feedback Messages** Throughout the interpersonal communication process, you exchange **feedback**—messages sent back to the speaker concerning reactions to what is said (Clement & Frandsen, 1976). Feedback tells the speaker what effect she or he is having on listeners. On the basis of this feedback, the speaker may adjust, modify, strengthen, de-emphasize, or change the content or form of the messages.

Feedback may come from yourself or from others. When you send a message—say, in speaking to another person—you also hear yourself. That is, you get feedback from your own messages: you hear what you say, you feel the way you move, you see what you write. In addition to this self-feedback, you get feedback from others. This feedback can take many forms. A frown or a smile, a yea or a nay, a pat on the back or a punch in the mouth are all types of feedback. Sometimes feedback is easy to identify, but sometimes it isn't (Skinner, 2002). Part of the art of effective communication is to discern feedback and adjust your messages on the basis of that feedback.

Feedback can be looked at in terms of five important dimensions: positive–negative; person focused–message focused; immediate–delayed; low monitoring–high monitoring; and supportive–critical. To use feedback effectively, you need to make educated choices along these dimensions.

**VIEWPOINT**

The "feedback theory of relationships" holds that satisfying friendships or romantic relationships may be characterized by feedback that is positive, person focused, immediate, low in monitoring, and supportive—and that unsatisfying relationships are characterized by feedback that is negative, self-focused, nonimmediate, high in monitoring, and critical. How effective is this theory in explaining relationships with which you're familiar?

**Positive–Negative** Feedback may be positive (you pay a compliment or pat someone on the back) or negative (you criticize someone or scowl). **Positive feedback** tells the speaker that he or she is on the right track and should continue communicating in essentially the same way. **Negative feedback** tells the speaker that something is wrong and that some adjustment should be made.

**Person Focused–Message Focused** Feedback may center on the person ("You're sweet" or "You have a great smile"). Or it may center on the message ("Can you repeat that number?" or "Your argument is a good one").

**Immediate–Delayed** In interpersonal situations, feedback is often sent immediately after the message is received; you smile or say something in response almost simultaneously with your receiving the message. In other communication situations, however, the feedback may be delayed. Instructor evaluation questionnaires completed at the end of a course provide feedback long after the class began. When you applaud or ask questions of a public speaker at the end of a lecture, the feedback is delayed. In interview situations, the feedback may come weeks afterward. In media situations, some feedback comes immediately through Nielsen ratings, and other feedback comes much later through viewing and buying patterns.

**Low Monitoring–High Monitoring** Feedback varies from the spontaneous and totally honest reaction (low-monitored feedback) to the carefully constructed response designed to serve a specific purpose (high-monitored feedback). In most interpersonal situations, you probably give feedback spontaneously; you allow your responses to show without any monitoring. At other times, however, you may be more guarded, as when your boss asks you how you like your job or when your grandfather asks what you think of his new earring.

**Supportive–Critical** Supportive feedback accepts the speaker and what the speaker says. It occurs, for example, when you console another, encourage him or her to talk, or otherwise confirm the person's definition of self. Critical feedback, on the other hand, is evaluative; it's judgmental. When you give critical feedback (whether positive or negative), you judge another's performance—as in, for example, coaching someone learning a new skill.

**Feedforward Messages**    **Feedforward** is information you provide before sending your primary message (Richards, 1951). Feedforward reveals something about the message to come. Examples of feedforward include the preface or table of contents of a book, the opening paragraph of a chapter, movie previews, magazine covers, and introductions in public speeches. Feedforward may serve a variety of functions: to open the channels of communication, to preview the message, to disclaim, and to altercast.

### To Open the Channels of Communication

In his influential essay "The Problem of Meaning in Primitive Languages," anthropologist Bronislaw Malinowski (1923) coined the phrase **phatic communion** to refer to messages that open the channels of communication rather than communicate information. Phatic communion (also referred to as phatic communication) is a perfect example of feedforward. It's information that tells you that the normal, expected, and accepted rules of interaction will be in effect. It tells you another person is willing to communicate. It's the "How are you" and "Nice weather" greetings that are designed to maintain rapport and friendly relationships (Placencia, 2004; Burnard, 2003). Similarly, listeners' short comments that are unrelated to the content of the conversation but that indicate interest and attention may also be considered phatic communication. (McCarthy, 2003). Not surprisingly, phatic communication is important not only in face-to-face interaction but also in e-mail (Bloch, 2002).

### To Preview the Message

Feedforward messages frequently preview other messages. They may, for example, preview the content ("I'm afraid I have bad news for you"), the importance ("Listen to this before you make a move"), the form or style ("I'll tell you all the gory details"), and the positive or negative quality of subsequent messages ("You're not going to like this, but here's what I heard"). The subject heading on your e-mail well illustrates this function of feedforward, as do the phone numbers and names that come up on your cell phone or call-waiting device.

### To Disclaim

The **disclaimer** is a statement that aims to ensure that your message will be understood as you want it to be and that it will not reflect negatively on you. For example, you might use a disclaimer when you think that what you're going to say may be met with opposition. Thus, you say "I'm not against immigration, but . . ." or "Don't think I'm homophobic, but . . . ." (Disclaimers, as they function to prevent conversational problems, are discussed in Chapter 9.)

### To Altercast

Feedforward is often used to place the receiver in a specific role and to request responses in terms of this assumed role, a process called **altercasting** (Weinstein & Deutschberger, 1963; McLaughlin, 1984). For example, you might altercast by asking a friend, "As a future advertising executive, what would you think of corrective advertising?" This question casts your friend in the role of advertising executive (rather than parent, Democrat, or Baptist, for example) and asks that she or he answer from a particular perspective.

**Message Overload**    Message overload—often called information overload in business—is one of the greatest obstacles to achieving communication efficiency and has even been linked to health problems in corporate managers (Lee, 2000). The ease with which e-mail and Internet messages can be copied or forwarded to large numbers of people with a few taps of the keyboard has obviously contributed to message overload, as have the junk mail and spam that seems to grow every day. Invariably, you must select certain messages to attend to and other messages to ignore. Today, for example, the American worker is exposed to more messages in one year than a person living in 1900 was in his or her entire life. Today, the average employee receives more than 50 e-mails daily. And in one day, the average manager sends and receives more than 100 documents.

One of the problems with message overload is that it absorbs an enormous amount of time. The more messages you have to deal with, the less time you have for those messages or tasks that are central to your purposes. Similarly, under conditions of message overload, errors are more likely, simply because you cannot devote the needed time to any one item. The more rushed you are, the more likely you are to make mistakes. In addition, research shows that under conditions of message overload you're more likely to respond to the simpler messages and to generate simpler responses (Jones, Ravid, & Rafaeli, 2004).

A major problem is that the overabundance of messages may make it difficult for you to determine efficiently which messages need immediate attention and which don't, which messages may be discarded and which must be retained.

Consider your own ways of dealing with message overload (Uris, 1986). Do you

❶ Think before passing on messages, realizing that not all messages must be passed on, that not everyone needs to know everything?

❷ Use the messages as they come to you and then throw them out? For example, do you write the relevant dates for a meeting on your calendar and then throw out the announcement or delete the e-mail?

❸ Organize your messages? Have you created folders to help you store and quickly retrieve the information you need?

❹ Get rid of extra copies? When you receive multiple copies do you get rid of all but the one you need?

❺ Distinguish between messages that you should save and messages that are only cluttering up your space?

## Channel

The communication **channel** is the medium through which messages pass. It's a kind of bridge connecting source and receiver. Communication rarely takes place over only one channel; two, three, or four channels are often used simultaneously. For example, in face-to-face interaction, you speak and listen (vocal–auditory channel), but you also gesture and receive signals visually (gestural–visual channel), and you emit odors and smell those of others (chemical–olfactory channel). Often you communicate through touch (cutaneous–tactile channel). Another way to think about channels is to consider them as the means of communication: for example, face-to-face contact, telephone, e-mail and snail mail, chat groups, instant messaging, news postings, film, television, radio, smoke signals, or fax.

Note that the channel imposes different restrictions on your message construction. For example, in CMC you can pause to think of the right word or phrase, you can go on for as short or as long a time as you want without any threat of interruption or contradiction, and you can edit your speech/message more easily.

At times one or more channels may be damaged. For example, in blind individuals the visual channel is impaired, so adjustments have to be made. Table 1.3 gives you an idea of how such adjustments between blind and sighted persons can make interpersonal communication more effective.

## Noise

Technically, **noise** is anything that distorts the message, anything that prevents the receiver from receiving the message. At one extreme, noise may prevent a message from getting from source to receiver. A roaring noise or line static can easily prevent entire messages from getting through to your telephone receiver. At the other extreme, with virtually no noise interference, the message of the source and the message received are almost identical.

**⏱ TABLE 1.3    INTERPERSONAL COMMUNICATION TIPS**

## Between Blind and Sighted People

People vary greatly in their visual abilities; some are totally blind, some are partially sighted, and some have unimpaired vision. Ninety percent of the people who are "legally blind" have some vision. All people, however, have the same need for communication and information. Here are some tips for making communication between blind and sighted people more effective:

**If you're the sighted person and are talking with a blind person:**

1. Identify yourself. Don't assume the blind person will recognize your voice.
2. Face your listener; you'll be easier to hear. Don't shout. Most people who are visually impaired are not hearing impaired. Speak at your normal volume.
3. Because your gestures, eye movements, and facial expressions cannot be seen by the visually impaired listener, encode into speech all the meanings you wish to communicate.
4. Use audible turn-taking cues. When you pass the role of speaker to a person who is visually impaired, don't rely on nonverbal cues; instead, say something like "Do you agree with that, Joe?"
5. Use normal vocabulary and discuss topics that you would discuss with sighted people. Don't avoid terms like "see" or "look" or even "blind." Don't avoid discussing a television show or the way your new car looks; these are normal topics for all people.

**If you are a visually impaired person, interacting with a sighted person:**

1. Help the sighted person meet your special communication needs. If you want your surroundings described, ask. If you want the person to read the road signs, ask.
2. Be patient with the sighted person. Many people are nervous talking with people who are visually impaired for fear of offending. Put them at ease in a way that also makes you more comfortable.

*Sources:* These suggestions were drawn from a variety of sources: http://www.cincyblind.org/what_do_you_do_.htm, http://www.abwa.asn.au/, and http://www.dol.gov (all accessed March 26, 2005).

---

Most often, however, noise distorts some portion of the message a source sends as it travels to a receiver.

Noise comes in a variety of forms (see Table 1.4). Noise may be physical (others talking loudly, cars honking, illegible handwriting, "garbage" on your computer screen), physiological (deafness, visual impairment, articulation disorders), psychological (preconceived ideas, wandering thoughts), or semantic (misunderstood meanings).

A useful concept in understanding noise and its importance in communication is **signal-to-noise ratio.** *Signal* refers to information that you'd find useful, and *noise* refers to information that is useless (to you). So, for example, a mailing list or newsgroup that contains lots of useful information would be high on signal and low on noise; messages that contain lots of useless information would be high on noise and low on signal.

Since messages may be visual as well as spoken, noise too may be visual. Sunglasses that prevent someone from seeing the nonverbal messages from your eyes would be considered noise, as would blurred type on a printed page.

All communications contain noise. Noise cannot be totally eliminated, but its effects can be reduced. Making your language more precise, sharpening your skills for sending and receiving nonverbal messages, and improving your listening and feedback skills are some ways to combat the influence of noise.

### Ask Yourself
#### The Consequences of Noise

Not only can noise distort message reception, but repeated exposure to noise from 90 to 140 decibels also can create permanent hearing loss. Amplified music at a concert can reach 120 to 130 decibels, and sounds from headphones can reach 100 decibels (*New York Times*, February 8, 2005, p. F5). Ask yourself: What might you do to protect your hearing in a culture in which loud noise is so common?

## ⏻ TABLE 1.4
### Four Types of Noise

The ability to both recognize and reduce noise is one of the most essential communication skills. What kinds of noise occur in settings such as the classroom, the workplace, and the family dining room? How can you combat the noise encountered in these settings?

| Types of Noise | Definition | Examples |
|---|---|---|
| Physical | Interference that is external to both speaker and listener | Screeching of passing cars, hum of computer, sunglasses, garbage on your computer, pop-ups and banner ads |
| Physiological | Physical barriers within the speaker or listener | Visual impairments, hearing loss, articulation problems, memory loss |
| Psychological | Cognitive or mental interference | Biases and prejudices in senders and receivers, closed-mindedness, inaccurate expectations, extreme emotionalism (anger, hate, love, grief) |
| Semantic | Speaker and listener assigning different meanings | People speaking different languages, use of jargon or overly complex terms not understood by listener, dialectical differences in meaning |

## Context

Communication always takes place in a **context** that influences the form and content of your messages. At times this context isn't obvious or intrusive; it seems so natural that it's ignored—like background music. At other times the context dominates, and the ways in which it restricts or stimulates your messages are obvious. Compare, for example, the differences among communicating in a funeral home, in a football stadium, in a formal restaurant, and at a rock concert. The context of communication has at least four dimensions, all of which interact with and influence each other.

The *physical dimension* is the tangible or concrete environment in which communication takes place—the room, hallway, or park, the boardroom or the family dinner table. The size of the space, its temperature, and the number of people present in the physical space would also be part of the physical dimension. In print media such as magazines or newspapers, context includes the positioning of stories and news articles; an article on page 37 is identified as less important than an article on page 1 or 2. Even the placement of passages within an article proves relevant. Recently, for example, the *New York Times* was criticized for putting information critical of the way it counted subscriptions (and thus set advertising rates) in the 30th paragraph of an article. Similarly, the political and social preferences of a newspaper can be identified, in part at least, by the physical context in which the editors place stories and news articles (Okrent, 2005).

The *temporal dimension* refers not only to the time of day and moment in history but also to where a particular message fits into the sequence of communication events. For example, a joke about illness told immediately after the disclosure of a friend's sickness will be received differently than the same joke told in response to a series of similar jokes. Also, some channels (for example, face-to-face, chat rooms, and instant messaging) allow for synchronous communication in which messages are sent and received simultaneously. Other channels (for example, letter writing, e-mail, and bulletin board posts) are asynchronous; messages are sent and received at different times.

The *social–psychological dimension* includes, for example, status relationships among the participants, roles and games that people play, norms of the society or group, and the friendliness, formality, or gravity of the situation.

The *cultural context* (Chapter 2) refers to the cultural beliefs and customs of the people communicating. When you interact with people from different cultures, you may each follow different rules of communication. This can result in confusion, unintentional insult,

# Ethics in Interpersonal Communication

## ETHICAL QUESTIONS

Because ethics is relevant to all forms of interpersonal communication, ethical issues are integrated throughout the text in these Ethics in Interpersonal Communication boxes. Here, as a kind of preview, are just a few of the ethical issues raised in these boxes. As you read these questions, think about your own ethical beliefs and how these beliefs influence the way you'd answer the questions.

■ What obligations do you have to keep a secret? Can you identify situations in which it would be unethical *not* to reveal information you promised to keep secret? See Ethics box, Chapter 3.

■ What are your ethical obligations as a listener? See Ethics box, Chapter 5.

■ Are ethical principles objective or subjective? For example, if lying is unethical, is it unethical in all situations? Or would your answer depend on the circumstances? See Ethics box, Chapter 6.

■ What are your ethical obligations when speaking? See Ethics boxes, Chapters 7 and 9.

■ Are there ethical and unethical ways to engage in conflict and conflict resolution? See Ethics box, Chapter 13.

### What would you do?

You're ready to enter into a permanent romantic relationship and are being pressured to talk about yourself. What can you ethically keep hidden? What types of information are you ethically obligated to reveal?

**◐ VIEWPOINT**

One study found that 80 percent of young adult women consider a spouse who can communicate his feelings more desirable than a man who earns a good living (www.gallup.com, accessed June 27, 2001). How important, compared to all the other factors you might take into consideration in choosing a partner, is the ability to communicate? What specific communication skills would you consider "extremely important" in a life partner?

inaccurate judgments, and a host of other miscommunications. Similarly, communication strategies or techniques that prove satisfying to members of one culture may prove disturbing or offensive to members of another. In fact, research shows that you lose more information in an intercultural situation (approximately 50 percent) than in an intracultural situation (approximately 25 percent) (Li, 1999).

## Ethics

Because communication has consequences, interpersonal communication also involves **ethics;** each communication act has a moral dimension, a rightness or wrongness (cf., Jaksa & Pritchard, 1994; Johannesen, 2001). Communication choices need to be guided by ethical considerations as well as by concerns with effectiveness and satisfaction. Some research finds important cross-cultural similarities in this regard; for example, it's been proposed that there are certain universal ethical principles that are held by all cultures, such as that you should tell the truth, have respect for another's dignity, and not harm the innocent (Christians & Traber, 1997). Ethics is therefore included as a universal of interpersonal communication and is presented in this text in "Ethics in Interpersonal Communication" boxes. These boxes cover issues such as the differences between subjective and objective approaches to ethics, whether the ends justify the means, the ethical obligations of speakers and listeners, lying, gossip, and unethical speech.

Table 1.5 presents some of the similarities and differences between face-to-face and computer-mediated communication. As you review the table, you may wish to add other similarities and differences—or to take issue with the ones identified here.

## Competence

Your ability to communicate effectively is your interpersonal **competence** (Spitzberg & Cupach, 1989; Wilson & Sabee, 2003). Communication

## Face-to-Face and Computer-Mediated Communication

Throughout this text face-to-face and computer-mediated interpersonal communication are discussed, compared, and contrasted. Here is a brief summary of some communication concepts indicating some of the ways in which face-to-face and computer-mediated communication (CMC) are similar and different. What other similarities and differences would you identify?

| Interpersonal Communication Element | Face-to-Face | CMC |
| --- | --- | --- |
| Sender (speaking turn, presentation of self, impression management) | Visual appearance communicates who you are; personal characteristics (sex, approximate age, race, etc.) are overt and open to visual inspection; receiver controls the order of what is attended to; disguise is difficult.<br><br>You compete for the speaker's turn and time with the other person(s); you can be interrupted. | You present the self you want others to see; personal characteristics are covert and are revealed when you want to reveal them; speaker controls the order of revelation; disguise or anonymity is easy.<br><br>It's always your turn; speaker time is unlimited; you can't be interrupted. |
| Receiver (number, interests, third party, impression formation) | One or a few who are in your visual field.<br><br>Receivers are limited to those you have the opportunity to meet; finding people who have the same interests you do can be difficult, especially in isolated communities with little mobility.<br><br>Your messages can be overheard by or repeated to third parties, but not verbatim and not with complete accuracy.<br><br>Impressions are based on the verbal and nonverbal cues receiver perceives. | One, a few, or as many as you find in a chat room, have on your e-mail list, or can address via bulletin board posts.<br><br>Receivers are virtually unlimited; you can more easily and quickly find people who match your interests.<br><br>Your messages can be retrieved by others or forwarded verbatim to a third party or to hundreds of third parties (with or without your knowledge).<br><br>Impressions are based (usually) on text messages receiver reads. |
| Context (physical, temporal, social-psychological, cultural) | Where you both are; together in essentially the same physical space.<br><br>Context happens as it happens; you have little control over the context once you're in a communication situation.<br><br>Communication is synchronous—messages are exchanged at the same time. | Where you and receiver each want to be, separated in space.<br><br>You can more easily choose the timing—when you want to respond.<br><br>Communication may be synchronous, as in chat rooms and instant messaging, or asynchronous—when messages are exchanged at different times, as in e-mail and bulletin board postings. |
| Channel | Channels are auditory + visual + tactile + proxemic.<br><br>Two-way channel enables immediate interactivity. | Channel is visual for text (though both auditory and visual for graphics and video are available).<br><br>Two-way channels; some enable immediate and some delayed interactivity. |
| Messages (verbal/nonverbal messages; permanence, purposes) | Spoken words along with gestures, eye contact, accent, paralinguistic cues, space, smell, touch, clothing, hair, and all the other nonverbal cues.<br><br>Messages are temporary unless recorded; speech signals fade rapidly.<br><br>Rarely are abbreviations verbally expressed. | Written words in purely text-based CMC, though that's changing.<br><br>Messages are permanent unless erased.<br><br>Limited nonverbal cues; some can be created with emoticons or words and some (like smells and touch) cannot.<br><br>CMC uses lots of abbreviations. |

*(continued)*

| | | |
|---|---|---|
| Feedforward | Feedforward is conveyed nonverbally and verbally early in the interaction. | In e-mail it's given in the headings and subject line as well as in the opening sentences. |
| Feedback | Usually immediate, though this can be delayed; immediacy is usually expected. | In e-mail, newsgroup, and discussion list communication, feedback is usually and easily delayed; some delay is expected. In chat and instant messaging it is immediate. |
| Purposes and Effects | All purposes (to learn, to relate, to influence, to play, to help) can be achieved. All effects can be achieved. Some purposes may be easier to achieve in face-to-face interaction; for example, affection or support. | All purposes (to learn, to relate, to influence, to play, to help) can be achieved. All effects can be achieved. Some purposes may be easier to achieve in CMC; for example, information. |
| Noise | Noise in the context; articulation, pronunciation, and grammatical errors. Physiological, psychological, and semantic noise are usually present to some extent. | Noise in your own surroundings; spelling and grammatical errors. Physiological, psychological, and semantic noise are usually present to some extent. |
| Ethics and Deception | Presentation of false physical self is difficult but not impossible; false psychological and social selves are easier to present. Nonverbal leakage cues often give you away when you're lying. | Presentation of false physical self as well as false psychological and social selves is relatively easy. Lying is probably easier. |
| Competence (oral, written, technological) | Effective speaking techniques. Oral skills aid in interaction management, empathy, other-orientation, etc. | Effective writing techniques. Writing skills aid in interaction management, empathy, other-orientation, etc. Technological skills aid in use of media. |

competence is a measure of the quality of your intellectual and physical interpersonal performance (Almeida, 2004). Your competence includes, for example, the knowledge that in certain contexts and with certain listeners one topic is appropriate and another isn't. Your knowledge about the rules of nonverbal behavior—for example, the appropriateness of touching, vocal volume, and physical closeness—is also part of your competence. In short, interpersonal competence includes knowing how to adjust your communication according to the context of the interaction, the person with whom you're interacting, and a host of other factors discussed throughout this text.

You learn communication competence much as you learn to eat with a knife and fork— by observing others, by explicit instruction, by trial and error. Some individuals learn better than others, though, and these are generally the people with whom you find it interesting and comfortable to talk. They seem to know what to say and how and when to say it.

Not surprisingly, there's a positive relationship between interpersonal competence on the one hand and success in college and job satisfaction on the other (Rubin & Graham, 1988; Wertz, Sorenson, & Heeren, 1988). So much of college and professional life depends on interpersonal competence—meeting and interacting with other students, teachers, or colleagues; asking and answering questions; presenting information or argument—that you should not find this connection surprising. Interpersonal competence also enables you to develop and maintain meaningful relationships in friendship, love, family, and work.

Such relationships, in turn, contribute to the lower levels of anxiety, depression, and loneliness observed in interpersonally competent people (Spitzberg & Cupach, 1989).

##  AXIOMS OF INTERPERSONAL COMMUNICATION

Now that the nature of interpersonal communication and its elements are clear, we can explore some of the more specific axioms or principles that are common to all or most interpersonal encounters. These axioms are largely the work of the transactional researchers Paul Watzlawick, Janet Helmick Beavin, and Don D. Jackson, presented in their landmark *Pragmatics of Human Communication* (1967; Watzlawick 1977, 1978).

### Interpersonal Communication Is a Transactional Process

A **transactional perspective** views interpersonal communication as (1) a process with (2) elements that are *inter*dependent. Figure 1.3 visually explains this transactional view and distinguishes it from two earlier views of how interpersonal communication works.

**Interpersonal Communication Is a Process**   Interpersonal communication is best viewed as an ever-changing process. Everything involved in interpersonal communication is in a state of flux: you're changing, the people you communicate with are changing, and your environment is changing. Sometimes these changes go unnoticed and sometimes they intrude in obvious ways, but they're always occurring.

The process of communication is circular: One person's message serves as the stimulus for another's message, which serves as a stimulus for the other person's message, and so on. Throughout this circular process, each person serves simultaneously as a speaker *and* a listener, an actor *and* a reactor. Interpersonal communication is a mutually interactive process.

**Elements Are Interdependent**   The elements in interpersonal communication are *inter*dependent. Each element—each part of interpersonal communication—is intimately

# Understanding Interpersonal Theory and Research
## COMMUNICATION THEORIES AND RESEARCH

A **theory** is a generalization that explains how something works—for example, gravity, blood clotting, interpersonal attraction, or communication. Academic writers usually reserve the term *theory* to refer to a well-established system of knowledge about how things work or how things are related that is supported by research findings.

The theories you'll encounter in this book explain how communication works—for example, how you accommodate your speaking style to your listeners, how communication works when relationships deteriorate, or how people self-disclose. Despite their many values, theories don't reveal truth in any absolute sense. Rather, theories reveal some degree of accuracy, some degree of truth. In the natural sciences (such as physics and chemistry), theories are extremely high in accuracy. In the social and behavioral sciences (such as communication, sociology, and psychology), the theories are far less accurate in describing or in predicting how things work.

Communication theories often have practical implications for developing your own skills. For example, theories of interpersonal attraction offer practical insight into how to make yourself more attractive to others; theories of nonverbal communication will help you use and decipher nonverbal behaviors more accurately. The more you know about the theories and research explaining how communication works, the more likely you'll be able to use them to build your own communication skills.

### Working with Theories and Research

Log on to your favorite electronic database and browse through issues of *Quarterly Journal of Speech, Communication Monographs, Communication Theory,* or *Journal of Communication* (or scan similar journals in your own field of study). You'll be amazed at the breadth and depth of academic research and theory.

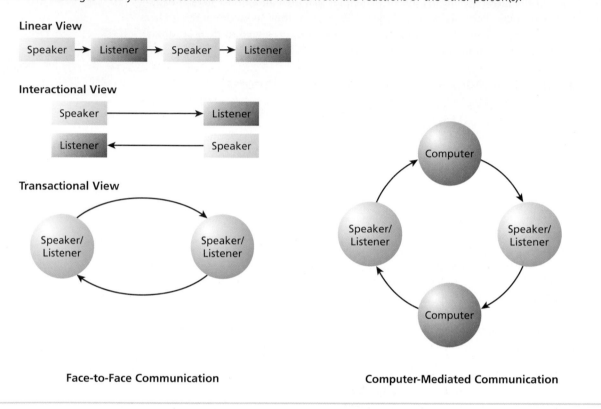

## FIGURE 1.3

### The Transactional View of Interpersonal Communication

The top figure represents a linear view of communication, in which the speaker speaks and the listener listens. The middle figure represents an interactional view, in which speaker and listener take turns speaking and listening; A speaks while B listens and then B speaks while A listens. The bottom figure represents a transactional view, in which each person serves simultaneously as speaker and listener; at the same time that you send messages, you also receive messages from your own communications as well as from the reactions of the other person(s).

**Linear View**

Speaker → Listener → Speaker → Listener

**Interactional View**

Speaker → Listener

Listener ← Speaker

**Transactional View**

Speaker/Listener ⟷ Speaker/Listener

Computer

Speaker/Listener

Speaker/Listener

Computer

**Face-to-Face Communication**          **Computer-Mediated Communication**

connected to the other parts and to the whole. For example, there can be no source without a receiver; there can be no message without a source; there can be no feedback without a receiver. Because of interdependency, a change in any one element causes changes in the others. For example, you're talking with a group of fellow students about a recent examination, and your teacher joins the group. This change in participants will lead to other changes—perhaps in the content of what you say, perhaps in the manner in which you express it. But regardless of what change is introduced, other changes result.

### Interpersonal Communication Is Ambiguous

An ambiguous message is a message that can be interpreted as having more than one meaning. Sometimes **ambiguity** occurs because people use words that can be interpreted differently. Informal time terms offer good examples; *soon, right away, in a minute, early, late,* and similar terms can easily be interpreted very differently by different people. The terms are ambiguous. A more interesting type of ambiguity is grammatical ambiguity. You can get a feel for this type of ambiguity by trying to paraphrase—rephrase in your own words—the following sentences:

- What has the cat in its paws?
- Visiting neighbors can be boring.
- They are frying chickens.

# Understanding Interpersonal Skills
## MINDFULNESS

**Mindfulness** is a state of mental awareness; in a mindful state you're conscious of your reasons for thinking or behaving in a particular way. Its opposite, **mindlessness,** is a lack of conscious awareness of your thinking or doing (Langer, 1989). To apply interpersonal skills appropriately and effectively, you need to be mindful of the unique communication situation you're in, of your available communication options, and of the reasons why one option is likely to prove better than the others (Langer, 1989; Elmes & Gemmill, 1990; Burgoon, Berger, & Waldron, 2000). You can look at this textbook and this course in interpersonal communication as means of awakening your mindfulness about the way you engage in interpersonal communication. After you complete this course and this text, you should be much more mindful about all your interpersonal interactions, and this heightened awareness will prove beneficial in your interpersonal communication and relationships (Carson, Carson, Gil, & Baucom, 2004; Sagula & Rice, 2004).

**Increasing Mindfulness.** To increase mindfulness, try the following suggestions (Langer, 1989):

- *Create and recreate categories.* Learn to see objects, events, and people as belonging to a wide variety of categories. Try to see, for example, your prospective romantic partner in a variety of roles—child, parent, employee, neighbor, friend, financial contributor, and so on. Avoid storing in memory an image of a person with only one specific label; if you do, you'll find it difficult to recategorize the person later.
- *Be open to new information and points of view,* even when these contradict your most firmly held stereotypes. New information forces you to reconsider what might be outmoded ways of thinking. New information can help you challenge long-held but now inappropriate beliefs and attitudes. Be willing to see your own and others' behaviors from a variety of viewpoints, especially the perspective of people very different from yourself.
- *Beware of relying too heavily on first impressions* (Chanowitz & Langer, 1981, Langer, 1989). Treat your first impressions as tentative—as hypotheses that need further investigation. Be prepared to revise, reject, or accept these initial impressions.
- *Think before you act.* Especially in delicate situations (e.g., when expressing anger or when conveying commitment messages), it's wise to pause and think over the situation mindfully (DeVito, 2003b). In this way you'll stand a better chance of acting and reacting appropriately.

Each of these ambiguous sentences can be interpreted and paraphrased in at least two different ways:

- What monster has the cat in its paws? What does the cat have in its paws?
- To visit neighbors is boring. Neighbors who visit are boring.
- Those people are frying chickens. Those chickens are for frying.

Although these examples are particularly striking—and are the work of linguists who analyze language—some degree of ambiguity exists in all interpersonal communication: All messages are ambiguous to some degree. When you express an idea you never communicate your meaning exactly and totally; rather, you communicate your meaning with some reasonable accuracy—enough to give the other person a reasonably clear idea of what you mean. Sometimes, of course, you're less accurate than you anticipated. Perhaps your listener "gets the wrong idea" or "gets offended" when you only meant to be humorous, or the listener "misunderstands your emotional meaning." Because of this inevitable uncertainty, you may qualify what you're saying, give an example, or ask, "Do you know what I mean?" These additional explanations help the other person understand your meaning and reduce uncertainty (to some degree).

## ASK Yourself
### Reducing Relationship Ambiguity

You've gone out with someone for several months and want to know where this relationship is going. You need to reduce your ambiguity about the future of the relationship and discover your partner's level of commitment. But you don't want to scare your partner. Ask yourself: What are some things you can say or do to find answers to your very legitimate questions?

Similarly, all relationships contain uncertainty. Consider your own close interpersonal relationships and ask yourself the following questions. Answer using a six-point scale with "1" meaning completely or almost completely uncertain to "6" meaning completely or almost completely certain. How certain are you about

❶ What you can or cannot say to each other in this relationship?
❷ Whether or not you and your partner feel the same way about each other?
❸ How you and your partner would describe this relationship?
❹ The future of the relationship?

It's very likely that you were not able to respond with 6s for all four questions, and equally likely that the same would be true for your relationship partner. These questions—adapted from a relationship uncertainty scale (Knoblock & Solomon, 1999)—and similar others illustrate that you probably experience some degree of uncertainty about the norms that govern your relationship communication (question 1), the degree to which you and your partner see the relationship in similar ways (question 2), the definition of the relationship (question 3), and the relationship's future (question 4).

The skills of interpersonal communication presented throughout this text may be looked at as means for appropriately reducing ambiguity and making your meaning as unambiguous as possible.

## Interpersonal Relationships May Be Symmetrical or Complementary

Interpersonal relationships can be described as either symmetrical or complementary (Bateson, 1972; Watzlawick, Beavin, & Jackson, 1967). In a **symmetrical relationship,** the two individuals mirror each other's behavior (Bateson, 1972). If one member nags, the other member responds in kind. If one member is passionate, the other member is passionate. If one member expresses jealousy, the other member also expresses jealousy. If one member is passive, so is the other. The relationship is one of equality, with the emphasis on minimizing the differences between the two individuals.

Note, however, the problems that can arise in this type of relationship. Consider the situation of a couple in which both members are very aggressive. The aggressiveness of one person fosters aggressiveness in the other, which fosters increased aggressiveness in the first individual. As this cycle escalates, the aggressiveness can no longer be contained, and the relationship is consumed by the aggression.

In a **complementary relationship,** the two individuals engage in different behaviors. The behavior of one serves as the stimulus for the other's complementary behavior. In complementary relationships, the differences between the parties are maximized. The people occupy different positions, one superior and the other inferior, one passive and the other active, one strong and the other weak. At times, cultures establish such relationships—for example, the complementary relationship between teacher and student or between employer and employee.

Early marriages are likely to be complementary relationships in which each person tries to complete him- or herself. When such couples separate and form new relationships, these new ones are more likely to be symmetrical and involve a kind of reconfirmation of the partner's own identities (Prosky, 1992). Generally, research finds that complementary couples have a poorer marital adjustment level than do symmetrical couples (Main & Oliver, 1988; Holden, 1991).

**⬆ VIEWPOINT**

What kinds of relationship ambiguity do you think are most damaging to a relationship's stability? Are there kinds of ambiguities that you think would solidify or enhance a relationship? Are there differences between the ways men and women look at relationship ambiguity?

# Interpersonal Communication Refers to Content and Relationship

Messages may make reference to the real world; for example, to the events and objects you see before you. At the same time, however, they also refer to the relationship between the people communicating. For example, a judge may say to a lawyer, "See me in my chambers immediately." This simple message has both a content aspect, which refers to the behavioral response expected (namely, that the lawyer will see the judge immediately), and a relationship aspect, which says something about the relationship between the judge and the lawyer and, as a result of this relationship, about how the communication is to be dealt with. Even the use of the simple command shows that there is a status difference between the two parties. This difference can perhaps be seen most clearly if you imagine the command being made by the lawyer to the judge. Such a communication appears awkward and out of place because it violates the normal relationship between judge and lawyer.

In any two communications, the content dimension may be the same, but the relationship aspect may be different, or the relationship aspect may be the same and the content dimension different. For example, the judge could say to the lawyer, "You had better see me immediately" or "May I please see you as soon as possible?" In both cases, the content is essentially the same; that is, the message about the expected behavioral response is the same. But the relationship dimension is quite different. The first message signifies a definite superior–inferior relationship; the second signals a more equal relationship, one that shows respect for the lawyer.

Similarly, at times the content may be different but the relationship is essentially the same. For example, a daughter might say to her parents, "May I go away this weekend?" or "May I use the car tonight?" The content of the two questions is clearly very different, but the relationship dimension is essentially the same. It clearly reflects a superior–inferior relationship in which permission to do certain things must be secured.

The major implications of these content and relationship dimensions center on conflict and its effective resolution. Many problems between people result from failure to recognize the distinction between the **content and relationship dimensions** of communication. For example, consider the couple arguing because Pat made plans to study with friends during the weekend without first asking Chris if that would be all right. Probably both would agree that to study over the weekend is the right decision. Thus, the argument isn't primarily concerned with the content level. It centers on the relationship level; Chris expected to be consulted about plans for the weekend. Pat, in not doing so, rejected this definition of their relationship. Similar situations occur when one member of a couple buys something, makes dinner plans, or invites a guest to dinner without first asking the other person. Even though the other person might have agreed with the decision, the couple argues because of the message communicated on the relationship level.

Let me give you a personal example. My mother came to stay for a week at a summer place I had. On the first day, she swept the kitchen floor six times, although I repeatedly said that it didn't need sweeping, that I would be tracking in dirt and mud from outside, and that all her effort was just wasted. But she persisted, saying that the floor was dirty and should be swept. On the content level, we were talking about the value of sweeping the kitchen floor, but on the relationship level, we were talking about something quite different: we were each saying, "This is my house." When I realized this (although, I confess, only after considerable argument), I stopped complaining about sweeping a floor that didn't need sweeping. Not surprisingly, she stopped sweeping.

Consider the following interchange:

| Dialogue | Comments |
| --- | --- |
| *He:* I'm going bowling tomorrow. The guys at the plant are starting a team. | He focuses on the content and ignores any relationship implications of the message. |

### A S K Yourself
#### Strengthening Similarities

You're dating a person you really like, but you are both so different—in values, politics, religion, and just about everything else. In fact, you're almost direct opposites. But you enjoy each other more than you do anyone else. Ask yourself: What can you do to encourage greater similarity while not losing the excitement created by the differences?

| | |
|---|---|
| *She:* Why can't we ever do anything together? | She responds primarily on a relationship level, ignores the content implications of the message, and expresses her displeasure at being ignored in his decision. |
| *He:* We can do something together anytime; tomorrow's the day they're organizing the team. | Again, he focuses almost exclusively on the content. |

This example reflects research findings that men generally focus more on the content while women focus more on the relationship dimensions of communication (cf. Pearson, West, & Turner, 1995; Wood, 1994; Ivy & Backlund, 2000). Once you recognize this difference, you may be better able to remove a potential barrier to communication between the sexes by being sensitive to the orientation of the opposite sex. Here is essentially the same situation but with added sensitivity:

| *Dialogue* | *Comments* |
|---|---|
| *He:* The guys at the plant are organizing a bowling team. I'd sure like to be on the team. Would it be a problem if I went to the organizational meeting tomorrow? | Although focused on content, he is aware of the relationship dimensions of his message and includes both in his comments—by acknowledging their partnership, asking if there would be a problem, and expressing his desire rather than his decision. |
| *She:* That sounds great, but I was hoping we could do something together. | She focuses on the relationship dimension but also acknowledges his content orientation. Note, too, that she does not respond as though she has to defend her emphasis on relationship aspects. |
| *He:* How about your meeting me at Joe's Pizza, and we can have dinner after the organizational meeting? | He responds to the relationship aspect—without abandoning his desire to join the bowling team—and incorporates it. |
| *She:* That sounds great. I'm dying for pizza. | She responds to both messages, approving of his joining the team and their dinner date. |

Arguments over the content dimension are relatively easy to resolve. Generally, you can look up something in a book or ask someone what actually took place. It is relatively easy to verify disputed facts. Arguments on the relationship level, however, are much more difficult to resolve, in part because you may not recognize that the argument is in fact a relational one. Once you realize that, you can approach the dispute appropriately and deal with it directly.

## Interpersonal Communication Is a Series of Punctuated Events

Communication events are continuous transactions. There is no clear-cut beginning and no clear-cut end. As participants in or observers of the communication act, you segment this continuous stream of communication into smaller pieces. You label some of these pieces causes or stimuli and others effects or responses.

Consider an example. A married couple is in a restaurant. The husband is flirting with another woman, and the wife is talking to her sister on her cell phone. Both are scowling at each other and are obviously in a deep nonverbal argument. Recalling the situation later, the husband might observe that the wife talked on the phone, so he innocently flirted with

## → FIGURE 1.4

### Punctuation and the Sequence of Events

In the figure, (A) shows the actual sequence of events as a continuous series of actions with no specific beginning or end. Each action (phoning and flirting) stimulates another action, but no initial cause is identified. (B) shows the same sequence of events as seen by the wife. She sees the sequence as beginning with the husband's flirting and her phoning behavior as a response to that stimulus. (C) shows the same sequence of events from the husband's point of view. He sees the sequence as beginning with the wife's phoning and his flirting as a response to that stimulus. Try using this three-part figure, discussed in the text, to explain what might go on when a supervisor complains that workers are poorly trained for their jobs and when workers complain that supervisors don't know how to supervise.

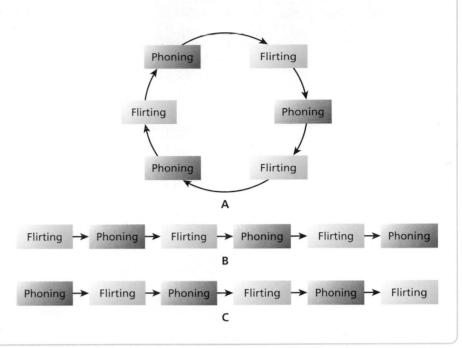

the other woman. The only reason for his behavior (he says) was his anger over her talking on the phone when they were supposed to be having dinner together. Notice that he sees his behavior as a response to her behavior. In recalling the same incident, the wife might say that she phoned her sister when he started flirting. The more he flirted, the longer she talked. She had no intention of calling anyone until he started flirting. To her, his behavior was the stimulus and hers was the response; he caused her behavior. Thus, the husband sees the sequence as going from phoning to flirting, and the wife sees it as going from flirting to phoning. This example is depicted visually in Figure 1.4 above and is supported by research which shows that, among marrieds at least, the individuals regularly see their partner's behavior as the cause of conflict (Schutz, 1999).

This tendency to divide communication transactions into sequences of stimuli and responses is referred to as **punctuation** (Watzlawick, Beavin, & Jackson, 1967). Everyone punctuates the continuous sequences of events into stimuli and responses for convenience. Moreover, as the example of the husband and wife illustrates, punctuation usually is done in ways that benefit the self and are consistent with a person's self-image.

Understanding how another person interprets a situation, how he or she punctuates, is a crucial step in interpersonal understanding. It is also essential in achieving empathy (feeling what the other person is feeling). In all communication encounters, but especially in conflicts, try to see how others punctuate the situation.

## Interpersonal Communication Is Inevitable, Irreversible, and Unrepeatable

Interpersonal communication cannot be prevented (is inevitable), cannot be reversed (is **irreversible**), and cannot be repeated (is unrepeatable). Let's look briefly at each of these qualities and their implications.

**Inevitability**     Often communication is thought of as intentional, purposeful, and consciously motivated. In many instances it is. But in other instances you're communicating even though you might not think you are or might not even want to be. Consider, for example, the new editorial assistant sitting at the desk with an "expressionless" face, perhaps staring out the window. Although this assistant might say that she or he is not communicating with the manager, the manager may derive any of a variety of messages from this behavior—for example, the assistant lacks interest, is bored, or is worried about something. In any event, the manager is receiving messages even though the assistant might not intend to communicate. In an interactional situation, all behavior is potentially communication. Any aspect of your behavior may communicate if the other person gives it message value. On the other hand, if the behavior (for example, the assistant's looking out the window) goes unnoticed, then no communication would have taken place (Watzlawick, Beavin, & Jackson, 1967; Motley, 1990a, 1990b; Bavelas, 1990; Beach, 1990).

Further, when you are in an interactional situation, your responses all have potential message value. For example, if you notice someone winking at you, you must respond in some way. Even if you don't respond openly, that lack of response is itself a response and it communicates (assuming it is perceived by the other person).

**Irreversibility**     The processes of some systems can be reversed. For example, you can turn water into ice and then reverse the process by melting the ice. Moreover, you can repeat this reversal of ice and water as many times as you wish. Other systems, however, are irreversible. In these systems, the process can move in only one direction; it cannot go back again. For example, you can turn grapes into wine, but you cannot reverse the process and turn the wine back into grapes.

Interpersonal communication is irreversible. What you have communicated remains communicated; you cannot *un*communicate. Although you may try to qualify, negate, or somehow reduce the effects of your message, once it has been sent and received, the message itself cannot be reversed. In interpersonal interactions (especially in conflict), you need to be especially careful that you don't say things you may wish to withdraw later. Similarly, commitment messages, such as "I love you," must be monitored lest you commit yourself to a position you may be uncomfortable with later.

Face-to-face communication is evanescent; it fades after you have spoken. There is no trace of your communications outside of the memories of the parties involved or of those who overheard your conversation. In computer-mediated communication, however, the messages are written and may be saved, stored, and printed. Both face-to-face and computer-mediated messages may be kept confidential or revealed publicly. But computer messages may be made public more easily and spread more quickly than face-to-face messages. Written messages provide clear evidence of what you have said and when you said it.

Because electronic communication often is permanent, you may wish to be cautious when employing it. E-mail messages probably are your most common form of computer communication, though the following cautions apply to all forms of electronic communication, including newsgroup postings and website messages:

- E-mails are difficult to destroy. Often e-mails you think you deleted will remain on servers and workstations and may be retrieved by a clever hacker.
- E-mails can easily be made public; the ease of forwarding e-mails to others or of posting your comments on websites makes it especially important to consider that what you intend for one person may actually be received by many.
- E-mails are not privileged communication and can easily be used against you, especially in the workplace. Criticism of others may one day be turned against you in accusations of discrimination.

- E-mails provide permanent records, making it impossible for you to say, for example, "That's not exactly what I said" because exactly what you said will be there in black and white.
- Personal e-mail files can be accessed by someone else—a nosy colleague at the next desk or a visiting neighbor—and then be sent to others.

**Unrepeatability**　In addition to being inevitable and irreversible, interpersonal communication is unrepeatable. The reason is simple: Everyone and everything is constantly changing. As a result, you can never recapture the exact same situation, frame of mind, or relationship dynamics that defined a previous interpersonal act. For example, you can never repeat the experience of meeting a particular person for the first time, comforting a grieving friend on the death of his or her mother, or resolving a specific conflict.

You can, of course, try again, as when you say, "I'm sorry I came off so forward; can we try again?" But notice that even when you say this, you don't erase the initial impression. Instead, you try to counteract the initial (and perhaps negative) impression by going through the motions once more. In doing so, you try to create a more positive impression, which you hope will lessen the original negative effect.

**A s к Yourself**
Lessening the Negative Impact

You write a gossipy e-mail about Ellen to your mutual friend Elle (revealing things about Ellen that you promised to keep secret) but inadvertently send the e-mail to Ellen herself.　Ask yourself:　What options do you have to correct this problem? What seems your best option?

## Reviewing　Key Terms and Concepts in Interpersonal Communication

This chapter introduced interpersonal communication, its importance, its elements, and some of its axioms or basic principles.

### The Importance of Interpersonal Communication

Why is interpersonal communication so important?

- It's crucial for the development and maintenance of interpersonal relationships.
- It's crucial for professional success and advancement.

### The Nature of Interpersonal Communication

What is interpersonal communication? At what point does communication become interpersonal?

- Interpersonal communication is communication between two or more connected individuals that involves dyadic primacy (the two-person unit is of central importance), dyadic coalitions (two-person groups form even in larger groups), and dyadic consciousness (the two persons think of themselves as a pair).
- Interpersonal communication can take place and interpersonal relationships can develop through face-to-face interactions as well as those you have on the Internet.
- Interpersonal communication serves a variety of purposes. It enables you to learn, relate, influence, play, and help.

### Elements of Interpersonal Communication

What are the essential elements of interpersonal communication?

- Source–receiver is the person who sends and receives interpersonal messages simultaneously.
- *Encoding–decoding* refers to the act of putting meaning into verbal and nonverbal messages and deriving meaning from the messages you receive from others.
- Messages are the signals that serve as stimuli for a receiver; metamessages are messages that refer to other messages.
  - Feedback messages are messages that are sent back by the receiver to the source in response to other messages.
  - Feedforward messages are messages that preface other messages and ask that the listener approach future messages in a certain way.
  - Message overload can hamper meaningful interaction.
- Channels are the media through which messages pass and which act as a bridge between source and receiver, for example, the vocal–auditory channel used in speaking or the cutaneous–tactile channel used in touch.
- Noise is the inevitable physical, physiological, psychological, and semantic interference that distorts a message.
- Context is the physical, social–psychological, temporal, and cultural environment in which communication takes place.
- Ethics is the moral dimension of communication, the study of what makes behavior moral or good as opposed to immoral and bad.
- Competence is the knowledge of and ability to use effectively your own communication system.

### Axioms of Interpersonal Communication

What general principles help explain what interpersonal communication is and how it works?

- Interpersonal communication is a transactional process.
  - Interpersonal communication is a process, an ongoing event, in which the elements are interdependent; communication is constantly occurring and changing.
  - Don't expect clear-cut beginnings or endings or sameness from one time to another.
- Interpersonal communication is ambiguous.
  - All messages are potentially ambiguous; different people will derive different meanings from the "same" message.
  - There is ambiguity in all relationships.
- Interpersonal relationships may be symmetrical or complementary.
  - Interpersonal interactions may stimulate similar or different behavior patterns, and relationships may be described as basically symmetrical or complementary.
  - Develop an awareness of symmetrical and complementary relationships.
- Interpersonal communication refers to content and relationship.

- All communications refer both to content and to the relationships between the participants.
  - Be aware of and respond to relationship messages as well as content messages.
- Interpersonal communication is a series of punctuated events.
  - Everyone separates communication sequences into stimuli and responses on the basis of his or her own perspective.
  - View punctuation as arbitrary, and adopt the other's point of view to increase empathy and understanding.
- Interpersonal communication is inevitable, irreversible, and unrepeatable.
  - When in an interactional situation, you cannot not communicate; you cannot uncommunicate; you cannot repeat exactly a specific message.
  - Seek to control as many aspects of your behavior as possible. In listening, seek out nonobvious messages. Beware of messages you may later wish to take back; for example, conflict and commitment messages.

## Applying Key Terms and Concepts in Interpersonal Communication

1 Can you identify any primary dyads in your extended family? What functions do these dyads serve?

2 How would you explain interpersonal communication or interpersonal relationships in terms of metaphors such as a seesaw, a ball game, a flower, ice skates, a microscope, a television sitcom, a work of art, a long book, a rubber band, or a software program?

3 What kinds of feedforward can you find in this book? What additional feedforward messages would you find useful in a textbook? In a lecture?

4 What characters in television sitcoms or dramas do you think demonstrate superior interpersonal competence?

What characters demonstrate obvious interpersonal incompetence?

5 How would you describe one of your interpersonal relationships in terms of symmetrical and complementary interactions? For example, is it a relationship defined by the differences or by the similarities between you? Is there equality between you, or is one of you superior? Are you dependent on each other or independent? Is the power shared, or is one person in control?

6 How would you describe the optimum level for relationship ambiguity? For example, would you want to be certain about everything? Be kept in the dark about certain things?

## Experiencing Key Terms and Concepts in Interpersonal Communication

Go to www.ablongman.com/devito.

*A variety of exercises will help you gain a deeper understanding of the concepts in this chapter and help you to apply this material to your own interpersonal interactions.*

❶ **Models of Interpersonal Communication** asks you to draw a model of interpersonal communication that will visualize and explain a specific interpersonal situation. ❷ **How Would You Give Feedback?** and ❸ **How Would You Give Feedforward?** provide practice in examining the types of feedback and feedforward you have available. ❹ **Ethics in Interpersonal Communication** asks you to consider what you feel is an ethical response in a variety of interpersonal situations. ❺ **How Can You Respond to Contradictory Messages?** looks at types of situations that may call for you to respond to contradictory meanings. ❻ **I'd Prefer to Be** is an icebreaker that will help you get to know others in the class and at the same time explore factors that can influence your interpersonal communication. ❼ **Applying the Axioms** and ❽ **Analyzing an Interaction** provide opportunities to examine how the axioms may be applied to actual interpersonal situations.

# Culture in Interpersonal Communication

⬆ *Hotel Rwanda* (2004)

*Hotel Rwanda* is the story of an attempted genocide by one cultural group, the Hutu, against another, the Tutsi, and of a hotel manager who fights to save as many Rwandans as he can. Although the film can be appreciated on many levels, one level clearly depicts the horrors that can result from a lack of cultural understanding and the absence of an appreciation for cultural diversity—some of the issues explored in this chapter.

> "Culture is communication, and communication is culture." —Edward T. Hall

A walk through any large city or through many small towns, through the schools and colleges, or into the business and manufacturing centers of the United States will convince you that this country is largely a collection of many different cultures. These cultures coexist somewhat separately but also with each influencing the others. This coexistence has led some researchers to refer to these cultures as cocultures (Schuter, 1990; Samovar & Porter, 2003, 2004; Jandt, 2004). Not surprisingly, culture has a significant impact on everyone and on just about every activity you might name. In this chapter we look at culture and its influence on interpersonal communication.

##  CULTURE AND INTERPERSONAL COMMUNICATION

Consider these facts (*The New York Times Almanac,* 2005; *The World Almanac and Book of Facts,* 2005):

The foreign-born population of the United States is increasing dramatically. In 1980 the foreign-born population was 14 million (about 6.2 percent of the total population), in 1990 it was 19.8 million (7.9 percent), and in 2000 it was 28.4 million (10.4 percent). Increasingly frequent communication in a multicultural context is inevitable.

In your more immediate environment, consider the number of foreign students who come to the United States to continue their education. For the years 2002–2003, according to the Institute of International Education (http://www.parstimes.com/news/archive/2003/washfile028.html, accessed February 8, 2005), there were 586,323 international students studying in the United States. The number of students from the top 10 countries, along with the percentage of increase or decrease from the previous year, were: India with 74,603 (up 12 percent), China with 64,757 (up 2 percent), South Korea with 51,519 (up 5 percent), Japan with 45,960 (down 2 percent), Taiwan with 28,017 (down 3 percent), Canada with 26,513 (unchanged), Mexico with 12,801 (up 2 percent), Turkey with 11,601 (down 4 percent), Indonesia with 10,432 (down 10 percent), and Thailand with 9,982 (down 14 percent). Students from the Middle East had declined the most—especially those from Saudia Arabia, Kuwait, and the United Arab Emirates—though the absolute numbers were still quite high: from 38,545 during the previous year to 34,803 for 2002–2003.

And if you're currently attending the University of Southern California, New York University, Columbia University, Purdue University, the University of Texas, or the University of Michigan, you're attending one of the six schools with the largest foreign student enrollment. In 2002–2003 there were 1,000 or more international students enrolled at each of 153 U.S. colleges and universities. And if you live in New York, Los Angeles, Boston, Washington D.C., Chicago, Philadelphia, San Jose, Houston, Dallas, or San Francisco, you're living in one of the 10 cities hosting the most international students. As you can see from even these few figures, frequent intercultural communication is an inevitable part of college life today.

Also, corporations in the United States are becoming more and more intercultural. Large and small corporations commonly announce that future growth will depend on expansion into foreign countries. U.S. manufacturing, media, information technology, and farming interests depend on foreign purchase. Business opportunities, therefore, have an increasingly international dimension, making cultural awareness and intercultural communication competence essential skills for professional success.

## The Nature of Culture

The word *culture* refers to the relatively specialized lifestyle of a group of people—consisting of their values, beliefs, artifacts, ways of behaving, and ways of communicating. Included in culture would be all that members of a social group have produced and developed—their language, modes of thinking, art, laws, and religion.

Culture is not synonymous with race or nationality. However, members of a particular race or country are often taught similar beliefs, attitudes, and values. This similarity makes it possible to speak of "Hispanic culture" or "African American culture." But, lest we be guilty of stereotyping, recognize that within any large culture—especially a culture based on race or nationality—there will be enormous differences. The Kansas farmer and the Wall Street executive may both be, say, German American, but they may differ widely in their attitudes and beliefs and in their general lifestyles. In some ways the Kansas farmer may be closer in attitudes and values to the Chinese farmer than to the Philadelphia lawyer.

Gender—although transmitted genetically and not by communication—is considered a cultural variable, largely because cultures teach boys and girls different attitudes, beliefs, values, and ways of communicating and relating to one another (Payne, 2001). You act like a man or a woman in part because of what your culture has taught you about how men and women should act. Further, you can view male–female communication as cross-cultural because of the numerous differences in the way men and women speak and listen (Eckstein & Goldman, 2001).

Culture is passed on from one generation to the next through communication, not through genes. Thus, the word *culture* does not refer to color of skin or shape of eyes. *Culture* does refer to beliefs in a supreme being, to attitudes toward success and happiness, and to the values placed on friendship, love, family, or money, since these are transmitted through communication.

**Enculturation** Culture is transmitted from one generation to another through **enculturation**, a process by which you learn the culture into which you're born (your native culture). Parents, peer groups, schools, religious institutions, and government agencies are the main teachers of culture. One instrument for spreading culture is of course the Internet. Because the Internet, although worldwide, is so dominated by the United States and by the English language and idiom, the culture of the Internet is dominated by the culture of the United States.

**Ethnic Identity** Through enculturation you develop an ethnic identity, a commitment to the beliefs and philosophy of your culture that, not surprisingly, can act as a protective shield against discrimination (Chung & Ting-Toomey, 1999; R. M. Lee, 2005). The degree to which you identify with your cultural group can be measured by your responses to questions such as the following (from Ting-Toomey, 1981).

Using a five-point scale with "1" meaning strongly disagree and "5" meaning strongly agree, indicate how true of you these statements are:

1. I am increasing my involvement in activities with my ethnic group.
2. I involve myself in causes that will help members of my ethnic group.
3. It feels natural being part of my ethnic group.
4. I have spent time trying to find out more about my own ethnic group.
5. I am happy to be a member of my ethnic group.
6. I have a strong sense of belonging to my ethnic group.
7. I often talk to other members of my group to learn more about my ethnic culture.

High scores (say 4s and 5s) indicate a strong commitment to your culture's values and beliefs; low numbers (1s and 2s) indicate a relatively weak commitment.

# Understanding Interpersonal Theory and Research

## THEORIES ABOUT CULTURE

Consider two theories of culture: cultural evolution and cultural relativism.

*Cultural evolution* (often called social Darwinism) holds that much as the human species evolved from earlier life forms to Homo sapiens, cultures also evolve. Consequently, some cultures may be considered advanced and others primitive. Most contemporary scholars reject this view, however, because the judgments that distinguish one culture from another have no basis in science and are instead based on individual values and preferences.

*Cultural relativism*, on the other hand, holds that all cultures are different but that no culture is either superior or inferior to any other (Berry, Poortinga, Segall, & Dasen, 1992). Today cultural relativism is generally accepted, and this view guides the infusion of cultural materials into contemporary textbooks on all academic levels (Jandt, 2004). But this position does not imply that all cultural practices are therefore equal or that you have to accept all cultural practices equally. There are many cultural practices popular throughout the world that you may find, quite logically and reasonably, unacceptable.

### Working with Theories and Research

Look up "culture" using your favorite electronic database. What can you add to the discussion in this chapter?

**Acculturation**   A different process of learning culture is **acculturation,** the process by which you learn the rules and norms of a culture different from your native culture (Chun, Organista & Marin, 2003). Through acculturation, your original or native culture is modified by direct contact with (or exposure to) a new and different culture. For example, when immigrants settle in the United States, the host country, their own culture becomes influenced by the host culture. Gradually, the values, ways of behaving, and beliefs of the host culture become more and more a part of the immigrants' culture. At the same time, the host culture changes as it interacts with the immigrants' culture. Generally, however, the culture of the immigrant changes more. The reasons for this are that the host country's members far outnumber the immigrant group, and the media are largely dominated by and reflect the values and customs of the host culture.

**Cultural Beliefs and Values**   Before exploring further the role of culture in communication, consider your own cultural values and beliefs by taking the accompanying self-test. This test will suggest how your own cultural values and beliefs might influence the messages you send and the messages you listen to in your interpersonal communication.

## TEST YOURSELF

### WHAT ARE YOUR CULTURAL BELIEFS AND VALUES?

The extremes of different cultural attitudes on six topics are identified below. For each topic indicate your own values. If your values are *very* similar to the extremes, select 1 or 7. If your values are *quite* similar to the extremes, select 2 or 6. If your values are *fairly* similar to the extremes, select 3 or 5. If you're in the middle, select 4.

| Men and women are equal and are entitled to equality in all areas. | **Gender Equality**<br>1 2 3 4 5 6 7 | Men and women should stick to their specific and different cultural roles. |
|---|---|---|
| Religion is the final arbiter of what is right and wrong; your obligation is to abide by your religion's rules. | **Religion**<br>1 2 3 4 5 6 7 | Religion is like any other social institution; it's not inherently moral or right just because it's a religion. |

| | | |
|---|---|---|
| Your first obligation is to your family; each person is responsible for the welfare of her or his family. | **Family**<br>1 2 3 4 5 6 7 | Your first obligation is to yourself; each person is responsible for her- or himself. |
| Work hard now for a better future. | **Time Orientation**<br>1 2 3 4 5 6 7 | Live in the present; the future may never come. |
| Money should be a major consideration in just about any decision you make. | **Money**<br>1 2 3 4 5 6 7 | Money should not enter into life's really important decisions such as what relationship to enter or what career to pursue. |
| The world is just; bad things happen to bad people and good things happen to good people. | **Belief in a<br>Just World**<br>1 2 3 4 5 6 7 | The world is random; bad and good things happen to people without reference to whether they're good or bad. |

**HOW DID YOU DO?** As demonstrated throughout this text and as research shows, your cultural values and beliefs influence your interpersonal communications as well as your decision making, your assessments of coworkers, your approach to teamwork, your level of trust in others, the importance you place on diversity in the workplace, and your attitudes toward the role of women in the workplace (Stephens & Greer, 1995; Bochner & Hesketh, 1994). For example, your beliefs and values about gender equality will influence the way in which you communicate with and about the opposite sex. Your beliefs about family will influence how you interact with family members.

**WHAT WILL YOU DO?** There are no right or wrong answers to this test. What makes this particular test of value for our purposes is that it asks you to examine your own cultural values and beliefs and hopefully stimulates you to go the next step and ask yourself how these values and beliefs influence your interpersonal communication. As you review your feelings about the six topics, try to identify at least one specific way in which your attitudes on each topic named in the self-test influence your interpersonal communication.

## The Relevance of Culture

There are lots of reasons for the cultural emphasis you'll find in this book.

**Demographic Changes** Among the reasons are demographic changes, sensitivity to cultural differences, economic and political interdependence, the spread of technology, and the culture-specific nature of interpersonal communication. Most obvious, perhaps, are the vast demographic changes taking place throughout the United States. Whereas at one time the United States was a country largely populated by Europeans, it's now a country greatly influenced by the enormous number of new citizens from Latin and South America, Africa, and Asia. Along with the aforementioned demographic shift so noticeable on college campuses, these changes have brought different interpersonal customs and the need to understand and adapt to new ways of looking at communication.

**Sensitivity to Cultural Differences** As a people we've become increasingly sensitive to cultural differences. American society has moved from an assimilationist attitude (people should leave their native culture behind and adapt to their new culture) to a perspective that values cultural diversity (people should retain their native cultural ways). With some notable exceptions—hate speech, racism, sexism, homophobia, and classism come quickly to mind—we are more concerned with saying the right thing and ultimately with developing a society where all cultures can coexist and enrich one another. The ability to interact effectively with members of other cultures often translates into financial gain and increased employment opportunities and advancement prospects as well.

# Ethics in Interpersonal Communication

## CULTURE AND ETHICS

One of the most shocking revelations to come to world attention after the events of September 11, 2001, was the way in which women were treated under Taliban rule in Afghanistan: Females could not be educated or even go out in public without a male relative escort, and when in public had to wear garments that covered their entire body.

Throughout history there have been cultural practices that today would be judged unethical. Sacrificing virgins to the gods, burning people who held different religious beliefs, and sending children to fight religious wars are obvious examples. But even today there are practices woven deep into the fabric of different cultures that you might find unethical. A few examples:

- bronco riding and bullfighting, practices involving inflicting pain and even causing the death of horses and bulls
- "female circumcision," whereby part or all of a young girl's genitals are surgically altered so that she can never experience sexual intercourse without extreme pain, a practice designed to keep her a virgin until marriage
- the belief and practice that a woman must be subservient to her husband's will
- the practice of wearing fur—which in some cases means killing wild animals and in others raising animals so they can be killed when their pelts are worth the most money

### What would you do?

You're talking with new work colleagues, and one of the above-mentioned practices is discussed with approval; your colleagues argue that each culture has a right to its own practices and beliefs. Given your own beliefs about these issues and about cultural diversity, what ethical obligations do you have to speak your mind without—you hope—jeopardizing your new position?

**Economic and Political Interdependence**  Today, most countries are economically dependent on one another. Our economic lives depend on our ability to communicate effectively across different cultures. Similarly, our political well-being depends in great part on that of other cultures. Political unrest in any part of the world—South Africa, Eastern Europe, Asia, and the Middle East, to take a few examples—affects our own security. Intercultural communication and understanding seem more crucial now than ever.

**Spread of Technology**  The rapid spread of technology has made intercultural communication as easy as it is inevitable. News from foreign countries is commonplace. You see nightly—in vivid detail—what is going on in remote countries, just as you see what's happening in your own city and state. Of course, the Internet has made intercultural communication as easy as writing a note on your computer. You can now communicate just as easily by e-mail with someone in Asia or Europe, for example, as you can with someone in another U.S. city or state (see Table 2.1).

**Culture-Specific Nature of Interpersonal Communication**  Still another reason culture is so important is that interpersonal competence is culture specific; what proves effective in one culture may prove ineffective in another. Many Asians, for example, often find that the values they were taught—values that promote cooperation and face-saving but discourage competitiveness and assertiveness—work against them in cultures that value competition and outspokenness (Cho, 2000). In another example, in the United States corporate executives get down to business during the first several minutes of a meeting. In Japan business executives interact socially for an extended period and try to find out something about one another. Thus, the communication principle influenced by U.S. culture would advise participants to get down to the meeting's agenda during the first five minutes. The principle influenced by Japanese culture would advise participants

### A S K Yourself

Putting Your Foot in Your Mouth

At work you tell a race-oriented joke, only to discover later that it has been resented and clearly violated the organizational norms for polite and unbiased talk.  Ask yourself:  What might you say to make this situation a little less awkward and less potentially damaging to your work experience?

## ⏺ TABLE 2.1
### Internet Usage by Country

The top 10 Internet-using countries appear here. In what ways do you think the numbers shown will change over the next several years?

| Country | Internet Users | Total Population | Percentage of Total Population |
| --- | --- | --- | --- |
| United States | 160,700,000 | 293,023,000 | 55 percent |
| Japan | 64,800,000 | 127,333,000 | 51 |
| China | 54,500,000 | 1,299,848,000 | 4 |
| Germany | 30,350,000 | 82,425,000 | 37 |
| United Kingdom | 27,150,000 | 60,271,000 | 45 |
| South Korea | 26,900,000 | 48,598,000 | 55 |
| Italy | 20,850,000 | 58,057,000 | 36 |
| Canada | 17,830,000 | 32,508,000 | 55 |
| France | 16,650,000 | 60,424,000 | 28 |
| India | 16,580,000 | 1,065,071,000 | 2 |

*Sources:* Figures for the number of Internet users are from *Time Almanac with Information Please,* 2005, p. 567; figures for total population are from *The World Almanac and Book of Facts,* 2005, pp. 848–849.

to avoid dealing with business until everyone has socialized sufficiently and feels well enough acquainted to begin negotiations. A third example: Giving a birthday gift to a close friend would be appreciated by many; but Jehovah's Witnesses would frown on this act, because they don't celebrate birthdays (Dresser, 1996). Neither principle is right, and neither is wrong. Each is effective within its own culture and ineffective outside its own culture.

## The Aim of a Cultural Perspective

Because culture permeates all forms of communication, it's necessary to understand its influences if you're to understand how communication works and master its skills. As illustrated throughout this text, culture influences communications of all types (Moon, 1996). It influences what you say to yourself and how you talk with friends, lovers, and family in everyday conversation (for example, Shibazaki & Brennan, 1998). It influences how you interact in groups and how much importance you place on the group versus the individual. It influences the topics you talk about and the strategies you use in communicating information or in persuading. It influences how you use the media and the credibility you attribute to them.

A cultural emphasis helps distinguish what is universal (true for all people) from what is relative (true for people in one culture and not true for people in other cultures) (Matsumoto, 1994). The principles for communicating information and for changing listeners' attitudes, for example, will vary from one culture to another. If you're to understand communication, then you need to know how its principles vary and how the principles must be qualified and adjusted on the basis of cultural differences.

A good example is that of age. If you were raised in the United States, you probably grew up with a youth bias (young is good, old is not so good)—an attitude the media reinforce daily—and might well assume that this preference for youth would be universal across all cultures. But it isn't; and if you assume it is, you may be in for intercultural difficulties. A good example is the case of the American journalist in China who remarked that the government official he was talking with was probably too young to remember a particular

### THE IMPORTANCE OF CULTURE IN INTERPERSONAL COMMUNICATION

**?** Culture seems to be a part of all my college courses. But I wonder: Is culture and intercultural communication that important today? Is this knowledge going to help me be more successful in my profession, whatever that will be?

Globalization has made the world more, not less complex, offering us many opportunities to interact with people of other cultures at home and abroad. Intercultural communication engages us at the individual and relational level. Our sense of efficacy in interaction depends to a large degree upon our training, knowledge, and willingness to be open to other cultures. This is the individual level; one may call it self-preparation for interaction. At the relational level we may be engaged in intercultural communication in several dimensions: advocacy, conversation, implementation of programs, deliberation, participation, presentation, and organization.

Knowledge of other cultures is fundamental to understanding how the world functions at the macro level. The more you build your capacity to engage different cultures, the greater your opportunity for success in your profession in the twenty-first century. Openness and humility are the keys to an effective interaction with others in your profession and in life.

**For more information** see Molefi Kete Asante, *Rhetoric, Race and Identity: The Architecton of Soul* (Amherst, MA: Prometheus Books, 2005) and Robert Shuter, "The Cultures of Rhetoric," in A Gonzales and D. Tanno (eds.), *Rhetoric in Intercultural Contexts* (Thousand Oaks, CA: Sage, 2000), pp. 11–17.

Molefi Kete Asante (Ph.D., University of California, Los Angeles) is Professor of Africana Studies at Temple University and the editor of the *Handbook of International and Intercultural Communication*. Dr. Asante is an international consultant on intercultural and international issues and the author of 60 books on culture and communication, including *Erasing Racism: The Survival of the American Nation* (Amherst, MA: Prometheus Books, 2003).

### ↑ VIEWPOINT

How would you describe the cultural makeup of your campus and your city? How would you describe intercultural communication on your campus and in your city?

event, a comment that would be taken as a compliment by most youth-oriented Americans. But to the Chinese official the comment appeared to be an insult, a suggestion that the official was too young to deserve respect (Smith, 2002).

This cultural understanding is needed to communicate effectively in the wide variety of intercultural situations. Success in interpersonal communication—at your job and in your social and personal life—will depend in great part on your understanding of and your ability to communicate effectively with persons who are culturally different from yourself. Daily the media bombard you with evidence of racial tensions; religious disagreements; sexual bias; and, in general, the problems caused when intercultural communication fails.

This emphasis on culture does not imply that you should accept all cultural practices or that all cultural practices are equal (Hatfield & Rapson, 1996). Consider this case in point (*Time*, December 2, 1993, p. 61). Assume you're a judge and the following case is presented to you: A Chinese immigrant killed his wife in New York because he suspected her of cheating. A "cultural defense" was offered, essentially claiming that infidelity so shames a man that he is uncontrollable in his anger. Would this cultural defense have influenced your judgment? In the actual case, influenced by an anthropologist's testimony that infidelity is so serious in Chinese culture that it pushed the defendant to commit the crime, the judge sentenced the defendant to five years' probation.

Further, a cultural emphasis does not imply that you have to accept or follow all of the practices of your own culture. For example, even if the majority in your culture find cockfighting acceptable, you need not agree with or follow the practice. Nor need you consider this practice equal to a cultural practice in which animals are treated kindly. You can reject capitalism or communism or socialism regardless of the culture in which you were raised. Of course, going against your culture's traditions and values is often very difficult. But it's important to realize that culture influences, it does not determine, your values or behavior. Often personality factors (your degree of assertiveness, extroversion, or optimism, for example) will prove more influential than culture (Hatfield & Rapson, 1996).

As demonstrated throughout this text, cultural differences exist throughout the interpersonal communication spectrum—from the way you use eye contact to the way you develop or dissolve a relationship (Chang & Holt, 1996). Culture even influences your level of happiness, which in turn influences your attitudes and the positivity and negativity of your messages (Kirn, 2005). But these should not blind you to the great number of similarities existing among even the most widely separated cultures. When discussing differences, remember that these are usually questions of degree rather than all-or-none. For example, most cultures value honesty, but some cultures give it greater emphasis than others. In addition, advances in media and technology and the widespread use of the Internet are influencing cultures and cultural change and are perhaps homogenizing different cultures to some extent, lessening differences and increasing similarities.

> **A s k Yourself**
> Misusing Linguistic Privilege
>
> You enter a group of racially similar people who are using terms normally considered offensive to refer to themselves. Trying to be one of the group, you too use such terms—but are met with extremely negative nonverbal feedback. Ask yourself: What are some things you might say to lessen this negative reaction and to let the group know that you don't normally use such racial terms?

# InterMedia

## CULTURAL IMPERIALISM

The term *Cultural imperialism* refers to a process whereby business and political practices, but especially media products, are exported to other cultures and come to extend the influence of the exporting culture over that of the importing culture. The theory argues that the media from developed countries such as the United States and western Europe have come to dominate the cultures of countries importing such media and at the same time to denigrate the customs and values of less technologically sophisticated local cultures (Folkerts & Lacy, 2005).

Media products from the United States are likely to emphasize this country's dominant attitudes and values; for example, our preference for competition, our emphasis on individuality, and our beliefs in capitalism and democracy. When American media products—movies, television programs, and music, for example—are consumed by other cultures, the values and attitudes embedded in these products can quickly become the values and attitudes of these other cultures.

Television programs, films, and music from the United States and western Europe are so popular and so in demand in developing countries that they may actually inhibit the growth of indigenous cultures' own talent. To combat this trend some countries (Canada, France, Taiwan, and South Korea among them) have imposed restrictions on the amount of U.S. television programming that can be imported (Rodman, 2001).

> **Follow Up**
>
> What do you think of the influence that media from the United States and western Europe are exerting on cultures throughout the world? How do you evaluate that influence? Do you see advantages? Disadvantages?

You'll see the cultural emphasis in this text in two ways. First, this chapter focuses on the role of culture in interpersonal communication, the ways cultures differ, and intercultural communication—especially the principles for increasing intercultural communication effectiveness. Second, cultural issues are integrated throughout the text as they relate to the topic being discussed. For example, when discussing self-disclosure or the meanings of nonverbal gestures, we also consider how different cultures view these forms of communication.

##  HOW CULTURES DIFFER

Cultures, of course, differ in a wide variety of ways; and for purposes of communication, the difference that probably comes to mind first is that of languages. Certainly, cultures do differ in the languages spoken and understood. In fact, one of the most popular theories in intercultural communication, the language relativity hypothesis, argued that the language you speak influences your thoughts and behaviors and that because cultures differ so widely in their languages, they also will differ in their ways of thinking and behaving.

Subsequent research and theory, however, did not support the extreme claims made by linguistic relativity researchers (cf. Pinker, 1994; Niemeier & Dirven, 2000; Durst, 2003). A more modified hypothesis is currently supported: The language you speak helps to *highlight* what you see and how you talk about it. For example, if you speak a language that is rich in color terms (English is a good example), you will find it easier to highlight and talk about nuances of color than will someone from a culture that has fewer color terms (some cultures distinguish only two or three or four parts of the color spectrum). This does not mean, however, that people *see* the world differently; only that their language helps (or doesn't help) them to focus on certain variations in nature and makes it easier (or more difficult) to talk about them. Nor does it mean that people speaking widely differing languages are doomed to misunderstanding each other. Translation enables us to understand a great deal of the meaning in a foreign-language message. We also have a ready arsenal of communication skills, which you'll encounter throughout this course, that can help bridge the communication gap between members of different cultures.

Language differences are not the only differences between cultures that will influence intercultural communication. Let's take a look at five such differences: power distances, masculine and feminine orientation, collectivism and individualism, high and low context, and time orientations (Gudykunst, 1991; Hall & Hall, 1987; Hofstede, 1997). As you review these differences, recognize that they are matters of degree. Characteristics aren't necessarily present in one culture and absent in the other; rather they're present in both but to different degrees. And that's what this discussion focuses on: degrees of differences, not absolute differences.

### Power Distances

In some cultures power is concentrated in the hands of a few, and there is a great difference in the power held by these people and that held by the ordinary citizen. These are called high-power-distance cultures; examples are Mexico, Brazil, India, and the Philippines (Hofstede, 1983, 1997). In low-power-distance cultures, power is more evenly distributed throughout the citizenry; examples include Denmark, New Zealand, Sweden, and to a lesser extent the United States. These differences affect interpersonal communication and relationships in a variety of ways.

Friendship and dating relationships will be influenced by the power distance between groups (Andersen, 1991). For example, in India (high power distance), friendships and romantic relationships are expected to take place within your cultural class; in Sweden (low power distance), a person is expected to select friends and romantic partners not on the basis of class or culture, but on individual factors such as personality, appearance, and the like.

In low-power-distance cultures there is a general feeling of equality that is consistent with acting assertively, and so you're expected to confront a friend, partner, or supervisor as-

sertively (Borden, 1991). In high-power-distance cultures, direct confrontation and assertiveness may be viewed negatively, especially if directed at a superior (Morrison, Chen, & Salgado, 2004).

In high-power-distance cultures you're taught to have great respect for authority; people in these cultures see authority as desirable and beneficial, and challenges to authority are generally not welcomed (Westwood, Tang, & Kirkbride, 1992; Bochner & Hesketh, 1994). For example, in one study Asian adolescents (high-power-distance culture) had greater difficulty discussing problems with their parents than did Caucasians (low-power-distance culture) (Rhee, Chang, & Rhee, 2003). In low-power-distance cultures, there's a certain distrust for authority; it's seen as a kind of necessary evil that should be limited as much as possible. This difference in attitudes toward authority can be seen right in the classroom. In high-power-distance cultures there's a great power distance between students and teachers; students are expected to be modest, polite, and totally respectful. In low-power-distance cultures students are expected to demonstrate their knowledge and command of the subject matter, participate in discussions with the teacher, and even challenge the teacher, something many high-power-distance culture members wouldn't even think of doing. The same is true for parents and their children's teachers; parents from high-power-distance cultures would be reluctant to question or even imply that they were questioning a teacher's decisions. A teacher who comes from a low-power-distance culture may see this parental behavior as a reluctance to get involved or as a lack of interest (Gibbs, 2005). The same differences can be seen in patient–doctor communication. Patients from high-power-distance cultures are less likely to challenge their doctors or admit that they don't understand the medical terminology than would patients in low-power-distance cultures.

High-power-distance cultures rely more on symbols of power. For example, titles (Dr., Professor, Chef, Inspector) are more important in high-power-distance cultures. Failure to include these in forms of address is a serious breach of etiquette. Low-power-distance cultures rely less on symbols of power, and less of a problem is created if you fail to use a respectful title (Victor, 1992). But even in low-power-distance cultures you may create problems if, for example, you call a medical doctor, police captain, military officer, or professor Ms. or Mr.

In the United States, two people quickly move from Title plus Last Name (Mr. or Ms. Smith) to First Name (Pat). In low-power-distance cultures less of a problem is created if you're too informal or if you presume to exchange first names before sufficient interaction has taken place. In high-power-distance cultures too great an informality—especially between those differing greatly in power—would be a serious breach of etiquette. Again, in even the lowest power-distance culture, you may still create problems if you call your English professor Pat.

Because the Internet and its information are available to vast numbers of people—not just to those in positions of power—it's been argued that power distances, especially in organizations, will change in the direction of becoming more egalitarian. Others have argued that this will not happen, simply because the hierarchical structure of most organizations serves them well; it's efficient and it encourages workers to climb the organizational ladder (Leavitt, 2005).

## Masculine And Feminine Cultures

A popular classification of cultures is in terms of their masculinity and femininity (Hofstede, 1997, 1998, 2000; Imwalle & Schillo, 2004). When denoting cultural orientations, the terms "masculine" and "feminine" should not be taken as perpetuating **stereotypes**, but as a reflection of some of the commonly held assumptions of a sizable number of people throughout the world. In a highly "masculine" culture men are viewed as assertive, oriented to material success, and strong; women on the other hand are viewed as modest, focused on the quality of life, and tender. In a highly "feminine" culture, both men and women are encouraged to be modest, oriented to maintaining the quality of life, and tender. The 10 countries with the highest masculinity score (beginning with the highest) are Japan, Austria, Venezuela, Italy, Switzerland, Mexico, Ireland, Jamaica, Great Britain, and Germany. The 10 countries with the highest femininity score (beginning with the highest) are Sweden, Norway, Netherlands, Denmark, Costa Rica, Yugoslavia, Finland, Chile, Portugal, and Thailand. Out of 53 countries ranked, the United States ranks 15th most masculine (Hofstede, 1997).

**Masculine cultures** emphasize success and socialize their people to be assertive, ambitious, and competitive. Members of masculine cultures are thus more likely to confront conflicts directly and to competitively fight out any differences; they're more likely to emphasize win–lose conflict strategies. **Feminine cultures** emphasize the quality of life and socialize their people to be modest and to emphasize close interpersonal relationships. Members of feminine cultures are thus more likely to emphasize compromise and negotiation in resolving conflicts; they're more likely to seek win–win solutions. Not surprisingly, people in feminine nations score significantly lower on depression levels (Arrindell, Steptoe, & Wardle, 2003).

Organizations also can be viewed in terms of masculinity or femininity. Masculine organizations emphasize competitiveness and aggressiveness. They focus on the bottom line and reward their workers on the basis of their contribution to the organization. Feminine organizations are less competitive and less aggressive. They're more likely to emphasize worker satisfaction and reward their workers on the basis of need; those who have large families, for example, may get better raises than the single people, even if the singles have contributed more to the organization.

## Individual and Collective Orientation

Cultures differ in the extent to which they promote individual values (for example, power, achievement, hedonism, and stimulation) versus collectivist values (for example, benevolence, tradition, and conformity). The countries with the highest individualist orientation (beginning with the highest) are the United States, Australia, Great Britain, Canada, Netherlands, New Zealand, Italy, Belgium, Denmark, Sweden, France, and Ireland. Countries with the highest collectivist orientation (beginning with the highest) are Guatemala, Ecuador, Panama, Venezuela, Colombia, Indonesia, Pakistan, Costa Rica, Peru, Taiwan, and South Korea (Hofstede, 1983, 1997; Hatfield & Rapson, 1996; Kapoor, Wolfe, & Blue, 1995). For the most part the individualist countries are wealthy and the collectivist countries are poor, but there are a few notable exceptions. For example, Japan and Hong Kong—which score in the middle—are wealthier than many of the most individualist countries.

One of the major differences between these two orientations is in the extent to which an individual's goals or the group's goals are given precedence. Individualist and collectivist tendencies are, of course, not mutually exclusive; this is not an all-or-none orientation but rather one of emphasis. You probably have both tendencies. For example, you may compete with other members of your basketball team for most baskets or most valuable player award (and thus emphasize individual goals). At the same time, however, you will—in a game—act in a way that will benefit the entire team (and thus emphasize group goals). In actual practice both individual and collective tendencies will help you and your team each achieve your goals. Yet most people and most cultures have a dominant orientation; they're more individually oriented (they see themselves as independent) or more collectively oriented (they see themselves as interdependent) in most situations, most of the time (cf. Singelis, 1994).

**A s k Yourself**
**Clashing Cultural Rules**

Your friend is pressed for time and asks you to do the statistical analyses for a term project. Your first impulse is to say yes, because in your culture it would be extremely impolite to refuse a favor to someone you've known for so long. Yet you're aware that doing work for others is considered unethical at colleges in the United States. **Ask yourself:** What might you say that would enable you to help your friend but would not involve behavior that would be considered deceitful and might be severely punished?

In some instances, however, these tendencies may come into conflict. For example, do you shoot for the basket and try to raise your own individual score, or do you pass the ball to another player who is better positioned to score and thus benefit the team as a whole? You make this distinction in popular talk when you call someone a team player (collectivist orientation) or an individual player (individualist orientation).

In an **individualist culture** members are responsible for themselves and perhaps their immediate family. In a **collectivist culture** members are responsible for the entire group.

In an individualist culture success is measured by the extent to which you surpass other members of your group; you would take pride in standing out from the crowd. Your heroes—in the media, for example—are likely to be those who are unique and who stand apart. In a collectivist culture success is measured by your contribution to the achievements of the group as a whole; you would take pride in your similarity to other members of your group. Your heroes are more likely to be team players who do not stand out from the rest of the group's members. Not surprisingly, advertisements in individualist cultures emphasize individual preferences and benefits, independence, and personal success; advertisements in collectivist cultures emphasize group benefits, family integrity, and group harmony (Han & Shavitt, 1994).

In an individualist culture you're responsible to your own conscience, and responsibility is largely an individual matter; in a collectivist culture you're responsible to the rules of the social group, and responsibility for an accomplishment or a failure is shared by all members. Competition is fostered in individualist cultures, whereas cooperation is promoted in collectivist cultures. Not surprisingly, people in collectivist cultures are more willing to forgive others than are those in individualist cultures (Fu, Watkins, & Hui, 2004).

In an individualist culture you might compete for leadership in a small group setting, and there would likely be a very clear distinction between leaders and members. In a collectivist culture leadership would be shared and rotated; there is likely to be little distinction between leader and members. These orientations will also influence the kinds of communication members consider appropriate in an organizational context. For example, individualist members will favor clarity and directness, whereas collectivists will favor "face-saving" and the avoidance of hurting others or arousing negative evaluations (Kim & Sharkey, 1995).

Distinctions between in-group members and out-group members are extremely important in collectivist cultures. In individualist cultures, which prize each person's individuality, the distinction is likely to be less important.

## High- and Low-Context Cultures

Cultures also differ in the extent to which information is made explicit or is assumed to be in the context or in the persons communicating. In a **high-context culture** much of the information in communication is in the context or in the person—for example, information that was shared through previous communications, through assumptions about one another, and through shared experiences. The information is thus known by all participants but isn't explicitly stated in the verbal messages. In **low-context-culture** most of the information is explicitly stated in the verbal message. In formal transactions it would be stated in written (or contract) form.

**⏏ VIEWPOINT**

In 1995 the Emma Lazarus poem inscribed on the Statue of Liberty was changed. The original last five lines of the poem, "The New Colossus," had been as follows, but in 1995 the words in brackets were deleted:

> Give me your tired, your poor,
> Your huddled masses yearning to breathe free,
> [The wretched refuse of your teeming shore,]
> Send these, the homeless, tempest-tost, to me:
> I lift my lamp beside the golden door.

The late Harvard zoologist Stephen Jay Gould, commenting on this change, noted that the poem no longer represented what Lazarus wrote. "The language police triumph and integrity bleeds," said Gould (1995). Yet it is true that calling immigrants "wretched refuse" is insulting; if Lazarus had been writing in 1995, she probably wouldn't have used that phrase. Would you have supported deleting the line?

To further appreciate the distinction between high and low context, consider giving directions ("Where's the voter registration center?") to someone who knows the neighborhood and to a newcomer to your city. With someone who knows the neighborhood (a high-context situation), you can assume that she or he knows the local landmarks. So you can give directions such as "next to the laundromat on Main Street" or "the corner of Albany and Elm." With the newcomer (a low-context situation), you can't assume that she or he shares any information with you. So you would have to use only those directions that a stranger would understand, for example, "make a left at the next stop sign" or "go two blocks and then turn right."

High-context cultures are also collectivist cultures (Gudykunst, Ting-Toomey, & Chua, 1988; Gudykunst & Kim, 1992). These cultures (Japanese, Arabic, Latin American, Thai, Korean, Apache, and Mexican are examples) place great emphasis on personal relationships and oral agreements (Victor, 1992). Low-context cultures are also individualist cultures. These cultures (German, Swedish, Norwegian, and American are examples) place less emphasis on personal relationships and more emphasis on verbalized, explicit explanation, and on written contracts in business transactions. The characteristics of individual–collective and high- and low-context cultures discussed here are summarized in Table 2.2.

Members of high-context cultures spend lots of time getting to know one another interpersonally and socially before any important transactions take place. Because of this prior personal knowledge, a great deal of information is shared by the members and therefore does not have to be explicitly stated. Members of low-context cultures spend much less time getting to know one another and hence don't have that shared knowledge. As a result everything has to be stated explicitly.

This difference between high- and low-context orientation is partly responsible for the differences observed in Japanese and American business groups (alluded to in Chapter 1). The Japanese spend lots of time getting acquainted before conducting actual business,

⊕ **TABLE 2.2**
## Differences between Individualist (Low-Context) and Collectivist (High-Context) Cultures

In every culture there will be variations in each of the characteristics listed here. View these, therefore, as general tendencies rather than as absolutes. Further, increased mobility, changing immigration patterns, and exposure to media from different parts of the world will gradually decrease the differences between these two sets of orientations.

| Individualist (Low-Context) Cultures | Collectivist (High-Context) Cultures |
|---|---|
| Your own goals are most important; you're responsible for yourself and to your own conscience. | The group's goals are most important; you're responsible for the entire group and to the group's values and rules. |
| Success depends on your surpassing others; competition is emphasized. | Success depends on your contribution to the group; cooperation is emphasized. |
| Clear distinction is made between group leaders and members. | Little distinction is made between leaders and members; leadership is normally shared. |
| In-group versus out-group distinctions are of little importance. | In-group versus out-group distinctions are of great importance. |
| Information is made explicit; little is left unsaid; directness is valued; face-saving is not vital. | Information is often left implicit, and much goes unsaid; indirectness is valued; face-saving is a major consideration. |
| Personal relationships are less important; hence, people spend little time getting to know one another at meetings and conferences. | Personal relationships are extremely important; hence, people spend much time getting to know one another at meetings and conferences. |

*Sources:* Based on the work of Hall (1983) and Hall & Hall (1987) and on interpretations by Gudykunst (1991) and Victor (1992).

whereas Americans get down to business very quickly. The Japanese (and members of other high-context cultures) want to get to know one another because important information isn't made explicit. They have to know you so they can read your nonverbals, for example (Sanders, Wiseman, & Matz, 1991). Americans can get right down to business because all important information will be stated explicitly.

To high-context cultural members, what is omitted or assumed is a vital part of the communication transaction. Silence, for example, is highly valued (Basso, 1972). To low-context cultural members, what is omitted creates ambiguity, but this ambiguity is simply something that will be eliminated by explicit and direct communication. To high-context cultural members, ambiguity is something to be avoided; it's a sign that the interpersonal and social interactions have not proved sufficient to establish a shared base of information (Gudykunst, 1983).

When this simple difference isn't understood, intercultural misunderstandings can easily result. For example, the directness characteristic of the low-context culture may seem insulting, insensitive, or unnecessary to the high-context cultural member. Conversely, to the low-context member, the high-context cultural member may appear vague, underhanded, or dishonest in his or her reluctance to be explicit or to engage in communication that a low-context member would consider open and direct.

Another frequent source of intercultural misunderstanding that can be traced to context differences can be seen in face-saving (Hall & Hall, 1987). High-context cultures place much more emphasis on face-saving; for example, they're more likely to avoid argument for fear of causing others to lose face. In contrast, low-context members (with their individualistic orientation) will readily use argument to win a point. Similarly, in high-context cultures criticism should take place only in private. Low-context cultures may not make this public–private distinction. Low-context managers who criticize high-context workers in public will find that their criticism causes interpersonal problems and does little to resolve the original difficulty (Victor, 1992).

Members of high-context cultures are reluctant to say no, for fear of offending and causing the person to lose face. Thus, it's necessary to be able to read when a Japanese executive's "yes" means yes and when it means no. The difference isn't in the words used but in the way in which they're used.

Members of high-context cultures also are reluctant to question the judgments of their superiors. In a company, for example, if a product were being manufactured with a defect, workers might be reluctant to communicate this back to management (Gross, Turner, & Cederholm, 1987). Similarly, workers might detect problems in procedures proposed by management but never communicate their concerns back to management. In an intercultural organization knowledge of this tendency would alert a low-context management to look more deeply into the absence of communication, especially the absence of messages that might appear critical or negative.

**SPEAKING**
**Interpersonal-E**

**Similarity.** You're more likely to help someone who is similar in race, attitude, and general appearance. Even the same first name is significant. For example, when an e-mail (asking receivers to fill out surveys of their food habits) identified the sender as one with the same name as the receiver, there was a greater willingness to comply with the request (Gueguen, 2003). Why do you think people do this? Do you do this?

# INTERCULTURAL COMMUNICATION

Understanding the role of culture in communication is an essential foundation for understanding intercultural communication as it occurs in an interpersonal context.

As a preface to this discussion, consider the following situations. How willing and open you would be to

- initiating a conversation with a culturally different person while waiting alone for a bus?
- having a close friendship with a culturally different person?
- having a long-term romantic relationship with a culturally different person?
- listening fairly to a conversation conducted by a culturally different person?
- ascribing a level of credibility to a culturally different person identical to that you would ascribe to a culturally similar person—all other things being equal?

## A Model of Intercultural Communication

The term **intercultural communication** refers to communication between persons who have different cultural beliefs, values, or ways of behaving. The model in Figure 2.1 illustrates this concept. The circles represent the cultures of the individual communicators. The inner squares identify the communicators (the sources/receivers). In this model each communicator is a member of a different culture. In some instances the cultural differences are relatively slight—say, between persons from Toronto and New York. In other instances the cultural differences are great—say, between persons from Borneo and Germany, or between persons from rural Nigeria and industrialized England.

Every message originates from a specific and unique cultural context, and that context influences the message's content and form. You communicate as you do largely as a result of your culture. Culture (along with the processes of enculturation and acculturation) influences every aspect of your communication experience.

## Principles for Improving Intercultural Communication

Murphy's Law ("Anything that can go wrong will go wrong") is especially applicable to intercultural communication. Intercultural communication is, of course, subject to all the same barriers and problems as are the other forms of communication discussed throughout this text. Drawing on the work of numerous intercultural researchers, let's consider several guidelines designed to counteract the barriers that are unique to intercultural communication (Barna, 1997; Ruben, 1985; Spitzberg, 1991).

**Educate Yourself**    There's no better preparation for intercultural communication than learning about the other culture. Fortunately, there are numerous sources to draw on. View a documentary or movie that presents a realistic view of the culture. Read material about the culture by persons from that culture as well as by "outsiders" (e.g., Foster, 2004). Scan magazines and websites from the culture. Talk with members of the culture. Chat in international chat rooms. Read materials addressed to people who need to communicate with those from other cultures. For example, books on the subject include: *Do's and Taboos of Hosting International Visitors* (Axtell, 1990), *Mind Your Manners: Managing Business Cultures in Europe* (Mole, 1998), *Do's and Taboos around the World* (Axtell, 1994), *The Executive Guide to Asia-Pacific Communications* (James, 1995), *How to Negotiate Anything with Anyone Anywhere around the World* (Acuff, 1993), *Internationally Yours: Writing and Communicating*

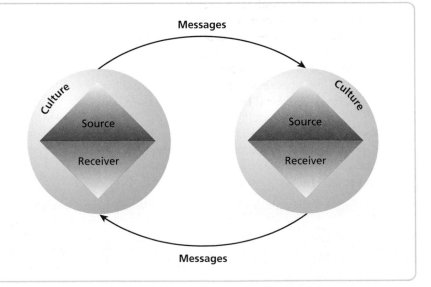

**➜ FIGURE 2.1**
## A Model of Intercultural Communication

This model of intercultural communication illustrates that culture is a part of every communication act. More specifically, it illustrates that the messages you send and the messages you receive will be influenced by your cultural beliefs, values, and attitudes.

*Successfully in Today's Global Marketplace* (DeVries, 1994), *International Business Etiquette in Europe: What You Need to Know to Conduct Business Abroad with Charm and Savvy* (Sabath, 1999), and *Global Etiquette Guide to Mexico and Latin America* (Foster, 2002).

Another part of this preparation is to recognize and face your own fears, which can stand in the way of effective intercultural communication (Gudykunst, 1994; Stephan & Stephan, 1985; Shelton & Richeson, 2005). For example, you may fear for your self-esteem. You may become anxious about your ability to control the intercultural situation, or you may worry about your own level of discomfort. You may fear saying something that will be considered politically incorrect or culturally insensitive and thereby losing face.

You may fear that you'll be taken advantage of by a member of another culture. Depending on your own stereotypes, you may fear being lied to, financially duped, or made fun of. You may fear that members of this other group will react to you negatively. You may fear, for example, that they will not like you or may disapprove of your attitudes or beliefs or perhaps even reject you as a person. Conversely, you may fear negative reactions from members of your own group. They might, for example, disapprove of your socializing with the culturally different.

Some fears, of course, are reasonable. In many cases, however, such concerns are groundless. Either way, they need to be assessed logically and their consequences weighed carefully. Then you'll be able to make informed choices about your communications.

**Reduce Uncertainty** All communication interactions involve uncertainty and ambiguity. Not surprisingly, uncertainty and ambiguity are greater when there are large cultural differences (Berger & Bradac, 1982; Gudykunst, 1989, 1993). Because of this greater uncertainty in intercultural communication, more time and effort are required to reduce it and thus to communicate meaningfully. Reducing your uncertainty about another person not only will make your communication more effective; it also will increase your liking for the person and make the interaction more satisfying (Neuliep & Grohskopf, 2000; Douglas, 1994). In situations of great uncertainty the techniques of effective communication (for example, active listening, perception checking, being specific, and seeking feedback) take on special importance.

Active listening (Chapter 5) and perception checking techniques (Chapter 4) help you to verify the accuracy of your perceptions and allow you to revise and amend any incorrect perceptions. Being specific reduces ambiguity and the chances of misunderstandings. For example, misunderstanding is a lot more likely in a conversation about "neglect" (a highly abstract concept) than in a discussion about "forgetting your last birthday" (a specific event).

Seeking feedback helps you to correct any possible misconceptions almost immediately. Seek feedback on whether you're making yourself clear ("Does that make sense?" "Do you see where to put the widget?"). Similarly, seek feedback to make sure you understand what the other person is saying ("Do you mean that you'll never speak with them again? Do you mean that literally?").

Although you're always in danger of misperceiving and misevaluating another person, you're in special danger in intercultural situations. Therefore, try to resist your natural tendency to judge others quickly and permanently. A judgment made early is likely to be based on too little information. Because of this, flexibility and a willingness to revise opinions are essential intercultural skills.

**⬆ VIEWPOINT**

One of the current controversies in education centers on the teaching of evolution (humans evolved from earlier forms of animals) versus creationism (God created humans as they are now). Although the scientific evidence and most scientists support evolution and argue that therefore this is what should be taught in the schools, many influential religious leaders have argued that creationism is an equally plausible explanation and have pressured some publishers to present evolution as just one theory and creationism as another (Lemonick, 2005b). How do you feel about this issue?

**Recognize Differences**   To communicate interculturally you need to recognize the differences between yourself and people from other cultures, the differences within the other cultural group, and the numerous differences in meaning.

### Differences between Yourself and the Culturally Different

A common barrier to intercultural communication occurs when you assume that similarities exist and that differences do not. This is especially true of values, attitudes, and beliefs. You might easily accept different hairstyles, clothing, and foods. In basic values and beliefs, however, you may assume that deep down all people are really alike. They aren't. When you assume similarities and ignore differences, you'll fail to notice important distinctions and when communicating will convey to others that your ways are the right ways and that their ways are not important to you. Consider this example. An American invites a Filipino coworker to dinner. The Filipino politely refuses. The American is hurt and feels that the Filipino does not want to be friendly. The Filipino is hurt and concludes that the invitation was not extended sincerely. Here, it seems, both the American and the Filipino assume that their customs for inviting people to dinner are the same when, in fact, they aren't. A Filipino expects to be invited several times before accepting a dinner invitation. When an invitation is given only once it's viewed as insincere.

Here's another example. An American college student hears the news that her favorite uncle has died. She bites her lip, pulls herself up, and politely excuses herself from the group of foreign students with whom she is having dinner. The Russian thinks: "How unfriendly." The Italian thinks: "How insincere." The Brazilian thinks: "How unconcerned." To many Americans, it's a sign of bravery to endure pain (physical or emotional) in silence and without any outward show of emotion. To members of other groups, such silence is often interpreted negatively to mean that the individual does not consider them friends who can share such sorrow. In other cultures, people are expected to reveal to friends how they feel.

### Differences within the Culturally Different Group

Within every cultural group there are vast and important differences. As all Americans are not alike, neither are all Indonesians, Greeks, Mexicans, and so on. When you ignore these differences—when you assume that all persons covered by the same label (in this case a national or racial label) are the same—you're guilty of stereotyping. A good example of this is seen in the use of the term "African American." The term stresses the unity of Africa and of those who are of African descent and is analogous to "Asian American" or "European American." At the same time, it ignores the great diversity within the African continent when, for example, it's used as analogous to "German American" or "Japanese American." More analogous terms would be "Nigerian American" or "Ethiopian American." Within each culture there are smaller cultures that differ greatly from each other and from the larger culture.

### Differences in Meaning

Meaning exists not in words but in people (a principle we'll return to in Chapter 6). Consider, for example, the differences in meaning that exist for words such as *woman* to an American and a Muslim, *religion* to a born-again Christian and an atheist, and *lunch* to a Chinese rice farmer and a Madison Avenue advertising executive. Even though the same word is used, its meanings will vary greatly depending on the listeners' cultural definitions.

Nonverbal differences in meaning also exist. For example, a left-handed American who eats with the left hand may be seen by a Muslim as obscene. To the Muslim, the left hand isn't used for eating or for shaking hands but to clean oneself after excretory functions. So using the left hand to eat or to shake hands is considered insulting and obscene.

# Understanding Interpersonal Skills
## CULTURAL SENSITIVITY

Cultural sensitivity is an attitude and way of behaving in which you're aware of and acknowledge cultural differences; it's crucial for such global goals as world peace and economic growth as well as for effective interpersonal communication (Franklin & Mizell, 1995). Without cultural sensitivity there can be no effective interpersonal communication between people who are different in gender or race or nationality or affectional orientation. So be mindful of the cultural differences between yourself and the other person. The techniques of interpersonal communication that work well with European Americans may not work well with Asian Americans; what proves effective in Japan may not in Mexico. The close physical distance that is normal in Arab cultures may seem too familiar or too intrusive in much of the United States and northern Europe. The empathy that most Americans welcome may be uncomfortable for most Koreans, Japanese, or Chinese.

**Increasing Cultural Sensitivity.** This chapter has identified many guidelines for more effective intercultural communication, and among them are recommendations that constitute the best advice for achieving cultural sensitivity:

- Prepare yourself. Read about and listen carefully for culturally influenced behaviors.
- Recognize and face your own fears of acting inappropriately toward members of different cultures.
- Recognize differences between yourself and culturally different individuals.
- Recognize that there are often enormous differences within any given cultural group.
- Recognize differences in meaning; words rarely mean the same thing to members of different cultures.
- Become conscious of the cultural rules and customs of others.

**Confront Your Stereotypes**    Stereotypes, especially when they operate below the level of conscious awareness, can create serious communication problems (Lyons & Kashima, 2003). Originally, the word *stereotype* was a printing term that referred to the plate that printed the same image over and over. A sociological or psychological stereotype is a fixed impression of a group of people. Everyone has attitudinal stereotypes—images of national groups, religious groups, or racial groups or perhaps of criminals, prostitutes, teachers, or plumbers. Consider, for example, if you have any stereotypes of, say, bodybuilders, the opposite sex, a racial group different from your own, members of a religion very different from your own, hard drug users, or college professors. It is very likely that you have stereotypes of several or perhaps even of all of these groups. Although we often think of stereotypes as negative ("They're lazy, dirty, and only interested in getting high"), stereotypes also may be positive ("They're smart, hardworking, and extremely loyal").

If you have these fixed impressions, you may, on meeting a member of a particular group, see that person primarily as a member of that group. Initially this may provide you with some helpful orientation. However, it creates problems when you apply to that person all the characteristics you assign to members of that group without examining the unique individual. If you meet a politician, for example, you may have a host of characteristics for politicians that you can readily apply to this person. To complicate matters further, you may see in the person's behavior the manifestation of various characteristics that you would not see if you did not know that the person was a politician. In online communication, because there are few visual and auditory cues, it's not surprising to find that people form impressions of online communication partners with a heavy reliance on stereotypes (Jacobson, 1999).

Consider, however, another kind of stereotype: You're driving along a dark road and are stopped at a stop sign. A car pulls up beside you and three teenagers jump out and rap on

### SPEAKING
### Interpersonal-E

**Differences.** People who interact in online political discussions see themselves as interacting with people very different from themselves. Yet, and contrary to the research showing that we communicate most with people we perceive as similar to ourselves, they enjoy this diversity of people and differences of opinions (Stromer-Gallery, 2003). Is this true of your own experiences in online discussions?

your window. There may be a variety of possible explanations. Perhaps they need help or they want to ask directions. Or they may be about to engage in carjacking. Your self-protective stereotype may help you decide on "carjacking" and may lead you to pull away and into the safety of a busy service station. In doing that, of course, you may have escaped being carjacked—or you may have failed to help people who needed assistance.

Stereotyping can lead to two major barriers. The tendency to group a person into a class and to respond to that person primarily as a member of that class can lead you to perceive that a person possesses certain qualities (usually negative) that you believe characterize the group to which he or she belongs. Then you will fail to appreciate the multifaceted nature of all people and all groups. For example, consider your stereotype of someone who is deeply into computers. Very likely your image is quite different from the research findings on such individuals, which show that in fact they are as often female as male and are as sociable, popular, and self-assured as their peers who are not into heavy computer use (Schott & Selwyn 2000).

Stereotyping also can lead you to ignore the unique characteristics of an individual; you therefore may fail to benefit from the special contributions each person can bring to an encounter.

**Adjust Your Communication**    Intercultural communication (in fact, all interpersonal communication) takes place only to the extent that you and the person you're trying to communicate with share the same system of symbols. Your communication will be hindered to the extent that your language and nonverbal systems differ. This **adjustment** principle takes on particular relevance when you realize that no two persons share identical symbol systems. Parents and children, for example, not only have different vocabularies but also, even more important, have different meanings for some of the terms they have in common. People in close relationships—either as intimate friends or as romantic partners—realize that learning the other person's signals takes a long time and, often, great patience. If you want to understand what another person means—by smiling, by saying "I love you," by arguing about trivial matters, by self-deprecating comments—you have to learn their system of signals.

This principle is especially important in intercultural communication, largely because people from different cultures use different signals and/or use the same signals to signify quite different things. Focused eye contact means honesty and openness in much of the United States. But in Japan and in many Hispanic cultures that same behavior may signify arrogance or disrespect if it occurs between a youngster and someone significantly older.

Part of the art of intercultural communication is learning the other person's signals, how they're used, and what they mean. Furthermore, you have to share your own system of signals with others so that they can better understand you. Although some people may know what you mean by your silence or by your avoidance of eye contact, others may not. You cannot expect others to decode your behaviors accurately without help.

An interesting theory largely revolving around adjustment is communication accommodation theory. This theory holds that speakers will adjust to or accommodate the speaking style of their listeners to gain, for example, social approval and greater communication efficiency (Giles, Mulac, Bradac, & Johnson, 1987). For example, research shows that when two people have a similar speech rate, they're attracted more to each other than to people with dissimilar rates (Buller, LePoire, Aune, & Eloy, 1992). Also, the speaker who uses language intensity or forcefulness similar to that of listeners is judged to have greater credibility than the speaker who uses intensity different from that of listeners (Aune & Kikuchi, 1993). Another study found that roommates who were similar in communication competence and low in verbal aggressiveness were highest in roommate liking and satisfaction (Martin & Anderson, 1995). People even accommodate in their e-mail. In still another study, for example, responses to messages that contained politeness cues were significantly more polite than responses to e-mails that did not contain such cues (Bunz & Campbell, 2004).

In some instances intermediaries may "broker" accommodation in an effort to make communication easier between two different groups. For example, among Chinese immigrants in New Zealand, many grandparents speak only Chinese and know only the Chinese culture, but their grandchildren speak only English and know only the New Zealand culture. In such situations the parents of the children (who know both languages and cultures) often serve as intermediaries or brokers between grandparents and grandchildren and help each group accommodate their communication toward the other (Ng, He, & Loong, 2004).

As you adjust your communications, recognize that each culture has its own rules and customs for communicating (Barna, 1997; Ruben, 1985; Spitzberg, 1991). These rules identify what is appropriate and what is inappropriate. Thus, for example, in American culture you would call a person you wished to date three or four days in advance; in certain Asian cultures you might call the person's parents weeks or even months in advance. In American culture you say, as a general friendly gesture and not as a specific invitation, "Come over and pay us a visit." To members of other cultures, this comment is sufficient for the listeners to actually visit at their convenience. In some cultures people show respect by avoiding direct eye contact with the person to whom they're speaking; in other cultures this same eye avoidance would signal disinterest. If a young American girl is talking with an older Indonesian man, for example, she's expected to avoid direct eye contact. Among Indonesians direct eye contact in this situation would be considered disrespectful. In some southern European cultures men walk arm in arm. In American culture this is considered inappropriate.

A good example of a series of rules for an extremely large and important culture appears in Table 2.3 "Interpersonal Communication Tips between People with and without Disabilities."

**Manage Culture Shock**   Culture shock is the psychological reaction you experience when you're in a culture very different from your own (Ward, Bochner, & Furnham, 2001; Wan, 2004). Culture shock is normal; most people experience it when entering a new and different culture. Nevertheless, it can be unpleasant and frustrating. Part of this results from feelings of alienation, conspicuousness, and difference from everyone else. When you lack knowledge of the rules and customs of the new society, you cannot communicate effectively. You're apt to blunder frequently and seriously. In your culture shock you may not know basic things:

- how to ask someone for a favor or pay someone a compliment
- how to extend or accept an invitation for dinner
- how early or how late to arrive for an appointment
- how long you should stay when visiting someone
- how to distinguish seriousness from playfulness and politeness from indifference
- how to dress for an informal, formal, or business function
- how to order a meal in a restaurant or how to summon a waiter

The amount of culture shock you undergo and the accompanying stress and difficulty you may experience seem proportional to the distance between your own culture and that of the new culture in which you now find yourself. Visiting a culture similar to your own will lead to less stress and fewer problems than visiting a culture very different from your own (Furnham, 2004). Interestingly, uncertainty reduction strategies (a person's prior international experience, the amount and types of intercultural training the person receives, and the time the person spends in the foreign culture) do not seem to facilitate emotional adjustment to a new culture (Taveggia & Santos, 2001).

Anthropologist Kalervo Oberg (1960), who first used the term *culture shock*, notes that it occurs in stages. These stages are useful for examining many encounters with the new and the different. Going away to college, moving in together, or joining the military, for example, can result in culture shock. Let's use the example of moving away from home into your own apartment to illustrate Kalervo's four stages:

*Stage One: The Honeymoon.* At first you experience fascination, even enchantment, with the new culture and its people. You finally have your own apartment. You're your own boss. Finally, on your own! When in groups of people who are culturally different, this stage is characterized by cordiality and friendship in these early and superficial relationships. Many tourists remain at this stage, because their stay in any one foreign country is so brief.

*Stage Two: The Crisis.* Here, the differences between your own culture and the new setting create problems. No longer do you find dinner ready for you unless you cook it yourself. Your clothes are not washed or ironed unless you do them yourself. Feelings of frustration and inadequacy come to the fore. This is the stage at which you experience the actual shock of the new culture. One study of foreign students coming from more than 100 countries and studying in 11 different countries found that 25 percent of the students experienced depression (Klineberg & Hull, 1979).

---

## ⟲ TABLE 2.3  INTERPERSONAL COMMUNICATION TIPS
## Between People With and Without Disabilities

Other "Tips" tables focus on visual impairment (Chapter 1), hearing loss (Chapter 5), and speech and language disorders (Chapter 9); here we look at communication between those with general disabilities—for example, people in wheelchairs or with, say, cerebral palsy—and those who have no such disability. The suggestions offered here are considered appropriate in the United States, although not necessarily in other cultures. For example, most people in the United States accept the phrase "person with mental retardation," but the term is considered offensive to many in the United Kingdom (Fernald, 1995).

### If you're the person without a general disability:

1. Avoid negative terms and terms that define the person as disabled, such as "the disabled man" or "the handicapped child." Instead say "person with a disability," always emphasizing the person rather than the disability. Avoid describing the person with a disability as abnormal; when you define people without disabilities as "normal," you in effect say that the person with a disability isn't normal.
2. Treat assistive devices such as wheelchairs, canes, walkers, or crutches as the personal property of the user. Don't move these out of your way; they're for the convenience of the person with the disability. Avoid leaning on a person's wheelchair; it's similar to leaning on a person.
3. Shake hands with the person with the disability if you shake hands with others in a group. Don't avoid shaking hands because the individual's hand is crippled, for example.
4. Avoid talking about the person with a disability in the third person. For example, avoid saying, "Doesn't he get around beautifully with the new crutches." Direct your comments directly to the individual.
5. Don't assume that people who have a disability are intellectually impaired. Slurred speech—such as may occur with people who have cerebral palsy or cleft palate—should never be taken as indicating a low-level intellect. So be especially careful not to talk down to such people as, research shows, many people do (Unger, 2001).
6. When you're not sure of how to act, ask. For example, if you're not sure if you should offer walking assistance, say, "Would you like me to help you into the dining room?" And, more important, accept the person's response. If he or she says no, then that means no; don't insist.
7. Maintain similar eye level. If the person is in a wheelchair, for example, it might be helpful for you to sit down or kneel down to get onto the same eye level.

### If you're the person with a general disability:

1. Let the other person know if he or she can do anything to assist you in communicating. For example, if you want someone to speak in a louder voice, ask. If you want to relax and have someone push your wheelchair, say so.
2. Be patient and understanding. Many people mean well but may simply not know how to act or what to say. Put them at ease as best you can.
3. Demonstrate your own comfort. If you detect discomfort in the other person, you might talk a bit about your disability to show that you're not uncomfortable about it—and that you understand that others may not know how you feel. But you're under no obligation to educate the public, so don't feel this is something you should or have to do.

*Sources:* These suggestions are based on a wide variety of sources, including http://www.empowermentzone.com/etiquet.txt (the website for the National Center for Access Unlimited), http://www.dol.gov/dol/odep/, http://www.drc.uga.edu, and http://www.ucpa.org/ (all accessed March 26, 2005).

*Stage Three: The Recovery.* During this period you gain the skills necessary to function effectively. You learn how to shop, cook, and plan a meal. You find a local laundry and figure you'll learn how to iron later. You learn the language and ways of the new culture. Your feelings of inadequacy subside.

*Stage Four: The Adjustment.* At this final stage, you adjust to and come to enjoy the new culture and the new experiences. You may still experience periodic difficulties and strains, but on a whole, the experience is pleasant. Actually, you're now a pretty decent cook. You're even coming to enjoy it. You're making a good salary, so why learn to iron?

People may also experience culture shock when they return to their original culture after living in a foreign culture, a kind of reverse culture shock (Jandt, 2004). Consider, for example, Peace Corps volunteers who work in rural and economically deprived areas. On returning to Las Vegas or Beverly Hills, they too may experience culture shock. A sailor who serves long periods aboard ship and then returns to an isolated farming community may experience culture shock. In these cases, however, the recovery period is shorter and the sense of inadequacy and frustration is less.

Among the ways to manage the inevitable culture shock, some strategies are to familiarize yourself with the host nation, form friendship networks to assist you in adjusting, interact with members of the culture and your hosts, and be open to seeking professional help in adjusting to cultural problems (Constantine, Anderson, Berkel, Caldwell, & Utsey, 2005; Britnell, 2004; Chapdelaine & Alexitch, 2004). Putting into practice the guidelines to effective intercultural communication outlined in this chapter also will help you manage your culture shock and make you a more effective intercultural communicator.

**SPEAKING**
**>> Interpersonal-E**

**Cultural Tours.** Virtual tours offer an interesting way to view a wide variety of areas. Popular tours that 54 million Americans already have taken include museums, vacation spots, schools, real estate, historical exhibits, parks, places such as the Taj Mahal and the White House, and hotels (Virtual Tours, Pew/Internet, Data Memo 202-419-4500, http://www.pewinternet.org, dated Decemeber 2004, accessed February 10, 2005). What are some virtual tours currently available that you might use to learn about different cultures?

## Reviewing    Key Terms and Concepts in Culture in Interpersonal Communication

This chapter explored the nature of culture and identified some key concepts and principles that explain the role of culture in interpersonal communication.

### Culture and Interpersonal Communication

What is culture and how is it transmitted?

- Culture is the relatively specialized lifestyle of a group of people (values, beliefs, artifacts, ways of behaving) that is passed from one generation to the next by means of communication (not genes).
- Ethnic Identity is a commitment to the ways and beliefs of your culture.
- Enculturation is the process through which you learn the culture into which you're born.
- Acculturation is the process by which you learn the rules and norms of a culture that is different from your native culture and that modifies your original or native culture.

### How Cultures Differ

How do cultures differ from one another? How do these differences affect interpersonal communication?

- In high-power-distance cultures, power is concentrated in the hands of a few and there is a great difference between those with and those without power. In low-power-distance cultures, the power is more equally shared throughout the citizenry.
- In highly masculine cultures, men are viewed as strong, assertive, and focused on success, whereas women are viewed as modest, tender, and focused on the quality of life. In highly feminine cultures, men and women are viewed more similarly.
- A collectivist culture emphasizes the group and subordinates the individual's goals to those of the group. An individualist culture emphasizes the individual and subordinates the group's goals to the individual's.
- In high-context cultures, much of the information is in the context; in low-context cultures, information is explicitly stated in the verbal message.

### Intercultural Communication

What is intercultural communication and what are its central principles?

- Intercultural communication is communication between people who have different cultures, beliefs, values, and ways of behaving.
- Some intercultural communication guidelines include: Prepare yourself; reduce uncertainty; recognize differences (between yourself and others, within the culturally different group, and in meanings); confront your stereotypes; adjust your communication; and manage culture shock.

**1** In this age of multiculturalism, how do you feel about Article II, Section 1 of the United States Constitution? The relevant section reads: "No person except a natural born citizen, or a citizen of the United States, at the time of the adoption of this Constitution, shall be eligible to the office of President."

**2** It's been argued that in the United States women are more likely to view themselves as interdependents, having a more collectivist orientation, whereas men are more likely to view themselves as independents, having a more individualist orientation (Cross & Madson, 1997). Does your experience support this?

**3** Informal time terms (for example, *soon, right away, early, in a while, as soon as possible*) seem to create communication problems because they're ambiguous; different people will often give the terms different meanings. How might you go about reducing or eliminating the ambiguity created by these terms?

**4** Has anyone ever assumed something untrue about you because you were a member of a particular culture? Did you find this disturbing?

**5** Consider how cultural differences underlie some of the most hotly debated topics in the news today. The following, for example, is a brief list of some of these topics. How would you respond to the various questions raised? How do your cultural attitudes, beliefs, and values influence your responses?

- Should Christian Science parents be prosecuted for preventing their children from receiving life-saving treatments such as blood transfusions? Some states, such as Connecticut and Arizona, grant Christian Scientists special rights in this regard. Should this special treatment be adopted by all states? Should it be eliminated?

- Should cockfighting be permitted in all states? Or should it be declared illegal as "cruelty to animals"? Some Latino Americans have argued that cockfighting is a part of their culture and should be permitted. Cockfighting is illegal in most of the United States, but in five states and in Puerto Rico, it is legal.)

- Should safe sex practices be taught in the elementary schools, or is this a matter for the home?

- Should those who commit hate or bias crimes be given harsher sentences?

- Should doctor-assisted suicides be legalized?

- In adoption decisions, should the race of the child and that of the adopting parents be an issue?

**6** In a small group, with the class as a whole, or in a brief paper, discuss how your beliefs, attitudes, and values were influenced by the culture in which you were raised. Were you taught that going against these beliefs, attitudes, and values would bring penalties?

# Experiencing  Key Terms and Concepts in Culture in Interpersonal Communication

Go to www.ablongman.com/devito.

*These exercises enable you to explore a wide variety of cultural issues and their relationships to interpersonal communication.*

❶ **Random Pairs** sets up specific intercultural dyads and asks you to consider how these dyads might influence communication. ❷ **Cultural Beliefs** asks you to examine some of your own cultural beliefs. ❸ **From Culture to Gender** explores the relationship of culture to gender beliefs. ❹ **Cultural Identities** lets you explore the strengths in the cultures represented by class members and others. ❺ **The Sources of Your Cultural Beliefs** explores the origins of your own beliefs about a wide variety of issues. ❻ **Confronting Intercultural Obstacles** presents situations that can cause intercultural conflict and asks you how you'd head off potential conflicts or resolve them.

# The Self in Interpersonal Communication

🔼 *Sideways* (2004)

*Sideways* depicts the lives of two college friends who have entirely different self-concepts. The film plays on the ways these self-concepts influence what the characters do and how they form relationships—topics considered here, along with other topics relating to the self and interpersonal communication.

Of all the elements in interpersonal communication, the self is the most important. In this chapter we focus on several aspects of the self: (1) three basic dimensions of the self: self-concept, self-awareness, and self-esteem; (2) self-disclosure; and (3) communication apprehension or fear of speaking.

##  DIMENSIONS OF THE SELF

Let's begin this discussion by focusing on several fundamental aspects of the self: self-concept (the way you see yourself), self-awareness (your insight into and knowledge about yourself), and self-esteem (the value you place on yourself). In these discussions you'll see how these dimensions influence and are influenced by the way you communicate.

### Self-Concept

You no doubt have an image of who you are; this is your **self-concept.** It consists of your feelings and thoughts about your strengths and weaknesses, your abilities and limitations, and your aspirations and worldview (Black, 1999). Your self-concept develops from at least four sources: (1) the image of you that others have and that they reveal to you, (2) the comparisons you make between yourself and others, (3) the teachings of your culture, and (4) the way you interpret and evaluate your own thoughts and behaviors (see Figure 3.1).

**Others' Images of You**    If you wished to see the way your hair looked, you would likely look in a mirror. But what would you do if you wanted to see how friendly or how assertive you are? According to Charles Horton Cooley's (1922) concept of the *looking-glass self,* you would look at the image of yourself that others reveal to you through the way they treat you and react to you (Hensley, 1996).

You'd look especially to those who are most significant in your life—to your *significant others.* As a child, you'd look to your parents and then to your teachers. As an adult, you might look to your friends, romantic partners, and colleagues at work. If these significant others think highly of you, you'll see this positive image of yourself reflected in their behaviors; if they think little of you, you'll see a more negative image. These reflections that you see in others help you define your self-concept.

**Social Comparisons**    Another way you develop your self-concept is by comparing yourself with others. When you want to gain insight into who you are and how effective or competent you are, you probably look to your peers. For example, after an examination you probably want to know how you performed relative to the other students in your class. If you play on a baseball team, it's important to know your batting average in comparison with others on the team. You gain an additional perspective when you see your score in comparison with the scores of your peers.

**Cultural Teachings**    Through your parents, teachers, and the media, your culture instills in you a variety of beliefs, values, and attitudes—about success (how you define it and how you should achieve it); about your religion, race, or nationality; about the ethical principles you should follow in business and in your personal life. These teachings provide bench-

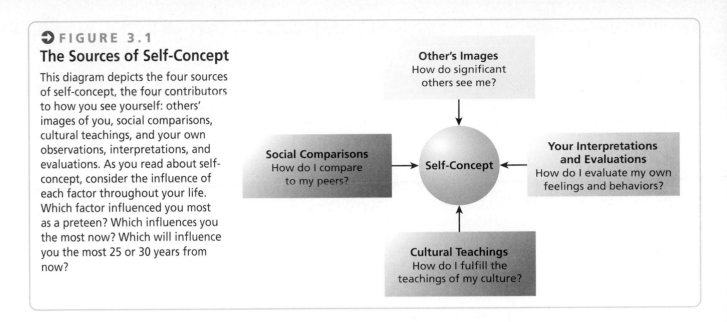

**→ FIGURE 3.1**

**The Sources of Self-Concept**

This diagram depicts the four sources of self-concept, the four contributors to how you see yourself: others' images of you, social comparisons, cultural teachings, and your own observations, interpretations, and evaluations. As you read about self-concept, consider the influence of each factor throughout your life. Which factor influenced you most as a preteen? Which influences you the most now? Which will influence you the most 25 or 30 years from now?

**Other's Images**
How do significant others see me?

**Social Comparisons**
How do I compare to my peers?

**Self-Concept**

**Your Interpretations and Evaluations**
How do I evaluate my own feelings and behaviors?

**Cultural Teachings**
How do I fulfill the teachings of my culture?

marks against which you can measure yourself. Your success in, for example, achieving what your culture defines as success will contribute to a positive self-concept. A perceived failure to achieve what your culture promotes (for example, not being married by the time you're 30) may contribute to a negative self-concept.

When you demonstrate the qualities that your culture (or your organization) teaches, you'll see yourself as a cultural success and will be rewarded by other members of the culture (or organization). Seeing yourself as culturally successful and getting rewarded by others will contribute positively to your self-concept. When you fail to demonstrate such qualities, you're more likely to see yourself as a cultural failure and to be punished by other members of the culture, contributing to a more negative self-concept.

You belong to a variety of cultures. Each of these cultures influences your attitudes and beliefs, and you may find that some of these influences contradict each other. For example, you may have been taught that it's important to be financially successful, but also that money is the root of all evil. You may have been taught to be the best in your field, but also to be cooperative and helpful to others, perhaps even those you are competing against. Such contradictory beliefs may easily cause intrapersonal conflicts. In extreme cases, you may decide to reject the attitudes and beliefs of one culture—often "the old world" culture—in favor of those of the culture with which you feel more comfortable.

**Your Own Interpretations and Evaluations**   Much in the way others form images of you based on what you do, you also react to your own behavior; you interpret and evaluate it. These interpretations and evaluations help to form your self-concept. For example, let us say you believe that lying is wrong. If you lie, you will evaluate this behavior in terms of your internalized beliefs about lying. You'll thus react negatively to your own behavior. You may, for example, experience guilt if your behavior contradicts your beliefs. In contrast, let's say you tutored another student and helped him or her pass a course. You would probably evaluate this behavior positively; you would feel good about this behavior and, as a result, about yourself.

## Self-Awareness

Your **self-awareness** represents the extent to which you know yourself. Understanding how your self-concept develops is one way to increase your self-awareness: The more you understand about why you view yourself as you do, the more you will understand who you are. Additional insight is gained by looking at self-awareness through the Johari model of the self, or your four selves (Luft, 1984).

**SPEAKING**
**>>Interpersonal-E**

**Online Ostracism.**
Ostracizing someone in face-to-face communication proves psychologically painful for the ignored person. One study argues that the same effects are present in online ostracism (Smith & Williams, 2004). How does online ostracism differ from face-to-face ostracism?

# Understanding Interpersonal Skills
## FLEXIBILITY

**Flexibility** is a quality of thinking and behaving in which you vary your messages based on the unique situation. One measure of flexibility asks you to consider how true you believe certain statements are—statements such as "People should be frank and spontaneous in conversation" or "When angry, a person should say nothing rather than say something he or she will be sorry for later." The "preferred" answer to all such questions is "sometimes true," underscoring the importance of flexibility in all interpersonal situations (Hart, Carlson, & Eadie, 1980). A more extensive test, by Matthew Martin and Rebecca Rubin (1994; also see Martin & Anderson, 1998) appears on the website at www.ablongman.com/devito.

**Increasing Flexibility.** Here are a few ways to cultivate flexibility.

- Realize that no two situations or people are exactly alike; ask yourself what is different about this situation or person and take these differences into consideration as you construct your messages.
- Realize that communication always takes place in a context (Chapter 1); ask yourself what is unique about this specific context and how this uniqueness should influence your messages.
- Realize that everything is in a state of flux. Just because the way you communicated last month was effective, doesn't mean it will be effective today or tomorrow. Realize too that sudden changes (the death of a lover or a serious illness) will influence what are and what are not appropriate messages.
- Realize that every situation offers you different options for communicating. Consider these options and try to predict the effects each option might have.

**Your Four Selves**   Self-awareness is neatly explained by the model of the four selves, the **Johari window.** This model, presented in Figure 3.2, has four basic areas, or quadrants, each of which represents a somewhat different self. The Johari model emphasizes that the several aspects of the self are not separate pieces but are interactive parts of a whole. Each part is dependent on each other part. Like that of interpersonal communication, this model of the self is transactional.

**The Open Self**   The *open self* represents all the information, behaviors, attitudes, feelings, desires, motivations, and ideas that you and others know. The type of information included here might range from your name, skin color, and sex to your age, political and religious affiliations, and financial situation. Your open self will vary in size, depending on the situation you're in and the person with whom you're interacting. Some people, for example, make you feel comfortable and supported; to them, you open yourself wide, but to others you may prefer to leave most of yourself closed.

Communication depends on the degree to which you open yourself to others and to yourself (Luft, 1969). If you don't allow other people to know you (thus keeping your open self small), communication between you and others becomes difficult, if not impossible. You can communicate meaningfully only to the extent that you know others and yourself. To improve communication, work first on enlarging the open self.

**The Blind Self**   The *blind self* represents all the things about yourself that others know but of which you're ignorant. These may vary from the relatively insignificant habit of saying "You know," rubbing your nose when you get angry, or having a distinct body odor, to things as significant as defense mechanisms, fight strategies, or repressed experiences.

Some people have a very large blind self; they seem totally oblivious to their faults and sometimes (though not as often) to their virtues. Others seem overly eager to have a small

## FIGURE 3.2
## The Johari Window

Visualize this model as representing your self. The entire model is of constant size, but each section can vary, from very small to very large. As one section becomes smaller, one or more of the others grows larger. Similarly, as one section grows, one or more of the others must get smaller. For example, if you reveal a secret and thereby enlarge your open self, this shrinks your hidden self. Further, this disclosure may in turn lead to a decrease in the size of your blind self (if your disclosure influences other people to reveal what they know about you but that you have not known). How would you draw your Johari window to show yourself when interacting with your parents? With your friends? With your college instructors? The name Johari, by the way, comes from the first names of the two people who developed the model, Joseph Luft and Harry Ingham.

*Source: Group Processes: An Introduction to Group Dynamics* by Joseph Luft, 1984, p. 60. Reprinted by permission of Mayfield Publishing Company, Mountain View, CA.

|  | Known to Self | Not Known to Self |
|---|---|---|
| **Known to Others** | **Open Self** Information about yourself that you and others know | **Blind Self** Information about yourself that you don't know but that others do know |
| **Not Known to Others** | **Hidden Self** Information about yourself that you know but others don't know | **Unknown Self** Information about yourself that neither you nor others know |

blind self. They seek therapy at every turn and join every self-help group. Some believe they know everything there is to know about themselves, that they have reduced the blind self to zero. Most of us lie between these extremes.

Communication and interpersonal relations are generally enhanced as the blind self becomes smaller. But be careful of trying to help someone else "discover" his or her blind self. This could cause serious problems. Such a revelation might trigger a breakdown in defenses; it might force people to admit their own jealousy or prejudice when they're not psychologically ready to deal with such information. Such revelations are best dealt with cautiously or under the guidance of trained professionals.

**The Hidden Self**     The *hidden self* contains all that you know of yourself and of others that you keep secret. In any interaction, this area includes everything you don't want to reveal, whether it's relevant or irrelevant to the conversation. At the extremes, we have the overdisclosers and the underdisclosers. The overdisclosers tell all. They tell you their marital difficulties, their children's problems, their financial status, and just about everything else. The underdisclosers tell nothing. They talk about you but not about themselves.

The problem with these extremes is that individuals don't distinguish between those who should and those who shouldn't be privy to such information. They also don't distinguish among the types of information they should or should not disclose. The vast majority of people, however, keep certain things hidden and disclose others; they make disclosures to some people and not to others. They're *selective* disclosers.

**The Unknown Self**     The *unknown self* represents truths about yourself that neither you nor others know. The existence of this self is inferred from a number of sources. Sometimes it's revealed through temporary changes brought about by special experimental conditions such as hypnosis or sensory deprivation. Sometimes this area is revealed by certain projective tests or dreams. Mostly, however, it's revealed by the fact that you're constantly learning things about yourself that you didn't know before (things that were previously in the unknown self)—for example, that you become defensive when someone asks you a question or voices disagreement, or that you compliment others in the hope of being complimented back.

Although you cannot easily manipulate this area, recognize that it does exist and that there are things about yourself and about others that you don't know and may never know.

**Increasing Self-Awareness**     You can increase your self-awareness in several ways: Ask yourself about yourself, listen to others, actively seek information about yourself, see your different selves, and increase your open self.

**Ask Yourself about Yourself**     One way to ask yourself about yourself is to take an informal "Who am I?" test (Bugental & Zelen, 1950; Grace & Cramer, 2003). Title a piece of paper "Who Am I?" and write 10, 15, or 20 times "I am. . . ." Then complete each of the sentences. Try not to give only positive or socially acceptable responses; just respond with what comes to mind first. Take another piece of paper and divide it into two columns; label one column "Strengths" and the other column "Weaknesses." Fill in each column as quickly as possible. Using these first two tests as a base, take a third piece of paper, title it "Self-Improvement Goals," and complete the statement "I want to improve my. . ." as many times as you can in five minutes. Because you're constantly changing, these self-perceptions and goals also change and so must be updated frequently.

Your cultural background will significantly influence your responses to this simple "Who Am I?" test. In one study, for example, participants from Malaysia (a collectivist culture) and from Australia and Great Britain (individualist cultures) completed this test. Malaysians produced significantly more group self-descriptions and fewer idiocentric self-descriptions than did the Australian or British respondents (Bochner, 1994; also see Radford, Mann, Ohta, & Nakane, 1993). If you completed the "Who Am I?" test, can you identify responses that were influenced by your individualist or collectivist orientation? Did other cultural factors influence your statements?

**Listen to Others**     You can learn a lot about yourself by seeing yourself as others do. Conveniently, others are constantly giving you the very feedback you need to increase self-awareness. In every interpersonal interaction, people comment on you in some way—on what you do, what you say, how you look. Sometimes these comments are explicit; most often they're discoverable in the way in which others look at you, in what they talk about, in their interest in what you say. Pay close attention to this kind of information (verbal and nonverbal) and use it to increase your own self-awareness.

**Actively Seek Information about Yourself**     Actively seek out information to reduce your blind self. You need not be so obvious as to say, "Tell me about myself" or "What do you think of me?" Also, you don't want to seek such information from just anyone. People who are overly negative, who have personal agendas, or who know you only slightly are generally poor sources. But you can use everyday situations to gain self-information: "Do you think I was assertive enough when asking for the raise?" Or "Would I be thought too forward if I invited myself for dinner?" Do not, of course, seek this information constantly; your friends would quickly find others with whom to interact. But you can make use of some situations—perhaps those in which you're particularly unsure of what to do or how you appear—to reduce your blind self and increase self-awareness.

**See Your Different Selves**     Each of your friends and relatives views you differently; to each you're a somewhat different person. Yet you are really all of these selves. Practice seeing yourself as do the people with whom you interact. For starters, visualize how you're seen by your mother, your father, your teachers, your best friend, the stranger you sat next to on the bus, your employer, your neighbor's child. Because you're a composite of all these views, it's important

# InterMedia

## USES AND GRATIFICATIONS THEORY

In much the same way that you communicate or enter relationships to gain some kind of reward, you also use the media to gain both immediate and delayed rewards. For example, you may watch a particular television program because it satisfies your immediate need for information or entertainment. Or you may read a book because it contributes to satisfying a long-range need you have to become a writer. Research claims you derive four general gratifications from media (Dominick, 2005):

- learning something—for example, finding out what the new tax laws will involve or how movie reviewers rate the film you want to see
- diversion—for example, watching a football game as a way to release emotional energy
- affiliation—for example, going to the movies together or talking about the developments on *Days of Our Lives* with friends or family
- withdrawal—for example, renting a DVD to escape temporarily from responsibilities and other people.

But different media require different amounts of effort. For example, there's less effort required—less expense, less investment of time—in watching television than in going to a movie. There's less effort involved in buying a book on the Internet than in driving to a brick-and-mortar bookstore.

Media researchers propose that you're more likely to select media that provide great rewards while requiring little effort and are less likely to select media that promise small rewards and require great effort. Internet service providers and online retailers seem to recognize the validity of this theory, called the uses and gratifications theory, and are highly motivated to make online access and buying effortless and enjoyable (Ruggiero, 2000).

### Follow Up

How do you use the media to get the rewards you want with the least possible effort? How adequately does this theory describe your own media behavior?

---

that you periodically see yourself through the eyes of others. The experience will give you new and valuable perspectives on yourself.

**Increase Your Open Self**  When you increase your open self and reveal yourself to others, you also reveal yourself to yourself. At the very least, you bring into clearer focus what you may have buried within. As you discuss yourself, you may see connections that you had previously missed, and with the aid of feedback from others you may gain still more insight. Also, by increasing the open self you increase the likelihood that a meaningful and intimate dialogue will develop; through such interactions you best get to know yourself. Do, however, consider the risks involved in such self-disclosures.

## Self-Esteem

How much do you like yourself? How valuable a person do you think you are? How competent do you think you are? The answers to these questions reflect your **self-esteem,** the value you place on yourself. People who have high self-esteem, for example, are going to communicate this throughout their verbal and nonverbal messages. The ways they phrase their ideas and questions or the way they hold their head and maintain eye contact are likely to differ greatly from the way the person with low self-esteem would communicate. Similarly, people with different views of themselves will develop and maintain relationships with friends, lovers, and family differently. As you read this chapter, think about your own relationships and how the way you see yourself influences them.

Self-esteem is important, it is thought, because success breeds success (but see the ViewPoint on the next page). When you feel good about yourself—about who you are and what you're capable of doing—you will perform better. When you think like a success, you're more likely to act like a success. When you think you're a failure, you're more likely to act like a failure. Increasing self-esteem will, therefore, help you to function more effectively in school, in interpersonal relationships, and in careers. Here are a few suggestions for increasing self-esteem.

**Attack Your Self-Destructive Beliefs** Being as honest with yourself as you can, ask yourself if you hold beliefs such as these:

① The drive *to be perfect:* Do you try to perform at unrealistically high levels at work, school, and home, acting as if anything short of perfection is unacceptable?

② The drive *to be strong:* Do you believe that weakness and any of the more vulnerable emotions like sadness, compassion, or loneliness are wrong?

③ The drive *to please:* Do you seek approval from others and assume that if you gain the approval of others, then you're a worthy and deserving person, but if others disapprove of you, then you're worthless and undeserving?

④ The drive *to hurry up:* Do you do things quickly and try to do more than can be reasonably expected in any given amount of time?

⑤ The drive *to try hard:* Do you take on more responsibilities than any one person can be expected to handle?

As you can see, these beliefs are unrealistic (Butler, 1981). While it would be nice to be perfect, it is not a logical or realistic goal. Similarly, it would be nice to be emotionally strong or to please others, but it is not always possible. Because these kinds of beliefs set up unattainable and unrealistic goals, they inevitably lead you to fail and consequently can damage your self-esteem and prevent you from building meaningful and productive relationships.

Recognizing that you may have internalized self-destructive beliefs is a first step toward eliminating them. A second step involves recognizing that these beliefs are unrealistic and self-defeating. Psychotherapist Albert Ellis (1988; Ellis & Harper, 1975) and other cognitive therapists (for example, Beck, 1988) would argue that you can accomplish this through cognitive restructuring—that is by understanding why these beliefs are unrealistic and substituting more realistic ones. For example, following Ellis, you might try replacing an unrealistic desire to please everyone in everything you do with a more realistic attitude that although it would be nice if others were pleased with you, it certainly is not essential. A third step is giving yourself permission to fail, to be less than perfect, to be normal.

Do recognize that it's the unrealistic nature of these "drivers" that creates problems. Drivers are unrealistic beliefs that may motivate you to act in ways that are self-defeating (Butler, 1981). Certainly, trying hard and being strong are not unhealthy when they're realistic. It's only when they become absolute—when you try to be everything to everyone—that they become impossible to achieve and create problems.

**Secure Affirmation** It's frequently recommended that you remind yourself of your successes—that you focus on your good acts; your good deeds; your positive qualities, strengths, and virtues; and your productive and meaningful

**⚓ VIEWPOINT**

Despite its intuitive value, self-esteem is not without its critics (for example, Bushman & Baumeister, 1998; Baumeister, Bushman, & Campbell, 2000; Bower, 2001; Coover & Murphy, 2000; Hewitt, 1998; Epstein, 2005). Some researchers argue that high self-esteem is not necessarily desirable: It does nothing to improve academic performance, does not predict success, and may even lead to antisocial (especially aggressive) behavior. Interestingly enough, a surprisingly large number of criminals and delinquents are found to have extremely high self-esteem. And conversely, many people who have extremely low self-esteem have become quite successful in all fields (Owens, Stryker, & Goodman, 2002). How do you feel about the benefits or liabilities of self-esteem?

relationships with friends, loved ones, and relatives (Aronson, Cohen, & Nail, 1998; Aronson, Wilson, & Akert, 1999).

The idea behind this advice is that the way you talk to yourself will influence what you think of yourself (Cottle, 2003). If you talk positively about yourself, you will come to feel more positive about yourself. If you tell yourself that you're a success, that others like you, that you will succeed on the next test, and that you will be welcomed when asking for a date, you will soon come to feel positive about yourself (Adler & Fagley, 2005). Self-affirmations such as the following are often recommended:

- I'm a worthy person.
- I'm responsible and can be depended upon.
- I'm capable of loving and being loved.
- I deserve good things to happen to me.
- I can forgive myself for mistakes and misjudgments.

However, not all researchers would agree with this advice. Some argue that such affirmations—although extremely popular in self-help books—may not be very helpful. If you have low self-esteem, you're not going to believe yourself, because you don't have a high opinion of yourself to begin with (Paul, 2001). The alternative to self-affirmation is to secure affirmation from others. You'd do this by, for example, becoming more interpersonally competent and by interacting with more positive people. In this way you'll get more positive feedback from others, which, it's argued, is more helpful than self-talk in raising self-esteem.

## Ask the Researcher

### UNDERSTANDING SELF-TALK

**?** I often find myself thinking pretty negative things about myself and telling myself I really can't do something well, even when I can. I think it must be something to do with my self-esteem, but I'm not sure. Can you tell me about it, maybe make some suggestions?

What you're describing is *negative self-talk*. It's a form of intrapersonal communication; it's communication within the self *about* the self. Most people self-talk, and it can be negative or positive.

Self-talk is evidence of the relationship a person has with self and therefore a pretty important part of building self-esteem. The first thing to do is to take time to really listen to yourself and get a sense of how often and how negative the self-talk is. The next step is to change the negative self-talk to positive talk. You can do this by talking to yourself (or thinking; it doesn't have to be out loud) the way you would to your best friend ("You look hot"). Try it for a week; it takes practice. Give it time and attention, like you give to relationships with others whom you care about. You can start by giving yourself this positive self-talk message: "Yeah, I can do that."

**For more information** see L. C. Lederman, "Internal Muzak: An Exploration of Intrapersonal Communication, from "*Information and Behavior,* reprinted in L. C. Lederman, D. Gibson, and M. Taylor (eds.), *Communication Theory: A Reader,* 2nd ed. (Dubuque, IA: Kendall Hunt, 2005).

Linda C. Lederman (Ph.D., Rutgers) is professor of communication at Arizona State University where she is professor of health communication. Her research examines the role of communication and experience, including intrapersonal communication, in health issues. Her most recent book, coauthored with Lea Stewart, is *Changing the Culture of College Drinking* (Cresskill, NJ: Hampton Press, 2005).

**Chapter 3** The Self in Interpersonal Communication

Your brother has entered a relationship with someone who constantly puts him down; this has lowered his self-esteem to the point where he has no self-confidence. If this continues you fear your brother may again experience severe bouts of depression.   Ask yourself:  What options do you have for dealing with this problem? What, if anything, would you do?

**Seek Out Nourishing People**   Psychologist Carl Rogers (1970) drew a distinction between *noxious* and *nourishing* people. Noxious people criticize and find fault with just about everything. Not surprisingly, these people are difficult to be around. More important, however, is that with time you may come to believe that their criticism and faultfinding are justified. When that happens, your self-esteem is likely to diminish.

Nourishing people, on the other hand, are positive. They're optimists. They reward you, they stroke you, they make you feel good about yourself. Here too, with time, you'll come to believe these compliments and positive statements; as a result, your self-esteem is likely to rise.

Identification with people similar to yourself also seems to increase self-esteem. For example, one study found that deaf people who identified with the larger deaf community had greater self-esteem than those who didn't so identify (Jambor & Elliott, 2005). Similarly, a person's sense of identification with his or her cultural group seems to foster positive self-esteem (McDonald, McCabe, Yeh, Lau, Garland, & Hough, 2005).

**Work on Projects That Will Result in Success**   Some people want to fail, or so it seems. Often, they select projects that will result in failure. Perhaps the projects are too large or too difficult. In any event, they're impossible. A more beneficial strategy is to select projects that will result in success. Each success helps build self-esteem. Each success makes the next success a little easier. This doesn't mean that you shouldn't dream big; only that in some cases you may be tempted to try the impossible and be hurt when you don't succeed.

When a project does fail, recognize that this doesn't mean that you're a failure. Everyone fails somewhere along the line. Failure is something that happens; it's not something inside you. Further, failing once does not mean that you will fail the next time. So put failure in perspective. Don't make it an excuse for not trying again.

# Understanding Interpersonal Theory and Research

## SOCIAL PRESENCE THEORY AND ONLINE COMMUNICATION

Social presence theory argues that the "bandwidth" (the number of message cues exchanged) of communication influences the degree to which the communication is personal or impersonal (Short, Williams, & Christie, 1976; Walther & Parks, 2002; Wood & Smith, 2005). When lots of cues are exchanged (especially nonverbal cues), as in face-to-face communication, you feel great social presence—the whole person (the real person) is there for you to communicate with and exchange messages. When the bandwidth is smaller (as in e-mail or chat communication), then the communication is more impersonal. So, for example, personal communication is easier to achieve in face-to-face situations (in which tone of voice, facial expressions, eye contact, and similar nonverbal cues come into play) than in computer-mediated communication, which essentially contains only written cues.

It's more difficult, the theory goes, to communicate supportiveness, warmth, and friendliness in text-based chat or e-mail exchanges because of the smaller bandwidth. Of course, as video and audio components become more widely used, this distinction will fade; for now, however, the proposition seems logical enough. But some researchers have questioned this theory. They have argued that factors such as attitude similarity and group identity among online participants can contribute mightily to personal communication and may even override the contribution of nonverbal cues. This controversy is likely to continue for some time.

### Working with Theories and Research

What has been your experience in online and face-to-face communication? Do you find that it's more difficult to communicate interpersonally and develop close relationships online because you don't have the nonverbal cues to guide your impressions?

# SELF-DISCLOSURE

One of the most important forms of interpersonal communication that you can engage in is talking about yourself, or **self-disclosure.** Self-disclosure means communicating information about yourself to another person. It may involve information about (1) your values, beliefs, and desires ("I believe in reincarnation"); (2) your behavior ("I committed grand larceny but was never caught"); or (3) your self-qualities or characteristics ("I'm dyslexic"). Overt and carefully planned statements about yourself as well as slips of the tongue would be classified as self-disclosing communications. Similarly, you could self-disclose nonverbally by, for example, wearing gang colors, a wedding ring, or a shirt with slogans that reveal your political or social concerns. Self-disclosure also may involve your reactions to the feelings of others: for example, when you tell your friend that you're sorry she was fired.

Self-disclosure occurs in all forms of communication, not just interpersonal. It frequently occurs in small group settings, in public speeches, and on television talk shows. As these examples make clear, self-disclosure can occur in face-to-face settings as well as through television and the Internet. In chat groups, for example, a great deal of self-disclosure goes on, as it does when people reveal themselves in personal e-mails and in newsgroup and listserv submissions. In fact, research finds that reciprocal self-disclosure occurs more quickly and at higher levels online than it does in face-to-face interactions (Levine, 2000; Joinson, 2001).

You probably self-disclose for a variety of reasons. Perhaps you feel the need for catharsis—a need to get rid of guilt feelings or to confess some wrongdoing. Or you might wish to make yourself look good, so you might self-disclose your good qualities by giving examples of your bravery or compassion or determination. You might also disclose to help the listener; to show the listener, for example, how you dealt with an addiction or succeeded in getting a promotion. Of course, you may self-disclose to encourage relationship growth, or to maintain or repair a relationship, or even as a strategy for ending a relationship.

Although self-disclosure may occur as a single message—for example, you tell a stranger on a train that you're thinking about getting a divorce—it's best viewed as a *developing* process in which information is exchanged between people in a relationship over the period of their relationship (Spencer, 1993, 1994). If we view it as a developing process, we can then appreciate how self-disclosure changes as the relationship changes; for example, as a relationship progresses from initial contact through involvement to intimacy and then perhaps to deterioration or dissolution. We can also appreciate how self-disclosure will differ depending on the type of relationship you have with another person; for example, depending on whether the other person is your friend, parent, child, or counselor.

Self-disclosure may involve information that you communicate to others freely or that you normally keep hidden. It may supply information ("I earn $45,000") or reveal feelings ("I'm feeling very blue").

Self-disclosure involves at least one other individual; it cannot be an *intra*personal communication act. To qualify as self-disclosure, the information must be received and understood by another individual. As you can appreciate, self-disclosure can vary from the relatively insignificant ("I'm a Sagittarius") to the highly revealing and deeply personal ("I'm currently in an abusive relationship" or "I'm almost always depressed").

The remaining discussion of this important concept will be more meaningful if you first consider your own willingness to self-disclose. How likely would you be to disclose the following items of information to, say, members of this class? Respond using a simple five-part scale (very likely, likely, not sure, unlikely, very unlikely):

1. Some of your personal characteristics that you're especially proud of and that give you satisfaction.
2. Some of the happiest moments in your life.
3. Aspects of your personality that you don't like.

④ Your most embarrassing moment.
⑤ Your sexual fantasies.
⑥ Your greatest fears.

Thinking about your willingness to disclose these types of information—and you can easily add other things about yourself that you would and would not disclose—should get you started examining your own self-disclosing behavior.

## Influences on Self-Disclosure

Many factors influence whether or not you disclose, what you disclose, and to whom you disclose. Among the most important factors are who you are, your culture, your gender, who your listeners are, and what your topic is.

**Who You Are**    Highly sociable and extroverted people self-disclose more than those who are less sociable and more introverted. People who are apprehensive about talking in general also self-disclose less than do those who are more comfortable in communicating.

Competent people and those with high self-esteem engage in self-disclosure more than less competent people and those with low self-esteem. Perhaps competent people have greater self-confidence and more positive things to reveal. Similarly, their self-confidence may make them more willing to risk possible negative reactions (McCroskey & Wheeless, 1976; Dolgin, Meyer, & Schwartz, 1991).

**Your Culture**    Different cultures view self-disclosure differently. People in the United States, for example, disclose more than do those in Great Britain, Germany, Japan, or Puerto Rico (Gudykunst, 1983). American students disclose more than do students from nine different Middle East countries (Jourard, 1971a). Americans also reported greater self-disclosure when communicating with other Americans than when communicating interculturally (Allen, Long, O'Mara, & Judd, 2003). Chinese students consider more topics to be

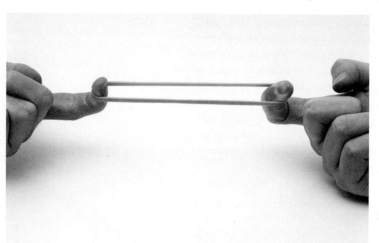

taboo and inappropriate for self-disclosure than do their British peers (Goodwin & Lee, 1994). Indians are reluctant to self-disclose for fear that what they say will reflect negatively on their reputation and family (Hastings, 2000). And in a study of Muslim, Druze, and Jewish adolescents in Israel, the Muslim students disclosed most, Jewish students next, and Druze students least (Shechtman, Hiradin, & Zina, 2003). Finally, in Japan it's considered undesirable for colleagues to reveal personal information, whereas in much of the United States it's expected (Barnlund, 1989; Hall & Hall, 1987).

In some cultures—for example, in Mexico—there is a strong emphasis on discussing all matters in a positive mode; this undoubtedly influences the way Mexicans approach self-disclosure as well. Negative self-disclosures, in contrast, are usually made to close intimates and then only after considerable time has elapsed in a relationship. This pattern is consistent with evidence showing that self-disclosure and trust are positively related (Wheeless & Grotz, 1977). Additional research finds that the Hispanic reluctance to disclose negative issues such as one's positive HIV status is creating serious problems in preventing and treating HIV infection (Szapocznik, 1995). Despite the generalization that many Latin Americans disclose less than people in the United States, however, one study found that Argentineans disclosed more than Americans (Horenstein & Downey, 2003).

There is some indication that the political climate today will influence the cross-cultural self-disclosure patterns of all people. Significant self-disclosures between Muslims and non-Muslim Americans, for example, are likely to be more guarded than before 9/11/2001 and the Iraq war, as are self-disclosures between recent immigrants and other Americans (Barry, 2003).

These differences aside, there are also important similarities across cultures. For example, people from Great Britain, Germany, the United States, and Puerto Rico are all more apt to disclose personal information—hobbies, interests, attitudes, and opinions on politics and religion—than information on finances, sex, personality, or interpersonal relationships (Jourard, 1968, 1971a, 1971b). Similarly, one study showed self-disclosure patterns between American males to be virtually identical to those between Korean males (Won-Doornink, 1991).

**Your Gender**    The popular stereotype of gender differences in self-disclosure emphasizes the male's reluctance to speak about himself. For the most part, research supports this view and shows that women disclose more than men. More specifically, women disclose more than men about their previous romantic relationships, their feelings about their closest same-sex friends, their greatest fears, and what they don't like about their partners (Sprecher, 1987). Women also seem to increase the depth of their self-disclosures as the relationship becomes more intimate, whereas men seem not to change their self-disclosure levels. Men, for example, have more taboo topics that they will not disclose to their friends than do women (Goodwin & Lee, 1994). Finally, women even self-disclose more to members of the extended family than do men (Komarovsky, 1964; Argyle & Henderson, 1985; Moghaddam, Taylor, & Wright, 1993).

There are exceptions to this general gender tendency, however. For example, in a study of Americans and Argentineans, males indicated a significantly greater willingness to self-disclose than females (Horenstein & Downey, 2003). Another notable exception occurs in initial encounters. Here men will disclose more intimately than women, perhaps "in order to control the relationship's development" (Derlega, Winstead, Wong, & Hunter, 1985).

Men and women give different reasons for avoiding self-disclosure (Rosenfeld, 1979), but one reason is shared by both genders: "If I disclose, I might project an image I don't want to project." In a society in which image is so important—in which a person's image is often the basis for success or failure—this fear is not surprising. Other reasons for avoiding self-disclosure, however, are unique to men or women. Among males' reasons for self-disclosure avoidance is the feeling that "If I disclose to you, I might project an image I don't want to project, which could make me look bad and cause me to lose control over you. This might go so far as to affect relationships I have with people other than you." Men's principal objective in avoiding self-disclosure is to maintain control. The general reason women avoid self-disclosure is that "If I disclose to you, I might project an image I don't want to project, such as my being emotionally ill, which you might use against me and which might hurt our relationship." Women's principal objective for avoiding self-disclosure is "to avoid personal hurt and problems with the relationship."

**Your Listeners**    Self-disclosure occurs more readily in small groups than in large groups. Dyads, or groups of two people, are the most hospitable groups for self-disclosure. With one listener, you can attend to the responses carefully. You can monitor the disclosures, continuing if there is support from your listener and stopping if there isn't. With more than one listener, such monitoring becomes difficult, because the listeners' responses are sure to vary. Interestingly enough, one study found that participants in computer-mediated communication used more direct strategies to reduce uncertainty and to elicit disclosures than they did in face-to-face encounters, which resulted in their judging the CMC conversations as more effective (Tidwell & Walther, 2002).

Because you disclose, generally at least, on the basis of the support you receive, you disclose to people you like (Collins & Miller, 1994; Derlega, Winstead, Greene, Serovich, & Elwood, 2004) and to people you trust and love (Wheeless & Grotz, 1977; Sprecher & Hendrick, 2004). You also come to like those to whom you disclose (Berg & Archer, 1983). Not surprisingly, you're more likely to disclose to people who are close to you in age

**Self-disclosure.** Some research indicates that self-disclosure occurs more quickly and at higher levels of intimacy online than in face-to-face situations (Joinson, 2001; Levine, 2000). Other research finds that people experience greater closeness and self-disclosure in face-to-face groups than in Internet chat groups (Mallen, Day, & Green, 2003). What has been your experience with self-disclosure in online and face-to-face situations?

(Parker & Parrott, 1995). Another finding is that most young men and women disclose more to their mothers than to their fathers, perhaps because mothers are seen to be more supportive than fathers; similarly, young men and women disclose their same-sex attraction more readily to their mothers than to their fathers (Savin-Williams & Ream, 2003).

At times more self-disclosure occurs in temporary than permanent relationships—for example, between strangers on a train or plane, a kind of "in-flight intimacy" (McGill, 1985). In this situation, two people set up an intimate self-disclosing relationship during a brief travel period, but they don't pursue it beyond that point. In a similar way, you might set up a relationship with one or several people on the Internet and engage in significant disclosure. Perhaps knowing that you'll never see these other people and that they will never know where you live or work or what you look like makes it a bit easier.

In American culture we're more likely to disclose when the person we're with discloses. This **dyadic effect** (what one person does, the other person does likewise) probably leads us to feel more secure and reinforces our own self-disclosing behavior. Disclosures are also more intimate when they're made in response to the disclosures of others (Berg & Archer, 1983). This dyadic effect is not universal across all cultures, however. For example, although Americans are likely to follow the dyadic effect and reciprocate with explicit, verbal self-disclosure, Koreans aren't (Won-Doornink, 1985). As you can appreciate, this can easily cause intercultural differences; for example, an American might be insulted if his or her Korean counterpart didn't reciprocate with self-disclosures that were similar in depth.

**Your Topic and Channel**   You're more likely to disclose about some topics than others. For example, you're probably more likely to self-disclose information about your job or hobbies than about your sex life or financial situation (Jourard, 1968, 1971a). You're also more likely to disclose favorable information than unfavorable information. Generally, the more personal and negative the topic, the less likely you will be to self-disclose.

Recently, research has addressed differences in self-disclosure depending on the channel; that is, whether disclosure takes place face-to-face or online. Some researchers have pointed to a "disinhibition effect" that occurs in online communication. We seem less inhibited in communicating in e-mail or in chat groups, for example, than we do face-to-face. Among the reasons for this seems to be the fact that in online communication there is a certain degree of anonymity and invisibility (Suler, 2004).

## Rewards of Self-Disclosure

Research shows that self-disclosure helps to increase self-knowledge, communication and relationship effectiveness, and physiological well-being.

**Self-Knowledge**   One reward of self-disclosure is that you gain a new perspective on yourself, a deeper understanding of your own behavior. Through self-disclosure you may bring to consciousness a great deal that you might otherwise keep from conscious analysis. For example, as Mark talks about the difficulties he had living with an alcoholic father, he may remember details of his early life or entertain new feelings.

Even self-acceptance is difficult without self-disclosure. You accept yourself largely through the eyes of others. Through self-disclosure and subsequent support, you may be in a better position to see the positive responses to you. Thus, you're more likely to respond by developing a more positive self-concept.

**Communication and Relationship Effectiveness**   Because you understand the messages of another person largely to the extent that you understand the person, self-disclosure is an essential condition for getting to know each other.

Couples who engage in significant self-disclosure are found to remain together longer than couples who don't (Sprecher, 1987). Self-disclosure helps you achieve a closer relationship with the person to whom you self-disclose and increases relationship satisfaction

(Schmidt & Cornelius, 1987; Meeks, Hendrick, & Hendrick, 1998). Within a sexual relationship, self-disclosure increases sexual rewards and general relationship satisfaction. These two benefits increase sexual satisfaction (Byers & Demmons, 1999). Without self-disclosure, meaningful relationships seem impossible to develop. Interestingly enough, you also come to increase your affection for your partner when you self-disclose.

**Physiological Health**   People who self-disclose are less vulnerable to illnesses (Pennebacker, 1991). Not surprisingly, health benefits also result from disclosing in e-mails (Sheese, Brown, & Graziano, 2004). For example, bereavement over the death of someone very close is linked to physical illness for those who bear this alone and in silence. But it's unrelated to any physical problems for those who share their grief with others. Similarly, women who suffer sexual trauma normally experience a variety of illnesses (among them, headaches and stomach problems). Women who keep these experiences to themselves, however, suffer these illnesses to a much greater extent than do those who talk with others about these traumas. The physiological effort required to keep your burdens to yourself seems to interact with the effects of the trauma to create a combined stress that can lead to a variety of illnesses.

## Dangers of Self-Disclosure: Risks Ahead

Realize that the more you reveal about yourself to others the more areas of your life you expose to possible attack. Especially in the competitive context of work (or even romance), the more that others know about you, the more they'll be able to use against you. This simple fact has prompted power watcher Michael Korda (1975, p. 302) to advise that you "never reveal all of yourself to other people; hold something back in reserve so that people are never quite sure if they really know you." This advice is not to suggest that you be secretive; rather, Korda is advocating "remaining slightly mysterious, as if [you] were always capable of doing something surprising and unexpected."

As you weigh your decision to self-disclose or not, keep Korda's advice in mind. Also, realize that there are considerable potential personal, relational, and professional risks to self-disclosure:

**Personal risks:** If you self-disclose aspects of your life that vary greatly from the values of those to whom you disclose, you may experience rejection by even the closest friends and family members. Men and women who disclose that they have cheated on their relationship partner, have stolen, or are suffering from protracted depression, for example, may find their friends and family no longer wanting to be quite as close as before.

**Relational risks:** Even in close and long-lasting relationships, self-disclosure can cause problems (Bochner, 1984). Total self-disclosure may prove threatening to a relationship by causing a decrease in mutual attraction, trust, or any of the bonds holding the individuals together. Self-disclosures concerning infidelity, romantic fantasies, past indiscretions or crimes, lies, or hidden weaknesses and fears could easily have such negative effects.

**Professional risks:** Revealing political views or attitudes toward different religious or racial groups may create problems on the job, as may disclosing any health problems, such as being HIV positive (Fesko, 2001). Teachers who disclose former or current drug use or cohabitation with students may find themselves denied tenure, teaching at undesirable hours, and eventually falling victim to "budget cuts." Teachers or students who, in the supportive atmosphere of their interpersonal communication course, disclose details about their sex lives or financial condition or reveal self-doubts, anxieties, and fantasies may find some less-than-sympathetic listeners using that information against them. Openly gay and lesbian personnel in the military, as well as in education, fire protection, law enforcement, or health care agencies, to cite

SPEAKING
**Interpersonal-E**

**Cookies.** Cookies—small files that keep track of the sites you visit and generally make surfing the Web more efficient—also collect information on your computer behavior that you may not want anyone to know about. You can easily delete cookies by going to Tools/Internet Options/General Tab/Settings/View Files and click on the cookie files you want to delete.

just a few examples, may find themselves confined to desk jobs, prevented from further advancement, or even charged with criminal behavior and fired.

In making your choice between disclosing and not disclosing, keep in mind—in addition to the advantages and dangers already noted—the irreversible nature of communication (discussed in Chapter 1). Regardless of how many times you may try to qualify something or take it back, once you have said something, you cannot withdraw it. You cannot erase the conclusions and inferences listeners have made on the basis of your disclosures.

## Guidelines for Self-Disclosure

Because self-disclosure is so important and so delicate a matter, guidelines are offered here for (1) deciding whether and how to self-disclose, (2) responding to the disclosures of others, and (3) resisting pressures to self-disclosure.

**Guidelines for Making Self-Disclosures**   In addition to weighing the potential rewards and dangers of self-disclosure already discussed, consider the following guidelines; they will help raise the right questions before you make what must be *your* decision.

**Consider the Motivation for the Self-Disclosure**   Self-disclosure should be motivated by a concern for the relationship, for the others involved, and for oneself. Some people self-disclose out of a desire to hurt the listener. Persons who tell their parents that they never loved them or that the parents hindered rather than helped their emotional development may be disclosing out of a desire to hurt and perhaps punish rather than to improve the relationship. Neither should self-disclosure be used to punish oneself, perhaps because of some guilt feeling or unresolved conflict. Self-disclosure should serve a useful and productive function for all persons involved.

**Consider the Appropriateness of the Self-Disclosure**   Self-disclosure should be appropriate to the context and to the relationship between you and your listener. Before making any significant self-disclosure, ask whether this is the right time and place. Could a better time and place be arranged? Ask, too, whether this self-disclosure is appropriate to the relationship. Generally, the more intimate the disclosures, the closer the relationship should be. It's probably best to resist intimate disclosures (especially negative ones) with nonintimates or casual acquaintances, or in the early stages of a relationship.

**Consider the Disclosures of the Other Person**   During your disclosures, give the other person a chance to reciprocate with his or her own disclosures. If reciprocal disclosures are not made, reassess your own self-disclosures. It may be a signal that for this person at this time and in this context, your disclosures are not welcome or appropriate. It's generally best to disclose gradually and in small increments. When you disclose too rapidly and all at once, you can't monitor your listener's responses and retreat if they're not positive enough. Further, you prevent the listener from responding with his or her own disclosures and thereby upset the natural balance that is so helpful in this kind of communication exchange.

**Consider the Possible Burdens Self-Disclosure Might Entail**   Carefully weigh the potential problems that you may incur as a result of your disclosure. Can you afford to lose your job if you disclose your arrest record? Are you willing to risk relational difficulties if you disclose your infidelities? Also, ask yourself whether you're making unreasonable demands on the listener. For example, consider the person who swears his or her mother-in-law to secrecy and then self-discloses having an affair with a neighbor. This disclosure places an unfair burden on the mother-in-law, who is now torn between breaking her promise of secrecy and allowing her child to believe a lie. Parents often place unreasonable burdens on their children by self-disclosing relationship problems, financial difficulties, or self-doubts, not realizing that the children may be too young or too emotionally involved to deal effectively with this information.

**Guidelines for Facilitating and Responding to Self-Disclosures**   When someone discloses to you, it's usually a sign of trust and affection. In serving this most important receiver function, keep the following guidelines in mind. These guidelines will also help you facilitate the disclosures of another person.

**Practice the Skills of Effective and Active Listening**   The skills of effective listening (Chapter 5) are especially important when you are listening to self-disclosures: Listen actively, listen for different levels of meaning, listen with empathy, and listen with an open mind. Paraphrase the speaker so that you can be sure you understand both the thoughts and the feelings communicated. Express an understanding of the speaker's feelings to allow the speaker the opportunity to see them more objectively and through the eyes of another. Ask questions to ensure your own understanding and to signal your interest and attention.

**Support and Reinforce the Discloser**   Express support for the person during and after the disclosures. Try to refrain from evaluation. Concentrate on understanding and empathizing with the discloser. Allow the discloser to choose the pace; don't rush the discloser with the too-frequent "So how did it all end?" response. Make your supportiveness clear to the discloser through your verbal and nonverbal responses: Maintain eye contact, lean toward the speaker, ask relevant questions, and echo the speaker's thoughts and feelings.

**Be Willing to Reciprocate**   When you make relevant and appropriate disclosures of your own in response to the other person's disclosures, you're demonstrating your understanding of the other's meanings and at the same time showing a willingness to communicate on this meaningful level.

**Keep the Disclosures Confidential**   When a person discloses to you, it's because she or he wants you to know the feelings and thoughts that are communicated. If you reveal these disclosures to others, negative effects are inevitable. Revealing what was said will probably inhibit future disclosures by this individual in general, and to you in particular; it's likely that your relationship will suffer considerably. But most importantly, betraying a confidence is unfair. It debases what could be and should be a meaningful interpersonal experience.

It's interesting to note that one of the netiquette rules of e-mail is that you shouldn't forward mail to third parties without the writer's permission. This rule is a useful one for self-disclosure generally: Maintain confidentiality; don't pass on disclosures made to you to others without the person's permission.

**Don't Use the Disclosures against the Person**   Many self-disclosures expose some kind of vulnerability or weakness. If you later turn around and use disclosures against the person who made them, you betray the confidence and trust invested in you. Regardless of how angry you may get, resist the temptation to use the disclosures of others as weapons—the relationship is sure to suffer and may never fully recover.

**Guidelines for Resisting Self-Disclosure**   You may, on occasion, find yourself in a position where a friend, colleague, or romantic partner pressures you to self-disclose. In such situations, you may wish to weigh the pros and cons of self-disclosure and then make your decision as to whether and what you'll disclose. If your decision is not to disclose and you're still being pressured, then you need to say something. Here are a few suggestions.

**A s к Yourself**
Discouraging Self-Disclosure

Your colleague at work reveals too much private information for your liking. You're really not interested in this person's sex life, financial woes, and medical problems.   Ask yourself: What can you do to eliminate this too-personal self-disclosure, at least to you?

Chapter 3   The Self in Interpersonal Communication

# Ethics in Interpersonal Communication

## KEEPING SECRETS

In *Secrets* (1983), ethicist Sissela Bok identifies three types of situations in which she argues it would be unethical to reveal the secrets of another person. According to Bok:

- It is unethical to reveal information that you promised to keep secret.
- It is unethical to talk about another person when you know the information to be false.
- It is unethical to invade the privacy to which everyone has a right, to reveal information that no one else has a right to know; and it is especially unethical when such disclosures can hurt the individual involved.

### What would you do?

As Bok suggests, consider an 18-year-old student with whom you're friendly who confides that he intends to commit suicide. Using these guidelines, how would you evaluate the ethics involved in revealing this secret? What ethical justification might be offered for revealing such a secret? If you were the student's friend, what would you do in this situation?

---

### ASK Yourself
#### Refusing to Self-Disclose

You've dated this person three or four times, and each time you're pressured to self-disclose past experiences and personal information you're simply not ready to talk about—at least, not at this early stage of the relationship. Ask yourself: What are some of the things you can say or do to resist this pressure to self-disclose? What might you say to discourage further requests that you reveal yourself?

**Don't Be Pushed**  Although there may be certain legal or ethical reasons for disclosing, generally, if you don't want to disclose, you don't have to. Don't be pushed into disclosing because others are doing it or because you're asked to. Realize that you're in control of what you reveal to whom and when. Remember that self-disclosure has significant consequences. If you're not sure you want to reveal something, at least not until you've had additional time to think about it, then don't.

**Be Assertive in Your Refusal to Disclose**  Say, very directly, "I'd rather not talk about that now" or "Now is not the time for this type of discussion." More specific guidelines for communicating assertiveness are offered in Chapter 6.

**Be Indirect and Move to Another Topic**  Avoid the question and change the subject. This is a polite way of saying, "I'm not talking about it," and may be the preferred choice in certain situations. Most often people will get the hint and understand your refusal to disclose. If they don't, then you may have to use a more direct approach.

##  COMMUNICATION APPREHENSION

Communication apprehension is one of the most extensively researched variables in the field of interpersonal communication, so we know a great deal about this problem that many people experience. First, let's look at the nature of communication apprehension, define it, and consider the factors that influence our level of apprehension. Second, we'll examine some of the theories of apprehension and see how, on the basis of these theories, you can more effectively manage or control it. These discussions will prove more valuable if you first take the following brief self-test, "How Apprehensive Are You?"

This questionnaire is composed of six statements concerning your feelings about communicating in interpersonal conversations. Please indicate in the space provided the degree to which each statement applies to you. Use the following scale: 1 = strongly agree, 2 = agree, 3 = undecided, 4 = disagree, 5 = strongly disagree. There are no right or wrong answers. Many of the statements are similar to other statements; do not be concerned about this. Work quickly; record your first impression.

_____ 1. While participating in a conversation with a new acquaintance, I feel very nervous.
_____ 2. I have no fear of speaking up in conversations.
_____ 3. Ordinarily I am very tense and nervous in conversations.
_____ 4. Ordinarily I am very calm and relaxed in conversations.
_____ 5. While conversing with a new acquaintance, I feel very relaxed.
_____ 6. I'm afraid to speak up in conversations.

**HOW DID YOU DO?**  Compute your score as follows:

1. Begin with the number 18; this is used as a base so that you won't wind up with negative numbers.
2. To 18, add your scores for items 2, 4, and 5.
3. Subtract your scores for items 1, 3, and 6 from your step 2 total.
4. The result (which should be somewhere between 6 and 30) is your apprehension score for interpersonal conversations. The higher the score, the greater your apprehension. A score above 18 indicates some degree of apprehension.

**WHAT WILL YOU DO?**  First try to identify those interpersonal situations that create the greatest apprehension for you. What factors can you identify that contribute to heightening apprehension? What can you do to reduce the impact of those factors?

_Source:_ From James C. McCroskey, _Introduction to Rhetorical Communication,_ 8th ed. (Boston: Allyn & Bacon, 2001). Copyright © 2001 by Pearson Education. Reprinted/adapted by permission of the publisher.

## The Nature of Communication Apprehension

Now that you have a general idea of your own communication apprehension, it may interest you to know that "communication apprehension is probably the most common handicap . . . suffered by people in contemporary American society" (McCroskey & Wheeless, 1976). According to surveys of college students, between 10 percent and 20 percent suffer "severe, debilitating communication apprehension," while another 20 percent suffer from "communication apprehension to a degree substantial enough to interfere to some extent with their normal functioning."

The terms **communication apprehension** and **shyness** (also known as unwillingness to communicate, stage fright, or reticence) refer to a state of fear or anxiety about communication interaction. People develop negative feelings and predict negative results as a function of engaging in communication interactions. They may fear making mistakes and being humiliated (Bippus & Daly, 1999). They feel that whatever gain would accrue from engaging in communication would be outweighed by the fear. To those with high communication apprehension, the communication interaction just isn't worth the fear it engenders.

**Trait apprehension** is fear of communication generally, regardless of the specific situation. It appears in dyadic, small group, public speaking, and mass communication situations. **State apprehension,** in contrast, is specific to a given communication situation. For example, a speaker may fear public speaking but have no difficulty with dyadic communication, or a speaker may fear job interviews but have no fear of public speaking. State apprehension is extremely common; it's experienced by most people in some situations.

Communication apprehension exists on a continuum. People are not either apprehensive or unapprehensive. We all experience some degree of apprehension. Some people are extremely apprehensive and become incapacitated in a communication situation. They suffer a great deal in a society oriented, as ours is, around communication—a society in which success depends on the ability to communicate effectively. Others are so mildly apprehensive that they appear to experience no fear at all when confronted by communication situations; they actively seek out communication experiences and rarely feel any significant apprehension. Most of us fall between these two extremes.

**Apprehensive Behaviors**   Generally, apprehension leads to a decrease in the frequency, strength, and likelihood of engaging in communication transactions. High apprehensives avoid communication situations; when forced to participate, they do so as little as possible. This reluctance to communicate shows itself in a variety of forms. For example, one study found those with high apprehension to be less willing to communicate, to volunteer, and to work with the terminally ill than were those who were low in apprehension (Ayres & Hopf, 1995). Your communication apprehension will even influence your satisfaction with dating (Powers & Love, 2000).

Consider the following statements about your own feelings about communicating with your dating partner. Are they basically true (yes) or basically false (no)?

❶ I am comfortable in developing intimate conversations with my partner.
❷ I feel I am an open communicator with my partner.
❸ I am hesitant to develop a "deep" conversation with my partner.
❹ Even in casual conversations with my partner, I feel I must guard what I say.

If you responded "yes" to statements 1 and 2 and "no" to statements 3 and 4, then, research shows, you're more likely to experience interpersonal communication satisfaction. If, on the other hand, you responded "no" to statements 1 and 2 and "yes" to statements 3 and 4, then you're likely to experience a lack of satisfaction. In small group situations, apprehensives not only talk less but also avoid the seats of influence—for example, those in the group leader's direct line of sight. High apprehensives are less likely to be seen as leaders in small group situations regardless of their actual behaviors. Even in classrooms, they avoid seats where they can be easily called on, and they maintain little direct eye contact with the instructor, especially when a question is likely to be asked. Related to this is the finding that apprehensives have more negative attitudes toward school, earn poorer grades, and are more likely to drop out of college (McCroskey, Booth-Butterfield, & Payne, 1989).

Teachers and students consider apprehensives to be less desirable social choices. Apprehensives disclose little and avoid occupations with heavy communication demands (for example, teaching or public relations). Within their occupation, they're less desirous of advancement, largely because advancement would bring an associated increase in communication. High apprehensives feel less satisfied with their jobs, probably because they're less successful in advancing and in developing interpersonal relationships. High apprehensives are even less likely to get job interviews. In the words of one article, in the United States we value "rugged individualism and the conquering of new environments, whether in outer space or in overseas markets. Personal attributes held high in our social esteem are leadership, assertiveness, dominance, independence, and risk taking. Hence a stigma surrounding shyness" (Carducci & Zimbardo, 1966, p. 66). Another reason why shyness is negatively evaluated is that many shy people don't detect and so can't respond appropriately to the emotional cues of others, perhaps conveying the impression that they don't care about or are uninterested in other people (*New York Times*, January 4, 2005, p. A16).

All this does not mean that apprehensives are ineffective or unhappy people. Most apprehensives have learned or can learn to deal with their communication anxiety.

**Influences on Communication Apprehension**   Research has identified several factors that increase communication apprehension (McCroskey & Daly, 1987; Beatty, 1988;

**SPEAKING**
**>> Interpersonal-E**

**Online shyness.** In face-to-face communication a shy person is highly sensitive to rejection cues from others. In computer-mediated communication, however, these cues are not as easily detected; so the shy person may feel more comfortable communicating online than in face-to-face situations (Stritzke, Nguyen, & Durkin, 2004). From your experience with your own level of shyness or with shy people you know, do you think this finding is generally true? If so, what implications can you draw for helping shy people communicate online (Scealy, Phillips, & Stevenson, 2002)?

Richmond & McCroskey, 1998). A knowledge of these factors will help you to increase your understanding and control of your own apprehension.

- *Degree of evaluation:* The more you perceive the situation as one in which you will be evaluated, the greater your apprehension is likely to be. Employment interviews, for example, provoke anxiety largely because they're highly evaluative.
- *Subordinate status:* When you feel that others are better communicators than you are or that they know more than you do, your apprehension increases. For example, shy students report particular difficulty in speaking with authorities (Zimbardo, 1977).
- *Degree of conspicuousness:* The more conspicuous you are, the more likely you are to feel apprehensive. This is why delivering a speech to a large audience is more anxiety provoking than speaking in a small group: You're more conspicuous before the large group—you stand out, and all attention is on you.
- *Degree of unpredictability:* The more unpredictable the situation, the greater your apprehension is likely to be. Ambiguous and new situations are unpredictable; you cannot know beforehand what they will be like, so you become anxious. A similar condition seems to increase people's shyness when interacting with strangers; 70 percent of shy students surveyed said they were especially shy with strangers (Zimbardo, 1977).
- *Degree of dissimilarity:* When you feel you have little in common with your listeners, you're likely to feel anxious.
- *Prior successes and failures:* Your experience in similar situations greatly influences the way you respond to new ones. Prior success generally (though not always) reduces apprehension, whereas prior failure generally (though not always) increases apprehension. There is no mystery here: Prior success says that you can succeed this time as well; prior failure warns that you may fail again.
- *Lack of communication skills and experience:* If you lack skills in typing, you can hardly expect to type very well. If you have never asked for a raise and have no idea how to go about doing it, for example, it's perfectly reasonable that you will feel apprehension.

**Culture and Communication Apprehension**    Apprehension, shyness, and the willingness to communicate vary from one culture to another (Breidenstein-Cutspec & Goering, 1989). For example, in one study of shyness, Israelis were found to be the least shy; only 24 percent reported they were currently experiencing shyness, compared to Mexicans (39 percent), Americans (42 percent), Germans (50 percent), Taiwanese (55 percent), and Japanese (60 percent) (Carducci & Zimbardo, 1996). In a study of the willingness to communicate, American college students indicated the highest willingness to communicate, whereas students from Micronesia indicated the lowest. Micronesian students also indicated the highest degree of shyness in this study, and Puerto Ricans reported the lowest (McCroskey & Richmond, 1990; Richmond & McCroskey, 1998). Other research finds similarities between different cultures, however; for example, Argentineans and Americans show similar degrees of apprehension (Sarquisse, Butler, & Pryor, 2003).

When the interpersonal communication is intercultural communication, additional uncertainty, fear, and anxiety, all of which are intimately related to communication apprehension (Stephan & Stephan, 1985), may enter in. When you're in an intercultural situation—say your coworkers are largely people of cultures very different from your own—you're more uncertain about the situation and about their possible responses, and you're more likely to experience heightened communication apprehension. Not surprisingly, most people react negatively to high uncertainty and develop a decreased attraction for these other people (Gudykunst & Nishida, 1984; Gudykunst, Yang, & Nishida, 1985). When you're sure of the situation and can predict what will happen, you're more likely to feel comfortable and at ease. But when the situation is uncertain and you cannot predict what will happen, you become more apprehensive (Gudykunst & Kim, 1992).

There are also gender differences in apprehension. For example, men report greater communication apprehension about intercultural communication than do women. Men also

Shyness researchers have argued that the people we single out as heroes are those who call attention to themselves—rock stars and media personalities, for example—because "people who are most likely to be successful are those who are able to obtain attention and feel comfortable with it" (Carducci & Zimbardo, 1996, p. 66). Who are your heroes? Are they people who call attention to themselves? Are any of your heroes high in communication apprehension or shy?

report greater ethnocentrism and less willingness to communicate interculturally than do women (Lin & Rancer, 2003a, 2003b).

## Theories of Communication Apprehension Management

Following communication researchers Virginia Richmond and James McCroskey (1998), we can distinguish three theoretical (and eminently practical) approaches to understanding and managing communication apprehension: cognitive restructuring, systematic desensitization, and skill acquisition.

**Cognitive Restructuring**   The cognitive restructuring theory, introduced earlier in this chapter, holds that your own unrealistic beliefs generate a fear of failure. Because you set unachievable goals ("Everyone must love me, I have to be thoroughly competent, I have to be the best in everything"), you logically fear failure. This fear of failure (and the irrational beliefs behind it) are at the foundation of your apprehension (for example, Markway, Carmin, Pollard, & Flynn, 1992). Cognitive restructuring, then, advises you to change your irrational beliefs and substitute more rational ones ("It would be nice if everyone loved me, but I don't need that to survive. I can fail. Although it would be nice, I don't have to be the best in everything."). Your last step is to practice your new, more rational beliefs (Ellis & Harper, 1975; Ellis, 1988).

The process may go something like this: Unrealistic beliefs give rise to anxiety because you know that you can never achieve these unrealistically high goals and are bound to fail at some point. There's not a speaker in the world who wouldn't fail given these unrealistic beliefs. You then focus on the inevitable failure; you can almost see yourself failing. This image leads to a loss of confidence and further visions of failure.

A special type of cognitive restructuring is *performance visualization,* designed specifically to reduce the outward manifestations of communication apprehension and also to reduce negative thinking (Ayres & Hopf, 1993; Ayres, Ayres, Grudzinskas, Hopf, et al., 1995). This technique, not surprisingly, has been shown to be significantly more effective with those who can create vivid mental images (Ayres, Hopf, & Ayres, 1994). The first part of performance visualization is to develop a positive attitude and a positive self-perception. This involves visualizing yourself in the role of, say, the effective employment interviewee. Visualize yourself walking into the interview—fully and totally confident. You scan the room and sit down. Throughout the interview you're fully in control of the situation. The interviewer is in rapt attention as you ask and respond to questions and, at the end, begs you to take the job. Throughout this visualization, avoid all negative thoughts. As you visualize yourself interviewing effectively, take special note of how you walk, look at the interviewer, respond to questions, and especially how you feel about the whole experience.

The second part of performance visualization is designed to help you model your performance on that of an especially effective communicator. Here you would view a particularly competent interviewee on video and make a mental movie of it. As you review the actual and the mental movie, you begin to shift yourself into the role of the interviewee. You, in effect, become this effective individual.

**Systematic Desensitization**   Systematic desensitization is a technique for dealing with many kinds of fears, including communication apprehension (Wolpe, 1958); it has even been found to reduce dating anxiety (Allen, Bourhis, Emmers-Sommer, & Sahlstein, 1998). The general assumption of systematic desensitization is that apprehension is learned—and that because it is learned, it can be unlearned. The procedure involves creating a hierarchy of behaviors leading up to the desired but feared behavior (say, asking for a date). One specific hierarchy might look like this:

4. Asking for the date
3. Making small talk
2. Introducing yourself to your prospective date
1. Dialing the phone

You would begin at the *bottom* of this hierarchy and mentally rehearse the first behavior (in this example, dialing the phone) until you can clearly visualize doing it without any uncomfortable anxiety. Once you can accomplish this, you can move to the second level. Here you would visualize the somewhat more threatening (here, introducing yourself to your prospective date). Once you can do this, you can move to the third level, and so on until you get to the desired behavior.

**Skill Acquisition**     The third general approach to communication apprehension holds that you develop apprehension largely because you see yourself as having inadequate skills. So you logically fear failing. The strategy for managing apprehension, therefore, is to acquire the specific skills involved in any given behavior. For example, the skills for business communication would involve a set of specific skills. These more specific skills would be mastered individually and then put together into the process of, say, talking with subordinates and supervisors. For example, some such skills would include presenting a positive self-image, complimenting the work of others, and tactfully criticizing another's performance. Other types of skills might be using deep breathing to relax yourself, creative visualization to help you see yourself as successful, or self-affirmation to help you feel better about yourself. Here are some additional suggestions for building skills:

**Prepare and Practice**     The more preparation and practice you put into something, the more comfortable you feel with it, and consequently the less apprehension you feel. If you're apprehensive telling jokes, then practice the joke you wish to tell. Rehearse it mentally and perhaps aloud until you're comfortable with it. In this way you'll acquire the very communication skills and experiences you'll need to help you master the tasks at which you want to be effective.

**Focus on Success**     Think positively. Concentrate your energies on doing the very best job you can in whatever situation you are in. Visualize yourself succeeding, and you stand a good chance of doing just that. Remember that having failed in the past does not mean that you must fail again in the future. You now have new skills and new experiences, and they increase your chances for success. But even if you do have a setback, put the setback and the apprehension in perspective; the world will not cave in if you don't succeed in any given communication situation.

**Familiarize Yourself with the Situation**     The more familiar you are with the situation, the better. The reason is simple: When you're familiar with the situation and with what will be expected of you, you're better able to predict what will happen. This will reduce ambiguity and make you feel more comfortable.

**Relax**     Apprehension is reduced when you're physically and mentally relaxed. For example, knowing that you have acquired new communication skills and that you have prepared yourself for the task of asking for a raise should help alleviate your normal anxiety.

> **A s k Yourself**
> *Lessening Apprehension*
>
> You've heard people say that you're not sociable. In truth, you'd love to be more sociable, but you're extremely apprehensive, especially when meeting new people or people you think you might become romantically interested in. Ask yourself: What are some of the things you can do to lessen your apprehension in social situations?

This chapter looked at the self in interpersonal communication and focused on three basic topics: dimensions of the self (self-concept, self-awareness, and self-esteem), self-disclosure, and communication apprehension.

## Dimensions of the Self

What are self-concept, self-awareness, and self-esteem, and how do they influence interpersonal communication?

- Self-concept is the image you have of who you are.
  - Sources of self-concept include others' images of you, social comparisons, cultural teachings, and your own interpretations and evaluations.
- Self-awareness is your knowledge of yourself; the extent to which you know who you are.
  - A useful way of looking at self-awareness is with the Johari window, which consists of four parts. The open self holds information known to self and others; the blind self holds information known only to others; the hidden self holds information known only to self; and the unknown self holds information known to neither self nor others.
  - To increase self-awareness, ask yourself about yourself, listen to others, actively seek information about yourself, see your different selves, and increase your open self.
- Self-esteem is the value you place on yourself; your perceived self-worth.
  - To increase self-esteem, try attacking your self-destructive beliefs, seeking affirmation, seeking out nourishing people, and working on projects that will result in success.

## Self-Disclosure

What is self-disclosure? What influences self-disclosure? What are its potential rewards and dangers? What guidelines are useful in making decisions to self-disclose and in listening to the disclosures of others?

- Self-disclosure is revealing information about yourself to others, information that is normally hidden.
- Self-disclosure is influenced by a variety of factors: who you are, your culture, your gender, your listeners, and your topic and channel.

- Among the rewards of self-disclosure are self-knowledge, ability to cope, communication effectiveness, meaningfulness of relationships, and physiological health. Among the dangers are personal risks, relational risks, professional risks, and the fact that communication is irreversible; once something is said, you can't take it back.
- In self-disclosing consider your motivation, the appropriateness of the disclosure to the person and context, the disclosures of others (the dyadic effect), and the possible burdens that the self-disclosure might impose on others and on yourself.
- In responding to the disclosures of others, listen effectively, support and reinforce the discloser, keep disclosures confidential, and don't use disclosures as weapons.
- In some situations you'll want to resist self-disclosing by being determined not to be pushed into it, being assertive and direct, or being indirect.

## Communication Apprehension

What is communication apprehension? How can you effectively manage your own apprehension?

- Communication apprehension is a state of fear or anxiety about communication situations. Trait apprehension is a fear of communication generally. State apprehension is a fear of communication that is specific to a situation (for example, an interview or public speaking situation).
- Theories and management of communication apprehension include cognitive restructuring, systematic desensitization, and skill acquisition.
  - Cognitive restructuring focuses on unrealistic beliefs and seeks to substitute more realistic ones.
  - Systematic desensitization attempts to train you to respond without apprehension to increasingly more anxiety-provoking situations.
  - Skill acquisition focuses on developing mastery of the skills involved in situations that normally provoke apprehension. To build skills: Prepare and practice, focus on success, familiarize yourself with the situation, and relax.

1 How satisfied are you with your self-concept? How satisfied are you with your current level of self-esteem? If you're unsatisfied, what are you going to do about it?

2 Do you engage in downward social comparison (comparing yourself to those you know are inferior to you in some way) or in upward social comparison (comparing yourself to those who you think are better than you) (Aspinwall & Taylor, 1993)? What are the purposes of these comparisons?

3 To what extent are you willing to manipulate the image of yourself that you present to other people? For example, would you be willing to deceive people by being friendly when you really disliked them? Or suppose you were anxious to date a particular person. If you knew the kind of person your prospective date liked, and you had the ability to communicate that you were this kind of person, would it be ethical for you to do this? What if the situation were at a job interview? Would it be ethical

for you to communicate an image of yourself that the interviewer wanted but that wasn't really you? In general, how authentic must you be to be ethical?

**4** The word *outing* refers to disclosure of something hidden by some third party. Originally used to mean revealing that someone is gay, the term now can refer to any type of disclosure of information that someone wishes to keep hidden. How do you feel about outing? What guidelines should the media follow in dealing with issues that individuals wish to keep private? At what point should the media be allowed to consider a person to be a public figure and hence without the right to privacy?

**5** One response that is seldom mentioned in discussions of disclosure is to say that you simply don't want to hear the disclosure. What kinds of disclosures are you most apt to *not* want to hear? How might you communicate this refusal to listen? Under what conditions would such refusals be appropriate?

**6** Research finds that in the classroom, increased instructor clarity and immediacy (language that creates a connection between sender and receiver) helps to reduce receiver apprehension (the fear people have that they won't be able to understand the message they're listening to). What might health care professionals do to help reduce receiver apprehension among patients (Chesebro & McCroskey, 1998)?

## Experiencing Key Terms and Concepts of the Self in Interpersonal Communication

Go to www.ablongman.com/devito.

*These exercises enable you to further explore the concepts of the self, especially self-disclosure and communication apprehension, discussed in this chapter.*

❶ **How Can You Attack Self-Defeating Drivers?** asks you to consider your own drivers and how you deal with them. ❷ **What Do You Have a Right to Know?** explores a different perspective on self-disclosure, namely the obligation to reveal parts of yourself. ❸ **Disclosing Your Hidden Self** presents an exciting class experience on the types of behaviors people keep hidden and the potential reactions to their disclosures. ❹ **Weighing the Rewards and Dangers of Self-Disclosure** presents a variety of scenarios of impending self-disclosure and asks you to consider the advantages and disadvantages of disclosing. ❺ **Time for Self-Disclosure** explores the appropriateness of time in revealing certain information. ❻ **Using Performance Visualization to Reduce Apprehension** and ❼ **Reducing Apprehension with Systematic Desensitization** provide guided experience in using these techniques to reduce communication apprehension. ❽ **How Flexible Is Your Communication?** provides an interesting self-test on your own flexibility.

# Perception in Interpersonal Communication

⬆ *Star Wars: Episode III: Revenge of the Sith* (2005)
*Star Wars: Episode III: Revenge of the Sith* (like all six films in the series)
challenges your initial perceptions and forces you to see dramatic changes
in various characters. As you'll see in this chapter, however, your perceptions of other people (and their perceptions of you) are extremely resistant
to change—a good reason to make favorable first impressions.

This chapter looks at perception—what it is and how it occurs, the processes that influence it, and the steps you can take to make your perceptions more accurate and more reliable.

**Perception** is the process by which you become aware of objects, events, and especially people through your senses: sight, smell, taste, touch, and hearing. Perception is an active, not a passive process. Your perceptions result from what exists in the outside world and from your own experiences, desires, needs and wants, loves and hatreds. Among the reasons perception is so important in interpersonal communication is that it influences your communication choices. The messages you send and listen to will depend on how you see the world, on how you size up specific situations, on what you think of the people with whom you interact.

##  STAGES OF PERCEPTION

**Interpersonal perception** is a continuous series of processes that blend into one another. For convenience of discussion we can separate interpersonal perception into five stages: (1) You sense, you pick up some kind of stimulation; (2) you organize the stimuli in some way; (3) you interpret and evaluate what you perceive; (4) you store it in memory; and (5) you retrieve it when needed.

### Stage One: Stimulation

At this first stage, your sense organs are stimulated—you hear a new CD, see a friend, smell someone's perfume, taste an orange, feel another's sweaty palm. Naturally, you don't perceive everything; rather, you engage in *selective perception,* a general term that includes selective attention and selective exposure. In selective attention, you attend to those things that you anticipate will fulfill your needs or will prove enjoyable. For example, when daydreaming in class, you don't hear what the instructor is saying until your name is called. Your selective attention mechanism then focuses your senses on your name.

Through **selective exposure** you expose yourself to people or messages that will confirm your existing beliefs, contribute to your objectives, or prove satisfying in some way. For example, after you buy a car, you're more apt to read and listen to advertisements for the car you just bought, because these messages tell you that you made the right decision. At the same time, you would avoid advertisements for the cars that you considered but eventually rejected, because these messages would tell you that you made the wrong decision.

You're also more likely to perceive stimuli that are greater in intensity than surrounding stimuli and those that have novelty value. For example, television commercials normally play at a greater intensity than regular programming to ensure that you'll take special notice. You're also more likely to notice the coworker who dresses in a novel way than you are to notice the one who dresses like everyone else. You will quickly perceive someone who shows up in class wearing a tuxedo or at a formal party in shorts.

## Stage Two: Organization

At the second stage, you organize the information your senses pick up. Three interesting ways in which people organize their perceptions are by rules, by schemata, and by scripts. Let's look at each briefly.

**Organization by Rules**   One frequently used rule of perception is that of *proximity* or physical closeness: Things that are physically close together constitute a unit. Thus, using this rule, you would perceive people who are often together, or messages spoken one immediately after the other, as units, as belonging together. You also assume that the verbal and nonverbal signals sent at about the same time are related and constitute a unified whole. That is, you assume they follow a *temporal* rule: Things occurring together in time belong together.

Another rule is *similarity:* Things that are physically similar, things that look alike, belong together and form a unit. This principle of similarity would lead you to see people who dress alike as belonging together. Similarly, you might assume that people who work at the same jobs, who are of the same religion, who live in the same building, or who talk with the same accent belong together.

The rule of *contrast* is the opposite of similarity: When items (people or messages, for example) are very different from each other, you conclude that they don't belong together; they're too different from each other to be part of the same unit. If you're the only one who shows up at an informal gathering in a tuxedo, you'd be seen as not belonging to the group because you contrast too much with other members.

**Organization by Schemata**   Another way you organize material is by creating **schemata**, mental templates or structures that help you organize the millions of items of information you come into contact with every day as well as those you already have in memory. (*Schemata* is the plural of *schema.*) Schemata may thus be viewed as general ideas about people (e.g., about Pat and Chris, Japanese, Baptists, or New Yorkers); about yourself (your qualities, abilities, and even liabilities); or about social roles (the characteristics of a police officer, professor, or multibillionaire CEO).

Stereotypes—discussed in Chapter 2—are a type of schema. As we saw in that discussion, stereotypes (and other schemata) can lead you to filter out positive information if the stereotype is negative or to filter out negative information if the stereotype is positive.

You develop schemata from your own experience—actual as well as via television, reading, and hearsay. You might have a schema for college athletes, for example, and this might include that they're strong, ambitious, academically weak, and egocentric. You've probably developed schemata for different religious, racial, and national groups, for men and women, and for people of different affectional orientations. Each group that you have some familiarity with will be represented in your mind in some kind of schema. Schemata help you organize your perceptions by allowing you to classify millions of people into a manageable number of categories or classes. As we'll see below, however, schemata can also create problems and influence you to see what is not there or to miss seeing what is there.

**Organization by Scripts**   A **script** is really a type of schema, but because it's a different type, it's given a different name. A script is an organized body of information about some action, event, or procedure. It's a general idea of how some event should play out or unfold; it's the rules governing events and their sequence. For example, you probably have a script for eating in a restaurant, with the actions organized into a pattern something like this: enter, take a seat, review the menu, order from the menu, eat your food, ask for the bill, leave a tip, pay the bill, exit the restaurant. Similarly, you probably have scripts for how you do laundry, how an interview is to be conducted, the stages you go through in introducing someone to someone else, and the way you ask for a date.

## Stage Three: Interpretation–Evaluation

The interpretation–evaluation step (a combined term because the two processes cannot be separated) is inevitably subjective and is greatly influenced by your experiences, needs, wants, values, beliefs about the way things are or should be, expectations, physical and emotional state, and so on. Your interpretation–evaluation will be influenced by your rules, schemata, and scripts as well as by your gender; for example, women have been found to view others more positively than men (Winquist, Mohr, & Kenny, 1998).

For example, on meeting a new person who is introduced to you as Ben Williams, a college football player, you're likely to apply your schema to this person and view him as strong, ambitious, academically weak, and egocentric. You will, in other words, see this person through the filter of your schema and evaluate him according to your schema for college athletes. Similarly, when viewing someone performing some series of actions (say, eating in a restaurant), you apply your script to this event and view the event through the script. You will interpret the actions of the diner as appropriate or inappropriate depending on your script for this behavior and the ways in which the diner performed the sequence of actions.

## Stage Four: Memory

Your perceptions and their interpretations–evaluations are put into memory; they're stored so that you may ultimately retrieve them at some later time. So, for example, you have in memory your schema for college athletes and the fact that Ben Williams is a football player. Ben Williams is then stored in memory with "cognitive tags" that tell you that he's strong, ambitious, academically weak, and egocentric. Despite the fact that you've not witnessed Ben's strength or ambitions and have no idea of his academic record or his psychological profile, you still may store your memory of Ben along with the qualities that make up your schema for "college athletes."

Let's say that at different times you hear that Ben failed Spanish I, normally an A or B course at your school; that Ben got an A in Chemistry (normally a tough course), and that Ben is transferring to Harvard as a theoretical physics major. Schemas act as filters or gatekeepers; they allow certain information to get stored in relatively objective form, much as you heard or read it, and may distort or prevent other information from getting stored. As a result, these three items of information about Ben may get stored very differently in your memory.

For example, you might readily store the information that Ben failed Spanish, because it's consistent with your schema; it fits neatly into the template you have of college athletes. Information that's consistent with your schema—such as in this example—will strengthen your schema and make it more resistant to change (Aronson, Wilson, & Akert, 1999). Depending on the strength of your schema, you might also store in memory (even though you didn't hear it) that Ben did poorly in other courses as well. The information that Ben got an A in chemistry, because it contradicts your schema (it just doesn't seem right), might easily be distorted or lost. The information that Ben is transferring to Harvard, however, is a bit different. This information is also inconsistent with your schema, but it is so

**VIEWPOINT**

In making evaluations of events or people, it would seem logical that we would first think about the event or person and then make the evaluation. Some research claims, however, that we really don't think before assigning any perception a positive or negative value. This research argues that all perceptions have a positive or negative value attached to them and that these evaluations are most often automatic and involve no conscious thought. Immediately upon perceiving a person, idea, or thing, we attach a positive or negative value (*New York Times,* August 8, 1995, pp. C1, C10). What do you think of this? One bit of evidence against this position would be the ability to identify several things, ideas, or people about which you feel *completely* neutral. Can you do it?

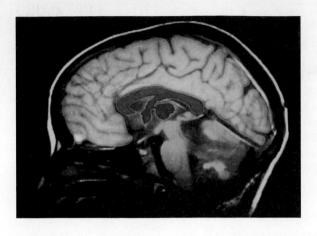

drastically inconsistent that you begin to look at this mindfully and may even begin to question your schema or perhaps view Ben as an exception to the general rule. In either case, you're going to etch Ben's transferring to Harvard very clearly in your mind.

### Stage Five: Recall

At some later date, you may want to recall or access the information you have stored in memory. Let's say you want to retrieve your information about Ben because he's the topic of discussion among you and a few friends. As we'll see in our discussion of listening in the next chapter, memory isn't reproductive; you don't simply reproduce what you've heard or seen. Rather, you reconstruct what you've heard or seen into a whole that is meaningful to you—depending in great part on your schemata and scripts—and it's this reconstruction that you store in memory. When you want to retrieve this information, you may recall it with a variety of inaccuracies:

- You're likely to recall information that is consistent with your schema; in fact, you may not even be recalling the specific information (say, about Ben) but may actually just be recalling your schema (which contains information about college athletes and, because of this, also about Ben).
- But you may fail to recall information that is inconsistent with your schema; you have no place to put that information, so you easily lose it or forget it.
- However, you may recall information that drastically contradicts your schema, because it forces you to think (and perhaps rethink) about your schema and its accuracy; it may even force you to revise your schema for college athletes in general.

## Implications of the Model of Perception

Before moving on to the more specific processes involved in interpersonal perception, let's spell out some of the implications of this five-stage model.

1. Everyone relies on shortcuts—rules, schemata, and scripts, for example, are all useful shortcuts to simplify your understanding, remembering, and recalling information about people and events. They also enable you to generalize, make connections, and otherwise profit from previously acquired knowledge. If you didn't have these shortcuts, you'd have to treat every person, role, or action differently from each other person, role, or action. This would make every experience a new one, totally unrelated to anything you already know.

2. Shortcuts, however, may mislead you; they may contribute to your remembering things that are consistent with your schemata (even if they didn't occur) and distorting or forgetting information that is inconsistent.

3. What you remember about a person or an event isn't an objective recollection but is more likely heavily influenced by your preconceptions or your schemata about what belongs and what doesn't belong, what fits neatly into the templates in your brain and what doesn't. Your reconstruction of an event or person contains a lot of information that was not in the original sensory experience—and may omit a lot that was in this experience.

4. Judgments about members of other cultures are often ethnocentric; because your schemata and scripts are created on the basis of your own cultural beliefs and experiences, you can easily (but inappropriately) apply these to members of other cultures. And so it's easy to infer that when members of other cultures do things that conform to your scripts, they're right, and when they do things that contradict your scripts, they're wrong—a classic example of ethnocentric thinking. This tendency can easily contribute to intercultural misunderstandings.

# Ethics in Interpersonal Communication

## PERSPECTIVES ON ETHICS

Are ethical principles objective or subjective?

- An *objective* view argues that morality is absolute and exists apart from the values or beliefs of any individual or culture: Standards apply to all people in all situations at all times. If lying, false advertising, using illegally obtained evidence, or revealing secrets is unethical, then any such behavior is considered unethical regardless of the circumstances surrounding it or the context in which it occurs. In a strict objective view the end doesn't justify the means; you cannot justify an unethical act regardless of how good or beneficial its results (or ends) might be.
- A *subjective* view argues that what is or is not ethical depends on the culture's values and beliefs as well as the particular circumstances. Thus, a subjective position would claim that lying may be wrong to win votes or sell cigarettes, but that white lies may be quite ethical if their purpose is to make someone feel better and the deceptions do no harm.

### What would you do?

After an examination, the instructor accuses a student of cheating and asks you if you witnessed it. Although you believe that both cheating and lying are unethical and you did witness the cheating, you don't want to make trouble for the student (or for yourself). Besides, the examination wasn't announced in advance, and it only counted a few points toward the final grade. What would you do in this situation?

---

5. A similar problem arises when you base your scripts for different cultural groups on stereotypes that you may have derived from television or movies. For example, you may have schemata for religious Muslims that you derived from the stereotypes presented in the media. If you apply these schemata to all Muslims, you risk seeing what conforms to your schemata but failing to see or distorting what does not conform.
6. Memory is especially unreliable when the information can be interpreted in different ways, when it's ambiguous. Thus, for example, consider the statement that "Ben didn't do as well in his other courses as he would have liked." If your schema of Ben was "brilliant" then you might "remember" that Ben got Bs. But if, as in our example, your schema was of the academically weak athlete, you might "remember" that Ben got Ds. Conveniently, but unreliably, schemata reduce ambiguity.

##  PERCEPTUAL PROCESSES

Before reading about the specific processes that you use in perceiving other people, examine your own perception strategies by taking the accompanying self-test, "How Accurate Are You at People Perception?"

## TEST YOURSELF

### HOW ACCURATE ARE YOU AT PEOPLE PERCEPTION?

Respond to each of the following statements with T if the statement is usually or generally true (accurate in describing your behavior) or with F if the statement is usually or generally false (inaccurate in describing your behavior).

_____ 1. I make predictions about people's behaviors that generally prove to be true.

_____ 2. When I know some things about another person, I can pretty easily fill in what I don't know.

_____ 3. Generally my expectations are borne out by what I actually see; that is, my later perceptions usually match my initial expectations.

4. I base most of my impressions of people on the first few minutes of our meeting.
5. I generally find that people I like possess positive characteristics and people I don't like possess negative characteristics.
6. I generally attribute people's attitudes and behaviors to their most obvious physical or psychological characteristic.

**HOW DID YOU DO?** This brief perception test was designed to raise questions to be considered in this chapter, not to provide you with a specific perception score. All statements refer to perceptual processes that many people use but that often get us into trouble, leading us to form inaccurate impressions. The questions refer to several processes to be discussed below: self-fulfilling prophecy (Statement 1), implicit personality theory (2), perceptual accentuation (3), primacy–recency (4), and consistency (5). Statement 6 refers to overattribution, one of the problems we encounter as we attempt to determine motives for other people's and even our own behaviors.

**WHAT WILL YOU DO?** As you read this chapter, think about these processes and consider how you might use them more accurately and not allow them to get in the way of accurate and reasonable people perception. At the same time, recognize that situations vary widely and that strategies for clearer perception will prove useful most of the time but not all of the time. In fact, you may want to identify situations in which you shouldn't follow the suggestions that this text will offer.

## Self-Fulfilling Prophecy

A **self-fulfilling prophecy** is a prediction that comes true because you act on it as if it were true. Put differently, a self-fulfilling prophecy occurs when you act on your schema as if it were true and in doing so make it true. Self-fulfilling prophecies occur in such widely different situations as parent–child relationships, educational settings, and business (Merton, 1957; Rosenthal, 2002; Madon, Guyll, & Spoth, 2004; Tierney & Farmer, 2004). There are four basic steps in the self-fulfilling prophecy:

1. You make a prediction or formulate a belief about a person or a situation. For example, you predict that Pat is friendly in interpersonal encounters.
2. You act toward that person or situation as if that prediction or belief were true. For example, you act as if Pat were a friendly person.
3. Because you act as if the belief were true, it becomes true. For example, because of the way you act toward Pat, Pat becomes comfortable and friendly.
4. You observe your effect on the person or the resulting situation, and what you see strengthens your beliefs. For example, you observe Pat's friendliness, and this reinforces your belief that Pat is in fact friendly.

The self-fulfilling prophecy also can be seen when you make predictions about yourself and fulfill them. For example, suppose you enter a group situation convinced that the other members will dislike you. Almost invariably you'll be proved right; the other members will appear to you to dislike you. What you may be doing is acting in a way that encourages the group to respond to you negatively. In this way, you fulfill your prophecies about yourself.

A widely known example of the self-fulfilling prophecy is the **Pygmalion effect**. In perhaps the classic study, teachers were told that certain pupils were expected to do exceptionally well, that they were late bloomers. The names of these students were actually selected at random by the experimenters. The results, however, were not random. The students whose names were given to the teachers actually performed at a higher level than the others. In fact, these students' IQ scores even improved more than did the other students'. The teachers' expectations probably prompted them to give extra attention to the selected students, thereby positively affecting their performance (Rosenthal & Jacobson, 1968; Insel & Jacobson, 1975; Rosenthal, 2002). The same general effect is found in military training and business settings in which trainees and workers perform better when their supervisors are given positive information about them (McNatt, 2001). The Pygmalion effect also is seen in such areas as leadership, athletic coaching, and effective stepfamilies and in employee creativity (Eden, 1992; Solomon et al., 1996; Einstein, 1995; Tierney & Farmer, 2004). Findings such as these have led one researcher to suggest applying the Pygmalion effect to improve worker productivity. The idea is that companies could boost productivity by creating positive attitudes about employees in supervisors and by helping employees to feel that their supervisors and the organizations as a whole value them highly (McNatt, 2001).

Self-fulfilling prophecies can short-circuit critical thinking and influence others' behavior (or your own) so that it conforms to your prophecies. As a result, you may see what you predicted rather than what is really there (for example, you may perceive yourself as a failure because you have predicted it rather than because of any actual failures).

## Implicit Personality Theory

Each person has a subconscious or implicit theory that says which characteristics of an individual go with other characteristics. Consider, for example, the following brief statements.

Note the word in parentheses that you think best completes each sentence.

1. Carlo is energetic, eager, and (intelligent, stupid).
2. Kim is bold, defiant, and (extroverted, introverted).
3. Joe is bright, lively, and (thin, heavy).
4. Eve is attractive, intelligent, and (likable, unlikable).
5. Susan is cheerful, positive, and (outgoing, shy).
6. Angel is handsome, tall, and (friendly, unfriendly).

What makes some of these choices seem right and others wrong is your **implicit personality theory**, the system of rules that tells you which characteristics go with which other characteristics. Your theory may, for example, have told you that a person who is energetic and eager is also intelligent, not stupid—although there is no logical reason why a stupid person could not be energetic and eager.

The widely documented **halo effect** is a function of the implicit personality theory (Dion, Berscheid, & Walster, 1972; Riggio, 1987). If you believe a person has some positive qualities, you're likely to infer that she or he also possesses other positive qualities. There is also a *reverse halo* (or *"horns") effect*: If you know a person possesses several negative qualities, you're more likely to infer that the person also has other negative qualities. For example, you're more likely to perceive attractive people as more generous, sensitive, trustworthy, and interesting than those less attractive. And the "horns effect" or "reverse halo effect" will lead you to perceive those who are unattractive as mean, dishonest, antisocial, and sneaky (Katz, 2003).

In using implicit personality theories, apply them carefully and critically so as to avoid perceiving qualities in an individual that your theory tells you should be present when they actually are not. For example, you may see "goodwill" in a friend's "charitable" acts when a tax deduction may have been the real motive. Similarly, be careful of ignoring or distorting qualities that don't conform to your theory but that are actually present in the individual, as research shows many people do (Plaks, Grant, & Dweck, 2005). For example, you may ignore negative qualities in your friends that you would easily perceive in your enemies.

### ⬆ VIEWPOINT

Racial profiling (the practice whereby the police focus on members of specific races as possible crime suspects) has been widely reported and widely condemned as racist. In the aftermath of the attack on the World Trade Center and the Pentagon on September 11, 2001, profiling of Muslims and of people who looked "Arab" became viewed by many as necessary for preventing further acts of terrorism. How do you feel about racial, ethnic, or religious profiling?

As might be expected, the implicit personality theories that people hold differ from culture to culture, group to group, and even person to person. For example, the Chinese have the concept *shi gu*, which refers to "someone who is worldly, devoted to his or her family, socially skillful, and somewhat reserved" (Aronson, Wilson, & Akert, 1999, p. 117). In English, on the other hand, we have a concept of the "artistic type," a generalization that seems absent in Chinese. Thus, although it is easy for speakers of English or Chinese to refer to specific concepts—such as "socially skilled" or "creative"—each language creates its own generalized categories. Thus, in Chinese the qualities that make up *shi gu* are more easily seen as going together than they might be for an English speaker; they're part of the implicit personality theory of more Chinese speakers than English speakers.

## Perceptual Accentuation

When poor and rich children were shown pictures of coins and later asked to estimate their size, the poor children's size estimates were much greater than the rich children's. Similarly, hungry people need fewer visual cues to perceive food objects and food terms than do people who are not hungry. This process, called **perceptual accentuation**, leads you to see what you expect or want to see. You see people you like as better looking and smarter than those you don't like. You magnify or accentuate what will satisfy your needs and desires: The thirsty person sees a mirage of water, the sexually deprived person sees a mirage of sexual satisfaction.

Perceptual accentuation can lead you to perceive what you need or want to perceive rather than what is really there, and to fail to perceive what you don't want to perceive. For example, you may not perceive signs of impending problems because you are focusing on what you want to perceive.

Perceptual accentuation also can lead you to perceive and remember positive qualities more than negative ones (a phenomenon referred to as the *Pollyanna effect*) and thus can distort your perceptions of others.

# Ask the Researcher

## MEDIA AND INTERNET VIOLENCE

 My two children (ages 11 and 13) love to watch TV shows and play computer games that I consider violent. Will this alter their perceptions of the real world? Is there anything I can or should do about this?

You are right to be concerned about the effects of watching violent television programs and playing aggressive video games. Research has found that these activities are associated with shifted perceptions of the world. Your children might come to believe that the world is a more violent place than it really is, or they might become desensitized to violence in the real world. Talking to your children can help mitigate these negative effects. Have some conversations with them about how the programs and game scenarios are and aren't realistic. Get them to think about the suffering of real crime victims and their families. Research shows that media content is less likely to have effects when the audience understands that it is unrealistic.

**For more information** see E. M. Perse, *Media Effects and Society* (Mahwah, NJ: Lawrence Erlbaum, 2001).

Elizabeth M. Perse (Ph.D., Kent State University) is professor and chair of communication at the University of Delaware and teaches courses in mass communication theory and effects. Her research focuses on the uses and effects of television and new communication technologies. She serves on the editorial boards of six communication journals and was recently listed among the top 100 most prolific scholars in the field of communication.

Another interesting distortion created by perceptual accentuation is that you may perceive certain behaviors as indicative that someone likes you simply because you want to be liked. For example, general politeness and friendly behavior used as a persuasive strategy (say, by a salesperson) are frequently seen as indicating genuine personal liking.

## Primacy–Recency

Assume for a moment that you're enrolled in a course in which half the classes are extremely dull and half extremely exciting. At the end of the semester, you evaluate the course and the instructor. Would your evaluation be more favorable if the dull classes occurred in the first half of the semester and the exciting classes in the second? Or would it be more favorable if the order were reversed? If what comes first exerts the most influence, you have a *primacy effect*. If what comes last (or most recently) exerts the most influence, you have a *recency effect*.

In the classic study on the effects of **primacy–recency** in interpersonal perception, college students perceived a person who was described as "intelligent, industrious, impulsive, critical, stubborn, and envious" more positively than a person described as "envious, stubborn, critical, impulsive, industrious, and intelligent" (Asch, 1946). Clearly, there's a tendency to use early information to get a general idea about a person and to use later information to make this impression more specific. The initial information helps you form a schema for the person. Once that schema is formed, you're likely to resist information that contradicts it.

One interesting practical implication of primacy–recency is that the first impression you make is likely to be the most important—and is likely to be made very quickly (Sunnafrank & Ramirez, 2004). The reason for this is that the schema that others form of you functions as a filter to admit or block additional information about you. If the initial impression or schema is positive, others are likely to readily remember additional positive information, because it confirms this original positive image or schema; to easily forget or distort negative information, because it contradicts this original positive schema; and to interpret ambiguous information as positive. You win in all three ways—if the initial impression is positive.

The tendency to give greater weight to early information and to interpret later information in light of early impressions can lead you to formulate a total picture of an individual on the basis of initial impressions that may not be typical or accurate. For example, if you judge a job applicant as generally nervous when he or she may simply be showing normal nervousness at being interviewed for a much-needed job, you will have misperceived this individual.

Similarly, this tendency can lead you to discount or distort subsequent perceptions so as not to disrupt your initial impression or upset your original schema. For example, you may fail to see signs of deceit in someone you like because of your early impressions that this person is a good and honest individual.

## Consistency

The tendency to maintain balance among perceptions or attitudes is called **consistency** (McBroom & Reed, 1992). You expect certain things to go together and other things not to go together.

On a purely intuitive basis, for example, respond to the following sentences by noting your expected response.

- ❶ I expect a person I like to (like, dislike) me.
- ❷ I expect a person I dislike to (like, dislike) me.
- ❸ I expect my friend to (like, dislike) my friend.
- ❹ I expect my friend to (like, dislike) my enemy.
- ❺ I expect my enemy to (like, dislike) my friend.
- ❻ I expect my enemy to (like, dislike) my enemy.

**SPEAKING**
**>> Interpersonal-E**

**Primacy and Recency Online.** How would you characterize the operation of primacy and recency in online communication? That is, which seems the more important in influencing your perceptions of others online—their earliest messages or their more recent messages?

According to most consistency theories, your expectations would be as follows: You would expect a person you liked to like you (1) and a person you disliked to dislike you (2). You would expect a friend to like a friend (3) and to dislike an enemy (4). You would expect your enemy to dislike your friend (5) and to like your other enemy (6). All these expectations are intuitively satisfying.

Further, you would expect someone you liked to possess characteristics you like or admire and would expect your enemies not to possess characteristics you like or admire. Conversely, you would expect people you liked to lack unpleasant characteristics and those you disliked to possess unpleasant characteristics.

Uncritically assuming that an individual is consistent can lead you to ignore or distort your perceptions of behaviors that are inconsistent with your picture of the whole person. For example, you may misinterpret Karla's unhappiness because your image of Karla is "happy, controlled, and contented." Consistency can also lead you to see certain behaviors as positive if you have interpreted other behaviors positively (the halo effect) or as negative if you have interpreted other behaviors negatively (the reverse halo effect).

## Attribution

Think about each of the following situations:

1. A woman is begging in the street.
2. A store owner kills a thief.
3. A father leaves his children.

To what do you attribute the causes of these situations? Did the begging, killing, and abandonment result from something within the person or from within the situation? The way you would answer these questions is neatly explained in **attribution** theory. Attribution theory explains the process you go through in trying to understand people's behaviors, particularly the reasons or motivations for these behaviors. Attribution—including **self-attribution**, in the case of your own behavior—helps you to impose order and logic and to better understand the possible causes of the behaviors you observe.

Attribution also helps you to make predictions about what will happen, what others are likely or unlikely to do. If you can be reasonably sure that Pat gave money out of a desire to help the poor (that is, if you can attribute the behavior to a desire to help), then you can make predictions about Pat's future behaviors that are more likely to be correct than predictions made without this initial attribution to guide you.

**Attribution Processes**    In trying to discover the causes of another's behavior, your first step is to determine whether the individual or some outside factor is responsible. That is, you must first determine whether the cause is *internal* (for example, due to some personality trait) or *external* (for example, due to some situational factor). Your assessment of someone's behavior as internally or externally motivated will greatly influence your evaluation of that person. If you judge people's cooperative behavior as internally caused (that is, as motivated by their personality), you're more apt to form a positive evaluation of them and, eventually, to like them. In contrast, if you judge that very same behavior to be externally caused (the watchful eye of the boss is forcing someone to behave cooperatively, for example), you're more apt to form a negative evaluation and, eventually, to dislike the person (because he or she isn't "really" cooperative).

Consider another example. You look at a cultural anthropology instructor's grade book and observe that the instructor gave 10 students Fs for the course. In an attempt to discover what this reveals about the instructor, you first have to discover whether the instructor was in fact responsible for the assignment of the 10 Fs or whether the grading could be attributed to external factors. Let's say you discover that the examinations on which the grades were based had been made up by a faculty committee, which also set the standards for passing or failing. In this case, you could not attribute any particular motives to this individual instructor because the behavior was not internally caused.

On the other hand, let's assume the following: This instructor made up the examination without any assistance, no departmental or university standards were used, and the instructor created a personal set of standards for passing and failing. Now you would be more apt (though perhaps not fully justified) to attribute the 10 Fs to internal causes. You would be strengthened in your beliefs that there was something within this instructor, such as some personality characteristic, that led to this behavior if you discovered that (1) no other instructor in anthropology gave nearly as many Fs, (2) this particular instructor frequently gives Fs in cultural anthropology, (3) this instructor frequently gives Fs in other courses as well, and (4) this instructor is the only one responsible for assigning grades and could have assigned grades other than F. These four bits of added information would lead you to conclude that there was something within this instructor that motivated the behavior. In forming such causal judgments, which you make every day, you use four principles: (1) consensus, (2) consistency, (3) distinctiveness, and (4) controllability.

**Consensus: Similarity with Others**   When you use the principle of consensus, you ask, "Do other people behave in the same way as the person on whom I'm focusing?" That is, is the person acting in accordance with the consensus, the majority? If the answer is no, you're more likely to attribute the behavior to some internal cause and conclude: "This person is different." In the instructor example, you would be strengthened in your belief that something internal caused the Fs to be given if you learned that other instructors didn't do this; that is, there was low consensus. When only one person acts contrary to the norm, you're more likely to attribute that person's behavior to internal motivation. If all instructors gave many Fs (that is, if there was high consensus), you'd be more likely to look for causality outside the individual instructor; you might conclude that the anthropology department uses a particular curve in determining grades or that the students were not very bright—or any other reason external to the specific instructor.

**Consistency: Similarity over Time**   When you use the principle of consistency, you ask if this person repeatedly (consistently) behaves in the same way in similar situations. If the answer is yes, there's high consistency, and you're likely to attribute the behavior to internal motivation. If you knew that this instructor frequently gives Fs in cultural anthropology, it would lead you to attribute the cause to the instructor rather than to outside sources. If, on the other hand, there was low consistency—that is, if this instructor rarely gives Fs—you'd be more likely to look for external reasons. Again, you might conclude, for example, that the students in this specific class were not very bright or that the department required the instructor to start giving out Fs.

**Distinctiveness: Similarity in Different Situations**   When you use the principle of distinctiveness, you ask if this person reacts in similar ways in different situations. If the answer is yes, there is low distinctiveness, and you're likely to conclude that the behavior has an internal cause. If the instructor reacted the same way (gave lots of Fs) in different situations (other courses), it would lead you to conclude that this particular class was not distinctive and that the motivation for the behavior could not be found in the unique situation. You'd further conclude that this behavior is likely due to the instructor's inner motivation. Consider the alternative: If this instructor gave all high grades and no Fs in other courses (that is, if the cultural anthropology class situation was highly distinctive), you'd conclude that the motivation for the failures was to be found in sources outside the instructor and for reasons unique to this class.

**Controllability: Behavior Control**   Let's say your friend is an hour late for a dinner appointment (cf. Weiner, Amirkhan, Folkes, & Verette, 1987). How would you feel about the following two possible excuses?

**Excuse 1:** I was reading this book, and I just couldn't put it down. I had to find out who the killer was.

**Excuse 2:** I was stuck on the subway for two hours; a water main broke, killing all the electricity.

It's likely you'd resent the first and accept the second excuse. The first excuse says that the reason for the lateness was controllable: Your friend chose to be late by completing the novel. You'd therefore hold your friend responsible for wasting your time and for a lack of consideration. The second excuse says that the reason was uncontrollable: Your friend couldn't help being late. Here you'd not hold your friend responsible. This, by the way, is why excuses involving uncontrollable factors are more effective than those involving controllable factors.

Think about your own tendency to make similar judgments based on controllability. For example, how you would respond to situations such as the following?

- Doris fails her midterm history exam.
- Sidney's car is repossessed because he failed to make the payments.
- Thomas's wife has just filed for divorce and he is feeling depressed.

Very probably you'd be sympathetic to each of these people if you felt they were not in control of what happened—for example, if the examination was unfair, if Sidney lost his job because of employee discrimination, and if Thomas's wife is leaving him for a billionaire. On the other hand, you might blame these people for their problems if you felt that they were in control of the situation—for example, if Doris partied instead of studying, if Sidney gambled his payments away, and if Thomas had been repeatedly unfaithful and his wife finally gave up trying to change him.

In perceiving other people, and especially in evaluating their behavior, you frequently ask if the person was in control of the behavior. Generally, research shows that if you feel people are in control of negative behaviors, you'll come to dislike them. But you'll feel sorry for someone you feel isn't in control of negative behaviors, and you won't blame the person for his or her negative circumstances.

Low consensus, high consistency, low distinctiveness, and high controllability lead to an attribution of internal causes. As a result, you praise or blame the person for his or her behaviors. High consensus, low consistency, high distinctiveness, and low controllability lead to an attribution of external causes. Table 4.1 summarizes these four principles of attribution.

**Attribution Errors**   Our efforts to attribute causality face several major barriers. Three such barriers are the self-serving bias, **overattribution,** and the fundamental attribution error.

**SPEAKING**

**Interpersonal-E**

**Online Attributions.**   It may be argued that the cues that enable you to make attributions of the social status of the other person in face-to-face communication are absent or fewer in Internet communication (Nowak, 2003). If this is so, how do you make judgments of the social status of your online communication partners?

⭘ **TABLE 4.1**

## A Summary of Causal Attribution

Situation: John has been fired from a job he began a few months ago. On what basis will you decide whether this outcome is internally caused (John is responsible) or externally caused (John isn't responsible)?

| Internal If | External If |
|---|---|
| No one else was fired (low consensus). | Lots of others were fired (high consensus). |
| John has been fired from lots of other jobs (high consistency). | John has never been fired from any other job (low consistency). |
| John has failed at many other things (low distinctiveness). | John has always been successful (high distinctiveness). |
| John could have been retained if he had agreed to move to another shop (high controllability). | John was not given any alternatives (low controllability). |

# InterMedia

## THE THIRD-PERSON EFFECT

How effective are the media in influencing you as compared to a group of your peers? Are you influenced less than your peers, about the same as your peers, or more than your peers? In a variety of studies conducted on college students, researchers found that students believed that they were influenced less by the media than were their peers (Davison, 1983; Reid & Hogg, 2005). Whether the topic was political advertising, rap music, or pornography, students felt they were less susceptible to media influence than were their peers (Hoffner et al., 2001). This belief, called the third-person effect, is especially strong when the media message is negative or socially unacceptable; for example, people think that messages of violence, racism, or sexism influence them much less than they influence their peers. The effect is weakened but still present when the message is more acceptable (for example, public service announcements).

### Follow Up

Try testing out this theory. For example, survey 10 or 20 people and ask them how influenced they feel they are by, say, media violence or racism. Then ask them if their friends and relatives are more influenced than they are. Then do likewise with a more socially acceptable issue such as media campaigns on the value of education or the importance of proper diet. Follow this up by questions about how influenced they feel their friends and relatives are by these same messages. Do you find a third-person effect?

**The Self-Serving Bias**    The **self-serving bias** is a mechanism designed to preserve self-esteem that seems pervasive throughout the general population (Mezulis, Abramson, Hyde, Hydge & Hankin, 2004; Kudo & Numazaki, 2003). You are guilty of the self-serving bias when you take credit for the positive and deny responsibility for the negative. For example, you're more likely to attribute your positive outcomes (say, you get an A on an exam) to internal and controllable factors—to your personality, intelligence, or hard work (Bernstein, Stephan, & Davis, 1979). You're more likely to attribute your negative outcomes (say, you get a D) to external and uncontrollable factors—to the exam's being exceptionally difficult or unfair. In other examples, you're even more likely to take credit for your computer's effective performance and to blame the device for negative outcomes (Moon, 2003). You're more likely to attribute your own group's successful outcomes to internal factors and its negative outcomes to external factors (Sherman & Kim, 2005). And you are likely to predict that your own behavior will be more positive than the behaviors of others. For example, when people were asked to indicate the changes that they would make if they won the lottery, they indicated that their own changes would be significantly more positive than the changes that would take place in other people (Nelson & Beggan, 2004).

The self-serving bias also influences the way you view conflict (Schutz, 1999). For example, you're likely to describe your opponent's negative behavior as internally motivated and your own negative behavior as externally caused ("I couldn't help it" or "They made me do it"). Similarly, you're more likely to make excuses and justify your own behavior than to do the same for your opponent's. Even young children, when reporting conflicts, will attribute positive actions to themselves and less positive actions to their siblings (Ross, Smith, Spielmacher, & Recchia, 2004).

There is some evidence (though it's not overwhelming) that we explain the behaviors of in-group and out-group members differently (Berry, Poortinga, Segall, & Dasen, 1992). For example, you're more likely to explain your group's members' positive behavior as internally motivated and nonmembers' positive behaviors as externally motivated. Thus, you would be more apt to explain, say, a high record of charitable contributions for members of your own culture with something like "We're a charitable people; we believe in helping others." If this is shown to be true for members of another culture, you'd be more apt to say something like "They're rich; they need tax deductions."

**SPEAKING**
**>> Interpersonal-E**

**Third-Person Effect.**
Consistent with the research on the third-person effect is the finding that most people believe Internet pornography has less of a negative effect on themselves than on others (Lo & Wei, 2002). What are the implications of this finding for the attitudes people have about Internet pornography?

# Understanding Interpersonal Theory and Research
## THE JUST WORLD HYPOTHESIS

Many people believe that the world is just: Good things happen to good people and bad things happen to bad people (Aronson, Wilson, & Akert, 1999; Hunt, 2000). Put differently, you get what you deserve! Even when you mindfully dismiss this assumption, you may use it mindlessly when perceiving and evaluating other people. Consider a particularly vivid example: If a woman is raped in certain cultures (for example, in Bangladesh, Iran, or Yemen) she is considered by many in that culture (certainly not all) to have disgraced her family and to be deserving of severe punishment—in many cases, even death. And although you may claim that this is unfair, much research shows that even in this country many people do in fact blame the victim for being raped, especially if the victim is male (Adams-Price, Dalton, & Sumrall, 2004; Anderson, 2004).

The belief that the world is just creates perceptual distortions by leading us to de-emphasize the influence of situational factors and to overemphasize the influence of internal factors in our attempts to explain the behaviors of other people or even our own behaviors.

### Working with Theories and Research

Using the psychology, sociology, and/or communication databases of Research Navigator (www.researchnavigator.com) or another online database, search for "just world." Scan some of the articles. What can you add to the discussion presented here?

Alternatively, you're likely to explain the negative behavior of members of your own culture as externally or situationally caused but to explain the very same behavior of members of other cultures as internally motivated. Thus, for example, you would be more apt to attribute a high college dropout rate in your own cultural group (a negatively evaluated behavior) to external sources such as instructors who were not motivating or irrelevant educational programs. If, on the other hand, the dropouts were members of another culture, then you'd be more apt to attribute the problem to internal sources ("The people aren't interested in education; they lack motivation").

### ASK Yourself
#### Overattributing

Your friends seem to (over)attribute everything you do to your being deaf. You need to set them straight. **Ask yourself:** What can you say to make your friends realize that being deaf does not influence everything you do or say?

**Overattribution**  Overattribution is the tendency to single out one or two obvious characteristics of a person and attribute everything that person does to these characteristics. For example, if the person had alcoholic parents or is blind or was born into great wealth, there's often a tendency to attribute everything that person does to such factors. So you might say Sally has difficulty forming meaningful relationships because she grew up in a home of alcoholics, Alex overeats because he's blind, or Lillian is irresponsible because she never had to work for her money. To prevent overattribution, recognize that most behaviors and personality characteristics result from lots of factors. You almost always make a mistake when you select one factor and attribute everything to it. When you make a judgment, ask yourself if other factors might be operating here: Are there other factors that might be making it difficult for Sally to form relationships, for Alex to control his eating habits, or for Lillian to behave responsibly?

**The Fundamental Attribution Error**  The **fundamental attribution error** occurs when you overvalue the contribution of internal factors and undervalue the influence of external factors. It's the tendency to conclude that people do what they do because that's the kind of people they are and not because of the situation they're in. When Pat is late for an appointment, this error may lead you to conclude that Pat is inconsiderate or irresponsible rather than attributing the lateness to the bus breaking down or to a traffic accident.

When you explain your own behavior, you also favor internal explanations, although not to as great an extent as when explaining the behaviors of others. One reason for giving greater weight to external factors in explaining your own behavior than you do in explaining the behavior of others is that you know the situation surrounding your own behavior. You know, for example, what's going on in your love life and you know your financial condition, so you naturally see the influence of these factors. But you rarely know as much about others, and thus you're likely to give less weight to the external factors in their cases.

This fundamental attribution error is at least in part culturally influenced. For example, in the United States people are more likely to explain behavior by saying that people did what they did because of who they are. But when Hindus in India were asked to explain why their friends behaved as they did, they gave greater weight to external factors than did Americans in the United States (Miller, 1984; Aronson, Wilson, & Akert, 1999). Further, Americans have little hesitation in offering causal explanations of a person's behavior ("Pat did this because . . ."). Hindus, on the other hand, are generally reluctant to explain a person's behavior in causal terms (Matsumoto, 1994).

Let's return to the three examples with which we opened this discussion of attribution as a way of summarizing the principles of consensus, consistency, distinctiveness, and controllability. Generally, you would consider the three actions—begging, killing, and abandonment—to result from something inherent in the begging woman, the store owner, and the father if other people behaved differently in situations similar to these (low consensus), if these people had engaged in these behaviors in the past (high consistency), if these people behaved similarly in other situations (low distinctiveness), and if these people were in control of their own behaviors (high controllability). Under these conditions, you'd probably conclude that the persons bear the responsibility for their behaviors.

Alternatively, you would consider these actions to have resulted from something external to the persons if many other people reacted the same way in similar situations (high consensus), if these people had never behaved in this way before (low consistency), if these people never engaged in these behaviors in different situations (high distinctiveness), and if these people were not in control of their own behavior (low controllability). Under these conditions, you'd probably conclude that these actions resulted from external factors, that these people had little or no control, and that, therefore, they're not personally responsible.

**⌖ VIEWPOINT**

Some people feel that media portrayals of cultural groups often perpetuate stereotypes. Thus, for example, *The Sopranos*, the HBO series pictured here, has been accused of perpetuating the stereotype of Italian Americans as gangsters or of gangsters as Italian. How do you feel about the media's portrayals of your own cultural groups? Do the media create and perpetuate stereotypes of your groups? If so, are they basically positive or negative?

## ▪ INCREASING ACCURACY IN INTERPERSONAL PERCEPTION

Successful interpersonal communication depends largely on the accuracy of your interpersonal perception. We've already identified the potential barriers that can arise with each of the perceptual processes; in the area of attribution, for example, we've looked at the self-serving bias, overattribution, and the fundamental attribution error. There are, however, additional ways to increase your accuracy in interpersonal perception.

### Analyze Perceptions

When you become aware of your perceptions, you'll be able to subject them to logical analysis, to critical thinking. Here are two suggestions.

- *Recognize your own role in perception.* Your emotional and physiological state will influence the meaning you give to your perceptions. A movie may seem hysterically funny when you're in a good mood but just plain stupid when you're in a bad mood or when you're preoccupied with family problems. Beware of your own biases. Know when your perceptual evaluations are unduly influenced by your own biases; for example, whether you tend to perceive only the positive in people you like and only the negative in people you don't like. Even your gender will influence your perceptions. Women consistently evaluate other people more positively than do men on factors such as agreeableness, conscientiousness, and emotional stability (Winquist, Mohr, & Kenny, 1998).

- *Avoid early conclusions.* On the basis of your observations of behaviors, formulate hypotheses to test against additional information and evidence rather than drawing conclusions you then look to confirm. Delay formulating conclusions until you have had a chance to process a wide variety of cues. Similarly, avoid the one-cue conclusion. Look for a variety of cues pointing in the same direction. The more cues point to the same conclusion, the more likely your conclusion will be correct. Be especially alert to contradictory cues that seem to refute your initial hypotheses. It's relatively easy to perceive cues that confirm your hypotheses but more difficult to acknowledge contradictory evidence. At the same time, seek validation from others. Do others see things in the same way you do? If not, ask yourself if your perceptions may be distorted in some way.

### Check Perceptions

**Perception checking** is another way to reduce uncertainty and to make your perceptions more accurate. The goal of perception checking is to further explore the thoughts and feelings of the other person, not to prove that your initial perception is correct. With this simple technique, you lessen your chances of misinterpreting another's feelings. At the same

# Understanding Interpersonal Skills
## OTHER-ORIENTATION

**Other-orientation** is a quality of interpersonal effectiveness that includes the ability to adapt your messages to the other person. It involves communicating attentiveness to and interest in the other person and genuine interest in what the person says.

**Communicating Other-Orientation.** You'll recognize the following behaviors in those with whom you enjoy talking.

- Show consideration and respect; ask if it's all right to dump your troubles on someone before doing so, or ask if your phone call comes at a good time.
- Acknowledge the other person's feelings as correct and legitimate: Expressions such as "You're right" or "I can understand why you're so angry" help focus the interaction on the other person and confirm that you're listening.
- Acknowledge the presence and the importance of the other person. Ask the other person for suggestions, opinions, and clarification as appropriate. This will ensure that you understand what the other person is saying from that person's point of view.
- Focus your messages on the other person. Use open-ended questions to involve the other person in the interaction (as opposed to questions that merely ask for a yes or no answer), and make statements that directly address the person. Use focused eye contact and appropriate facial expressions; smile, nod, and lean toward the other person.
- Grant the other person permission to express (or to not express) her or his feelings. A simple statement such as "I know how difficult it is to talk about feelings" opens up the topic of feelings and gives the other person permission either to pursue such a discussion or to say nothing.

time, you give the other person an opportunity to elaborate on his or her thoughts and feelings. In its most basic form, perception checking consists of two steps.

**ASK Yourself**
Checking Perceptions

Your friend just had a baby and has been acting strangely—she doesn't communicate with friends, rarely goes out of the house, and seems depressed generally. You think she could be suffering from postpartum depression and you'd like to help. **Ask yourself:** What can you say to check your perceptions before you offer any specific advice or support?

1. Describe what you see or hear, recognizing that descriptions are not really objective but are heavily influenced by who you are, your emotional state, and so on. At the same time, you may wish to describe what you think is happening. Try to do this as descriptively (not evaluatively) as you can. Sometimes you may wish to offer several possibilities.

   ▦ You've called me from work a lot this week. You seem concerned that everything is all right at home.

   ▦ You've not wanted to talk with me all week. You say that my work is fine but you don't seem to want to give me the same responsibilities that other editorial assistants have.

2. Seek confirmation: Ask the other person if your description is accurate. Avoid mind reading. Don't try to read the thoughts and feelings of another person just from observing their behaviors. Regardless of how many behaviors you observe and how carefully you examine them, you can only *guess* what is going on in someone's mind. A person's motives are not open to outside inspection; you can only make assumptions based on overt behaviors. So be careful that your request for confirmation does not sound as though you already know the answer. Avoid phrasing your questions defensively, as in, for example, "You really don't want to go out, do you? I knew you didn't when you turned on that lousy television." Instead, ask for confirmation in as supportive a way as possible.

   ▦ Would you rather watch TV?
   ▦ Are you worried about me or the kids?
   ▦ Are you displeased with my work? Is there anything I can do to improve my job performance?

## Reduce Uncertainty

Reducing uncertainty enables us to achieve greater accuracy in perception. In large part we learn about uncertainty and how to deal with it from our culture. In some cultures people do little to avoid uncertainty and have little anxiety about not knowing what will happen next; uncertainty to them is a normal part of life and is accepted as it comes. Members of these cultures don't feel threatened by unknown situations. Examples of such low-anxiety cultures include Singapore, Jamaica, Denmark, Sweden, Hong Kong, Ireland, Great Britain, Malaysia, India, the Philippines, and the United States. Other cultures do much to avoid uncertainty and have a great deal of anxiety about not knowing what will happen next; uncertainty is seen as threatening and something that must be counteracted. Examples of such high-anxiety cultures include Greece, Portugal, Guatemala, Uruguay, Belgium, El Salvador, Japan, Yugoslavia, Peru, France, Chile, Spain, and Costa Rica (Hofstede, 1997; Shuper, Sorrentino, Otsubo, & Walker, 2004).

The potential for communication problems can be great when people come from cultures with different attitudes toward uncertainty. For example, managers from cultures with weak uncertainty avoidance will accept workers who work only when they have to and will not get too upset when workers are late. Managers from cultures with strong uncertainty avoidance will expect workers to be busy at all times and will have little tolerance for lateness.

Because weak-uncertainty-avoidance cultures have great tolerance for ambiguity and uncertainty, they minimize the importance of rules governing communication and relationships (Hofstede, 1997; Lustig & Koester, 2005). People who don't follow the same rules as the cultural majority are readily tolerated. Different approaches and perspectives may even be encouraged in cultures with weak uncertainty avoidance. Strong-uncertainty-avoidance cultures create very clear-cut rules for communication that must not be broken.

Students from weak-uncertainty-avoidance cultures appreciate freedom in education and prefer vague assignments without specific timetables. These students will want to be rewarded for creativity and will easily accept an instructor's lack of knowledge in some areas. Students from strong-uncertainty-avoidance cultures prefer highly structured experiences where there is little ambiguity; they prefer specific objectives, detailed instructions, and definite timetables. These students expect to be judged on the basis of the right answers and expect the instructor to have all the answers all the time (Hofstede, 1997).

A variety of strategies can help reduce uncertainty (Berger & Bradac, 1982; Gudykunst, 1993).

- Observing another person while he or she is engaged in an active task, preferably interacting with others in an informal social situation, will often reveal a great deal about the person, as people are less apt to monitor their behaviors and more likely to reveal their true selves in informal situations.

- You can sometimes manipulate situations so as to observe the person in more specific and revealing contexts. Employment interviews, theatrical auditions, and student teaching are some situations that can enable observer to see how a person might act and react and thus can help reduce uncertainty about the person.

- When you log on to an Internet chat group for the first time and lurk, reading the exchanges between the other group members before saying anything yourself, you're learning about the people in the group and about the group itself, thus reducing uncertainty. When uncertainty is reduced, you're more likely to make contributions that will be appropriate to the group and less likely to violate the group's norms; in short, you're more likely to communicate effectively.

- You can collect information about a person through asking others. You might inquire of a colleague if a third person finds you interesting and might like to have dinner with you.

- Interact with the individual. For example, you can ask questions: "Do you enjoy sports?" "What did you think of that computer science course?" "What would you do if you got fired?" You also gain knowledge of another by disclosing information about yourself. Your disclosures will help to create an environment that encourages disclosures from the person about whom you wish to learn more.

## Increase Cultural Sensitivity

Recognizing and being sensitive to cultural differences will help increase your accuracy in perception. For example, Russian or Chinese artists such as ballet dancers will often applaud their audience by clapping. Americans seeing this may easily interpret this as egotistical. Similarly, a German man will enter a restaurant before the woman in order to see if the place is respectable enough for the woman to enter. This simple custom can easily be interpreted as rude when viewed by people from cultures in which it's considered courteous for the woman to enter first (Axtell, 1994).

Within every cultural group there are wide and important differences. As all Americans are not alike, neither are all Indonesians, Greeks, or Mexicans. When you make assumptions that all people of a certain culture are alike, you're thinking in stereotypes. Recognizing differences between another culture and your own, and among members of the same culture, will help you perceive situations more accurately.

Cultural sensitivity will help counteract the difficulty most people have in understanding the nonverbal messages of people from other cultures. For example, it's easier to interpret the facial expressions of members of your own culture than those of members of other cultures (Weathers, Frank, & Spell, 2002). This "in-group advantage" will assist your perceptional accuracy for members of your own culture but will often hinder your accuracy for members of other cultures (Elfenbein & Ambady, 2002).

The suggestions for improving intercultural communication offered in Chapter 2 are applicable to increasing your cultural sensitivity in perception; they are listed here to refresh your memory.

- Prepare yourself.
- Reduce uncertainty.
- Recognize differences (between yourself and people from other cultures, among members of other cultures, and between your meanings and the meanings that people from other cultures might have).
- Confront your stereotypes.
- Adjust your communication.
- Manage culture shock.

## Reviewing  Key Terms and Concepts in Interpersonal Perception

This chapter examined perception, a fundamental process in all interpersonal communication encounters, and looked at the stages you go through in perceiving people, the processes that influence your perceptions, and some of the ways in which you can make your perceptions more accurate.

### Stages of Perception

What is perception and how does it work?

- Perception is the process by which you become aware of objects and events in the external world.
- Perception occurs in five stages: (1) stimulation, (2) organization, (3) interpretation–evaluation, (4) memory, and (5) recall.

### Perceptual Processes

What influences your interpersonal perceptions?

- Your self-fulfilling prophecies may influence the behaviors of others.
- Your implicit personality theory allows you to conclude that certain characteristics go with certain other characteristics.
- Perceptual accentuation may lead you to perceive what you expect to perceive instead of what is really there.
- Perceptions may be affected by primacy–recency. Your tendency to give extra importance to what occurs first (a primacy effect) may lead you to see what conforms to this judgment and to distort or otherwise misperceive what contradicts it.

First impressions often serve as filters, as schemata, for more recent information. In some cases, you may give extra weight to what occurs last (a recency effect).
- The tendency to seek and expect consistency may influence you to see what is consistent and to not see what is inconsistent.
- Attributions of causality, the process through which you try to understand the behaviors of others (and your own behaviors, in self-attribution), particularly the reasons or motivations for these behaviors, are made on the basis of consensus, consistency, distinctiveness, and controllability. Errors of attribution include the self-serving bias, overattribution, and the fundamental attribution error.

### Increasing Accuracy in Interpersonal Perception

How might you increase your accuracy in perception?

- Perceive critically: For example, recognize your role in perception, avoid early conclusions, and avoid mind reading.
- Check your perceptions: Describe what you see or hear and ask for confirmation.
- Reduce uncertainty: For example, lurk before actively participating in an Internet chat group, collect information about the person or situation, interact, and observe the situation.
- Be culturally sensitive: Recognize the differences between you and others and also the differences among people from other cultures.

## Applying  Key Terms and Concepts in Interpersonal Perception

1 Although most of the research on the self-fulfilling prophecy illustrates its distorting effect on behavior, consider how you might go about using the self-fulfilling prophecy to encourage behaviors you want to increase in strength and frequency. For example, what might you do to encourage persons who are high in communication apprehension to speak up with greater confidence? What might you do to encourage people who are reluctant to self-disclose to reveal more of their inner selves?

2 Do you engage in selective perception when listening to people talk about you? For example, are you more likely to attend to the positives than the negatives?

3 Using the concepts of attribution—especially controllability—how would you explain the attitudes that many people have about homeless people? About drug addicts or alcoholics? About successful politicians, scientists, or millionaires?

**4** Writers to advice columnists generally attribute their problems to external sources, whereas the columnists' responses often focus on internal sources, and their advice is therefore directed at the writer (you shouldn't have done that; apologize; get out of the relationship) (Schoeneman & Rubanowitz, 1985). Do you find this true when people discuss their problems with you, whether face-to-face, in letters, or in e-mail? Do you generally respond as would the columnists?

**5** What one suggestion for increasing perceptual accuracy do you wish others would follow more often when they make judgments about you?

**6** For the next several days, record all examples of people perception on your part—all instances in which you drew a conclusion about another person. Try to classify these in terms of the processes identified in this chapter; for example, processes such as implicit personality theory and attribution. Record also the specific context in which the instances occurred. After you've identified the various processes, share your findings in groups of five or six or with the entire class. As always, disclose only what you wish to disclose. What processes most frequently characterize your perceptions? Do these processes create any barriers to accurate perception?

## Experiencing  Key Terms and Concepts in Interpersonal Perception

Go to www.ablongman.com/devito.

*These exercises focus on sensitizing you to the influences on your perceptions and on helping you make your perceptions more accurate.*

❶ **Perceiving My Selves** invites you to consider how you see yourself and how you think others see you. This exercise is also an excellent icebreaker. ❷ **How Might You Perceive Others' Perceptions?** presents a variety of situations in which people are likely to see things very differently and sensitizes you to the variety of perceptions possible from the "same" event. ❸ **How Do You Make Attributions?** looks at a few specific situations and asks how you might make attributions in explaining the reasons for the behaviors. ❹ **Barriers to Accurate Perception** presents a dialogue containing a variety of perceptual errors and asks you to identify them. ❺ **Perspective Taking** asks you to take positive and negative perspectives on the same situations to help you explore the different conclusions people may draw from the same incident.

# Listening in Interpersonal Communication

**↑** *Cellular* (2004)

The movie *Cellular* tells the story of a high school science teacher (played by Kim Basinger) who is kidnapped and locked in an attic. With only a broken phone she tries to find someone who will listen to her and come to her rescue and save her son. The discussion to follow also focuses on listening—but not as a way to save your life. This chapter has a more modest goal: to make your interpersonal communication more effective.

> “Most of the successful people
> I've known are the ones who
> do more listening than talking.”
>
> —Bernard Baruch

Before reading about listening in interpersonal communication, examine your own listening habits and tendencies by taking the accompanying self-test, "How Well Do You Listen?"

## TEST YOURSELF

### HOW WELL DO YOU LISTEN?

Respond to each question using the following scale: 1 = always, 2 = frequently, 3 = sometimes, 4 = seldom, and 5 = never.

_____ 1. I listen to what the speaker is saying and feeling; I try to feel what the speaker feels.

_____ 2. I listen objectively; I focus on the logic of the ideas rather than on the emotional meaning of the message.

_____ 3. I listen without judging the speaker.

_____ 4. I listen critically, evaluating the speaker and what the speaker is saying.

_____ 5. I listen to the literal meanings that a speaker communicates; I don't look too deeply into hidden meanings.

_____ 6. I look for the hidden meanings, the meanings that are revealed by subtle verbal or nonverbal cues.

_____ 7. I listen actively, communicate acceptance of the speaker, and prompt the speaker to further explore his or her thoughts.

_____ 8. I listen without active involvement; I generally remain silent and take in what the other person is saying.

**HOW DID YOU DO?** These statements focus on the ways of listening discussed in this chapter, each of which is appropriate at some times but not at others. The only responses that are inappropriate are "always" and "never." Effective listening is listening that is tailored to the specific communication situation.

**WHAT WILL YOU DO?** Consider how you might use these statements to begin to improve your listening effectiveness. A good way to begin doing this is to review these statements and try to identify situations in which each statement would be appropriate and situations in which each statement would be inappropriate.

If you measured the importance of activities by the time you spent on them, then—according to the research studies available—listening would be your most important communication activity. Studies conducted from 1929 to 1980 showed listening to be the most often used form of communication, followed by speaking, reading, and writing (Rankin, 1929; Werner, 1975; Barker, Edwards, Gaines, Gladney, & Holley, 1980; Steil, Barker, & Watson, 1983; Wolvin & Coakley, 1996). This was true of high school and college students as well as of adults from a wide variety of fields. Because of the growth of the Internet,

these studies are now dated and their findings of limited value. Your communication patterns are very different from those of someone raised and educated before widespread use of home computers. However, anecdotal evidence (certainly not conclusive in any way) suggests that listening is probably still your most frequent communication activity. Just think of how you spend your day; listening probably occupies a considerable amount of time.

And effective listening is an important skill. It's interesting to note that the effective listener—to take just a few examples—is likely to emerge as a more effective group leader, salesperson, health care worker, or manager (Johnson & Bechler, 1998; Kramer, 1997; Castleberry & Shepherd, 1993; Lauer, 2003; Stein & Bowen, 2003; Levine, 2004). In recent years medical educators, claiming that doctors are not trained to listen to patients, have introduced what they call "narrative medicine" to teach doctors how to listen to their patients, and to help doctors recognize how their perceptions of their patients are influenced by their own emotions (Smith, 2003).

Another way to appreciate the importance of listening is to consider its many benefits. Here are some, built around the purposes of human communication identified in Chapter 1. Listening enables you:

- *To learn:* To acquire knowledge of others, the world, and yourself, so as to avoid problems and make more reasonable decisions. For example, listening to Peter tell about his travels to Cuba will help you learn more about Peter and about life in another country. Listening to your sales staff discuss their difficulties may help you offer more pertinent sales training.
- *To relate:* To gain social acceptance and popularity. Others will increase their liking of you once they see the genuine concern for them that you communicate through attentive and supportive listening.
- *To influence:* To change the attitudes and behaviors of others. For example, workers are more likely to follow your advice once they feel you've really listened to their insights and concerns.
- *To play:* To enjoy yourself and share pleasurable thoughts and feelings. Listening to the anecdotes of coworkers will allow you to gain a more comfortable balance between the world of work and the world of play.
- *To help:* To assist others in some way. For example, listening to your child's complaints about her teacher will increase your ability to help your child cope with school and her teacher.

 ## STAGES OF LISTENING ✓

**Listening** is not the same as hearing. Hearing is a physiological process that occurs when you're in the vicinity of vibrations in the air and these vibrations impinge on your eardrum. Hearing is basically a passive process that occurs without any attention or effort on your part. Listening is different.

Listening involves a series of five steps: receiving, understanding, remembering, evaluating, and responding (Figure 5.1). Note that the listening process is circular. The responses of one person serve as the stimuli for the other person, whose responses in turn serve as the stimuli for the first person, and so on.

### Stage One: Receiving

Listening begins with receiving the messages the speaker sends. The messages are both verbal and nonverbal; they consist of words as well as gestures, facial expressions, and variations in volume and rate.

## FIGURE 5.1

### A Five-Stage Model of Listening

Recognize that at each stage there will be lapses. Thus, for example, at the receiving stage a listener receives part of the message and, because of noise and perhaps for other reasons, fails to receive other parts. Similarly, at the stage of understanding, a listener understands part of the message and, because of each person's inability to share another's meanings exactly, fails to understand other parts. The same is true for remembering, evaluating, and responding. This model draws on a variety of previous models that listening researchers have developed (for example, Alessandra, 1986; Barker, 1990; Brownell, 2002).

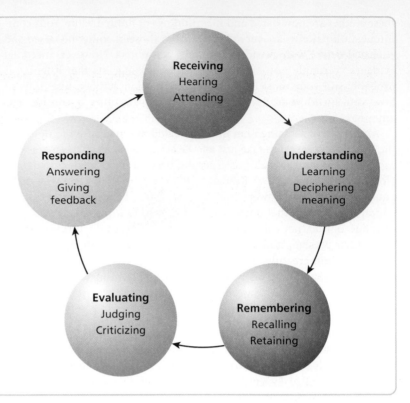

At this stage, you note not only what is said (verbally and nonverbally) but also what is omitted. You receive, for example, your boss's summary of your accomplishments as well as the omission of your shortcomings.

Analyze your own receiving. Do you

❶ Focus your attention on the speaker's verbal and nonverbal messages, on what is said and on what isn't said?
❷ Avoid distractions in the environment; if necessary, shut off the stereo or tell your assistant to hold your calls?
❸ Focus your attention on the speaker rather than on what you'll say next?
❹ Maintain your role as listener and avoid interrupting?

In this brief discussion of receiving—and, in fact, in this entire chapter on listening—the unstated assumption is that both individuals can receive auditory signals without difficulty. But for the many people who have hearing impairments, listening presents a variety of problems. Table 5.1 provides tips for communicating between deaf and hearing people.

### ASK Yourself

**Respecting Communication Norms**

As a gift for your three roommates, you buy each of them a lottery ticket. Big surprise: One of them wins (more than $250,000) but says nothing beyond "thank you"; nothing about sharing the winnings or even taking you out to dinner. None of the other roommates has said anything. Ask yourself: What might you do to get some understanding and closure on this without wrecking the friendships?

### Stage Two: Understanding

Understanding is the stage at which you learn what the speaker means—at which you grasp the thoughts and emotional tone expressed.

In understanding, do you

❶ Avoid assuming you understand what the speaker is going to say before he or she actually says it?
❷ Relate the new information the speaker is giving to what you already know?
❸ See the speaker's messages from the speaker's point of view; avoid judging the message until you fully understand it as the speaker intended it?

## Between Deaf and Hearing People

People with hearing loss differ greatly in their hearing ability: Some are totally deaf and can hear nothing, others have some hearing loss and can hear some sounds, and still others have impaired hearing but can hear most speech. Although people with profound hearing loss can speak, their speech may appear labored and may be less clear than the speech of those with unimpaired hearing. Here are some suggestions for more effective communication between deaf and hearing people.

### If you have unimpaired hearing:

1. *Set up a comfortable context.* Reduce the distance between yourself and the person with a hearing impairment. Reduce the background noise. Turn off the television and even the air conditioner.
2. *Avoid interference.* Make sure the visual cues from your speech are clearly observable; for example, face the person squarely and avoid smoking, chewing gum, or holding your hand over your mouth. Make sure the lighting is adequate.
3. *Speak with an adequate volume.* But avoid shouting, which can distort your speech and may insult the person. Be careful to avoid reducing volume at the ends of your sentences.
4. *Phrase ideas in different ways.* Because some words are easier to lip-read than others, it often helps if you can rephrase your ideas in different words.
5. *Avoid overlapping speech.* When in group situations, only one person should speak at a time. Similarly, direct your comments to the person with hearing loss himself or herself; don't talk to the person through a third party. Elementary school teachers, for example, have been found to direct fewer comments to deaf children than to hearing students (Cawthon, 2001).
6. *Ask for additional information.* Ask the person if there is anything you can do to make it easier for him or her to understand you.
7. *Don't avoid common terms.* Use terms like *hear, listen, music,* or *deaf* when they're relevant to the conversation. Trying to avoid these common terms will make your speech sound artificial.
8. *Use nonverbal cues.* Nonverbals can help communicate your meaning; gestures indicating size or location and facial expressions indicating emotions and feelings are often helpful.

### If you have impaired hearing:

1. *Do your best to eliminate background noise.*
2. *Move closer to the speaker if this helps you hear better.* Alert the speaker that this closer distance will help you hear better.
3. *Ask for adjustments.* If you feel the speaker can make adjustments to ease your comprehension, ask. For example, ask the speaker to repeat a message, to speak more slowly or more distinctly, or to increase his or her volume.
4. *Position yourself for best reception.* If you hear better in one ear than another, position yourself accordingly and, if necessary, clue the speaker in to this fact.
5. *Ask for additional cues.* If necessary, ask the speaker to write down certain information, for example, phone numbers or website addresses. Carrying a pad and pencil will prove helpful for this and in the event that you wish to write something down for others.

*Sources:* These suggestions were drawn from a variety of sources: *Tips for Communicating with Deaf People* (Rochester Institute of Technology, National Technical Institute for the Deaf, Division of Public Affairs), http://www.his.com/~lola/deaf.html, http://www.zak.co.il/deaf-info/old/comm_strategies.html, http://www.agbell.org/, http://www.dol.gov/odep/pubs/fact/comucate.htm, and http://spot.pcc.edu/~rjacobs/career/communication_tips.htm (all websites accessed April 9, 2005).

④ Ask questions for clarification, if necessary; ask for additional details or examples if they're needed?

⑤ Rephrase (paraphrase) the speaker's ideas in your own words?

## Stage Three: Remembering

For effective listening to take place, you need to remember the messages. For example, when Susan says she is planning to buy a new car, the effective listener remembers this and at later meetings asks about the car. When Joe says his mother is ill, the effective listener remembers this and inquires about her health later in the week.

In some small group and public speaking situations, you can augment your memory by taking notes or by taping the messages. In most interpersonal communication situations, however, note taking is inappropriate, although you often do write down a telephone

# InterMedia

## GATEKEEPING

"Gatekeeping" in interpersonal communication, introduced as a concept by Kurt Lewin in his *Human Relations* (1947), involves both the *process* by which a message passes through various gates and the *people or groups* (gatekeepers) that allow the message to pass.

As you were growing up, your parents gave you certain information and withheld other information (Fagan & Barnett, 2003). Depending on the culture in which you were raised, you may have been told about Santa Claus and the Tooth Fairy but not about cancer or mutual funds. When you went to school, your teachers served a similar function. They taught you about certain historical events but not others. Textbook authors serve a similar gatekeeping function. For example, there has been controversy over the trend in Japanese high school textbooks to downplay crimes committed by Japan against its neighbors, particularly the Chinese and the Koreans (Onishi, 2005b). Editors of newspapers, periodicals, publishing houses, and websites are also gatekeepers (Lewis 1995; Bodon, Powell, & Hickson, 1999).

The media, usually on the basis of their own codes and sometimes because of legal regulations, censor what gets through. Often, of course, media organizations gatekeep to increase profits; for example, they may emphasize (open the gates for) stories of celebrities, violence, and sex because these sell and deemphasize (close the gates on) minority issues, classical drama, or any issues that reflect negatively on their own biases. Television controls, with their capability to lock out channels or programs based on movie or TV ratings, now make it extremely easy for parents to serve as gatekeepers over the programs their children watch.

### Follow Up

Consider how one, two, or three of the following function as gatekeepers in relation to your ability to acquire information: The editor of your college newspaper, Oprah Winfrey, your best friend, the president of the United States, network news shows, or the advertising department of a large corporation.

### ⬆ VIEWPOINT

The term *false memory syndrome* refers to a phenomenon in which a person "remembers" past experiences that never actually occurred. Most of the studies on false memory syndrome have centered on erroneous recollections of abuse and other traumatic experiences. Often these false memories are implanted by therapists and interviewers, whose persistent questioning over a period of time can create such a realistic scenario that an individual comes to believe these things actually occurred (Porter, Brit, Yuille, & Lehman, 2000). In what other, less dramatic ways can false memory syndrome occur?

number, an appointment, or directions. And in many work situations, taking notes is common and may even be expected.

What you remember is actually not what was said but what you think (or remember) was said. Memory for speech isn't reproductive; you don't simply reproduce in your memory what the speaker said. Rather, memory is reconstructive; you actually reconstruct the messages you hear into a system that makes sense to you.

In remembering, do you

1. Identify the central ideas and the major support advanced?
2. Summarize the message in a more easily retained form, but take care not to ignore crucial details or qualifications?
3. Repeat names and key concepts to yourself or, if appropriate, aloud?

### Stage Four: Evaluating

**Evaluating** consists of judging the messages in some way. At times you may try to evaluate the speaker's underlying intentions or motives. Often this evaluation process goes on without much conscious awareness. For example, Elaine tells you that she is up for a promotion and is really excited about it. You may then try to judge her intention: Perhaps she wants

## CUES TO LYING

In normal listening you assume the speaker is telling the truth. When you do question the speaker's truthfulness, it may be because the speaker exhibits cues that often accompany lying. Research has identified numerous such cues. Typically liars smile less; respond with shorter answers, often a simple yes or no; use fewer specifics and more generalities, such as "we hung out"; shift their posture more; use more self-touching movements; use more and longer pauses; avoid direct eye contact with the listener and blink more often than normal; appear less friendly and attentive; and make more speech errors (Knapp & Hall, 2002; O'Hair, Cody, Goss, & Krayer, 1988; Bond & Atoum, 2000; Al-Simadi, 2000; Burgoon & Bacue, 2003). Be careful, however, that you don't fall into the trap of thinking that just because someone emits some or all of these cues, he or she is therefore lying. These cues are often used by truth-tellers as well as liars. In one study, in fact, people who held stereotypical views of how liars behave (for example, "liars don't look at you" or "liars fidget") were *less* effective in detecting lying than were those who did not hold such beliefs (Vrij & Mann, 2001).

### Working with Theories and Research

Recall a situation in which you assumed, on the basis of such cues (or others), that someone was lying. What happened? Should you want to learn more about lying, log on to Research Navigator (www.researchnavigator.com) or another online database and search for lying, deception, and similar terms. It's a fascinating subject of study.

you to use your influence with the company president, or she's preoccupied with the promotion and so tells everyone, or she's looking for a compliment.

In other situations your evaluation is more in the nature of critical analysis. For example, in listening to proposals advanced in a business meeting, you might ask: Are they practical? Will they increase productivity? What's the evidence? Is there contradictory evidence?

In evaluating, do you

1. Resist evaluation until you fully understand the speaker's point of view?
2. Assume that the speaker is a person of goodwill, and give the speaker the benefit of any doubt by asking for clarification on positions to which you feel you might object?
3. Distinguish facts from inferences (see Chapter 7), opinions, and personal interpretations by the speaker?
4. Identify any biases, self-interests, or prejudices that may lead the speaker to slant unfairly what is presented?

### Stage Five: Responding

Responding occurs in two phases: responses you make while the speaker is talking and responses you make after the speaker has stopped talking. These responses are feedback—information that you send back to the speaker and that tells the speaker how you feel and what you think about his or her messages. Responses made while the speaker is talking should be supportive and should acknowledge that you're listening to the speaker. These responses include what nonverbal researchers call **back-channeling cues**—comments such as "I see," "yes," "uh-huh," and similar signals that let the speaker know you're listening.

Responses made after the speaker has stopped talking are generally more elaborate and might include expressing empathy ("I know how you must feel"), asking for clarification ("Do you mean that this new health plan is to replace the old one?"), challenging ("I think your evidence is weak here"), or agreeing ("You're absolutely right on this; I'll support your proposal").

In responding, do you

1. Support the speaker throughout the speaker's talk by using and varying your back-channeling cues?
2. Express support for the speaker in your final responses?
3. Act honestly? The speaker has a right to expect honest responses, even if they express disagreement.
4. Own your responses? State your thoughts and feelings as your own, and use I-messages.
5. Resist (as men are often accused of doing) "responding to another's feelings" with "solving the person's problems" (Tannen, 1990)? It's usually more productive to view your task in more limited terms: to encourage the person to express and perhaps to clarify his or her feelings and to provide a supportive atmosphere.

## Implications of the Model of Listening

A few general comments on the model of listening presented here will round out the presentation of the five steps in listening.

1. Listening involves a collection of skills: attention and concentration (receiving), learning (understanding), memory (remembering), critical thinking (evaluation), and competence in giving feedback (responding). Listening can go wrong at any stage—but you can improve your listening ability by strengthening the skills needed at each step of the listening process.
2. All five listening stages overlap; when you listen, you're performing all five processes at essentially the same time. For example, when listening in conversation, you're not only remaining attentive to what the other people are saying but also critically evaluating what they just said and perhaps giving feedback of approval.
3. Listening is never perfect. There are lapses in attention, misunderstandings, lapses in memory, inadequate critical thinking, and inappropriate responding. The goal is to reduce these obstacles as best you can.

# Ethics in Interpersonal Communication

## ETHICAL LISTENING

As a listener you have at least these two ethical obligations.

- You owe it to the speaker to give an *honest hearing,* without prejudgment, putting aside prejudices and preconceptions as best you can. At the same time, you owe the speaker your best effort at understanding emotionally as well as intellectually what he or she means.
- Second, you owe the speaker *honest responses.* Just as you should be honest with the listener when speaking, you should be honest with the speaker when listening. This means giving open and honest feedback and also reflecting honestly on the questions that the speaker raises.

### What would you do?

Your friend begins revealing deeply personal secrets—problems at home, a lack of money, no friends, and on and on. You don't want to hear all this; it depresses you. You want to avoid these disclosures by making excuses to cut the conversation short or change the subject. At the same time, however, you wonder if you have an ethical obligation to listen openly and respond honestly to your friend. What would you do in this situation?

**TABLE 5.2**

## Problem-Causing Listening Responses

| Listener Type | Listening (Responding) Behavior | (Mis)interpreting Thoughts |
|---|---|---|
| The static listener | Gives no feedback, remains relatively motionless, reveals no expression. | Why isn't she reacting? Am I not producing sound? |
| The monotonous feedback giver | Seems responsive, but the responses never vary; regardless of what you say, the response is the same. | Am I making sense? Why is he still smiling? I'm being dead serious |
| The overly expressive listener | Reacts to just about everything with extreme responses. | Why is she so expressive? I didn't say anything that provocative. She'll have a heart attack when I get to the punchline. |
| The reader/writer | While "listening" reads or writes about matters having nothing to do with what the speaker is saying; only occasionally glances up. | Am I that boring? Is last week's student newspaper more interesting than me? |
| The eye avoider | Looks all around the room and at others but never at you. | Why isn't he looking at me? Do I have spinach on my teeth? |
| The preoccupied listener | Listens to other things at the same time, often with headphones with the sound so loud that it interferes with your own thinking. | When is she going to shut that music off and really listen? Am I so boring that my talk needs background music? |
| The waiting listener | Listens for a cue to take over the speaking turn. | Is he listening to me or rehearsing his next interruption? |
| The thought-completing listener | Listens a little and then finishes your thought. | Am I that predictable? Why do I bother saying anything? He already knows what I'm going to say. |

4. Listening is situational; your style of listening should vary with the circumstances. You listen differently depending on your purpose, your conversational partners, and the type of message; for example, in some situations you'll need to be especially critical and in others especially supportive. The next section will elaborate on this concept and explain the major styles of listening and how you might use them most effectively depending on the situation.

Table 5.2 identifies some types of difficult listeners and their problem-causing ways of responding. Review this table and see if it includes some of your own listening behaviors.

## STYLES OF EFFECTIVE LISTENING

As stressed throughout this chapter, listening is situational; the type of listening that is appropriate will vary with the situation, and each situation will call for a somewhat different combination of listening styles. The art of effective listening is largely one of making appropriate choices along the following four dimensions: (1) empathic versus objective listening, (2) nonjudgmental versus critical listening, (3) surface versus depth listening, and (4) active versus inactive listening. Let's take a look at each of these dimensions.

### Empathic and Objective Listening

If you're to understand what a person means and what a person is feeling, you need to listen with some degree of empathy (Rogers,

> **ASK Yourself**
>
> *Giving Listening Cues*
>
> Often you're asked by a speaker if he or she is getting through or making sense. It seems as if speakers doubt that you're listening. But, usually at least, you are.   Ask yourself: What might you do to show people you're listening to them and interested in what they're saying?

1970; Rogers & Farson, 1981). To empathize with others is to feel with them, to see the world as they see it, to feel what they feel. Only when you achieve this can you fully understand another person's meaning. Empathic listening will also help you enhance your relationships (Barrett & Godfrey, 1988; Snyder, 1992).

Although for most communication situations empathic listening is the preferred mode of responding, there are times when you need to go beyond it to measure meanings and feelings against some objective reality. It's important to listen to Peter tell you how the entire world hates him and to understand how Peter feels and why he feels this way. But then you need to look a bit more objectively at Peter and perhaps see the paranoia or the self-hatred. Sometimes you have to put your empathic responses aside and listen with objectivity and detachment.

In adjusting your empathic and objective listening, keep the following recommendations in mind:

- Punctuate from the speaker's point of view (Chapter 1). That is, if you want to understand the speaker's perspective, see the sequence of events as the speaker does and try to figure out how this can influence what the speaker says and does.
- Engage in equal, two-way conversation. To encourage openness and empathy, try to eliminate any physical or psychological barriers to equality (for example, step from behind the large desk separating you from your employees). Avoid interrupting the speaker—which sends the signal that what you have to say is more important.
- Seek to understand both thoughts and feelings. Don't consider your listening task finished until you've understood what the speaker is feeling as well as thinking.
- Avoid "offensive listening," the tendency to listen to bits and pieces of information that will enable you to attack the speaker or find fault with something the speaker has said (Floyd, 1985).
- Strive to be objective when listening to friends and foes alike. Your attitudes may lead you to distort messages—to block out positive messages about a foe and negative messages about a friend. Guard against "expectancy hearing," when you fail to hear what the speaker is really saying and hear what you expect to hear instead.

## Nonjudgmental and Critical Listening

Effective listening includes both nonjudgmental and critical responses. You need to listen nonjudgmentally—with an open mind with a view toward understanding. You also need to listen critically—with a view toward making some kind of evaluation or judgment. Clearly listen first for understanding while suspending judgment. Only after you've fully understood the relevant messages should you evaluate or judge.

Supplement open-minded listening with critical listening. Listening with an open mind will help you understand messages better; listening with a critical mind will help you analyze and evaluate the messages. In adjusting your nonjudgmental and critical listening, focus on the following guidelines:

- Keep an open mind. Avoid prejudging. Delay your judgments until you fully understand the intention and the content the speaker is communicating. Avoid both positive and negative evaluation until you have a reasonably complete understanding.
- Avoid filtering out or oversimplifying complex messages. Similarly, avoid filtering out undesirable messages. You don't want to hear that something you believe in is untrue, that people you care for are unkind, or that ideals you hold are self-destructive. Yet it's important that you reexamine your beliefs by listening to these messages.
- Recognize your own biases. These may interfere with accurate listening and cause you to distort message reception through the process of assimilation—the tendency to integrate and interpret what you hear or think you hear to fit your own biases, prejudices, and expectations. For example, are your ethnic, national, or religious biases preventing you from appreciating a speaker's point of view?
- Be sure to listen critically to the entire message when you need to make evaluations and judgments. Recognize and combat the natural human tendency to sharpen—a

process in which one or two aspects of the message become highlighted, emphasized, and perhaps embellished. Often the concepts that are sharpened are incidental remarks that somehow stand out from the rest of the message.

- Recognize some of the popular but fallacious forms of reasoning, such as the following (Lee & Lee, 1972, 1995; Pratkanis & Aronson, 1991):
  - *Name-calling* involves giving an idea, a group of people, or a political philosophy a bad name ("atheist," "Neo-Nazi," "cult"). In the opposite of name-calling, the speaker tries to make you accept some idea by associating it with things you value highly ("democracy," "free speech," "academic freedom"). Remember that although labels are useful most of the time, they often can obscure the actual person or idea. Listen first to evidence and argument; never take labels as evidence or reasons for judgment.
  - *Testimonial* involves using the image associated with some person to gain your approval (if you respect the person) or your rejection (if you don't respect the person). This technique is used by advertisers who use people dressed up to look like doctors or plumbers or chefs to sell their products. Listen carefully to the person's credentials; be suspicious when you hear such phrases as "experts agree," "scientists say," "good cooks know," or "dentists advise." Ask yourself exactly who these experts are and what the source of their expertise is.
  - *Bandwagon* is a technique that tries to persuade you to accept or reject an idea or proposal on the grounds that "everybody is doing it," so you should "jump on the bandwagon." You'll hear this technique used frequently during election time, when campaigns cite poll results in an effort to get you to join the group and vote for one person or another. Again, listen to the evidence; 50,000 Frenchmen—as the saying goes—can be wrong.
  - *Agenda-setting* involves claiming that a particular issue is crucial and all others are unimportant and insignificant. This technique is used frequently in interpersonal conflict situations: Each person may claim that her or his viewpoint is the accurate and important one and that the other person's is less accurate and less important. In almost all situations, and especially in interpersonal conflict situations, there are many issues and many sides to each issue.
  - *Attack* involves accusing another person (usually an opponent) of some serious wrongdoing so that the issue under discussion never gets examined; for example "How can I ever believe you after you lied?" Although a person's reputation and past behavior are often relevant, listen most carefully to the issue at hand. When personal attack draws attention away from other issues, then it becomes fallacious.

**⬆ VIEWPOINT**

Although empathy is almost universally considered positive, there is some evidence to show that it also can have a negative side. For example, people are most empathic with those who are similar—racially and ethnically as well as in appearance and social status. The more empathy you feel toward your own group, the less empathy—possibly even the more hostility—you feel toward other groups. The same empathy that increases your understanding of your own group decreases your understanding of other groups. So although empathy may encourage group cohesiveness and identification, it also can create dividing lines between your group and "them" (Angier, 1995b). Have you ever experienced or witnessed these negative effects of empathy?

## Surface and Depth Listening

In Shakespeare's *Julius Caesar,* Marc Antony, in giving the funeral oration for Caesar, says: "I come to bury Caesar, not to praise him. / The evil that men do lives after them; / The good is oft interred with their bones." And later: "For Brutus is an honourable man; / So are they all, all honourable men." If we listen beyond the surface of Marc Antony's words, we can see that he does comes to praise Caesar, and to convince the crowd that

# Understanding Interpersonal Skills

## OPENNESS

**Openness** in interpersonal communication is a person's willingness to self-disclose—to reveal information about himself or herself that might normally be kept hidden—provided that such disclosure is appropriate (as discussed in Chapter 3). Openness also includes a willingness to listen openly to and to react honestly to the messages of others.

**Communicating Openness.** Consider these few ideas.

- Self-disclose when appropriate. Be mindful about your disclosures, remembering that there are benefits and dangers to this form of communication.
- Respond to those with whom you're interacting with spontaneity and with appropriate honesty—though also with an awareness of what you're saying and of what the possible outcomes of your messages might be.
- Own your own feelings and thoughts. Take responsibility for what you say. Use **I-messages** instead of **you-messages**. Instead of saying, "You make me feel stupid when you don't ask my opinion," own your feelings and say, for example, "I feel stupid when you ask everyone else what they think but don't ask me." When you own your feelings and thoughts—when you use I-messages—you say, in effect, "This is how *I* feel," "This is how *I* see the situation." I-messages make explicit the fact that your feelings result from the interaction between what is going on outside your skin (what others say, for example) and what is going on inside your skin (your preconceptions, attitudes, and prejudices, for example).

Brutus was dishonorable—despite the fact that at first glance his words seem to say quite the opposite.

In most messages there's an obvious meaning that you can derive from a literal reading of the words and sentences. But there's often another level of meaning. Sometimes, as in *Julius Caesar,* it's the opposite of the literal meaning; at other times it seems totally unrelated. Consider some frequently heard types of messages. For example, Carol asks you how you like her new haircut. On one level the meaning is clear: Do you like the haircut? But there's also another, perhaps more important, level: Carol is asking you to say something positive about her appearance. In the same way, the parent who complains about working hard at the office or in the home may, on a deeper level, be asking for an expression of appreciation. The child who talks about the unfairness of the other children in the playground may be asking for comfort and love.

To appreciate these other meanings you need to engage in depth listening. If you respond only to the surface-level communication (the literal meaning), you miss the opportunity to make meaningful contact with the other person's feelings and needs. If you say to the parent, "You're always complaining. I bet you really love working so hard," you fail to respond to the call for understanding and appreciation. In regulating your surface and depth listening, consider the following guidelines:

- *Focus on both verbal and nonverbal messages.* Recognize both consistent and inconsistent "packages" of messages and use these as guides for drawing inferences about the speaker's meaning. Ask questions when in doubt. Listen also to what is omitted. Remember that speakers communicate by what they leave out as well as by what they include.
- *Listen for both content and relational messages.* The student who constantly challenges the teacher is, on one level, communicating disagreement over content. However, on another level—the relationship level—the student may be voicing objections to the

instructor's authority or authoritarianism. The instructor needs to listen and respond to both types of messages.

- *Make special note of statements that refer back to the speaker.* Remember that people inevitably talk about themselves. Whatever a person says is, in part, a function of who that person is. Attend carefully to those personal, self-referential messages.
- *At the same time, don't disregard the literal meaning of interpersonal messages in trying to uncover the hidden meaning.* Balance your listening between the surface and the underlying meaning. Respond to the different levels of meaning in the messages of others as you would like others to respond to yours—be sensitive but not obsessive. Be attentive but not too eager to uncover hidden messages.

## Active and Inactive Listening

One of the most important communication skills you can learn is that of active listening (Gordon, 1975). Consider the following interaction. You're disappointed that you have to redo your entire report, and you say: "I can't believe I have to rewrite this entire budget report. I really worked hard on this project and now I have to do it all over again." To this, you get three different responses:

**APOLLO:**  That's not so bad; most people find they have to redo their first reports. That's the norm here.

**ATHENA:**  You should be pleased that all you have to do is a simple rewrite. Peggy and Michael both had to completely redo their entire projects.

**DIANA:**  You have to rewrite that report you've worked on for the last three weeks? You sound really angry and frustrated.

All three listeners are probably trying to make you feel better. But they go about it in very different ways and, you can be sure, with very different results. Apollo tries to lessen the significance of the rewrite. This well-intended response is extremely common but does little to promote meaningful communication and understanding. Athena tries to give the situation a positive spin. With these responses, however, both these listeners are also suggesting that you should not be feeling the way you do. They're implying that your feelings are not legitimate and should be replaced with more logical feelings.

Diana's response, however, is different from the others. Diana uses **active listening.** Active listening owes its development to Thomas Gordon (1975), who made it a cornerstone of his P-E-T (Parent Effectiveness Training) technique; it is a process of sending back to the speaker what you as a listener think the speaker meant—both in content and in feelings. Active listening, then, is not merely repeating the speaker's exact words, but rather putting together your understanding of the speaker's total message into a meaningful whole.

Active listening serves several important functions. First, it helps you as a listener check your understanding of what the speaker said and, more important, of what he or she meant. Reflecting back perceived meanings to the speaker gives the speaker an opportunity to offer clarification and correct any misunderstandings.

Second, through active listening you let the speaker know that you acknowledge and accept his or her feelings. In the sample responses given, the first two listeners challenged the speaker's feelings. Diana, the active listener, accepted what you were feeling. In addition, she also explicitly identified your feelings: "You sound angry and frustrated," allowing you an opportunity to correct her interpretation if necessary.

Third, active listening stimulates the speaker to explore feelings and thoughts. Diana's response encourages you to elaborate on your feelings, and helps you deal with them by talking them through.

A word of caution: In communicating your understanding back to the person, be especially careful to avoid sending what Gordon (1975) calls "solution messages"—messages that tell the person how he or she *should* feel or what he or she *should* do. Four types of messages send solutions, and you'll want to avoid them in your active listening:

**SPEAKING**
**>> Interpersonal-E**

**Internet Noise.** Spam and pop-ups are visual noise and, like any kind of noise, interfere with your receiving the messages you want to receive. Check out the ways your ISP allows you to block unwanted messages. It will help you attend to the desired messages.

- ordering messages: "*Do this. . . .*" "*Don't touch that. . . .*"
- warning and threatening messages: "*If you don't do this, you'll. . . .*" "*If you do that, you'll. . . .*"
- preaching and moralizing messages: "*People should all. . . .*" "*We all have responsibilities. . . .*"
- advising messages: "*Why don't you. . . .*" "*I think you should. . . .*"

Three simple techniques may prove useful in learning the process of active listening: Paraphrase the speaker's meaning, express understanding, and ask questions.

- *Paraphrase the speaker's meaning.* Stating in your own words what you think the speaker means and feels helps ensure understanding and also shows interest in the speaker. Paraphrasing gives the speaker a chance to extend what was originally said. Thus, when Diana echoes your thoughts, you're given the opportunity to elaborate on why rewriting the budget report means so much to you. In paraphrasing, be objective; be especially careful not to lead the speaker in the direction you think he or she should go.

  Also, be careful that you don't overdo paraphrase; only a very small percentage of statements need paraphrasing. Paraphrase when you feel there's a chance for misunderstanding or when you want to express support for the other person and keep the conversation going.
- *Express understanding of the speaker's feelings.* Echo the feelings the speaker expressed or implied ("You must have felt horrible"). This expression of feelings will help you further check your perception of the speaker's feelings. This will also allow the speaker to see his or her feelings more objectively (especially helpful when they're feelings of anger, hurt, or depression) and to elaborate on them.
- *Ask questions.* Asking questions ensures your own understanding of the speaker's thoughts and feelings and secures additional information ("How did you feel when you read your job appraisal report?"). Ask questions to provide just enough stimulation and support for the speaker to feel he or she can elaborate on these thoughts and feelings. These questions should further confirm your interest and concern for the speaker but not pry into unrelated areas or challenge the speaker in any way.

Active listening, then, is not merely repeating the speaker's exact words, but rather putting together into some meaningful whole your understanding of the speaker's total message. And incidentally, when combined with empathic listening, it proves the most effective mode for success as a salesperson (Comer & Drollinger, 1999).

Once again, the type of listening that is appropriate varies with the situation. You can visualize a listening situation as one in which you have to make choices among the four dimensions of listening discussed in this section. Each listening situation should call for a somewhat different configuration of listening responses; the art of effective listening is largely one of making appropriate choices along the four dimensions of empathic–objective, nonjudgmental–critical, surface–depth, and active–inactive listening.

## CULTURE, GENDER, AND LISTENING

Listening is difficult, in part, because of the inevitable differences in the communication systems between speaker and listener. Because each person has had a unique set of experiences, each person's meaning system is going to be different from every other person's. When speaker and listener come from different cultures or are of different genders, the differences and their effects are naturally much greater. Consider culture first.

## Culture and Listening

In a global environment in which people from very different cultures work together, it's especially important to understand the ways in which cultural differences can influence listening. Three such factors may be singled out: (1) language and speech, (2) nonverbal behaviors, and (3) feedback.

**Language and Speech**    Even when speaker and listener speak the same language, they speak it with different meanings and different accents. No two speakers speak exactly the same language. Speakers of the same language will, at the very least, have different meanings for the same terms because they have had different experiences.

Speakers and listeners who have different native languages and who may have learned English as a second language will have even greater differences in meaning. Translations never fully capture the meaning in the other language. If your meaning for the word *house* was learned in a culture in which everyone lived in their own house with lots of land around it, then communicating with someone for whom the meaning of *house* was learned in a neighborhood of high-rise tenements is going to be difficult. Although you'll each hear the same word, the meanings you'll each develop will be drastically different. In adjusting your listening—especially in an intercultural setting—understand that the speaker's meanings may be very different from yours even though you're speaking in the same language.

In many classrooms throughout the United States, there will be a wide range of accents. Students whose native language is a tonal one, such as Chinese (in which differences in pitch signal important meaning differences), may speak English with variations in pitch that may be puzzling to others. Those whose native language is Japanese may have trouble distinguishing *l* from *r*, as Japanese does not include this distinction. The native language acts as a filter and influences the accent given to the second language.

**Nonverbal Behaviors**    Speakers from different cultures have different display rules—cultural rules that govern what nonverbal behaviors are appropriate or inappropriate in a public setting. As you listen to other people, you also "listen" to their nonverbal cues. If nonverbals are drastically different from what you expect on the basis of the verbal message, you may experience them as a kind of noise or interference or even as contradictory messages. Also, of course, different cultures may give very different meanings to the same nonverbal gesture. For example, the thumb and forefinger forming a circle means "OK" in most of the United States; but it means "money" in Japan, "zero" in some Mediterranean countries, and "I'll kill you" in Tunisia.

**Feedback**    Members of some cultures give very direct and very frank feedback. Speakers from these cultures—the United States is a good example—expect feedback to be an honest reflection of what their listeners are feeling. In other cultures—Japan and Korea are good examples—it's more important to be positive than to be truthful, and so people may respond with positive feedback (say, in commenting on a business colleague's proposal) even though they don't agree with what is being said. Listen to feedback, as you would all messages, with a full recognition that various cultures view feedback very differently.

## Gender and Listening

Men and women learn different styles of listening, just as they learn different styles for using verbal and nonverbal messages. Not surprisingly, these different styles can create

⬆ **VIEWPOINT**

The popular belief is that men listen in the way they do to prove themselves superior and that women listen as they do to ingratiate themselves. Although there is no evidence to show that these images are valid, they persist in the assumptions that people make about the opposite sex. What do you believe accounts for the differences in the way men and women listen?

major difficulties in opposite-sex interpersonal communication. According to Deborah Tannen (1990) in her best-selling *You Just Don't Understand: Women and Men in Conversation,* women seek to build rapport and establish closer relationships and use listening to achieve these ends. Men, on the other hand, will play up their expertise, emphasize it, and use it in dominating the interaction. Women play down their expertise and are more interested in communicating supportiveness. Tannen argues that the goal of a man in conversation is to be given respect, so he seeks to show his knowledge and expertise. A woman, on the other hand, seeks to be liked, so she expresses agreement.

Men and women also show that they're listening in different ways. In conversation, a woman is more apt to give lots of listening cues—interjecting "Yeah" or "Uh-huh," nodding in agreement, and smiling. Women also make more eye contact when listening than do men, who are more apt to look around and often away from the speaker (Brownell, 2002). A man is more likely to listen quietly, without giving lots of listening cues as feedback. Subsequent research seems to confirm Tannen's position. For example, an analysis of calls to a crisis center in Finland revealed that calls received by a female counselor were significantly longer for both men and women callers (Salminen & Glad, 1992). It's likely that the greater number of listening cues given by the women encouraged the

## Ask the Researcher

### LISTENING TO GENDER DIFFERENCES

 If women and men do appear to listen differently, what can I do to make sure the other person is really listening in ways that I need?

That women appear to be better listeners is probably due to the fact that women, not men, are typically socialized to provide prosocial listening cues and to solve problems. As this chapter suggests, the responsibility to ensure that the other party is listening appropriately is a shared one. To ensure meaningful listening:

1. Determine your listening needs. Do you want *advice* on how to solve a personal or professional problem? Do you need an *empathic* ear to vent your frustration about a disappointment? Is it *action* such as help that you are seeking?
2. Evaluate the timing and place. Important conversations should take place when both parties can devote sufficient time in a setting free of extraneous distractions.
3. Make your needs clear. "I'd like your advice about . . ." or "I need your feedback on . . ." provide critical cues that orient the listener. During interaction, both the speaker and the listener need to check that they are being heard and understood accurately.

**For more information** see Deborah Borisoff and Dan Hahn, "Gender and Listening: Values Revalued," in M. Purdy and D. Borisoff (eds.), *Listening in Everyday Life: A Personal & Professional Approach,* 2nd ed. (Lanham, MD: University Press of America, 1997); and Judi Brownell, *Listening: Attitudes, Principles and Skills,* 2nd ed. (Boston; Allyn & Bacon, 2002).

Deborah Borisoff (Ph.D., New York University) is professor of culture and communication at New York University and teaches courses and conducts research in the areas of gender and communication, conflict, listening, and organizational communication. Dr. Borisoff also serves as a consultant to various business organizations and educational institutions.

callers to keep talking. This same study also found that male callers were helped by "just listening," whereas women callers were helped by "empathic understanding."

Tannen argues, however, that men listen less to women than women listen to men. The reason, says Tannen, is that listening places the person in an inferior position, whereas speaking places the person in a superior position. Men may seem to assume a more argumentative posture while listening, as if getting ready to argue. They also may appear to ask questions that are more argumentative or that seek to puncture holes in your position as a way to play up their own expertise. Women are more likely to ask supportive questions and perhaps offer criticism that is more positive than men. Women let the speaker see that they're listening. Men, on the other hand, use fewer listening cues in conversation. Men and women act this way to both men and women; their customary ways of talking don't seem to change depending on whether the listener is male or female.

There is no evidence to show that these differences represent any negative motives on the part of men (to prove themselves superior) or of women (to ingratiate themselves). Rather, these differences in listening seem largely the result of the way in which men and women have been socialized.

Further, not all researchers agree that there is sufficient evidence to make the claims that Tannen and others make about gender differences (Goldsmith & Fulfs, 1999). Gender differences are changing drastically and quickly; it's best to take generalizations about gender as starting points for investigation and not as airtight conclusions.

## Reviewing  Key Terms and Concepts in Interpersonal Listening

This chapter focused on the nature of listening, the dimensions of listening that you need to consider for effective listening, and the influence of culture and gender on listening.

### Stages of Listening

What is listening? What purposes does listening serve?

- Listening is an active process of receiving, understanding, remembering, evaluating, and responding to communications.
- Listening enables you (1) to learn, to acquire information; (2) to relate, to help form and maintain relationships; (3) to influence, to have an effect on the attitudes and behaviors of others; (4) to play, to enjoy yourself; and (5) to help, to assist others.

### Styles of Effective Listening

What are your listening options?

- *Empathic–objective listening* refers to the extent to which you focus on feeling what the speaker is feeling.

- *Nonjudgmental–critical listening* refers to the extent to which you accept and support the speaker.
- *Surface–depth listening* refers to the extent to which you focus on the obvious surface meanings.
- *Active–inactive listening* refers to the extent to which you reflect back on what you think the speaker means in content and feeling.

### Culture, Gender, and Listening

How is listening influenced by culture and gender?

- Members of different cultures vary on a number of communication dimensions that influence listening: speech and language, nonverbal behavioral differences, and approaches to feedback.
- Men and women may listen differently; generally, women give more specific listening cues to show they're listening than do men.

## Applying  Key Terms and Concepts in Interpersonal Listening

**1** Are some people more deserving of empathy than others? What makes a person deserving of your empathic listening? For example, would you find it more difficult to empathize with someone who was overjoyed because of winning the lottery for $7 million or with someone who was overcome with sadness because of the death of a loved one? How easy would it be for you to empathize with someone who was depressed because an expected bonus of $60,000 turned out to be only $35,000?

**2** What types of listening would you use (and which types would you definitely not use) in each of the following situations: *(a)* Your steady dating partner for the last five years tells you that spells of depression are becoming more frequent and more long lasting. *(b)* An instructor lectures on the contributions of Ancient China to modern civilization. *(c)* A physician discusses your recent physical tests and makes recommendations. *(d)* A salesperson tells you the benefits of the new computer. *(e)* A gossip columnist details the secret life of your favorite movie star.

**3** Using the four dimensions of listening effectiveness discussed in this chapter (empathic–objective, nonjudgmental–critical, surface–depth, and active–inactive), how would you describe yourself as a listener when listening in class? When listening to your best friend? When listening to a romantic partner? When listening to parents? When listening to superiors at work?

**4** Here are a few situations in which you might want to use paraphrasing to ensure that you understand the speaker's thoughts and feelings. For each situation, (1) identify the thoughts you feel the speaker is expressing, (2) identify the feelings you think the speaker is experiencing, and (3) put these thoughts and feelings into a paraphrase.

■ Did you hear I got engaged to Jerry? Our racial and religious differences are really going to cause difficulties for both of us. But we'll work it through.

■ I got a C on that paper. That's the worst grade I've ever received. I just can't believe that I got a C. This is my major. What am I going to do?

■ That rotten, inconsiderate pig just up and left. He never even said goodbye. We were together for six months and after one small argument he leaves without a word. And he even took my bathrobe—that expensive one he bought for my last birthday.

**5** Consider this dialogue and note the active listening techniques used throughout:

**PAT:** That jerk demoted me. He told me I wasn't an effective manager. I can't believe he did that, after all I've done for this place.

**CHRIS:** I'm with you. You've been manager for three or four months now, haven't you?

**PAT:** A little over three months. I know it was probationary, but I thought I was doing a good job.

**CHRIS:** Can you get another chance?

**PAT:** Yes, he said I could try again in a few months. But I feel like a failure.

**CHRIS:** I know what you mean. It sucks. What else did he say?

**PAT:** He said I had trouble getting the paperwork done on time.

**CHRIS:** You've been late filing the reports?

**PAT:** A few times.

**CHRIS:** Is there a way to delegate the paperwork?

**PAT:** No, but I think I know now what needs to be done.

**CHRIS:** You sound as though you're ready to give that manager's position another try.

**PAT:** Yes, I think I am, and I'm going to let him know that I intend to apply in the next few months.

**6** What would be an appropriate active listening response for each of these situations?

■ Your friend Phil has just broken up a love affair and is telling you about it. "I can't seem to get Chris out of my mind," he says. "All I do is daydream about what we used to do and all the fun we used to have."

■ A young nephew tells you that he can't talk with his parents. No matter how hard he tries, they don't listen. "I tried to tell them that I can't play baseball and I don't want to play baseball," he confides. "But they ignore me and tell me that all I need is practice."

■ Your mother has been having a difficult time at work. She was recently passed up for a promotion and received one of the lowest merit raises given in the company. "I'm not sure what I did wrong," she tells you. "I do my work, mind my own business, don't take my sick days like everyone else. How could they give that promotion to Helen, who's only been with the company for two years? Maybe I should just quit."

# Experiencing    Key Terms and Concepts in Interpersonal Listening

Go to www.ablongman.com/devito.

*This group of listening experiences will help you gain new insights into listening and will help to sharpen your listening skills.*

❶ **Listening to Other Perspectives** and ❷ **How Might You Listen to New Ideas?** present two creative thinking tools to sharpen a variety of skills, especially listening. ❸ **Regulating Your Listening Perspective** presents different scenarios that call for different types of listening to heighten your awareness of potential listening choices. ❹ **Experiencing Active Listening** asks you how you'd listen in a variety of situations calling for active listening. ❺ **Sequential Communication**, which you might recognize as the game of telephone, will help you identify some of the major errors made in listening. ❻ **Reducing Barriers to Listening** asks how you'd listen effectively in difficult situations. ❼ **Typical Man, Typical Woman** explores some of the differences in the way we think of men and women as listeners. ❽ **Paraphrasing to Ensure Understanding** and ❾ **How Can You Express Empathy?** provide practice in essential listening skills.

CHAPTER

# 6

# Universals of Verbal and Nonverbal Messages

⬆ *Ray* (2004)
The financial and critical success of *Ray* was clearly due in great part to the effective combination of verbal and nonverbal messages used by Jamie Foxx to depict the life and music of Ray Charles. Here we look at verbal and nonverbal messages and how they interact to yield effective interpersonal interactions.

This chapter introduces verbal and nonverbal communication and explains (1) some of the ways in which such messages interact, (2) basic principles of meaning, and (3) fundamental principles of messages.

## THE INTERACTION OF VERBAL AND NONVERBAL MESSAGES

In face-to-face communication, you blend verbal and nonverbal messages to best convey your meanings. There is also evidence to show that you blend verbal and nonverbal messages to help you think and remember (Iverson & Goldin-Meadow, 1999). Identifying the six major ways in which nonverbal messages interact with verbal messages will help to highlight this important verbal–nonverbal connection and will serve as a useful introduction to the various characteristics of meanings and messages.

Nonverbal communication is often used to *accent*, to emphasize some part of the verbal message. You might, for example, raise your voice to underscore a particular word or phrase, bang your fist on the desk to stress your commitment, or look longingly into someone's eyes when saying "I love you."

Nonverbal communication may be used to *complement*, to add nuances of meaning not communicated by your verbal message. Thus, you might smile when telling a story (to suggest that you find it humorous) or frown and shake your head when recounting someone's deceit (to suggest your disapproval).

You may deliberately *contradict* your verbal messages with nonverbal movements, for example, by crossing your fingers or winking to indicate that you're lying.

Nonverbal movements may be used to *control*, or to indicate your desire to control, the flow of verbal messages, as when you purse your lips, lean forward, or make hand movements to indicate that you want to speak. You might also put up your hand or vocalize your pauses (for example, with "um") to indicate that you have not finished and aren't ready to relinquish the floor to the next speaker.

You can *repeat* or restate the verbal message nonverbally. You can, for example, follow your verbal "Is that all right?" with raised eyebrows and a questioning look, or you can motion with your head or hand to repeat your verbal "Let's go."

You may also use nonverbal communication to *substitute* for verbal messages. You can, for example, signal "OK" with a hand gesture. You can nod your head to indicate yes or shake your head to indicate no.

When you communicate electronically, of course, your message is communicated by means of typed letters without facial expres-

### ASK Yourself
#### Confronting a Lie

You ask about the previous night's whereabouts of your romantic partner of two years and are told something you know beyond any doubt to be false. You don't want to break up the relationship over this, but you do want the truth and an opportunity to resolve the problems that contributed to this situation.   Ask yourself: What are some of the things you might say to achieve your purposes? What are some types of messages you'd want to avoid?

sions or gestures that normally accompany face-to-face communication and without the changes in rate and volume that are a part of normal telephone communication. To compensate for this lack of nonverbal behavior, the emoticon was created. Sometimes called a "smiley" after the ever-present :), the emoticon is a typed symbol that communicates through a keyboard the nuances of the message normally conveyed by nonverbal expression and changes in vocal expression. The absence of the nonverbal channel through which you can clarify your message—for example, smiling or winking to communicate sarcasm or humor—make such typed symbols extremely helpful. Researchers have investigated the factors influencing the use of emoticons and the effects they have (Rezabeck & Cochenour, 1995). Here are some of the more popular emoticons used in computer talk.

| | |
|---|---|
| : - ) | = smile; I'm only kidding |
| : - ( | = frown; I'm feeling sad; this saddens me |
| * | = kiss |
| :- | = male |
| >- | = female |
| { } | = hug |
| {{{***}}} | = hugs and kisses |
| ; - ) | = sly smile |
| _this is important_ | = underlining, adds emphasis |
| *this is important* | = asterisks, adds emphasis |
| ALL CAPS | = shouting, emphasizing |
| <G> or <grin> | = grin |

Not surprisingly, these symbols aren't used universally (Pollack, 1996). For example, because it's considered impolite for a Japanese woman to show her teeth when she smiles, the Japanese emoticon for a woman's smile is (^ . ^) where the dot signifies a closed mouth. A man's smile is written (^ _ ^). Other emoticons popular in Japan but not used in Europe or the United States are (^ ^ ;) for "cold sweat," (^ o ^ ; Ò) for "excuse me," and (^ o ^) for "happy."

##  MEANING PRINCIPLES ✓

Meaning is an active process created in cooperation between source and receiver, speaker and listener, writer and reader. Understanding what meanings are and how they're passed from one person to another will help maximize your own verbal and nonverbal message potential.

### Meanings Are in People

Meaning depends not only on messages (whether verbal, nonverbal, or both) but also on the interaction of these messages and the receiver's own thoughts and feelings. You don't "receive" meaning; you create meaning. You construct meaning out of the messages you receive combined with your own social and cultural perspectives (beliefs, attitudes, and values, for example) (Berger & Luckmann, 1980; Delia, 1977; Delia, O'Keefe, & O'Keefe, 1982). Words don't mean; people mean. Consequently, to discover meaning, you need to look into people and not merely into words.

To illustrate the implications of the principle that meanings are in people, record your meanings for the terms listed below on the seven-point scales. Write each term's first letter in the appropriate space for the various dimensions of meaning provided, depending on how close you feel the term's meaning is to the adjectives in the scale. Thus, if you feel that a concept is extremely good or extremely bad, then place the term's first letter on the space closest to good or bad. If you feel that the concept is quite good or quite bad, then place the term's first letter in the second or the seventh position. If you feel that the concept is fairly good or fairly bad, then place the letter in the third or the fifth position. If you feel that the concept is neither good nor bad, then place the letter in the middle position. Do likewise for all six scales and for all five terms.

*Terms:* (a) abortion, (b) biological warfare, (c) college, (d) death penalty, (e) euthanasia

| | | |
|---|---|---|
| good | __:__:__:__:__:__:__ | bad |
| ugly | __:__:__:__:__:__:__ | beautiful |
| weak | __:__:__:__:__:__:__ | strong |
| active | __:__:__:__:__:__:__ | passive |
| large | __:__:__:__:__:__:__ | small |
| hot | __:__:__:__:__:__:__ | cold |

If you have the opportunity, compare your meanings with those of others in small groups or in the class as a whole. Are there large differences between your meanings and those of others? How would you describe these differences in terms of connotation and denotation? What accounts for the differences in meanings? That is, what factors contribute to your meanings for these terms? Put differently, how did you acquire the meanings you indicated on these scales? What does this experience illustrate about the principle that meanings are in people?

## Meanings Are More Than Words and Gestures

When we want to communicate a thought or feeling to another person, we do so with relatively few symbols. These symbols represent just a small part of what we're thinking or feeling, much of which remains unspoken. If we were to try to describe every feeling in detail,

# Understanding Interpersonal Skills

## METACOMMUNICATION

**Metacommunication** is communication that refers to other communications; it's communication about communication. Both verbal and nonverbal messages can be metacommunicational. Verbally, for example, you can say, "Do you understand what I'm trying to say?" Nonverbally you can hug someone you're consoling.

Interpersonal effectiveness often hinges on the ability to metacommunicate. For example, in conflict situations it's often helpful to talk about the way you fight. In romantic relationships, it's often helpful to talk about what each of you means by "steady" or "really care." On the job, it's often necessary to talk about the way orders are delegated or the way criticism should be expressed.

**Metacommunicating.** Here are a few suggestions for increasing your metacommunicational effectiveness:

- Explain the feelings that go with your thoughts.
- Give clear feedforward to help the other person get a general picture of the messages that will follow.
- Paraphrase your own complex messages so as to make your meaning extra clear. Similarly, check on your understanding of another's message by paraphrasing what you think the other person means.
- Ask for clarification if you have doubts about another's meaning.
- Use metacommunication when you want to clarify the communication patterns between yourself and another person: "I'd like to talk about the way you talk about me to our friends" or "I think we should talk about the way we talk about sex."

we would never get on with the job of living. The meanings we seek to communicate are much more than the sum of the words and nonverbal behaviors we use to represent them.

Because of this, you can never fully know what another person is thinking or feeling. You can only approximate it on the basis of the meanings you receive—which, as already noted, are greatly influenced by who you are and what you are feeling. Conversely, others can never fully know you; they, too, can only approximate what you're feeling. Failure to understand another person or to be understood is not an abnormal occurrence.

## Meanings Are Unique

Because meanings are derived from both the messages communicated and the receiver's own thoughts and feelings, no two people ever derive the same meanings. Similarly, because people change constantly, no one person can derive the same meanings on two separate occasions. Who you are can never be separated from the meanings you create. As a result, check your perceptions of another's meanings by asking questions, echoing what you perceive to be the other person's feelings or thoughts, seeking elaboration and clarification, and in general practicing the skills identified in the discussions of effective interpersonal perception and listening (Chapters 4 and 5).

Also recognize that as you change, you also change the meanings you create out of past messages. Thus, although the message sent may not have changed, the meanings you created from it yesterday and the meanings you create today may be quite different. Yesterday, when a special someone said, "I love you," you created certain meanings. But today, when you learn that the same "I love you" was said to three other people or when you fall in love with someone else, you drastically change the meanings you perceive from these words.

## Meanings Are Context-Based

Verbal and nonverbal communications exist in a context that, to a large extent, determines the meaning of any verbal or nonverbal behavior. The same words or behaviors may have totally different meanings when they occur in different contexts. For example, the greeting, "How are you?" means "Hello" to someone you pass regularly on the street but means "Is your health improving?" when said to a friend in the hospital. A wink to an attractive person on a bus means something completely different from a wink that signifies a put-on or a lie. Similarly, the meaning of a given signal depends on the other behavior it accompanies or is close to in time. Pounding a fist on the table during a speech in support of a politician means something quite different from that same gesture in response to news of a friend's death. Divorced from the context, signals alone cannot reveal what meaning was intended. Of course, even if you know the context in detail, you still may not be able to decipher the meaning of the message.

Especially important is the cultural context, which is emphasized throughout this text. The cultural context will influence not only the meaning assigned to speech and gesture but whether a meaning is friendly, offensive, lacking in respect, condescending, sensitive, and so on.

**SPEAKING**
**Interpersonal-E**

**Irony.** One prediction frequently made about computer-mediated versus face-to-face interaction has been that irony (subtle sarcasm, such as calling a poorly reasoned argument a "brilliant deduction" or a dead-end job the "fast track") would be used less in CMC, largely because of the absence of nonverbal cues and the greater likelihood of miscommunication. However, at least one study found the exact opposite (Hancock, 2004). What reasons might you offer to account for this counterintuitive result?

# MESSAGE PRINCIPLES ✓

You'll be in a better position to control the message process once you understand how interpersonal messages work and the principles they follow. Here we consider seven basic principles of messages: Interpersonal messages occur in packages; they are governed by rules; and they vary in abstraction, politeness, inclusion, directness, and assertiveness.

## Messages Are Packaged ✓

The sounds you make with your mouth or the gestures you make with your hands or eyes usually occur in "packages" in which the verbal and nonverbal behaviors reinforce each other. Usually, all parts of the message system work together to communicate a unified

# Ask the Researcher

## TALKING ABOUT DIFFICULT TOPICS

**?** Do you have any suggestions for talking about really difficult relationship topics, like the use of condoms, infidelity, different religious beliefs, and the like?

The key when talking about difficult issues is not being evaluative of the other person or their attitudes—face-saving should always be allowed. Try to be as descriptive and empathic as possible—try to talk about and understand different positions without implying that your attitude is better or that there's something wrong with the other person or their attitudes. Bringing up condom use in any way other than implying that the other person has likely done something wrong usually works. Religious beliefs can be talked about by indicating you're interested in the person's beliefs without implying that yours are better. Infidelity is tough, in that it's a moral issue that implies that someone has done something wrong—betrayed someone else. Even this topic, however, can be discussed with a focus on trying to understand the other person's perspective rather than telling them what they've done wrong. Saving face is harder here. . . .

**For more information** see B. Reel and T. L. Thompson, "Is It a Matter of Politeness?: Face-saving Techniques in Discussions of Safer sex," *Southern Speech Communication Journal* 69 (2004): 99–120; R. Agne, T. L. Thompson, and L. P. Cusella, "Stigma in the Line of Face: Self-Disclosure of Patients' HIV Status to Health Care Providers," *Journal of Applied Communication Research* 28 (2000): 235–261; and B. W. Reel and T. L. Thompson, "A Test of the Effectiveness of Strategies for Talking about AIDS and Condom Use," *Journal of Applied Communication Research* 22 (1994): 127–140.

Teresa L. Thompson (Ph.D., 1980, Temple University) is professor of communication at the University of Dayton. She teaches courses in health communication, interpersonal communication, communication theory, and research methods (Thompson@udayton.edu) She edits the journal *Health Communication*.

meaning. When you speak words of anger, you also communicate anger through your body and face by tensing, scowling, and perhaps assuming a fighting posture. You often fail to notice this "packaging" in others' messages because it seems so natural. But when the nonverbal messages of someone's posture or face contradict what is said verbally, you take special notice. For example, the person who says, "I'm so glad to see you," but avoids direct eye contact and looks around to see who else is present is sending contradictory messages. You also see contradictory or mixed messages when couples say they love each other but seem to go out of their way to hurt each other nonverbally—for example, being late for important dates, flirting with others, or avoiding touching each other.

An awareness of the packaged nature of communication, then, suggests a warning against the too-easy interpretation of another's meaning, especially as revealed in nonverbal behaviors. Before you identify or guess the meaning of any bit of behavior, look at the entire package or cluster of which it's a part, the way in which the cluster is a response to its context, and the role of the specific nonverbal behavior within that cluster. That attractive person winking in your direction may be giving you the come-on; however, don't rule out the possibility of ill-fitting contact lenses.

## Messages Are Rule-Governed

The rule-governed nature of verbal communication is well known. Every language has rules (the rules of grammar), which native speakers follow in producing and understanding sentences even though they may be unable to state such rules explicitly. Nonverbal communication also is regulated by a system of rules or norms that state what is and what is not appropriate, expected, and permissible in specific social situations. You learned these rules by observing the behaviors of the adult community. For example, you learned how to express sympathy along with the rules that your culture has established for expressing it appropriately. You learned that touch is permissible under certain circumstances but not under others. You learned which types of touching are permissible and which aren't. You learned that women may touch each other in public; for example, they may hold hands, walk arm in arm, engage in prolonged hugging, and even dance together. You also learned that men may not do these things, at least not without inviting social criticism. Further, perhaps most obvious, you learned that certain parts of the body may not be touched and others may. As a relationship changes, so do the rules for touching. As you become more intimate, the rules for touching become less restrictive.

Of course, these nonverbal rules vary greatly from one culture to another. Rules are cultural (and relative) institutions; they're not universal laws. In the United States, for example, direct eye contact usually signals openness and honesty. Among some Latin Americans and Native Americans, however, direct eye contact between, say, a teacher and a student is considered inappropriate, perhaps aggressive; appropriate student behavior is to avoid eye contact with the teacher. From this simple example it's easy to see how miscommunication can take place. To a teacher in the United States, avoidance of eye contact by a Latin American or Native American could signify guilt, lack of interest, or disrespect when in fact the student was following her or his own culturally established rules. Table 6.1, drawn from Axtell (1994) and Sabath (1999), gives you an idea of the problems that can arise when you assume that the rules governing message behavior in one culture are the same rules used in other cultures.

## ⬇ TABLE 6.1
### Some Nonverbal Taboos

These are only a small number of the nonverbal taboos that exist throughout the world. Can you add any nonverbal taboos to this list?

| Nonverbal Behavior | Taboo |
| --- | --- |
| Blinking your eyes | Considered impolite in Taiwan |
| Folding your arms over your chest | Considered disrespectful in Fiji |
| Putting your hands in your pockets | Considered impolite in Malaysia |
| Waving your hand | Insulting in Nigeria and Greece |
| Gesturing with the thumb up | Considered rude in Australia |
| Tapping your two index fingers together | In Egypt, means that a couple is sleeping together or represents a request to sleep together |
| Pointing with the index finger | Considered impolite in many Middle-Eastern countries, China, and Indonesia |
| Bowing to a lesser degree than your host | Implies that you're superior in Japan |
| With a clenched fist, inserting your thumb between your index and middle finger (called the *fig*) | Considered obscene in some southern European countries |
| Using your left hand to eat or shake hands | Considered impolite in a wide variety of cultures; for example, in Malaysia, Indonesia, and Arab countries |
| Pointing at someone with your index and third fingers | Means you're wishing evil on the person in some African countries |
| Resting your feet on a table or chair | Insulting in some Middle Eastern countries |

**Chapter 6** Universals of Verbal and Nonverbal Messages

# Ethics in Interpersonal Communication

## LYING

Lying occurs when you send messages designed to make others believe what you know to be untrue (Ekman, 1985; Burgoon & Hoobler, 2002). You can lie by commission (by making explicitly false statements or even by being evasive or misleading) or by omission (by omitting relevant information and so allowing others to draw incorrect inferences). Similarly, you can lie verbally (in speech or writing) or nonverbally (wearing an innocent facial expression instead of acknowledging the commission of some wrong, or nodding knowingly instead of expressing honest ignorance) (O'Hair, Cody, & McLaughlin, 1981). Lies range from "white lies" and truth stretching to lies that form the basis of relationship infidelity, libel, and perjury. And, not surprisingly, lies have ethical implications.

- Some lies may be considered ethical (for example, lying to a child to protect a fantasy belief in Santa Claus or the tooth fairy, or publicly agreeing with someone to enable the person to save face).

- Some lies may be considered not only ethical but required (for example, lying to protect someone from harm).

- Other lies are always considered unacceptable and unethical (for example, lying to defraud investors or to falsely accuse someone).

### What would you do?

You've been asked to serve as a witness in the trial of someone suspected of robbing a local grocery store. You don't want to get involved—yet you wonder if you can ethically refuse and say you didn't see anything (although you did). There are other witnesses, and your testimony is not likely to make a significant difference. What would you do?

## Messages Vary in Abstraction

Consider the following list of terms:

> entertainment
> film
> American film
> classic American film
> *All about Eve*

At the top is the general or abstract term *entertainment*. Note that entertainment includes all the items on the list plus various others—television, novels, drama, comics, and so on. *Film* is more specific and concrete. It includes all of the items below it as well as various other items such as Indian film or Russian film. It excludes, however, all entertainment that is not film. *American film* is again more specific than film and excludes all films that aren't American. *Classic American film* further limits American film to a relatively small group of highly acclaimed films. *All about Eve* specifies concretely the one item to which reference is made.

The more general term—in this case, *entertainment*—conjures up many different images. One person may focus on television, another on music, another on comic books, and still another on radio. To some, the word *film* may bring to mind the early silent films. To others, it brings to mind high-tech special effects. To still others, it recalls Disney's animated cartoons. *All about Eve* guides the listener still further—in this case to one film. But note that even though *All about Eve* identifies one film, different listeners are likely to focus on different aspects of the film, perhaps its character development, perhaps its love story, perhaps its financial success.

Effective verbal messages include words at many levels of abstraction. At times an abstract, general term may suit your needs best; at other times a more concrete, specific term

### SPEAKING
### Interpersonal-E

**Low-Order Abstraction.** In much the same way that you use specific terms to direct your face-to-face listeners' attention to exactly what you want them to focus on, you also use specific terms to direct an Internet search engine to narrow its focus to (ideally) just those items you want to access.

may serve better. Generally, however, the specific term will prove the better choice. As you get more specific—less abstract—you more effectively guide the images that will come into your listeners' minds.

## Messages Vary in Politeness

**Politeness** is a desirable trait across most cultures (Brown & Levinson, 1988). Cultures differ, however, in how they define politeness. For example, among English speakers politeness involves showing consideration for others and presenting yourself with confidence and polish. In Japanese it involves showing respect, especially for those in higher-status positions, and presenting yourself with modesty (Haugh, 2004). Cultures also vary in how important they consider politeness as compared with, say, openness or honesty. And, of course, cultures differ in the rules for expressing politeness or impoliteness and in the punishments for violating the accepted rules (Mao, 1994; Strecker, 1993). For example, Asian cultures, especially Chinese and Japanese, are often singled out because they emphasize politeness and mete out harsher social punishments for violations than would people in the United States or western Europe (Fraser, 1990).

In the business world politeness is now recognized as an important part of interpersonal interactions. In one study some 80 percent of employees surveyed believed that they did not get respect at work, and 20 percent felt they were victims of weekly incivility. Rudeness in the workplace, it's been argued, reduces performance effectiveness, hurts creativity, and leads to increased worker turnover—all of which is costly for the organization (Tsiantar, 2005). On an international level, politeness is big business; firms that teach Americans the rules of international politeness are flourishing, charging upwards of $10,000 per day to teach corporate executives how to behave politely in foreign cultures (Peltier, 2005).

There are large gender differences in the expression of politeness (Holmes, 1995). Generally, studies from various different cultures show, women's speech is more polite than men's speech, even on the telephone (Brown, 1980; Wetzel, 1988; Holmes, 1995; Smoreda & Licoppe, 2000). Women more often seek areas of agreement in conversation and even in conflict situations than do men. Similarly, young girls are more apt to try to modify disagreements, whereas young boys are more apt to express "bald disagreements" (Holmes, 1995). Women also use more polite speech when seeking to gain another person's compliance than men do (Baxter, 1984).

Yet there are also similarities across genders. For example, both men and women in the United States and New Zealand seem to pay compliments in similar ways (Manes & Wolfson, 1981; Holmes, 1986, 1995), and men and women use similar politeness strategies when communicating bad news in an organization (Lee, 1993).

Culture and gender are not the only factors influencing politeness, of course. Your personality and your professional training will influence your degree of politeness and how you express politeness (Edstrom, 2004). Politeness also seems to vary with the type of relationship. One researcher, for example, has proposed that politeness varies among strangers, friends, and intimates as depicted in Figure 6.1. And the context of communication will influence politeness; formal situations in which there is considerable power difference call for greater politeness than informal circumstances in which the power differences are minimal (Mullany, 2004). Surprising as it may seen, there is even evidence that shows you express politeness when you talk to your computer (Nass, 2004).

**Netiquette**  The Internet has very specific rules for politeness, called *netiquette* (Kallos, 2005). Much as the rules of etiquette provide guidance in communicating in social situations, the rules of netiquette provide guidance in communicating over the Net and are of major concern to just about everyone using computer-mediated communication (Berry, 2004; Fuller, 2004; Ford, 2003; Conlin, 2002; Dereshiwsky, Moan, & Guhungu, 2002). These rules are helpful for making Internet communication more pleasant and easier and also for

## FIGURE 6.1
### Wolfson's Bulge Model of Politeness

This figure depicts a proposed relationship between the levels of politeness and intimacy. Politeness, according to this model, is greatest with friends and significantly less with strangers and intimates. On another dimension, how polite is your communication with people in positions of authority—say, professors, supervisors, or police officers—compared with your communication with people in positions similar to your own—say, other students, colleagues, or neighbors? Can you phrase this comparison in the form of a communication rule?

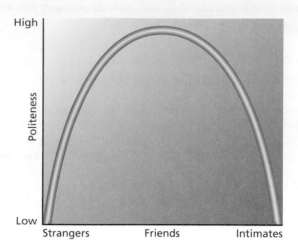

achieving greater personal efficiency. They also help to lessen the strain on the system and on other users. Here are several netiquette guidelines:

- *Read the FAQs.* Before asking questions about the system, read the Frequently Asked Questions. Your question has probably been asked before, and you'll put less strain on the system.
- *Don't shout.* WRITING IN CAPS IS PERCEIVED AS SHOUTING. It's okay to use caps occasionally to achieve emphasis. If you wish to give emphasis, highlight _like this_ or *like this*.
- *Lurk before speaking.* Lurking is reading posted notices and conversations without contributing anything. In computer communication, lurking is good, not bad. Lurking will help you learn the rules of the particular group and will help you avoid saying things you'd like to take back.
- *Don't contribute to traffic jams.* Try connecting during off hours whenever possible. If you're unable to connect, try later. In securing information, try local information sources before trying more distant sources; it requires fewer connections and less time. Be economical in using files (for example, photographs) that may tie up lines for long periods of time.
- *Be brief.* Communicate only the information that is needed; communicate clearly, briefly, and in an organized way.
- *Treat newbies kindly.* Remember you were once a newbie yourself.
- *Don't send commercial messages to those who didn't request them.* Junk mail is junk; but on the Internet, the receiver often has to pay for the time it takes to read and delete these unwanted messages.
- *Don't spam.* Spamming occurs when you send someone unsolicited mail, repeatedly send the same mail, or posting the same message to lots of newsgroups, even when the message is irrelevant to the focus of the group. Spam may cost people money (to maintain the Internet connection needed to download the e-mail they didn't want in the first place), and it costs them time. Also, it clogs the system, slowing it down for everyone.
- *Don't flame.* Flaming is making personal attacks on other users. As in face-to-face conflict, personal attacks are best avoided on the Internet. So avoid flaming and participating in flame wars.
- *Avoid offensive language.* Refrain from expressions that would be considered offensive to others, such as sexist or racist terms.

As you may know, software is now available that will scan your e-mail, alert you if you may have broken an organizational rule, and give you a chance to revise your potentially offensive e-mail (Schwartz, 2005).

The Internet also has specific rules for what is and is not ethical, an issue that is tackled in the Chapter 9 Ethics box, "Communicating in Cyberspace."

## Messages Vary in Inclusion

Some messages are inclusive; they include all people present and acknowledge the relevance of others. Other messages exclude specific people and in some cases entire cultural groups.

You see messages of exclusion in the use of in-group language in the presence of an out-group member. When doctors get together and discuss medicine, there is no problem. But when they get together with someone who isn't a doctor, they often fail to adjust to this new person. Instead, they simply continue with discussions of procedures, symptoms, medications, and all the talk that excludes others present.

Excluding talk also occurs when people of the same nationality get together within a larger, more heterogeneous group and use the language of their nationality—sometimes just isolated words, sometimes sentences, and sometimes even entire conversations. Similarly, references to experiences not shared by all (common topics include having children, exotic vacations, and people we know) can serve to include some and exclude others. The use of these terms and experiences in the presence of nonmembers emphasizes their status as outsiders and excludes these people from full participation in the communication act (cf. Sizemore, 2004).

Another form of excluding talk is the use of the terms of your own cultural group as universal, as applying to everyone. In using such terms, you exclude others. For example, *church* refers to the place of worship for specific religions, not all religions. Similarly, *Bible* refers to the Christian religious scriptures and is not a general term for *religious scriptures*. Nor does *Judeo-Christian tradition* include the religious traditions of everyone. Similarly, the terms *marriage, husband,* and *wife* refer to some heterosexual relationships and exclude others; in most of the world they also exclude gay and lesbian relationships.

Consider the vast array of alternative terms that are inclusive rather than exclusive. For example, the Association of American University Presses (Schwartz et al., 1995) recommends using *place of worship* instead of *church* when you wish to include the religious houses of worship of all people. Similarly, *committed relationship* is more inclusive than *marriage, couples therapy* is more inclusive than *marriage counseling,* and *life partner* is more inclusive than *husband* or *wife. Religious scriptures* is more inclusive than *Bible.* Of course, if you're referring to, say, a specific Baptist church or married heterosexual couples, then the terms *church* and *marriage* are perfectly appropriate.

In general, instead of trying to emphasize the exclusion of one or more members, consider the principle of **inclusion.** Regardless of the type of communication situation we are in, everyone needs to be included in the interaction. Even if job-related issues have to be discussed in the presence of someone who is not a work colleague, that person can be included in a variety of ways; for example, the group can seek the nonmember's perspective or suggest an analogy from his or her field.

Another way to practice inclusion is to fill in relevant details discussed by the group for those who may be unaware. For example, when people, places, or events are mentioned in a group discussion, briefly identify them for those to whom they may be unfamiliar. Brief parenthetical identifying phrases are usually sufficient: "Margo—she's Jeff's daughter—loved San Francisco State."

When someone asks a question or makes a comment requiring a response, be sure to respond in some way, even if you're talking, attending to someone else, or otherwise engaged. Acknowledge the comment—verbally, if possible, or nonverbally with a nod or smile, for example. Practicing inclusion is so easy that it's surprising that the principle is violated so blatantly and so often. When inclusion is practiced, everyone gains a great deal more satisfaction from the interaction.

## Messages Vary in Directness

Consider your own tendency to be direct or indirect. Imagine you're talking with a friend. Would you be more likely to use the sentences from Column A or from Column B to communicate essentially the same information?

| *Column A* | *Column B* |
|---|---|
| Would you like to watch *The West Wing*? | I'd like to watch *The West Wing*. |
| I'd really like some ice cream. | Would you get me a bowl of ice cream? |
| Isn't it chilly in here? | Jenny, please close the window. |
| It must have been expensive. | How much did you pay? |
| I really need to find someone to watch the dog for the weekend. | Would you mind watching my dog next weekend? |
| Are you doing anything this weekend? | I'd like to go to the movies this weekend; want to come? |
| The phone's ringing. | Would you please answer the phone? |

The statements in Column A are relatively indirect; they're attempts to get the listener to say or do something without committing the speaker. The statements in Column B, on the other hand, are direct; they state the speaker's preferences and/or ask the listener to do or say something. Direct and indirect messages can also be nonverbal. For example, you may use an indirect message such as glancing at your watch to communicate that it's late, or you may use a more direct message such as getting up and putting on your jacket. Indirect messages have both advantages and disadvantages.

### Advantages of Indirect Messages
Indirect messages allow you to express a desire without insulting or offending anyone; they allow you to observe the rules of polite interaction. So instead of saying, "I'm bored with this group," you say, "It's getting late and I have to get up early tomorrow," or you look at your watch and pretend to be surprised by the time. Instead of saying, "This food tastes like cardboard," you say, "I just started my diet" or "I just ate." In each instance you're stating a preference but are saying it indirectly so as to avoid offending someone.

Sometimes indirect messages allow you to ask for compliments in a socially acceptable manner, such as saying, "I was thinking of getting my eyes done." You hope to get the desired compliment: "Your eyes? They're perfect as they are."

### Disadvantages of Indirect Messages
Indirect messages can create problems. Consider the following dialogue in which an indirect request is made:

**PAT:** You wouldn't like to have my parents over for dinner this weekend, would you?
**CHRIS:** I really wanted to go to the beach and just relax.
**PAT:** Well, if you feel you have to go to the beach, I'll make the dinner myself. You go to the beach. I really hate having them over and doing all the work myself. It's such a drag shopping, cooking, and cleaning all by myself.

Given this situation, Chris has two basic alternatives. One is to stick with the plan to go to the beach and relax. In this case Pat is going to be upset and Chris is going to be made to feel guilty for not helping with the dinner. A second alternative is to give in to Pat, help with the dinner, and not go to the beach. In this case Chris is going to have to give up a much desired plan and is likely to resent Pat's "manipulative" tactics. Regardless of which decision is made, one person wins and one person loses. This win–lose situation creates resentment, competition, and often an "I'll get even" attitude. With direct requests, this type of situation is much less likely to develop. Consider:

**PAT:** I'd like to have my parents over for dinner this weekend. What do you think?

**CHRIS:** Well, I really wanted to go to the beach and just relax.

Regardless of what develops next, both individuals are starting out on relatively equal footing. Each has clearly and directly stated a preference. Although at first these preferences seem mutually exclusive, it might be possible to meet both persons' needs. For example, Chris might say, "How about going to the beach this weekend and having your parents over next weekend? I'm really exhausted; I could use the rest." Here is a direct response to a direct request. Unless there is some pressing need to have Pat's parents over for dinner this weekend, this response may enable each to meet the other's needs.

**Gender and Cultural Differences in Directness**  The popular stereotype in much of the United States holds that women tend to be indirect in making requests and in giving orders, and that through this indirectness women communicate powerlessness, a discomfort with their own authority. Men, the stereotype continues, are direct, sometimes to the point of being blunt or rude. This directness communicates men's power and comfort with their own authority.

Deborah Tannen (1994b) provides an interesting perspective on these stereotypes. Women are, it seems, more indirect in giving orders; they are more likely to say, for example, "It would be great if these letters could go out today" than "Have these letters out by three." But Tannen (1994b, p. 84) argues that "issuing orders indirectly can be the prerogative of those in power" and in no way shows powerlessness. Power, to Tannen, is the ability to chose your own style of communication.

Men, however, are also indirect, but in different situations (Rundquist, 1992). According to Tannen, men are more likely to use indirectness when they express weakness, reveal a problem, or admit an error. Men are more likely to speak indirectly in expressing emotions other than anger. Men are also more indirect when they refuse expressions of increased romantic intimacy. Men are thus indirect, the theory goes, when they're saying something that goes against the masculine stereotype.

Many Asian and Latin American cultures stress the value of indirectness, largely because it enables people to save face by avoiding criticism and contradictions (Kapoor, Hughes, Baldwin, & Blue, 2003). A somewhat different kind of indirectness is seen in the greater use of intermediaries to resolve conflict among the Chinese than among North Americans, for example (Ma, 1992). In most of the United States, however, directness is preferred. "Be up front" and "tell it like it is" are commonly heard communication guidelines. Contrast these with the following two principles of indirectness found in the Japanese language (Tannen, 1994b):

🔇 **VIEWPOINT**

In the classic film *The Graduate,* there's a particularly good example of direct and indirect messages. Benjamin, the graduate (played by Dustin Hoffman) and Mrs. Robinson (Anne Bancroft) are having an affair. Because of the age difference and the fact that Benjamin is actually in love with Mrs. Robinson's daughter, their affair is uncomfortable and awkward. Mrs. Robinson, contrary to the research evidence showing that women are indirect, is very direct in expressing what she wants and what she doesn't want. Benjamin, also contrary to the research, is very indirect, often failing even to voice his feelings. More recently, on *Desperate Housewives*, you see teenager John calling the woman who employs him as a gardener—but with whom he's also having sex—not Gabrielle but "Mrs. Solis." Under what other types of circumstances would you think this direct/indirect pattern would be reversed, with men being the more indirect and women being more direct?

*omoiyari,* close to empathy, says that listeners need to understand the speaker without the speaker's being specific or direct. This style obviously places a much greater demand on the listener than would a direct speaking style.

*sassuru* advises listeners to anticipate a speaker's meanings and use subtle cues from the speaker to infer his or her total meaning.

Interestingly, in one study American males were found to be less direct than a similar group of Egyptian males (Nelson, Al Batal, & El Bakary, 2002). Comparisons like these among Americans, Japanese, and Egyptians are especially helpful in illustrating how difficult it is to draw generalizations concerning the communication tendencies of any one culture.

In thinking about direct and indirect messages, it's important to realize how easily misunderstandings can occur. For example, a person who uses an indirect style of speech may be doing so to be polite and may have been taught this style by his or her culture. If you assume, instead, that the person is using indirectness to be manipulative, because your culture regards it so, then miscommunication is inevitable.

## Messages Vary in Assertiveness

If you disagree with other people in a group, do you speak your mind? Do you allow others to take advantage of you because you're reluctant to say what you want? Do you feel uncomfortable when you have to state your opinion in a group? Questions such as these speak to your degree of assertiveness. Before reading further about this aspect of communication, take the self-test "How Assertive Are Your Messages?"

In addition to identifying some specific assertive behaviors (as in the self-test), we can further clarify the nature of assertive communication by distinguishing it from nonassertiveness and aggressiveness (Alberti, 1977).

# Understanding Interpersonal Theory and Research

## THEORIES OF GENDER DIFFERENCES

Throughout this text, gender differences are discussed in a wide variety of contexts. One researcher distinguishes three broad sets of reasons or theories to explain gender differences in communication (Holmes, 1995):

- Gender differences are due to innate biological differences. Thus, gender differences in communication such as in politeness or in listening behavior are the result of inherited biological factors that have evolved over millions of years.
- Gender differences are due to different patterns of socialization. Thus, the gender differences that you observe in communication are due to the ways in which boys and girls are raised and taught.
- Gender differences are due to inequalities in social power. For example, because of women's lesser social power, they're more apt to communicate with greater deference and politeness than are men.

### Working with Theories and Research

Recently Lawrence Summers, the president of Harvard University, observed that the low representation of women in the sciences at universities might be due to innate differences between the sexes (Traub, 2005; Murray, 2005; Judson, 2005). Although some people saw this as a reasonable statement, many people felt this comment was sexist, and Summers was severely criticized in most of the media. How do you feel about this? You may wish to research this incident by examining some of the many newspaper and magazine articles that appeared in January 2005.

# TEST YOURSELF

## HOW ASSERTIVE ARE YOUR MESSAGES?

Indicate how true each of the following statements is about your own communication. Respond instinctively rather than in the way you feel you should respond. Use the following scale: 5 = always or almost always true; 4 = usually true; 3 = sometimes true, sometimes false; 2 = usually false; and 1 = always or almost always false.

_____ 1. I would express my opinion in a group even if my view contradicted the opinions of others.
_____ 2. When asked to do something that I really don't want to do, I can say no without feeling guilty.
_____ 3. I can express my opinion to my superiors on the job.
_____ 4. I can start up a conversation with a stranger on a bus or at a business gathering without fear.
_____ 5. I voice objection to people's behavior if I feel it infringes on my rights.

**HOW DID YOU DO?**  All five items in this test identified characteristics of assertive communication. So high scores (say about 20 and above) would indicate a high level of assertiveness. Low scores (say about 10 and below) would indicate a low level of assertiveness.

**WHAT WILL YOU DO?**  The remaining discussion in this chapter clarifies the nature of assertive communication and offers guidelines for increasing your own assertiveness. Consider these suggestions as ways to increase your own assertiveness and at the same time to reduce your aggressive tendencies when appropriate.

## Nonassertiveness, Aggressiveness, and Assertiveness

*Nonassertiveness* refers to a lack of assertiveness in certain types of or in all communication situations. People who are nonassertive fail to assert their rights. In many instances, these people do what others tell them to do—parents, employers, and the like—without questioning and without concern for what is best for them. They operate with a "You win, I lose" philosophy; they give others what they want without concern for themselves (Lloyd, 2001). Nonassertive people often ask permission from others to do what is their perfect right. Social situations create anxiety for these individuals, and their self-esteem is generally low.

*Aggressiveness* is the other extreme. Aggressive people operate with an "I win, you lose" philosophy; they care little for what the other person wants and focus only on their own needs. Some people communicate aggressively only under certain conditions or in certain situations (for example, after being taken advantage of over a long period of time); others communicate aggressively in all or at least most situations. Aggressive communicators think little of the opinions, values, or beliefs of others and yet are extremely sensitive to others' criticisms of their own behavior. Consequently, they frequently get into arguments with others.

*Assertiveness*—behavior that enables you to act in your own best interests without denying or infringing

**◑ VIEWPOINT**

When asked what they would like to change about the communication patterns of the opposite sex, men said they wanted women to be more direct, and women said they wanted men to stop interrupting and offering advice (Noble, 1994). What one change would you like to see in the communication system of the opposite sex? Of your own sex?

upon the rights of others—is the generally desired alternative to nonassertiveness or aggressiveness (Alberti, 1977; Alberti & Emmons, 2001). Assertive communication is especially useful in making interpersonal contact and in interpersonal conflict (Fodor & Collier, 2001). Assertive people operate with an "I win, you win" philosophy; they assume that both parties can gain something from an interpersonal interaction, even from a confrontation. Assertive people are more positive and score lower on measures of hopelessness than do nonassertive people (Velting, 1999). Assertive people are willing to assert their own rights. Unlike their aggressive counterparts, however, they don't hurt others in the process. Assertive people speak their minds and welcome others' doing likewise.

People who are assertive in interpersonal communication display four major characteristics (Norton & Warnick, 1976). To what extent do these characteristics apply to you?

1. Do you engage in frank and open expression of your feelings to people in general as well as to those for whom you may have romantic feelings?
2. Do you readily volunteer opinions and beliefs, deal directly with interpersonal communication situations that may be stressful, and question others without fear?
3. Do you stand up and argue for your rights, even if this might entail a certain degree of disagreement or conflict with relatives or close friends?
4. Do you make up your mind based on evidence and argument instead of just accepting what others say?

Research shows that people who are assertive would answer yes to these questions. Assertive people are more open, less anxious, more contentious, and less likely to be intimidated or persuaded. Assertive people also are more positive and more hopeful than are nonassertive people

# InterMedia

## HATE SPEECH

Hate speech is speech that is hostile, offensive, degrading, or intimidating to a particular group of people. Women, African Americans, Muslims, Jews, Asians, Hispanics, and gay men and lesbians are among the major targets of hate speech in the United States. Because the media are so powerful in influencing opinions, and because the media reach so many people, the issue of hate speech in the media takes on special importance (Ruscher, 2001).

Hate speech occurs in all forms of communication. Some examples:

- People utter insults to someone passing by.
- Posters and fliers degrade specific groups.
- Radio talk shows denigrate members of certain groups.
- Computer games are configured to target members of minority groups.
- Websites insult and demean certain groups and at the same time encourage hostility toward members of these groups (Rivlin, 2005).

Some colleges are instituting "hate speech codes," written statements that spell out what constitutes hate speech and what the penalties for hate speech will be. Proponents of such codes argue that they teach students that hate speech is unacceptable, is harmful to all people (but especially to minority members who are the targets of such attacks), and may be curtailed in the same way as other undesirable acts (for example, child pornography or rape). Opponents argue that such codes fail to address the underlying prejudices and biases that give rise to hate speech; that they stifle free expression and violate the First Amendment's guarantee of free speech; and that they may be used unfairly by the majority to silence minority opinion and dissent.

### Follow Up

Using your favorite electronic database, look up "hate speech" and "campus codes." After reading about hate speech and the codes that have been developed, formulate your own position on campus codes for hate speech. What reasons can you develop in support of your position?

(Velting, 1999). On the somewhat negative side, people high in assertiveness (especially males) also are more likely to engage in online flaming (Alonzo & Aiken, 2004). In contrast, people who are not assertive would probably say no to each question. Unassertive people are less open, more anxious, less contentious, more likely to be intimidated, and more easily persuaded.

Do realize that as with many other aspects of communication, there will be wide cultural differences when it comes to assertiveness. For example, the values of assertiveness are more likely to be extolled in individualist cultures than in collectivist cultures. Assertiveness will be valued more by those cultures that stress competition, individual success, and independence. It will be valued much less by those cultures that stress cooperation, group success, and interdependence of all members on one another. American students, for example, are found to be significantly more assertive than Japanese or Korean students (Thompson, Klopf, & Ishii, 1991; Thompson & Klopf, 1991). Thus, for some situations, assertiveness may be an effective strategy in one culture, but may create problems in another culture. Assertiveness with an elder in many Asian and Hispanic cultures may be seen as insulting and disrespectful.

**Principles for Increasing Assertive Communication**    Most people are nonassertive in certain situations. If you're one of these people and if you wish to modify your behavior, there are steps you can take to increase your assertiveness (Windy & Constantinou, 2005; Bower & Bower, 2005). (If you are always nonassertive and are unhappy about this, then you may need to work with a therapist to change your behavior.)

**Analyze Assertive Communications**    The first step in increasing your assertiveness skills is to understand the nature of assertive communications. Observe and analyze the messages of others. Learn to distinguish the differences among assertive, aggressive, and nonassertive messages. Focus on what makes one behavior assertive and another behavior nonassertive or aggressive. Table 6.2 reviews some of the verbal and nonverbal messages that distinguish assertive from nonassertive or aggressive communication.

After you've gained some skills in observing the behaviors of others, turn your analysis to yourself. Analyze situations in which you're normally assertive and situations in which you're more likely to act nonassertively or aggressively. What characterizes these situations? What do the situations in which you're normally assertive have in common? How do you speak? How do you communicate nonverbally?

**⊕ VIEWPOINT**

On your college campus, which would be most likely to be considered hate speech: sexist, heterosexist, racist, or ageist language? Which would be the least likely? How do you respond when you hear other students using sexist language? Heterosexist language? Racist language? Ageist language?

**Rehearse Assertive Communications**    Select a situation in which you're normally nonassertive. Build a hierarchy that begins with a relatively nonthreatening message and ends with the desired communication. For example, let's say that you have difficulty voicing your opinion to your supervisor at work. The desired behavior, then, is to tell your supervisor your opinions. You would construct a hierarchy of situations leading up to this desired behavior. Such a hierarchy might begin with visualizing yourself talking with your boss. Visualize this scenario until you can do it without any anxiety or discomfort. Once you have mastered this visualization, visualize a step closer to your goal, such as walking into your boss's office. Again, do this until your visualization creates no discomfort. Continue with these successive visualizations until you can visualize yourself telling your boss your opinion. As with the other visualizations, do this until you can do it while totally relaxed. This is the mental rehearsal.

You might add a vocal dimension to this by actually acting out (with voice and gesture) your telling your boss your opinion. Again, do this until you experience no difficulty or discomfort. Next, try doing this in front of a trusted and supportive friend or group of friends. Ideally this interaction will provide you with useful feedback. After this rehearsal, you're probably ready for the next step.

## Assertive and Aggressive Messages

As you read this table, consider your customary ways of interacting, especially when you feel angry or threatened. How often do you use assertive messages? How often do you use aggressive messages?

| Assertive Messages | Aggressive Messages |
|---|---|
| I-messages that accept responsibility for your own feelings (*I feel angry when you . . .*) | You-messages that attribute your feelings to others (*You make me angry when you. . .*) |
| Descriptive and realistic expressions (*Last Saturday, you . . .*) | Allness and extreme expressions (*You never . . . ; you always . . .*) |
| Equality messages that recognize the essential equality of oneself and others (*We need to . . .*) | Inequality messages that may be insulting or condescending (*You don't know . . .*) |
| Relaxed and erect body posture | Tense or overly rigid posture |
| Expressive and genuine facial expressions; focused but nonthreatening eye contact | Unexpressive or overly hostile facial expressions; intense eye contact or excessive eye contact avoidance |
| Normal vocal volume and rhythm pattern | Overly soft or overly loud and accusatory tone |

**Communicate Assertively**    This step is naturally the most difficult but obviously the most important. Here's a generally effective pattern to follow in communicating assertively:

- Describe the problem; don't evaluate or judge it. *We're all working on this advertising project together. You're missing half our meetings and you still haven't produced your first report.* Be sure to use I-messages and to avoid messages that accuse or blame the other person.
- State how this problem affects you; tell the person how you feel. *My job depends on the success of this project, and I don't think it's fair that I have to do extra work to make up for what you're not doing.*
- Propose solutions that are workable and that allow the person to save face. Describe or visualize the situation if your solution were put into effect. *If you can get your report to the group by Tuesday, we'll still be able to meet our deadline. I could give you a call on Monday to remind you.*
- Confirm understanding. *It's clear that we can't produce this project if you're not going to pull your own weight. Will you have the report to us by Tuesday?*

Keep in mind that assertiveness is not always the most desirable response. Assertive people are assertive when they want to be, but they can be nonassertive if the situation calls for it. For example, you might wish to be nonassertive in a situation in which assertiveness might emotionally hurt the other person. Let's say that an older relative wishes you to do something for her or him. You could assert your rights and say no, but in doing so you would probably hurt this person; it might be better simply to do as asked. Of course, there are limits that should be observed. You should be careful, in such a situation, that you're not hurt instead. For example, if your parents want you to continue to live at home until marriage, they may be hurt by your assertive behavior in refusing. Yet the alternative is to hurt yourself by living with your parents when you're ready to be on your own.

After communicating, get feedback from others. Start with people who are generally supportive. They should provide you with the social reinforcement everyone needs in learning new behavioral patterns. This feedback is particularly important, because your intention and others' perception of your behavior may be totally different. For example, you may behave in certain ways with the intention of communicating confidence, but an observer may perceive arrogance. Thus, another person's perception of your behavior can often help you to see yourself as others do.

In all behaviors, but especially with new behaviors, recognize that you may at first fail. You might, for example, try to answer the teacher's question and find not only that you have the wrong answer but that you don't even understand the question. You might raise your hand and find yourself at a loss for words when you're recognized. Such incidents should not discourage you; realize that in all attempts to change behaviors, you will experience both failure and success.

A note of caution should be added to this discussion. It's easy to visualize a situation in which, for example, people are talking behind you in a movie, and with your newfound enthusiasm for assertiveness, you tell them to be quiet. It's also easy to see yourself getting smashed in the teeth as a result. In applying the principles of assertive communication, be careful that you don't go beyond what you can handle effectively.

**A S K Yourself**
Talking Assertively

Everyone tells you that you are unassertive and that that is the reason why you've been passed over for raises and promotion; you're not perceived to have leadership potential. Ask yourself: What might you do to begin to make your communication more assertive?

## Reviewing  Key Terms and Concepts in Verbal and Nonverbal Messages

This chapter introduced the message system and examined the interaction and basic principles of verbal and nonverbal messages.

### The Interaction of Verbal and Nonverbal Messages

How do nonverbal messages interact with verbal messages? Noverbals can

- accent, or emphasize a verbal message
- complement, or add nuances of meaning
- contradict, or deny the verbal message
- control, or manage the flow of communication
- repeat, or restate the message
- substitute, or take the place of a verbal message

### Meaning Principles

What is meaning, and what principles regulate the communication of meaning from one person to another?

- Meanings are in people, in their thoughts and feelings, not just in their words.
- Meaning is more than words and gestures; meaning includes what speaker and listener bring to interpersonal interaction.

- Meaning is unique; no two people experience exactly the same meaning.
- Meanings are context-based; the context heavily influences the meanings that words and gestures are given.

### Message Principles

What are the major characteristics of verbal and nonverbal messages?

- Messages are packaged; they occur in clusters and usually reinforce one another but also may contradict one another.
- Messages are rule-governed; they follow the rules of the culture.
- Messages vary in abstraction; they vary from very specific to highly abstract and general.
- Messages vary in politeness from rude to extremely polite.
- Messages vary in inclusion and may include or exclude other people.
- Messages vary in assertiveness; you can increase your assertiveness by analyzing the communications around you, rehearsing assertive communication, and communicating with assertive messages.

## Applying  Key Terms and Concepts in Verbal and Nonverbal Messages

**1** A weasel is a slippery rodent; just when you're going to catch it, it slips away. Weasel words are words whose meanings are difficult to pin down. For example, an ad claiming that a certain drug works better than Brand X doesn't specify how much better or in what respect the drug performs better. It's possible that it performs better in one respect and less effectively on nine other measures. "Better" is a weasel word. "Like" is another word often used for weaseling, as when a claim is made that "Brand X will make you feel like a new man." Other weasel words are "helped," "virtually," "as much as," and "more economical." How many weasel words can you identify in a half-hour television show's commercials?

**2** Most often people lie to gain some benefit or reward (for example, to increase desirable relationships, to protect their self-esteem, or to obtain money) or to avoid punishment. In an analysis of 322 lies, researchers found that 75.8 percent benefited the liar, 21.7 percent benefited the person who was told the lie, and 2.5 percent benefited a third party (Camden, Motley, & Wilson, 1984). Are lies told to benefit others less unethical than lies told to benefit yourself?

**3** How would you state the rules for the appropriateness of such common nonverbal messages as *(a)* smiling, *(b)* winking, and *(c)* shaking hands?

**4** Consider the differences in meaning for such words as *woman* to an American and an Iranian, *religion* to a born-again Christian and an atheist, and *lunch* to a Chinese rice farmer and a Wall Street executive. What principles might help such diverse groups understand the different meanings?

**5** Many people who practice direct communication see those who communicate indirectly as being manipulative. According to Tannen (1994b, p. 92), however, "'manipulative' is often just a way of blaming others for our discomfort with their styles." Do you agree with Tannen? Or do you think that indirectness is often intentionally manipulative?

**6** A widely held assumption in anthropology, linguistics, and communication is that the importance of a concept to a culture can be measured by the number of words the language has for talking about the concept. So, for example, in English there are lots of words for money or for transportation or communication. With this principle in mind, consider the findings of Julia Stanley, for example. Stanley researched English-language terms indicating sexual promiscuity and found 220 terms referring to a sexually promiscuous woman but only 22 terms for a sexually promiscuous man (Thorne, Kramarae, & Henley, 1983). What does this finding suggest about our cultures' attitudes and beliefs about promiscuity in men and women?

## Experiencing    Key Terms and Concepts in Verbal and Nonverbal Messages

Go to www.ablongman.com/devito.

*This group of experiences will help clarify the interaction and basic principles of verbal and nonverbal messages.*

❶ **Integrating Verbal and Nonverbal Messages** explores some of the connections between verbal and nonverbal messages. ❷ **Climbing the Abstraction Ladder** and ❸ **Using the Abstraction Ladder as a Creative Thinking Tool** will clarify the nature of the abstraction process and explain a useful creative thinking technique. ❹ **How Can You Vary Directness for Greatest Effectiveness?** provides practice in varying directness. ❺ **How Can You Rephrase Clichés?** identifies some of the many clichés and provides an opportunity to replace these with more creative and meaningful expressions. ❻ **Who?** is a class game–experience that asks you to identify characteristics of other people on the basis of their various verbal and nonverbal messages. This exercise can be used as an introduction to the messages section or as a conclusion. ❼ **Analyzing Assertiveness** provides practice scenarios calling for assertiveness.

# CHAPTER

# 7 | Verbal Messages

🔺 *Finding Neverland* (2004)

*Finding Neverland* tells the story of James Barrie, the creator of Peter Pan. Entirely through words Barrie brought to life characters (among them Tinkerbelle and Captain Hook) that have lived in the minds of children—and adults—ever since. Words have tremendous power and can enable you to accomplish a great deal, as you'll discover in the pages to follow.

This chapter continues the exploration of messages and focuses on the verbal message system, identifying several fundamental principles of language and their implications for interpersonal communication: (1) Language symbolizes reality; (2) language expresses both facts and inferences; (3) language expresses both denotation and connotation; (4) language can criticize and praise; (5) language can obscure distinctions; and (6) language can confirm and disconfirm. Taken together these principles illustrate the range of language and demonstrate how you can use it more effectively.

## LANGUAGE SYMBOLIZES REALITY

**Language** symbolizes reality; of course, it's not the reality itself. Consider: Have you ever reacted to the way something was labeled or described rather than to the actual item? Have you ever bought something because of its name rather than because of the actual object? If so, you were probably responding as if language were the reality, a distortion called intensional orientation.

### Intensional Orientation

The term **intensional orientation** refers to the tendency to view people, objects, and events in terms of how they're talked about or labeled rather than in terms of how they actually exist. **Extensional orientation** is the opposite: the tendency to look first at the actual people, objects, and events and then at the labels. It's the tendency to be guided by what you see happening rather than by the way something or someone is talked about or labeled.

Intensional orientation occurs when you act as if the words and labels were more important than the things they represent—as if the map were more important than the territory. In its extreme form, intensional orientation is seen in the person who is afraid of dogs and who begins to sweat when shown a picture of a dog or when hearing people talk about dogs. Here the person is responding to a label as if it were the actual thing. In its more common form, intensional orientation occurs when you see people through your schemata instead of on the basis of their specific behaviors. For example, it occurs when you think of a professor as an unworldly egghead before getting to know the specific professor.

The corrective to intensional orientation is to focus first on the object, person, or event and then on the way in which the object, person, or event is talked about. Labels are certainly helpful guides, but don't allow them to obscure what they're meant to symbolize.

**Cultural Identifiers** The fact that the word is not the thing does not mean that words may be chosen at random or that all words are equal. Consider *cultural identifiers*—the preferred terms peo-

# Understanding Interpersonal Theory and Research

## THE THEORY OF E-PRIME

**E-prime** is normal English without the verb *to be* in any form; it's English without such words as *is, are, was, were, am.* The theory of E-prime holds that when you communicate without the verb *to be* (that is, in E-prime), you describe events more accurately (Bourland, 1965–66; Bourland, 2004; Wilson, 1989; Klein, 1992; Maas, 2002).

For example, when you say, "Johnny is a failure," the verb *to be* implies that "failure" is *in* Johnny rather than in your observation or evaluation of Johnny. The verb *to be* also implies permanence. That is, the implication is that because failure is *in* Johnny, it will always be there; Johnny will always be a failure. A more accurate and descriptive statement might be "Johnny failed his last two math exams."

When you say, for example, "I'm not a good conversationalist" or "I'm unpopular" or "I'm lazy," you imply that these qualities are *in* you. But these are simply evaluations that may be incorrect or, if at least partly accurate, may change (Joyner, 1993).

### Working with Theories and Research

With this concept of E-prime in mind, how would you describe your own language behavior when thinking and talking about yourself? About others? Might E-prime prove useful?

---

ple use to identify their cultural origins. Always, when in doubt about using a cultural identifier, find out. The preferences and many of the specific examples identified here are drawn largely from the findings of the Task Force on Bias-Free Language of the Association of American University Presses. Do realize that not everyone would agree with these recommendations; they're presented here—in the words of the Task Force—"to encourage sensitivity to usages that may be imprecise, misleading, and needlessly offensive" (Schwartz et al., 1995, p. ix).

Generally, the term *girl* should be used only to refer to very young females and is equivalent to *boy.* Neither term should be used for people older than, say, 13 or 14, though some popular uses extend the terms through high school age. *Girl* is never used to refer to a grown woman, nor is *boy* used to refer to persons in blue-collar positions, as it once was. *Lady* is negatively evaluated by many because it connotes the stereotype of the prim and proper woman. *Woman* or *young woman* is preferred. *Older person* is preferred to *elder, elderly, senior,* or *senior citizen* (which technically refers to someone older than 65).

Generally, *gay* is the preferred term to refer to a man who has an affectional preference for another man and *lesbian* is the preferred term for a woman who has an affectional preference for another woman. (*Lesbian* means "homosexual woman" so the phrase *lesbian woman* is redundant.) This preference for the term *lesbian* is not universal among homosexual women; in one survey, for example, 58 percent preferred *lesbian;* 34 percent preferred *gay* (Lever, 1995). *Homosexual* refers to both gay men and lesbians but more often to a sexual orientation to members of one's own sex. *Gay* and *lesbian* refer to a lifestyle and not just to sexual orientation. *Gay* as a noun, although widely used, may prove offensive in some contexts; for example, "We have two gays on the team." Although used within the gay community in an effort to remove the negative stigma through frequent usage, the term *queer*—as in *queer power*—is often resented when used by outsiders. Because most scientific thinking holds that a person's sexuality is genetically determined rather than being a matter of choice, the term *sexual orientation* rather than *sexual preference* or *sexual status* (which is also vague) is preferred.

Generally, most African Americans prefer *African American* to *black* (Hecht, Jackson, & Ribeau, 2003) though *black* is often used with *white* and is used in a variety of other contexts (for example, Department of Black and Puerto Rican Studies, the *Journal of Black History,* and Black History Month). The American Psychological Association recommends that both terms be capitalized, but *The Chicago Manual of Style* (the manual used by most publishing houses) recommends using lowercase. The terms *Negro* and *colored,* although used in the names of some organizations (for example, the United Negro College Fund and the National Association for the Advancement of Colored People) aren't used outside of these contexts.

*White* is generally used to refer to those whose roots are in European cultures and usually does not include Hispanics. Similar to *African American* is the phrase *European American.* Few European Americans, however, would want to be called that; most prefer their national origins be emphasized; for example, *German American* or *Greek American.* This preference may well change as Europe moves into a more cohesive and united entity. *People of color*—a more literary-sounding term appropriate perhaps to public speaking but awkward in most conversations—is preferred to *nonwhite*, which implies that whiteness is the norm and non-whiteness is a deviation from that norm. The same is true of the term *non-Christian.*

Generally, *Hispanic* is used to refer to anyone who identifies himself or herself as belonging to a Spanish-speaking culture. *Latina* (female) and *Latino* (male) refer to those whose roots are in one of the Latin American countries, such as the Dominican Republic, Nicaragua, or Guatemala. *Hispanic American* refers to those United States residents whose ancestry is a Spanish culture and includes Mexican, Caribbean, and Central and South Americans. In emphasizing a Spanish heritage, the term is really inadequate as an identifier for the many people in the Caribbean and in South America whose origins are French or Portuguese. *Chicana* (female) and *Chicano* (male) refer to those with roots in Mexico, though it often connotes a nationalist attitude (Jandt, 2004) and is considered offensive by many Mexican Americans. *Mexican American* is preferred.

*Inuk* (pl. *Inuit*) was officially adopted at the Inuit Circumpolar Conference to refer to the indigenous peoples of Alaska, northern Canada, Greenland, and eastern Siberia. This term is preferred to *Eskimo* (a term the United States Census Bureau uses), which was applied to the indigenous peoples of Alaska by Europeans and derives from a term that means "raw meat eaters" (Maggio, 1997).

*Indian* refers only to someone from India and is incorrectly used when applied to members of other Asian countries or to the indigenous peoples of North America. In the United States *American Indian* or *Native American* is preferred, even though many Native Americans refer to themselves as *Indians* and *Indian people* and the Bureau of Indian Affairs is still so named. In Canada "First People" is the preferred designation for indigenous people. The term *native American* (with a lowercase *n*) is most often used to refer to persons born in the United States. Although the term technically could refer to anyone born in North or South America, people outside the United States generally prefer more specific designations such as *Argentinean, Cuban,* or *Canadian.* The term *native* means an indigenous inhabitant; it's not used to mean "someone having a less developed culture."

*Muslim* is the preferred form (rather than the older *Moslem*) to refer to a person who adheres to the religious teachings of Islam. *Quran* (rather than *Koran*) is the preferred term for the scriptures of Islam. The terms *Mohammedan* and *Mohammedanism* aren't considered appropriate, because they imply worship of Muhammad, the prophet, which is "considered by Muslims to be a blasphemy against the absolute oneness of God" (Maggio, 1997, p. 277).

Although there is no universal agreement, generally *Jewish people* is preferred to *Jews*, and *Jewess* (a Jewish female) is considered derogatory. *Jew* should only be used as a noun and is never correctly used as a verb or an adjective (Maggio, 1997).

### A S K Yourself
#### Using Inappropriate Cultural Identifiers

Your parents use cultural identifiers that would be considered inappropriate among most social groups—not because of prejudice but mainly through ignorance and habit. You want to avoid falling into these patterns yourself. Ask yourself: What steps might you take to help you achieve your goal of developing culturally sensitive language?

When in the United States history was being written from a European perspective, it was taken as the focal point and the rest of the world was defined in terms of its location from Europe. Thus, Asia became the *East* or the *Orient,* and Asians became *Orientals*—a term that is today considered inappropriate or Eurocentric. People from Asia are *Asians,* just as people from Africa are *Africans* and people from Europe are *Europeans.*

## Allness

Another way in which messages can fail to recognize that language only partially symbolizes reality is known as **allness.** The world is infinitely complex, and because of this you can never say all there is to say about anything—at least not logically. This is particularly true when you are dealing with people. You may think you know all there is to know about certain individuals or about why they did what they did, yet clearly you don't know all. You can never know all the reasons you yourself do something, so there is no way you can know all the reasons your parents, friends, or enemies did something.

You may, for example, be assigned to read a textbook. Because previous texts have been dull and perhaps the first chapter of this one is dull, you may infer that the rest of the book will likewise be dull. Of course, the rest of a book is often even worse than its beginning. Yet it could be that the rest of the book would prove exciting were it read with an open mind. The problem here is that you run the risk of judging an entire text in such a way as to preclude any other possibilities. If you tell yourself that the book is going to be dull, it will probably seem dull; if you say a required course will be useless, it will be extremely difficult for the instructor to make the course anything but what you have defined it to be. Only occasionally do people allow themselves to be proved wrong.

The parable of the six blind men and the elephant is an excellent example of an "allness orientation"—the tendency to judge the whole on the basis of experience with part of the whole—and its attendant problems. You may recall from elementary school the poem by John Saxe that concerns six learned blind men of Indostan who came to examine an elephant, an animal they had only heard about. The first blind man touched the elephant's side and concluded that an elephant was like a wall. The second felt the tusk and said an elephant must be like a spear. The third held the trunk and concluded that an elephant was much like a snake. The fourth touched the knee and knew an elephant was like a tree. The fifth felt the ear and said an elephant was

like a fan. The sixth grabbed the tail and concluded that an elephant was like a rope. Each of these learned men reached his own conclusion regarding what an elephant was really like. Each argued that he was correct and that the others were wrong.

Each, of course, was correct; at the same time, however, all were wrong. The point this parable illustrates is that you can never see all of anything; you can never experience anything fully. You see part of an object, event, or person—and on that limited basis, you conclude what the whole is like. This procedure is universal, and you follow it because you cannot possibly observe everything. Yet recognize that when making judgments of the whole based on only a part, you're actually making inferences that can later be proved wrong. If you assume that you know everything there is to know about something or someone, you fall into the pattern of misevaluation called allness.

Famed British prime minister Disraeli once said that "to be conscious that you are ignorant is a great step toward knowledge." This observation is an excellent example of a **nonallness** attitude. If you recognize that there is more to learn, more to see, more to hear, you leave yourself open to this additional information, and you're better prepared to assimilate it.

A useful **extensional device** that can help you avoid allness is to end each statement, sometimes verbally but always mentally, with an **"etc."** (et cetera)—a reminder that there is more to learn, know, and say; that every statement is inevitably incomplete. To be sure, some people overuse the et cetera. They use it as a substitute for being specific, which defeats its purpose. Instead, it should be used to mentally remind yourself that there is more to know and more to say.

# LANGUAGE EXPRESSES BOTH FACTS AND INFERENCES

Language enables you to form statements of facts and inferences without making any linguistic distinction between the two. Similarly, when you listen to such statements you often don't make a clear distinction between statements of facts and statements of inference. Yet there are great differences between the two. Barriers to clear thinking can be created when inferences are treated as facts, a tendency called **fact–inference confusion.**

For example, you can make statements about things that you observe, and you can make statements about things that you have not observed. In form or structure these statements are similar; they cannot be distinguished from each other by any grammatical analysis. For example, you can say, "She is wearing a blue jacket" as well as "She is harboring an illogical hatred." If you diagrammed these sentences, they would yield identical structures, and yet you know that they're different types of statements. In the first sentence, you can observe the jacket and the blue color; the sentence constitutes a **factual statement.** But how do you observe "illogical hatred"? Obviously, this is not a descriptive statement but an **inferential statement,** a statement that you make not solely on the basis of what you observe but on the basis of what you observe plus your own conclusions.

There's no problem with making inferential statements; you must make them if you're to talk about much that is meaningful. The problem arises when you act as though those inferential statements are factual statements. Consider, for example, the following anecdote (Maynard, 1963):

> A woman went for a walk one day and met her friend, whom she had not seen, heard from, or heard of in ten years. After an exchange of greetings, the woman said, "Is this your little boy?" and her friend replied, "Yes. I got married about six years ago." The woman then asked the child, "What is your name?" and the little boy replied, "Same as my father's." "Oh," said the woman, "then it must be Peter."

The question, of course, is how did the woman know the boy's father's name? The answer is obvious, but only after you recognize that in reading this short passage you have, quite unconsciously, made an inference that is preventing you from arriving at the answer. You have inferred that the woman's friend is a woman. Actually, the friend is a man named Peter.

Perhaps the classic example of this type of fact–inference confusion concerns the case of the "empty" gun that unfortunately proves to be loaded. With amazing frequency, we find in the newspapers examples of people who are so sure that the guns are empty that they point them at someone else and fire. Often, of course, they're empty. But unfortunately, often they're not. Too often someone draws the inference that the gun is empty but acts as if it were a fact and fires the gun.

You may wish to test your ability to distinguish facts from inferences by taking the self-test "Can You Distinguish Facts from Inferences?"

# TEST YOURSELF
## CAN YOU DISTINGUISH FACTS FROM INFERENCES?

Carefully read the following account, modeled on a report developed by William Haney (1973), and the observations based on it. Indicate whether you think the observations are true, false, or doubtful on the basis of the information presented in the report. Circle T if the observation is definitely true, F if the observation is definitely false, and ? if the observation may be either true or false. Judge each observation in order. Don't reread the observations after you have indicated your judgment, and don't change any of your answers.

*A well-liked college teacher had just completed making up the final examinations and had turned off the lights in the office. Just then a tall, broad figure appeared and demanded the examination.*

*The professor opened the drawer. Everything in the drawer was picked up and the individual ran down the corridor. The dean was notified immediately.*

T  F  ?   1. The thief was tall and broad.
T  F  ?   2. The professor turned off the lights.
T  F  ?   3. A tall figure demanded the examination.
T  F  ?   4. The examination was picked up by someone.
T  F  ?   5. The examination was picked up by the professor.
T  F  ?   6. A tall figure appeared after the professor turned off the lights in the office.
T  F  ?   7. The man who opened the drawer was the professor.
T  F  ?   8. The professor ran down the corridor.
T  F  ?   9. The drawer was never actually opened.
T  F  ?  10. Three persons are referred to in this report.

**HOW DID YOU DO?**   After you answer all 10 questions, form small groups of five or six and discuss the answers. Look at each statement from each member's point of view. For each statement, ask yourself "How can you be absolutely certain that the statement is true or false?" You should find that only one statement can be clearly identified as true and only one as false; eight should be marked "?".

**WHAT WILL YOU DO?**   As you read this chapter try to formulate specific guidelines that will help you distinguish facts from inferences as a speaker and as a listener.

This test is designed to trap you into making inferences and treating them as facts. Statement 3 is true (it's in the report); statement 9 is false (the drawer was opened); but all other statements are inferences and should have been marked "?". Review the remaining eight statements to see why you cannot be certain that any of them are either true or false.

A related communication barrier is created by the tendency to draw **pragmatic implications.** Consider the following: The sales manager has been replaced. You know that this manager was not doing a particularly good job and that many sales representatives complained about poor leadership. On the basis of this knowledge, you draw a pragmatic implication—an inference that is probably but not necessarily true—and conclude that the sales manager was fired. This type of situation occurs every day. You see your supervisor in a romantic restaurant with the new sales manager. You draw the pragmatic conclusion that they're having an affair. You might even further infer that the reason the old sales manager was fired was because of the supervisor's affair with the new manager.

Some of the essential differences between factual and inferential statements are summarized in Table 7.1. Distinguishing between these two types of statements does not imply

⬇ **TABLE 7.1**
## Differences between Factual and Inferential Statements

These differences highlight the important distinctions between factual and inferential statements and are based on the discussions of Haney (1973) and Weinberg (1959). As you go through this table, consider how you would classify such statements as: "God exists," "Democracy is the best form of government," "This paper is white," "The Internet will grow in size and importance over the next 10 years," and "This table is based on Haney and Weinberg."

| Factual Statements | Inferential Statements |
| --- | --- |
| May be made only after observation | May be made at any time |
| Are limited to what has been observed | Go beyond what has been observed |
| May be made only by the observer | May be made by anyone |
| May be about only the past or the present | May be about any time—past, present, or future |
| Approach certainty | Involve varying degrees of probability |
| Are subject to verifiable standards | Are not subject to verifiable standards |

# Understanding Interpersonal Skills

## CONFIDENCE

**Confidence** is a person's belief that he or she is an effective and competent communicator and the person's ability to project this competence when interacting with others. Researchers find that a relaxed posture communicates a sense of control, superior status, and power (Spitzberg & Cupach, 1984, 1989). Tenseness, rigidity, and discomfort, on the other hand, signal a lack of self-control, which in turn signals an inability to control the environment or perhaps to manage or lead others.

**Communicating Confidence.** Here are a few suggestions for communicating confidence in interpersonal interactions.

- Take the initiative in introducing yourself to others and in introducing topics of conversation.
- Demonstrate the nonverbal behavior of confidence, which is relaxed (not rigid), flexible (not locked into one or two vocal ranges or body movements), and controlled (not shaky or awkward).
- Control your emotions. Once your emotions get the best of you, you'll appear to have lost confidence. A confident person approaches situations and makes decisions on the basis of logic and evidence, not on the basis of emotions.
- Admit your mistakes. Only a confident person can openly admit mistakes and not worry about what others will think.
- Avoid turning normally declarative sentences into questions by a rising intonation (for example, "I'll arrive at nine?"). Asking for agreement often communicates a lack of confidence.

that one type is better than the other. Both types of statements are useful; both are important. The problem arises when you treat an inferential statement as if it were fact. Phrase your inferential statements as tentative. Recognize that such statements may be wrong. Leave open the possibility of other alternatives.

## LANGUAGE EXPRESSES BOTH DENOTATION AND CONNOTATION

Consider a word such as "death." To a doctor this word might mean the point at which the heart stops beating. This is denotative meaning, a rather objective description of an event. To a mother whose son has just died, however, the word means much more. It recalls the son's youth, his ambitions, his family, his illness, and so on. To her, the word is emotional, subjective, and highly personal. These emotional, subjective, and personal associations are the word's connotative meaning. The **denotation** of a word is its objective definition; the **connotation** is its subjective or emotional meaning.

Now consider a simple nod of the head in answer to the question, "Do you agree?" This gesture is largely denotative and simply says yes. What about a wink, a smile, or an overly rapid speech rate? These nonverbal expressions are more connotative; they express your feelings rather than objective information.

The denotative meaning of a message is general or universal; most people would agree with the denotative meanings and would give similar definitions. Connotative meanings, however, are extremely personal, and few people would agree on the precise connotative meaning of a word or nonverbal behavior.

"Snarl words" and "purr words" may further clarify the distinction between denotative and connotative meaning (Hayakawa & Hayakawa, 1989; Hoffmann, 2005). Snarl words are highly negative ("She's an idiot," "He's a pig," "They're a bunch of losers"). Sexist, racist, and heterosexist language and hate speech provide lots of other examples. Purr words are highly positive ("She's a real sweetheart," "He's a dream," "They're the greatest"). Although they may sometimes seem to have denotative meaning and refer to the "real world," snarl and purr words are actually connotative in meaning. They don't describe people or events; rather, they reveal the speaker's feelings about these people or events.

##  LANGUAGE CAN CRITICIZE AND PRAISE

Throughout your communication experiences, you're expected to criticize, to evaluate, and otherwise to render judgment on some person or on something someone did or created. Especially in helping professions, such as teaching, nursing, or counseling, criticism is an important and frequently used skill. The problem arises when criticism is used outside of its helping function; when it's inappropriate or excessive. An important interpersonal skill is to develop a facility for detecting when a person is asking for criticism and when that person is simply asking for a compliment. For example, when a friend asks how you like his or her new apartment, the friend may be searching for a compliment rather than wanting you to itemize all the things wrong with the place. Similarly, the person who says, "Do I look okay?" may be asking for a compliment.

Sometimes the desire to be liked (or perhaps the need to be appreciated) is so strong that we go to the other extreme and paint everything with praise. The most ordinary jacket, the most common thought, the most average meal are given extraordinary praise, way beyond their merits. Both overly critical and the overly complimentary individuals soon find that their comments are no longer met with concern or interest.

As an alternative to excessive criticism or praise, consider the principle of honest appraisal. Tell the truth—but note that there is an art to truth telling, just as there is an art to all other forms of effective communication. First, distinguish between instances in which an honest appraisal is sought and those in which the individual needs a compliment. Respond to the appropriate level of meaning. Second, if an honest appraisal is desired and if yours is a negative one, give some consideration to how you should phrase your criticism.

In giving criticism focus on the event or the behavior rather than on personality; for example, say "This paper has four typos and has to be redone" rather than "You're a lousy typist; do this over." In offering criticism, be specific. Instead of saying "This paper is weak," as some English teachers might, say "I think the introduction wasn't clear enough. Perhaps a more specific statement of purpose would have worked better."

Try to state criticism positively, if at all possible. Rather than saying, "You look terrible in black," it might be more helpful to say, "You look much better in bright colors." In this way, you're also being constructive; you're explaining what could be done to make the situation better. If you do express criticism that seems to prove destructive, it may be helpful to offer a direct apology or to disclaim any harmful intentions (Baron, 1990). In your positive statement of criticism, try to demonstrate that your criticism stems from your caring and concern for the other person (Hornsey, Bath, & Gunthorpe, 2004). Instead of saying, "The introduction to your report is boring," say, "I really want your report to be great; I'd open with some humor to get the group's attention." Say, "I want you to make a good impression. I think the dark suit would work better."

Own your thoughts and feelings. Instead of saying, "Your report was unintelligible," say, "I had difficulty following your ideas." At the same time, avoid mind reading. Instead of saying, "Don't you care about the impression you make? This report is terrible," say, "I think I would use a stronger introduction and a friendlier writing style."

Be clear. Many prefer to phrase their criticism ambiguously thinking that this will hurt less. Research suggests, however, that although ambiguous criticism may appear more polite, it also will appear less honest, less competent, and not necessarily more positive (Edwards & Bello, 2001).

Avoid ordering or directing the other person to change; try identifying possible alternatives. Instead of saying, "Don't be so forward when you're first introduced to someone," consider saying, "I think they might respond better to a less forward approach." Also, whether with workplace colleagues or in relationships, generally avoid what one writer has called "microinequities"—subtle putdowns, sarcastic remarks, and gestures that imply a lack of concern or interest (Lubin, 2004).

Consider the context of the criticism. Generally, it's best to express criticism in situations where you can interact with the person and express your attitudes in dialogue rather than monologue. By this principle, then, your first choice would be to express criticism face-to-face, your second choice would be by telephone, and a distant third choice by letter, memo, or e-mail. Also, try to express your criticism in private. This is especially important when dealing with members from cultures where public criticism could result in a serious loss of face.

In expressing praise, keep the following in mind:

- *Use I-messages.* Instead of saying "That report was good," say "I thought that report was good" or "I liked your report."
- *Make sure your affect (facial movement) communicates your positive feelings.* Often, when people praise others simply because it's the socially correct response, they may betray their lack of conviction with too little or inappropriate affect.
- *Name the behavior you're praising.* Instead of saying "That was good," say "I enjoyed your speech" or "I thought your introduction was great."
- *Take culture into consideration.* Many Asians, for example, feel uncomfortable when praised, because they may interpret praise as a sign of veiled criticism (Dresser, 1996).

##  LANGUAGE CAN OBSCURE DISTINCTIONS

Language can obscure distinctions among people or events that are covered by the same label but are really quite different (indiscrimination) by making it easy to focus on extremes rather than on the vast middle ground between opposites (polarization) and by ignoring the inevitable process of change (static evaluation).

### Indiscrimination

Nature seems to abhor sameness at least as much as vacuums, for nowhere in the universe can you find identical entities. Everything is unique. Language, however, provides common nouns, such as *teacher, student, friend, enemy, war, politician, liberal,* and the like, that may lead you to focus on similarities. Such nouns can lead you to group together all teachers, all students, and all friends and perhaps divert attention from the uniqueness of each individual, object, and event.

The misevaluation known as **indiscrimination**—a form of stereotyping (see Chapter 2)—occurs when you focus on classes of individuals, objects, or events and fail to see that each is unique and needs to be looked at individually. Indiscrimination can be seen in such statements as these:

- He's just like the rest of them: lazy, stupid, a real slob.
- I really don't want another ethnic on the board of directors. One is enough for me.
- Read a romance novel? I read one when I was 16. That was enough to convince me.

A useful antidote to indiscrimination is the extensional device called the **index,** a spoken or mental subscript that identifies each individual in a group as an individual even though all members of the group may

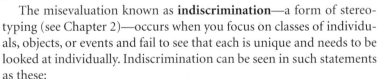

be covered by the same label. For example, when you think and talk of an individual politician as just a "politician," you may fail to see the uniqueness in this politician and the differences between this particular politician and other politicians. However, when you think with the index—when you think not of politician but of politician$_1$ or politician$_2$ or politician$_3$—you're less likely to fall into the trap of indiscrimination and more likely to focus on the differences among politicians. The same is true with members of cultural, national, or religious groups; when you think and even talk of Iraqi$_1$ and Iraqi$_2$, you'll be reminded that not all Iraqis are the same. The more you discriminate *among* individuals covered by the same label, the less likely you are to discriminate *against* any group.

**Ethnocentrism**    To gain interesting perspective on indiscrimination, let's look briefly at ethnocentrism. Before reading about this important concept, examine your own ethnocentrism by taking the accompanying self-test.

---

# TEST YOURSELF
## HOW ETHNOCENTRIC ARE YOU?

Here are 18 statements representing your beliefs about your culture. For each statement indicate how much you agree or disagree, using the following scale: 5 = strongly agree, 4 = agree, 3 = neither agree nor disagree, 2 = disagree, 1 = strongly disagree.

_____ 1. Most cultures are backward compared to my culture.
_____ 2. My culture should be the role model for other cultures.
_____ 3. Lifestyles in other cultures are just as valid as those in my culture.
_____ 4. Other cultures should try to be like my culture.
_____ 5. I'm not interested in the values and customs of other cultures.
_____ 6. People in my culture could learn a lot from people in other cultures.
_____ 7. Most people from other cultures just don't know what's good for them.
_____ 8. I have little respect for the values and customs of other cultures.
_____ 9. Most people would be happier if they lived like people in my culture.
_____ 10. People in my culture have just about the best lifestyles of anywhere.
_____ 11. Lifestyles in other cultures are not as valid as those in my culture.
_____ 12. I'm very interested in the values and customs of other cultures.
_____ 13. I respect the values and customs of other cultures.
_____ 14. I do not cooperate with people who are different.
_____ 15. I do not trust people who are different.
_____ 16. I dislike interacting with people from different cultures.
_____ 17. Other cultures are smart to look up to my culture.
_____ 18. People from other cultures act strange and unusual when they come into my culture.

**HOW DID YOU DO?**   This test was presented to give you the opportunity to examine some of your own cultural beliefs, particularly those cultural beliefs that contribute to ethnocentrism. The person low in ethnocentrism would have high scores (4s and 5s) for items 3, 6, 12, and 13 and low scores (1s and 2s) for all the others. The person high in ethnocentrism would have low scores for items 3, 6, 12, and 13 and high scores for all the others.

**WHAT WILL YOU DO?**   Use this test to bring your own cultural beliefs to consciousness so you can examine them logically and objectively. Ask yourself if your beliefs are productive beliefs that will help you achieve your professional and social goals, or if they're counterproductive beliefs that will actually hinder your progress.

*Source:* This test is taken from James W. Neuliep, Michelle Chaudoir, and James C. McCroskey (2001). A cross-cultural comparison of ethnocentrism among Japanese and United States college students. *Communication Research Reports* 18 (Spring):137–146. Used by permission of Eastern Communication Association.

---

As you've probably gathered from taking this test, **ethnocentrism** is the tendency to evaluate the values, beliefs, and behaviors of your own culture as being more positive, logical, and natural than those of other cultures. Although normally thought of negatively, ethnocentrism has its positive aspects. For example, if a group is under attack, ethnocentrism will help create cohesiveness. It has also been argued that it forms the basis of patriotism and a willingness to sacrifice for the benefit of the group (Neuliep & McCroskey, 1997).

But ethnocentrism also can create considerable problems. Although the research is not conclusive, it appears that it may create obstacles to communication with those who are culturally different from you. It can also lead to hostility toward outside groups and may blind you to seeing other perspectives, other values, other ways of doing things (Neuliep & McCroskey, 1997; Cashdan, 2001; Jörn, 2004).

Ethnocentrism exists on a continuum (see Table 7.2). People aren't either ethnocentric or not ethnocentric; rather, most are somewhere between these polar opposites. Of course, your degree of ethnocentrism varies, depending on the group on which you focus. For example, if you're Greek American, you may have a low degree of ethnocentrism when dealing with Italian Americans but a high degree when dealing with Turkish Americans or Japanese Americans. Most important for our purposes is that your degree of ethnocentrism (and we are all ethnocentric to at least some degree) will influence your interpersonal interactions.

There is nothing wrong with classifying. In fact, it's an extremely useful method of dealing with any complex matter; it puts order into thinking. The problem arises not from classification itself but from applying an evaluative label to a class and using that label as an "adequate" map for each and every individual in the group.

## ⤴ VIEWPOINT

Ethnocentrism gives people pride in their culture and its achievements and contributes to a willingness to sacrifice for the culture. At the same time, however, it may lead people to see other cultures and members of other cultures as inferior and to be unwilling to profit from the insights and contributions of other cultures. How would you describe the influence of ethnocentrism on the events of September 11, 2001, and on developments that followed over the next several months? For example, did you become more ethnocentric after these events? Less ethnocentric?

## ⤵ TABLE 7.2
## The Ethnocentrism Continuum

This table summarizes some of the interconnections between ethnocentrism and communication. In this table, five degrees of ethnocentrism are identified; in reality, there are as many degrees as there are people. The "communication distances" are general terms that highlight the attitude that dominates that level of ethnocentrism. Under "communications" are some of the major ways people might interact given their particular degree of ethnocentrism. Can you identify your own ethnocentrism on this table? For example, are there groups to which you have low ethnocentrism? Middle? High? What accounts for these differences? This table draws on the work of several intercultural researchers (Lukens, 1978; Gudykunst & Kim, 1992; Gudykunst, 1991).

| Degree of Ethnocentrism | Communication Distance | Communications |
|---|---|---|
| Low | Equality | You treat others as equals; you view different customs and ways of behaving as equal to your own. |
| | Sensitivity | You want to decrease distance between yourself and others. |
| | Indifference | You lack concern for others; you prefer to interact in a world of similar others. |
| | Avoidance | You avoid and limit communications, especially intimate ones with interculturally different others. |
| High | Disparagement | You engage in hostile behavior and belittle others; you view different cultures and ways of behaving as inferior to your own. |

# Ethics in Interpersonal Communication

## LIBEL, SLANDER, AND MORE

The First Amendment to the U.S. Constitution states:

> Congress shall make no law . . . abridging the freedom of speech, or of the press; or the right of the people peaceably to assemble and to petition the Government for a redress of grievances.

But speech is not always free; at times it's unlawful, and at times it's unethical. For example, it's unlawful to yell *fire* in a movie house when there's no fire, plot the overthrow of the government, plan terrorist attacks, burn the flag, or send materials resembling disease-carrying substances through the mail.

Often speech is unethical. For example, it's considered unethical to defame another person—to falsely attack the person's reputation and thereby cause damage to it. When this attack is done in print or in pictures, it's *libel;* when done through speech or gesture, it's *slander*.

Whereas just decades ago using sexist, homophobic, racist, or ageist terms in conversation, demeaning another person because of that person's gender, age, race, nationality, affectional orientation, physical condition, or religion, or speaking in ethnic or cultural stereotypes would have gone unnoticed, today it would be considered inappropriate and unethical.

### What would you do?

You join colleagues at the water cooler, only to discover that they're telling racist jokes. You don't want to criticize them, for fear that you'll become unpopular and that these colleagues will make it harder for you to get ahead. At the same time, however, you don't want to remain silent, for fear it will imply that you accept this type of talk. What would you do in this situation?

## Polarization

**Polarization,** often referred to as the fallacy of "either/or," is the tendency to look at the world and to describe it in terms of extremes—good or bad, positive or negative, healthy or sick, brilliant or stupid, rich or poor, and so on. Polarized statements come in many forms, for example:

- After listening to the evidence, I'm still not clear who the good guys are and who the bad guys are.
- Well, are you for us or against us?
- College had better get me a good job. Otherwise, this has been a big waste of time.

### ASK Yourself
### Discouraging Ethnocentricity

You've been dating a wonderful person for the last few months, but increasingly you are discovering that your "ideal" partner is extremely ethnocentric and sees little value in other religions, other races, other nationalities. Ask yourself: What are some things you can do to educate your possible life partner?

Most people exist somewhere between the extremes of good and bad, healthy and sick, brilliant and stupid, rich and poor. Yet there seems to be a strong tendency to view only the extremes and to categorize people, objects, and events in terms of these polar opposites.

You can easily demonstrate this tendency by filling in the opposites for each of the following words:

Opposite

tall ___:___:___:___:___:___    _____

heavy ___:___:___:___:___:___    _____

strong ___:___:___:___:___:___    _____

happy ___:___:___:___:___:___    _____

legal ___:___:___:___:___:___    _____

Filling in the opposites should have been relatively easy and quick. The words should also have been fairly short. Further, if various different people supplied the opposites, there would be a high degree of agreement among them.

Now try to fill in the middle positions with words meaning, for example, "midway between tall and short," "midway between heavy and light," and so on. Do this before reading any farther.

These midway responses (compared to the opposites) were probably more difficult to think of and took you more time. The responses should also have been long words or phrases of several words. Further, different people would probably agree less on these midway responses than on the opposites.

This exercise clearly illustrates the ease with which you can think and talk in opposites and the difficulty you have in thinking and talking about the middle. But recognize that the vast majority of cases exist between extremes. Don't allow the ready availability of extreme terms to obscure the reality of what lies in between (Read, 2004).

In some cases, of course, it's legitimate to talk in terms of two values. For example, either this thing you're holding is a book or it isn't. Clearly, the classes "book" and "not-book" include all possibilities. There is no problem with this kind of statement. Similarly, you may say that a student either will pass this course or will not, as these two categories include all the possibilities.

You create problems when you use this either/or form in situations where it's inappropriate; for example, "The supervisor is either for us or against us." Note that these two choices don't include all possibilities: The supervisor may be for us in some things and against us in others, or he or she may be neutral. During the Vietnam War there was a tendency to categorize people as either "hawk" or "dove," but clearly many people were neither, and many were probably both—hawks on certain issues and doves on others. More recently, you see examples of polarization in opinions about the war in the Middle East, with some people entirely and totally supportive of one side and others entirely and totally supportive of the other side.

# Ask the Researcher

## ACCURACY IN LANGUAGE

 I realize that there are many shades of gray, but do I really have to talk with middle terms and qualify my statements? They make me sound wishy-washy and less powerful than I'd like to appear.

You may sound powerful today, but at the cost of appearing unreliable or untrustworthy tomorrow. Reality is complex and multifaceted, and our senses can only take in a fraction of what is going on at any given time. When we put our experiences into words, the medium of language further distorts and oversimplifies the world, inevitably leading to error. While we can never completely overcome human fallibility, we can minimize our mistakes by communicating precisely and concretely. Scientists understand that all knowledge is tentative, and adjust their communication to avoid describing the world in abstract and absolute terms. And they have achieved extraordinary success by being highly specific in their language use. General semantics recommends that we make a science of living, that we be as careful in our everyday communication as scientists are when they communicate their findings. By representing reality as accurately as possible, and acknowledging our own subjectivity, we can communicate more reliably, and live saner lives.

**For more information** see S. I. Hayakawa and Alan R. Hayakawa, *Language in Thought and Action,* 5th ed. (San Diego: Harcourt Brace, 1990); and Neil Postman, *Crazy Talk, Stupid Talk* (New York: Delacorte, 1976).

Lance Strate (Ph.D., New York University) is associate professor of communication and media studies at Fordham University and teaches courses in language, media, and culture (strate @ Fordham.edu). Professor Strate is president of the Media Ecology Association, editor of the journal *Explorations in Media Ecology,* and a member of the editorial board of *ETC.: A Review of General Semantics.*

## Static Evaluation

Another distinction language often obscures is that of change. Language changes very slowly, especially when compared to the rapid pace at which people and things change. When you retain an evaluation, despite the changes in the person or thing, you're engaging in **static evaluation.**

Alfred Korzybski (1933) used an interesting illustration in this connection: In a tank there is a large fish and many small fish that are its natural food source. Given freedom in the tank, the large fish will eat the small fish. After some time, the tank is partitioned, with the large fish on one side and the small fish on the other, divided only by glass. For a time, the large fish will try to eat the small fish but will fail; each time it tries, it will knock into the glass partition. After some time, it will learn that trying to eat the small fish means difficulty, and it will no longer go after them. Now, however, the partition is removed, and the small fish swim all around the big fish. But the big fish does not eat them and in fact will die of starvation while its natural food swims all around. The large fish has learned a pattern of behavior, and even though the actual territory has changed, the map remains static.

While you would probably agree that everything is in a constant state of flux, the relevant question is whether you act as if you know this. Do you act in accordance with the notion of change, instead of just accepting it intellectually? Do you treat your little sister as if she were 10 years old, or do you treat her like the 20-year-old woman she has become? Your evaluations of yourself and others must keep pace with the rapidly changing real world. Otherwise you'll be left with attitudes and beliefs—static evaluations—about a world that no longer exists.

To guard against static evaluation, use a device called the **date:** Mentally date your statements and especially your evaluations. Remember that Gerry Smith$_{2002}$ is not Gerry Smith$_{2006}$; academic abilities$_{2003}$ are not academic abilities$_{2006}$. T. S. Eliot, in *The Cocktail Party,* said that "what we know of other people is only our memory of the moments during which we knew them. And they have changed since then . . . at every meeting we are meeting a stranger."

# InterMedia

## THINKING CRITICALLY ABOUT THE MEDIA

Watching a televised news show, reading a post on the Internet, or reading a newspaper or newsmagazine has to involve serious critical thinking. This chapter's discussions of ways to use verbal messages effectively offer useful critical thinking guidelines that you can easily apply to the media. For example:

- **Beware of intensional orientation.** Distinguish between the way the media present and talk about something and what exists in reality.
- **Beware of allness.** The media cannot say all about anything; always assume there is more to be said, more to learn.
- **Beware of fact–inference confusion.** Distinguish between facts and inferences, and treat them differently.
- **Beware of static evaluation.** The world and people are constantly changing; what was true in a news broadcast six months ago may no longer be true today, so update your conclusions frequently.
- **Beware of indiscrimination.** No two things, people, or cultures are the same. In their effort to simplify, the media frequently oversimplify and often present people and cultures in stereotypes.
- **Beware of polarization.** The media, in their need to grab attention, often present people and events in their most extreme manifestations (Gamson, 1998). But extremes don't represent the majority of people.

### Follow Up

From a few evenings' television, record as many examples as you can find of each of the critical thinking errors listed here (in dramas, sitcoms, and talk shows as well as in news and information programming). What one critical thinking principle do you find violated most often?

# LANGUAGE CAN CONFIRM AND DISCONFIRM

The language behaviors known as confirmation and disconfirmation have to do with the extent to which you acknowledge another person. Consider this situation. You've been living with someone for the last six months and you arrive home late one night. Your partner, let's say Pat, is angry and complains about your being so late. Of the following responses which are you most likely to give?

❶ Stop screaming. I'm not interested in what you're babbling about. I'll do what I want, when I want. I'm going to bed.

❷ What are you so angry about? Didn't you get in three hours late last Thursday when you went to that office party? So knock it off.

❸ You have a right to be angry. I should have called to tell you I was going to be late, but I got involved in a serious debate at work, and I couldn't leave until it was resolved.

In response 1, you dismiss Pat's anger and even indicate dismissal of Pat as a person. In response 2, you reject the validity of Pat's reasons for being angry, although you do not dismiss either Pat's feelings of anger or of Pat as a person. In response 3, you acknowledge Pat's anger and the reasons for being angry. In addition, you provide some kind of explanation and, in doing so, show that both Pat's feelings and Pat as a person are important and that Pat has the right to know what happened. The first response is an example of disconfirmation, the second of rejection, and the third of confirmation.

Psychologist William James once observed that "no more fiendish punishment could be devised, even were such a thing physically possible, than that one should be turned loose in society and remain absolutely unnoticed by all the members thereof." In this often-quoted observation, James identifies the essence of disconfirmation (Watzlawick, Beavin, & Jackson, 1967; Veenendall & Feinstein, 1995).

**Disconfirmation** is a communication pattern in which you ignore a person's presence as well as that person's communications. You say, in effect, that the person and what she or he has to say aren't worth serious attention. Disconfirming responses often lead to loss of self-esteem (Sommer, Williams, Ciarocco, & Baumeister, 2001).

Note that disconfirmation is not the same as **rejection.** In rejection, you disagree with the person; you indicate your unwillingness to accept something the other person says or does. In disconfirming someone, however, you deny that person's significance; you claim that what this person says or does simply does not count.

**Confirmation** is the opposite communication pattern. In confirmation, you not only acknowledge the presence of the other person but also indicate your acceptance of this person, of this person's definition of self, and of your relationship as defined or viewed by this other person. Confirming responses often lead to gains in self-esteem and have been shown to reduce student apprehension in the classroom and indirectly to increase motivation and learning (Ellis, 2004). You can communicate both confirmation and disconfirmation in a wide variety of ways; Table 7.3 shows just a few.

## Talking with the Grief Stricken

Talking with the grief stricken provides an interesting perspective on confirmation. Grief is something everyone experiences at some time. It may be experienced because of illness or death, the loss of a highly valued relationship (for example, a romantic breakup), the loss of certain physical or mental abilities, or the loss of material possessions (your house burning down or stock market losses). Consider the following example of one attempt to talk with a grief-stricken individual.

**A s k Yourself**
Discouraging Disconfirmation

For the last several months you've noticed how disconfirming your neighbors are toward their preteen children; it seems the children can never do anything to the parents' satisfaction. Ask yourself: What are some of the things you might say (if you do decide to get involved) to make your neighbors more aware of their communication patterns and the possible negative effects these might have?

## ⟳ TABLE 7.3
## Confirmation and Disconfirmation

This table identifies some specific confirming and disconfirming messages. As you review this table, try to imagine a specific illustration for each of the ways of communicating disconfirmation and confirmation (Pearson, 1993; Galvin, Bylund, & Brommel, 2004).

| Confirmation | Disconfirmation |
| --- | --- |
| Acknowledge the presence and the contributions of the other person by either supporting or taking issue with what he or she says. | Ignore the presence or contributions of the other person; express indifference to what the other person says. |
| Make nonverbal contact by maintaining direct eye contact and, when appropriate, touching, hugging, kissing, and otherwise demonstrating acknowledgment of the other. | Make no nonverbal contact; avoid direct eye contact; avoid touching and general nonverbal closeness. |
| Engage in dialogue (communication in which both persons are speakers and listeners; both are involved; both are concerned with and have respect for each other). | Engage in monologue (communication in which one person speaks and one person listens; there is no real interaction; there is no real concern or respect for each other). |
| Demonstrate understanding of what the other person says and means and reflect your understanding in what you say, or when in doubt ask questions. | Jump to interpretation or evaluation rather than working at understanding what the other person means. |
| Acknowledge the other person's requests; answer the other person's questions; return phone calls and e-mails. | Ignore the other person's requests; fail to answer questions; don't return phone calls or reply to e-mails. |
| Encourage the other person to express his or her thoughts and feelings by showing interest and asking questions. | Interrupt or otherwise make it difficult for the other person to express himself or herself. |
| Respond directly and exclusively to what the other person says. | Avoid responding, or respond tangentially by acknowledging the other person's comment but shifting the focus of the message in another direction. |

I just heard that Harry died—I mean, passed away. I'm so sorry. I know exactly how you feel. But you know, it's for the best. I mean the man was suffering. I remember seeing him last month; he was so weak he could hardly stand. And he looked so sad. He must have been in constant pain. It's better this way. He's at peace. You'll get over it. You'll see. Time heals all wounds. It was the same way with me, and you know how close we were. I mean we were devoted to each other. Everyone said we were the closest pair they had ever seen. And I got over it. So how about we go to dinner tonight? We'll talk about old times. Come on. Come on. Don't be a spoilsport. I really need to get out. I've been in the house all week. Come on, do it for me. After all, you have to forget; you have to get on with your own life. I won't take no for an answer. I'll pick you up at seven.

To avoid the kind of communication illustrated above and to make this often difficult form of communication easier, confirm the other person and the person's feelings. "You must miss him a great deal" confirms the person's feelings, for example. Avoid expressions that are disconfirming: "You'll see, things will be better tomorrow." Give the grieving person permission to grieve. Let the person know that it's acceptable for him or her to grieve in the ways that feel most comfortable—for example, crying or talking about old times.

Encourage the grieving person to express feelings and talk about the loss. Most people who experience grief welcome the opportunity to talk about it. However, don't try to force the person to talk about experiences or feelings she or he may not be ready to share. At the same time, avoid trying to force the grief-stricken individual to focus on the bright side; she or he may not be ready. Avoid expressions such as "You're so lucky you still have some vision left" or "It's better this way; Pat was suffering so much."

Empathize with the grief-stricken person and communicate this empathic understanding. Let the person know that you can understand what he or she is feeling. Don't assume, though, that your feelings (however empathic) are the same in depth or in kind. If, having never experienced this tragedy, you say to a parent who has lost a child, "I know exactly what you're feeling," you risk arousing resentment.

Be especially sensitive to **leave-taking cues**—signals that the person is ready to conclude the conversation. Don't try to force your presence on someone who is grief stricken or press the person to stay with you or a group of people. When in doubt, ask.

These concepts of confirmation and disconfirmation also give unique insight into a wide variety of offensive language practices, language that alienates and separates, language that disconfirms. Four offensive language practices are sexism, heterosexism, racism, and ageism.

## Sexism

Attitudes toward **sexist language**—language that tends to disconfirm members of one gender, usually women—probably stem from attitudes toward women generally. Those with negative attitudes toward women are less likely to detect sexist language in others and are more likely to use sexist language themselves (Parks & Roberton, 2004; Swim, Mallett, & Stangor, 2004). The same may well be true of those who use language that is heterosexist, racist, or ageist.

In regard to sexism, the National Council of Teachers of English (NCTE) has proposed guidelines for nonsexist (gender-free, gender-neutral, or sex-fair) language. These concern the use of generic *man,* the use of generic *he* and *his,* and sex-role stereotyping (Penfield, 1987).

**Generic Man**   The word *man* refers most clearly to an adult male. To use the term to refer to both men and women emphasizes "maleness" at the expense of "femaleness." Similarly the terms *mankind* or *the common man* or even *cavemen* imply a primary focus on adult males. Gender-neutral terms can easily be substituted. Instead of *mankind,* you can say *humanity, people,* or *human beings.* Instead of *the common man,* you can say *the average person* or *ordinary people.* Instead of *cavemen,* you can say *prehistoric people* or *cave dwellers.*

Similarly, the use of such terms as *policeman* or *fireman* and other terms that presume maleness as the norm and femaleness as a deviation from this norm are clear and common examples of sexist language. Consider using nonsexist alternatives (for example, *police officer* and *firefighter*) for these and similar terms; make these alternatives a part of your active vocabulary. What alternatives can you offer for each of these terms: chairman, the common man, countryman, doorman, man, mankind, manmade, mailman, manpower, repairman, fireman, freshman, salesman, stewardess, waitress, Web master, and womanizer?

**Generic He and His**   The use of the masculine pronoun to refer to any individual regardless of sex is certainly declining. But only a generation ago, as recently as 1975, all college textbooks, for example, used the masculine pronoun as generic. There seems to be no legitimate reason the feminine pronoun could not alternate with the masculine pronoun in referring to hypothetical individuals, or why such terms as *he and she* or *her and him* could not be used instead of just *he* or *him.* Alternatively, you can restructure your sentences to eliminate any reference to gender. For example, the NCTE Guidelines (Penfield, 1987) suggest that instead of saying, "The average student is worried about his grades," you say, "The average student is worried about grades." Instead of saying, "Ask the student to hand in his work as soon as he is finished," say, "Ask students to hand in their work as soon as they're finished."

**Sex-Role Stereotyping**   The words you use often reflect a sex-role bias, the assumption that certain roles or professions belong to men and others belong to women. Not surprisingly, sex-role stereotyping is especially prevalent in traditionally male-dominated areas of work (Irizarry, 2004). In eliminating sex-role stereotyping, avoid, for example, making the

hypothetical elementary school teacher female and the college professor male. Avoid referring to doctors as male and nurses as female. Avoid noting the gender of a professional with terms such as "female doctor" or "male nurse." When you're referring to a specific doctor or nurse, the person's gender will become clear when you use the appropriate pronoun: "Dr. Smith wrote the prescription for her new patient" or "The nurse recorded the patient's temperature himself."

Here are a few additional examples. How would you rephrase these?

1. You really should get a second doctor's opinion. Just see what he says.
2. Johnny went to school today and met his kindergarten teacher. I wonder who she is?
3. Everyone needs to examine his own conscience.
4. The effective communicator is a selective self-discloser; he discloses to some people about some things some of the time.
5. The effective waitress knows when her customers need her.
6. The history of man is largely the story of how technology has replaced his manual labor.

## Heterosexism

A close relative of sexism is heterosexism (Perez, 2005). The term *heterosexist language* is a relatively new addition to our list of linguistic prejudices. **Heterosexist language** is language that disparages lesbians and gay men (Rothblum & Bond, 1996). As in the case of sexist language, we see heterosexism both in derogatory terms used for lesbians and gay men and in more subtle forms. For example, when we qualify a description of a profession—as in "gay athlete" or "lesbian doctor"—we are in effect stating that athletes and doctors are not normally gay or lesbian. Further, we are highlighting the affectional orientation of the athlete or the doctor in a context in which it may have no relevance. This practice is, of course, the same as qualifying by gender, as already noted. You even see heterosexist attitudes communicated in the "startled eye blink" with which some people react to gay couples (Mahaffey, Bryan, & Hutchison, 2005).

Still another instance of heterosexism is the presumption of heterosexuality. Usually, people assume that the person they're talking to or about is heterosexual. Usually, they're correct, because the majority of the population is heterosexual. At the same time, however, note that heterosexism denies lesbians and gay males their true identity. The practice of assuming that a person is heterosexual is very similar to the presumption of whiteness and maleness that we have made significant progress toward eliminating.

### VIEWPOINT

What do you feel is the current status of sexism and sexist language in your area of the world? Can you identify specific types of sexism that you've observed? In what types of situations is sexism seen most clearly (for example, on the job, in schools, in the military, in the ministry)?

Perhaps the most important step in eliminating heterosexism in communication is to avoid any offensive nonverbal mannerisms that parody stereotypes when talking about gays and lesbians. At the same time, avoid "complimenting" gay men and lesbians by saying they "don't look it." To gays and lesbians, that is not a compliment. Similarly, expressing disappointment that a person is gay—for example, saying "What a waste!"—and meaning it as a compliment is not really complimentary.

Avoid, too, assuming that every gay man or lesbian knows what every other gay man or lesbian is thinking. To make such an assumption is very similar to asking someone from Japan why Sony is investing heavily in the United States, or as one comic put it, asking an African American, "What do you think Jesse Jackson meant by that last speech?" Similarly, saying things like "Lesbians are so loyal" or "Gay men are so open with their feelings"—statements that ignore the wide individual differences within any group—are potentially insulting to members of either group.

Avoid *overattribution*, the tendency to attribute just about everything a person does, says, and believes to his or her being gay or lesbian. As discussed in Chapter 4, overattribution distorts perception and helps to recall and perpetuate stereotypes.

Remember that relationship milestones are important to all people. Ignoring the anniversary of your uncle and his same-sex partner or forgetting that partner's birthday while remembering and celebrating similar milestones of another uncle and his opposite-sex partner is unfair and will be resented.

As you think about heterosexism, recognize that heterosexist language will create barriers to communication—but that its absence will foster more meaningful communication: greater comfort, an increased willingness to disclose personal information, and a greater willingness to engage in future interactions (Dorland & Fisher, 2001).

## Racism

According to Andrea Rich (1974), "any language that, through a conscious or unconscious attempt by the user, places a particular racial or ethnic group in an inferior position is racist." **Racist language** reflects and expresses racist attitudes. It also contributes to the development of racist attitudes in those who use or hear such language. Even when racism is subtle, unintentional, and even unconscious, its effects are systematically damaging (Dovidio, Gaertner, Kawakami, & Hodson, 2002).

Racist terms are used by members of one culture to disparage members of other cultures—their customs or their accomplishments. Racist language emphasizes differences rather than similarities and separates rather than unites members of different cultures. Traditionally, racist language has been used by the dominant group to establish and maintain power over other groups. Today, however, it is used by racists (or the racist-talking) in all groups. The social consequences of racist language in terms of employment, education, housing opportunities, and general community acceptance are well known.

It's interesting to note that the terms denoting some of the major movements in art—for example, "impressionism" and "cubism"—were originally applied negatively. The terms were adopted by the artists themselves and eventually became positive. A parallel can be seen in the use of the word "queer" by some lesbian and gay organizations. Their purpose in using the term is to cause it to lose its negative connotation.

It has often been pointed out (Davis, 1973; Bosmajian, 1974; Purnell, 1982) that some aspects of language may be inherently racist. For example, Davis's examination of English found 134 synonyms for "white." Of these, 44 have positive connotations (for example, "clean," "chaste," and "unblemished") and only 10 have negative connotations (for example, "whitewash" and "pale"); the remaining synonyms are relatively neutral. Of the 120 synonyms for "black," 60 were found to have unfavorable connotations ("unclean," "foreboding," and "deadly") and none to have positive connotations.

Consider such phrases as the following:

the Korean doctor
the Latino prodigy
the African American mathematician
the white rapper
the American Indian physicist

Often, such identifiers are used to emphasize that the combination of race and occupation (or talent or accomplishment) is rare and unexpected, that this member of a racial or ethnic group is an exception. It also implies that racial factors are somehow important in the context. In some cases, of course, you may want to include the racial identifier because it's relevant to the conversation. For example, in commenting on the changes in Hollywood, you might say, "This is the first year that both best acting Oscars were won by African Americans."

# Ageism

**Ageism** is discrimination based on age. Most researchers in the area would accept the definition of ageism as "any attitude, action, or institutional structure which subordinates a person or group because of age or any assignment of roles in society purely on the basis of age" (Traxler, 1980, p. 14). In the United States and throughout much of the industrialized world, ageism signifies discrimination against old people and against aging in general. But ageism also can involve prejudice against other age groups. For example, if you refer to teenagers as selfish and undependable, you're discriminating against a group purely because of their age and thus are ageist in your statements. In some cultures—some Asian and some African cultures, for example—the old are revered and respected. They are sought after for advice on relationship matters, economic questions, and ethical concerns.

Popular language is replete with examples of ageist phrases; *little old lady, old hag, old-timer, over the hill, old coot,* and *fogy* are just some examples. As it is with racist language, ageist language can crop up when you qualify or describe the abilities of an older person. For example, when you refer to a "quick-witted 75-year-old" or an "agile 65-year-old" or a "responsible teenager," you are saying that these qualities in persons of these ages are unusual and need special mention. You're saying that "quick-wittedness" and "75 years of age" do not normally go together. You imply the same abnormality for "agility" and "being 65" and for "responsible" and "teenager." The problem with this is that it's simply wrong. There are many 75-year-olds who are extremely quick-witted—and many 30-year-olds who aren't.

You also communicate ageism when you speak to older people in overly simple words or explain things to them that don't need explaining (Brown & Draper, 2003), especially if you draw the attention of others in the area to the fact that you are talking down to the older person. Nonverbally, you engage in ageist communication when, for example, you avoid touching an older person but touch others, or when you avoid making direct eye contact with the older person but readily do so with others. Sometimes people speak to older people at an overly high volume, as if all older people had hearing difficulties.

And, of course, the media perpetuate ageist stereotypes by picturing older people as unproductive, complaining, and unromantic. Rarely, for example, do the media portray older people who are productive workers, who are cooperative and pleasant, and who are involved in romantic and sexual relationships. To counteract such stereotyping, some 40 U.S. medical schools are increasing students' contacts with older people as one way to help the students understand that older individuals are not necessarily dependent or frail (Bernard, 2004).

One useful way to avoid ageist language is to recognize illogical ageist stereotypes. How many of these stereotypes do you hold, perhaps mindlessly?

- *"Older people are mentally slow."* In fact most people remain mentally alert well into old age. Avoid talking down to a person because he or she is older.
- *"Older people can't remember anything."* They can remember, and they do. So don't assume you have to refresh their memory each time you see them.
- *"Older people are not interested in relationships."* They are. Avoid implying that what was important earlier is now no longer.
- *"Older people all are hard of hearing and visually impaired."* Most older people hear and see quite well, sometimes with hearing aids or glasses. Don't speak at an abnormally high volume or maintain an overly close physical distance.
- *"Older people are not interested in the world around them."* They are. Engage them in conversation as you would wish to be engaged.

Of course, although you want to avoid ageist communication, there are times when you may wish to make adjustments in your communication when talking with older people who do have language or communication difficulties. The American Speech and Hearing Association offers several useful suggestions (http://www.asha.org/speech/development/communicating-better-with-older-people.htm, accessed January 31, 2003):

- Reduce as much background noise as you can.
- Ease into the conversation; begin with familiar, casual topics and then move into more unfamiliar topics. Stay with each topic for a while; avoid jumping too quickly from one idea to another.
- Speak in relatively short sentences and questions.
- Give the person added time to respond. Some older people react more slowly and need extra time.
- Listen actively. Practice the skills of active listening discussed in Chapter 5.

## Sexist, Heterosexist, Racist, and Ageist Listening

Just as sexist, heterosexist, racist, and ageist attitudes will influence your language, they also can influence your listening. In this type of listening you hear what the speaker is saying through the stereotypes you hold; you listen differently to a person because of his or her gender, affectional orientation, race, or age even when these characteristics are irrelevant to the message.

Sexist, heterosexist, racist, and ageist listening occur in a wide variety of situations. For example, when you dismiss a valid argument or attribute validity to an invalid argument because the speaker is of a particular gender, affectional orientation, race, or age, you're listening with prejudice.

To be sure, there are instances in which these characteristics are relevant and pertinent to your evaluation of the message. For example, the gender of a speaker talking about pregnancy, fathering a child, or birth control is, most would agree, probably relevant to the message. In such cases it is not sexist to take the gender of the speaker into consideration. It is, however, sexist to assume that only a member of one gender can be an authority on a particular topic or that the opinions of all members of one gender are without value. The same is true of listening that is influenced by stereotypes about affectional orientation, race, or age.

## Reviewing Key Terms and Concepts in Verbal Messages

This chapter covered some of the barriers to effective interpersonal communication.

### Language Symbolizes Reality

What is intensional orientation, and how can you combat it? What is allness, and how can you correct it?

- Intensional orientation is the tendency to view the world in the way it's talked about or labeled. To combat intensional orientation, respond to things first; look for the labels second.
- Allness is the tendency to describe the world in extreme terms that imply one knows all or is saying all there is to say. To combat allness, remind yourself that you can never know all or say all about anything; use a mental and sometimes verbal "etc."

### Language Expresses Both Facts and Inferences

How do facts and inferences differ? How can you distinguish them more clearly?

- Fact–inference confusion is the tendency to confuse factual and inferential statements and to respond to inferences as if they were facts.
- To combat such confusions, distinguish facts from inferences and respond to inferences as inferences, not as facts.

### Language Expresses Both Denotation and Connotation

What is the difference between denotation and connotation?

- The denotative meaning is the dictionarylike, objective meaning of a word or sentence.
- Connotation is the subjective and personal meaning of a word or sentence.

### Language Can Criticize and Praise

How can you more effectively communicate both criticism and praise?

- Excessive criticism or praise is talk that is basically dishonest and in many instances manipulative.
- The principle of honest appraisal calls for saying what you feel, but gently and kindly.

### Language Can Obscure Distinctions

What are indiscrimination and ethnocentrism, and how can you reduce them? What is polarization, and what can you do to eliminate it? What is static evaluation, and how can you eliminate it?

- Indiscrimination is the tendency to group unique individuals or items because they're covered by the same term or label.

To combat indiscrimination, recognize uniqueness, and index each individual in a group (teacher$_1$, teacher$_2$).

- Polarization is the tendency to describe the world in terms of extremes or polar opposites. To combat polarization use middle terms and qualifiers.
- Static evaluation is the tendency to describe the world in static terms, denying constant change. To combat static evaluation, recognize the inevitability of change; date statements and evaluations, realizing, for example, that Gerry Smith$_{2002}$ is not Gerry Smith$_{2006}$.

## Language Can Confirm and Disconfirm

What are disconfirmation and confirmation (and the related sexist, heterosexist, racist and ageist communications)?

- Disconfirmation is communication that ignores another, that denies the other person's definition of self.
- Confirmation expresses acknowledgment and acceptance of others and avoids sexist, heterosexist, racist, and ageist expressions that are disconfirming.

## Applying Key Terms and Concepts in Verbal Messages

**1** Do the media give greater attention to ideas phrased in extremes than to ideas phrased more logically as somewhere between the extremes? What are the implications of this?

**2** Visualize yourself seated with a packet of photographs of strangers before you. You're asked to scratch out the eyes in each photograph. As you go through the photos, scratching out the eyes, you come upon a photograph of your mother. Are you able to scratch out the eyes as you have done with the pictures of the strangers? Are you responding intensionally or extensionally?

**3** What cultural identifiers do you prefer people to use in relation to you? How can you let other people know the cultural descriptions that you want them to use?

**4** Describe a situation in which someone committed indiscrimination against you or someone you know by assuming that you (or a person you know) believed something or behaved in a particular way because of gender, race, nationality, religion, or affectional orientation.

**5** Do you agree with the proposition that everyone is ethnocentric to some degree? If so, where would you place yourself on the ethnocentric continuum when the "other" is a person of the opposite sex? A person of a different affectional orientation? A person of a different race? A person of a different religion?

**6** Watch television for one evening and try to identify as many as possible of the misevaluations (or conceptual distortions) discussed in this chapter. Try to find at least one example of intensional orientation, allness, fact–inference confusion, indiscrimination, polarization, and static evaluation. How are these resolved in the sitcom or drama?

## Experiencing Key Terms and Concepts in Verbal Messages

Go to www.ablongman.com/devito.

*This group of experiences deals with verbal messages and ways to use such messages more critically.*

❶ **Identifying the Barriers to Communication** provides a dialogue containing the various barriers discussed in this chapter. ❷ **How Do You Talk? As a Woman? As a Man?** and ❸ **Recognizing Gender Differences** look at gender differences in language and at our perceptions of the speech of others. ❹ **Thinking with E-Prime** focuses on the difficulties that can be created when you use and think with the verbal "to be." ❺ **How Do You Talk about the Middle?** illustrates the ways in which our language makes it easy to polarize. ❻ **Confirming, Rejecting, and Disconfirming** looks at specific examples of these varied messages. ❼ **"Must Lie" Situations** examines scenarios in which many people would consider it ethical, even necessary, to lie.

# Nonverbal Messages

*House of Flying Daggers* (2004)
With little plot, *House of Flying Daggers* engages you with its visual display. It is the power of the nonverbal messages that maintains your interest and attention—much as it does in interpersonal communication, the subject of this chapter.

> **"What we learn only through the ears makes less impression upon our minds than what is presented to the trustworthy eye."** —Horace

**Nonverbal communication** is communication without words. You communicate nonverbally when you gesture, smile or frown, widen your eyes, move your chair closer to someone, wear jewelry, touch someone, or raise your vocal volume, or even when you say nothing. The crucial aspect of nonverbal communication is that the message you send is in some way received by one or more other people. If you gesture while alone in your room and no one is there to see you, then, most theorists would argue, communication has not taken place. The same, of course, is true of verbal messages: If you recite a speech and no one hears it, then communication has not taken place.

Your ability to use nonverbal communication effectively can yield two major benefits (Burgoon & Hoobler, 2002). First, the greater your ability to send and receive nonverbal signals, the higher your attraction, popularity, and psychosocial well-being are likely to be. Second, the greater your nonverbal skills, the more successful you're likely to be at influencing (or deceiving) others. Skilled nonverbal communicators are highly persuasive; this persuasive power can be used to help or support another or it can be used to deceive and fool.

Research shows that women are the better senders and receivers of nonverbal messages (Hall, 1998; Burgoon & Hoobler, 2002). Although this superiority does not hold in all contexts, it does hold in most. For example, in a review of 21 research studies, 71 percent found women to be superior nonverbal senders. And in a review of 61 studies on decoding, 84 percent found women superior receivers (Hall, 1998).

##  NONVERBAL COMMUNICATION FUNCTIONS

Although nonverbal communication serves the same general functions as verbal communication, several specific functions have been singled out by nonverbal researchers as especially significant: (1) impression management, (2) forming and defining relationships, (3) structuring conversation, (4) influencing, and (5) expressing emotions (Burgoon, Buller, & Woodall, 1996; Burgoon & Hoobler, 2002).

### Impression Formation and Management

It is largely through the nonverbal communications of others that you form impressions of them. Based on a person's body size, skin color, and dress, as well as the way the person smiles, maintains eye contact, and expresses himself or herself facially, you form impressions—you judge who the person is and what the person is like. One nonverbal researcher argues that these impressions may be grouped into four categories:

- credibility, or how competent and believable you find the person
- likability, or how much you like or dislike the person
- attractiveness, or how physically appealing you find the person
- dominance, or how powerful the individual is (Leathers, 1997)

Of course, you reveal yourself largely through the same nonverbal signals you use to size up others. But not only do you communicate your true self nonverbally; you also manage the impression that you present to others, perhaps endeavoring to appear brave when you're really scared or happy when you're really sad.

## Forming and Defining Relationships

Much of your relationship life is lived nonverbally. Largely through your nonverbal signals, you communicate your relationship to another person and that person communicates nonverbally to you. Holding hands, looking longingly into each other's eyes, and even dressing alike are ways in which you communicate closeness in your interpersonal relationships.

You also use nonverbal signals to communicate your relationship dominance and status (Knapp & Hall, 2002). A large corner office with a huge desk communicates high status, just as a basement cubicle communicates low status.

## Structuring Conversation and Social Interaction

When you're in conversation, you give and receive turn-taking cues—signals that you're ready to speak, to listen, to comment on what the speaker just said. It is these cues that regulate and structure the interaction. Turn-taking cues may be verbal (as when you say, "What do you think?") but most often they're nonverbal; a nod of the head in the direction of someone else, for example, signals that you're ready to give up your speaking turn and want the other person to say something.

You also show that you're listening and that you want the conversation to continue (or that you're not listening and want the conversation to end) largely through nonverbal signals.

## Influence

Much as you influence others by what you say, you also influence others by your nonverbal signals. A focused glance that says you're committed, gestures that further explain what you're saying, and appropriate dress that says, "I'll easily fit in with this company" are a few examples of how you influence others with nonverbal signals.

And, of course, with the ability to influence comes the ability to deceive—to lie, to mislead another person into thinking something is true when it's false or that something is false when it's true. Using your eyes and facial expressions to communicate a liking for other people when you're really interested only in gaining their support for your promotion is an often-seen example of nonverbal deception. Not surprisingly, you also use nonverbal signals to detect deception in others. For example, you may suspect a person of lying if he or she avoids eye contact, fidgets, or uses inconsistent verbal and nonverbal messages.

## Emotional Expression

Although **emotions** are often explained and revealed verbally, nonverbal expressions communicate a great part of your emotional experience. It is largely through facial expressions that you reveal your level of happiness or sadness or confusion, for example. Of course, you also reveal your feelings by posture (for example, whether tense or relaxed), gestures, and eye movements—and even by the extent to which your pupils dilate.

People often use nonverbal messages to communicate unpleasant messages—messages they might feel uncomfortable saying in words (Infante, Rancer, & Womack, 2003). For example, you might avoid eye contact and maintain large distances between yourself and someone with whom you don't want to interact, or with whom you want to decrease the intensity of your relationship.

# NONVERBAL COMMUNICATION CHANNELS

Focusing on the channels of nonverbal communication, we can distinguish a wide variety of nonverbal messages. Let's look in detail at each nonverbal channel: (1) body communication, (2) facial communication, (3) eye communication, (4) touch communication, (5) paralanguage and silence, (6) spatial messages, (7) artifactual communication, and (8) temporal communication.

## Body Communication

Generally, we can consider body communication in two parts—the gestures you make with your body and your body's appearance.

**Body Gestures**     An especially useful classification in **kinesics,** or the study of communication through body movement, identifies five types: emblems, illustrators, affect displays, regulators, and adaptors (Ekman & Friesen, 1969). Table 8.1 summarizes and provides examples of these five types of movements.

**Emblems**     **Emblems** are substitutes for words; they're body movements that have rather specific verbal translations, such as the nonverbal signs for "OK," "Peace," "Come here," "Go away," "Who, me?" "Be quiet," "I'm warning you," "I'm tired," and "It's cold." Emblems are as arbitrary as any words in any language. Consequently, your present culture's emblems are not necessarily the same as your culture's emblems of 300 years ago or the same as the emblems of other cultures. For example, the sign made by forming a circle with the thumb and index finger may mean "nothing" or "zero" in France, "money" in Japan, and something sexual in certain southern European cultures. But just as the English language is spreading throughout the world, so, too, is the English nonverbal language. The American use of this emblem to mean "OK" is spreading as fast, for example, as English technical and scientific terms.

**Illustrators**     **Illustrators** accompany and literally illustrate verbal messages. Illustrators make your communications more vivid and help to maintain your listener's attention. They

 **TABLE 8.1**
### Five Types of Body Movements

Can you identify similar gestures that mean different things in different cultures and that might create interpersonal misunderstandings?

| | Name and Function | Examples |
|---|---|---|
| | **Emblems** directly translate words or phrases. | "OK" sign, "Come here" wave, hitchhiker's sign |
| | **Illustrators** accompany and literally "illustrate" verbal messages. | Circular hand movements when talking of a circle, hands far apart when talking of something large |
| | **Affect displays** communicate emotional meaning. | Expressions of happiness, surprise, fear, anger, sadness, disgust |
| | **Regulators** monitor, maintain, or control the speaking of another. | Facial expressions and hand gestures indicating "Keep going," "Slow down," or "What else happened?" |
| | **Adaptors** satisfy some need. | Scratching head |

also help to clarify and intensify your verbal messages. In saying, "Let's go up," for example, you probably move your head and perhaps your finger in an upward direction. In describing a circle or a square, you more than likely make circular or square movements with your hands. Research points to another advantage of illustrators: that they increase your ability to remember. People who illustrated their verbal messages with gestures remembered some 20 percent more than those who didn't gesture (Goldin-Meadow, Nusbaum, Kelly, & Wagner, 2001).

We are aware of illustrators only part of the time; at times, they may have to be brought to our attention. Illustrators are more universal than emblems; illustrators will be recognized and understood by members of more different cultures than will emblems.

**Affect Displays** **Affect displays** are the movements of the face that convey emotional meaning—the expressions that show anger and fear, happiness and surprise, eagerness and fatigue. They're the facial expressions that give you away when you try to present a false image and that lead people to say, "You look angry. What's wrong?" We can, however, consciously control affect displays, as actors do when they play a role. Affect displays may be unintentional (as when they give you away) or intentional (as when you want to show anger, love, or surprise). A particular kind of affect display is the poker player's "tell," a bit of nonverbal behavior that communicates bluffing; it's a nonverbal cue that tells others that a player is lying. In much the same way that you may want to conceal certain feelings from friends or relatives, the poker player tries to conceal any such tells.

**Regulators** **Regulators** monitor, maintain, or control the speaking of another individual. When you listen to another, you're not passive; you nod your head, purse your lips, adjust your eye focus, and make various paralinguistic sounds such as "mm-mm" or "tsk." Regulators are culture-bound: Each culture develops its own rules for the regulation of conversation. Regulators also include such broad movements as shaking your head to show disbelief or leaning forward in your chair to show that you want to hear more.

Regulators communicate what you expect or want speakers to do as they're talking: for example, "Keep going," "Tell me what else happened," "I don't believe that. Are you sure?" "Speed up," and "Slow down." Speakers often receive these nonverbal signals without being consciously aware of them. Depending on their degree of sensitivity, speakers modify their speaking behavior in accordance with these regulators.

**Adaptors** **Adaptors** satisfy some need and usually occur without conscious awareness; they're unintentional movements that usually go unnoticed. Nonverbal researchers identify three types of adaptors based on their focus, direction, or target: self-adaptors, alter-adaptors, and object-adaptors (Burgoon, Buller, & Woodall, 1996).

**Self-adaptors** usually satisfy a physical need, generally serving to make you more comfortable; examples include scratching your head to relieve an itch, moistening your lips because they feel dry, or pushing your hair out of your eyes. When these adaptors occur in private, they occur in their entirety: You scratch until the itch is gone. But in public these adaptors usually occur in abbreviated form. When people are watching you, for example, you might put your fingers to your head and move them around a bit but probably not scratch with the same vigor as when in private.

**Alter-adaptors** are the body movements you make in response to your current interactions. Examples include crossing your arms over your chest when someone unpleasant approaches or moving closer to someone you like.

**Object-adaptors** are movements that involve your manipulation of some object. Frequently observed examples include punching holes in or drawing on a styrofoam coffee cup, clicking a ballpoint pen, or chewing on a pencil. Object-adaptors are usually signs of negative feelings; for example, you emit more adaptors when feeling hostile than when feeling friendly. Further, as anxiety and uneasiness increase, so does the frequency of object-adaptors (Burgoon, Buller, & Woodall, 1996).

**Body Appearance** Of course, the body communicates even without movement. For example, others may form impressions of you from your general body build; from your height and weight; and from your skin, eye, and hair color. Assessments of your power, your attractiveness, and your suitability as a friend or romantic partner are often made on the basis of your body appearance (Sheppard & Strathman, 1989).

Height, for example, is significant in a wide variety of situations. Tall presidential candidates have a much better record of winning elections than do their shorter opponents. Tall people seem to be paid more and are favored by interviewers over shorter applicants (Keyes, 1980; Guerrero, DeVito, & Hecht, 1999; Knapp & Hall, 2002; Jackson & Ervin, 1992). Taller people also have higher self-esteem and greater career success than do shorter people (Judge & Cable, 2004).

Your body reveals your race, through skin color and tone, and also may give clues as to your more specific nationality. Your weight in proportion to your height will communicate messages to others, as will the length, color, and style of your hair.

**⬆ VIEWPOINT**

On a 10-point scale, with 1 indicating "not at all important" and 10 indicating "extremely important," how important is body appearance to your own romantic interest in another person? Do the men and women you know conform to the stereotypes that say males are more concerned with the physical and females more concerned with personality?

Your general attractiveness also is a part of body communication. Attractive people have the advantage in just about every activity you can name. They get better grades in school, are more valued as friends and lovers, and are preferred as coworkers (Burgoon, Buller, & Woodall, 1996). Although we normally think that attractiveness is culturally determined—and to some degree it is—research seems to indicate that definitions of attractiveness are becoming universal (Brody, 1994). That is, a person rated as attractive in one culture is likely to be rated as attractive in other cultures—even in cultures whose people are widely different in appearance.

## Facial Communication

Throughout your interpersonal interactions, your face communicates, especially signaling your emotions. In fact, facial movements alone seem to communicate the degree of pleasantness, agreement, and sympathy a person feels; the rest of the body doesn't provide any additional information. For other aspects, however—for example, the intensity with which an emotion is felt—both facial and bodily cues are used (Graham, Bitti, & Argyle, 1975; Graham & Argyle, 1975).

Some nonverbal communication researchers claim that facial movements may communicate at least the following eight emotions: happiness, surprise, fear, anger, sadness, disgust, contempt, and interest (Ekman, Friesen, & Ellsworth, 1972). Others propose that, in addition, facial movements may communicate bewilderment and determination (Leathers, 1997).

Try to communicate surprise using only facial movements. Do this in front of a mirror, and try to describe in as much detail as possible the specific movements of the face that make up surprise. If you signal surprise as most people do, you probably exhibit raised and curved eyebrows, long horizontal forehead wrinkles, wide-open eyes, dropped-open mouth, and lips parted with no tension. Even if there were differences—and clearly there would be from one person to another—you could probably recognize the movements listed here as indicative of surprise.

Of course, some emotions are easier to communicate and to decode than others. For example, in one study, happiness was judged with an accuracy ranging from 55 percent to 100 percent, surprise from 38 percent to 86 percent, and sadness from 19 percent to 88 percent (Ekman, Friesen, & Ellsworth, 1972). Research finds that women and girls are more accurate judges of facial emotional expression than men and boys (Hall, 1984; Argyle, 1988).

As you've probably experienced, you may interpret the same facial expression differently depending on the context in which it occurs. For example, in a classic study, when a smiling face was presented looking at a glum face, the smiling face was judged to be vicious and taunting. But, when the same smiling face was presented looking at a frowning face, it was judged peaceful and friendly (Cline, 1956). In general, not surprisingly, people who smile are judged to be more likable and more approachable than people who don't smile or people who pretend to smile (Gladstone & Parker, 2002; Kluger, 2005).

**Facial Management**    As you learned the nonverbal system of communication, you also learned certain **facial management techniques** that enable you to communicate your feelings to achieve the effect you want—for example, to hide certain emotions and to emphasize others. Consider your own use of such facial management techniques. As you do so, think about the types of interpersonal situations in which you would use each of these facial management techniques (Malandro, Barker, & Barker, 1989; Metts & Planalp, 2002). Would you

- *intensify*, as when you exaggerate surprise when friends throw you a party to make your friends feel better?
- *deintensify*, as when you cover up your own joy in the presence of a friend who didn't receive such good news?
- *neutralize*, as when you cover up your sadness to keep from depressing others?
- *mask*, as when you express happiness in order to cover up your disappointment at not receiving the gift you expected?
- *simulate*, as when you express an emotion you don't feel?

These facial management techniques help you display emotions in socially acceptable ways. For example, when someone gets bad news in which you may secretly take pleasure,

the display rule dictates that you frown and otherwise nonverbally signal your sorrow. If you place first in a race and your best friend barely finishes, the display rule requires that you minimize your expression of pleasure in winning and avoid any signs of gloating. If you violate these display rules, you'll be judged as insensitive. So although facial management techniques may be deceptive, they're also expected—and, in fact, required by the rules of polite interaction.

**Facial Feedback**    In one interesting study, participants held a pen in their teeth to simulate a sad expression. They then rated photographs. Results showed that mimicking sad expressions actually increased the degree of sadness the subjects reported feeling when viewing the photographs (Larsen, Kasimatis, & Frey, 1992). This finding is an example of the **facial feedback hypothesis**, which holds that your facial expression influences physiological arousal (Lanzetta, Cartwright-Smith, & Kleck, 1976; Zuckerman, Klorman, Larrance, & Spiegel, 1981).

Further support for this hypothesis comes from a study that compared participants who feel emotions such as happiness and anger with those who both feel and express these emotions. In support of the facial feedback hypothesis, subjects who felt and expressed the emotions became emotionally aroused faster than did those who only felt the emotion (Hess, Kappas, McHugo, & Lanzetta, 1992). So not only does your facial expression influence the judgments and impressions that others have of you; it also influences your level of emotional arousal (Cappella, 1993).

# Eye Communication

The messages communicated by the eyes vary depending on the duration, direction, and quality of the eye behavior. For example, in every culture there are rather strict, though unstated, rules for the proper duration for eye contact. In much of England and the United States, for example, the average length of gaze is 2.95 seconds. The average length of mutual gaze (two persons gazing at each other) is 1.18 seconds (Argyle, 1988; Argyle & Ingham, 1972). When the duration of eye contact is shorter than 1.18 seconds, you may think the person is uninterested, shy, or preoccupied. When the appropriate amount of time is exceeded, you may perceive this as showing high interest.

In much of the United States direct eye contact is considered an expression of honesty and forthrightness. But the Japanese often view eye contact as a lack of respect. The Japanese will glance at the other person's face rarely and then only for very short periods (Axtell, 1994). In many Hispanic cultures, direct eye contact signifies a certain equality and so should be avoided by, say, children when speaking to a person in authority. Try visualizing the potential misunderstandings that eye communication alone could create when people from Tokyo, San Francisco, and San Juan try to communicate.

The direction of the eye also communicates. Generally, in communicating with another person, you will glance alternatively at the other person's face, then away, then again at the face, and so on. When these directional rules are broken, different meanings are communicated—abnormally high or low interest, self-consciousness, nervousness over the interaction, and so on. The quality of the gaze—how wide or how narrow your eyes get during interaction—also communicates meaning, especially interest level and such emotions as surprise, fear, and disgust.

**Eye Contact**   You use eye contact to serve several important functions (Knapp & Hall, 1992; Malandro, Barker, & Barker, 1989; Marshall, 1983; Marsh, 1988). You can use eye contact to *monitor feedback*. For example, when you talk with someone, you look at the person intently, as if to say, "Well, what do you think?" or "React to what I've just said." You also look at speakers to let them know that you're listening. Studies show that listeners gaze at speakers more than speakers gaze at listeners (Knapp & Hall, 2002). The percentage of interaction time spent gazing while listening, for example, ranges from 62 percent to 75 percent; the percentage of time spent gazing while talking, however, ranges from 38 percent to 41 percent. When these percentages are reversed—when a speaker gazes at the listener for longer than "normal" periods or when a listener gazes at the speaker for shorter than "normal" periods—the conversational interaction becomes awkward. You may wish to try this with a friend. Even with mutual awareness, you'll notice the discomfort caused by this seemingly minor communication change.

When you speak with two or three other people, you maintain eye contact to *secure the attention and interest* of your listeners. When someone fails to pay the attention you want, you probably increase your eye contact, hoping your focus on this person will increase attention.

Eye communication also can *regulate or control the conversation*. For example, with eye movements you can inform the other person that the channel of communication is open and that she or he should now speak. A clear example of this occurs in the college classroom, where the instructor asks a question and then locks eyes with a student. Without any verbal message, it's assumed that the student should answer the question. Similarly, when you're nearing the end of what you want to say, you'll probably focus eye contact on the person you think wants to speak next and then turn over the conversation to that person.

Eye communication also helps to *signal the nature of the relationship* between two people—for example, to indicate positive or negative regard. In the United States, when you like someone, you increase your eye contact. When eye contact exceeds 60 percent in an interaction, the people are probably more interested in each other than in the verbal messages being exchanged (Argyle, 1988). Some researchers note that eye contact serves to enable gay men and lesbians to signal their homosexuality and perhaps their interest in someone—an ability referred to as "gaydar" (Nicholas, 2004).

**SPEAKING**
**>> Interpersonal-E**

**Immediacy.** How would you establish psychological closeness in face-to-face and in computer-mediated communication? After you've developed your responses, take a look at O'Sullivan, Hunt, and Lippert (2004).

Eye contact in humans (and in other higher primates) is often used to *signal status and aggression*. Among many younger people, prolonged eye contact from a stranger is taken to signify aggressiveness and frequently prompts physical violence—merely because one person looked perhaps a little longer than was considered normal in that specific culture (Matsumoto, 1996). A less extreme way to assert one's position is with **visual dominance** behavior (Exline, Ellyson, & Long, 1975). As mentioned earlier, the average person maintains a higher level of eye contact while listening and a lower level while speaking. When people want to signal dominance, they may reverse this pattern and maintain a high level of eye contact while talking but a much lower level while listening. If you visualize a manager criticizing a subordinate, you'll probably picture the manager maintaining direct eye contact with the subordinate while criticizing—and maintaining little eye contact when listening to excuses he or she considers inadequate. Another way people try to signal dominance is to lower their eyebrows. Research does support this general interpretation of the behavior. For example, faces with lowered eyebrows, in both cartoons and photographs, were judged to communicate greater dominance than faces with raised eyebrows (Keating, Mazur, & Segall, 1977). Eye movements also may signal whether the relationship between two people is amorous, hostile, or indifferent.

Eye movements are often used to *compensate for increased physical distance*. By making eye contact we overcome psychologically the physical distance between us. When we catch someone's eye at a party, for example, we become psychologically close even though we may be separated by considerable physical distance. Eye contact and other expressions of psychological closeness, such as self-disclosure and intimacy, have been found to vary in proportion to each other.

**Eye Avoidance** The eyes, sociologist Erving Goffman observed in *Interaction Ritual* (1967), are "great intruders." When you avoid eye contact or avert your glance, you allow

# Understanding Interpersonal Skills
## IMMEDIACY

**Immediacy** is the creation of a sense of togetherness, of oneness, between speaker and listener. When you communicate immediacy you convey a sense of interest and attention, a liking for and an attraction to the other person. People respond to communication that is immediate more favorably than to communication that is not. There is much evidence demonstrating the effectiveness of immediacy in a variety of communication situations (Moore, Masterson, Christophel, & Shea, 1996; Witt & Wheeless, 2001; Wilson & Taylor, 2001; Baringer & McCroskey, 2000).

**Communicating Immediacy.** Here are a few suggestions for communicating immediacy.

- Express psychological closeness and openness by, for example, maintaining physical closeness and arranging your body to exclude third parties. Maintain appropriate eye contact and limit looking around at others.
- Smile and express your interest in the other person.
- Use the other person's name: for example, say, "Joe, what do you think?" instead of "What do you think?"
- Focus on the other person's remarks. Make the speaker know that you heard and understood what was said, and give the speaker appropriate verbal and nonverbal feedback.
- Express immediacy with cultural sensitivity. In the United States immediacy behaviors are generally seen as friendly and appropriate. In other cultures, however, the same immediacy behaviors may be viewed as overly familiar—as presuming that a relationship is close when only acquaintanceship exists (Axtell, 1994).

others to maintain their privacy. You probably do this when you see a couple arguing in the street or on a bus. You turn your eyes away, as if to say, "I don't mean to intrude; I respect your privacy." Goffman refers to this behavior as **civil inattention.**

Eye avoidance also can signal lack of interest—in a person, a conversation, or some visual stimulus. At times, like the ostrich, we hide our eyes to try to cut off unpleasant stimuli. Notice, for example, how quickly people close their eyes in the face of some extreme unpleasantness. Interestingly enough, even if the unpleasantness is auditory, we tend to shut it out by closing our eyes. At other times, we close our eyes to block out visual stimuli and thus to heighten our other senses; for example, we often listen to music with our eyes closed. Lovers often close their eyes while kissing, and many prefer to make love in a dark or dimly lit room.

**Pupil Dilation**    In the fifteenth and sixteenth centuries, Italian women used to put drops of belladonna (which literally means "beautiful woman") into their eyes to enlarge the pupils so that they would look more attractive. Research in the field of **pupillometrics** supports the intuitive logic of these women: Dilated pupils are in fact judged more attractive than constricted ones (Hess, 1975; Marshall, 1983).

In one study, for example, photographs of women were retouched (Hess, 1975). In one set of photographs the pupils were enlarged, and in the other they were made smaller. Men were then asked to judge the women's personalities from the photographs. The photos of women with small pupils drew responses such as cold, hard, and selfish; those with dilated pupils drew responses such as feminine and soft. However, the male observers could not verbalize the reasons for the different perceptions. Both **pupil dilation** itself and people's reactions to changes in the pupil size of others seem to function below the level of conscious awareness.

Pupil size also reveals your interest and level of emotional arousal. Your pupils enlarge when you're interested in something or when you're emotionally aroused. When homosexuals and heterosexuals were shown pictures of nude bodies, the homosexuals' pupils dilated more when viewing same-sex bodies, whereas the heterosexuals' pupils dilated more when viewing opposite-sex bodies (Hess, Seltzer, & Schlien, 1965). These pupillary responses are unconscious and are even observed in persons with profound mental retardation (Chaney, Givens, Aoki, & Gombiner, 1989). Perhaps we find dilated pupils more attractive because we judge them as indicative of a person's interest in us. That may be why models, Beanie Babies, and Teletubbies have exceptionally large pupils.

Although belladonna is no longer used, the cosmetics industry has made millions selling eye enhancers—eye shadow, eyeliner, false eyelashes, and tinted contact lenses that change eye color. These items function (ideally, at least) to draw attention to these most powerful communicators.

## Touch Communication

**Tactile communication** or communication by touch, also referred to as **haptics,** is perhaps the most primitive form of communication. Developmentally, touch is probably the first sense to be used; even in the womb, the child is stimulated by touch. Soon after birth the child is fondled, caressed, patted, and stroked. In turn, the child explores its world through touch. In a very short time, the child learns to communicate a wide variety of meanings through touch. Not surprisingly, touch also varies with your relationship stage. In the early stages of a relationship, you touch little; in intermediate stages (involvement and intimacy), you touch a great deal; and at stable or deteriorating stages, you again touch little (Guerrero & Andersen, 1991).

**The Meanings of Touch**    Touch may communicate five major meanings (Jones & Yarbrough, 1985). *Positive emotions* may be communicated by touch, mainly between intimates or others who have a relatively close relationship. Among the most important of

**ASK Yourself**
Touching

Your supervisor touches just about everyone. You don't like it and want it to stop—at least as far as you're concerned.   Ask yourself:  What are some ways you can nonverbally show your aversion to this unwanted touching?

these positive emotions are support, appreciation, inclusion, sexual interest or intent, and affection. Additional research found that touch communicated such positive feelings as composure, immediacy, trust, similarity and quality, and informality (Burgoon, 1991). Touch also has been found to facilitate self-disclosure (Rabinowitz, 1991).

Touch often communicates *playfulness,* either affectionately or aggressively. When touch is used in this manner, the playfulness deemphasizes the emotion and tells the other person that it's not to be taken seriously. Playful touches lighten an interaction.

Touch also may *control* the behaviors, attitudes, or feelings of the other person. Such control may communicate various different kinds of messages. To ask for compliance, for example, we touch the other person to communicate "Move over," "Hurry," "Stay here," or "Do it." Touching to control may also communicate status and dominance (Henley, 1977; DiBaise & Gunnoe, 2004). The higher-status and dominant person, for example, initiates touch. In fact, it would be a breach of etiquette for the lower-status person to touch the person of higher status.

*Ritualistic* touching centers on greetings and departures. Shaking hands to say hello or goodbye is perhaps the clearest example of ritualistic touching, but we might also hug, kiss, or put an arm around another's shoulder.

*Task-related* touching is associated with the performance of a function, such as removing a speck of dust from another person's face, helping someone out of a car, or checking someone's forehead for fever. Task-related touching seems generally to be regarded positively. In studies on the subject, for example, book borrowers had a more positive attitude toward the library and the librarian when touched lightly, and customers gave larger tips when lightly touched by the waitress (Marsh, 1988). Similarly, diners who were touched on the shoulder or hand when being given their change in a restaurant tipped more than diners who were not touched (Crusco & Wetzel, 1984; Stephen & Zweigenhaft, 1986).

**Touch Avoidance**   Much as we have a need and desire to touch and be touched by others, we also have a tendency to avoid touch from certain people or in certain circumstances (Andersen & Leibowitz, 1978). Before reading about the research findings on **touch avoidance,** you may wish to take the accompanying touch avoidance self-test.

# TEST YOURSELF
## DO YOU AVOID TOUCH?

This instrument is composed of 18 statements concerning how you feel about touching other people and being touched. Please indicate the degree to which each statement applies to you by indicating whether you: 1 = strongly agree, 2 = agree, 3 = are undecided, 4 = disagree, or 5 = strongly disagree.

_____ 1. A hug from a same-sex friend is a true sign of friendship.
_____ 2. Opposite-sex friends enjoy it when I touch them.
_____ 3. I often put my arm around friends of the same sex.
_____ 4. When I see two friends of the same sex hugging, it revolts me.
_____ 5. I like it when members of the opposite sex touch me.

_____ 6. People shouldn't be so uptight about touching persons of the same sex.

_____ 7. I think it is vulgar when members of the opposite sex touch me.

_____ 8. When a member of the opposite sex touches me, I find it unpleasant.

_____ 9. I wish I were free to show emotions by touching members of the same sex.

_____ 10. I'd enjoy giving a massage to an opposite-sex friend.

_____ 11. I enjoy kissing a person of the same sex.

_____ 12. I like to touch friends that are the same sex as I am.

_____ 13. Touching a friend of the same sex does not make me uncomfortable.

_____ 14. I find it enjoyable when my date and I embrace.

_____ 15. I enjoy getting a back rub from a member of the opposite sex.

_____ 16. I dislike kissing relatives of the same sex.

_____ 17. Intimate touching with members of the opposite sex is pleasurable.

_____ 18. I find it difficult to be touched by a member of my own sex.

**HOW DID YOU DO?** To score your touch avoidance questionnaire:

1. Reverse your scores for items 4, 7, 8, 16, and 18. Use these reversed scores in all future calculations.
2. To obtain your same-sex touch avoidance score (the extent to which you avoid touching members of your sex), total the scores for items 1, 3, 4, 6, 9, 11, 12, 13, 16, and 18.
3. To obtain your opposite-sex touch avoidance score (the extent to which you avoid touching members of the opposite sex), total the scores for items 2, 5, 7, 8, 10, 14, 15, and 17.
4. To obtain your total touch avoidance score, add the subtotals from steps 2 and 3.

The higher the score, the higher the touch avoidance—that is, the greater your tendency to avoid touch. In studies by Andersen and Leibowitz (1978), who constructed this test, average opposite-sex touch avoidance scores were 12.9 for males and 14.85 for females. Average same-sex touch avoidance scores were 26.43 for males and 21.70 for females. How do your scores compare with the college students in Andersen and Leibowitz's research? Is your touch avoidance likely to be higher when interacting with persons who are culturally different from you? Can you identify types of people and types of situations in which your touch avoidance would be especially high? Especially low?

**WHAT WILL YOU DO?** Are you satisfied with your score? Would you like to change your touch avoidance tendencies? What might you do about them?

_Source:_ Adapted from Peter Andersen and Ken Liebowitz, "The Development and Nature of the Construct Touch Avoidance," _Environmental Psychology and Nonverbal Behavior_ 3 (1978):89–106. Copyright © 1978. Adapted with kind permission from Springer Science and Business Media.

Among the important findings is that touch avoidance is positively related to communication apprehension: People who fear oral communication also score high on touch avoidance. (You may wish to compare your scores on this touch avoidance test with your scores on the communication apprehension test presented in Chapter 3.) Touch avoidance also is high among those who self-disclose little; touch and self-disclosure are intimate forms of communication, and people who are reluctant to get close to another person by self-disclosure also seem reluctant to get close through touch.

Older people have higher touch avoidance scores for opposite-sex persons than do younger people. Apparently, as we get older we are touched less by members of the opposite sex, and this decreased frequency of touching may lead us to avoid touching. Males score higher than females on same-sex touch avoidance. This accords well with our stereotypes: Men avoid touching other men, but women may and do touch other women. Women, it is found, have higher touch avoidance scores for opposite-sex touching than do men.

## Paralanguage and Silence

Two aspects of nonverbal communication that are often considered together, because they involve manipulating sound, are paralanguage and silence. Let's consider paralanguage first.

**Paralanguage**   **Paralanguage** is the vocal but nonverbal dimension of speech. It has to do with the manner in which you say something rather than with what you say. An old exercise used to increase a student's ability to express different emotions, feelings, and attitudes was to have the student say the following sentence while accenting or stressing different words: "Is this the face that launched a thousand ships?" Significant differences in meaning are easily communicated, depending on where the stress is placed. Consider, for example, the following variations:

① *Is* this the face that launched a thousand ships?
② Is *this* the face that launched a thousand ships?
③ Is this the *face* that launched a thousand ships?
④ Is this the face that *launched* a thousand ships?
⑤ Is this the face that launched a *thousand ships*?

Each of these five sentences communicates something different. Each, in fact, asks a totally different question, even though the words used are identical. All that distinguishes the sentences is variation in stress, one of the aspects of paralanguage.

In addition to stress, paralanguage includes such vocal characteristics as **rate** and **volume.** Paralanguage also includes the vocalizations we make when laughing, yelling, moaning, whining, and belching; vocal segregates—sound combinations that aren't words—such as "uh-uh" and "shh"; and **pitch,** the highness or lowness of vocal tone (Argyle, 1988; Trager 1958, 1961).

A good way to appreciate the workings of paralanguage is to examine your own vocal behavior when communicating different meanings. Try reading each of the sentences below first to communicate praise and then to communicate criticism. What changes in your vocal expression communicate the differences in meaning?

1. Now that looks good on you.
2. That was some meal.
3. You're an expert.
4. You're so sensitive.
5. Are you ready?

**People Perception and Paralanguage**  When listening to people—regardless of what they're saying—we form impressions based on their paralanguage as to what kind of people they are. It does seem that certain voices are symptomatic of certain personality types or problems and, specifically, that the personality orientation gives rise to the vocal qualities. Our impressions from paralanguage cues span a broad range and consist of physical impressions (perhaps about body type and certainly about gender and age), personality impressions (they sound shy, they appear aggressive), and evaluative impressions (they sound like good people, they sound evil and menacing, they have vicious laughs).

One of the most interesting findings on voice and personal characteristics is that listeners can accurately judge the socioeconomic status (high, middle, or low) of speakers after hearing a 60-second voice sample. In fact, many listeners reported that they made their judgments in less than 15 seconds. It has also been found that the speakers judged to be of high status were rated as being of higher credibility than those rated of middle or low status.

It's interesting to note that listeners agree with one another about the personality of the speaker even when their judgments are in error. Listeners seem to have stereotyped ideas about the way vocal characteristics and personality characteristics are related, and they use these stereotypes in their judgments.

**Persuasion and Paralanguage**  The rate of speech is the aspect of paralanguage that has received the most research attention—because speech rate is related to persuasiveness. Therefore, it's of interest to the advertiser, the politician, and, anyone else who wants to convey information or to influence others orally, especially when time is limited or expensive. The research on rate of speech shows that in one-way communication situations, persons who talk fast are more persuasive and are evaluated more highly than those who talk at or below normal speeds (MacLachlan, 1979). This greater persuasiveness and higher regard holds true whether the person talks fast naturally or the speech is sped up electronically (as in time-compressed speech).

In one experiment, subjects were asked to listen to taped messages and then to indicate both the degree to which they agreed with the message and their opinions as to how intelligent and objective they thought the speaker was (MacLachlan, 1979). Rates of 111, 140, and 191 words per minute were used. (The average speaking rate is about 130 to 150 words per minute.) Subjects agreed most with the fastest speech and least with the slowest speech. Further, they rated the fastest speaker as the most intelligent and objective and the slowest speaker as the least intelligent and objective. Even in experiments in which the speaker was known to have something to gain personally from persuasion (as would, say, a salesperson), the speaker who spoke at the fastest rate was the most persuasive. Research also finds that faster speech rates increase listeners' perceptions of speaker competence and dominance (Buller, LePoire, Aune, & Eloy, 1992).

These general findings need to be qualified in two ways. First, there are cultural differences. For example, among Koreans the opposite effect was found: Male speakers who spoke rapidly were given unfavorable credibility ratings (Lee & Boster, 1992). Researchers have suggested that in individualist societies a rapid-rate speaker is seen as more competent than a slow-rate speaker, whereas in collectivist cultures a speaker who uses a slower rate is judged to be more competent.

SPEAKING
>> **Interpersonal-E**

**Adjusting Volume.**  Much as you have a preference for a certain volume of speech, you probably also have a preference for the size of computer screen text with which you're most comfortable. You can easily adjust the text size by going to View/Text Size/ and select your desired text size.

**Paralanguage.** When you are speaking and have lots to communicate in a short time, the best you can do is to increase your speech rate. When you have a lot to communicate electronically, you can significantly compress your files to reduce the time they take to send and receive and to reduce the amount of storage space they take up. For instructions on how to do this, see www.winzip.com.

Second, whether or not rapid speech rate is more persuasive depends on whether the speaker is speaking for or against your existing position (Smith & Shaffer, 1991, 1995). The rapid speaker who speaks *against* your existing attitudes is generally more effective than the speaker who speaks at a normal rate. But, the rapid speaker who speaks *in favor of* your existing attitudes (say, in an attempt to strengthen them) is actually less effective than the speaker who speaks at a normal rate. The reason for this is quite logical. In the case of the speaker speaking against your attitudes, the rapidity of speech doesn't give you the time you need to think of counterarguments to rebut the speaker's position. So you're more likely to be persuaded by the speaker's position, because you don't have the time to consider why the speaker may be incorrect. In the case of the speaker speaking in favor of your attitudes, the rapidity of speech doesn't give you the time you need to mentally elaborate on the speaker's arguments. Therefore, they don't carry as much persuasive force as they would if spoken more slowly, giving you the time to think of reasons to agree with the speaker.

Rapid speech also has the advantage in comprehension. Subjects who listened to speeches at 201 words per minute (about 140 is average) comprehended 95 percent of the message, and those who listened to speeches at 282 words per minute (that is, double the normal rate) comprehended 90 percent. Even though the rates increased dramatically, the comprehension rates fell only slightly. These 5 percent and 10 percent losses are more than offset by the increased speed and thus make the faster rates much more efficient in communicating information. If the speech speeds are increased more than 100 percent, however, comprehension falls dramatically.

Exercise caution in applying this research to your own interpersonal interactions (MacLachlan, 1979). Realize that while the speaker is speaking, the listener is generating and framing a reply. If the speaker talks too rapidly, there may not be enough time to compose this reply, and resentment may be generated. Furthermore, the increased rate may seem so unnatural that the listener may come to focus on the speed of speech rather than the thought expressed.

**Silence**    "Speech," wrote Thomas Mann, "is civilization itself. The word, even the most contradictory word, preserves contact; it's silence which isolates." Philosopher Karl Jaspers, on the other hand, observed that "the ultimate in thinking as in communication is silence," and philosopher Max Picard noted that "silence is nothing merely negative; it's not the mere absence of speech. It's a positive, a complete world in itself."

# Ethics in Interpersonal Communication

## INTERPERSONAL SILENCE

In the U.S. legal system you have the right to remain silent and to refuse to incriminate yourself. But you don't have the right to refuse to reveal information about the criminal activities of others that you may have witnessed. Rightly or wrongly, however (and this in itself is an ethical issue), psychiatrists and lawyers are often exempt from this general rule. Similarly, a wife can't be forced to testify against her husband nor a husband against his wife.

But in interpersonal situations there aren't any written rules, so it's not always clear if or when silence is ethical. For example, most people (but not all) would agree that you have the right to withhold information that has no bearing on the matter at hand. Thus, your previous relationship history, affectional orientation, or religion is usually irrelevant to your ability to function as a doctor or police officer and may thus be kept private in most job-related situations.

### What would you do?

At the supermarket you witness a mother who is verbally abusing her small child. Your first impulse is to speak up and tell this woman that verbal abuse can have lasting effects on the child and often leads to physical abuse. At the same time, you don't want to interfere with a mother's right to say what she wants to her child; nor do you want to aggravate a mother who may later take out her frustration on the child. What is your ethical obligation in this case? What would you do in this situation?

The one thing on which these contradictory observations agree is that **silence** communicates. Your silence communicates just as intensely as anything you verbalize (see Jaworski, 1993). Like words and gestures, silence serves important communication functions. Silence allows the speaker *time to think,* time to formulate and organize his or her verbal communications. Before messages of intense conflict, as well as those confessing undying love, there is often silence. Again, silence seems to prepare the receiver for the importance of these future messages.

Some people use silence as a weapon *to hurt* others. We often speak of giving someone "the silent treatment." After a conflict, for example, one or both individuals might remain silent as a kind of punishment. Silence used to hurt others also may take the form of refusing to acknowledge the presence of another person, as in disconfirmation (see Chapter 7); here silence is a dramatic demonstration of the total indifference one person feels toward the other.

Sometimes silence is used as a *response to personal anxiety,* shyness, or threats. You may feel anxious or shy among new people and prefer to remain silent. By remaining silent you preclude the chance of rejection. Only when you break your silence and attempt to communicate with another person do you risk rejection.

Silence may be used *to prevent communication* of certain messages. In conflict situations, silence is sometimes used to prevent certain topics from surfacing and to prevent one or both parties from saying things they may later regret. In such situations, silence often allows us time to cool off before expressing hatred, severe criticism, or personal attacks that we know are irreversible.

Like the eyes, face, or hands, silence can also be used to *communicate emotional responses* (Ehrenhaus, 1988). Sometimes silence communicates a determination to be uncooperative or defiant; by refusing to engage in verbal communication, you defy the authority or the legitimacy of the other person's position. Silence is often used to communicate annoyance, usually accompanied by a pouting expression, arms crossed in front of the chest, and nostrils flared. Silence may express affection or love, especially when coupled with long and longing gazes into each other's eyes.

Silence may also be used strategically, to *achieve specific effects.* The pause before making what you feel is an important comment or after hearing about some mishap may be strategically positioned to communicate a desired impression—to make your idea stand out among others or perhaps to give others the impression that you care a lot more than you really do. In some cases a prolonged silence after someone voices disagreement may give the appearance of control and superiority. It's a way of saying, "I can respond in my own time." Generally, research finds that people use silence strategically more with strangers than they do with close friends (Hasegawa & Gudykunst, 1998).

Of course, you also may use silence when you simply have *nothing to say,* when nothing occurs to you, or when you don't want to say anything. James Russell Lowell expressed this well: "Blessed are they who have nothing to say, and who cannot be persuaded to say it."

## Spatial Messages

Space is an especially important factor in interpersonal communication, although we seldom think about it. Edward T. Hall (1959, 1963, 1966), who pioneered the study of spatial communication, called this area **proxemics.** We can examine this broad area by looking at proxemic distances, the theories about space, and territoriality.

**Proxemic Distances**   Four proxemic distances correspond closely to the major types of relationships. They are intimate, personal, social, and public distances (see Table 8.2).

**Intimate Distance**   Within **intimate distance,** ranging from the close phase of actual touching to the far phase of 6 to 18 inches, the presence of the other person is unmistakable.

## TABLE 8.2

### Relationships and Proxemic Distances

Note that these four distances can be further divided into close and far phases and that the far phase of one level (say, personal) blends into the close phase of the next level (social). Do your relationships also blend into one another? Or are, say, your personal relationships totally separate from your social relationships?

| Relationship | Distance |
|---|---|
| Intimate relationship | Intimate distance<br>0 ——————————— 18 inches<br>close phase　　　　　far phase |
| Personal relationship | Personal distance<br>1½ ——————————— 4 feet<br>close phase　　　　　far phase |
| Social relationship | Social distance<br>4 ——————————— 12 feet<br>close phase　　　　　far phase |
| Public relationship | Public distance<br>12 ——————————— 25+ feet<br>close phase　　　　　far phase |

You experience the sound, smell, and feel of the other's breath. The close phase is used for lovemaking and wrestling, for comforting and protecting. In the close phase, the muscles and the skin communicate, while actual words play a minor role. The far phase allows people to touch each other by extending their hands. The individuals are so close that this distance is not considered proper for strangers in public. Because of the feeling of inappropriateness and discomfort (at least for some Americans), if strangers are this close (say, on a crowded bus), their eyes seldom meet but remain fixed on some remote object.

**Personal Distance**　You carry a protective bubble defining your **personal distance,** which allows you to stay protected and untouched by others. Personal distance ranges from 18 inches to about 4 feet. In the close phase, people can still hold or grasp each other, but only by extending their arms. You can then take into your protective bubble certain individuals—for example, loved ones. In the far phase, you can touch another person only if you both extend your arms. This far phase is the extent to which you can physically get your hands on things; hence, it defines, in one sense, the limits of your physical control over others. At times, you may detect breath odor, but generally at this distance etiquette demands that you direct your breath to some neutral area.

**Social Distance**　At the **social distance,** ranging from 4 to 12 feet, you lose the visual detail you had at the personal distance. The close phase is the distance at which you conduct impersonal business or interact at a social gathering. The far phase is the distance at which you stand when someone says, "Stand away so I can look at you." At this distance, business transactions have a more formal tone than they do when conducted in the close phase. In the offices of high officials, the desks are often positioned so that clients are kept at least this distance away. Unlike the intimate distance, where eye contact is awkward, the far phase of the social distance makes eye contact essential—otherwise, communication is lost. The voice is generally louder than normal at this level. This distance enables you to avoid constant interaction with those with whom you work without seeming rude.

### Public Distance

**Public distance** ranges from 12 to more than 25 feet. In the close phase, a person seems protected by space. At this distance, you're able to take defensive action should you feel threatened. On a public bus or train, for example, you might keep at least this distance from a drunk. Although you lose the fine details of the face and eyes, you're still close enough to see what is happening.

At the far phase, you see others not as separate individuals but as part of the whole setting. People automatically establish a space of approximately 30 feet around important public figures, and they seem to do this whether or not there are guards preventing their coming closer. The far phase is the distance by which actors on stage are separated from their audience; consequently, their actions and voices have to be somewhat exaggerated.

The specific distance that you'll maintain between yourself and any given person depends on a wide variety of factors (Burgoon, Buller, & Woodall, 1996; Burgoon & Bacue, 2003). Among the most significant are *gender* (women sit and stand closer to each other than do men in same-sex dyads, and people approach women more closely than they approach men); *age* (people maintain closer distances with similarly aged others than they do with those much older or much younger); and *personality* (introverts and highly anxious people maintain greater distances than do extroverts). Not surprisingly, you'll maintain shorter distances with people you're familiar with than with strangers, and with people you like than with those you don't like.

### Theories about Space

Researchers studying nonverbal communication have offered numerous explanations as to why people maintain the distances they do. Prominent among these explanations are protection theory, equilibrium theory, and expectancy violation theory—rather complex names for simple and interesting concepts.

### Protection Theory

**Protection theory** holds that you establish a body buffer zone around yourself as protection against unwanted touching or attack (Dosey & Meisels, 1976). When you feel that you may be attacked, your body buffer zone increases; you want more space around you. For example, if you found yourself in a dangerous neighborhood at night, your body buffer zone would probably expand well beyond what it would be if you were in familiar and safe surroundings. If someone entered this buffer zone, you would probably feel threatened and seek to expand the distance by walking faster or crossing the street.

In contrast, when you're feeling secure and protected, your buffer zone becomes much smaller. For example, if you're with a group of close friends and feel secure, your buffer zone shrinks, and you may welcome close proximity and mutual touching.

### Equilibrium Theory

**Equilibrium theory** holds that intimacy and interpersonal distance vary together: The greater the intimacy, the closer the distance; the lower the intimacy, the greater the distance. This theory says that you maintain close distances with those with whom you have close interpersonal relationships and that you maintain greater distances with those with whom you do not have close relationships (Argyle & Dean, 1965; Bailenson, Blascovich, Beall, & Loomis, 2001).

At times, of course, your interpersonal distance does not accurately reflect your level of intimacy. When this happens, you make adjustments. For example, let's say that you have an intimate relationship with someone, but for some reason you're separated—perhaps because you could not get concert seats next to each other or you're at a party and have each been led to different parts of a large banquet hall. When this happens, you probably try to preserve your psychological closeness by maintaining frequent eye contact or perhaps by facing each other.

**A s k Yourself**
Inviting and Discouraging Conversation

Sometimes you want to encourage people to come into your office and chat, and at other times you want to be left alone. Ask yourself: What might you do nonverbally to achieve each goal?

At other times, however, you're forced into close distances with someone with whom you're not intimate (or may even dislike)—for example, on a crowded bus or in the dentist's chair. In these situations, you also compensate, but in such cases you seek to make the psychological distance greater. Consequently, you might avoid eye contact and turn in an opposite direction. In the dentist's chair, you probably close your eyes to decrease this normally intimate distance. If seated to the right of a stranger, you might cross your legs and turn your torso to the left.

**Expectancy Violations Theory**   **Expectancy violations theory** explains what happens when you increase or decrease the distance between yourself and another in an interpersonal interaction (Burgoon & Hoobler, 2002; Burgoon & Bacue, 2003). Each culture has certain expectancies for the distance people are to maintain in their conversations. Of course, each person has certain idiosyncrasies. Together, these determine "expected distance." What happens when these expectations are violated?

If you violate the expected distance to a great extent—small violations most often go unnoticed—then the relationship itself comes into focus. The other person begins to turn attention away from the topic of conversation and toward you and your relationship with him or her. It's also interesting to note that those who violate normal expected spatial relationships are judged to be less truthful than those who didn't commit such violations (Feeley & deTurck, 1995).

If the other person perceives you positively—for example, if you're a high-status person or you're particularly attractive—then you'll be perceived even more positively if you violate the norm. If, however, you're perceived negatively and you violate the norm, you'll be perceived even more negatively. Thus, the positively evaluated person will be perceived more positively if he or she violates the norm, whereas the negatively evaluated person will be more positively perceived if the distance norm is not violated.

**Territoriality**   Another type of communication having to do with space is **territoriality,** the possessive reaction to an area or to particular objects. You interact basically in three types of territories (Altman, 1975):

- **Primary territories,** or **home territories,** are areas that you might call your own; these areas are your exclusive preserve and might include your room, your desk, or your office.
- **Secondary territories** are areas that don't belong to you but that you have occupied; thus, you're associated with them. Secondary territories might include the table in the cafeteria that you regularly eat at, your classroom seat, or your neighborhood turf.
- **Public territories** are areas that are open to all people; they may be owned by some person or organization, but they are used by everyone. Examples include a movie house, a restaurant, or a shopping mall.

When you operate in your own primary territory, you have an interpersonal advantage, often called the **home field advantage.** In their own home or office, people take on a kind of leadership role: They initiate conversations, fill in silences, assume relaxed and comfortable postures, and in conversations maintain their positions with greater conviction. Because the territorial owner is dominant, you stand a better chance of getting your raise, your point accepted, and the contract resolved in your favor if you're in your own territory (your office, your home) rather than in someone else's (your supervisor's office, for example) (Marsh, 1988).

Like animals, humans mark both their primary and secondary territories to signal ownership. Some teenagers—perhaps because they can't yet own territories—use markers to indicate pseudo-ownership or appropriation of someone else's space, or of a public territory, for their own use (Childress, 2004). Graffiti and the markings of gang boundaries come quickly to mind as examples. In general, three types of **markers** may be identified:

central, boundary, and ear markers (Goffman, 1971). **Central markers** are items you place in a territory to reserve it for you—for example, a drink at the bar, books on your desk, or a sweater over a library chair.

**Boundary markers** set boundaries that divide your territory from that of others. In the supermarket checkout line, the bar that is placed between your groceries and those of the person behind you is a boundary marker, as are fences, the armrests separating chairs, and the contours of the molded plastic seats on a bus.

**Ear markers**—a term taken from the practice of branding animals on their ears—are identifying marks that indicate your possession of a territory or object. Trademarks, nameplates, and monograms are all examples of ear markers.

Markers are important in giving you a feeling of belonging. For example, students in college dormitories who marked their rooms by displaying personal items stayed in school longer than did those who didn't personalize their spaces (Marsh, 1988).

Again, like animals, humans use territory to signal their status. For example, the size and location of your territory (your home or office, say) indicates something about your status. Status is also signaled by the unwritten law granting the right of invasion, or **territorial encroachment.** Higher-status individuals have a "right" to invade the territory of lower status persons, but the reverse is not true. The boss of a large company, for example, can barge into the office of a junior executive, but the reverse would be unthinkable. Similarly, a teacher may invade a student's personal space by looking over her or his shoulder as the student writes, but the student cannot do the same to the teacher.

## Artifactual Communication

Artifactual communication concerns the messages conveyed by objects that are made by human hands. Thus, aesthetics, color, clothing, jewelry, and hairstyle, as well as scents such as perfume, cologne, or incense, all are considered artifactual. We look briefly at each of these.

**Space Decoration**   That the decoration or surroundings of a place exert influence on perceptions should be obvious to anyone who has ever entered a hospital, with its sterile walls and furniture, or a museum, with its imposing columns, glass-encased exhibits, and brass plaques. Even the way a room is furnished exerts influence on us. In a classic study, researchers attempted to determine if the aesthetic conditions of a room would influence the judgments people made in it (Maslow & Mintz, 1956; Mintz, 1956). Three rooms were used: one was beautiful, one average, and one ugly. The beautiful room had large windows, beige walls, indirect lighting, and attractive, comfortable furnishings. The average room was a professor's office with mahogany desks and chairs, metal bookcases and filing cabinets, and window shades. The ugly room was painted battleship gray; lighting was provided by an overhead bulb with a dirty, torn shade. The room was furnished to give the impression of a janitor's storeroom in horrible condition. The ashtrays were filled and the window shades torn.

In the three different rooms, students rated art prints in terms of the fatigue/energy and displeasure/well-being depicted in them. As predicted, the students in the beautiful room rated the prints as more energetic and as displaying well-being; the prints judged in the ugly room were rated as displaying fatigue and displeasure, while those judged in the average room were perceived as somewhere between these two extremes.

The way you decorate your private spaces communicates something about who you are. The office with a mahogany desk, bookcases, and oriental rugs communicates importance and status within the organization, just as a metal desk and bare floor communicate a status much farther down in the hierarchy. At home, the cost of your furnishings may communicate your status and wealth, and their coordination may communicate your sense of style. The magazines may communicate your interests. The arrangement of chairs around a television set may reveal how important watching television is. Bookcases lining the walls reveal the importance of reading. In fact, there is probably little in your home that does not send messages to others and that others do not use for making inferences about you. Computers, wide-screen televisions, well-equipped kitchens, and oil paintings of great grandparents, for example, all say something about the people who own them. Likewise, the absence of certain items will communicate something about you. Consider, for example, what messages you would get from a home in which there was no television, telephone, or books.

People also will form opinions about your personality on the basis of room decorations. Research, for example, finds that people will make judgments as to your openness to new experiences (distinctive decorating usually communicates this, as do different types of books and magazines and travel souvenirs) and as to your conscientiousness, emotional stability, degree of extroversion, and agreeableness. Not surprisingly, bedrooms prove more revealing than offices (Gosling, Ko, Mannarelli, & Morris, 2002).

### Color Communication

When you're in debt, you speak of being "in the red"; when you make a profit, you're "in the black." When you're sad, you're "blue"; when you're healthy, you're "in the pink"; when you're covetous, you're "green with envy." To be a coward is to be "yellow," and to be inexperienced is to be "green." When you talk a great deal, you talk "a blue streak"; when you're angry, you "see red." As revealed through these timeworn clichés, language abounds in color symbolism.

**Color communication** takes place on many levels. For example, there is some evidence that colors affect us physiologically. Respiratory movements increase in the presence of red light and decrease in the presence of blue light. Similarly, eye blinks increase in frequency when eyes are exposed to red light and decrease when exposed to blue. This seems consistent with our intuitive feelings that blue is more soothing and red more provocative. After a school changed the paint on its walls from orange and white to blue, the students' blood pressure decreased and their academic performance improved.

Colors surely influence our perceptions and behaviors (Kanner, 1989). People's acceptance of a product, for example, is largely determined by its package. In one study, for example, the very same coffee taken from a yellow can was described as weak, from a dark brown can as too strong, from a red can as rich, and from a blue can as mild. Even our acceptance of a person may depend on the colors worn. Consider, for example, the comments of one color expert (Kanner, 1989): "If you have to pick the wardrobe for your defense lawyer heading into court and choose anything but blue, you deserve to lose the case." Black is so powerful that it can work against the lawyer with the jury. Brown lacks sufficient authority. Green will probably elicit a negative response.

### Clothing and Body Adornment

Clothing serves a variety of functions. It protects you from the weather and, in sports like football, from injury. It helps you conceal parts of your body and so serves a modesty function. In the business world it may communicate your position within the hierarchy and your willingness and desire to conform to the clothing norms of the organization. It also may communicate your professionalism, which seems to be the reason why some organizations favor dress codes (Smith, 2003). Clothing also serves as a form of **cultural display** (Morris, 1977). It communicates your cultural and subcultural affiliations. In the United States, where there are so many different ethnic groups, you regularly see examples of dress that indicate what country the wearers are from.

The very poor and the very rich don't dress in the same way, nor do white- and blue-collar workers or the young and the old (Lurie, 1983). People dress, in part at least, to identify with the groups of which they are or want to be members.

Similarly, college students will perceive an instructor dressed informally as friendly, fair, enthusiastic, and flexible, and the same instructor dressed formally as prepared, knowledgeable, and organized (Malandro, Barker, & Barker, 1989).

**A s k Yourself**

Criticizing with Kindness

A close friend is going to an important job interview dressed totally inappropriately and asks, "How do I look?" Ask yourself: What are some of the ways of expressing your response that will help your friend with the interview presentation but also bolster your friend's self-esteem?

Clothing also seems to influence your own behavior and the behavior of groups. For example, it has been argued that people who dress casually act more informally (Morand, cited in *Psychology Today,* March/April 1995, p. 16). Therefore, meetings with such casually dressed people are more likely to involve a freer exchange of thoughts and ideas, which in turn may stimulate creativity. This casual attire seems to work well in companies that must rely heavily on creative developments, such as computer software companies. A decade ago IBM, for example, relaxed its conservative dress code and allowed some measure of informal dress among its workers (*New York Times,* 7 February 1995, p. B1). But banks and insurance companies, which traditionally have resisted change, may prefer a more formal attire that creates distance between workers as well as between employees and customers.

Your jewelry, too, communicates messages about you. Wedding and engagement rings are obvious examples of jewelry designed to communicate very specific messages. College rings and political buttons also communicate specific information. If you wear a Rolex watch or large precious stones, others are likely to infer that you're rich. Men with earrings will be judged differently from men without earrings.

Today body piercings are popular, especially among the young. Nose and nipple rings and tongue and belly-button jewelry send a variety of messages. Although people wearing such jewelry may wish to communicate meanings of their own, those interpreting these messages seem to infer that the wearer is communicating an unwillingness to conform to social norms and a willingness to take greater risks than those without such piercings (Forbes, 2001). It's worth noting that in a study of employers' perceptions, applicants with eyebrow piercings were rated and ranked significantly lower than those without such piercings (Acor, 2001). In another study, nose-pierced job candidates were given lower scores on measures of credibility such as character and trust as well as sociability and hirability (Seiter & Sandry, 2003). And in relation to health, tattoos and piercings may communicate such undesirable traits as impulsiveness, unpredictability, and a tendency toward recklessness or violence (Rapsa & Cusack, 1990; Smith, 2003).

Tattoos—temporary or permanent ones—likewise communicate a variety of messages, often the name of a loved one or some symbol of allegiance or affiliation. Tattoos also communicate to the wearers themselves. For example, tattooed students see themselves (and perhaps others do as well) as more adventurous, creative, individualistic, and risk-prone than those without tattoos (Drews, Allison, & Probst, 2000).

The way you wear your hair communicates who you are. Your hair may communicate a concern for being up-to-date, a desire to shock, or perhaps a lack of concern for appearances. Men with long hair will generally be judged as less conservative than men with shorter hair.

In a study on interpersonal attraction, slides of male and female models were shown with and without glasses and were evaluated by men and women. Results indicated that persons with glasses were rated more negatively than the very same persons without glasses (Hasart & Hutchinson, 1993).

**Scent**   Smell is a peculiar aspect of nonverbal communication and is discussed in widely different ways by different writers. Here, because the emphasis is on using scents (for example, perfume or cologne), it's grouped with artifactual communication. But recognize that body odor also communicates, and perhaps that part of smell is best thought of as a form of body communication. You also use smells to make yourself feel better. When the smells are pleasant, you feel better about yourself; when the smells are unpleasant, you feel less good about yourself. In fact, research finds that smells can influence your body's chemistry, which, in turn, influences your emotional state. For example, the smell of chocolate results in the reduction of theta brain waves, which produces a sense of relaxation and a reduced level of attention (Martin, 1998).

**Olfactory communication,** or olfactics, is extremely important in a wide variety of situations. Scientists estimate that you can smell some 10,000 different odors (Angier, 1995a). Smell is now big business (Kleinfield, 1992). There is some, though not conclusive, evidence showing that the smell of lemon contributes to a perception of health; the smells of lavender and eucalyptus seem to increase alertness, and the smell of rose oil seems to reduce blood pressure. Findings such as these have contributed to the growth of aromatherapy and to the profession of aromatherapist (Furlow, 1996). Because humans possess "denser skin concentrations of scent glands than almost any other mammal," it has been argued that it only remains for us to discover how we use scent to communicate a wide variety of messages (Furlow, 1996, p. 41). Some of the most important messages scent seems to communicate involve attraction, taste, memory, and identification.

In many animal species the female gives off a scent that draws males, often from far distances, and thus ensures the continuation of the species. Humans, too, emit sexual *attractants* called sex pheromones, body secretions that arouse sexual desire. Humans, of course, supplement pheromones with perfumes, colognes, after-shave lotions, powders, and the like to further enhance attractiveness and sexuality. Although we often think of women as the primary users of perfumes and scents, increasingly men are using them as well—not only cologne and after-shave lotions but body sprays, which have become big business with a market estimated at $180 million (Dell, 2005). Not surprisingly, biotechnology companies are busily at work with the aim of bottling human sex pheromones as well (Bishop, 1993). Women, research finds, prefer the scent of men who bear a close genetic similarity to themselves—a finding that may account in part for our attraction to people much like ourselves (Ober, Weitkamp, Cox, Dytch, Kostyu, & Elias, 1997; Wade, 2002).

Without smell, *taste* would be severely impaired. For example, it would be extremely difficult to taste the difference between a raw potato and an apple without the sense of smell. Street vendors selling hot dogs, sausages, and similar foods are aided greatly by the smells that stimulate the appetites of passersby.

Smell is a powerful *memory* aid; you can often recall situations from months and even years ago when you happen upon a similar smell. One reason smell can so effectively recall a previous situation is that it's often associated with significant emotional experiences (Rubin, Groth, & Goldsmith, 1984; Malandro, Barker, & Barker, 1989).

Smell is often used to create an image or an *identity* for a product. Advertisers and manufacturers spend millions of dollars each year creating scents for cleaning products and toothpastes, for example. These scents have nothing to do with the products' cleaning power. Instead, they function solely to help create product images or identities. There also is evidence that we can identify specific significant others by smell. For example, infants find their mothers' breasts through smell, and mothers can identify their newborns solely through smell. In one study young children were able to identify the T-shirts of their brothers and sisters solely on the basis of smell (Porter & Moore, 1981; Angier, 1995a). One researcher goes so far as to advise: "If your man's odor reminds you of Dad or your brother, you may want genetic tests before trying to conceive a child" (Furlow, 1996, p. 41).

## Temporal Communication

**Temporal communication** consists of the messages communicated by your time orientation and treatment of time. Shortly we'll consider the cultural dimension of time differences. Here, let's look at another dimension of time, psychological time. The study of the communicative function of time is often referred to as **chronemics.**

The term **psychological time** refers to a person's emphasis on, or orientation toward, the past, present, or future. In a *past orientation,* you give particular reverence to the past; you might relive old times and regard old methods as the best. Events are seen as circular and recurring, so that the wisdom of yesterday is applicable also to today and tomorrow. In a *present orientation,* you live in the present and for the present. Present activities command your attention; you engage in them not for their future rewards or their past significance but because they're happening now. In its extreme form, this orientation is hedonistic. In a *future orientation,* you give primary attention to the future. You save today, work hard in college, and deny yourself certain enjoyments and luxuries, all because you're preparing for the future.

Researchers have provided some interesting correlations to these different time orientations (Gonzalez & Zimbardo, 1985; Rappaport, Enrich, & Wilson, 1985). Before reading their conclusions, you may wish to take the self-test "What Time Do You Have?"

## TEST YOURSELF

### WHAT TIME DO YOU HAVE?

For each statement, indicate whether the statement is true (T) of your general attitude and behavior, or untrue (F) of your general attitude and behavior. (A few statements are purposely repeated to facilitate scoring and analyzing your responses.)

_____ 1. Meeting tomorrow's deadlines and doing other necessary work comes before tonight's partying.

_____ 2. I meet my obligations to friends and authorities on time.

_____ 3. I complete projects on time by making steady progress.

_____ 4. I am able to resist temptations when I know there is work to be done.

_____ 5. I keep working at a difficult, uninteresting task if it will help me get ahead.

_____ 6. If things don't get done on time, I don't worry about it.

_____ 7. I think that it's useless to plan too far ahead because things hardly ever come out the way you planned anyway.

_____ 8. I try to live one day at a time.

_____ 9. I live to make better what is rather than to be concerned about what will be.

_____ 10. It seems to me that it doesn't make sense to worry about the future, since fate determines that whatever will be, will be.

_____ 11. I believe that getting together with friends to party is one of life's important pleasures.

_____ 12. I do things impulsively, making decisions on the spur of the moment.

_____ 13. I take risks to put excitement in my life.

_____ 14. I get drunk at parties.

_____ 15. It's fun to gamble.

_____ 16. Thinking about the future is pleasant to me.

_____ 17. When I want to achieve something, I set subgoals and consider specific means for reaching these goals.

_____ 18. It seems to me that my career path is pretty well laid out.

_____ 19. It upsets me to be late for appointments.

_____ 20. I meet my obligations to friends and authorities on time.

_____ 21. I get irritated at people who keep me waiting when we've agreed to meet at a given time.

_____ 22. It makes sense to invest a substantial part of my income in insurance premiums.

_____ 23. I believe that "a stitch in time saves nine."

_____ 24. I believe that "a bird in the hand is worth two in the bush."

_____ 25. I believe it is important to save for a rainy day.

_____ 26. I believe a person's day should be planned each morning.

_____ 27. I make lists of things I must do.

_____ 28. When I want to achieve something, I set subgoals and consider specific means for reaching those goals.

_____ 29. I believe that "a stitch in time saves nine."

**HOW DID YOU DO?**  This time test measures seven different factors. If you selected true (T) for all or most of the questions within any given factor, you're high on that factor. If you selected untrue (F) for all or most of the questions within any given factor, you're low on that factor.

The first factor, measured by questions 1–5, is a future, work motivation, perseverance orientation. These people have a strong work ethic and are committed to completing a task despite difficulties. The second factor (questions 6–10) is a present, fatalistic, worry-free orientation. High scorers on this factor live one day at a time, not necessarily to enjoy the day but to avoid planning for the next day.

The third factor (questions 11–15) is a present, pleasure-seeking, partying orientation. These people enjoy the present, take risks, and engage in a variety of impulsive actions. The fourth factor (questions 16–18) is a future, goal-seeking, and planning orientation. These people derive pleasure from planning and achieving a variety of goals.

The fifth factor (questions 19–21) is a time-sensitivity orientation. People who score high are especially sensitive to time and its role in social obligations. The sixth factor (questions 22–25) is a future, practical action orientation. These people do what they have to do—take practical actions—to achieve the future they want.

The seventh factor (questions 26–29) is a future, somewhat obsessive daily planning orientation. High scorers make daily "to do" lists and devote great attention to detail.

**WHAT WILL YOU DO?**  Now that you have some idea of how you treat time, consider how these attitudes and behaviors work for you. For example, will your time orientations help you achieve your social and professional goals? If not, what might you do about changing these attitudes and behaviors?

*Source:* From A. Gonzalez and P. Zimbardo, "Time in Perspective," *Psychology Today,* March 1985. Reprinted with permission from *Psychology Today Magazine.* Copyright © 1985 by Sussex Publishers, Inc.

One of the findings of the time research is that future income is positively related to future orientation. The more future oriented a person is, the greater that person's income is likely to be. Present orientation is strongest among lowest-income males.

The time orientation that people develop depends a great deal on their socioeconomic class and personal experiences. Gonzalez and Zimbardo (1985) observe: "A child with parents in unskilled and semi-skilled occupations is usually socialized in a way that promotes a present-oriented fatalism and hedonism. A child of parents who are managers, teachers, or other professionals learns future-oriented values and strategies designed to promote achievement."

Different time perspectives also account for much intercultural misunderstanding, because different cultures often teach their members drastically different time orientations. The future-oriented person who works for tomorrow's goals will frequently regard the present-oriented person who focuses on enjoying today as lazy and poorly motivated. In turn, the present-oriented person may see those with strong future orientations as obsessed with accumulating wealth or rising in status.

 ## NONVERBAL COMMUNICATION AND CULTURE

Throughout this chapter we've seen a few cultural and gender differences in nonverbal communication. Cultural variations in certain channels of nonverbal communication, however, have become the focus of sustained research. Here we consider just a sampling of research on the relationship between culture and nonverbal communication expressed through facial expressions, color, touch, silence, and time.

### Culture and Facial Expression

The wide variations in facial communication that we observe in different cultures seem to reflect which reactions are publicly permissible rather than a fundamental difference in the way emotions are facially expressed. In one study, for example, Japanese and American students watched a film of a surgical operation (Ekman, 1985). The students were videotaped

# Understanding Interpersonal Theory and Research
## THE THEORY OF THE SOCIAL CLOCK

Your culture maintains a *social clock*—a time schedule for the right time to do various important things, such as starting dating, finishing college, buying your own home, or having a child. The social clock tells you if you're keeping pace with your peers, are ahead of them, or are falling behind (Neugarten, 1979; Greene, 2003). On the basis of this social clock, which you learned as you grew up, you evaluate your own social and professional development. If you're keeping pace with the rest of your peers (for example, you started dating at the "appropriate" age or you're finishing college at the "appropriate" age), you'll feel well adjusted, competent, and a part of the group. If you're late, you'll probably experience feelings of dissatisfaction. Although today the social clock is becoming more flexible and more tolerant of deviations from the acceptable timetable than it was in past decades, it still exerts pressure on each of us to keep pace with our peers (Peterson, 1996).

### Working with Theories and Research

How important is the social clock to you? Have you ever felt out of step with your peers in some area? Did your feeling influence your behavior in any way?

---

both during an interview about the film and alone while watching the film. When alone, the students showed very similar reactions; but in the interview the American students displayed facial expressions indicating displeasure, whereas the Japanese students did not show any great emotion. Similarly, it's considered "forward" or inappropriate for Japanese women to reveal broad smiles, so many Japanese women will hide their smile, sometimes with their hands (cf. Ma, 1996). Women in the United States, on the other hand, have no such restrictions and so are more likely to smile openly. Thus, the difference may not be in the way different cultures express emotions but rather in the society's **cultural display rules,** or rules about the appropriate display of emotions in public (cf. Matsumoto, 1991).

Cultural differences also exist in the ways people decode the meanings of facial expressions. For example, American and Japanese students judged the meaning of a smiling and a neutral facial expression. The Americans rated the smiling face as more attractive, more intelligent, and more sociable than the neutral face. In contrast, the Japanese rated the smiling face as more sociable but not as more attractive. They did, however, rate the neutral face as more intelligent (Matsumoto & Kudoh, 1993).

## Culture and Colors

Colors vary greatly in their meanings from one culture to another. Some of these cultural differences are illustrated in Table 8.3—but before looking at the table, think about the meanings of such colors as red, green, black, white, blue, yellow, and purple in your own culture or cultures.

### ask Yourself
#### Demonstrating Credibility

At work people don't attribute any credibility to you, although you're probably as competent as anyone else. You need to increase the credibility cues you give off.   Ask Yourself: What nonverbal cues communicate competence and ability? How might you begin to integrate these into your own communication?

## Culture and Touch

The several functions and examples of touching discussed earlier in this chapter were based on studies in North America; in other cultures these functions are not served in the same way. In some cultures, for example, some task-related touching is viewed negatively and is to be avoided. Among Koreans it is considered disrespectful for a store owner to touch a customer in, say, handing back change; it is considered too intimate a gesture. A member of another culture who is used to such touching may consider the Korean's behavior cold and aloof. Muslim children are socialized not to touch members of the opposite sex; their behavior can easily be interpreted as unfriendly by American children who are used to touching one another (Dresser, 1996).

## ⬇ TABLE 8.3
## Some Cultural Meanings of Color

This table, constructed from research reported by various culture watchers, illustrates only some of the different meanings that colors may communicate and especially how they are viewed in different cultures (Dreyfuss, 1971; Hoft, 1995; Dresser, 1996; Singh & Pereira, 2005). As you read this table consider the meanings you give to these colors and where your meanings came from.

| Color | Cultural Meanings and Comments |
|---|---|
| Red | In China red signifies prosperity and rebirth and is used for festive and joyous occasions; in France and the United Kingdom it indicates masculinity, in many African countries blasphemy or death, and in Japan anger and danger. Red ink, especially among Korean Buddhists, is used only to write a person's name at the time of death or on the anniversary of the person's death; this can create problems when American teachers use red ink to mark homework. |
| Green | In the United States green signifies capitalism, go ahead, and envy; in Ireland patriotism; among some Native Americans femininity; to the Egyptians fertility and strength; and to the Japanese youth and energy. |
| Black | In Thailand black signifies old age, in parts of Malaysia courage, and in much of Europe death. |
| White | In Thailand white signifies purity, in many Muslim and Hindu cultures purity and peace, and in Japan and other Asian countries death and mourning. |
| Blue | In Iran blue signifies something negative, in Ghana joy; among the Cherokee it signifies defeat, for the Egyptian virtue and truth, and for the Greek national pride. |
| Yellow | In China yellow signifies wealth and authority, in the United States caution and cowardice, in Egypt happiness and prosperity, and in many countries throughout the world femininity. |
| Purple | In Latin America purple signifies death, in Europe royalty, in Egypt virtue and faith, in Japan grace and nobility, in China barbarism, and in the United States nobility and bravery. |

In one study on touch, college students in Japan and in the United States were surveyed (Barnlund, 1975). Students from the United States reported being touched twice as much as did the Japanese students. In Japan there is a strong taboo against strangers' touching, and the Japanese are therefore especially careful to maintain sufficient interpersonal distance.

Some cultures—including many in southern Europe and the Middle East—are contact cultures; others are noncontact cultures, such as those of northern Europe and Japan. Members of contact cultures maintain close distances, touch one another in conversation, face each other more directly, and maintain longer and more focused eye contact. Members of noncontact cultures maintain greater distance in their interactions, touch each other rarely (if at all), avoid facing each other directly, and maintain much less direct eye contact. As a result, of these differences, problems may occur. For example, northern Europeans and Japanese may be perceived as cold, distant, and uninvolved by southern Europeans—who may in turn be perceived as pushy, aggressive, and inappropriately intimate.

## Culture, Paralanguage, and Silence

Cultural differences also need to be taken into consideration when we evaluate the results of the studies on speech rate, because different cultures view speech rate differently. For example, investigators found that Korean male speakers who spoke rapidly were given unfavorable credibility ratings, unlike Americans who spoke rapidly (Lee & Boster, 1992). Researchers have suggested that in individualist societies a rapid-rate speaker is seen as more competent than a slow-rate speaker, whereas in collectivist cultures a speaker who uses a slower rate is judged more competent.

Similarly, not all cultures view silence as functioning in the same way (Vainiomaki, 2004). In the United States, for example, people often interpret silence negatively. At a business meeting or even in an informal social group, others may wonder if the silent member is not listening, has nothing interesting to add, doesn't understand the issues, is insensitive, or is too self-absorbed to focus on the messages of others.

Other cultures, however, view silence more positively. In many situations in Japan, for example, silence is a response that is considered more appropriate than speech (Haga, 1988). And in this country the traditional Apache regard silence very differently than do European Americans (Basso, 1972). Among the Apache mutual friends do not feel the need to introduce strangers who may be working in the same area or on the same project. The strangers may remain silent for several days. This period enables people to observe one another and to come to a judgment about the other individuals. Once this assessment is made, the individuals talk. When courting, especially during the initial stages, Apache couples remain couples silent for hours; if they do talk, they generally talk very little. Only after a couple has been dating for several months will they have lengthy conversations. These periods of silence are generally attributed to shyness or self-consciousness. The use of silence is explicitly taught to Apache women, who are especially discouraged from engaging in long discussions with their dates. Silence during courtship is a sign of modesty to many Apache.

## Culture and Time

Culture influences our attitudes toward time in a variety of ways. Here we look at two dimensions of **cultural time:** formal versus informal time and monochronism versus polychronism. Another cultural dimension of time, the social clock, is discussed in the Understanding Interpersonal Theory and Research box on page 187.

**Formal and Informal Time**   In the United States and in most of the world, *formal time* communication has to do with seconds, minutes, hours, days, weeks, months, and years. Some cultures, however, may use seasons or phases of the moon to demarcate their most important time periods. In the United States, if your college is on the semester system, your courses are divided into 50- or 75-minute periods that meet two or three times a week for 14-week periods. Eight semesters of 15 or 16 periods per week equal a college education. As

# InterMedia

## THE SPIRAL OF SILENCE

The "spiral of silence" theory argues that you're more likely to voice agreement than disagreement (Noelle-Neumann, 1973, 1980, 1991; Severin & Tankard, 2001; Scheufele & Moy, 2000). The theory claims that when a controversial issue arises, you estimate public opinion and figure out which views are popular and which are not, largely by attending to the media (Gonzenbach, King, & Jablonski, 1999). You also estimate the punishments you're likely to get for expressing minority opinions. You then use these estimates to regulate your expression of opinions.

Generally, you're more likely to voice your opinions when you agree with the majority than when you disagree. And there's evidence to show that this effect is stronger for minority group members (Bowen & Blackmon, 2003). You may do this to avoid being isolated from the majority or for fear of being proved wrong. Or you may simply assume that the majority, because they're a majority, must be right.

According to the theory of the spiral of silence, as people with minority views remain silent, the media position gets stronger (because those who agree with it are the only ones speaking). When you hear opinions from the media, you're likely to assume that nearly everyone is in agreement—after all, those who disagree aren't voicing their opinions. So, as the media's position grows stronger, the silence of the opposition also grows, and the situation becomes an ever-widening spiral.

### Follow Up

The Internet may in some ways act as a counteragent to the spiral of silence, because it provides so many free ways for you to express minority viewpoints (anonymously if you wish) and to quickly find like-minded others (McDevitt, Kiousis, & Wahl Jorgenen, 2003). Do you find the Internet a hospitable place for minority views? What types of media are the least hospitable to minority views?

these examples illustrate, formal time units are arbitrary. The culture establishes them for convenience.

*Informal time* communication involves the use of **informal time terms**—for example, expressions such as "forever," "immediately," "soon," "right away," "as soon as possible." This type of time communication creates the most problems, because informal terms have different meanings for different people. This is especially true when these terms are used interculturally. For example, what does "late" mean when applied to a commuter train that is not on time? Apparently, it depends on your culture. In the New York area, "late" means arriving six minutes or more after the scheduled time; in Britain it means five minutes or more. But in Japan it means one minute. The deadly train crash that killed 90 people in Japan in 2005—the most deadly crash in Japan in 40 years—was attributed to the Japanese concern (or obsession) with time (Onishi, 2005a).

Not only in concepts of lateness but in other respects as well, attitudes toward time vary from one culture to another. In one study, for example, researchers measured the accuracy of clocks in six cultures—in Japan, Indonesia, Italy, England, Taiwan, and the United States. Japan had the most accurate and Indonesia had the least accurate clocks. The investigators also measured the speed at which people in these six cultures walked; results showed that the Japanese walked the fastest, the Indonesians the slowest (LeVine & Bartlett, 1984).

**Monochronism and Polychronism**   Another important distinction is that between **monochronic** and **polychronic time orientations** (Hall, 1959, 1976; Hall & Hall, 1987). Monochronic people or cultures—such as those of the United States, Germany, Scandinavia, and Switzerland—schedule one thing at a time. In these cultures time is compartmentalized and there is a time for everything. On the other hand, polychronic people or cultures—such as those of Latin Americans, Mediterranean peoples, and Arabs—schedule multiple things at the same time. Eating, conducting business with several different people, and taking care of family matters all may occur at the same time.

No culture is entirely monochronic or polychronic; rather, these are general tendencies that are found across a large part of the culture. Some cultures combine both time orientations; for example, both orientations are found in Japan and in parts of American culture. Table 8.4 identifies some of the distinctions between these two time orientations.

⬇ TABLE 8.4
## Monochronic and Polychronic Time

As you read this table, based on Hall and Hall (1987), note the potential for miscommunication that these differences might create when M-time and P-time people interact. Have any of these differences ever created interpersonal misunderstandings for you?

| The Monochronic-Time Person | The Polychronic-Time Person |
|---|---|
| does one thing at a time | does several things at once |
| treats time schedules and plans very seriously; feels they may be broken only for the most serious of reasons | treats time schedules and plans as useful (not sacred); feels they may be broken for a variety of causes |
| considers the job the most important part of life, ahead of even family | considers the family and interpersonal relationships more important than the job |
| considers privacy extremely important; seldom borrows or lends to others; works independently | is actively involved with others; works in the presence of and with lots of people at the same time |

This chapter explored nonverbal communication and identified several functions that research has focused on, the varied channels of nonverbal communication, and the influence of culture on nonverbal messages.

## Nonverbal Communication Functions

What functions of nonverbal communication has research investigated?

- impression formation and management: how nonverbal messages allow people to form impressions of you and you of them
- forming and defining relationships: how you express the state of your relationship nonverbally
- structuring conversation and social interaction: how nonverbal messages regulate speaking and listening in conversation
- influence: how nonverbal messages can persuade
- emotional expression: how nonverbal messages reveal feelings

## Nonverbal Communication Channels

What channels do nonverbal messages pass through?

- body communication
  - Among body gestures are emblems, which translate words and phrases rather directly; illustrators, which accompany and illustrate verbal messages; affect displays, which convey emotional meaning; regulators, which monitor or control the speaking of the other person; and adaptors, which serve some need and usually are performed only partially in public.
  - General body appearance (e.g., height, weight, level of attractiveness, and skin color) can communicate a person's power, attractiveness, and suitability as a friend or romantic partner.
- facial communication
  - Facial movements express emotions, such as happiness, surprise, fear, anger, sadness, disgust/contempt, interest, bewilderment, and determination.
  - Some facial movements manage the meanings being communicated by means of intensifying, deintensifying, neutralizing, and masking.
- eye communication
  - Through eye contact we monitor feedback, maintain interest/attention, signal conversational turns, signal the nature of relationships, compensate for physical distance.
  - Through eye avoidance we give others privacy, signal disinterest, cut off unpleasant stimuli, heighten other senses.
  - Pupil dilation indicates interest/arousal, increases attractiveness.
- touch communication
  - Among the meanings touch can communicate are positive affect, playfulness, control, ritual functions, and task-relatedness.

- paralanguage and silence
  - Paralanguage cues help people form impressions; identify emotional states; and make judgments of speakers' credibility, intelligence, and objectivity.
  - Silence can communicate varied meanings and is greatly influenced by culture.
- spatial messages
  - The major types of distance that correspond to types of relationships are intimate distance (touching to 18 inches), personal distance (18 inches to 4 feet), social distance (4 to 12 feet), and public distance (12 or more feet).
  - Theories about space include protection theory (you maintain spatial distance to protect yourself); equilibrium theory (you regulate distance according to the intimacy level of your relationship); and expectancy violations theory (increasing or decreasing the expected distance between yourself and another can send important messages).
  - Your territories may be identified as primary (areas you own), secondary (areas that you occupy regularly), and public (areas open to everyone). Like animals, humans often mark their territories with central, boundary, and ear markers as proof of ownership. Your territory (its appearance and the way it's used) also communicates status.
- artifactual communication
  - Space decoration influences people's perceptions of energy, time, status, and personal characteristics.
  - Colors communicate different meanings depending on the culture.
  - Clothing and body adornment serve especially as cultural display and communicate messages about status and social thinking.
  - Scents can communicate messages related to attraction, taste, memory, and identification.
- temporal communication
  - Three main time orientations can be distinguished: past, present, and future.
  - These orientations influence a wide variety of behaviors, such as your willingness to plan for the future, your tendency to party, and even your potential income.

## Nonverbal Communication and Culture

How does culture influence nonverbal communication?

- Culture influences the rules for expressing emotions facially and the meanings given to such facial expressions.
- Cultures attribute different meanings to colors.
- Cultures have different preferences for touch behavior, some encouraging lots of touching and some discouraging it.
- Paralinguistic variations and silence are interpreted differently in different cultures.
- Cultures vary in the way they deal with formal and informal time and also vary in the way they schedule events (monochronism and polychronism).

1 Research shows that women are perceived to be and are in reality more skilled at both encoding and decoding nonverbal messages (Briton & Hall, 1995a). Do you notice this in your own interactions? Do these differences give women an advantage in conversation? In negotiation? In conflict resolution?

2 The "Pygmalion gift" is a gift that is designed to change the recipient into what the donor wants that person to become. For example, the parent who gives a child books or science equipment may be asking the child to be a scholar or a scientist. What messages have you recently communicated in your gift-giving behavior? What messages do you think others have communicated to you by the gifts they gave you?

3 Another type of time is biological time; the term refers to your body clock, the ways your body functions differently at different times. Your intellectual, physical, and emotional lives, according to theories of biorhythms, are lived in cycles that influence your effectiveness. Detailed explanations and instructions for calculating your own intellectual, physical, and emotional cycles can be found in DeVito (1989), or even better, you can visit a website that will compute your biorhythms (for example, www.bio-chart.com or (www.core2.com/biorhythms/index.html) (accessed 8/11/05).

4 A popular defense tactic in sex crimes against women, gay men, and lesbians is to blame the victim by referring to the way the victim was dressed and implying that the victim, by wearing certain clothing, provoked the attack. Currently New York and Florida are the only states that prohibit defense attorneys from referring to the way a sex-crime victim was dressed at the time of the attack (*New York Times,* July 30, 1994, p. 22). What do you think of this? If you don't live in New York or Florida, have there been proposals in your state to similarly limit this defense tactic?

5 Here are a few findings from research on nonverbal gender differences (Burgoon, Buller, & Woodall, 1996; Guerrero, DeVito, & Hecht, 1999; Gamble & Gamble, 2003; Stewart, Cooper, Stewart, with Friedley, 2003; KroLøkke & Sørensen, 2006): (1) Women smile more than men. (2) Women stand closer to each other than do men and are generally approached more closely than men. (3) Both men and women, when speaking, look at men more than at women. (4) Women both touch and are touched more than men. (5) Men extend their bodies more, taking up greater areas of space, than women. What problems might these differences create when men and women communicate with each other?

6 Test your ability to identify these emotions on the basis of verbal descriptions. Try to "hear" the following voices and to identify the emotions being communicated. Do you hear affection, anger, boredom, or joy (Davitz, 1964)?

- This voice is soft, with a low pitch, a resonant quality, a slow rate, and a steady and slightly upward inflection. The rhythm is regular, and the enunciation is slurred.
- This voice is loud, with a high pitch, a moderately blaring quality, a fast rate, an upward inflection, and a regular rhythm.
- This voice is loud, with a high pitch, a blaring quality, a fast rate, and an irregular up-and-down inflection. The rhythm is irregular, and the enunciation is clipped.
- This voice is moderate to low in volume, with a moderate-to-low pitch, a moderately resonant quality, a moderately slow rate, and a monotonous or gradually falling inflection. The enunciation is somewhat slurred.

Go to www.ablongman.com/devito.

*This group of experiences deals with nonverbal messages and provides opportunities to work with these various channels of communication.*

❶ **Facial Expressions** and ❷ **Eye Contact** focus on the various meanings the face and the eyes communicate. ❸ **Interpersonal Interactions and Space** and ❹ **Sitting at the Company Meeting** look at the meanings communicated by the way you use space. ❺ **The Meanings of Color** helps sensitize you to the various meanings that different colors communicate. ❻ **Communicating Emotions Nonverbally** and ❼ **Praising and Criticizing** look at how a variety of meanings can be communicated without words. ❽ **Artifacts and Culture: The Case of Gifts** illustrates the vast cultural differences in what is considered appropriate gift-giving.

# Messages and Conversation

*Phone Booth* (2002)

In *Phone Booth* you see a man confined to talking on the telephone in his desperate effort to prevent his own death. Although conversation is not usually a matter of life or death, it does have considerable consequences, as you'll discover in the following discussion.

**Conversation** can be defined as "relatively informal social interaction in which the roles of speaker and hearer are exchanged in a nonautomatic fashion under the collaborative management of all parties" (McLaughlin, 1984). Examining conversation provides an excellent opportunity to look at verbal and nonverbal messages as they're used in day-to-day communications and thus serves as a useful culmination for this second part of the text.

##  THE CONVERSATION PROCESS

It's convenient to divide up conversation into chunks or stages and to view each stage as requiring a choice as to what you'll say and how you'll say it. Here we divide the sequence into five steps: opening, feedforward, business, feedback, and closing (see Figure 9.1). These stages and the way people follow them will vary depending on the personalities of the communicators, their culture, the context in which the conversation occurs, the purpose of the conversation, and the entire host of factors considered throughout this text.

When reading about the process of conversation, keep in mind that not everyone speaks with the fluency and ease that many textbooks often assume. Speech and language disorders, for example, can seriously disrupt the conversation process when some elementary guidelines aren't followed. Table 9.1 offers suggestions for making such conversations run more smoothly.

➲ FIGURE 9.1

**A Five-Stage Model of Conversation**

This model of the stages of conversation is best seen as a way of talking about conversation and not as a hard-and-fast depiction of stages all conversations follow. As you review the model, consider how accurately it depicts conversation as you experience it. Can you develop a more accurate and more revealing model?

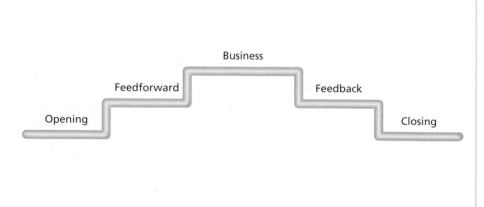

## ↻ TABLE 9.1 INTERPERSONAL COMMUNICATION TIPS
### Between People With and Without Speech and Language Disorders

Speech and language disorders vary widely—from fluency problems such as stuttering, to indistinct articulation, to difficulty in finding the right word, or aphasia. Following a few simple guidelines can facilitate communication between people with and without speech and language disorders.

**If you're the person without a speech or language disorder:**

1. Avoid finishing another's sentences. Although you may think you're helping the person who stutters or has word-finding difficulty, finishing the person's sentences may communicate the idea that you're impatient and don't want to spend the extra time necessary to interact effectively.
2. Avoid giving directions to the person with a speech disorder. Saying "slow down" or "relax" will often seem insulting and will make further communication more difficult.
3. Maintain eye contact. Show interest and at the same time avoid showing any signs of impatience or embarrassment.
4. Ask for clarification as needed. If you don't understand what the person said, ask him or her to repeat it. Don't pretend that you understand when you don't.
5. Don't treat people who have language problems like children. A person with aphasia, say, who has difficulty with names or nouns generally, is in no way childlike.

**If you're the person with a speech or language disorder**

1. Let the other person know what your special needs are. For example, if you stutter, you might tell others that you have difficulty with certain sounds and so they need to be patient.
2. Demonstrate your own comfort. Show that you have a positive attitude toward the interpersonal situation. If you appear comfortable and positive, others will also.

*Source:* These suggestions were drawn from a variety of sources: http://wwww.nsastuter.org/documents/listenrs.html, http://www.aphasia.org/NAAcommun.html, http://spot.pcc.edu/~rjacobs/career/communication_tips.htm, and http://www.dol.gov/odep/pubs/fact/comucate.htm (all accessed April 4, 2005).

## Opening

The first step is to open the conversation, usually with some kind of greeting: "Hi. How are you?" "Hello, this is Joe." The greeting is a good example of **phatic communion** (see Chapter 1). It's a message that establishes a connection between two people and opens up the channels for more meaningful interaction. Openings, of course, may be nonverbal as well as verbal. A smile, kiss, or handshake may be as clear an opening as "Hello." Greetings are so common that they often go unnoticed. But when they're omitted—as when the doctor begins the conversation by saying, "What's wrong?"—you may feel uncomfortable and thrown off guard.

In normal conversation, the greeting is reciprocated with a greeting similar in degree of formality and intensity. When it isn't—when the other person turns away or responds coldly to your friendly "Good morning"—you know that something is wrong.

Openings are also generally consistent in tone with the main part of the conversation; a cheery "How ya doing today, bud?" is not normally followed by news of a family death, and a friendly conversation is not begun with insensitive openers: "Wow, you've gained a few pounds haven't you?"

> **A s k Yourself**
> **Prefacing to Extremes**
>
> A friend whom you talk to on the phone fairly regularly seems to take phatic communication to a new level—the preface is so long that it makes you want to get off the phone, and frequently you make excuses to do just that. **Ask yourself:** What are some things you might do to change this communication pattern?

## Feedforward

At the second step, you usually provide some kind of feedforward (see Chapter 1), which gives the other person a general idea of the conversation's focus: "I've got to tell you about Jack," "Did you hear what happened in class yesterday?" or "We need to talk about our

vacation plans." Feedforward also may identify the tone of the conversation ("I'm really depressed and need to talk with you") or the time required ("This will just take a minute") (Frentz, 1976; Reardon, 1987).

Conversational awkwardness often occurs when feedforwards are used inappropriately. For example, using overly long feedforwards may make the listener wonder whether you'll ever get to the business at hand and may make you seem disorganized and lacking in focus. Omitting feedforward before a truly shocking message (for example, the terminal illness of a friend or relative) can make you seem insensitive or uncaring.

Often the feedforward is combined with the opening, as when you see someone on campus, for example, and say, "Hey, listen to this" or when, in a work situation, someone says, "Well, folks, let's get the meeting going."

## Business

The third step is the "business," the substance or focus of the conversation. The term *business* is used to emphasize that most conversations are goal directed. That is, you converse to fulfill one or several of the general purposes of interpersonal communication: to learn, relate, influence, play, or help (see Chapter 1). The term is also sufficiently general to incorporate all kinds of interactions. Not surprisingly, however, each culture has certain conversational **taboos**— topics or language that should be avoided, especially by "outsiders" (see Table 9.2). In any case, the business is conducted through an exchange of speaker and listener roles. Brief, rather than long, speaking turns characterize most satisfying conversations.

In the business stage, you talk about Jack, what happened in class, or your vacation plans. This is obviously the longest part of the conversation and the reason for the opening and the feedforward.

## Feedback

The fourth step is feedback (see Chapter 1), the reverse of the second step. Here you reflect back on the conversation to signal that, as far as you're concerned, the business is completed: "So you want to send Jack a get-well card," "Wasn't that the craziest class you ever heard of?" or "I'll call for reservations, and you'll shop for what we need."

Of course, the other person may not agree that the business has been completed and may therefore counter with, for example, "But what hospital is he in?" When this happens, you normally go back a step and complete the business.

## Closing

The fifth and last step, the opposite of the first step, is the closing, the goodbye, which often reveals how satisfied the persons were with the conversation: "I hope you'll call soon" or "Don't call us, we'll call you." The closing also may be used to schedule future conversations: "Give me a call tomorrow night" or "Let's meet for lunch at twelve." When closings are indefinite or vague, conversation often becomes awkward; you're not quite sure if you should say goodbye or if you should wait for something else to be said.

In a way similar to the opening and the feedforward being combined, the closing and the feedback might be combined, as when you say: "Look, I've got to think more about this commitment, okay?"

## ⏺ TABLE 9.2
## Conversational Taboos around the World

This table lists several examples of topics that Roger Axtell (in *Do's and Taboos around the World,* 1994) recommends that visitors from the United States avoid when in other countries. These examples are not intended to be exhaustive, but rather should serve as a reminder that each culture defines what is and what is not an appropriate topic of conversation. Note that this list was published in 1993. How would you revise this list to better represent today's conversational taboos?

| Country | Conversational Taboos |
| --- | --- |
| Belgium | Politics, language differences between French and Flemish, religion |
| Norway | Salaries, social status |
| Spain | Family, religion, jobs, criticism of bullfighting |
| Egypt | Middle Eastern politics |
| Nigeria | Religion |
| Libya | Politics, religion |
| Iraq | Religion, Middle Eastern politics |
| Japan | World War II |
| Pakistan | Politics |
| Philippines | Politics, religion, corruption, foreign aid |
| South Korea | Internal politics, socialism or communism, criticism of the government |
| Bolivia | Politics, religion |
| Colombia | Politics, criticism of bullfighting |
| Mexico | Mexican–American war, illegal aliens |
| Caribbean nations | Race, local politics, religion |

Before reading about the process of conversation management, think of your own conversations, recalling both conversations that were satisfactory and some that were unsatisfactory. Think of a specific recent conversation as you respond to the self-test "How Satisfying Is Your Conversation?" Taking this test now will help highlight the characteristics of conversational behavior and the aspects that make some conversations satisfying and others unsatisfying.

# TEST YOURSELF
## HOW SATISFYING IS YOUR CONVERSATION?

Respond to each of the following statements by recording the number best representing your feelings, using this scale: 1 = strongly agree, 2 = moderately agree, 3 = slightly agree, 4 = neutral, 5 = slightly disagree, 6 = moderately disagree, 7 = strongly disagree.

_____ 1. The other person let me know that I was communicating effectively.

_____ 2. Nothing was accomplished.

_____ 3. I would like to have another conversation like this one.

_____ 4. The other person genuinely wanted to get to know me.

_____ 5. I was very dissatisfied with the conversation.

_____ 6. I felt that during the conversation I was able to present myself as I wanted the other person to view me.

_____ 7. I was very satisfied with the conversation.
_____ 8. The other person expressed a lot of interest in what I had to say.
_____ 9. I did *not* enjoy the conversation.
_____ 10. The other person did *not* provide support for what he or she was saying.
_____ 11. I felt I could talk about anything with the other person.
_____ 12. We each got to say what we wanted.
_____ 13. I felt that we could laugh easily together.
_____ 14. The conversation flowed smoothly.
_____ 15. The other person frequently said things which added little to the conversation.
_____ 16. We talked about something I was *not* interested in.

**HOW DID YOU DO?**   To compute your score, follow these steps:

1. Add the scores for items 1, 3, 4, 6, 7, 8, 11, 12, 13, and 14.
2. Reverse the scores for items 2, 5, 9, 10, 15, and 16 such that 7 becomes 1, 6 becomes 2, 5 becomes 3, 4 remains 4, 3 becomes 5, 2 becomes 6, and 1 becomes 7.
3. Add the reversed scores for items 2, 5, 9, 10, 15, and 16.
4. Add the totals from steps 1 and 3 to yield your communication satisfaction score.

You may interpret your score along the following scale:

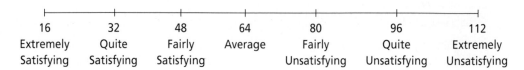

| 16 | 32 | 48 | 64 | 80 | 96 | 112 |
|----|----|----|----|----|----|-----|
| Extremely Satisfying | Quite Satisfying | Fairly Satisfying | Average | Fairly Unsatisfying | Quite Unsatisfying | Extremely Unsatisfying |

**WHAT WILL YOU DO?**   Before reading the remainder of this chapter, try to identify those qualities that make a conversation satisfying for you. What interpersonal qualities are most important to making a person a satisfying conversational partner? How might you cultivate these qualities? Table 9.3 identifies some unsatisfying conversational partners that you'll likely want to avoid in your own conversations.

*Source:* This test was developed by Michael Hecht and appeared in "The Conceptualization and Measurement of Interpersonal Communication Satisfaction," *Human Communication Research* 4 (1978): 253–264. It is reprinted by permission of the author.

 # CONVERSATIONAL MANAGEMENT

Speakers and listeners have to work together to make conversation an effective and satisfying experience. **Conversational management** includes initiating, maintaining, and closing conversations.

## Initiating Conversations

Several approaches to opening a conversation can be derived from the elements of the interpersonal communication process discussed in Chapter 1:

- *Self-references* say something about yourself. Such references may be of the "name, rank, and serial number" type—for example: "My name is Joe. I'm from Omaha." On the first day of class, students might say, "I'm worried about this class" or "I took this instructor last semester; she was excellent."
- *Other-references* say something about the other person or ask a question: "I like that sweater." "Didn't we meet at Charlie's?" Of course, there are pitfalls here. Generally, it's best not to comment on the person's race ("My uncle married a Korean"), the person's affectional orientation ("Nice to meet you; I have a gay brother"), or physical disability ("It must be awful to be confined to a wheelchair").

# InterMedia

## THE DIFFUSION OF INNOVATIONS

The *diffusion of innovation* theory focuses on the way media influence people to adopt something new or different. In this context the term *diffusion* refers to the passage of an innovation through society. *Innovation* refers to anything new; examples include soft contact lenses, laptop computers, personal data assistants, and PowerPoint aids for public speaking. Research distinguishes five types of adopters of innovations (see the figure below).

- *Innovators* (approximately 3 percent of the population) are not necessarily the originators of any given new idea, but they're the people who first introduce the innovation on a reasonably broad scale.
- *Early adopters* (approximately 14 percent) legitimize the innovation and make it acceptable to people in general.
- The *early majority* (approximately 34 percent) follows the early adopters and further legitimates the innovation.
- The *late majority* (approximately 34 percent) adopts the innovation after about half the population has adopted it.
- *Laggards* (approximately 14 percent) are the last group to adopt the innovation.

One final group, *diehards,* never adopt the innovation. Present-day examples of diehards include accountants who continue to do tax returns without the aid of computer software and lawyers or doctors who never use computerized databases.

### Follow Up

What is the role of the media in influencing your adoptions? What is the role of interpersonal conversation in influencing your adoptions? How do the media and interpersonal messages interact to influence your decisions about adopting innovations?

### The Five Types of Adopters

The five types of adopters as represented in the population according to the diffusion of innovations theory.

*Source:* Reprinted with the permission of The Free Press, an imprint of Simon & Schuster Adult Publishing Group, from *The Diffusion of Innovations,* Fourth Edition, by Everett M. Rogers. Copyright © 1995 by Everett M. Rogers. Copyright © 1962, 1971, 1983 by The Free Press. All rights reserved.

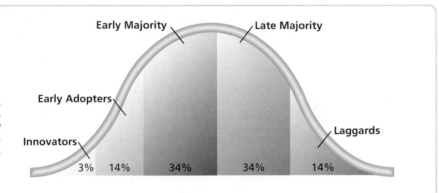

- *Relational references* say something about the two of you: for example, "May I buy you a drink?" "Would you like to dance?" or simply "May I join you?"
- *Context references* say something about the physical, social–psychological, cultural, or temporal context. The familiar "Do you have the time?" is a reference of this type. But you can be more creative and say, for example, "This restaurant seems very friendly" or "This Dali is fantastic."

As you know from experience, conversations are most satisfying when they're upbeat and positive. So it's generally best to lead off with something positive rather than something negative. Say, for example, "I like the music here" instead of "Don't you just hate this place?" Also, it's best not to be too revealing; disclosing too much too early in an interaction can make the other person feel uncomfortable.

## ⏷ TABLE 9.3

### Unsatisfying Conversational Partners and How Not to Become One of Them

As you read this table, consider your own conversations. Have you met any of these people? Have you ever been one of these people?

| Unsatisfying Conversational Partners | How Not to Become One of Them |
|---|---|
| The **Detour Taker** begins to talk about a topic and then goes off pursuing a totally different subject. | Follow a logical pattern in conversation, and avoid frequent and long detours. |
| The **Complainer** has many complaints and rarely tires of listing each of them. | Be positive; emphasize what's good before what's bad. |
| The **Moralist** evaluates and judges everyone and everything. | Avoid evaluation and judgment; see the world through the eyes of the other person. |
| The **Inactive Responder** gives no reaction regardless of what you say. | Respond overtly with verbal and nonverbal messages; let the other person see and hear that you're listening. |
| The **Story Teller** tells stories, too often substituting them for two-way conversation. | Talk about yourself in moderation; be other-oriented. |
| The **Interrogator** asks questions about everything, even about matters that are obvious or irrelevant. | Ask questions in moderation—to secure needed information and not to get every imaginable detail. |
| The **Egotist** talks only about topics that are self-related. | Be other-oriented; focus on the other person; listen as much as you speak. |
| The **Doomsayer** is the ultimate negative thinker; everything is a problem. | Be positive; talk about the good as well as the bad. |
| The **Arguer** listens only to find something to take issue with. | Be supportive, but argue and disagree when it's appropriate. |
| The **Thought Completer** "knows" exactly what you're going to say and so says it for you. | Don't interrupt; assume that the speaker wants to finish her or his own thoughts. |
| The **Self-Discloser** discloses more than you need or want to hear. | Disclose selectively, in ways appropriate to your relationship with the listener. |
| The **Advisor** regularly and consistently gives advice, whether you want it or not. | Don't assume that the expression of a problem is a request for a solution. |
| The **Psychiatrist** analyzes everything you say and mindreads your motives. | Avoid playing the therapist as a regular role; be a friend, lover, or parent. |

Another way of looking at the process of initiating conversations is to examine the infamous "opening line," the opener designed to begin a romantic relationship.

Consider your own opening lines (or the opening lines that have been used on you). Let's say you're at a club and want to strike up a conversation—and perhaps spark a relationship. Which of the following are you most likely to use (Kleinke, 1986; Kleinke & Dean, 1990)?

❶ *Cute–flippant openers* are humorous, indirect, and ambiguous as to whether or not the one opening the conversation really wants an extended encounter. Examples: "Is that really your hair?" "Bet I can outdrink you."

❷ *Innocuous openers* are highly ambiguous as to whether these are simple comments that might be made to just anyone or whether they're in fact openers designed to initiate an extended encounter. Examples: "What do you think of the band?" "Could you show me how to work this machine?"

❸ *Direct openers* demonstrate clearly the speaker's interest in meeting the other person. Examples: "I feel a little embarrassed about this, but I'd like to meet you." "Would you like to have a drink after dinner?"

One advantage of *cute-flippant* openers is that they're indirect enough to cushion any rejection. These are also, however, the lines least preferred by both men and women.

In contrast, both men and women generally like *innocuous* openers; they're indirect enough to allow for an easy out if the other person doesn't want to talk.

On *direct* openers, however, genders differ. Men like direct openers that are very clear in meaning, possibly because men are not used to having another person initiate a meeting. Women prefer openers that aren't too strong and that are relatively modest.

In e-mail conversations the situation is a bit different. Even before your message is opened, the receiver knows who the sender is, when the message was composed, and, from the title or subject line, something about the nature of your message. In addition to this general hint at the nature of the message, most e-mail users begin their e-mail with a kind of orientation or preface to what will follow, for example, "I'm writing to ask the name of your acupuncturist" or "I want to fill you in as to what happened at the party." Generally, such openers are direct and relate closely to what is to follow.

## Maintaining Conversations

In maintaining conversations you follow a variety of principles and rules. Here we'll consider first the principles and maxims you follow in conversation, and second the ways in which the speaker and listener exchange turns in conversation.

**The Principle of Cooperation**   During conversation you probably follow the principle of **cooperation,** implicitly agreeing with the other person to cooperate in trying to understand what each is saying (Grice, 1975; Lindblom, 2001). You cooperate largely by using four

# Understanding Interpersonal Skills

## EXPRESSIVENESS

**Expressiveness** is the skill of communicating genuine involvement; it involves, for example, taking responsibility for your thoughts and feelings, encouraging expressiveness or openness in others, and providing appropriate feedback.

**Communicating Expressiveness.** Here are a few suggestions for communicating expressiveness.

- Vary your vocal rate, pitch, volume, and rhythm to convey involvement and interest. Vary your language; avoiding clichés and trite expressions, which signal a lack of originality and personal involvement.
- Use appropriate gestures, especially gestures that focus on the other person rather than yourself. Maintain eye contact and lean toward the person; at the same time, avoid self-touching gestures or directing your eyes to others in the room.
- Give verbal and nonverbal feedback to show that you're listening. Such feedback promotes relationship satisfaction.
- Communicate expressiveness in ways that are culturally sensitive. Some cultures (Italian, for example) encourage expressiveness and teach children to be expressive. Other cultures (Japanese and Thai, for example) encourage a more reserved response style (Matsumoto, 1996). Some cultures (Arab and many Asian cultures, for example) consider expressiveness by women in business settings to be inappropriate (Lustig & Koester, 2006; Axtell, 1994; Hall & Hall, 1987).

conversational maxims—principles that speakers and listeners in the United States and in many other cultures follow in conversation. Although the names for these maxims may be new, the principles themselves will be easily recognized from your own experiences.

**The Maxim of Quantity**   Be as informative as necessary to communicate the intended meaning. Thus, in keeping with the **quantity maxim,** you include information that makes the meaning clear but omit what does not; you give neither too little nor too much information. You see people violate this maxim when they try to relate an incident and digress to give unnecessary information. You find yourself thinking or saying, "Get to the point; so what happened?" This maxim is also violated when necessary information is omitted. In this situation, you find yourself constantly interrupting to ask questions: "Where were they?" "When did this happen?" "Who else was there?"

This simple maxim is frequently violated in e-mail communication. Here, for example, are three ways in which e-mail often violates the maxim of quantity and some suggestions on how to avoid these violations.

- Chain e-mails often violate the maxim of quantity by sending people information they don't really need or want. Some people maintain lists of e-mail addresses and send all these people the same information. It's highly unlikely that everyone on these lists needs or wants to read the long list of jokes you find so funny. *Suggestion:* Avoid chain e-mail (at least most of the time). When something comes along that you think someone you know would like to read, send it on to the specific one, two, or three people you know would like to receive it.
- When chain e-mails are used, they often contain the e-mail addresses of everyone on the chain. These extensive headers clog the system and also reveal e-mail addresses that some people may prefer to keep private or to share with others at their own discretion. *Suggestion:* When you do send chain e-mails (and in some situations, they serve useful purposes), conceal the e-mail addresses of your recipients by using some general description such as "undisclosed recipients."
- Lengthy attachments take time to download and often create problems for people who do not have the latest technology. Not everyone wants to see the two hundred photos of your last vacation. *Suggestion:* Use attachments in moderation; find out first who would like to receive photos and who would not.

**The Maxim of Quality**   Say what you know or assume to be true, and do not say what you know to be false. When you're in conversation, you assume that the other person's information is true—at least as far as he or she knows. When you speak with people who frequently violate the **quality maxim** by lying, exaggerating, or minimizing major problems, you come to distrust what such individuals are saying and wonder what is true and what is fabricated.

**The Maxim of Relation**   Talk about what is relevant to the conversation. Thus, the **relation maxim** states, if you're talking about Pat and Chris and say, for example, "Money causes all sorts of relationship problems," it's assumed by others that your comment is somehow related to Pat and Chris. This principle is frequently violated by speakers who digress widely or frequently interject irrelevant comments, causing you to wonder how these comments are related to what you're discussing.

**The Maxim of Manner**   Be clear, avoid ambiguities, be relatively brief, and organize your thoughts into a meaningful sequence. Thus, in accordance with the **manner maxim,** you use terms that the listener understands and clarify terms that you suspect the listener will not understand. When talking with a child, for example, you simplify your vocabulary. Similarly, you adjust your manner of speaking on the basis of the information you and the listener share. When talking to a close friend, for example, you can refer to mutual acquaintances and to experiences you've had together. When talking to a stranger, however, you'll either omit such references or explain them.

# Ethics in Interpersonal Communication

## COMMUNICATING IN CYBERSPACE

Because of the explosion in computer communication, nethics (the ethics of Internet communication) has become an important part of ethical communication generally. Of course, the same principles that govern ethical face-to-face interaction also should prevail when you communicate on the Internet. Here, however, are a few ethical principles with special relevance to computer communication. It is unethical to:

- invade the privacy of others; for example, to read the files of another person or break into files you're not authorized to read
- harm others or their property; for example, to create computer viruses, publish instructions for making bombs, or create websites that promote violence
- spread falsehoods about other people, about the powers of medical or herbal treatments, or about yourself
- plagiarize, appropriating the work of another as your own
- steal passwords, PIN numbers, or authorization codes that belong to others
- copy software programs that you haven't paid for

### What Would You Do?

As an experiment you develop a computer virus that can destroy websites. Recently you've come across a variety of websites that you feel promote child pornography. You wonder if you can ethically destroy these websites. And, further, you wonder if not destroying them might actually be more unethical than using your newly developed virus.

---

The four maxims just discussed aptly describe most conversations as they take place in much of the United States. Recognize, however, that maxims will vary from one culture to another. Here are two maxims appropriate in cultures other than that of the United States, but also appropriate to some degree throughout the United States:

- In Japanese conversations and group discussions, a maxim of *preserving peaceful relationships* with others may be observed (Midooka, 1990). Thus, for example, it would be considered inappropriate to argue and to directly demonstrate that another person is wrong. It would be inappropriate to contribute to another person's embarrassment or, worse, loss of face.
- The maxim of *self-denigration,* observed in the conversations of Chinese speakers, may require that you avoid taking credit for some accomplishment or make less of some ability or talent you have (Gu, 1990). To put yourself down in this way is a form of politeness that seeks to elevate the person to whom you're speaking.

**The Principle of Dialogue**    Think about your own communication tendencies. Which of the following paired statements *generally* characterizes your interpersonal interactions?

| | |
|---|---|
| ❶ You frequently use negative criticism ("I didn't like that explanation") and negative personal judgments ("You're not a very good listener, are you?"). | ❶ You avoid negative criticism and negative personal avoid judgments; you practice using positive criticism ("I like those first two explanations best; they were really well reasoned"). |
| ❷ You frequently use dysfunctional communication, such as expressing unwillingness to talk, or use messages that are unrelated to the topic of discussion ("There's no sense discussing this; I can see you're not rational"). | ❷ You keep the channels of communication open ("I really don't know what I did that offended you, but tell me. I don't want to hurt you again"). |
| ❸ You rarely demonstrate through paraphrase or summary that you understand the other person's meaning. | ❸ You frequently paraphrase or summarize what the other person has said to ensure accurate understanding. |

### SPEAKING
### >> Interpersonal-E

**Gender Differences.** In the mid-1990s men used the Internet much more than women. Although the differences are lessening today, women still remain less frequent and less intense users than men (Ono & Zavodny, 2003). How would you describe the ways in which men and women use the Internet?

④ You rarely request clarification of the other person's perspectives or ideas.

⑤ You frequently request personal positive statements or statements of self-approval ("How did you like the way I told that guy off? Clever, no?").

④ You request clarification as necessary and ask for the other person's point of view because of a genuine interest in the other person's perspective.

⑤ You avoid requesting self-approval statements.

The statements in the left column are examples of monologue. The statements on the right are examples of dialogue. **Monologue** is communication in which one person speaks and the other listens; there's no real interaction among participants. The term *monologic communication* is an extension of this basic definition and refers to communication in which there is no genuine interaction, in which you speak without any real concern for the other person's feelings or attitudes. The monologic communicator is concerned only with his or her own goals and is interested in the other person only insofar as that person can be used to achieve those goals. In monologic interaction, you communicate what will advance your own goals, prove most persuasive, and benefit you.

Not surprisingly, effective communication is based not on monologue but on its opposite, *dialogue* (Buber, 1958; Brown & Keller, 1979; Thomlison, 1982; Yau-fair Ho, Chan, Peng, & Ng, 2001; McNamee & Gergen, 1999). In **dialogue,** there is two-way interaction. Each person is both speaker and listener, sender and receiver. In *dialogic communication* there is deep concern for the other person and for the relationship between the two people. The objective of dialogue is mutual understanding and empathy. There is respect for the other person, not because of what this person can do or give, but simply because this person is a human being and therefore deserves to be treated honestly and sincerely.

In a dialogic interaction, you respect the other person enough to allow that person the right to make his or her own choices without coercion, without the threat of punishment, without fear or social pressure. A dialogic communicator respects other people enough to believe that they can make their own decisions and implicitly or explicitly lets them know that whatever choices they make, they will still be respected as people.

# Understanding Interpersonal Theory and Research

## SOCIAL INFORMATION PROCESSING AND ONLINE COMMUNICATION

Social information processing (SIP) theory argues—contrary to social presence theory (see the Understanding Interpersonal Theory and Research box in Chapter 3, p. 64)—that whether you're communicating face-to-face or online, you can communicate the same degree of personal involvement and develop similar close relationships (Walther, 1992; Walther & Parks, 2002). The idea behind this theory is that communicators are clever people and that whatever channel people have available to send and receive messages, they will make adjustments to communicate what they want and to develop the relationships they want. It is true that when communication time is limited—as it is in many research studies—it is probably easier to communicate and develop relationships in face-to-face interaction than in online situations. But when the interaction occurs over an extended time, as it often does in ongoing chat groups and in repeated e-mail exchanges, then the communication and the relationships can be as personal as those you develop in face-to-face situations.

### Working with Theories and Research

How would you compare the level of closeness that you can communicate in face-to-face and in online situations? Do you feel it's more difficult (or even impossible) to communicate, say, support, warmth, and friendship in online communication than in face-to-face communication?

**The Principle of Turn Taking**   The defining feature of conversation is that the speaker and listener exchange roles throughout the interaction. You accomplish this through a wide variety of verbal and nonverbal cues that signal **conversational turns**—the changing (or maintaining) of the speaker or listener role during the conversation. In hearing people, turn taking is regulated by both audio and visual signals. Among blind speakers, the turn taking is governed in larger part by audio signals and often touch. Among deaf speakers, turn-taking signals are largely visual and also may involve touch (Coates & Sutton-Spence, 2001). Combining the insights of a variety of communication researchers (Duncan, 1972; Burgoon, Buller, & Woodall, 1996; Pearson & Spitzberg, 1990), let's look more closely at conversational turns in terms of cues that speakers use and cues that listeners use.

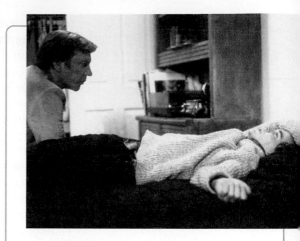

**↑ VIEWPOINT**

In dialogic interaction between, say, a fluent speaker and a person who has a severe physical or psychological communication problem, the more fluent speaker often tries to help the speaker with the problem communicate more effectively. In fact, some researchers have argued that the more competent communicator has an ethical responsibility to "equalize" the interaction by helping the other person to better convey his or her meaning (von Tetzchner & Jensen, 1999). Do you consider this an ethical responsibility?

**Speaker Cues**   As a speaker, you regulate conversation through two major types of cues: turn-maintaining and turn-yielding. *Turn-maintaining cues* are designed to help you maintain the speaker's role. You can do this with a variety of cues; for example, by audibly inhaling to show that you have more to say, continuing a gesture or gestures to show that you have not completed the thought, avoiding eye contact with the listener so there's no indication that you're passing the speaking turn to him or her, sustaining your intonation pattern to indicate that you intend to say more, or vocalizing pauses ("er," "um") to prevent the listener from speaking and to show that you're still talking (Duncan, 1972; Burgoon, Buller, & Woodall, 1996). In most cases, speakers are expected to maintain relatively brief speaking turns and to turn over the speaking role willingly to the listener (when so signaled by the listener).

With *turn-yielding cues* you tell the listener that you're finished and wish to exchange the role of speaker for that of listener. These cues tell the listener (sometimes a specific listener) to take over the role of speaker. For example, at the end of a statement you might add some paralinguistic cue such as "eh?" that asks one of the listeners to assume the role of speaker. You can also indicate that you've finished speaking by dropping your intonation, by prolonged silence, by making direct eye contact with a listener, by asking some general question, or by nodding in the direction of a particular listener.

In much the same way that you expect a speaker to yield the role of speaker, you also expect the listener to willingly assume the speaking role. Those who don't may be regarded as reticent or unwilling to involve themselves and take equal responsibility for the conversation. For example, in an analysis of turn-taking violations in the conversations of marrieds, the most common violation found was that of no response. Forty-five percent of the 540 violations identified involved a lack of response to an invitation to assume the speaker role. Of these "no response" violations, 68 percent were committed by men and 32 percent by women. Other turn-taking violations include interruptions, delayed responses, and inappropriately brief responses. From this it's been argued that by means of these violations, all of which are committed more frequently by men, men often silence women in marital interactions (DeFrancisco, 1991).

**Listener Cues**   As a listener, you can regulate the conversation by using a variety of cues. *Turn-requesting cues* let the speaker know that you'd like to take a turn as speaker. Sometimes you can do this by simply saying, "I'd like to say something," but often you do it more subtly through some vocalized "er" or "um" that tells the mindful speaker that you'd now like to speak. This request to speak is also often made with facial and mouth gestures. You can,

**Turn Taking in Chat Rooms.**
Because responses in chat rooms are posted in the order in which they are received, traditional turn taking does not appear to be followed. How would you describe the rules of turn taking in chat rooms?

for example, indicate a desire to speak by opening your eyes and mouth widely as if to say something, by beginning to gesture with your hand, or by leaning forward.

You can also indicate your reluctance to assume the role of speaker by using *turn-denying cues*. For example, intoning a slurred "I don't know" or a brief grunt signals you have nothing to say. Other ways to refuse a turn are to avoid eye contact with the speaker who wishes you to take on the role of speaker or to engage in some behavior that is incompatible with speaking—for example, coughing or blowing your nose.

*Back-channeling cues* are used to communicate various types of information back to the speaker without your assuming the role of speaker. Some researchers call these "acknowledgment tokens"—brief utterances such as "mm-hm," "uh-huh," and "yeah," the three most often used such tokens—that tell the speaker you're listening (Schegloff, 1982; Drummond & Hopper, 1993). You can communicate a variety of messages with these back-channeling cues; four such types are included in Table 9.4.

Some back-channeling cues are actually *interruptions*. These interruptions, however, are generally confirming rather than disconfirming. They tell the speaker that you're listening and are involved (Kennedy & Camden, 1988). Other interruptions are not as confirming and simply take the speaking turn away from the speaker, either temporarily or permanently. Sometimes the interrupter may apologize for breaking in; at other times he or she may not even seem aware of interrupting.

Interruptions can serve a variety of specific functions. For example, interruptions may be used to change the topic ("I gotta tell you this story before I bust"), to correct the speaker ("You mean four months, not years, don't you?"), to seek information and perhaps interject a question of clarification ("Do you mean Jeff's cousin?"), or to introduce essential information ("Your car's on fire"). Of course, you can interrupt to end the conversation ("I hate to interrupt, but I really have to get back to the office").

Not surprisingly, research finds that superiors (bosses, supervisors) and those in positions of authority (police officers, interviewers) interrupt those in inferior positions more than the other way around (Carroll, 1994; Ashcraft, 1998). In fact, it would probably strike you as strange to see a worker repeatedly interrupting a supervisor or a student repeatedly interrupting a professor.

## ↻ TABLE 9.4
## Functions of Back-Channeling Cues

Although you're probably seldom mindful of using back-channeling cues, you would miss them sorely if your listeners didn't use them. As you read through this table, consider how you communicate these various functions and how responsive you are to the back-channeling cues of others. This table is based on the excellent research summaries of Burgoon, Buller, and Woodall (1996) and Pearson and Spitzberg (1990).

| Functions | Examples |
|---|---|
| To indicate agreement or disagreement | Smiles, nods of approval, brief comments such as "Right" and "Of course," or a vocalization like "uh-huh" signal agreement. Frowning, shaking your head, or making comments such as "No" or "Never" signal disagreement. |
| To indicate degree of involvement | An attentive posture, forward leaning, and focused eye contact tell the speaker that you're involved in the conversation. An inattentive posture, backward leaning, and avoidance of eye contact communicate a lack of involvement. |
| To pace the speaker | Ask the speaker to slow down by raising your hand near your ear and leaning forward or to speed up by continued nodding of your head. Cue the speaker verbally by asking the speaker to slow down or to speed up. |
| To ask for clarification | Puzzled facial expressions, perhaps coupled with a forward lean, or direct interjection of "Who?," "When?," or "Where?" signal your need for clarification. |

Another and even more often studied aspect of interruption is that of gender difference. Do men or women interrupt more? Research here is conflicting. These few research findings will give you an idea of the differing results (Pearson, West, & Turner, 1995):

- The more malelike the person's gender identity—regardless of the person's biological sex—the more likely it is that the person will interrupt (Drass, 1986).
- There are no significant differences between boys and girls aged two to five in interrupting behavior (Greif, 1980).
- Fathers interrupt their children more than mothers do (Greif, 1980).
- Women more than men judge "simultaneous talk" as being interruptions (Bresnahan & Cai, 1996).
- Men interrupt more than women do (Zimmerman & West, 1975; West & Zimmerman, 1977).
- Men and women do not differ in their interrupting behavior (Roger & Nesshoever, 1987).
- No single linguistic feature has been found that definitely identifies a message as an interruption (Coon & Schwanenflugel, 1996).

The various turn-taking cues and how they correspond to the conversational wants of speaker and listener are summarized in Figure 9.2.

## Closing Conversations

Closing a conversation is often a difficult task. It can be an awkward and uncomfortable part of interpersonal interaction. Here are a few suggestions you might consider:

- Reflect back on the conversation and briefly summarize it so as to bring it to a close. For example: "I'm glad I ran into you and found out what happened at that union meeting. I'll probably be seeing you at the meetings next week."
- Directly state the desire to end the conversation and to get on with other things. For example: "I'd like to continue talking, but I really have to run. I'll see you around."
- Refer to future interaction. For example: "Why don't we get together next week sometime and continue this discussion?"
- Ask for closure. For example: "Have I explained what you wanted to know?"
- State that you enjoyed the interaction. For example: "I really enjoyed talking with you."

### ASK Yourself
#### Interrupting

You're supervising a group of six people who are working to revise your college's website. But one member of the group interrupts so much that other members have simply stopped contributing. It's become a one-person group, and you can't have this. Ask yourself: What are some of the things that you might say to correct this situation without coming across as the bossy supervisor?

---

### → FIGURE 9.2
### Turn Taking and Conversational Wants

Quadrant 1 represents the speaker who wishes to speak (continue to speak) and uses turn-maintaining cues; quadrant 2, the speaker who wishes to listen and uses turn-yielding cues; quadrant 3, the listener who wishes to speak and uses turn-requesting cues; and quadrant 4, the listener who wishes to listen (continue listening) and uses turn-denying cues. Back-channeling cues would appear in quadrant 4, as they are cues that listeners use while they continue to listen. Interruptions would appear in quadrant 3, though they're not so much cues that request a turn as takeovers of the speaker's position. Does this model allow for the representation off all conversational cues? Are there other types of cues that are not represented here?

|  | Conversational Wants | |
|---|---|---|
|  | **To Speak** | **To Listen** |
| **Speaker** | 1 Turn-maintaining cues | 2 Turn-yielding cues |
| **Listener** | 3 Turn-requesting cues | 4 Turn-denying cues |

## COMPUTER-MEDIATED COMMUNICATION

 I'm just getting into CMS (I know I'm late) and I really don't know how to alter my normal face-to-face conversational style to fit CMC—or even if I should alter it. I don't want to appear like the beginner I really am. Any suggestions?

If you're late to using CMC, it can be confusing following the conversational flow. It's like walking into a party where a number of people are talking at the same time. Before joining in, you should spend time reading and watching what other people are saying. Orient yourself to the conversation already taking place. Be aware that conversations often reference earlier messages and "RE" in the title means the message is part of a conversational "thread." Some lists have archives you can read to catch up with the group.

In Instant Messenging (IM) and chat environments, you will probably notice conversations that contain acronyms, playful spelling, and emoticons. It may take a while to get used to reading this new Internet shorthand. But dictionary guides for acronyms and emoticons are available on the Web to help you better understand this new style of language. Also, it is helpful to ask a friend who is familiar with Internet conversations for help.

**For further information** see S. B. Barnes, *Computer-Mediated Communication: Human-to-Human Communication across the Internet* (Boston: Allyn & Bacon, 2003) or visit http://emoticons.muller-godschalk.com/.

Susan B. Barnes (Ph.D, New York University) is an associate professor in the Department of Communication at Rochester Institute of Technology and teaches courses in electronic communication and computer-mediated communication, while researching social media and electronic forms of communication. Dr. Barnes (Susan.Barnes@rit.edu) also is the associate director of the Social Computing Lab at RIT (social.it.rit.edu).

## SPEAKING
## Interpersonal-E

**Relationship Communication in E-mail.** Women are more likely to use e-mail for relational purposes (e.g., for keeping in touch with family and friends) than are males—a finding that replicates the gender differences found in face-to-face communication and that demonstrates that it's easier for women to expand their social networks (Boneva, Kraut, & Frohlich, 2001). Do you find that women are more relational in their communication than men?

Closing a conversation in e-mail follows the same principles as closing a face-to-face conversation. But exactly when you end the e-mail exchange is often not clear, partly because the absence of nonverbal cues creates ambiguity. For example, if you ask someone a question and the other person answers, do you then e-mail again and say "thanks"? If so, should the other person e-mail you back and say "It was my pleasure"? And, if so, should you then e-mail back and say "I appreciate your willingness to answer my questions"? And, if so, should the other person then respond with something like "It was no problem"?

On the one hand, you don't want to prolong the interaction more than necessary; on the other, you don't want to appear impolite. So how do you signal (politely) that the e-mail exchange should stop? Here are a few suggestions (Cohen, 2002).

- Include in your e-mail the notation NRN (No Reply Necessary).
- If you're replying with information the other person requested, end your message with something like "I hope this helps."
- Title or head your message FYI (For Your Information), indicating that your message is just to keep someone in the loop.
- When you make a request for information, end your message with "thank you in advance."

With any of these closings, it should be clear to the other person that you're attempting to end the conversation. Obviously, you will have to use more direct methods with those who don't take these subtle hints or don't realize that both persons are responsible for the interpersonal interaction and for bringing it to a satisfactory close.

# CONVERSATIONAL PROBLEMS: PREVENTION AND REPAIR

In conversation you may anticipate a problem and seek to prevent it. Or you may discover that you said or did something that will lead to disapproval, and you may seek to excuse yourself. Here we'll look at just one example of a device to prevent potential conversational problems (the disclaimer) and one example of a device to repair conversational problems (the excuse). The purpose of these examples is simply to illustrate the complexity of these processes, not to present an exhaustive list of the ways conversational problems may be prevented or repaired.

## Preventing Conversational Problems: The Disclaimer

Let's say, for example, that you fear your listeners will at first think a comment you're about to make is inappropriate, that they may rush to judge you without hearing your full account, or that they will think you're not in full possession of your faculties. In these cases, you may use some form of disclaimer. A *disclaimer* (see Chapter 1) is a statement that aims to ensure that your message will be understood and will not reflect negatively on you (Hewitt & Stokes, 1975; McLaughlin, 1984). There are several types of disclaimer.

*Hedging* helps you to separate yourself from the message so that if your listeners reject your message, they need not reject you (for example, "I may be wrong here, but . . ."). If a hedge is seen as indicating a lack of certainty or conviction because of some inadequacy, it will decrease the attractiveness of both women and men (Wright & Hosman, 1983). However, it will will be more positively received if it is seen as indicating a lack of belief in allness (as indicating that no one can know all about any subject) as well as a belief that tentative statements are all a person can reasonably make (Hosman, 1989; Pearson, Turner, & Todd-Mancillas, 1991).

*Credentialing* helps you establish your special qualifications for saying what you're about to say ("Don't get me wrong, I'm not homophobic" or "As someone who telecommutes, I . . ."). *Sin licenses* ask listeners for permission to deviate in some way from some normally accepted convention ("I know this may not be the place to discuss business, but . . ."). *Cognitive disclaimers* help you make the case that you're in full possession of your faculties ("I know you'll think I'm crazy, but let me explain the logic of the case"). *Appeals for the suspension of judgment* ask listeners to hear you out before making a judgment ("Don't hang up on me until you hear my side of the story").

Generally, disclaimers are effective when you think you might offend listeners in telling a joke ("I don't usually like these types of jokes, but . . ."). In one study, for example, 11-year-old children were read a story about someone whose actions created negative effects. Some children heard the story with a disclaimer, and others heard the same story without the disclaimer. When the children were asked to indicate how the person should be punished, those who heard the story with the disclaimer recommended significantly lower punishments (Bennett, 1990).

Disclaimers, however, can also get you into trouble. For example, to preface remarks with "I'm no liar" may well lead listeners to think that perhaps you are lying. Also, if you use too many disclaimers, you may be perceived as someone who doesn't have any strong convictions or as one who wants to avoid responsibility for just about everything. This seems especially true of hedges.

In responding to statements containing disclaimers, it's often necessary to respond to both the disclaimer and to the statement. By doing so, you let the speaker know that you heard the disclaimer and that you aren't going to view this communication negatively. Appropriate responses might be: "I know you're no sexist, but I don't agree that . . ." or "Well, perhaps we should discuss the money now even if it doesn't seem right."

**Driving and the Cell Phone.** One of the great advantages of cell phone communication is that you can talk wherever you are. However, talking on the cell while driving creates problems—as both common sense and research findings agree (Charlton, 2004; Gugerty, Rakauskas, & Brooks, 2004). What can you do to guard against the dangers of driving while talking on the phone? Would you support passing laws banning cell phone use by drivers, as has been done in some municipalities?

## Repairing Conversational Problems: The Excuse

At times you may say the wrong thing; then, because you can't erase the message (communication really is irreversible), you may try to account for it. Perhaps the most common method for doing so is the excuse. You learn early in life that when you do something that others will view negatively, an excuse is in order to justify your performance. **Excuses,** central to all forms of communication and interaction, are "explanations or actions that lessen the negative implications of an actor's performance, thereby maintaining a positive image for oneself and others" (Snyder, 1984; Snyder, Higgins, & Stucky, 1983).

Excuses seem especially in order when you say or are accused of saying something that runs counter to what is expected, sanctioned, or considered "right" by the people with whom you're talking. Ideally, the excuse lessens the negative impact of the message.

**Some Motives for Excuse Making**    The major motive for excuse making seems to be to maintain your self-esteem, to project a positive image to yourself and to others. Excuses also represent an effort to reduce stress: You may feel that if you can offer an excuse—especially a good one that is accepted by those around you—it will reduce the negative reaction and the subsequent stress that accompanies a poor performance.

Excuses also may enable you to maintain effective interpersonal relationships even after some negative behavior. For example, after criticizing a friend's behavior and observing the negative reaction to your criticism, you might offer an excuse such as, "Please forgive me; I'm really exhausted. I'm just not thinking straight." Excuses enable you to place your messages—even your possible failures—in a more favorable light.

**Types of Excuses**    Think of the recent excuses you have used or heard. Did they fall into any of these three classes (Snyder, 1984)?

❶ *I didn't do it:* Here you deny that you have done what you're being accused of. You may then bring up an alibi to prove you couldn't have done it, or perhaps you may accuse another person of doing what you're being blamed for ("I never said that" or "I wasn't even near the place when it happened"). These "I didn't do it" types are the worst excuses, because they fail to acknowledge responsibility and offer no assurance that this failure will not happen again.

❷ *It wasn't so bad:* Here you admit to doing it but claim the offense was not really so bad or perhaps that there was justification for the behavior ("I only padded the expense account, and even then only modestly" or "Sure, I hit him, but he was asking for it").

❸ *Yes, but:* Here you claim that extenuating circumstances accounted for the behavior; for example, that you weren't in control of yourself at the time or that you didn't intend to do what you did ("It was the liquor talking" or "I never intended to hurt him; I was actually trying to help").

**Good and Bad Excuses**    The most important question for most people is what makes a good excuse and what makes a bad excuse (Snyder, 1984; Slade, 1995). How can you make good excuses and thus get out of problems, and how can you avoid bad excuses that only make matters worse? Good excuse makers use excuses in moderation; bad excuse makers rely on excuses too often. Good excuse makers avoid blaming others, especially those they work with; bad excuse makers blame even their work colleagues. In a similar way, good excuse makers don't attribute their failure to others or to the company; bad excuse makers do. Good excuse makers acknowledge their own responsibility for the failure by noting that they did something wrong (not that they lack competence); bad excuse makers refuse to accept any responsibility for their failures. Excuse makers who accept responsibility will be perceived as more credible, competent, and likable than those who deny responsibility (Dunn & Cody, 2000).

What makes one excuse effective and another ineffective will vary from one culture to another and will depend on factors already discussed such as the culture's individualism–collectivism, its power distance, the values it places on assertiveness, and various other cultural tendencies (Tata, 2000). But, at least in the United States, researchers seem to agree that the best excuses contain five elements (Slade, 1995; Coleman, 2002).

1. You demonstrate that you really understand the problem and that your partner's feelings are legitimate and justified. Avoid minimizing the issue or your partner's feelings ("It was only $100; you're overreacting," "I was only two hours late").

2. You acknowledge your responsibility. If you did something wrong, avoid qualifying your responsibility ("I'm sorry *if* I did anything wrong") or expressing a lack of sincerity ("Okay, I'm sorry; it's obviously my fault—*again*"). On the other hand, if you can demonstrate that you had no control over what happened and therefore cannot be held responsible, your excuse is likely to be highly persuasive (Heath, Stone, Darley, & Grannemann, 2003).

3. You acknowledge your own displeasure at what you did; you make it clear that you're not happy with yourself for having done what you did.

4. You request forgiveness for what you did. Be explicit about this.

5. You make it clear that your misdeed will never happen again.

Table 9.5 provides examples of excuses you might use in romantic and business situations.

**⏻ TABLE 9.5**
### Excuses in Romantic and Workplace Relationships

Here are five intended excuse messages along with some specific examples. As you read this table, visualize a specific situation in which you recently made an excuse. Can what you said (or should have said) be organized into this five-step plan?

| Intended Message | In Romantic Relationships | At Work |
| --- | --- | --- |
| 1. I see. | I should have asked you first; you have a right to be angry. | I understand that we lost the client because of this. |
| 2. I did it. | I was totally responsible. | I should have acted differently. |
| 3. I'm sorry. | I'm sorry that I didn't ask you first. | I'm sorry I didn't familiarize myself with the client's objections to our last offer. |
| 4. Forgive me. | Forgive me? | I'd really like another chance. |
| 5. I'll do better. | I'll never lend anyone money without first discussing it with you. | This will never happen again. |

# GOSSIP AND THE GRAPEVINE

Two additional forms of conversation need to be mentioned: gossiping and grapevine conversation. These two forms of conversation are especially interesting—both because they occupy such a large part of our conversational time and because they can create problems when some simple principles are not followed. Let's consider gossip first.

## Gossip

Gossip is social talk that involves making evaluations about persons who are not present during the conversation; it generally occurs when two people talk about a third party (Eder & Enke, 1991). As you obviously know, a large part of your conversation at work and in social situations is spent gossiping (Lachnit, 2001; Waddington, 2004; Carey, 2005). In fact, one study estimates that approximately two-thirds of people's conversation time is devoted to social topics, and that most of these topics can be considered gossip (Dunbar, 2004). Gossiping seems universal among all cultures (Laing, 1993), and among some it's a commonly accepted ritual (Hall, 1993).

Lots of reasons have been suggested for the popularity and persistence of gossip. One reason often given is that gossip bonds people together and solidifies their relationship; it creates a sense of camaraderie (Greengard, 2001; Hafen, 2004). At the same time, of course, it helps to create an in-group (those doing the gossiping) and an out-group (those being gossiped about). Gossip also serves a persuasive function in teaching people the **cultural rules** of their society. That is, when you gossip about the wrong things that so-and-so did, you're in effect identifying the rules that should be followed and perhaps even the consequences that follow when the rules are broken. Gossip enables you to learn what is and what is not acceptable behavior (Baumeister, Zhang, & Vohs, 2004). Within an organization, gossip helps to regulate organization behavior: Gossip enables workers to learn who the organizational heroes are, what they did, and how they were rewarded—and carries an implicit exhortation to do likewise. And, of course, negative gossip enables workers to learn who broke the rules and what punishments resulted from such rule-breaking—again, with an accompanying implicit admonition to avoid such behaviors (Hafen, 2004).

People often engage in gossip for some kind of reward; for example, to hear more gossip, gain social status or control, have fun, cement social bonds, or make social comparisons (Rosnow, 1977; Miller & Wilcox, 1986; Leaper & Holliday, 1995; Wert & Salovey, 2004). Research is not consistent on the consequences of gossip for the person gossiping. One research study argues that gossiping leads others to see you more negatively, regardless of whether your gossip is positive or negative and whether you're sharing this gossip with strangers or friends (Turner, Mazur, Wendel, & Winslow, 2003). Another study finds that positive gossip leads to acceptance by your peers and greater friendship intimacy (Cristina, 2001).

As you might expect, gossiping often has ethical implications, and in many instances gossip would be considered unethical. Some such instances: when gossip is used to unfairly hurt another person, when you know it's not true, when no one has the right to such personal information, or when you've promised secrecy (Bok, 1983).

## The Grapevine

A particular kind of gossip that occurs in organizational settings is that of grapevine conversation. **Grapevine messages** don't follow any of the formal lines of communication established in an organization; rather, they seem to have a life of their own and may be concerned with personal and social matters or with job-related issues that you want to discuss in a more interpersonal setting. Not surprisingly, the grapevine also grows as the size of the organization increases.

The grapevine is most likely to be used when there are important subjects to be discussed, when formal management communication is lacking, and when people perceive the situation as threatening or insecure (Crampton, Hodge, & Mishra, 1998). In fact, one research study notes that during crises workers spend between 65 and 70 percent of their time on the grapevine. Even in noncrisis times, workers spend 10 to 15 percent of their time on grapevine conversation (Smith, 1996). The grapevine also is surprisingly accurate, with estimates of accuracy ranging from 75 to 95 percent (Davis, 1980; Hellweg, 1992; Smith, 1996).

Grapevine conversation is not simply frivolous; it's an essential part of effective business communication, though it's interesting to note that in one study more than 92 percent of organizations surveyed had no policy for dealing with grapevine messages (Crampton, Hodge, & Mishra, 1998). Here are a few useful suggestions for dealing with this unique kind of conversation:

- Understand the variety of purposes the grapevine serves. Its speed and general accuracy make it an ideal medium to carry a great deal of the social communications that so effectively bind workers together.
- Although grapevine information is generally accurate, it's often incomplete and may contain crucial distortions. So if you learn something through the grapevine, treat the information as tentative, as possibly not necessarily true.
- Tap into the grapevine. Whether you're a worker or in management, it's important to hear grapevine information. It may clue you in to events that will figure into your future with the organization, and it will help you network with others in the organization.
- Always assume that what you say in grapevine communication will be repeated to others (Smith, 1996; Hilton, 2000). Always be mindful of your organizational communications; the potentially offensive joke that you e-mail a colleague can easily be forwarded to the very people who may take offense.

## Reviewing  Key Terms and Concepts in Conversation

This chapter reviewed the process of conversation and focused on its stages, on rules and principles for effective management, is on ways to cope with conversational problems, and on gossip and the grapevine—two special forms of conversation.

### The Conversation Process

What are the major stages in conversation?

- The *opening* initiates and begins the conversation.
- The *feedforward* previews or prefaces the major part of the conversation that is to follow.
- The *business* is the major part of the conversation; it's the reason for the conversation.
- The *feedback* summarizes or reflects back on the conversation.
- The *closing* brings the conversation to an end.

### Conversational Management

How do you go about initiating, maintaining, and closing conversations so that they're effective and satisfying?

- Initiating conversations is often accomplished by means of self-references, other-references, relational references, and context references.

- Maintaining conversations depends on the principle of cooperation; the maxims of quantity, quality, relation, and manner; the principle of dialogue; and the principle of turn taking.
- Ways to close conversations include reflecting back on the conversation, directly stating the desire to end the conversation, referring to future interactions, asking for closure, and expressing pleasure with interaction.

### Conversational Problems: Prevention and Repair

How may conversational problems be prevented and repaired?

- One way to prevent conversational problems is to use the disclaimer, a statement that helps to ensure that your message will be understood and will not reflect negatively on you. Disclaimer types include hedging, credentialing, sin licenses, cognitive disclaimers, and appeals for the suspension of judgment.
- Conversational repair often involves the excuse, an explanation designed to lessen the negative impact of a speaker's messages. Excuses generally come in three types: *I didn't do it, It wasn't so bad,* and *Yes, but.*

**1** Try collecting examples of disclaimers from your interpersonal interactions as well as from the media. Consider, for example, what type of disclaimer is being used. Why is it being used? Is the disclaimer appropriate? What other kinds of disclaimers could have been used more effectively?

**2** Another way of looking at conversational rule violations is as breaches of etiquette. When you fail to follow the rules of etiquette, you're often breaking a conversational rule. A variety of websites focus on etiquette in different communication situations. For the etiquette of online conversation see http://www.internetiquette.org/; for Web etiquette see http://www.w3.org/Provider/Style/Etiquette.html; and for cell phone etiquette see http://www.cell-phone-etiquette.com/index.htm. Visit one or more of these websites and record any rules you find particularly applicable to interpersonal communication and conversation.

**3** As explained in the text, research shows that hedging reflects negatively on both male and female speakers when it indicates a lack of certainty or conviction resulting from some inadequacy on the speaker's part. The hedging will be more positively received, however, if listeners feel it reflects the speaker's belief that tentative statements are the only kinds a person can reasonably make (Wright & Hosman, 1983; Hosman, 1989;

Pearson, West, & Turner, 1995). Do you find this to be true from your experience in using and listening to hedges?

**4** As we've seen, each culture has its own conversational taboos; some examples are presented in Table 9.2 (p. 197). What are some of the conversational taboos you find operating in the classroom? In informal groups with other students? At work?

**5** An analysis of 43 published studies on interruptions and gender differences showed that men interrupted significantly more than women (Anderson, 1998). Among the reasons offered to explain why men interrupt more is the proposition that men who interrupt are seeking to shift the conversational focus to areas of their competence and away from areas of incompetence and to maintain power and control. What is your own experience with gender differences and interruptions? Do you find that your own experience supports these findings on gender differences? Based on your experiences, how would you explain the reasons for interrupting?

**6** Given your understanding of turn-taking and the ways in which blind and sighted people communicate (you may wish to revisit Table 1.3 in this connection), what suggestions would you advance for improving communication between blind and sighted individuals?

Go to www.ablongman.com/devito.

*This group of experiences deals with the conversation process and with a special type of conversational situation, namely communicating emotions.*

❶ **How Do You Open a Conversation?** and ❷ **How Do You Close a Conversation?** provide practice in beginning and ending conversations effectively. ❸ **Conversational Analysis: A Chance Meeting** provides a dialogue that you can analyze for the elements and principles of conversation covered in this chapter. ❹ **Giving and Taking Directions** is a gamelike experience that will illustrate the difficulties in giving and taking directions and suggest how these difficult communication situations can be made more effective. ❺ **Communicating Your Emotions,** ❻ **Expressing Negative Feelings,** ❼ **Communicating Emotions Effectively,** and **Emotional Advice** provide experience in communicating your emotions to others. ❾ **Gender and the Topics of Conversation** looks at gender differences in conversation. ❿ **Responding Effectively in Conversation** and **The Qualities of Effectiveness** are summary-type exercises that provide the opportunity to apply the qualities of effectiveness that you've already encountered to conversation. **Formulating Excuses** provides practice in developing and expressing excuses.

CHAPTER

# 10 | Universals of Interpersonal Relationships

⬆ *Kinsey* (2004)

One of the most influential people in bringing to light the sexual and relationship practices of ordinary people was Alfred Kinsey, whose life and contributions are depicted in the film *Kinsey*. This chapter looks at relationships and describes their characteristics, their stages, and the ways in which they are influenced by culture and technology.

> **"Communication is to a relationship what breathing is to maintaining life. "** —Virginia Satir

Contact with other human beings is so important that when you're deprived of it for long periods, depression sets in, self-doubt surfaces, and you may find it difficult to manage even the basics of daily life. Research shows clearly that the most important contributor to happiness—outranking money, job, and sex—is a close relationship with one other person (Freedman, 1978; Laroche & deGrace, 1997; Lu & Shih, 1997). The desire for relationships is universal; interpersonal relationships are important to men and to women, to homosexuals and to heterosexuals, to young and to old (Huston & Schwartz, 1995).

Interpersonal relationships come in a variety of forms. Although the romantic relationship perhaps comes to mind most quickly, interpersonal relationships exist between friends, mentors and protégés, family members, and work team colleagues, for example. The quality that makes a relationship interpersonal is interdependency: The actions of one person affect the other; one person's actions have consequences for the other person. The actions of a stranger, such as working overtime or flirting with a coworker, will have no impact on you; you and the stranger are independent—your actions have no effect on the other person. If, however, you were in an interpersonal relationship and your partner worked overtime or flirted with a coworker, it would have an impact on you and on the relationship in some way.

##  CHARACTERISTICS OF INTERPERSONAL RELATIONSHIPS

Relationships may be viewed on a continuum, from the impersonal at one end to the highly personal (that is, interpersonal) at the other end. We can distinguish interpersonal relationships from impersonal relationships on the basis of three main factors: psychological data, explanatory knowledge, and personally established rules.

### Psychological Data

In impersonal relationships, people respond to each other chiefly as members of the class or group to which each belongs. For example, initially you respond to a particular college professor as you respond to college professors in general. Similarly, the college professor responds to you as he or she responds to students generally. As your relationship becomes more personal, however, both of you begin to respond to each other not as members of groups but as unique individuals. Put differently, in impersonal relationships, the social or cultural role of the person governs your interaction; in personal or interpersonal relationships, the psychological uniqueness of the person tells you how to interact.

This progression from social to psychological data happens in the United States and in most European cultures. In many Asian and African cultures, however, the individual's group membership is always important; it never recedes into the background. Thus, in these cultures, a person's group membership (the person's social data)—even in the closest intimate relationships—is always important, often more important than the person's individual or psychological characteristics (Moghaddam, Taylor, & Wright, 1993).

## Explanatory Knowledge

In impersonal relationships, you can do little more than *describe* a person or a person's way of communicating. As you get to know someone a bit better, you can *predict* his or her behavior. If you get to know the person even better, you'll become able to *explain* the behavior. The college professor, in an impersonal relationship, may be able to describe, say, your lateness; perhaps he or she also can predict that you'll be five minutes late to class each Friday. In an interpersonal situation, however, the professor can go beyond these levels to explain the behavior—in this case, give reasons why you're late.

## Personally Established Rules

In impersonal relationships, the rules of interaction are set down by social norms. Students and professors behave toward one another—in impersonal situations—according to the social norms established by their culture and society. However, as the relationship between student and professor becomes interpersonal, the social rules no longer totally regulate the interaction. Student and professor begin to establish rules of their own, largely because they begin to see each other as unique individuals rather than merely as members of the social categories of "student" and "professor."

A good way to begin the study of interpersonal relationships is to examine your own relationships (past, present, or those you look forward to) by taking the self-test "What Do Your Relationships Do for You?" It highlights the advantages and the disadvantages that relationships serve.

# TEST YOURSELF
## WHAT DO YOUR RELATIONSHIPS DO FOR YOU?

Focus on your own relationships in general (friendship, romantic, family, and work), or focus on one particular relationship (say, your relationship with your life partner, your child, or your best friend), or focus on one type of relationship (say, friendships) and respond to the following by indicating the extent to which your relationship(s) serve each of these functions. Use a 10-point scale with 1 indicating that your relationship(s) never serves this function, 10 indicating that your relationship(s) always serves this function, and the numbers in between indicating levels between these extremes.

_____ 1. My relationships help to lessen my loneliness.
_____ 2. My relationships increase my obligations.
_____ 3. My relationships help me gain in self-knowledge and in self-esteem.
_____ 4. My relationships prevent me from developing other relationships.
_____ 5. My relationships maximize my pleasures and minimize my pains.
_____ 6. My relationships scare me, because they may be difficult to dissolve.

**HOW DID YOU DO?** The numbers from 1 to 10 that you used to respond to each statement should give you some idea of how strongly your relationships serve these advantages. The odd-numbered statements (1, 3, and 5) express what most people would consider advantages of interpersonal relationships.

(1) One of the major benefits of relationships is that they help to lessen loneliness and depression (Rokach, 1998; Morahan-Martin & Schumacher, 2003; Wallis, 2005; Lansford, Antonucci, Akiyama, & Takahashi, 2005). They make you feel that someone cares, that someone likes you, that someone will protect you, that someone ultimately will love you.

(2) Close relationships increase your obligations to these other people, sometimes to great extents. Your time is no longer entirely your own. And although you enter relationships to spend more time with these special people, you also incur time (and perhaps financial) obligations with which you may not be happy.

(3) Through contact with others you learn about yourself and see yourself from different perspectives and in different roles, as a child or parent, as a coworker, as a manager, as a best friend. Healthy

interpersonal relationships help enhance self-esteem and self-worth. Simply having a friend or romantic partner (at least most of the time) makes you feel desirable and worthy.

(4) Close relationships can result in your abandoning other relationships. Sometimes, it involves someone you like but your partner can't stand. More often, however, it's simply a matter of time and energy; relationships take a lot of both, and you have less to give to these other and less intimate relationships.

(5) The most general function served by interpersonal relationships, and one that encompasses all the others, is that of maximizing pleasure and minimizing pain. Your good friends, for example, will make you feel even better about your good fortune and less hurt when you're confronted with hardships.

(6) The closer your relationship, the more emotionally difficult it is to dissolve, a feeling that may be uncomfortable for some people. If the relationship is deteriorating, you may feel distress or depression. In some cultures, for example, religious pressures may prevent married couples from separating. And, if lots of money is involved, dissolving a relationship often can mean giving up the assets you've spent your life accumulating.

The even-numbered statements (2, 4, and 6) express what most people consider disadvantages of interpersonal relationships:

**WHAT WILL YOU DO?**   One way to use this self-test is to consider how you might lessen the disadvantages of your interpersonal relationships. Consider, for example, if your own behaviors are contributing to the disadvantages. For example, do you bury yourself in one or two relationships and discourage the development of others? At the same time, consider how you can maximize the advantages that your relationships currently provide.

 ## STAGES IN INTERPERSONAL RELATIONSHIPS

You and another person don't become intimate friends immediately upon meeting. Rather, you build an intimate relationship gradually, through a series of steps or stages. The same is true of most relationships. Of course, the "love at first sight" phenomenon creates a

# Understanding Interpersonal Theory and Research
## RELATIONSHIP DIALECTICS THEORY

**Relationship dialectics theory** argues that people in a relationship experience ongoing tensions between conflicting pairs of opposite motives or desires. Research generally finds three such opposites (Baxter, 2004; Baxter & Simon, 1993; Rawlins, 1989, 1992).

- You have a desire for both closedness and openness. That is, you want both to be in an exclusive relationship and, on the other hand, to be free to connect with different people. You want the security of an exclusive relationship but also the excitement of new and different relationships.
- You want to be both autonomous and connected; you want to remain an autonomous, independent individual but also to connect intimately to another person and to a relationship (Sahlstein, 2004).
- You want both novelty and predictability; you want newness, different experiences, and adventure on the one hand and sameness, stability, and predictability on the other.

These tensions influence your behavior. For example, if you find your primary relationship (see Chapter 12) overwhelmingly predictable, you may seek novelty elsewhere, perhaps through trips to exotic places, perhaps through contacts with different partners. If you find the relationship too connected (even "suffocating"), you may crave physical and psychological space to meet your autonomy needs.

### Working with Theories and Research

Analyze your own relationships in terms of the opposing needs and wants noted here. How would you describe your own needs for closedness–openness, autonomy–connection, and novelty–predictability? How do these needs influence your relationship behavior?

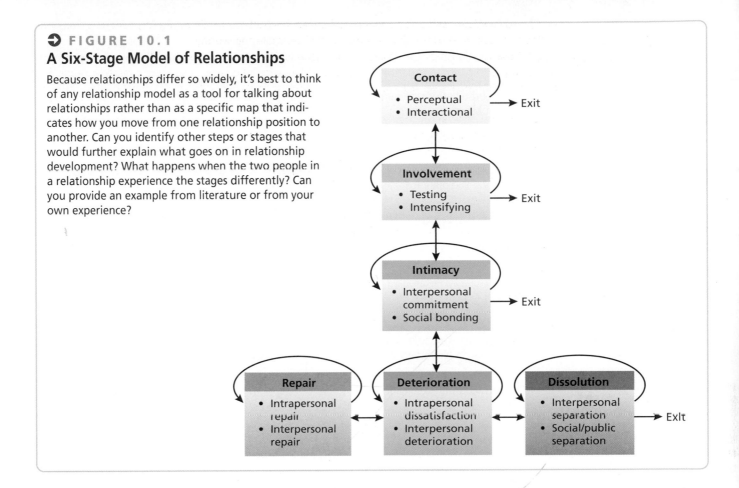

### ◑ FIGURE 10.1
### A Six-Stage Model of Relationships

Because relationships differ so widely, it's best to think of any relationship model as a tool for talking about relationships rather than as a specific map that indicates how you move from one relationship position to another. Can you identify other steps or stages that would further explain what goes on in relationship development? What happens when the two people in a relationship experience the stages differently? Can you provide an example from literature or from your own experience?

**Contact**
- Perceptual
- Interactional
→ Exit

**Involvement**
- Testing
- Intensifying
→ Exit

**Intimacy**
- Interpersonal commitment
- Social bonding
→ Exit

**Repair**
- Intrapersonal repair
- Interpersonal repair

**Deterioration**
- Intrapersonal dissatisfaction
- Interpersonal deterioration

**Dissolution**
- Interpersonal separation
- Social/public separation
→ Exit

problem for a stage model of relationships. So, rather than argue that such love cannot occur (my own feeling is that it can and frequently does), it seems wiser simply to claim that the stage model characterizes most relationships for most people most of the time.

The six-stage model in Figure 10.1 describes the main stages in most relationships. For a particular relationship, you might wish to modify the basic model. But as a general description of **relationship development,** the stages seem fairly standard. Do realize, of course, that both partners may not perceive their relationship in the same way; one person, for example, may see the relationship as intimate whereas the other does not.

As shown in the figure, the six stages of face-to-face or "real-world" relationships are contact, involvement, intimacy, deterioration, repair, and dissolution. Each stage has an early and a late phase. These stages describe relationships as they are; they don't evaluate or prescribe how relationships should be. Online relationships are somewhat different; see Table 10.1 for an example of the stages of an Internet relationship.

## Contact

At the initial phase of the **contact** stage, there is some kind of *perceptual contact*—you see, hear, read a message from or perhaps smell the person. From this you form a mental and physical picture—gender, approximate age, beliefs and values, height, and so on. After this perception, there is usually *interactional contact.* Here the contact is superficial and relatively impersonal. This is the stage at which you exchange basic information that is preliminary to any more intense involvement ("Hello, my name is Joe"). Here you initiate interaction ("May I join you?") and engage in invitational communication ("May I buy you a drink?"). According to some researchers, it's at this stage—

## Online Relationship Stages

This table represents one attempt to identify the stages that people go through in Internet relationships. As you read down the table, consider how accurately this represents what you know of online relationships. How would you describe the way Internet relationships develop?

| Stage | Behavior |
|---|---|
| 1. Curiosity | You explore and search for individuals through chat rooms and other online sources. |
| 2. Investigation | You find out information about the individual. |
| 3. Testing | You introduce various topics, looking for common ground. |
| 4. Increasing frequency of contact | You increase the breadth and depth of your relationship. |
| 5. Anticipation | You anticipate face-to-face interaction and wonder what that will bring. |
| 6. Fantasy integration | You create a fantasy of what the person looks like and how the person behaves. |
| 7. Face-to-face meeting | You meet face-to-face, and reality and fantasy meet. |
| 8. Reconfiguration | You adjust the fantasy to the reality; you may decide to end the relationship or pursue it more vigorously. |
| 9. Already separated | If you decide to maintain the relationship, you explore ways you can maintain a long-distance relationship through other means of communication. |
| 10. Long-term relationship | You negotiate the new relationship, whether it will continue in its online form or change into a new face-to-face form. |

*Source:* This table is adapted from Leonard J. Shedletsky and Joan E. Aitken, *Human Communication on the Internet* (Boston: Allyn & Bacon, 2004), p. 159. Copyright © by Pearson Education. Adapted by permission of the publisher.

within the first four minutes of initial interaction—that you decide whether you want to pursue the relationship (Zunin & Zunin, 1972).

At the contact stage in face-to-face interaction, physical appearance is especially important, because it's the characteristic most readily seen. Yet through verbal and nonverbal behaviors, qualities such as friendliness, warmth, openness, and dynamism also are revealed. In contrast, in computer-mediated contact, attitudinal sameness and wanting essentially the same things may be most influential in the beginning. This distinction, however, gets cloudy at times. For example, at least one online bulletin board contains a "missed connections" section where people post messages such as "I saw you on the bus and thought we connected, but you got off before I could say anything"—in the hope that the other person also felt a "missed connection" and also is hoping to make contact (J. Lee, 2005).

## Involvement

At the **involvement** stage, a sense of mutuality, of being connected develops. Here you experiment and try to learn more about the other person. At the initial phase of involvement, a kind of *testing* goes on. You want to see whether your initial judgment proves reasonable. So you may ask questions: "Where do you work?" "What are you majoring in?" If you want to get to know the person even better, you might continue your involvement by intensifying your interaction by beginning to reveal yourself, though in a preliminary way. In a dating relationship, you might, for example, use a variety of strategies to help you move to the next stage and perhaps to intimacy. For example, you might increase contact with your partner; give your partner tokens of affection such as gifts, cards, or flowers; increase your own personal attractiveness; do things that suggest intensifying the relationship, such as flirting or making your partner jealous; and become more sexually intimate (Tolhuizen, 1989).

# Ethics in Interpersonal Communication

## YOUR OBLIGATION TO REVEAL YOURSELF

If you're in a close relationship, your influence on your partner is considerable, so you may have an obligation to reveal certain things about yourself. Conversely, you may feel that the other person—because he or she is so close to you—has an ethical obligation to reveal certain information to you.

| Romantic Partner | Friend | At what point do you have an ethical obligation to reveal: |
|---|---|---|
| _____ | _____ | Age |
| _____ | _____ | History of family genetic disorders |
| _____ | _____ | HIV status |
| _____ | _____ | Past sexual experiences |
| _____ | _____ | Marital history |
| _____ | _____ | Annual salary and net financial worth |
| _____ | _____ | Affectional orientation |
| _____ | _____ | Attitudes toward other races and nationalities |
| _____ | _____ | Religious beliefs |
| _____ | _____ | Past criminal activity or incarceration |

### What would you do?

At what point in a relationship—if any—do you feel you would have an ethical obligation to reveal each of the 10 items of information listed here? Visualize a relationship as existing on a continuum from initial contact at 1 to extreme intimacy at 10, and use the numbers from 1 to 10 to indicate at what point you would feel your romantic partner or friend had a right to know each type of information about you. If you feel you would never have the obligation to reveal this information, use 0. As you respond to these items, ask yourself, What gives one person the right to know personal information about another person?

Throughout the relationship process, but especially during the involvement and early intimacy stages, you test your partner; you try to find out how your partner feels about the relationship. Among the strategies you might use are these (Baxter & Wilmot, 1984; Bell & Buerkel-Rothfuss, 1990):

- *Directness:* You ask your partner directly how he or she feels, or you disclose your own feelings on the assumption that your partner will also self-disclose.
- *Indirect suggestion:* You joke about a shared future together, touch more intimately, or hint that you're serious about the relationship, for example. Similar responses from your partner will mean that he or she wishes to increase the intimacy of the relationship.
- *Public presentation:* You may introduce your partner as your "boyfriend" or "girl-friend," for example, and see how your partner responds.
- *Separation:* You separate yourself physically to see how the other person responds. If your partner calls, then you know he or she is interested in the relationship.
- *Third party:* You ask mutual friends about your partner's feelings and intentions.

## Intimacy

At the **intimacy** stage, you commit yourself still further to the other person and establish a relationship in which this individual becomes your best or closest friend, lover, or companion. You also come to share each other's social networks, a practice followed by members of widely different cultures (Gao & Gudykunst, 1995).

### ASK Yourself
#### Refusing a Gift Positively

You're becoming friendly with a coworker whom you think you might like to date. Without any warning, your coworker gives you a very intimate gift—it's too much, too soon. Ask yourself: What might you say to refuse the gift but not close off the possibility of dating?

Not surprisingly, your relationship satisfaction also increases with the move to this stage (Siavelis & Lamke, 1992). One research study defined intimacy as the feeling that you could be honest and open when talking about yourself, your thoughts, and your feelings that you don't reveal in other relationships (Mackey, Diemer, & O'Brien, 2000).

The intimacy stage usually divides itself into two phases. In the *interpersonal commitment* phase the two people commit themselves to each other in a private way. In the *social bonding* phase the commitment is made public—perhaps to family and friends, perhaps to the public at large. Here you and your partner become a unit, an identifiable pair.

When the intimacy stage involves a lifetime partnership, you face three main anxieties (Zimmer, 1986). A *security anxiety* leads you to worry that your partner may leave you for someone else or that he or she will be sexually unfaithful. A *fulfillment anxiety* involves concerns that you may not be able to achieve a close, warm, and special rapport or that you won't be able to have an equal relationship. An *excitement anxiety* makes you worry that boredom and routine may set in or that you'll lose your freedom and become trapped.

Of course, not everyone strives for intimacy (Bartholomew, 1990; Thelen, Sherman, & Borst, 1998; Bumby & Hansen, 1997). Some people are so fearful of the consequences of intimacy that they actively avoid it. Others dismiss intimacy and defensively deny their need for more and deeper interpersonal contact. And still others, of course, are happy without an intimate relationship.

**Intimacy and Risk**    To some people, relational intimacy is extremely risky. To others, it involves only low risk.

Consider your own view of relationship risk by responding to the following questions.

1. Is it dangerous to get really close to people?
2. Are you afraid to get really close to someone because you might get hurt?
3. Do you find it difficult to trust other people?
4. Do you believe that the most important thing to consider in a relationship is whether you might get hurt?

People who answer yes to these and similar questions see intimacy as involving considerable risk (Pilkington & Richardson, 1988). Such people have fewer close friends, are less likely to have a romantic relationship, have less trust in others, have a low level of dating assertiveness, have lower self-esteem, are more possessive and jealous in their love, and are generally less sociable and extroverted than those who see intimacy as involving little risk (Pilkington & Woods, 1999).

**VIEWPOINT**

Some cultures consider sexual relationships to be undesirable outside of marriage; others see sex as a normal part of intimacy and chastity as undesirable. Intercultural researchers (Hatfield & Rapson, 1996, p. 36) recall a meeting at which colleagues from Sweden and the United States were discussing ways of preventing AIDS. When members from the United States suggested teaching abstinence, Swedish members asked, "How will teenagers ever learn to become loving, considerate sexual partners if they don't practice?" "The silence that greeted the question," note the researchers, "was the sound of two cultures clashing." How have your cultural beliefs and values influenced what you consider appropriate relationship behavior?

**Intimacy and Social Penetration**    As you progress from contact through involvement to intimacy, **social penetration** is likely to increase. That is both the **breadth** or **depth** or number of topics you talk about and the **depth** or degree of "personalness" with which you pursue them increase (Altman & Taylor, 1973; Hensley, 1996; DerLega, 2004). Such increases are influenced greatly by attitude similarity; when you perceive attitude similarity between yourself and another person, you're more likely to increase social penetration than if you didn't see this similarity (Hammer, 1986). Visualize an individual as a circle divided into various parts (to represent the topics of interpersonal communication or the breadth of the relationship) and into layers (to represent the degree of personalness with which you talk or the depth of the relationship). For illustration, see Figure 10.2. Each circle in the figure contains eight topic areas to depict breadth (identified A through H) and five levels of intimacy to depict depth (represented by the concentric circles). Note that in circle 1, only three topic areas are penetrated. Of these, one is penetrated only to the first level and two to the second. In

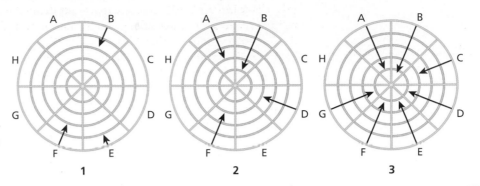

**→ FIGURE 10.2**

## Models of Social Penetration

How accurately do the concepts of breadth and depth express your communication in relationships of different intensities? Can you identify other aspects of messages that change as you go from talking to an acquaintance, to a friend, or to an intimate?

this type of interaction, three topic areas are discussed, and only at rather superficial levels. This is the type of relationship you might have with an acquaintance. Circle 2 represents a more intense relationship, one that has greater breadth and depth; more topics are discussed and to deeper levels of penetration. This is the type of relationship you might have with a friend. Circle 3 represents a still more intense relationship. Here there is considerable breadth (seven of the eight areas are penetrated) and depth (most of the areas are penetrated to the deepest levels). This is the type of relationship you might have with a lover or a parent.

All relationships—with friends, lovers, families—may be described in terms of breadth and depth, concepts that are central to the theory of social penetration (Altman & Taylor, 1973; DerLega, 2004). In its initial stage a relationship is normally characterized by narrow breadth (few topics are discussed) and shallow depth (the topics are discussed only superficially). As the relationship grows in intensity and intimacy, breadth and depth increase. Equally important, these increases are seen as comfortable, normal, and natural progressions. At the same time, communication becomes more personalized, more synchronized, and easier (Gudykunst, Nishida, & Chua, 1987).

## Deterioration

The **relationship deterioration** stage is characterized by a weakening of the bonds between the friends or lovers. The first phase of deterioration is usually *intrapersonal dissatisfaction:* You begin to experience personal dissatisfaction with everyday interactions and begin to view the future with your partner more negatively. If this dissatisfaction grows, you pass to the second phase, *interpersonal deterioration.* You withdraw and grow farther and farther apart. You share less of your free time. When you're together, there are more awkward silences, fewer disclosures, less physical contact, and a lack of psychological closeness. Conflicts become more common and their resolution more difficult.

When a relationship begins to deteriorate, the breadth and depth (which increase as the relationship becomes more intimate) will often reverse themselves—a process of **depenetration,** sometimes referred to as the *reversal hypothesis.* For example, in the process of terminating a relationship, you may eliminate certain topics from your interpersonal interactions and at the same time discuss acceptable topics in less depth. You may reduce the level of your disclosure, revealing less and less of your inner feelings. This reversal does not always occur (Baxter, 1983). There is some evidence to show, for example, that, among friends, although depth decreases in the early stages of deterioration, it may later increase (Tolhuizen, 1986).

## Repair

The **relationship repair** stage is not always pursued. Some relational partners may pause during deterioration and try to repair their relationship. Others, however, may progress—without stopping, without thinking—to dissolution.

At the first repair phase, *intrapersonal repair*, you may analyze what went wrong and consider ways of solving your relational difficulties. You might at this stage consider changing your behaviors or perhaps changing your expectations of your partner. You might also evaluate the rewards of your relationship as it is now and the rewards to be gained if your relationship ended.

Should you decide that you wanted to repair your relationship, you might discuss this with your partner at the *interpersonal repair* phase—you might talk about the problems in the relationship, the changes you wanted to see, and perhaps what you'd be willing to do and what you'd want your partner to do. This is the stage of negotiating new agreements and new behaviors. You and your partner might try to repair your relationship by yourselves, or you might seek the advice of friends or family or perhaps go for professional counseling.

## Dissolution

At the **relationship dissolution** stage, the bonds between the individuals are broken. In the beginning, dissolution usually takes the form of *interpersonal separation*, in which you may move into separate apartments and begin to lead lives apart from each other. If this separation proves acceptable and if the original relationship isn't repaired, you enter the phase of *social or public separation*. If the relationship is a marriage, this phase corresponds to divorce. In some cases the former partners change the definition of their relationship; for ex-

# Understanding Interpersonal Skills
## POSITIVENESS

**Positiveness** in interpersonal communication has to do with the use of positive rather than negative messages. For example, instead of the negative "I wish you wouldn't ignore my opinions," consider the positive alternative: "I feel good when you ask my opinions." Instead of the negative "You look horrible with long hair" consider the positive: "I think you look great with short hair." As you can expect, positive messages are important to creating and maintaining relationship satisfaction and are used more often by women, both in face-to-face and in computer-mediated communication, than by men (Gattis, Berns, Simpson, & Christensen, 2004; Adrianson, 2001).

**Communicating Positiveness.** Here are a few suggestions for communicating positiveness.

- Look for the positive in the person or in the person's work and compliment it. Compliment specifics; overly general compliments ("Your project was interesting") are rarely as effective as those that are specific and concrete ("Your proposal will boost efficiency and produce a great financial saving . . .").
- Express satisfaction nonverbally when communicating with others. For example, use friendly facial expressions, maintain a reasonably but appropriately close distance, and focus eye contact and avoid glancing away from the other person for long periods of time. At the same time, avoid negative teasing, which has been shown to lower satisfaction among couples (Horvath, 2004).
- Express positiveness with a recognition of cultural differences (Dresser, 1996; Chen, 1992). For example, in the United States it's considered appropriate for a supervisor to compliment a worker for doing an exceptional job. But in many collectivist cultures this would be considered inappropriate, because it singles out one individual and separates that person from the group.

ample, the "ex-lovers" become "friends" or "business partners." Avoidance of each other and a return to being "single" are among the primary characteristics of dissolution.

Dissolution also is the stage during which the ex-partners begin to look upon themselves as individuals rather than halves of a pair. They try to establish a new and different life, either alone or with another person. Some people, it's true, continue to live psychologically with a relationship that has already been dissolved; they frequent old meeting places, reread old love letters, daydream about all the good times, and fail to extricate themselves from a relationship that has died in every way except in their memory.

In cultures that emphasize continuity from one generation to the next and in which being "old-fashioned" is evaluated positively—as in, say, China—interpersonal relationships are likely to be long lasting and permanent. Those who maintain long-term relationships tend to be rewarded, and those who break relationships tend to be punished. But in cultures in which change is seen as positive and being old-fashioned as negative—as in, say, the United States—interpersonal relationships are likely to be more temporary (Moghaddam, Taylor, & Wright, 1993). Here the rewards for long-term relationships and the punishments for broken relationships will be significantly less.

## Implications of the Model of Relationships

Before moving on to a discussion of relationship types, consider some of the implications of this model of relationships.

1. Because relationships differ so widely, it's best to think of any relationship model as a tool for talking about relationships rather than as a specific map that indicates how you move from one relationship position to another. The model presented here is certainly not the only way you can look at relationships. Table 10.2 presents a somewhat different model to give you a different perspective on how to view relationships.

2. Within each relationship and within each relationship stage, there are dynamic tensions between several pairs of competing opposite desires. The assumption made by relationship dialectics theory (discussed in the Understanding Interpersonal Theory and Research box, p. 218) is that all relationships can be defined by these opposites; for example, by the tensions between wishes for autonomy and connection, novelty and predictability, and closedness and openness. These tensions influence the movement from one relationship stage to another. For example, your desire for autonomy may lead you away from moving toward greater intimacy, whereas your need for connection will move you close to intimacy.

3. A more obvious type of movement is depicted in Figure 10.1 (see p. 219) by the different types of arrows. The exit arrows show that each stage offers the opportunity to exit the relationship. After saying "hello" you can say "goodbye" and exit. The vertical or movement arrows going to the next stage and back again represent the fact that you can move to another stage: either to a stage that is more intense (say, from involvement to intimacy) or to a stage that is less intense (say, from intimacy to deterioration). The self reflexive arrows—the arrows that return to the beginning of the same level or stage—signify that any relationship may become stabilized at any point. You may, for example, continue to maintain a relationship at the intimate level without its deteriorating or going back to a less intense stage of involvement. Or you may remain at the "Hello, how are you?" stage—the contact stage—without getting any further involved.

4. Movement through the various stages usually is a gradual process; you don't jump from contact to involvement to intimacy. Rather, you progress gradually, a few degrees at a time. Yet there are leaps that must and do take place. For example, during

↑ **VIEWPOINT**
Throughout the life of a relationship, there exist "turning points," those jumps or leaps that project you from one relationship level to another. Do men and women, homosexuals and heterosexuals, and young and old see turning points in the same way? In what ways might different groups see turning points differently? Which turning points would be the most important to you?

## ⏷ TABLE 10.2
### Knapp's Model of Relationship Stages

This model of relationships contains 10 stages: 5 stages that bring people together and 5 that separate them. How accurately does this model describe your own relationships or those with which you're familiar?

| The first five stages refer to the processes of coming together and moving toward greater connection and intimacy. | |
|---|---|
| Stage 1: **Initiation** | You perceive and interact with the other person; you try to present yourself in a positive light and to open the channels of communication. |
| Stage 2: **Experimenting** | You try to learn about the other person. |
| Stage 3: **Intensifying** | You interact on a more personal and intimate level; your speech becomes more informal and includes lots of terms that have meaning only for the two of you. |
| Stage 4: **Integrating** | You come together; you cultivate mutual opinions and attitudes. |
| Stage 5: **Bonding** | You name the relationship for others; for example, you choose marriage or domestic partnership or designate yourselves as "exclusive partners." |

| The next five stages refer to the stages of coming apart and moving away from intimacy. | |
|---|---|
| Stage 6: **Differentiating** | You begin to think of yourselves as different and distinct from each other. |
| Stage 7: **Circumscribing** | You restrict communication, perhaps to topics that are safe and will not cause conflict. |
| Stage 8: **Stagnating** | Your communication becomes relatively inactive; when you do communicate, it's with difficulty and awkwardness. |
| Stage 9: **Avoiding** | You physically separate; there is little or no face-to-face interaction. |
| Stage 10: **Terminating** | You break the bonds that once held the relationship together. |

*Sources:* This model of relationship is adapted from Mark L. Knapp, *Social Intercourse: From Greeting to Goodbye* (Boston: Allyn & Bacon, 1978) and Mark L. Knapp and Anita L. Vangelisti, *Interpersonal Communication and Human Relationships*, 5th ed. (Boston: Allyn & Bacon, 2005), pp. 34–47. Copyright © by Pearson Education. Adapted by permission of the publisher.

the involvement stage of a romantic relationship, the first kiss or the first sexual encounter requires a leap. It requires a change in the kind of communication and in the kind of intimacy experienced by the two people. Before you take these leaps, you probably first test the waters. Before the first kiss, for example, you may hold each other, look longingly into each other's eyes, and perhaps caress each other's face. You may do this (in part) to discover if the leap—the kiss, for example—will be met with a favorable response. No one wants rejection—especially of romantic advances.

5. Movement from one stage to another depends largely on your communication skills—your abilities to initiate and open a relationship, to present yourself as likable, to express affection, to self-disclose appropriately, and in fact all the interpersonal skills you've been acquiring throughout this course (cf. Dindia & Timmerman, 2003).

### ASK Yourself
#### Moving through Relationship Stages

Your recent romantic partner seems to be moving too fast for your liking. You want to take things a lot slower, yet you don't want to turn this person off; this may be The One. Ask yourself: What might you say (and where might you say it) to get your partner to proceed more slowly?

## RELATIONSHIPS IN A CONTEXT OF CULTURE AND TECHNOLOGY

The research and theory discussed here and in the next two chapters derive in great part from research conducted on heterosexual couples in the United States and on face-to-face interaction. Although we've paused at many points to note cultural differences and the role of the Internet in relationships, it's helpful to bring the influences of culture and technology together now that we've covered a significant part of our relationship discussion.

# Ask the Researcher

## HOMOSEXUAL AND HETEROSEXUAL RELATIONSHIPS

**?** I'm gay, and I'm wondering just how this interpersonal relationship material applies to me. It seems most of the research concerns heterosexual relationships. Is any of this stuff really relevant to me?

Definitely. Researchers find more similarities than differences in the communication patterns of homosexual and heterosexual partners. For example, while gay and lesbian couples are more likely than heterosexual couples to value equality and reciprocity in their relationships, homosexual and heterosexual couples are similar in the average length of their romantic relationships; their desires for affection, companionship, and commitment; and the behaviors used to maintain their relationships, such as sharing tasks, talking about the relationship, sharing time together, assuring the other, and interacting with supportive social networks.

Additionally, all people in close relationships, both homosexual and heterosexual, construct and continuously reconstruct their relationships through their exchange of verbal and nonverbal messages. Communication is the glue that holds people in a relationship. Because both partners make choices about how they'll communicate, they explicitly and implicitly "negotiate" the nature of their relationship in their exchanges. This process gives partners the ability to construct very traditional relationships or very unique and highly complex relationships.

**For further information** see S. M. Haas and L. Stafford, "An Initial Examination of Maintenance Behaviors in Gay and Lesbian Relationships," *Journal of Social and Personal Relationships* 15 (1998): 846–855, and L. A. Baxter and B. M. Montgomery, *Relating: Dialogues and Dialectics* (New York: Guilford Press, 1996).

Barbara Montgomery (Ph.D., Purdue University) is provost and vice president for academic affairs at Colorado State University–Pueblo. Dr. Montgomery applies interpersonal communication theories and research findings daily in university administration and in higher education consulting.

## Relationships and Culture

In the model and in the discussion of relationship development so far, it has been asssumed that you voluntarily choose your relationship partners—that you consciously choose to pursue certain relationships and not others. In some cultures, however, your romantic partner is chosen for you by your parents. In some cases your husband or wife is chosen to solidify two families or to bring some financial advantage to your family or village. An arrangement such as this may have been entered into by your parents when you were an infant or even before you were born. In Kyrgyzstan, to take an example that's very different from what most of us are familiar with, at least one-third of wives are snatched against their will by their future husbands in a practice called *ala kachuu* (meaning something similar to "grab and run"). The reason given by the men who engage in this practice is that it's easier and less expensive than paying the standard bride price, which may be as high as $800 and a cow (Smith, 2005). At a less extreme level, of course, in most cultures there's pressure to marry "the right" person and to be friends with certain people and not with others.

In the United States, researchers study and textbook authors write about dissolving relationships and how to survive relationship breakups. It's assumed that you have the right to exit an undesirable relationship. But in some cultures you simply cannot dissolve a relationship once it's formed or once there are children. In the practice of Roman Catholicism, once people are validly married, they're always married and cannot dissolve that relationship. In many Muslim cultures only the man may initiate the

**A s k Yourself**
Meeting the Parents

You're dating someone from a very different culture and have been invited to meet the parents and have a traditional ethnic dinner. Ask yourself: What might you do to make this potentially difficult situation go smoothly?

**⊙ VIEWPOINT**

What are your feelings about office romance? What do you see as the advantages and the disadvantages of dating and perhaps mating with someone with whom you work?

dissolution of a marriage. More important to such cultures may be such issues as "How do you maintain a relationship that has problems?" "What can you do to survive in this unpleasant relationship?" "How can you repair a troubled relationship?" (Moghaddam, Taylor, & Wright, 1993).

Further, the culture will influence the difficulty that you go through when relationships break up. For example, married persons whose religion forbids divorce and remarriage will experience religious disapproval and condemnation as well as the same economic and social difficulties everyone else goes through. In the United States child custody almost invariably goes to the woman, and this presents an added emotional burden for the man. In Iran child custody goes to the man, which presents added emotional burdens for the woman. In India women experience greater difficulty than men in divorce because of their economic dependence on men, the cultural beliefs about women, and the patriarchal order of the family (Amato, 1994). And it was only in 2002 that the first wife in Jordan was granted a divorce. Before then, only men had been granted divorces (*New York Times,* May 15, 2002, p. A6).

In most of the United States, interpersonal friendships are drawn from a relatively large pool. Out of all the people you come into regular contact with, you choose relatively few of these as friends. With online chat groups the number of friends you can have has increased enormously, as has the range from which these friends can be chosen. In rural areas and in small villages throughout the world, however, you have very few choices. The two or three other children your age become your friends; there's no real choice because these are the only possible friends you could make.

Most cultures assume that relationships should be permanent or at least long lasting. Consequently, it's assumed that people want to keep relationships together and will expend considerable energy to maintain relationships. Because of this bias, there has been little research that has studied how to move effortlessly from one intimate relationship to another or that advises you how to do this more effectively and efficiently.

Culture influences heterosexual relationships by assigning different roles to men and women. In the United States, men and women are supposed to be equal—at least that is the stated ideal. As a result, both men and women can initiate relationships and both can dissolve them. Both men and women are expected to derive satisfaction from their interpersonal relationships; and when that satisfaction isn't present, either may seek to exit the relationship.

Gay and lesbian relationships are accepted in some cultures and condemned in others. In some areas of the United States, "domestic partnerships" may be registered, and these grant gay men, lesbians, and (in some cases) unmarried heterosexuals rights that were formerly reserved only for married couples, such as health insurance benefits and the right to make decisions when one member is incapacitated. In the United States as of this writing, only one state, Massachusetts, has issued marriage licenses to same-sex couples. In many countries same-sex couples would be considered criminals and could face severe punishment—in some cultures death. In Norway, Sweden, Canada, and Denmark, on the other hand, same-sex relationship partners have essentially the same rights as married partners.

## Relationships and Technology

Perhaps even more obvious than the impact of culture is the influence of technology on interpersonal relationships. And although one might argue, as one researcher has, that face-to-face interaction is still both primal and primary (Turner, 2002)—and although it's true that the growth rate of online relationships has slowed somewhat over the last decade (Williams, 2004)—there can be no doubt that online relationships are here to stay and have and will exert enormous influence on all interpersonal relationships (Hardey, 2004). The number of Internet users is rapidly increasing, and commercial websites devoted to meeting other people are proliferating, making it especially easy to develop online relationships. Books currently (August 20, 2005) high on Amazon.com list include such titles as *Online Dating for Dummies* (Silverstein & Lasky, 2004), *I Can't Believe I'm Buying This Book: A Commonsense Guide to Successful Internet Dating* (Katz, 2004), and *Meet Me Don't Delete Me: Internet Dating: I've Made All the Mistakes so You Don't Have To* (Bacon, 2004). These and numerous others attest to the importance of online relationships. The afternoon television talk shows frequently focus on computer relationships, especially on getting people together who have established a relationship online but who have never met. Clearly, many are turning to the Internet to find a friend or romantic partner. In one study of MOOs (online role-playing games), 93.6 percent of the users formed ongoing friendship and romantic relationships (Parks & Roberts, 1998). Some people use the Internet as their only means of interaction; others use it as a way of beginning a relationship and intend to supplement computer talk later with photographs, phone calls, and face-to-face meetings.

In research on online relationships, almost two-thirds of newsgroup users had formed new acquaintances, friendships, or other personal relationships with someone they met on the Internet. Almost one-third said that they communicated with their partner at least three or four times a week; more than half communicated on a weekly basis (Parks & Floyd, 1996).

Women, it seems, are more likely to form relationships on the Internet than men. In the same study about 72 percent of women and 55 percent of men had formed personal

SPEAKING
>> Interpersonal-E

**Advantages of Online Relationships.** Among the advantages of online relationships is that they reduce the importance of physical characteristics and instead emphasize such factors as rapport, similarity, and self-disclosure and in the process promote relationships that are based on emotional intimacy rather than physical attraction (Cooper & Sportolari, 1997). What do you see as the main advantages of online relationships?

# InterMedia

## PARASOCIAL RELATIONSHIPS

Parasocial relationships are relationships that audience members perceive themselves to have with media personalities (Rubin & McHugh, 1987; Giles, 2001; Giles & Maltby, 2004). At times viewers develop these relationships with real media personalities—Katie Couric, Regis Philbin, Ellen DeGeneres, or Dr. Phil, for example. As a result they may watch these people faithfully and communicate with the individuals in their own imaginations. At other times the relationship is with a fictional character—an investigator on *CSI*, a lawyer on *Law and Order*, or a doctor on a soap opera. In fact, actors who portray doctors frequently get mail asking for medical advice. When a character with whom people have a parasocial relationship dies, some people exhibit significant negative reactions, in some cases similar to those experienced when a real relationship ends (Cohen, 2003, 2004). Obviously, most people don't go quite this far.

Parasocial relationships develop from an initial attraction to the character's social and task roles, to a perceived relationship, and finally to a sense that this relationship is an important one (Rubin & McHugh, 1987). The more you can predict the behavior of a character, the more likely you are to develop a parasocial relationship with that character (Perse & Rubin, 1989). As you can imagine, these parasocial relationships are most important to those who spend a great deal of time with the media and who have few real-life interpersonal relationships (Rubin, Perse, & Powell, 1985; Cole & Leets, 1999).

### Follow Up

Some research indicates that parasocial relationships actually facilitate interpersonal interaction (May, 1999). How might parasocial relationships do this? Conversely, can you think of ways in which parasocial relationships might hinder interpersonal interaction?

relationships online (Parks & Floyd, 1996). Not surprisingly, those who communicated more frequently formed more relationships.

As relationships develop on the Internet, network convergence occurs; that is, as a relationship between two people develops, they begin to share their network of other communicators with each other (Parks, 1995; Parks & Floyd, 1996). This, of course, is similar to relationships formed through face-to-face contact. Online work groups are also on the increase and have been found to be more task oriented and more efficient than face-to-face groups (Lantz, 2001). Online groups also provide a sense of belonging that may once have been thought possible only through face-to-face interactions (Silverman, 2001).

There are lots of advantages to establishing relationships online. For example, online relationships are safe in terms of avoiding the potential for physical violence or sexually transmitted diseases. Unlike relationships established in face-to-face encounters, in which physical appearance tends to outweigh personality, on the Internet your inner qualities are communicated first. Rapport and mutual self-disclosure become more important than physical attractiveness in promoting intimacy (Cooper & Sportolari, 1997). And, contrary to some popular opinions, online relationships rely just as heavily on the ideals of trust, honesty, and commitment as do face-to-face relationships (Whitty & Gavin, 2001). Friendship and romantic interaction on the Internet are a natural boon to shut-ins and the extremely shy, for whom traditional ways of meeting someone are often difficult. Computer talk also can be empowering for those with "physical disabilities or disfigurements," from whom face-to-face interactions often are superficial and frequently end with withdrawal (Lea & Spears, 1995; Bull & Rumsey, 1988). By eliminating the physical cues, computer talk equalizes the interaction and doesn't put the disabled or disfigured person at an immediate disadvantage in a society where physical attractiveness is so highly valued. You're free to reveal as much or as little about your physical self as you wish, when you wish.

Another obvious advantage is that the number of people you can reach is so vast that it's relatively easy to find someone who matches what you're looking for. The situation is like finding a book that covers just what you need from a library of millions of volumes rather than from a collection of only several thousand. Still another advantage for many is that the socioeconomic and educational status of people on the Net is significantly higher than you're likely to find in a bar or singles group.

Of course, there are also disadvantages. For one thing, you can't see the person. Unless you exchange photos or meet face-to-face, you won't know what the person looks like. Even if photos are exchanged, how certain can you be that the photos are of the person or that they were taken recently? In addition, you can't hear the person's voice, and this too hinders you in formulating a total picture of the other person. Of course, you can always add an occasional phone call to give you this added information.

Online, people can present a false self with little chance of detection. For example, minors may present themselves as adults; and adults may present themselves as children in order to begin illicit and illegal sexual communications and, perhaps, to arrange meetings. Similarly, people can present themselves as poor when they're rich, as mature when they're immature, as serious and committed when they're just enjoying the experience. Although you can also misrepresent yourself in face-to-face relationships, the fact that it's easier to do online probably accounts for greater misrepresentation in computer relationships (Cornwell & Lundgren, 2001).

Another potential disadvantage—though some might argue it is actually an advantage—is that computer interactions may become all consuming and may substitute for face-to-face interpersonal relationships.

## ASK Yourself
### Coming Clean

You're getting ready to meet someone you've only communicated with over the Internet, and you're going to have to admit that you lied about your age and a few other things. Ask yourself: What do you have to come clean with most immediately? What are your options for expressing this? What seems the best option?

This chapter introduced interpersonal relationships and focused on three areas: the advantages and disadvantages of relationships, the stages you go through in developing and perhaps dissolving relationships, and the influence of culture and technology on interpersonal relationships.

### Characteristics of Interpersonal Relationships

How do interpersonal relationships differ from impersonal relationships?

- Among the differences: In interpersonal relationships people base their predictions on psychological (rather than sociological) data, explanatory (rather than descriptive) knowledge, and personally established (rather than socially established) rules.
- Interpersonal relationships have both advantages and disadvantages. Some advantages are that interpersonal relationships help alleviate loneliness, enable you to secure stimulation, help you to gain self-knowledge and enhance your self-esteem, and enable you to maximize pleasure and minimize pain. Some of the disadvantages are that interpersonal relationships put pressure on you to reveal yourself to others; impose significant financial, emotional, and temporal obligations; may lead to increased isolation from former friends; and may present difficulties in dissolving.

### Stages in Interpersonal Relationships

What are the stages that a relationship goes through?

- At the *contact* stage you make perceptual contact and later interact with the person.

- At the *involvement* stage you test your potential partner and, if this proves satisfactory, move on to intensifying your relationship.
- At the *intimacy* stage you may make an interpersonal commitment and later enter the stage of social bonding, in which you publicly reveal your relationship status.
- At the *deterioration* stage the bonds holding you together begin to weaken. Intrapersonal dissatisfaction later becomes interpersonal, when you discuss it with your partner and perhaps others.
- At the *repair* stage you first engage in intrapersonal repair, analyzing what went wrong and perhaps what you can do to set things right; later you may engage in interpersonal repair, in which you and your partner consider ways to mend your deteriorating relationships.
- At the *dissolution* stage you separate yourself from your partner and later perhaps separate socially and publicly.

### Relationships in a Context of Culture and Technology

In what ways do culture and technology influence interpersonal relationships?

- Culture influences the beliefs you have about relationships, the purposes and values you feel relationships should serve, the choices involved in developing and in dissolving relationships, the rules that relationships should follow, and the roles that are considered appropriate in relationships.
- Technology has now assumed a major role in all interpersonal relationships, especially their development and maintenance.

1. It was only as recently as 1967—after nine years of trials and appeals—that the U.S. Supreme Court forbade any state laws against interracial marriage (Crohn, 1995). How would you describe the state of interracial romantic relationships today? What obstacles do such relationships face? What advantages do they offer?

2. Research finds that relationship dissolution is a significant influence on men who commit suicide, but not on women (Kposowa, 2000). Can you suggest any reasons for this finding?

3. At least one research study shows that in face-to-face relationships romanticism seems to increase on the basis of the amount of choice you have in selecting a partner. In countries where there is much choice, as in the United States and Europe, romanticism is high; in countries where there is less choice (as in India and parts of Africa), romanticism is lower (Medora, Larson, Hortacsu, & Dave, 2002). Internet dating provides greater choice than do face-to-face interactions, so does it follow that romanticism will be higher in Internet interactions?

4. According to some theories of gender differences in relationships, particularly evolutionary psychology or social Darwinism, men focus on youth and attractiveness in selecting a partner with whom to have children; women, on the other hand, seek men who have wealth and power in an attempt to achieve security. Some research casts doubt on this theory and suggests that both men and women who see themselves as especially attractive will seek partners who are also attractive. Similarly, those who are wealthy will seek others who have similar wealth (Angier, 2003). Which theory do you believe is more valid?

5. Can you supply personal examples that illustrate the three types of movement among the relationship stages—one example of a relationship that moved from one stage to another, one that remained at one stage for a long period, and one that ended?

6. Is the six-stage model presented here an adequate way to describe most interpersonal relationships as you understand them? How would you describe the stages of interpersonal relationships?

Go to www.ablongman.com/devito.

*The following exercises focus on interpersonal relationships and the communication that takes place at each stage.*

❶ **Analyzing Stage Talk** and ❷ **Learning to Hear Stage Talk** provide opportunities to look at the various cues to the different relationship stages. ❸ **Giving Repair Advice** looks at relationship difficulties and encourages you to offer relationship repair advice based on the discussions in this chapter. ❹ **'Til This Do Us Part** is an exercise that looks at some of the relationship issues that can break up the relationship.

# CHAPTER 1

# Interpersonal Relationships: Growth and Deterioration

*Closer* (2004)

*Closer* describes the lives of two couples—their relationships' growth and deterioration and the changes that take place in their interpersonal communication. All of these topics closely reflect the discussion in this chapter.

> "After all, my erstwhile dear,
> My no longer cherished.
> Need we say it was not love,
> Just because it perished?"
>
> —Edna St. Vincent Millay

Now that we have a general idea of the functions that relationships serve and the various stages relationships go through, we can explore relationship development and relationship deterioration in greater detail.

##  RELATIONSHIP DEVELOPMENT

Numerous theories offer insight into why you develop your relationships. Several theories bearing directly on relationship development have already been discussed:

- **Uncertainty reduction theory** (Chapter 4) describes relationship development as a process of reducing uncertainty about each other (Berger & Calabrese, 1975). For example, the theory predicts that high uncertainty prevents intimacy, whereas low uncertainty creates intimacy. The more relationship uncertainty you have, the more topics you're likely to avoid sharing with each other, as you can't predict how the topics will be received (Knobloch & Carpenter-Theune, 2004). High uncertainty decreases liking for another person, whereas low uncertainty increases liking.
- *Social penetration theory* (Chapter 10) describes the progression of a relationship along the communication dimensions of breadth and depth. As a relationship moves to greater intimacy, relationship depth and breadth increase; as a relationship moves away from intimacy, relationship depth and breadth decrease (usually).
- *Relationship dialectics theory* (Chapter 10) describes relationships in terms of tensions between competing desires or motivations, such as the desire for autonomy and the desire to belong to someone, desires for novelty and predictability, and desires for closeness and openness.
- *Rules theory* (discussed more fully on pp. 242–243) describes relationships as interactions governed by series of rules that couples agree to follow. When the rules are followed, a relationship is maintained; when they're broken, the relationship experiences difficulty and perhaps deteriorates or even dissolves.

In this chapter, three additional theories are singled out: *attraction theory, social exchange theory,* and *equity theory.* The theories offer interesting perspectives on relationships. They help explain what happens in interpersonal relationships (and in interpersonal communication generally) during the stages of development, maintenance, deterioration, and repair. They shed light on important interpersonal processes—for example, power and conflict—and on significant interpersonal relationships, such as those of friendship, love, and family.

### Attraction Theory

You're no doubt attracted to some people and not attracted to others. In a similar way, some people are attracted to you and some aren't. If you were to examine the people to whom you're attracted and those to whom you're not attracted, you would probably see patterns in your judgments, even though many of them seem unconsciously motivated. **Attraction theory** holds that you develop relationships with others on the basis of three major factors: attractiveness, proximity, and similarity.

**Attractiveness**    **Attractiveness** has to do with both appearance and personality. When you say, "I find that person attractive," you probably mean either that you find that person physically attractive or that you find that person's personality or behavior attractive. For the most part, you probably like physically attractive rather than physically unattractive people. And what's especially interesting is that some research indicates that the preference for "pretty" faces is inborn. In one study 100 infants were presented with two images side by side: One image was of an attractive face and the other an unattractive face. Interestingly enough the infants spent approximately 80 percent of their time looking at the attractive face and hardly glanced at the unattractive face. Adults seem to have similar preferences, even when they differ culturally. For example, Africans looking at two European faces select as more attractive the same face that Europeans select, and Europeans looking at two African faces select as more attractive the same image that Africans select (Slater et al., 1998). And you probably like people who possess a pleasant rather an unpleasant personality. Generally, you attribute positive characteristics to people you find attractive and negative characteristics to people you find unattractive.

Supporting the popular belief, research—in Bulgaria, Nigeria, Indonesia, Germany, and the United States—finds that men consider physical attractiveness in their partner more important than do women (Buss & Schmitt, 1993). Similarly, in a study of gay male dating behavior, the physical attractiveness of a person's partner was the most important factor in influencing how much the person enjoyed his date and how much he wished to date that person again (Sergios & Cody, 1985). The more attractive you find someone, the more you are apt to exaggerate your good qualities in order to get a date with that person (Rowatt, Cunningham, & Druen, 1999). Apparently, such exaggeration is seen as more acceptable when the goal is a date with an exceptionally attractive person but less acceptable when the prospective date is less attractive.

Note that the factor of physical appearance enters the face-to-face relationship through nonverbal cues—you see the person's eyes, face, body—and that you perceive attractiveness immediately. In online relationships, in contrast, physical attractiveness can be signaled only through words and self-descriptions (Levine, 2000). And generally this attractiveness is revealed only gradually. As you can appreciate, the face-to-face encounter favors those who are physically attractive, whereas the online encounter favors those who are verbally adept at self-presentation and thus can offer an advantage to less-attractive individuals. Often you'd reveal your physical self online in increments: first some general verbal descriptions ("I'm six feet tall, brown hair, brown eyes"), then perhaps a photo, and then perhaps a face-to-face meeting. It seems reasonable to assume that physical attractiveness will prove most important when it's immediate and less important when it's revealed after a period of acquaintanceship.

Those who are perceived as attractive are also seen as competent; and conversely, those who are perceived as competent—say, as a team member working on a project or in social situations—are also seen as more attractive (Duran & Kelly, 1988). Similarly, you'll find those with whom you have positive interactions more attractive than those with whom you have negative interactions (Albada, 2002).

You can easily understand that people like physically attractive people more than they like physically unattractive people. What seems less intuitive is the fact that we also think that more attractive people are more familiar to us than are less attractive people; in other words, we're more likely to think we've met a person before if that person is attractive (Monin, 2003). Also, although

**A s k Yourself**

Projecting an Image

You're entering a new job and want to be perceived as likable and friendly but also as serious and conscientious.   Ask yourself:  What types of messages might help you achieve your dual goal? Which might you try first?

culture influences what people think constitutes physical attractiveness and what doesn't, some research indicates that certain facial features seem to be thought attractive in all cultures—that there is a kind of universal attractiveness (Brody, 1994). For example, a study comparing the very different cultures of England and Japan found that for long-term relationships both men and women preferred opposite-sex faces that were on the feminized side; these faces were seen as more sensitive and honest (Penton-Voak, Jacobson, & Trivers, 2004). This finding fits neatly with other research indicating that, contrary to popular opinion, nice guys don't finish last but instead are seen as more attractive than men described as "less nice" (Urbaniak & Kilmann, 2003).

**Proximity**    If you look around at people you're attracted to, you'll probably notice that they're people who live or work close to you. For example, in a study of friendships in a student housing development, researchers found that the closer students' rooms were to each other, the better the chances that the occupants would become friends (Festinger, Schachter, & Back, 1950). The people who became friends were those who had the greatest opportunity to interact. One reason **proximity,** or closeness, influences attraction is that it allows you to get to know the other person. You come to like people you know because you can better predict their behavior; perhaps because of this they seem less frightening than complete strangers do (Berger & Bradac, 1982).

Another approach argues that "mere exposure" to others leads you to develop positive feelings for them (Zajonc, 1968). In one study a female stranger attended some classes 5 times, some classes 10 times, some classes 15 times, and some classes not at all (Moreland & Beach, 1992). At the end of the semester the students in the classes rated this woman (who never spoke but just sat where people could see her) in terms of how attractive they felt she was and how much they liked her. Consistent with the **mere exposure hypothesis,** the woman was liked least and considered least attractive in the class in which she never appeared, liked more and seen as more attractive in the class in which she appeared 5 times, still more in the class in which she appeared 10 times, and most in the class in which she appeared 15 times. How can you account for these results except by "mere exposure"? Exposure increases attraction when the initial interaction is favorable or neutral. When the initial interaction is negative, however, repeated exposure may actually decrease attraction.

**Similarity**    If you could construct your ideal mate, he or she would probably look, act, and think very much like you. By being attracted to people like yourself, you validate yourself; you tell yourself that you're worthy of being liked. Although there are exceptions, the **similarity** factor probably means that you will be attracted to your own mirror image: to people who are similar to you in nationality, race, ability, physical characteristics, intelligence, attitudes, and so on.

If you were to ask a group of friends, "To whom are you attracted?" they would probably name very attractive people; in fact, they would probably name the most attractive people they know. But if you were to observe these friends, you would find that they go out with and establish relationships with people who are about equal in physical attractiveness. The **matching hypothesis** predicts that although you may be attracted to the most physically attractive people, you will date and mate with people who are at about your level of physical attractiveness (Walster, Walster, & Berscheid, 1978; Smith & Weber, 2005). Intuitively, this seems satisfying. In some cases, however, you notice discrepancies: for example, an attractive person dating someone much less attractive. In cases such as these, you would probably look for compensating factors, for qualities that compensate for the lack of physical attractiveness. Prestige, money, power, intelligence, youth, and various personality characteristics are obvious factors that compensate for a lack of attractiveness.

In addition to physical similarity, you're likely attracted to people who have attitudes similar to your own, who like what you like, and who dislike what you dislike. The more significant the attitude, the more important the similarity. Marriages between people with great dissimilarities are more likely to end in divorce than marriages between people whose attitudes are similar (Blumstein & Schwartz, 1983).

Attitude similarity as an essential element in attraction has been found in such diverse cultures as the United States, India, Japan, and Mexico, and is especially significant in initial attraction (Hatfield & Rapson, 1992). It also seems to predict relationship success. People who are similar in attitude become more attracted to each other over time, whereas people who are dissimilar in attitude become less attracted to each other over time (Neimeyer & Mitchell, 1988; Honeycutt, 1986). Also, the more intellectually similar people are and the more they see the world similarly, the greater their attraction to each other (Neimeyer & Neimeyer, 1983). You're also more likely to find those who are culturally similar more attractive than those who are culturally different (Pornpitakpan, 2003). And you're more likely to help someone who is similar in race, attitude, and general appearance.

Even the same first name is significant. For example, when an e-mail (asking recipients to fill out surveys of their food habits) identified the sender as having the same name as the addressee, recipients showed a greater willingness to comply with the request (Gueguen, 2003).

Although most people would argue that "birds of a feather flock together" (the similarity position), others argue that "opposites attract." This concept, called **complementarity,** argues that people are attracted to dissimilar others—at least in certain situations. For example, the submissive student may get along especially well with an assertive teacher but may not get along with an assertive romantic partner. Theodore Reik (1944), in his classic *A Psychologist Looks at Love,* takes a complementarity position when he argues that you fall in love with people who possess characteristics that you do not possess and actually envy. The introvert, for example, if displeased with being shy, might be attracted to an extrovert. Most research, however, clearly supports the greater importance of similarity as opposed to difference.

### Affinity-Seeking Strategies

Attractiveness, proximity, and similarity are factors that influence interpersonal attraction apart from anything you may do or say. In addition, however, you can increase your attractiveness by using **affinity-seeking strategies.** These strategies are derived from studies in which some people were asked to list the things that people can say or do to get others to like them and others were asked to list the things that lead others to dislike them. Thus, the strategies represent what people *think* makes them attractive to others, what people *think* makes people like them, and what people *think* makes others feel positive toward them. As you can see from examining the list of strategies that follows, their use is likely to increase your attractiveness. Such strategies are especially important in initial interactions, and their use by teachers has even been found to increase student motivation (Martin & Rubin, 1998; Myers & Zhong, 2004). Here are the major strategies found in the research (Bell & Daly, 1984):

Be of help to Other (the other person).

Appear to be "in control" as a leader, as one who takes charge.

### ⊙ VIEWPOINT

It's been argued that you don't actually develop attraction to those who are similar to you but rather are repulsed by those who are dissimilar (Rosenbaum, 1986). For example, you may be repulsed by those who disagree with you and therefore exclude them from those with whom you might develop a relationship. You're therefore left with a pool of possible partners whose attitudes are similar to yours. What do you think of this "repulsion hypothesis"? Do you and your relationship history more closely follow the predictions of repulsion theory or of attraction theory? Or might both dynamics be operating?

Present yourself as socially equal to Other.

Present yourself as comfortable and relaxed when with Other.

Allow Other to assume control over relational activities.

Follow the cultural rules for polite, cooperative conversation with Other.

Appear active, enthusiastic, and dynamic.

Stimulate and encourage Other to talk about himself or herself; reinforce disclosures and contributions of Other.

Ensure that activities with Other are enjoyable and positive.

Include Other in your social activities and groupings.

Show that your relationship with Other is closer than it really is.

Listen to Other attentively and actively.

Communicate interest in Other.

Engage in self-disclosure with Other.

Appear optimistic and positive rather than pessimistic and negative.

Appear to Other as an independent and freethinking individual.

Appear to Other as being as physically attractive as possible.

Appear to Other as an interesting person to get to know.

Appear as one who is able to administer rewards to Other for associating with you.

Show respect for Other, and help Other to feel positively about himself or herself.

Arrange circumstances so that you and Other come into frequent contact.

Communicate warmth and empathy to Other.

Demonstrate that you share significant attitudes and values with Other.

Communicate supportiveness in Other's interpersonal interactions.

Appear to Others as honest and reliable.

## Social Exchange Theory

**Social exchange theory,** based on an economic model of profits and losses, claims that you develop social and professional relationships that enable you to maximize your profits (Gergen, Greenberg, & Willis, 1980; Thibaut & Kelley, 1959; Brandes, Ravi & Wheatley, 2004).

**Profits, Rewards, and Costs**    The theory begins with the following equation:

$$\text{Profits} = \text{Rewards} - \text{Costs}$$

Rewards are anything that you want, that you enjoy, and that you'd be willing to incur costs to obtain. For example, to acquire the reward of financial gain, you might have to work rather than play. To earn an A in an interpersonal communication course, you might have to write a term paper or study more than you want to. To gain a promotion, you might have to do unpleasant tasks or work overtime. Love, affection, status, money, gifts, security, social acceptance, companionship, friendship, and intimacy are just a few examples of rewards for which you would be willing to work (that is, incur costs).

Costs are those things that you normally try to avoid—things you consider unpleasant or difficult. Working overtime, washing dishes and ironing clothes, watching a television show that your partner enjoys but you find boring, dressing in ways that are physically uncomfortable, and doing favors for people you dislike might all be considered costs.

Using this basic economic model, social exchange theory claims that you seek to develop relationships (friendship and romantic) in which the rewards are greater than the costs. The preferred relationships, according to this theory, are those that are most profitable—that give you the greatest rewards with the least costs.

**Comparison Levels**   You enter a relationship with a general idea of the kinds of profit you ought to get out of it. This is your *comparison level,* your realistic expectation of what you feel you deserve from a relationship. For example, in a study of couples, it was found that most people expect reasonably high levels of trust, mutual respect, love, and commitment. Their expectations are significantly lower for time spent together, privacy, sexual activity, and communication (Sabatelli & Pearce, 1986). When the rewards you get equal or surpass this comparison level, you feel satisfied with your relationship.

You also have a *comparison level for alternatives.* That is, you probably compare the profits you get from your current relationships with the ones you think you can get from alternative relationships. For example, if you believe you'll not be able to find another suitable partner, you're more likely to stay in your relationship, even if it's an abusive one (Berscheid, 1985). If you see that the profits from your present relationship are less than the profits you could get from an alternative relationship, you might decide to leave your current relationship and enter this new and potentially more profitable connection (Crawford, Feng, Fisher, & Diana, 2003).

## Equity Theory

**Equity theory** uses the concepts of social exchange but goes a step farther. It claims that you develop and maintain relationships in which your ratio of rewards to costs is approximately equal to your partner's (Walster, Walster, & Berscheid, 1978; Messick & Cook, 1983). An equitable relationship, then, is one in which participants derive rewards that are proportional to their costs. If you work harder for the relationship than your partner does, then equity demands that you should get greater rewards than your partner. If you work equally hard, then equity demands that each of you should get approximately equal rewards. Much research finds that people want equity and feel that relationships should be characterized by equity (Ueleke et al., 1983). Further, equity contributes significantly to relationship satisfaction (Larsen, 2004). The idea behind this is that if you're underbenefited (if you get less than you put in), you'll be angry. If, on the other hand, you're overbenefited (if you get more than you put in), you'll feel guilty (Walster, Walster, & Traupman, 1978). However, some research has questioned this rather neat but intuitively unsatisfying assumption and finds that the overbenefited person is often quite happy and contented; guilt deriving from getting more than you deserve seems easily forgotten (Noller & Fitzpatrick, 1993; Sprecher & Schwartz, 1994).

**Relationship Satisfaction and Equity**   Equity theory puts into clear focus the sources of relational dissatisfaction you see every day. For example, in a traditional marriage, husband and wife may have full-time jobs, but the wife may also do the major share of the household chores. Thus, although both may be deriving equal rewards—they have equally good cars, they live in the same three-bedroom house, and so on—the wife is paying more of the costs. According to equity theory, she will be dissatisfied because of this lack of equity. Further, romantic relationships that are inequitable (in the partners' emotional contributions and in their sharing of power and decision making) tend to create greater psychological problems—especially for women—than will equitable relationships (Galliher, Rostosky, Welsh, & Kawaguchi, 1999). In work situations you see the same dynamic. For example, suppose there are two management trainees. Each does an equal amount of work, but one trainee gets a bonus of $5,000 and the other a bonus of $20,000. Clearly, there is inequity, and there will be dissatisfaction and less effectiveness on the job (Taris, Van Horn, & Schaufeli, 2004).

**Equity, Culture, and Gender**   Equity theory is consistent with the capitalistic orientation of Western culture, in which each person is paid, for example, according to his or her contributions. The

> **A s k Yourself**
> Achieving Equity
>
> After thinking about equity, you realize that you put in a lot of effort into your present relationship than your partner; that is, you pay much more than half the costs. You want this imbalance to be corrected.   Ask yourself:  What might you say to help to make the relationship more equitable?

more you contribute to the organization or the relationship, the more rewards you should get out of it. In other cultures, however, a principle of equality or need might operate. According to the principle of equality, each person would get equal rewards, regardless of their individual contribution. According to the principle of need, each person would get rewards according to individual need (Moghaddam, Taylor, & Wright, 1993). People from India are, for example, more likely to distribute rewards on the basis of need than are Americans; Americans are more likely to distribute rewards on the basis of equity, on the basis of the costs paid into the relationship (Berman, Murphy-Berman, & Singh, 1985; Moghaddam, Taylor, & Wright, 1993). It's not surprising to find that in the United States equity is highly correlated with relationship satisfaction and with relationship duration (Schafer & Keith, 1980). In much of Europe, on the other hand, equity seems to be unrelated to satisfaction or duration (Lujansky & Mikula, 1983).

As has been argued and as is supported by some research, women and men generally remain unequal at home and in the workplace, despite the advances in equality that have been made in the last 30 or 40 years (cf. Hendrick, 2004). And women are more likely to engage in extramarital affairs when they perceive their relationship as inequitable (Prins, Buunk, & Van Yperen, 1994). (Perceptions of inequity by men, in contrast, do not influence their likelihood of engaging in extramarital affairs.) Further, women are more likely than men to break up a relationship as a result of their own extrarelational affair (Janus & Janus, 1993).

##  RELATIONSHIP MAINTENANCE

**Relationship maintenance** behaviors are behaviors that serve to continue (maintain, retain) your relationship. (Behaviors directed at mending badly damaged or even broken relationships are considered under the topic of *repair*, pp. 250–254.) Of course, maintenance behaviors can serve a variety of functions. Some examples:

- to keep the relationship intact: to retain the semblance of a relationship, to prevent dissolution of the relationship
- to keep the relationship at its present stage: to prevent it from moving too far toward either less or greater intimacy
- to keep the relationship satisfying: to maintain an appropriate balance between rewards and penalties

Some people, after entering a relationship, assume that it will continue unless something catastrophic happens. Consequently, although they may seek to prevent any major mishaps, they're unlikely to engage in much maintenance behavior. Others will be ever on the lookout for something wrong and will seek to patch it up as quickly and as effectively as possible. In between lie most people, who will engage in maintenance behaviors when things are going wrong and when there is the possibility that the relationship can be improved.

Not surprisingly, a great deal of relationship maintenance takes place through e-mail (Stafford, Kline, & Dimmick, 1999; Howard, Rainie, & Jones, 2001). Because many relationships develop online, and because online contact is so easy to maintain even when partners are widely separated geographically, the use of e-mail is likely to increase in frequency and importance. The use of e-mail to maintain relationships is more common among women than men; women also find such e-mail contact more gratifying than do men (Boneva, Kraut, & Frohlich, 2001).

**⊙ VIEWPOINT**

How would you feel if you were in a relationship in which you and your partner contributed an equal share of the costs (that is, you each worked equally hard), but your partner derived significantly greater rewards? How would you feel if you and your partner contributed an equal share of the costs, but you derived significantly greater rewards?

## Reasons for Maintaining Relationships

The reasons for maintaining relationships are as numerous and as varied as the reasons for beginning them. Before looking at the specific reasons, let's look at what the theories predict.

*Attraction theory* holds that relationships are maintained when there is significant attraction, generally of the kind that led to the development of the relationship. Although both individuals, as well as their definitions of what constitutes attractiveness, may have changed, the importance of attraction—however defined—is likely to continue throughout the life of the relationship.

*Social exchange theory* holds that relationships will be maintained as long as the relationship is profitable—as long as the rewards exceed the costs. Note, of course, that what constitutes a reward and how significant that reward is can be defined only by the individual. More specifically, you're likely to maintain a relationship when it's more rewarding than what you expected (your comparison level). You're also likely to maintain your present relationship even when it falls short of your comparison level, as long as it's still higher than what you feel you could get elsewhere (your comparison level for alternatives). So even though you may think you deserve more, if you can't get more, then you're likely to stay put.

*Equity theory* holds that you maintain a relationship when you perceive relative equity. If you feel that you're getting rewards from the relationship proportional to the costs you're paying, then you're likely to maintain the relationship. If either person—but especially the person who is being shortchanged—perceives a lack of equity, the relationship may experience difficulty.

**SPEAKING**
**>> Interpersonal-E**

**Relationship Maintenance and E-Mail.** E-mail is one of the major ways in which people maintain meaningful relationships (Stafford, Kline, & Dimmick, 1999). In what specific ways can you envision e-mail's being used to communicate relationship maintenance messages?

# Understanding Interpersonal Theory and Research
## RELATIONSHIP COMMITMENT

An important factor influencing the course of relationship deterioration (as well as relationship maintenance) is the degree of commitment that you and your relationship partner have toward each other and toward the relationship. Not surprisingly, commitment is especially strong when individuals are satisfied with their relationship and grows weaker as individuals become less satisfied (Hirofumi, 2003). Three types of commitment are often distinguished and can be identified from your answers to the following questions (Johnson, 1973, 1982, 1991; Knapp & Taylor, 1994; Kurdek, 1995; Knapp & Vangelisti, 2005):

- Do I want to stay in this relationship? Do I have a *desire* to keep this relationship going?
- Do I have a moral *obligation* to stay in this relationship?
- Do I have to stay in this relationship? Is it a *necessity* for me to stay in this relationship?

All relationships are held together, in part, by commitment based on desire, obligation, or necessity, or on some combination of these factors. And the strength of the relationship, including its resistance to possible deterioration, is related to your degree of commitment. When a relationship shows signs of deterioration and yet there's a strong commitment to preserving it, you may well surmount the obstacles and reverse the process. For example, couples with high relationship commitment will avoid arguing about minor grievances and also will demonstrate greater supportiveness toward each other than will those with lower commitment (Roloff & Solomon, 2002). Similarly, those who have great commitment are likely to experience greater jealousy in a variety of situations (Rydell, McConnell, & Bringle, 2004). When commitment is weak and the individuals doubt that there are good reasons for staying together, the relationship deteriorates faster and more intensely.

**Working with Theories and Research**

Has commitment or the lack of it (on the part of either or both of you) ever influenced the progression of one of your relationships? What happened?

In addition to these theoretical predictions, let's look at some of the more popular and frequently cited reasons for relationship maintenance.

**Staying Together.** One study found that of people who meet on the Internet, those who meet in places of common interests, who communicate over a period of time before they meet in person, who manage barriers to greater closeness, and who manage conflict well are more likely to stay together than couples who do not follow this general pattern (Baker, 2002). Based on your own experiences, how would you predict which couples would stay together and which would break apart?

- *Emotional attachment:* Often you maintain a relationship because you love each other, you want to preserve your relationship, and you don't find alternative couplings as inviting or as potentially enjoyable.
- *Convenience:* The difficulties involved in finding another person to live with, another business partner, or another social escort may make it more convenient to stay together than to break up.
- *Children:* A couple may stay together because they feel, rightly or wrongly, that it's in the best interests of the children; or the children may provide a socially acceptable excuse to mask the real reason—convenience, financial advantage, fear of being alone, and so on.
- *Fear:* People may fear venturing into the outside world, being alone, facing others as "single," or even making it on one paycheck and so may elect to preserve their current relationship as the better alternative.
- *Inertia:* Some relationships are maintained because of inertia (the tendency for a body at rest to remain at rest and a body in motion to remain in motion); change seems too much trouble.
- *Commitment:* People may have a strong commitment to each other or to the relationship (Yela, 2000). In fact, recent research finds that women's commitment is more closely related to relationship maintenance and stability than any other factor (Sprecher, 2001).

## Rules for Maintaining Relationships

You gain an interesting perspective by looking at interpersonal relationships in terms of the rules that govern them. The general assumption of **rules theory** is that in a wide variety of cultures relationships—friendship and love in particular—are held together by mutual adherence to certain rules (Argyle, 1986; Argyle, Henderson, Bond, Iizuka, et al., 1986). When those rules are broken, the relationships may deteriorate and eventually dissolve.

Relationship rules help distinguish successful from destructive relationship behavior. They help pinpoint why relationships break up and how they may be repaired. Further, if you know what the rules are, you'll be better able to learn (and teach) the social skills involved in relationship development and maintenance. As you'll see below, rules of loyalty, openness, honesty, and respect are especially important and regulate both friendship and romantic relationships (Baxter, Dun, & Sahlstein, 2001).

**Friendship Rules**    The left half of Table 11.1 presents some of the most important rules of friendship (Argyle & Henderson, 1984). When these rules are followed, the friendship is strong and mutually satisfying. When these rules are broken, interpersonal conflict is likely to occur (Samter & Cupach, 1998). Sometimes rule breaking creates problems that cannot be fixed, and so the friendship dies. The right half of Table 11.1 presents the abuses that are most significant in breaking up a friendship (Argyle & Henderson, 1984). Note that some of the rules for maintaining a friendship directly correspond to the abuses that break up friendships. For example, it's important to "demonstrate emotional support" to maintain a friendship; when emotional support is not shown, the friendship will prove less satisfying and may well break up. The general assumption here is that friendships break down when a significant friendship rule is violated. The maintenance strategy depends on your knowing the rules and having the ability to apply the appropriate skills (Trower, 1981; Blieszner & Adams, 1992).

**Romantic Rules**    Other research has identified the rules that couples in romantic relationships establish and follow. Here, for example, drawn from two research studies, are rules that both keep the relationship together and, when broken, lead to deterioration and even-

## TABLE 11.1
### Rules for Maintaining and Breaking Up a Friendship

Have you seen these rules in operation in your own friendships? Are there other important rules that you would add to the list presented here?

| Maintaining a Friendship | Breaking Up a Friendship |
|---|---|
| Stand up for your friend in his or her absence. | Be intolerant of your friend's friends. |
| Share information and feelings about successes. | Criticize your friend in public. |
| Demonstrate emotional support. | Discuss confidences between yourself and your friend with others. |
| Trust each other; confide in each other. | Don't display any positive regard for your friend. |
| Offer to help your friend in time of need. | Don't demonstrate any positive support for your friend. |
| Try to make your friend happy when the two of you are together. | Nag your friend. |
| Don't criticize in public. | Don't trust or confide in your friend. |
| Keep confidences. | Don't volunteer to help your friend in time of need. |
| Don't be jealous or negative about other relationships. | Be jealous or critical of your friend's other relationships. |
| Respect your friend's privacy. | Feel free to take up as much of your friend's time as you want. |

tually to dissolution (Baxter, 1986; Kline & Stafford, 2004). If you have had a serious romantic relationship, think about it as you examine the rules that follow; if you have not had such a relationship, think about the relationship you want. As you read the list, consider your own relationship behaviors. Do you and your partner

- acknowledge each other's individual identities and lives beyond the relationship?
- express similar attitudes, beliefs, values, and interests?
- enhance each other's self-worth and self-esteem?
- remain loyal and faithful to each other?
- have substantial shared time together?
- attempt to make your interactions enjoyable?
- listen and try not to judge?
- act cheerful and positive?
- compliment each other's achievements?
- try to avoid embarrassing each other?

## Communication for Maintaining Relationships

One reason relationships last is that partners employ effective **relationship communication** to make them work. Interestingly enough, among married couples, the wives' use of maintenance strategies has a more significant effect on the satisfaction, love, and commitment that couples experience than does the husbands' use of such strategies (Weigel & Ballard-Reisch, 1999). This is not to say that men's maintenance strategies are ineffective; it's merely to say that in the average heterosexual married relationship, the couple is more influenced by the wife's maintenance behaviors.

There is conflicting research evidence on the value of electronic communication in maintaining relationships. In one study, for example, the researchers found that 55 percent of Internet users claimed that e-mail strengthened their family ties and 66 percent claimed that it improved their connections with close friends. Related to this is the finding that

# Ethics in Interpersonal Communication

## INFORMATION ETHICS

The approach to ethics taken in this book from its inception has been information ethics. This position argues that people have the right to information relevant to the choices they make. From this basic premise several corollaries follow:

- Communications are ethical when they facilitate people's freedom of choice by presenting them with accurate information. Communications are unethical when they prevent people from securing such information or give them false or misleading information that will lead them to make choices they would not make if they had more accurate information.

- You have the right to information about yourself that others possess and that may influence the choices you make. Thus, for example, you have the right to face your accusers, to know the witnesses who will testify against you, to see your credit ratings, and to know what Social Security benefits you'll receive. On the other hand, you do not have the right to information that is none of your business, such as information about whether your neighbors are happy or argue a lot or receive food stamps.

- You have an obligation to reveal information that you possess that bears on the choices of other people and of your society. Thus, for example, you have an obligation to identify wrongdoing that you witness, to identify someone in a police lineup, to report criminal activity, and to testify at a trial when you possess pertinent information. This information is judged essential for society to accomplish its purposes and to make its legitimate choices.

### What would you do?

Your best friend's husband is currently having an extramarital affair with a 15-year-old. Your friend suspects this is going on and asks if you know anything about it. Would it be ethical for you to lie and say you know nothing, or are you obligated to tell your friend what you know? Are you obligated to tell the police? What would you do in this situation?

---

Internet users seem to experience significantly less social isolation than those who don't use the Internet. Only 8 percent of Internet users noted that they felt socially isolated, while 18 percent of nonusers reported feelings of social isolation (Raney, 2000). Another study reported contrary findings, claiming that the more people use the Internet the less they communicate with family members in their home, the smaller their social circle, and the more they experience loneliness and depression (Kraut et al., 1999). The only reasonable conclusion seems to be that for some users the Internet strengthens social connections with friends and family, but for others it substitutes for face-to-face social interactions and connections.

Many researchers have focused on the maintenance strategies people use in their various relationships (Ayres, 1983; Dindia & Baxter, 1987; Dainton & Stafford, 1993; Guerrero, Eloy, & Wabnik, 1993; Canary, Stafford, Hause, & Wallace, 1993; Canary & Stafford, 1994). Here are some examples of how people maintain their relationships, presented in the form of suggestions for maintaining relationships.

- *Be nice.* Researchers call this *prosocial behavior.* You're polite, cheerful, and friendly; you avoid criticism; and you compromise even when it involves self-sacrifice. Prosocial behavior also includes talking about a shared future; for example, talking about a future vacation or buying a house together. It also includes acting affectionately and romantically.

- *Communicate.* You call just to say, "How are you?" or send cards or letters. Sometimes communication is merely "small talk" that is insignificant in itself but is engaged in because it preserves contact. Also included would be talking about the honesty and openness in the relationship and talking about shared feelings. Responding constructively in a conflict (even when your partner may act in ways harmful to the relationship) is another type of communicative maintenance strategy (Rusbult & Buunk, 1993).

- *Be open.* You engage in direct discussion and listen to the other—for example, you self-disclose, talk about what you want from the relationship, give advice, and express empathy.
- *Give assurances.* You assure the other person of the significance of the relationship—for example, you comfort the other, put your partner first, and express love.
- *Share joint activities.* You spend time with the other—for example, playing ball, visiting mutual friends, doing specific things as a couple (even cleaning the house), and sometimes just being together and talking with no concern for what is done. Controlling (eliminating or reducing) extrarelational activities would be another type of togetherness behavior (Rusbult & Buunk, 1993). Also included here would be ceremonial behaviors; for example, celebrating birthdays and anniversaries, discussing past pleasurable times, and eating at a favorite restaurant.
- *Be positive.* You try to make interactions pleasant and upbeat—for example, holding hands, giving in to make your partner happy, and doing favors. At the same time, you would avoid certain issues that might cause arguments.
- *Focus on improving yourself.* For example, you work on making yourself look especially good and attractive to the other person.

 ## RELATIONSHIP DETERIORATION

In **relationship deterioration,** as discussed in Chapter 10, there is a weakening of the bonds that hold people together. The process of deterioration may be gradual or sudden. For example, gradual deterioration may occur in a situation in which one of the parties in a relationship develops close ties with a new intimate, and this new relationship gradually

# Understanding Interpersonal Skills
## EMPATHY

**Empathy** is feeling what another person feels from that person's point of view without losing your own identity. Empathy enables you to understand emotionally what another person is experiencing. (To sympathize, in contrast, is to feel *for* the person—to feel sorry or happy for the person, for example.)

**Communicating Empathy.** Here are a few suggestions to help you communicate empathy effectively (Authier & Gustafson, 1982).

- Make it clear that you're trying to understand, not to evaluate, judge, or criticize.
- Focus your concentration: Maintain eye contact, an attentive posture, and physical closeness. Express involvement through facial expressions and gestures.
- Reflect back to the speaker the feelings that you think are being expressed, in order to check the accuracy of your perceptions and to show your commitment to understanding the speaker. Offer tentative statements about what you think the person is feeling; for example, "You seem really angry with your father" or "I hear some doubt in your voice."
- When appropriate, use your own self-disclosures to communicate your understanding; but be careful that you don't refocus the discussion on yourself.
- Address mixed messages so as to foster more open and honest communication. For example, if your friend verbally expresses contentment but shows nonverbal signs of depression, it may be prudent to question the possible discrepancy.

**Virtual Infidelity.** Online infidelity is a relatively new problem with which couples must cope. Generally such infidelity is seen as a consequence of a failure in communication between the couple (Young, Griffin-Shelley, Cooper, O'Mara, & Buchanan, 2000). How would you describe online infidelity? What warning signs would lead you to suspect your partner of engaging in a secretive online relationship?

pushes out the old. Sudden deterioration may occur when a rule that was essential to the relationship (for example, the rule of complete fidelity) is broken and both parties realize that the relationship cannot be sustained.

In terms of the theories introduced earlier, relationship deterioration can occur when you no longer find your partner attractive physically and in personality, when you no longer experience closeness, or when the differences become more important than the similarities. When relationships break up, it's generally the more attractive person who leaves (Blumstein & Schwartz, 1983). There is no denying the power of attractiveness in the development of relationships and the influence of its loss in the deterioration of relationships. According to social exchange, deterioration can set in when the costs begin to exceed the rewards. Similarly, a relationship may deteriorate when you feel that you could do better with someone else. Even if your relationship is less than you expected it to be, you probably will not dissolve it unless you perceive that another relationship (or being alone) will provide a greater profit. In terms of equity, deterioration can occur when you feel that you're putting more into the relationship than you're getting out of it or that your partner is benefiting from the relationship disproportionately.

## Causes of Relationship Deterioration

There are as many reasons for relationship deterioration as there are people in relationships. It is, therefore, extremely difficult to identify specific causes for any specific relationship deterioration. Still, some general causes—applicable to a wide variety of relationship breakups—may be identified.

As a preface, recall that the factors that are important in establishing relationships (discussed in Chapter 10) may, when no longer present, contribute to deterioration. For example, when loneliness is no longer reduced by the relationship (when one or both individuals feel lonely frequently or for prolonged periods), the relationship may well be on the road to decay, because it's not serving a function it was entered into to serve. Similarly, when relationships no longer provide stimulation, gains in knowledge and esteem, enhancement of physical and emotional health, or maximizing of pleasures and minimizing of pain, they are likely to be in trouble.

**Beliefs about Relationships**    The beliefs you have about relationships will greatly influence the course of your relationships. For example, if you and your partner have similar beliefs—and if these beliefs are realistic—then your relationship is likely to be strengthened by your similar belief systems. If, on the other hand, you and your partner hold widely different beliefs about, say, gender or financial expectations, then your relationship is more likely to experience instability and interpersonal distancing than if you both held similar beliefs (Pasley, Kerpelman, & Guilbert, 2001). Similarly, if one of you holds unrealistic or dysfunctional beliefs, then the quality of your relationship is likely to diminish (Goodwin & Gaines, 2004). This role of unrealistic beliefs is well illustrated in the self-test "What Do You Believe about Relationships?"

# TEST YOURSELF
## WHAT DO YOU BELIEVE ABOUT RELATIONSHIPS?

On the line next to each statement, indicate whether you think the statement is TRUE (you agree with the statement to some extent) or FALSE (you disagree with the statement to some extent).

_____    1. If a person has any questions about the relationship, then it means there is something wrong with it.

_____    2. If my partner truly loved me, we would not have any quarrels.

_____    3. If my partner really cared, he or she would always feel affection for me.

_____ 4. If my partner gets angry at me or is critical in public, this indicates he or she doesn't really love me.

_____ 5. My partner should know what is important to me without my having to tell him or her.

_____ 6. If I have to ask for something that I really want, it spoils it.

_____ 7. If my partner really cared, he or she would do what I ask.

_____ 8. A good relationship should not have any problems.

_____ 9. If people really love each other, they should not have to work on their relationship.

_____ 10. If my partner does something that upsets me, I think it is because he or she deliberately wants to hurt me.

_____ 11. When my partner disagrees with me in public, I think it is a sign that he or she doesn't care for me very much.

_____ 12. If my partner contradicts me, I think that he or she doesn't have much respect for me.

_____ 13. If my partner hurts my feelings, I think that it is because he or she is mean.

_____ 14. My partner always tries to get his or her own way.

_____ 15. My partner doesn't listen to what I have to say.

**HOW DID YOU DO?**  Aaron Beck, one of the leading theorists in cognitive therapy and the author of the popular _Love Is Never Enough,_ claims that all of these beliefs are unrealistic and may create problems in your interpersonal relationships. The test was developed to help people identify potential sources of difficulty for relationship development and maintenance. The more statements that you indicated you agree with, the more unrealistic your expectations are.

**WHAT WILL YOU DO?**   If you hold any of these beliefs and you agree that they are counterproductive, what can you do about them? You may want to begin this analysis by reviewing the list—individually or in small groups—and identifying with hypothetical or real examples why each belief is unrealistic (or realistic).

_Source:_ This test was taken from Aaron Beck, _Love Is Never Enough_, pp. 67–68. Copyright © 1988 by Aaron T. Beck, M.D. Reprinted by permission of Harper Collins Publishers, Inc. and Arthur Pine Associates, Inc. Beck notes that this test was adapted in part from the Relationship Belief Inventory of N. Epstein, J. L. Pretzer, and B. Fleming, "The Role of Cognitive Appraisal in Self-Reports of Marital Communication," _Behavior Therapy_ 18 (1987): 51–69.

**Excessive Intimacy Claims**    In most relationships—especially intense ones—the members make intimacy claims on each other (Blood, 1973). Such claims may include expectations that the partner will sympathize and empathize, attend to self-disclosures with total absorption, or share the other's preferences with equal intensity. These intimacy claims often restrict personal freedom and may take the form of possessiveness. To be always responsive, always sympathetic, always loving, always attentive is more than many can manage. In some relationships the intimacy claims and demands are so great that the partners' individual identities may be in danger of being absorbed or destroyed.

**Third-Party Relationships**    People establish and maintain relationships to maximize their pleasure and minimize their pain. When these goals cease to be met, the relationship stands little chance of survival. These needs are so great that when they're not met within the existing relationship, their fulfillment will be sought elsewhere. When a new relationship serves these needs better, the old relationship may deteriorate. At times, this may be a romantic interest; at other times, the new relationship may be with a parent or, frequently, a child. When one partner's need for affection or attention, once supplied by the other person, is now supplied by a friend or a child, the primary relationship may be in trouble.

**Relationship Changes**    The development of incompatible attitudes, vastly different intellectual interests and abilities, or major goal changes may contribute to relationship deterioration. Similarly, changes in behavior may create difficulties. For example, if you once devoted lots of time to your partner and to the relationship and now are totally absorbed

with business or school, your relationship is going to face significant repercussions. The person who develops an addiction (to drugs, alcohol, or even stamp collecting) will likewise present the relationship with a serious problem.

### Undefined Expectations
Unresolved expectations over who is in charge are a frequent cause of relationship difficulties (Lederer, 1984). Often, conflicts over such trivial issues as who does the dishes or who walks the dog mask resentment and hostility concerning some more significant unresolved expectation.

At times, the expectations each person has of the other may be unrealistic; difficulties may then arise when reality enters the relationship. This type of situation often occurs early in a relationship, when, for example, the individuals think they will want to spend all their time together. When it's discovered that neither one does, each resents this "lessening" of feeling in the other. The resolution of such problems lies in demonstrating that the original expectations were unrealistic and that realistic and satisfying ones can be substituted.

### Sex-Related Problems
Few relationships are free of sexual differences and problems. In fact, sexual problems rank among the top three problems in almost all studies of newlyweds (Blumstein & Schwartz, 1983). When these same couples are surveyed later in their relationship, the sexual problems have not gone away; they're just discussed less. Apparently, people resign themselves to living with the problems.

Although sexual frequency isn't related to relationship breakdown, sexual satisfaction is. It's the quality of the sexual relationship, not the quantity of sexual encounters, that is crucial. When the quality is poor, outside affairs may be sought, and these contribute significantly to breakups for all couples, whether married or cohabiting.

### Work-Related Problems
Problems associated with either partner's job often lead to difficulties within the relationship. This is true for all types of couples. With heterosexual couples (both marrieds and cohabitants), if the man is disturbed about the woman's job—for example, if she earns a great deal more than he does or devotes a great deal of time to the job—the relationship is in considerable trouble. This is true whether the relationship is in its early stages or is well established (Blumstein & Schwartz, 1983). One research study found that husbands whose wives worked were less satisfied with their own jobs and lives than were men whose wives didn't work (Staines, Pottick, & Fudge, 1986). This personal dissatisfaction will naturally have negative effects on the relationship. Another study found that men and women who retire while their spouses continue to work experience considerable marital conflict, regardless of gender (Moen, Jim, & Hofmeister, 2001).

The research bearing on the effects of workaholism on interpersonal relationships is conflicting. One study, for example, argues that workaholics do not seem to have lower relationship adjustment than nonworkaholics (McMillan, O'Driscoll, & Brady, 2004). Another study, however, argues that workaholism is similar to alcoholism and has a negative impact on interpersonal relationships (Porter, 1996).

With homosexual relationships the situation is a bit different. Gay men, like heterosexual men, are career oriented. Because of this, work-related problems may be magnified, because both partners devote considerable time to work and have less time available for the more relational concerns. Lesbians, on the other hand, are less career oriented than gay men and are more relationship oriented. This may be one reason lesbian relationships seem to last longer than gay male relationships (Blumstein & Schwartz, 1983; Huston & Schwartz, 1995).

**Financial Difficulties**   In surveys of problems among couples, financial difficulties loom large. Money is a major taboo topic for couples beginning a relationship, yet it proves to be the cause of major problems as people settle into their relationship. One-fourth to one-third of all couples rank money as their primary problem; almost all rank it as one of their major problems (Blumstein & Schwartz, 1983).

Money is so important in relationships because of its close connection with power. Money brings power in relationships, as it does in business. The person bringing in the most money wields the most power. This person has the final say, for example, on the purchase of expensive items as well as on decisions having nothing to do with money. The power that money brings quickly spreads to nonfinancial issues as well.

Money also creates problems because men and women view it differently (Blumstein & Schwartz, 1983). To many men, money is power. To many women, it's security and independence. To men, money is accumulated to exert power and influence. To women, money is accumulated to achieve security and reduce dependence on others. Conflicts over the way the couple's money is to be spent or invested can easily result from such different views. Further, when the wife earns a high income, marital conflict increases and the husband's satisfaction with the relationship decreases (Harrell, 1990).

## Effects of Relationship Deterioration

When relationships deteriorate or break up, a variety of things happen. Although we're conditioned to view relationship breakup as something negative, it's certainly not always negative and, in fact, may bring some positive benefits as well. On the negative side, perhaps the most obvious is a loss of all the benefits or rewards you enjoyed as a result of the relationship. Regardless of how unsatisfying the relationship may ultimately have been, it probably also had many good aspects. These are now lost.

There is also, generally, a loss of self-esteem. You may feel unworthy or perhaps guilty. You may blame yourself for doing the wrong things, for not doing the right things, or for being responsible for the losses you now confront. Of course, there are likely to be friends and family members who will give you a hard time, often implying that you're to blame.

There also are practical issues. Most relationship breakups have financial implications, and you may now encounter money problems. Paying the rent, tuition, or outstanding loans by yourself may prove difficult. If the relationship is a marriage, then there are legal and perhaps religious implications of the breakup. If there are children, the situation becomes even more complicated.

Nevertheless, not all relationships should be sustained. Not all breakups are bad; and few, if any, bad breakups are entirely bad. In the midst of a breakup, this may be difficult to appreciate. In retrospect, it's almost always true.

Some relationships are unproductive for one or both parties, and a breakup is often the best alternative. A breakup may provide an opportunity for the individuals to regain their independence and to become self-reliant again. Some relationships are so absorbing that there is little time for reflection on oneself, on others, and on the relationship. Sometimes distance helps. A breakup also may allow you to develop new associations and to explore different types of relationships with different types of people. Relational deterioration need not have only negative consequences; it's up to you to take away the positive lessons from a decaying relationship.

Relationship deterioration involves special communication patterns. These patterns are in part a response to the deterioration; you communicate the way you do because you feel that your relationship is in trouble. However, these patterns are also causative: The communication patterns you use largely determine

the fate of your relationship. Here are a few communication patterns that are seen during relationship deterioration.

- *Withdrawal:* Nonverbally, withdrawal is seen in the greater space you need and the speed with which tempers and other signs of disturbance arise when that space is invaded. Other nonverbal signs of withdrawal include a decrease in eye contact, and touching, less similarity in clothing, and fewer displays of items associated with the other person, such as bracelets, photographs, and rings (Miller & Parks, 1982; Knapp & Vangelisti, 2000). Verbally, withdrawal is marked by a decreased desire to talk and especially to listen. At times, you may use small talk not as a preliminary to serious conversation but as an alternative, perhaps to avoid confronting the serious issues.

- *Decline in self-disclosure:* Self-disclosing communications decline significantly. If the relationship is dying, you may think self-disclosure not worth the effort. Or you may limit your self-disclosures because you feel that the other person may not accept them or can no longer be trusted to be supportive and empathic.

- *Deception:* Deception increases as relationships break down. Sometimes this takes the form of clear-cut lies, which you or your partner may use to avoid arguments over such things as staying out all night, not calling, or being seen in the wrong place with the wrong person. At other times, lies may be used because of a feeling of shame; you may not want the other person to think less of you. One of the problems with deception is that it has a way of escalating, eventually creating a climate of distrust and disbelief.

- *Positive and negative messages:* During deterioration there's an increase in negative and a decrease in positive messages. Once you praised the other's behaviors, but, now you criticize them. Often the behaviors have not changed significantly; what has changed is your way of looking at them. What once was a cute habit now becomes annoying; what once was "different" now becomes inconsiderate. When a relationship is deteriorating, requests for pleasurable behaviors decrease ("Will you fix me my favorite dessert?") and requests to stop unpleasant or negative behaviors increase ("Will you stop monopolizing the phone?") (Lederer, 1984). Even the social niceties that accompany requests get lost as they deteriorate from "Would you please make me a cup of coffee, honey?" to "Get me some coffee, will you?" to "Where's my coffee?"

Figure 11.1 summarizes the changes in communication (discussed in this chapter and in Chapter 10) that take place as you move toward or away from intimacy. The general and most important point this figure makes is that communication effectiveness and satisfaction increase as you move toward intimacy and decrease as you move away from intimacy.

## RELATIONSHIP REPAIR

If you wish to save a relationship, you may try to do so by changing your communication patterns and, in effect, putting into practice the insights and skills learned in this course. First, we'll look at some general ways to repair a relationship, and second, we'll examine ways to deal with repair when you are the only one who wants to change the relationship.

### Interpersonal Repair

We can look at the strategies for repairing a relationship in terms of the following six suggestions, whose first letter conveniently spell out the word *REPAIR*, a useful reminder that repair is not a one-step but a multistep process (see Figure 11.2).

## → FIGURE 11.1
### Communication in Relationships

This summary of some of the changes that accompany increased intimacy and some that accompany decreased intimacy contains many of the findings discussed here and in Chapter 10. Changes related to the major theories discussed in this chapter are noted here in boldface. As you read down the list, try to identify examples that influenced your own relationships. Did any factors listed here produce effects on your relationships different from those predicted here? For example, did one of the factors listed here as leading to greater intimacy actually result in decreased intimacy? What else happens as a relationship moves toward intimacy? Toward deterioration? How would you go about testing the validity of these movement predictions?

| The Movement Is Toward Intimacy When: | | The Movement Is Away from Intimacy When: |
|---|---|---|
| attractiveness of alternatives decreases | Contact | attractiveness of alternatives increases |
| other-orientation increases | | other-orientation decreases |
| withdrawal decreases | | withdrawal increases |
| empathy expressions increase | | empathy expressions decrease |
| positive exchanges increase | | negative exchanges increase |
| loving/liking becomes less conditional | Involvement | loving/liking becomes more conditional |
| interpersonal breadth increases | | interpersonal breadth decreases |
| interpersonal depth increases | | interpersonal depth decreases |
| uncertainty decreases | | uncertainty increases |
| self-disclosure and openness increase | | self-disclosure and openness decrease |
| **attraction increases** | Intimacy | **attraction decreases** |
| **reinforcement increases** | | **reinforcement decreases** |
| **profits increase** | | **profits decrease** |
| **equity increases** | | **equity decreases** |
| use of private language increases | | use of private language decreases |
| defensiveness decreases and supportiveness increases | | defensiveness increases and supportiveness decreases |
| behavioral similarity increases | Deterioration | behavioral similarity decreases |
| deception decreases | | deception increases |
| negative request behaviors decrease and positive request behaviors increase | | negative request behaviors increase and positive request behaviors decrease |
| power to punish and reward increases | | power to punish and reward decreases |
| immediacy increases | | immediacy decreases |
| cherishing behaviors increase | Dissolution | cherishing behaviors decrease |
| nonverbal communication carries more meaning | | nonverbal communication carries less meaning |
| commitment increases | | commitment decreases |

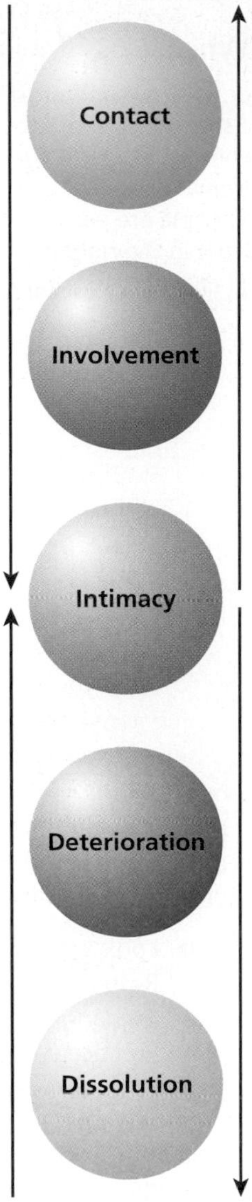

**Recognize the Problem**   Your first step is to identify the problem and to recognize it both intellectually and emotionally. Specify what is wrong with your present relationship (in concrete terms) and what changes would be needed to make it better (again, in specific terms). Create a picture of your relationship as you would want it to be, and compare that picture to the way the relationship looks now. Specify the changes that would have to take place if the ideal picture were to replace the present picture.

Try also to see the problem from your partner's point of view and to have your partner see the problem from yours. Exchange these perspectives, empathically and with open minds. Try, too, to be descriptive when discussing grievances, taking special care to avoid such troublesome terms as "always" and "never." Own your feelings and thoughts; use I-messages and take responsibility for your feelings instead of blaming your partner.

**Engage in Productive Communication and Conflict Resolution**   Interpersonal communication skills such as those considered throughout the text (for example, other-

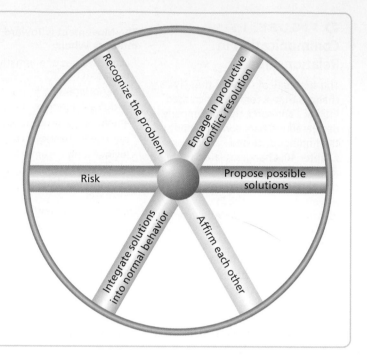

**→ FIGURE 11.2**

## The Relationship Repair Wheel

The wheel seems an apt metaphor for the repair process; the specific repair strategies—the spokes—all work together in constant process. The wheel is difficult to get moving, but once in motion it becomes easier to turn. Also, it's easier to start when two people are pushing, but it is not impossible for one to move it in the right direction. What metaphor do you find helpful in thinking about relationship repair?

orientation, openness, confidence, immediacy, expressiveness, and empathy, considered in the Understanding Interpersonal Skills boxes throughout the text) are especially important during repair and are an essential part of any repair strategy. Do you generally follow these productive conflict strategies? Here are several suggestions to refresh your memory.

1. Look closely for relational messages that will help clarify motivations and needs. Respond to these messages as well as to the content messages.
2. Exchange perspectives and see the situation as your partner does.
3. Practice empathic and positive responses, even in conflict situations.
4. Own your feelings and thoughts. Use I-messages and take responsibility for these feelings.
5. Use active listening techniques to help your partner explore and express relevant thoughts and feelings.
6. Remember the principle of irreversibility; think carefully before saying things you may later regret.
7. Keep the channels of communication open. Be available to discuss problems, to negotiate solutions, and to practice new and more productive communication patterns.

Similarly, the skills of effective interpersonal conflict resolution are crucial in any attempt at relationship repair. If partners address relationship problems by deploying productive conflict resolution strategies, the difficulties may be resolved, and the relationship may actually emerge stronger and healthier. If, however, unproductive and destructive strategies are used, then the relationship may well deteriorate further. The nature and skills of conflict resolution are considered in depth in Chapter 13.

**Pose Possible Solutions**  After the problem is identified, you discuss solutions—possible ways to lessen or eliminate the difficulty. Look for solutions that will enable both of you to win. Try to avoid "solutions" in which one person wins and the other loses. With such win–lose solutions, resentment and hostility are likely to fester.

**Affirm Each Other**  Any strategy of relationship repair should incorporate supportiveness and positive evaluations. For example, happy couples engage in greater positive behav-

The media are currently teaching millions of people about interpersonal relationships. Whether for good or ill, millions of people tune in to the ubiquitous television talk shows to learn about friendship and romantic, family, and workplace relationships. Talk shows often present themselves as educational; as therapy; and as arbiters of how you, your parents, and your friends should develop and maintain relationships. Especially in the monologue that closes many of the shows, talk show hosts with little to no professional training dispense advice on interpersonal behavior.

And of course people also learn about how family members should communicate and relate to one another, how friends are supposed to behave, and how workplace colleagues should interact from situation comedies and dramas. Though the aim of these programs is simply to entertain, you can readily imagine what people learn and internalize from *Desperate Housewives, Boston Legal,* or *The Simpsons.*

Newspaper and magazine columnists offer advice without knowing even a modicum of information about who you are, what difficulties you may be experiencing, or what you really want and need. And astrology columns and psychic hotlines give you advice that has no basis in research.

### Follow Up

What media exert the most influence on your views about relationships? What role do talk shows, advice columns, and psychic hotlines play in your relational life and in the lives of your peers?

---

ior exchange: They communicate more agreement, approval, and positive affect than do unhappy couples (Dindia & Fitzpatrick, 1985). Clearly, these behaviors result from the positive feelings the partners have for each other. However, it can also be argued that these expressions help to increase the positive regard each person has for the other.

One way to affirm another is to talk positively. Reverse negative communication patterns. For example, instead of withdrawing, talk about the causes of and the possible cures for your disagreements and problems. Reverse the tendency to hide your inner self. Disclose your feelings. Compliments, positive stroking, and all the nonverbals that say "I care" are especially important when you wish to reverse negative communication patterns.

Cherishing behaviors are an especially insightful way to affirm another person and to increase favor exchange (Lederer, 1984). **Cherishing behaviors** are those small gestures you enjoy receiving from your partner (a smile, a wink, a squeeze, a kiss). Cherishing behaviors should be (1) specific and positive, (2) focused on the present and future rather than related to issues about which the partners have argued in the past, (3) capable of being performed daily, and (4) easily executed. People can make a list of the cherishing behaviors they each wish to receive and then exchange lists. Each person then performs the cherishing behaviors desired by the partner. At first, these behaviors may seem self-conscious and awkward. In time, however, they will become a normal part of interaction.

**Integrate Solutions into Normal Behavior**   Often solutions that are reached after an argument are followed for only a very short time; then the couple goes back to their previous, unproductive behavior patterns. Instead, integrate the solutions into your normal behavior; make them an integral part of your everyday relationship behavior. For example, make the exchange of favors, compliments, and cherishing behaviors a part of your normal relationship behavior.

**Risk**   Take risks in trying to improve your relationship. Risk giving favors without any certainty of reciprocity. Risk rejection by making the first move to make up or by saying you're sorry. Be willing to change, to adapt, to take on new tasks and responsibilities.

---

Risk the possibility that a significant part of the problem is you—that you're being unreasonable or controlling or stingy and that this is causing problems and needs to be changed.

## Intrapersonal Repair

One of the most important avenues to relationship repair originates with the principle of punctuation (see Chapter 1) and the idea that communication is circular rather than linear (see Chapter 1; Duncan & Rock, 1991). Let's consider an example involving Pat and Chris: Pat is highly critical of Chris; Chris is defensive and attacks Pat for being insensitive, overly negative, and unsupportive. If you view the communication process as beginning with Pat's being critical (that is, the stimulus) and with Chris's attacks being the response, you have a pattern such as occurs in Figure 11.3(A).

With this view, the only way to stop the unproductive communication pattern is for Pat to stop criticizing. But what if you are Chris and can't get Pat to stop being critical? What if Pat doesn't want to stop being critical?

You get a different view of the problem when you see communication as circular and apply the principle of punctuation. The result is a pattern such as appears in Figure 11.3(B).

Note that no assumptions are made about causes. Instead, the only assumption is that each response triggers another response; each response depends in part on the previous response. Therefore, the pattern can be broken at any point: Chris can stop Pat's criticism, for example, by not responding with attacks. Similarly, Pat can stop Chris's attacks by not responding with criticism.

In this view, either person can break an unproductive circle. Clearly, relationship communication can be most effectively improved when both parties change their unproductive patterns. Nevertheless, communication can be improved even if only one person changes and begins to use a more productive pattern. This is true to the extent that Pat's criticism depends on Chris's attacks and to the extent that Chris's attacks depend on Pat's criticism.

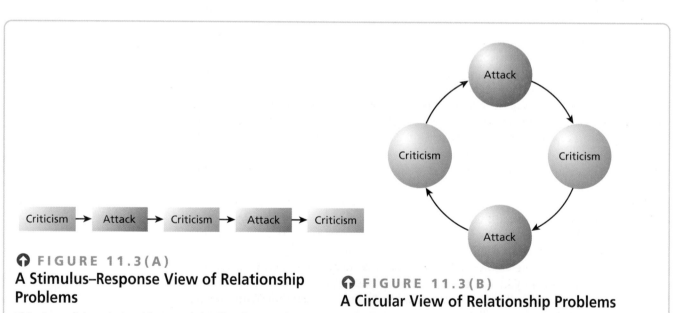

### ⬆ FIGURE 11.3(A)
## A Stimulus–Response View of Relationship Problems

This view of the relationship process implies that one behavior is the stimulus and one behavior is the response. It implies that a pattern of behavior can be modified only if you change the stimulus, which will produce a different (more desirable) response.

### ⬆ FIGURE 11.3(B)
## A Circular View of Relationship Problems

Note that in this view of relationships, as distinguished from that depicted in Figure 11.3(A), relationship behaviors are seen in a circular pattern; no specific behavior is singled out as a stimulus and none as a response. The pattern can thus be broken by interference anywhere along the circle.

## RELATIONSHIP DISSOLUTION

Some relationships, of course, do end. Sometimes there simply is not enough to hold the individuals together. Sometimes there are problems that cannot be resolved. Sometimes the costs are too high and the rewards too few, or the relationship is recognized as destructive and escape is the only alternative. As a relationship ends, you're confronted with two general issues: how to end the relationship, and how to deal with the inevitable problems that relationship endings cause.

### Strategies of Disengagement

When you wish to exit a relationship, you need some way of explaining this—to yourself as well as to your partner. You need a strategy for getting out of a relationship that you no longer find satisfying or profitable. Five such strategies are presented below (Cody, 1982). As you read down the list, note that the strategies depend on your goal. For example, you're more likely to remain friends if you use de-escalation than if you use justification or avoidance (Banks, Altendorf, Greene, & Cody, 1987).

Have you heard these used or used any of these yourself?

● The use of a positive tone to preserve the relationship and to express positive feelings for the other person. For example, "I really care for you a great deal, but I'm not ready for such an intense relationship."

## Ask the Researcher

### THE DEATH OF A RELATIONSHIP

 I recently lost my partner of 20 years in a car accident and am having lots of trouble dealing with this loss. Is there anything I can do to lessen the pain I feel?

The sudden loss of someone with whom you've had a long and intimate relationship can create lots of problems. The relationship has become part of your own identity, so losing your partner is like losing a part of your "self." You have lost not only your partner, but also your plans for the future, your emotional support, and perhaps even your financial support. Thus, you are now forced to be a different person than you were as a part of a relationship, and in this sense at least your loss is similar to the loss experienced by the dissolution of any intimate relationship. Your particular loss, however, is compounded because you didn't get to say good-bye. You may feel anger against the world, including the deceased, and you may even feel guilty that you were spared. Time may be the most important factor in healing such a loss; give yourself a chance to mourn and to learn to live alone.

For further information see C. A. Corr, C. M. Nabe, & D. M. Corr, *Death and Dying, Life and Living,* 2nd ed. (Pacific Grove, CA: Brooks/Cole, 1997); E. Kübler-Ross, *On Death and Dying* (New York: Macmillan, 1969, 1997); and H. S. Kushner, *When Bad Things Happen to Good People* (New York: Avon, 1981).

Shirlee A. Levin (M.A., University of Hawaii) is a professor of speech communication at the College of Southern Maryland, where she teaches courses in interpersonal communication, intercultural communication, groups and leadership, and the basic course. She has presented workshops for middle and high school students and faculty as well as for civic and religious groups. In 2003 she received the Community College Outstanding Educator Award from the National Communication Association, and she currently serves as president of the Maryland Communication Association.

❷ Negative identity management to blame the other person for the breakup and to absolve yourself of the blame for the breakup. For example, "I can't stand your jealousy, your constant suspicions, your checking up on me. I need my freedom."

❸ Justification to give reasons for the breakup. For example, "I'm going away to college for four years; there's no point in not dating others."

❹ Behavioral de-escalation to reduce the intensity of the relationship. For example, you might avoid the other person, cut down on phone calls, or reduce the amount of time you spend together.

❺ De-escalation to reduce the exclusivity and hence the intensity of the relationship. For example, "I'm just not ready for an exclusive relationship. I think we should see other people."

## Dealing with a Breakup

Regardless of the specific reason for the end of the relationship, relationship breakups are difficult to deal with; invariably they cause stress and emotional problems, and they may actually create as much pain in a person's brain as physical injuries (Eisenberger, Lieberman, & Williams, 2003). Women, it seems, experience greater depression and social dysfunction than men after relationship dissolution (Chung, Farmer, Grant, Newton, Payne, Perry, Saunders, Smith, & Stone, 2002). Consequently, it's important to give attention to self-repair. Here are a few suggestions to ease the difficulty that is sure to be experienced, whether the breakup is between friends or lovers or occurs because of death, separation, or the loss of affection and connection.

**Break the Loneliness–Depression Cycle**   The two most common feelings following the end of a relationship are loneliness and depression. These feelings are significant; treat them seriously. Realize that depression often leads to serious illness. In most cases, fortunately, loneliness and depression are temporary. Depression, for example, usually does not last longer than three or four days. Similarly, the loneliness that follows a breakup is generally linked to this specific situation and will fade when the situation changes. Grief—over the death of a loved one, say—may last a lot longer. When depression does last, is especially deep, or disturbs your normal functioning, it's time for professional help.

**Take Time Out**   Resist the temptation to jump into a new relationship while the old one is still warm or before a new one can be assessed with some objectivity. At the same time, resist swearing off all relationships. Neither extreme works well.

Take time out for yourself. Renew your relationship with yourself. If you were in a long-term relationship, you probably saw yourself as part of a team, as part of a couple. Now get to know yourself as a unique individual, standing alone at present but fully capable of entering a meaningful relationship in the near future.

**Bolster Self-Esteem**   When relationships fail, self-esteem often declines. This seems especially true for those who did not initiate the breakup (Collins & Clark, 1989). You may feel guilty for having caused the breakup or inadequate for not holding on to the relationship. You may feel unwanted and unloved. Your task is to regain a positive self-image.

Recognize, too, that having been in a relationship that failed—even if you view yourself as the main cause of the breakup—does not mean that you are a failure. Neither does it mean that you cannot succeed in a new and different relationship. It does mean that something went wrong with this one relationship. Ideally, it was a failure from which you have learned something important about yourself and about your relationship behavior.

**Remove or Avoid Uncomfortable Symbols**   After any breakup, there are a variety of reminders—photographs, gifts, and letters, for example. Resist the temptation to throw these out. Instead, remove them. Give them to a friend to hold or put them in a closet where you'll not see them. If possible, avoid places you frequented together. These symbols will bring back uncomfortable memories. After you have achieved some emotional distance, you can go back and enjoy these as reminders of a once pleasant relationship. Support for this suggestion comes from research showing that the more vivid your memory of a broken love affair—a memory greatly aided by these relationship symbols—the greater your depression is likely to be (Harvey, Flanary, & Morgan, 1986).

**Seek Support**   Many people feel they should bear their burdens alone. Men, in particular, have been taught that this is the only "manly" way to handle things. But seeking the support of others is one of the best antidotes to the unhappiness caused when a relationship ends. Tell your friends and family of your situation—in only general terms, if you prefer—and make it clear that you want support. Seek out people who are positive and nurturing. Avoid negative individuals who will paint the world in even darker tones. Make the distinction between seeking support and seeking advice. If you feel you need advice, seek out a professional.

**Avoid Repeating Negative Patterns**   Many people repeat their mistakes. They enter second and third relationships with the same blinders, faulty preconceptions, or unrealistic expectations with which they entered earlier involvements. Instead, use the knowledge gained from your failed relationship to prevent repeating the same patterns.

At the same time, don't become a prophet of doom. Don't see in every relationship vestiges of the old. Don't jump at the first conflict and say, "Here it goes all over again." Treat the new relationship as the unique relationship it is. Don't evaluate it through past experiences. Use past relationships and experiences as guides, not filters.

## Reviewing   Key Terms and Concepts in Interpersonal Relationships: Growth and Deterioration

### Relationship Development

What are some of the major theories that explain why you develop the relationships you do?

- Attraction theory holds that you develop relationships with those you consider attractive (physically and in personality), who are physically close to you, and who are similar to you.
- Social exchange theory holds that you develop relationships that enable you to maximize profits—relationships from which you derive more rewards than costs.
- Equity theory holds that you develop and maintain relationships in which your ratio of rewards compared to costs is approximately equal to your partner's.

### Relationship Maintenance

What are the reasons for relationship maintenance? What behaviors do people use to maintain their relationships?

- Reasons for maintaining a relationship include emotional attachment, convenience, children, fear, inertia, and commitment.
- Maintenance behaviors include being nice, communicating, being open, giving assurances, sharing joint activities, being positive, and improving yourself.

- Relationship maintenance can be achieved by following the rules for keeping the relationship, whether friendship or romance, together.

### Relationship Deterioration

What is relationship deterioration? Why do relationships deteriorate?

- Relationship deterioration involves the weakening of the bonds holding people together. It occurs when one or both parties are unhappy with the current state of the relationship.
- Among the causes of relationship deterioration are unrealistic beliefs about relationships, excessive intimacy claims, third-party relationships, relationship changes, undefined expectations, sex-related problems, work-related problems, and financial difficulties.
- Among the negative effects of relationship deterioration may be the loss of the good times and positive interactions, a loss of self-esteem, and financial problems. Positive effects may include an end to the relationship problems that precipitated the breakup, a renewed independence, and the opportunity to develop new relationships.
- Among the communication changes that occur during relationship deterioration are verbal and nonverbal withdrawal, a

decline in self-disclosure, an increase in deception, and an increase in negative messages and decrease in positive messages.

## Relationship Repair

What is relationship repair? What strategies can you use to repair a relationship?

- In relationship repair people endeavor to correct the problems that beset a relationship and to bring the relationship to a more intimate, more positive state.
- General repair strategies include recognizing the problem, engaging in productive communication and conflict resolution, posing possible solutions, affirming each other, integrating solutions into normal behavior, and risking.

- Repair isn't necessarily a two-person process; one person can break unproductive and destructive cycles.

## Relationship Dissolution

What is relationship dissolution? What strategies are used to dissolve relationships?

- Dissolution is the breaking or dissolving of the bonds that hold the relationship together.
- Among the strategies are positive tone, negative identity management, justification, behavioral de-escalation, and de-escalation of exclusivity.

## Applying Key Terms and Concepts in Interpersonal Relationships: Growth and Deterioration

**1** One way to improve communication during difficult times is to ask your partner to engage in positive behaviors rather than to stop negative behaviors. Consider how you might use this suggestion to replace such statements as the following: (1) "I hate it when you ignore me at business functions." (2) "I can't stand going to these cheap restaurants; when are you going to start spending a few bucks?" (3) "Stop being so negative; you criticize everything and everyone."

**2** Do you "comparison shop" (compare your own relationship against potential alternative relationships) regardless of the type of relationship you're in? Or do you stop "shopping" when the relationship reaches a certain level of commitment?

**3** Do a cost–benefit analysis of any one of your current relationships. In one column identify all the costs, and in the other column identify all the benefits you get from the relationship. Next, altercast: Playing the role of the person you just did an analysis of, do a cost–benefit analysis of yourself (as you think you might be seen by this person). What can you learn from this type of analysis?

**4** How would you feel if you were in a relationship in which you and your partner contributed an equal share of the costs (that is, you each worked equally hard) but your partner derived significantly greater rewards?

**5** What practical suggestions for dealing with relationship deterioration, repair, or dissolution do the theories of attraction, social exchange, and equity offer?

**6** How would you explain the finding that when relationships break up, it's the more attractive person who leaves first? What other factors might account for who leaves first?

## Experiencing Key Terms and Concepts in Interpersonal Relationships: Growth and Deterioration

Go to www.ablongman.com/devito.

*This group of experiences deals with interpersonal relationships and their development, maintenance, deterioration, repair, and dissolution.*

❶ **Interpersonal Relationships in Songs and Greeting Cards** explores the way cards and songs talk about relationships. ❷ **Applying Theories to Problems** provides an opportunity to apply the theories discussed in this chapter to common relationship problems. ❸ **Male and Female** looks at gender differences in relationships. ❹ **Changing the Distance between You** illustrates how relationship changes can be made. ❺ **Relational Repair from Advice Columnists** encourages you to critically examine the advice given by relationship columnists. ❻ **How Can You Get Someone to Like You?** looks at affinity-seeking strategies and how they're used to change people's perceptions. ❼ **How Might You Repair Relationships?** presents a variety of relationship problems and asks you to apply the insights gained here and from your own experience in suggesting repair strategies.

CHAPTER

# 12

# Interpersonal Relationships: Friendship, Love, Family, and Workplace

⬆ *Vera Drake* (2004)

On one level *Vera Drake* is the story of a woman who performs illegal abortions in London in the 1950s. On another level it is the story of a family and of how the family's members are all affected by what happens to one of them—a defining quality of relationships that are interpersonal. This chapter examines family as well as friendship, love, and work relationships.

**CHAPTER CONTENTS**

Friendship

Love

Family

Workplace Relationships

> "The easiest kind of relationship
> is with ten thousand people,
> the hardest is with one."
> 
> —Joan Baez

Now that the basic principles and stages of interpersonal relationships have been discussed, we can focus on specific relationship types. In this chapter we consider (1) friendship, (2) love, (3) family, and (4) workplace relationships, establishing what these are and exploring how interpersonal communication within each of these relationships can be made more effective.

## FRIENDSHIP

**Friendship** has engaged the attention and imagination of poets, novelists, and artists of all kinds. In television friendships have become almost as important as romantic pairings. And friendship also interests a range of interpersonal communication researchers (Samter, 2004). Throughout your life you'll meet many people, but out of this wide array you'll develop few relationships you would call friendships. Yet despite the low number of friendships you may form, their importance is great.

Friendship is an *interpersonal relationship* between two interdependent persons that is *mutually productive* and *characterized by mutual positive regard*. First, friendship is an interpersonal relationship; communication interactions must have taken place between the people. Further, the relationship involves a "personalistic focus" (Wright, 1978, 1984); friends react to each other as complete persons, as unique, genuine, and irreplaceable individuals.

Second, friendships must be mutually productive—they cannot be destructive to either person. Once destructiveness enters into a relationship, it can no longer be characterized as friendship. Lover relationships, marriage relationships, parent–child relationships, and just about any other possible relationship can be either destructive or productive, but friendship must enhance the potential of each person and can only be productive.

Third, friendships are characterized by mutual positive regard. Liking people is essential if we are to call them friends. Three major characteristics of friendship—trust, emotional support, and sharing of interests (Blieszner & Adams, 1992)—facilitate mutual positive regard.

When friends are especially close, the actions of one will impact more significantly on the other than they would if the friends were just casual acquaintances. The closer friends are, the more interdependent they become. At the same time, however, the closer friends are, the more independent they are of, for example, the attitudes and behaviors of others. Also, the less they are influenced by the societal rules that govern more casual relationships. Close friends are likely to make up their own rules for interacting with each other; they decide what they will talk about and when, what they can say to each other without offending and what they can't, when and for what reasons they can call each other, and so on.

In North America friendships clearly are a matter of choice; you choose—within limits—who your friends will be. And most researchers define friendship as a voluntary relationship, a relationship of choice (Samter, 2004). The density of the cities and the ease of communication and relocation makes many friendships voluntary. But in many parts of the world—for example, in small villages miles away from urban centers, where people are born, live, and die without venturing much beyond their community—relationships aren't voluntary. In these cases, you simply form relationships with those in your village. You don't have the luxury of selecting certain people to interact with and others to ignore. You must interact with and form friendships and romantic relationships with members of the community simply because these are the only people you come into contact with on a regular basis (Moghaddam, Taylor, & Wright, 1993).

## Friendship Types

Not all friendships are the same. But how do they differ? One way of answering this question is by distinguishing among three major types: friendships of reciprocity, receptivity, and association (Reisman, 1979, 1981).

The friendship of *reciprocity* is the ideal type, characterized by loyalty, self-sacrifice, mutual affection, and generosity. A friendship of reciprocity is based on equality: Each individual shares equally in giving and receiving the benefits and rewards of the relationship.

In the friendship of *receptivity,* in contrast, there is an imbalance in giving and receiving; one person is the primary giver and one the primary receiver. This is a positive imbalance, however, because each person gains something from the relationship. The different needs of both the person who receives and the person who gives affection are satisfied. This is the friendship that may develop between a teacher and a student or between a doctor and a patient. In fact, a difference in status is essential for the friendship of receptivity to develop.

The friendship of *association* is a transitory one. It might be described as a friendly relationship rather than a true friendship. Associative friendships are the kind we often have with classmates, neighbors, or coworkers. There is no great loyalty, no great trust, no great giving or receiving. The association is cordial but not intense.

Another way to look at friendship types is to compare face-to-face and online friendships. Not surprisingly, there is not yet enough research to draw clear distinctions between face-to-face and online friendships. Nevertheless, some differences are coming to light. For example, one study found that people viewed opposite-sex face-to-face friendships as more intimate than online friendships. Female–female online and face-to-face friendships, however, were rated equally—and male–male online friendships were rated as more intimate than face-to-face friendships (Haidar-Yassine, 2002). Another study found that face-to-face friendships involved more interdependence, greater breadth and depth, greater understanding, and greater commitment. Over time, however, as both types of friendships improved, the differences between face-to-face and online friendships decreased (Chan & Cheng, 2004).

For still another answer to the question of how friendships differ, consider the needs that friends serve. On the basis of your experiences or your predictions, you select as friends those who will help to satisfy your basic growth needs. Selecting friends on the basis of need satisfaction is similar to choosing a marriage partner, an employee, or any person who may be in a position to satisfy your needs. Thus, for example, if you need to be the center of attention or to be popular, you might select friends who allow you, and even encourage you, to be the center of attention or who tell you, verbally and nonverbally, that you're popular.

As your needs change, the qualities you look for in friendships also change. In many instances, old friends are dropped from your close circle to be replaced by new friends who better serve these new needs. One way to look at the needs that friendships serve is to look at the values or rewards that you seek to gain through your friendships (Wright 1978, 1984).

Consider the values you look for in a friend. Do you look for values such as these?

❶ *Utility:* Someone who may have special talents, skills, or resources that will prove useful to you in achieving your specific goals and needs. For example, might you become friends with someone who is particularly bright, because such a person might assist you in getting better grades, in solving problems, or in getting a better job?

❷ *Affirmation:* Someone who will affirm your personal value and help you to recognize your attributes. For example, might you develop a friendship with someone

**SPEAKING**
**Interpersonal-E**

**Some Reasons for Internet Friendships.** Research on young people aged 10 to 17 finds that among both girls and boys, those who form close online relationships are more likely to have low levels of communication with their parents and to be "highly troubled" than those who don't form such close online relationships (Wolak, Mitchell, & Finkelhor, 2003). Does your knowledge and memory of this age group corroborate that finding? What other characteristics do you think might differentiate young people who form close relationships online and those who don't?

because of that person's appreciation of your leadership abilities, your athletic prowess, or your sense of humor?

③ *Ego support:* Someone who behaves in a supportive, encouraging, and helpful manner. For example, would you seek friendships that would help you view yourself as worthy and competent?

④ *Stimulation:* Someone who introduces you to new ideas and new ways of seeing the world and helps you to expand your worldview. For example, would you form friendships with those who might bring you into contact with previously unfamiliar people, issues, religions, cultures, and experiences?

⑤ *Security:* Someone who does nothing to hurt you or to emphasize or call attention to your inadequacies or weaknesses. For example, would you select friends because you wouldn't have to worry about their betraying you or making negative comments about you?

## Friendship and Communication

Friendships develop over time in stages. At one end of the friendship continuum are strangers, or two persons who have just met, and at the other end are intimate friends. What happens between these two extremes?

As you progress from the initial contact stage to intimate friendship, the depth and breadth of communications increase (see Chapter 10). You talk about issues that are closer and closer to your inner core. Similarly, the number of communication topics increases as your friendship becomes closer. As depth and breadth increase, so does the satisfaction you derive from the friendship. This increase in depth and breadth can and does occur in all forms of communication—face-to-face as well as online. It's interesting to note that research has found that friendship is the primary goal for Internet communication among college students. In one study more than 60 percent of online users established successful online friendships, and about 50 percent felt more comfortable meeting someone online than in person (Knox, Daniels, Sturdivant, & Zusman, 2001). In another study 36 percent indicated that they had established an online friendship, compared to 22 percent who established an online romance (Nice & Katzev, 1998). Not surprisingly, instant messaging has been found to promote intimacy and to encourage online partners to meet face-to-face (Hu, Wood, Smith, & Westbrook, 2004).

Earlier (Chapter 10) we looked at the concept of dynamic tension in relationships, we looked at noting that there is a tension between, for example, autonomy and connection—the desire to be an individual but also to be connected to another person. Friendships also are defined by dynamic tensions (Rawlins, 1983). One tension is between the impulse to be open and to reveal personal thoughts and feelings on the one hand, and the impulse to protect yourself by not revealing personal information on the other. Also, there is the tension between being open and candid with your friend and being discreet. Because of these contradictory impulses, friendships don't always follow a straight path of increasing openness and candor. This is not to say that openness and candor don't increase as you progress from initial to casual to close friendships; they do. But the pattern does not follow a straight line; throughout the friendship development process, there are tensions that periodically restrict openness and candor.

There also are regressions that may temporarily pull the friendship back to a less intimate stage. Friendships stabilize at a level that is comfortable to both persons; some friendships will remain casual and others will remain close. Again, although friendship is presented in stages, the progression is not always a straight line to ever increasing intimacy.

With these qualifications in mind, we can discuss three stages of friendship development and integrate some of the characteristics of effective interpersonal communication identified in the Understanding Interpersonal Skills boxes (cf. Johnson, Wittenberg, Villagran, Mazur, & Villagran, 2003). The assumption made here is that as the friendship progresses from initial contact and acquaintanceship through casual friendship to close and intimate friendship, the qualities of effective interpersonal communication increase.

However, there is no assumption made that close relationships are necessarily the preferred type or that they're better than casual or temporary relationships. We need all types.

**Initial Contact and Acquaintanceship**    The first stage of friendship development is an initial meeting of some kind. This does not mean that what happened prior to the encounter is unimportant—quite the contrary. In fact, your prior history of friendships, your personal needs, and your readiness for friendship development are extremely important in determining whether the relationship will develop.

At the initial stage, the characteristics of effective interpersonal communication are usually present to only a small degree. You're guarded rather than open or expressive, lest you reveal aspects of yourself that might be viewed negatively. Because you don't yet know the other person, your ability to empathize with or to orient yourself significantly to the other is limited, and the relationship—at this stage, at least—is probably viewed as too temporary to be worth the effort. Because the other person is not well known to you, supportiveness, positiveness, and equality would all be difficult to manifest in any meaningful sense. The characteristics demonstrated are probably more the result of politeness than any genuine expression of positive regard.

At this stage, there is little genuine immediacy; the people see themselves as separate and distinct rather than as a unit. Any confidence that is demonstrated is probably more a function of the individual personalities than of the relationship. Because the relationship is so new and because the people don't know each other very well, the interaction often is characterized by awkwardness—for example, by overlong pauses, uncertainty over the topics to be discussed, and ineffective exchanges of speaker and listener roles.

**Casual Friendship**    In this second stage there is a dyadic consciousness, a clear sense of "we-ness," of togetherness; communication demonstrates a sense of immediacy. At this stage you participate in activities as a unit rather than as separate individuals. A casual friend is one we would go with to the movies, sit with in the cafeteria or in class, or ride home with from school.

At this casual friendship stage, the qualities of effective interpersonal interaction begin to be seen more clearly. You start to express yourself openly and become interested in the other person's disclosures. You begin to own your feelings and thoughts and respond openly to his or her communications. Because you're beginning to understand this person, you empathize and demonstrate significant other-orientation. You also demonstrate supportiveness and develop a genuinely positive attitude both toward the other person and toward mutual communication situations. As you learn this person's needs and wants, you can stroke more effectively.

There is an ease at this stage, a coordination in the interaction between the two persons. You communicate with confidence, maintain appropriate eye contact and flexibility in body posture and gesturing, and use few of the adaptors that signal discomfort.

**Close and Intimate Friendship**    At the stage of close and intimate friendship, there is an intensification of the casual friendship; you and your friend see yourselves more as an exclusive unit, and each of you derives greater benefits (for example, emotional support) from intimate friendship than from casual friendship (Hays, 1989).

Because you know each other well (for example, you know each other's values, opinions, and attitudes), your uncertainty about each other has been significantly reduced—you're able to predict each other's behaviors with considerable accuracy. This knowledge

**A S K Yourself**

Asking a Favor

You need to borrow $200 from your roommate, and you have no idea when you'll be able to pay it back.   Ask yourself:  What are some of the ways you might ask for this loan and at the same time not put your roommate into an awkward and uncomfortable position?

makes significant interaction management possible, as well as greater positivity, supportiveness, and openness (Oswald, Clark, & Kelly, 2004). Similarly, it would seem logical to predict that you would be able to read the other's nonverbal signals more accurately and could use these signals as guides to your interactions—avoiding certain topics at certain times or offering consolation on the basis of facial expressions. However, there is some evidence to suggest that less close friends are better at judging when someone is concealing sadness and anger than are close and intimate friends (Sternglanz & DePaulo, 2004). In any case, at this stage you exchange significant messages of affection: messages that express fondness, liking, loving, and caring for the other person. Openness, self-disclosure, and emotional support become more important than shared activities (Fehr, 2004).

You become more other-oriented and more willing to make significant sacrifices for the other person. You'll go far out of your way for the benefit of this friend, and the friend does the same for you. You empathize and exchange perspectives a great deal more, and you expect in return that your friend will also empathize with you. With a genuinely positive feeling for this individual, your supportiveness and positive stroking become spontaneous. Because you see yourselves as an exclusive unit, equality and immediacy are in clear evidence. You view this friend as one who is important in your life; as a result, conflicts—inevitable in all close relationships—are important to resolve through compromise and understanding rather than through, for example, refusal to negotiate or a show of force.

You're willing to respond openly, confidently, and expressively to this person and to own your feelings and thoughts. Your supportiveness and positiveness are genuine expressions of the closeness you feel for this person. Each person in an intimate friendship is truly equal; each can initiate and each can respond; each can be active and each can be passive; each speaks and each listens.

## Friendship, Culture, and Gender

Your friendships and the way you look at friendships will be influenced by your culture and your gender. Let's look first at culture. In the United States you can be friends with someone yet never really be expected to go much out of your way for this person. Many Middle Easterners, Asians, and Latin Americans would consider going significantly out of their way an absolutely essential ingredient in friendship; if you're not willing to sacrifice for your friend, then this person is not really your friend (Dresser, 1996).

Generally friendships are closer in collectivist cultures than in individualist cultures (see Chapter 2). In their emphasis on the group and on cooperating, collectivist cultures foster the development of close friendship bonds. Members of a collectivist culture are expected to help others in the group. When you help or do things for someone else, you increase your own attractiveness to this person, and this is certainly a good start for a friendship. Of course, the culture continues to reward these close associations.

Members of individualist cultures, on the other hand, are expected to look out for Number One, themselves. Consequently, they're more likely to compete and to try to do better than each other—conditions that don't support, generally at least, the development of friendships.

As noted in Chapter 2, these characteristics are extremes; most people have both collectivist and individualist values but have them in different degrees, and that is what we are talking about here—differences in degree of collectivist and individualist orientation.

Gender also influences your friendships—who becomes your friend and the way you look at friendships. Perhaps the best-documented finding—already noted in our discussion of self-disclosure—is that women self-disclose more than men (e.g., Dolgin, Meyer, & Schwartz, 1991). This difference holds throughout male and female friendships. Male friends self-disclose less often and with less intimate details than female friends do. Men generally don't view intimacy as a necessary quality of their friendships (Hart, 1990).

Women engage in significantly more affectional behaviors with their friends than do males; this difference may account for the greater difficulty men experience in beginning and maintaining close friendships (Hays, 1989). Women engage in more casual communication; they also share greater intimacy and more confidences with their friends than do men. Communication, in all its forms and functions, seems a much more important dimension of women's friendships.

When women and men were asked to evaluate their friendships, women rated their same-sex friendships higher in general quality, intimacy, enjoyment, and nurturance than did men (Sapadin, 1988). Men, in contrast, rated their opposite-sex friendships higher in quality, enjoyment, and nurturance than did women. Both men and women rated their opposite-sex friendships similarly in intimacy. These differences may be due, in part, to our society's suspicion of male friendships; as a result, a man may be reluctant to admit to having close relationship bonds with another man.

Men's friendships are often built around shared activities—attending a ball game, playing cards, working on a project at the office. Women's friendships, on the other hand, are built more around a sharing of feelings, support, and "personalism." Similarity in status, in willingness to protect a friend in uncomfortable situations, in academic major, and even in proficiency in playing the game Password were significantly related to the relationship closeness of male–male friends but not of female–female or female–male friends (Griffin & Sparks, 1990). Perhaps similarity is a criterion for male friendships but not for female or mixed-sex friendships.

The ways in which men and women develop and maintain their friendships will undoubtedly change considerably—as will all gender-related variables—in coming years. Perhaps there will be a further differentiation or perhaps an increase in similarities. In the meantime, given the present state of research in gender differences, we need to be careful not to exaggerate and to treat small differences as if they were highly significant. We need to avoid stereotypes, and we should not stress opposites to the neglect of the huge number of similarities between men and women (Wright, 1988; Deaux & LaFrance, 1998).

Further, friendship researchers warn that even when we find differences, the reasons for them aren't always clear (Blieszner & Adams, 1992). An interesting example is the finding that middle-aged men have more friends than middle-aged women and that women have more intimate friendships (Fischer & Oliker, 1983). But why is this so? Do men have more friends because they're friendlier than women, or because they have more opportunities to develop such friendships? Do women have more intimate friends because they have more opportunities to pursue such friendships or because they have a greater psychological capacity for intimacy?

##  LOVE

Of all the qualities of interpersonal relationships, none seems as important as love. "We are all born for love," noted famed British prime minister Benjamin Disraeli. "It is the principle of existence and its only end." **Love** is a feeling characterized by closeness and caring and by intimacy, passion, and commitment. It's also an interpersonal relationship developed, maintained, and sometimes destroyed through communication. And at the same time a relationship that can be greatly enhanced with communication skills (Dindia & Timmerman, 2004).

Although there are many theories about love, the one that captured the attention of interpersonal researchers and continues to receive research support is a conceptualization proposing that

**A s к Yourself**

From Friendship to Love

You have a great friendship with a colleague at work, but recently these feelings of friendship are turning to feelings of love.   Ask yourself: How can you move this friendship to love, or at least discover if the other person would be receptive to this change (cf. Marano, 2004)?

# Understanding Interpersonal Skills
## SUPPORTIVENESS

**Supportiveness** in communication is behavior that is descriptive rather than evaluative and provisional rather than certain (cf. Gibb, 1961). *Descriptive messages* state in relatively objective terms what you see or what you feel—as opposed to evaluative messages, which express your opinions and judgments. Descriptive messages may make others feel supported; judgmental or evaluative messages, on the other hand, may elicit **defensiveness**. This doesn't mean that all evaluative communications meet a defensive response, of course. For example, the would-be actor who wants to improve technique often welcomes both positive and negative evaluations.

*Provisional messages* express an open-minded attitude and a willingness to hear opposing viewpoints. Certainty messages, on the other hand, tolerate no differences of opinion and are likely to engender defensiveness.

**Communicating supportiveness.** Here are a few suggestions for communicating supportiveness by being descriptive and provisional, which will increase relationship satisfaction (Cramer, 2004).

- Avoid accusations or blame ("I should have stayed with my old job and not listened to your brother's advice").
- Avoid negative evaluative terms ("Didn't your sister look horrible in that red dress?")
- Avoid "preaching" ("You need to learn word processing and spreadsheet skills").
- Express your willingness to listen with an open mind and your readiness to consider changing your way of thinking and doing things.
- Ask for the opinions of others, and show that these are important to you. Resist the temptation to focus too much on your own way of seeing things.

there is not one but six types of love (Lee, 1976; Kanemasa, Taniguchi, Daibo & Ishimori, 2004). View the descriptions of each type as broad characterizations that are generally but not always true. As a preface to this discussion of the types of love, you may wish to respond to the self-test "What Kind of Lover Are You?"

# TEST YOURSELF
## WHAT KIND OF LOVER ARE YOU?

Respond to each of the following statements with T for true (if you believe the statement to be a generally accurate representation of your attitudes about love) or F for false (if you believe the statement does not adequately represent your attitudes about love).

_____ 1. My lover and I have the right physical "chemistry" between us.
_____ 2. I feel that my lover and I were meant for each other.
_____ 3. My lover and I really understand each other.
_____ 4. I believe that what my lover doesn't know about me won't hurt him or her.
_____ 5. My lover would get upset if he or she knew of some of the things I've done with other people.
_____ 6. When my lover gets too dependent on me, I want to back off a little.

_____ 7. I expect to always be friends with my lover.

_____ 8. Our love is really a deep friendship, not a mysterious, mystical emotion.

_____ 9. Our love relationship is the most satisfying because it developed from a good friendship.

_____ 10. In choosing my lover, I believed it was best to love someone with a similar background.

_____ 11. An important factor in choosing a partner is whether or not he or she would be a good parent.

_____ 12. One consideration in choosing my lover was how he or she would reflect on my career.

_____ 13. Sometimes I get so excited about being in love with my lover that I can't sleep.

_____ 14. When my lover doesn't pay attention to me, I feel sick all over.

_____ 15. I cannot relax if I suspect that my lover is with someone else.

_____ 16. I would rather suffer myself than let my lover suffer.

_____ 17. When my lover gets angry with me, I still love him or her fully and unconditionally.

_____ 18. I would endure all things for the sake of my lover.

**HOW DID YOU DO?** This scale, from Hendrick and Hendrick (1990), is based on the work of John Alan Lee (1976), as is the discussion of the six types of love that follows. The statements refer to the six types of love that we discuss below: eros, ludus, storge, pragma, mania, and agape. "True" answers represent your agreement and "false" answers your disagreement with the type of love to which the statements refer. Statements 1–3 are characteristic of the eros lover. If you answered true to these statements, you have a strong eros component to your love style. If you answered false, you have a weak eros component. Statements 4–6 refer to ludus love, 7–9 refer to storge love, 10–12 to pragma love, 13–15 to manic love, and 16–18 to agapic love.

**WHAT WILL YOU DO?** What things might you do to become more aware of the different love styles and to become a more well-rounded lover? How might you go about incorporating the qualities of effective interpersonal communication—for example, being more flexible, more polite, and more other-oriented—to become a more responsive, more exciting, more playful love partner?

_Source:_ From "A Relationship Specific Version of the Love Attitude Scale" by C. Hendrick and S. Hendrick, _Journal of Social Behavior and Personality 5,_ 1990. Reprinted by permission of Select Press.

## Love Types

Let's look at each of Lee's (1976) six types of love:

- _Eros: Beauty and sexuality._ Like Narcissus, who fell in love with the beauty of his own image, the erotic lover focuses on beauty and physical attractiveness, sometimes to the exclusion of qualities you might consider more important and more lasting. Also like Narcissus, the erotic lover has an idealized image of beauty that is unattainable in reality. Consequently, the erotic lover often feels unfulfilled. Not surprisingly, erotic lovers are particularly sensitive to physical imperfections in the ones they love.

- _Ludus: Entertainment and excitement._ Ludus love is experienced as a game, a fun. The better you can play the game, the greater the enjoyment. Love is not to be taken too seriously; emotions are to be held in check lest they get out of hand and make trouble; passions never rise to the point where they get out of control. A ludic lover is self-controlled, always aware of the need to manage love rather than allow it to be in control. Perhaps because of this need to control love, some researchers have proposed that ludic love tendencies may reveal tendencies to sexual aggression (Sarwer, Kalichman, Johnson, Early, et al., 1993). Not surprisingly, the ludic lover retains a partner only as long as the partner is interesting and amusing. When interest fades, it's time to change partners. Perhaps because love is a game, sexual fidelity is of little importance. In fact, recent research shows that people who score high on ludic love are more likely to engage in "extradyadic" dating and sex than those who score low on ludus (Wiederman & Hurd, 1999).

And, not surprisingly, ludic lovers score high on narcissism (Campbell, Foster, & Finkel, 2002).

- *Storge: Peaceful and slow.* Storge love (a word that come from the Greek for "familial love") lacks passion and intensity. Storgic lovers don't set out to find lovers but to establish a companionable relationship with someone they know and with whom they can share interests and activities. Storgic love is a gradual process of unfolding thoughts and feelings; the changes seem to come so slowly and so gradually that it's often difficult to define exactly where the relationship is at any point in time. Sex in storgic relationships comes late, and when it comes, it assumes no great importance.

- *Pragma: Practical and traditional.* The pragma lover is practical and seeks a relationship that will work. Pragma lovers want compatibility and a relationship in which their important needs and desires will be satisfied. They're concerned with the social qualifications of a potential mate even more than with personal qualities; family and background are extremely important to the pragma lover, who relies not so much on feelings as on logic. The pragma lover views love as a useful relationship that makes the rest of life easier. So the pragma lover asks such questions about a potential mate as "Will this person earn a good living?" "Can this person cook?" "Will this person help me advance in my career?" Pragma lovers' relationships rarely deteriorate. This is partly because pragma lovers choose their mates carefully and emphasize similarities. Another reason is that they have realistic romantic expectations.

- *Mania: Elation and depression.* Mania is characterized by extreme highs and extreme lows. The manic lover loves intensely and at the same time intensely worries about the loss of the love. This fear often prevents the manic lover from deriving as much pleasure as possible from the relationship. With little provocation, the manic lover may experience extreme jealousy. Manic love is obsessive; the manic lover must possess the beloved completely. In return, the manic lover wishes to be possessed, to be loved intensely. The manic lover's poor self-image seems capable of being improved only by love; self-worth comes from being loved rather than from any sense of inner satisfaction. Because love is so important, danger signs in a relationship are often ignored; the manic lover believes that if there is love, then nothing else matters.

- *Agape: Compassionate and selfless.* Agape is a compassionate, egoless, self-giving love. The agapic lover loves even people with whom he or she has no close ties. This lover loves the stranger on the road even though the two of them probably will never meet again. Agape is a spiritual love, offered without concern for personal reward or gain. This lover loves without expecting that the love will be reciprocated. Jesus, Buddha, and Gandhi preached this unqualified love, agape (Lee, 1976). In one sense, agape is more a philosophical kind of love than a love that most people have the strength to achieve. Not surprisingly people who believe in *yuan*, a Chinese concept that comes from the Buddhist belief in predestiny, are more likely to favor agapic (and pragmatic) love and less likely to favor erotic love (Goodwin & Findlay, 1997).

Each of these varieties of love can combine with others to form new and different patterns (for example, manic and ludic or storge and pragma). These six, however, identify the major types of love and illustrate the complexity of any love relationship. The six styles should also make it clear that different people want different things, that each person seeks satisfaction in a unique way. The love that may seem lifeless or crazy or boring to you may be ideal for someone else. At the same time, another person may see these very same negative qualities in the love you're seeking.

Love changes. A relationship that began as pragma may develop into ludus or eros. A relationship that began as erotic may develop into ma-

## ⊙ VIEWPOINT

Researcher Robert Sternberg defines love as a combination of intimacy, passion, and commitment (Sternberg, 1986, 1988; Lemieux & Hale, 1999, 2001). *Intimacy,* the emotional aspect of love, includes sharing, communicating, and mutual support. *Passion,* the motivational aspect, consists of physical attraction and romantic passion. *Commitment,* the cognitive aspect, consists of the decisions you make concerning your lover. When you have all three aspects to about equal degrees, you have complete or consummate love. How does this definition match the meaning that you have for "love"?

nia or storge. One approach sees this developmental process as having three major stages (Duck, 1986):

- First stage: Eros, mania, and ludus (initial attraction)
- Second stage: Storge (as the relationship develops)
- Third stage: Pragma (as relationship bonds develop)

In reading about the love styles, you may have felt that certain personality types are likely to favor one type of love over another. Here are personality traits that research finds people assign to each love style (Taraban & Hendrick, 1995). **Which personality characteristics do you think go with which love style (eros, ludus, storge, pragma, mania, or agape)?**

1. inconsiderate, secretive, dishonest, selfish, dangerous
2. honest, loyal, mature, caring, loving, understanding
3. jealous, possessive, obsessed, emotional, dependent
4. sexual, exciting, loving, happy, optimistic
5. committed, giving, caring, self-sacrificing, loving
6. family-oriented, planning, careful, hard-working, concerned

Very likely you perceived these personality factors in the same way as did the participants in the research from which these traits were drawn: 1 = ludus, 2 = storge, 3 = mania, 4 = eros, 5 = agape, and 6 = pragma. Do note, of course, that these results do not imply that ludus lovers *are* inconsiderate, secretive, and dishonest; they merely mean that people in general (and perhaps you in particular) *think* of ludus lovers as inconsiderate, secretive, and dishonest.

## Love and Communication

How do you communicate when you're in love? What do you say? What do you do nonverbally? According to research, you exaggerate your beloved's virtues and minimize his or her faults. You share emotions and experiences and speak tenderly, with an extra degree of courtesy, to each other; "please," "thank you," and similar polite expressions abound. You frequently use "personalized communication." This type of communication includes secrets you keep from other people and messages that have meaning only within your specific relationship (Knapp, Ellis, & Williams, 1980). You also create and use personal idioms (and pet names): words, phrases, and gestures that carry meaning only for the particular relationship and that say you have a special language that signifies your special bond (Hopper, Knapp, & Scott, 1981). When outsiders try to use personal idioms—as they sometimes do—the expressions seem inappropriate, at times even an invasion of privacy.

You engage in significant self-disclosure. There is more confirmation and less disconfirmation among lovers than among either nonlovers or those who are going through romantic breakups. Not surprisingly, you also use more constructive conflict resolution strategies (see Chapter 13) if you feel your relationship is threatened (Keltner, Londahl, & Smith, 2001). You're highly aware of what is and is not appropriate to say to the person you love. You know how to reward, but also how to punish, each other. In short, you know what to do to obtain the reaction you want.

Among your most often used means for communicating love are telling the person face-to-face or by telephone (in one survey 79 percent indicated they did it this way), expressing supportiveness, and talking things out and cooperating (Marston, Hecht, & Robers, 1987).

Nonverbally, you also communicate your love. Prolonged and focused eye contact is perhaps the clearest nonverbal indicator of love. So important is eye contact that its avoidance almost always triggers a "what's wrong?" response. You also have longer periods of silence than you do with friends (Guerrero, 1997). In addition, you display affiliative cues (signs that show you love the other person), including head nods, gestures, and forward leaning. And you give Duchenne smiles—smiles that are beyond voluntary control and that signal

**A s k Yourself**
Discovering Personal Information

You're becoming romantically involved with someone at work, but before this relationship goes any farther, you want to know about this person's HIV status and safe sex practices. Ask yourself: What are some of the things that you might say that will elicit truthful information but at the same time will not create a rift in the relationship?

# Understanding Interpersonal Theory and Research

## JEALOUSY

**Jealousy** is a reaction to relationship threat: If you feel that someone is moving in on your relationship partner, you may experience jealousy—especially if you feel that this interloper is succeeding. So what do you do when you experience jealousy? Communication researchers find several popular but generally negative interactive responses (Guerrero, Andersen, Jorgensen, Spitzberg, & Eloy, 1995; Dindia & Timmerman, 2003). You may:

- nonverbally express your displeasure; for example, cry or facially express hurt
- threaten to become violent or actually engage in violence
- direct verbal aggressiveness toward the partner; for example, be sarcastic or accusatory
- withdraw affection from your partner or be abnormally silent, sometimes denying that anything is wrong

On the more positive side are responses known as "integrative communication": messages that attempt to work things out with your partner, such as self-disclosing your feelings and being honest.

### Working with Theories and Research

Examine your own jealousy or the jealousy you witness in others and especially the ways in which you or they have expressed this jealousy. What types of responses seem to promote relationship satisfaction? What types seem to damage the relationship?

---

genuine joy (Gonzaga, Keltner, Londahl, & Smith, 2001). These smiles give you crow's-feet around the eyes, raise up your cheeks, and puff up the lower eyelids (Lemonick, 2005a).

You grow more aware not only of your loved one but also of your own physical self. Your muscle tone is heightened, for example. When you're in love you engage in preening gestures, especially immediately prior to meeting your lover, and you position your body attractively—stomach pulled in, shoulders square, legs arranged in appropriate masculine or feminine positions. Your speech may even have a somewhat different vocal quality. There is some evidence to show that sexual excitement enlarges the nasal membranes, which introduces a certain nasal quality into the voice (M. Davis, 1973).

You eliminate socially taboo adaptors, at least in the presence of the loved one. For example, you curtail scratching your head, picking your teeth, cleaning your ears, and passing wind. Interestingly enough, these adaptors often return after lovers have achieved a permanent relationship.

You touch more frequently and more intimately (Guerrero, 1997). You also use more "tie signs," nonverbal gestures that show that you're together, such as holding hands, walking with arms entwined, kissing, and the like. You may even dress alike. The styles of clothes and even the colors selected by lovers are more similar than those worn by nonlovers.

## Love, Culture, and Gender

Like friendship, love is heavily influenced by culture and gender (Dion & Dion, 1996). Let's consider first some of the cultural influences on the way you look at love and perhaps on the type of love you're seeking or maintaining. Although most of the research on six love styles has been done in the United States, some research has been conducted in other cultures (Bierhoff & Klein, 1991). Here is just a sampling of the research findings—just enough to illustrate that culture is an important factor in love.

Asians have been found to be more friendship oriented in their love style than are Europeans (Dion & Dion, 1993b). Members of individualist cultures (for example, Europeans) are likely to place greater emphasis on romantic love and on individual fulfillment. Members of collectivist cultures are likely to spread their love over a large network of relatives (Dion & Dion, 1993a). When compared to their Chinese counterparts, American men scored higher on ludic and agapic love and lower on erotic and pragma love. American men also are less likely to view emotional satisfaction as crucial to relationship maintenance (Sprecher & Toro-Morn, 2002).

One study finds a love style among Mexicans characterized as calm, compassionate, and deliberate (Leon, Philbrick, Parra, Escobedo, et al., 1994). In comparisons between love styles in the United States and France, it was found that people in the United States scored higher on storge and mania than the French; in contrast, the French scored higher on agape (Murstein, Merighi, & Vyse, 1991). In the United States Caucasian women, scored higher on mania than African American women, whereas African American women scored higher on agape. Caucasian and African American men, however, scored very similarly; no statistically significant differences were found (Morrow, Clark, & Brock, 1995).

Gender also influences love. In the United States the differences between men and women in love are considered great. In poetry, novels, and the mass media, women and men are depicted as acting very differently when falling in love, being in love, and ending a love relationship. As Lord Byron put it in *Don Juan,* "Man's love is of man's life a thing apart, / 'Tis woman's whole existence." Women are portrayed as emotional, men as logical. Women are supposed to love intensely; men are supposed to love with detachment.

Women and men seem to experience love to a similar degree, and research continues to find great similarities between men's and women's conceptions of love (Rubin, 1973; Fehr & Broughton, 2001). However, women indicate greater love than men do for their same-sex friends. This may reflect a real difference between the sexes, or it may be a function of the greater social restrictions on men. A man is not supposed to admit his love for another man. Women are permitted greater freedom to communicate their love for other women.

Men and women also differ in the types of love they prefer (Hendrick, Hendrick, Foote, & Slapion-Foote, 1984). For example, on one version of the love self-test presented earlier, men scored higher on erotic and ludic love, whereas women scored higher on manic, pragmatic, and storgic love. No difference was found for agapic love.

Women have their first romantic experiences earlier than men. In the United States the median age of first infatuation for women is 13 and for men 13.6; the median age for first time of being in love for women is 17.1 and for men 17.6 (Kirkpatrick & Caplow, 1945; Hendrick, Hendrick, Foote, & Slapion-Foote, 1984). Research on the age of first sexual experience show that gender differences vary from one culture to another (Singh, Wulf, Samara, & Cuca, 2000). For example, the median age in Ghana for the first sexual experience is 16.9 for females and 18.4 for males. In the United States the median age is 17.2 for females and 16.1 for males. And in Great Britain the differences are minimal (17.4 for females and 17.2 for males). In the United States females marry for the first time at a younger age than men; in 2003 the median age for first marriage was 25.3 for females and 27.1 for males (www.census.gov, accessed 8/19/2005). People of different experiences, cultures, and ages, for example, will probably see these figures very differently. Some will see these as much too high, others will see these as about right, and still others will see these as too low.

Much research finds that men place more emphasis on romance than women. For example, when college students were asked the question "If a man (woman) had all the other qualities you desired, would you marry this person if you were not in love with him (her)?" Approximately two-thirds of the men responded no, which seems to indicate that a high percentage were concerned with love and romance. However, less than one-third of the women responded no (LeVine,

🔂 **VIEWPOINT**

Men and women from different cultures were asked the following question: "If a man (woman) had all the other qualities you desired, would you marry this person if you were not in love with him (her)?" Results varied from one culture to another (Levine, Sato, Hashimoto, & Verma, 1994). For example, 50 percent of the respondents from Pakistan said yes, 49 percent of those from India said yes, and 19 percent from Thailand said yes. At the other extreme were those from Japan (only 2 percent said yes), the United States (only 3.5 percent said yes), and Brazil (only 4 percent said yes). How would you answer this question? How is your answer influenced by your culture?

Sato, Hashimoto, & Verma, 1994). Further, when men and women were surveyed concerning their view on love—whether it's basically realistic or basically romantic—it was found that married women had a more realistic (less romantic) conception of love than did married men (Knapp & Vangelisti, 2005).

Additional research also supports the view that men are more romantic. For example, "Men are more likely than women to believe in love at first sight, in love as the basis for marriage and for overcoming obstacles, and to believe that their partner and relationship will be perfect" (Sprecher & Metts, 1989). This difference seems to increase as the romantic relationship develops: Men become more romantic and women less romantic (Fengler, 1974).

One further gender difference may be noted, and that is the difference between men and women in breaking up a relationship (Blumstein & Schwartz, 1983; cf., Janus & Janus, 1993). Popular myth would have us believe that love affairs break up as a result of the man's outside affair. But the research does not support this. When surveyed as to the reason for breaking up, only 15 percent of the men indicated that it was their interest in another partner, whereas 32 percent of the women noted this as a cause of the breakup. These findings are consistent with their partners' perceptions as well: 30 percent of the men (but only 15 percent of the women) noted that their partner's interest in another person was the reason for the breakup.

In their reactions to broken romantic affairs, women and men exhibit similarities and differences. For example, the tendency for women and men to recall only pleasant memories and to revisit places with past associations was about equal. However, men engaged in more dreaming about the lost partner and in more daydreaming generally as a reaction to the breakup than did women.

# FAMILY

If you had to define the term **family,** you might reply that a family consists of a husband, a wife, and one or more children. When pressed, you might add that some families also include other relatives—in-laws, brothers and sisters, grandparents, aunts and uncles, and so on. But other types of relationships are, to their own members, "families." Table 12.1 provides a few statistics on the family as constituted in 1970 and in 2002.

One obvious example is the family without children which in 2002 totaled 52 percent of the families in the United States. About 28 percent of American families are headed by a single parent.

Another obvious example is people living together in an exclusive relationship who are not married. For the most part these cohabitants live as if they were married: There is an exclusive sexual commitment; there may be children; there are shared financial responsibilities, shared time, and shared space. These relationships mirror traditional marriages, except that in marriage the union is recognized by a religious body, the state, or both and only marrieds can profit from federal benefits and protections.

Another example is the gay or lesbian couple who live together as "domestic partners" or in a "civil union"—relatively new terms for people living in a committed relationship—in households that have all the characteristics of a family. Many of these couples have children from previous heterosexual unions, through artificial insemination, or by adoption. Although accurate statistics are difficult to secure, primary relationships among gays and lesbians seem more common than the popular media lead us to believe. According to *Time Almanac with Information Please* (2005), the number of homosexual partners sharing a household is approximately 1 percent of all households (or 594,391 same-sex partner households). And, most relational experts agree, being in a committed relationship is the goal of most people, regardless of affectional orientation (Patterson, 2000; Kurdek, 2000; 2004; Fitzpatrick & Caughlin, 2002).

**SPEAKING**
**Interpersonal-E**

**The Internet and Generational Conflict.** In South Korea, Internet use seems to be contributing further to the already significant generational conflict between children and parents (Rhee & Kim, 2004). Has computer-mediated communication contributed to generational communication gaps within your own family network?

## TABLE 12.1
### The Changing Face of the American Family

Here are a few statistics on the nature of the American family for 1970 and 2002, as reported by the *New York Times Almanac 2005* and *The World Almanac and Book of Facts 2005*, along with some trends these figures may indicate. What other trends do you see occurring in the family?

| Family Characteristic | 1970 | 2002 | Trends |
|---|---|---|---|
| Number of members in average family | 3.58 | 3.21 | Reflects the tendency toward smaller families |
| Families without children | 44.1% | 52% | Reflects the growing number of families that are opting not to have children |
| Families headed by married couples | 86.8% | 76.3% | Reflects the growing trend for heterosexual couples to live as a family without marriage, for singles to have children, and for gay men and lesbians to form families |
| Females as heads of households | 10.7% | 17.7% | Reflects the growing number of women who have children without marriage and the increase in divorce and separation |
| Married-couple families | 86.8% | 76.3% | Reflects the growing trend for couples to form families without being married |
| Single-parent families | 13% | 27.8% | Reflects the growing trend for women (especially) to maintain families without a partner |
| Households headed by never-married women with children | 248,000 | 4.3 million | Reflects the growing trend for women to have children and maintain a family without marriage |
| Children living with only one parent | 12% | 23% | Reflects the growing divorce rate and the increased number of children born to unwed mothers |
| Children between 25 and 34 living at home with parents | 8% (11.9 million) | 9.3% (19.2 million) | Reflects the increased economic difficulty of establishing a household and perhaps the increased divorce rate and later dates for marriage (especially true for men) |

The communication principles that apply to the traditional nuclear family (the mother–father–child family) also apply to these relationships. In the following discussion, the term **primary relationship** denotes the relationship between the two principal parties—the husband and wife, the lovers, the domestic partners, for example—and the term *family* denotes the broader constellation that includes children, relatives, and assorted significant others.

## Characteristics of Families

All primary relationships and families have several qualities that further characterize this relationship type: defined roles, recognition of responsibilities, shared history and future, shared living space, and established rules.

**Defined Roles**   Primary relationship partners have a relatively clear perception of the roles each person is expected to play in relation to the other and to the relationship as a whole. Each acquired the rules of his or her culture and social group; each knows approximately what his or her obligations, duties, privileges, and responsibilities are. The partners' roles might include those of wage earner, cook, house cleaner, child caregiver, social secretary,

## DYSFUNCTIONAL FAMILY PATTERNS

I come from a classic dysfunctional family, and I'm determined to leave that behind me. But I have heard that family patterns repeat themselves. Is there anything I can do to stop this cycle from repeating—and from preventing me from having a happy and productive family life myself?

Changing long-standing patterns of behavior is difficult. You've already taken a step toward changing when you became aware of the pattern. Now you need to take time to understand it—to figure out why family members engage in certain behaviors and avoid others. Understanding the pattern will help you recognize it when it crops up again. Another important step toward changing is being willing to differentiate yourself from your family. When you stop engaging in the pattern, you will be unlike other family members. You may feel marginalized and you may even be rejected. Before you can change, you need to be willing to be different. Finally, it is important to identify and practice an alternative pattern of behavior. It is easy to look at family members and see a pattern that is dysfunctional; it's much harder to come up with an alternative. Engaging in an alternative pattern will help prevent you from falling back into the old one.

**For further information** see L. Rubin, *The Transcendent Child: Tales of Triumph over the Past* (New York: Basic Books, 1996).

Anita L. Vangelisti (Ph.D., University of Texas at Austin) is professor of communication studies at the University of Texas at Austin. Her research focuses on the associations between communication and emotion in the context of close personal relationships. She is coeditor of the Cambridge University Press series on *Advances in Personal Relationships* and has served on the editorial boards of more than a dozen journals. Dr. Vangelisti has published numerous articles and chapters as well as several books.

home decorator, plumber, carpenter, food shopper, money manager, and so on. At times the roles may be shared, but even then it's generally assumed that one person has primary responsibility for certain tasks and the other person for others.

Most heterosexual couples divide the roles rather traditionally, with the man as primary wage earner and maintenance person and the woman as primary cook, child rearer, and housekeeper. This is less true among more highly educated couples and those in the higher socioeconomic classes, where changes in traditional role assignments are first seen. However, among gay and lesbian couples, clear-cut, stereotypical male and female roles are not found. One research review, for example, noted that scientific studies "have consistently debunked this myth. Most contemporary gay relationships do not conform to traditional 'masculine' and 'feminine' roles; instead, role flexibility and turn taking are more common patterns. . . . In this sense, traditional heterosexual marriage is not the predominant model or script for current homosexual couples" (Peplau, 1988).

**Recognition of Responsibilities** Family members see themselves as having certain obligations and responsibilities to one another. A single person does not have the same kinds of obligations to another as someone in a primary relationship. For example, individuals have an obligation to help each other financially. There are also emotional responsibilities: to offer comfort when our family members are distressed, to take pleasure in their pleasures, to feel their pain, to raise their spirits. Each person in a couple also has a temporal obligation to reserve some large block of time for the other. Time sharing seems important to all relationships, although each couple will define it differently.

**Shared History and Future**   Primary relationships have a shared history and the prospect of a shared future. For a relationship to become primary, there must be some history, some significant past interaction. This interaction enables the members to get to know each other, to understand each other a little better, and ideally to like and even love each other. Similarly, the individuals view the relationship as having a potential future. Despite researchers' prediction that 50 percent of couples now entering first marriages will divorce (the rate is higher for second marriages) and that 41 percent of all persons of marriageable age will experience divorce, most couples entering a relationship such as marriage view it—ideally, at least—as permanent.

**Shared Living Space**   In general American culture, persons in primary interpersonal relationships usually share the same living space. When living space is not shared, the situation is generally seen as "abnormal" or temporary, both by the culture as a whole and by the individuals involved in the relationship. Even those who live apart for significant periods probably perceive a shared space as the ideal and, in fact, usually do share some special space at least part of the time. In some other cultures, however, men and women don't share the same living space; the women may live with the children while the men live together in a communal arrangement (Harris, 1993).

Although shared living space is generally a goal of most primary relationships, in the United States, the number of long-distance relationships is increasing. Further, although living together is a goal, this does not mean that long-distance relationships are necessarily less satisfying. After a thorough review of the research, one researcher concludes that "there is little, if any, decrease in relationship satisfaction, intimacy, and commitment as long as lovers are able to reunite with some frequency (approximately once a month)" (Rohlfing, 1995, pp. 182–183).

Not surprisingly, research finds that lovers employ a variety of strategies to maintain long-distance relationships, acknowledging in their use of strategies that something extra has to be done to keep the relationships satisfying and together. Among these strategies are recognizing that long-distance relationships are common; establishing support systems while apart; and communicating in creative ways, such as via cards or videos (Westefeld & Liddell, 1982).

**Established Rules**   Family communication research points to the importance of rules in defining the family (Galvin & Brommel, 2000). You can view rules as concerning three main interpersonal communication issues (Satir, 1983): (1) What can you talk about? Can you talk about the family finances? Grandpa's drinking? Your sister's lifestyle? (2) How can you talk about something? Can you joke about your brother's disability? Can you directly address questions of family history or family skeletons? (3) To whom can you talk? Can you talk openly to extended family members such as cousins and aunts and uncles? Can you talk to close neighbors about family health issues?

All families teach rules for communication. Some of these are explicit, such as "Never contradict a family member in front of outsiders" or "Never talk finances with outsiders." Other rules are unspoken; you deduce them as you learn the communication style of your family. For example, if financial issues are always discussed in secret and in hushed tones, then you can infer that you shouldn't tell others about family finances.

These rules tell you which behaviors will be rewarded (and therefore what you should do) and which will be punished (and therefore what you should not do). Rules tell you what moves are permissible and what moves are not permissible. Rules also provide a kind of structure that defines the family as a cohesive unit and that distinguishes it from other similar families.

Not surprisingly, the rules a family develops are greatly influenced by the wider culture. Although there are many similarities among families throughout the world, there are also differences (Georgas et al., 2001). For example, members of collectivist cultures are more

**SPEAKING**
**>> Interpersonal-E**

**Students Away at College.** When students go away to college, they often maintain close connections with their family and high school friends through cell phones, e-mail, and instant messaging. What advantages does this ease of connection provide? Can you identify any problems it might create?

# InterMedia

## AGENDA-SETTING THEORY

Agenda-setting theory argues that the media establish your agenda by telling you—by virtue of what they cover—who is important and what events are significant (McCombs & Shaw, 1972, 1993). Agenda-setting theory emphasizes the media's influence, not in telling you *what* to think, but in telling you what to think *about* (Edelstein, 1993; McCombs, Lopez-Escobar, & Llamas, 2000).

Both salience and obtrusiveness influence the media's ability to establish your agenda (Folkerts & Lacy, 2004).

- *Salience* is the importance of an issue to you. For example, if you live in a high-crime city, then news of crime, crime deterrents, and crime statistics are probably important to you. If the media cover such salient issues, then their ability to establish your agenda is enhanced. If they fail to cover such issues, then you're less likely to set your agenda on the basis of media coverage.

- *Obtrusiveness* relates to your experience with an issue. If you have direct experience with an issue, then it's obtrusive; if you don't have direct experience, then it's unobtrusive. For example, if college tuition costs go up, then the issue is obtrusive, as you (presumably) have direct experience with it. But if a volcano erupts on some unknown island, it's unobtrusive. The media's agenda-setting influence is greater for unobtrusive issues, because you have no direct experience with those issues and hence have to rely on what the media tell you is or isn't important.

### Follow Up

What relationship issues have high salience for you? What relationship issues are obtrusive? How do the media help set your friendship, love, family, and workplace relationship agenda?

---

likely to keep family information from outsiders as a way of protecting the family than are members of individualist cultures. This tendency to protect the family can create serious problems in cases of wife abuse. Many women will not report spousal abuse because of this desire to protect the family image and not to let others know that things aren't perfect at home (Dresser, 1996).

Family communication theorists argue that rules should be flexible so that special circumstances can be accommodated; for example, there are situations that necessitate changing the family dinner time, vacation plans, or savings goals (Noller & Fitzpatrick, 1993). And rules should be negotiable so that all members can participate in their modification and feel a part of family government.

## ASK Yourself
### Establishing Family Communication Rules

You hope to begin your family in the very near future, and the notion of family communication rules seems intriguing. You begin to wonder what types of rules you'd like to see in your own soon-to-be family. Ask yourself: What goals do you want to achieve in your family communication? What rules would best contribute to achieving these goals? What rules would work against these goals?

## Family Types

Based on responses from more than 1,000 couples to questions concerning their degree of sharing, their space needs, their conflicts, and the time they spend together, researchers have identified three basic types of primary relationships: traditionals, independents, and separates (Fitzpatrick, 1983, 1988, 1991; Noller & Fitzpatrick, 1993).

*Traditional* couples share a basic belief system and philosophy of life. They see themselves as a blending of two persons into a single couple rather than as two separate individuals. They're interdependent and believe that each individual's independence must be sacrificed for the good of the relationship. Traditionals believe in mutual sharing and do little separately. This couple holds to the traditional gender roles, and there are seldom any role conflicts.

There are few power struggles and few conflicts in general, because each person knows and adheres to a specified role within the relationship. In their communications, traditionals are highly responsive to each other. Traditionals lean toward each other, smile, talk a lot, interrupt each other, and finish each other's sentences.

*Independent* couples stress their individuality. The relationship is important, but never more important than each person's individual identity. Although independents spend a great deal of time together, they don't ritualize it, for example, with schedules. Each individual spends time with outside friends. Independents see themselves as relatively androgynous—as individuals who combine the traditionally feminine and the traditionally masculine roles and qualities. The communication between independents is responsive. They engage in conflict openly and without fear. Their disclosures are quite extensive and include high-risk and negative disclosures that are typically absent among traditionals.

*Separate* couples live together but view their relationship more as a matter of convenience than a result of their mutual love or closeness. They seem to have little desire to be together and, in fact, usually are together only at ritual functions, such as mealtime or holiday get-togethers. It's important to these separates that each has his or her own physical as well as psychological space. Separates share little; each seems to prefer to go his or her own way. Separates hold relatively traditional values and beliefs about gender roles, and each person tries to follow the behaviors normally assigned to each role. What best characterizes this type, however, is that each person sees himself or herself as a separate individual and not as a part of a "we."

In addition to these three pure types, there also are combinations. For example, in the separate–traditional couple one individual is a separate and one a traditional. Another common pattern is the traditional–independent, in which one individual believes in the traditional view of relationships and one in autonomy and independence.

## Family and Communication

One helpful way to understand families and primary relationships is in terms of the communication patterns that dominate the relationship. Four general communication patterns are identified here; each interpersonal relationship may then be viewed as a variation on one of these basic patterns.

### The Equality Pattern
The equality pattern probably exists more in theory than in practice, but it's a good starting point for looking at communication in primary relationships. It exists more among same-sex couples than opposite-sex couples (Huston & Schwartz, 1995). In the equality pattern each person shares equally in the communication transactions; the roles played by each are equal. Thus, each person is accorded a similar degree of credibility; each is equally open to the ideas, opinions, and beliefs of the other; each engages in self-disclosure on a more or less equal basis. The communication is open, honest, direct, and free of the power plays that characterize so many other interpersonal relationships. There is no leader or follower, no opinion giver or opinion seeker; rather, both parties play these roles equally. Because of this basic equality, the communication exchanges themselves, over a substantial period, are equal. For example, the number of questions asked, the depth and frequency of self-disclosures, and the nonverbal behaviors of touching and eye gaze would all be about the same for both people.

Both parties share equally in decision-making processes—in insignificant decisions, such as which movie to attend, as well as in significant choices, such as where to send a child to school, whether to

**VIEWPOINT**

If you looked at the family from an evolutionary–Darwinian point of view, one research watcher notes, you'd have to conclude that families are "inherently unstable" and that it's necessity, not choice, that keeps them together. If they had better opportunities elsewhere, many family members would leave immediately (Goleman, 1995b). What do you see as the greatest advantages of family? What do you see as the greatest disadvantages?

attend religious services, or what house to buy. Conflicts may occur with some frequency in equality relationships, but they're not seen as threatening to the individuals or to the relationship. They're viewed, rather, as exchanges of ideas, opinions, and values. These conflicts tend to be about content rather than relational issues (Chapter 13), and the couple has few power struggles within the relationship domain.

Equal relationships also are equitable. According to equity theory, family or relationship satisfaction will be highest when there is equity—when each partner gets a proportional share of the costs and the rewards of the relationship (Chapter 11). Dissatisfaction over inequities can lead to a "balancing of the scales" reaction. For example, an underbenefited partner may seek an outside affair as a way to get more relationship benefits—more love, more consideration, more support (Walster, Walster, & Traupmann, 1978; Noller & Fitzpatrick, 1993).

**The Balanced Split Pattern**   In the balanced split pattern, an equality relationship is maintained, but each person has authority over different domains. Each person is seen as an expert or a decision maker in different areas. For example, in the traditional nuclear family, the husband maintains high credibility in business matters and perhaps in politics. The wife maintains high credibility in such matters as child care and cooking. These gender roles are breaking down in many cultures, but they still define many families throughout the world (Hatfield & Rapson, 1996).

Conflict is generally viewed as nonthreatening by individuals in balanced split families, because each has specified areas of expertise. Consequently, the outcome of any conflict is almost predetermined.

**The Unbalanced Split Pattern**   In the unbalanced split relationship, one person dominates: One person is seen as an expert in more than half the areas of mutual communication. In many unions this "expertise" equates with control. Thus, in the unbalanced split, one person is more or less regularly in control of the relationship. In some cases this person is the more intelligent or more knowledgeable, but in many cases he or she is the more physically attractive or the higher wage earner. The less attractive or lower-income partner compensates by giving in to the other person, allowing the other to win arguments or to have his or her way in decision making.

The person in control makes more assertions, tells the other person what should or will be done, gives opinions freely, plays power games to maintain control, and seldom asks for opinions in return. The noncontrolling person, conversely, asks questions, seeks opinions, and looks to the other for decision-making leadership.

**The Monopoly Pattern**   In a monopoly relationship, one person is seen as the authority. This person lectures rather than communicating. Rarely does this person seek others' advice, and he or she always reserves the right to have the final say. In this type of couple, arguments are few—because both individuals already know who is boss and who will win any argument that may arise. When the authority is challenged, however, there are arguments and bitter conflicts. One reason the conflicts are so bitter is that these individuals have had no rehearsal for adequate conflict resolution. They don't know how to argue or how to disagree agreeably, so their conflict strategies frequently take the form of hurting the other person.

The controlling person tells the partner what is and what is not to be. The controlling person talks more frequently and goes off the topic of conversation more than does the noncontrolling partner (Palmer, 1989). The noncontrolling person looks to the other to give permission, to voice opinion leadership, and to make decisions, almost as a child looks to an all-knowing, all-powerful parent.

# Ethics in Interpersonal Communication

## RELATIONSHIP ETHICS

The ethical issues and guidelines that operate within a friendship, romantic, family, or workplace relationship can be reviewed with the acronym ETHICS—empathy (Cheney & Tompkins, 1987), talk rather than force, honesty (Krebs, 1989), interaction management, confidentiality, and supportiveness (Johannesen, 2001).

- *Empathy:* People in relationships have an ethical obligation to try to understand what other individuals are feeling as well as thinking from those individuals' points of view.
- *Talk:* Decisions in a relationship should be arrived at by talk rather than by force—by persuasion, not by coercion.
- *Honesty:* Relationship communication should be honest and truthful.
- *Interaction management:* Relationship communication should be satisfying and comfortable and is the responsibility of all individuals.
- *Confidentiality:* People have a right to expect that what they say in confidence will not be revealed to others.
- *Supportiveness:* A supportive and cooperative climate should characterize the interpersonal interactions of people in relationships.

### What would you do?

You're managing a team to select an architect for your company's new office complex. The problem is that Jack doesn't do any work and misses most of the meetings. You spoke with him about it, and he confided that he's going through a divorce and can't concentrate on the project. You feel sorry for Jack and have been carrying him for the last few months but realize now that you'll never be able to bring the project in on time if you don't replace Jack. Also, you don't want to get a negative appraisal because of Jack. What would you do in this situation?

## WORKPLACE RELATIONSHIPS

The workplace is a context in which all forms of communication take place and, not surprisingly, all kinds of relationships may be seen. Here we'll look at three kinds of relationships that are especially important in the workplace: romantic, mentoring, and network relationships.

### Romantic Relationships

Unlike television depictions, in which workers are always best friends who would do anything for one another and in which the characters move in and out of office romances with little difficulty—at least with no difficulty that can't be resolved in 24 minutes—real-life office romance can be complicated.

Opinions vary widely concerning workplace romances. Some organizations, on the assumption that romantic relationships are basically detrimental to the success of the workplace, have explicit rules prohibiting such relationships. In some organizations (including the military), members can be fired for such relationships. In other organizations, the prohibitions are unwritten and informal but nevertheless clearly in opposition to office romances. In a recent high-profile example, the president and CEO of Boeing Aircraft, Harry Stonecipher, was asked to step down after he admitted he had had an affair with a female executive, despite the fact that under his leadership Boeing's stock price rose more than 30 percent. Boeing's reasons were that the affair "reflected poorly on his judgment" and that it was "inconsistent" with Boeing's code of conduct (http://cbs.marketwatch.com, accessed March 11, 2005). Yet in some other organizations the taboos against office romance are lessening, with a variety of business professionals supporting such relationships—or at

### SPEAKING
>> Interpersonal-E

**Online trust.** Some research finds that people who are more trusting in their daily lives may experience greater difficulty in developing trust online (Feng, Lazar, & Preece, 2004; Henderson & Gilding, 2004). What do you find to be the relationship between face-to-face trusting and online trusting?

least recognizing that such relationships are inevitable (Armour, 2003; Ward, 2003; Franklin, 2002).

On the positive side, the work environment seems a perfect place to meet a potential romantic partner. After all, by virtue of the fact that you're working in the same office, probably you both are interested in the same field, have similar training and ambitions, and will spend considerable time together—all factors that foster the development of a successful interpersonal relationship. Also, given that Americans are marrying later in life, they are less likely to meet prospective partners in school; so work seems the logical alternative. One study found that some 80 percent of workers in the United States have experienced some sort of office romance (Pierce & Aguinis, 2001). And another study of 31,000 workers, conducted by MSNBC and *Elle* magazine (www.elle.com/Contests/sex%20survey/statistics.asp, accessed May 20, 2002), found that the majority were willing to engage in office romance. Sixty-two percent of these respondents had had at least one office romance. And, of course, even Bill Gates met his wife at work.

Similarly, office romances can lead to greater work satisfaction. For example, if you're romantically attracted to another worker, it can make going to work, working together, and even working added hours more enjoyable and more satisfying. If the relationship is good and mutually satisfying, the individuals are likely to develop empathy for each other and to act in ways that are supportive, cooperative, and friendly; in short, the workers are more likely to show all the characteristics of effective communication noted throughout this book.

However, even when the relationship is good for the two individuals, it may not be good for other workers. Seeing the loving couple together every day may generate office gossip that may prove destructive. Others may think the lovers are a team that has to be confronted as a pair, and that you can't criticize one without incurring the wrath of the other.

Workplace romantic relationships may cause problems for management when, for example, a promotion is to be made or relocation decisions are necessary. Can you legitimately ask one lover to move to Boston and the other to move to San Francisco? Will it prove difficult for management to promote one lover who then becomes the supervisor of the other?

The workplace also puts pressure on the individuals. Most organizations, at least in the United States, are highly competitive; one person's success often means another's failure. In this competitive context, the normal self-disclosures that regularly accompany increased intimacy (which often reveal weaknesses, doubts, and misgivings) may actually prove a liability.

When the romance goes bad or when it's one-sided, there are even more disadvantages. One obvious problem is that it can be stressful for the former lovers to see each other regularly and perhaps to work together. Other workers may feel they have to take sides, being supportive of one partner and critical of the other. This can easily cause friction throughout the organization. In addition, when an office romance breaks up, it's usually the more competent and employable person who leaves for another job, leaving the firm with the less valuable employee and the need to retrain someone to take over the departed lover's functions (Jones, 2004). Still another and perhaps more serious issue is the potential for charges of sexual harassment, especially if the romance was between a supervisor and a worker. Whether the charges are legitimate or are the result of an unhappy love affair and unrelated to the organization, management will find itself in the middle, facing lawsuits and time and money lost from investigating and ultimately acting on the charges.

The generally negative attitude of management toward office love affairs and the problems in dealing with the normal stress of both work and romance seem to present significant obstacles to such relationships and to the workplace, so workers are generally advised by management not to romance their colleagues. Friendships, on the other hand, seem the much safer course. Companies often encourage

You've been asked to help mentor at-risk college freshmen—to help them adjust to the college experience and develop productive study habits. Ask yourself: What behaviors would contribute to effective mentoring in this situation? What behaviors should a mentor avoid in this situation?

friendships by setting up sports teams, dinners, and lounge and exercise areas. And, in fact, research finds that office friendships increase employees' job satisfaction and commitment to the organization and decrease turnover (Morrison, 2004).

## Mentoring Relationships

In a **mentoring relationship** an experienced individual helps to train someone who is less experienced. (Mullen, 2005). Having a mentor, some organizational experts argue, is crucial for rising in a hierarchy and for developing your skills (Dahle, 2004). An accomplished teacher, for example, might mentor a younger teacher who has newly arrived or who has never taught before. The mentor guides the new person through the organization maze, teaches the strategies and techniques for success, and otherwise communicates his or her accumulated knowledge and experience to this "mentee."

The mentoring relationship provides an ideal learning environment. The relationship may be face-to-face or online (Purcell, 2004); either way, it's usually a one-on-one relationship between expert and novice, a relationship that is supportive and trusting. There's a mutual and open sharing of information and thoughts about the job. The relationship enables the novice to try out new skills under the guidance of an expert, to ask questions, and to obtain the feedback so necessary in learning complex skills. Mentoring is perhaps best characterized as a relationship in which the experienced and powerful mentor empowers the novice, giving the novice the tools and techniques for gaining the same power the mentor holds.

The mentoring relationship has been found to be one of the three primary paths for career achievement among African American men and women (Bridges, 1996). And in a study of middle-level managers, those who had mentors and participated in mentoring relationships were found to get more promotions and higher salaries than those who didn't have mentors (Scandura, 1992).

At the same time, the mentor benefits from clarifying his or her thoughts, seeing the job from the perspective of a newcomer, and considering and formulating answers to a variety of questions. Much as a teacher learns from teaching, a mentor learns from mentoring.

## Networking Relationships

In the popular mind, **networking** is often viewed simply as a technique for securing a job. But it actually has much broader applications and can be viewed as a process of using other people to help you solve your problems, or at least to offer insights that bear on your problem—for example, how to publish your manuscript, where to look for low-cost auto insurance, how to find an affordable apartment, or how to empty your cache.

Networking comes in at least two forms: informal and formal. Informal networking is what we do every day when we find ourselves in a new situation or are unable to answer questions. Thus, for example, if you're new at a school, you might ask someone in your class where to eat or where to shop for new clothes or who's the best teacher for interpersonal communication. In the same way, when you enter a new work environment, you might ask more experienced workers how to perform certain tasks or whom you should approach—or avoid—when you have questions.

Formal networking is the same thing, except that it's much more systematic and strategic. It's the establishment of connections with people who can help you—answer your questions, get you a job, help you get promoted, help you relocate or accomplish any task you want to accomplish.

At the most obvious level, you can network with people you already know. If you review the list of people in your acquaintance, you'll probably discover that you know a great number of people with very specialized knowledge who can be of assistance to you in

> ### ASK Yourself
> **Apologizing**
>
> You've been very successful in the stock market; so when you got the best tip ever, you shared it with three of your friends at work. Unfortunately, the stock tanked, your colleagues lost several thousand dollars each, and the situation at work is uncomfortable at best. Ask yourself: What might you say to these colleagues to reduce the tension and get things back to the way they were?

a wide variety of ways. In some cultures (Brazil is one example) friendships are established in part because of potential networking connections (Rector & Neiva, 1996). You also can network with people who know people you know. Thus, you may contact a friend's friend to find out if the firm he or she works for is hiring. Or you may contact people you have no connection with. Perhaps you've read something that someone wrote or you've heard the person's name raised in connection with an area in which you're interested and you want to get more information. With e-mail addresses so readily available, it's now quite common to e-mail individuals who have particular expertise and ask them questions you might have.

The great value of networking, of course, is that it provides you with access to a wealth of specialized information. At the same time, it often makes accessing that information a lot easier than if you had to find it all by yourself.

In networking it's often recommended that you try to establish relationships that are mutually beneficial. After all, much as others are useful sources of information for you, you're likely to be a useful source of information for others. If you can provide others with helpful information, it's more likely that they will provide helpful information for you. In this way, a mutually satisfying and productive network is established.

Some networking experts advise you to develop files and directories of potentially useful sources that you can contact for needed information. For example, if you're a freelance artist, you might develop a list of people who might be in positions to offer you work or who might lead you to others who might offer such work. Authors, editors, art directors, administrative assistants, people in advertising, and a host of others might eventually provide useful leads for such work. Creating a directory of such people and keeping in contact with them on a fairly regular basis can often simplify your obtaining freelance work.

Formal networking requires that you take an active part in locating and establishing these connections. Be proactive; initiate contacts rather than waiting for them to come to you. Of course, this can be overdone; you don't want to rely on people to do work you can easily do yourself. Yet if you're also willing to help others, there is nothing wrong in asking these same people to help you. If you're respectful of their time and expertise, it's likely that your networking attempts will be responded to favorably. Following up your requests with thank-you notes will help you establish networks that can be ongoing, productive relationships rather than one-shot affairs.

## ASK Yourself
### Networking

You want to establish a small mail-order business selling framed prints; you plan to buy the frames and prints separately and inexpensively at yard sales, restore them, and sell them. Ask yourself: What types of network connections might be appropriate in this situation? How would you go about the actual networking?

## Reviewing    Key Terms and Concepts in Friendship, Love, Family, and Workplace Relationships

This chapter explored some major kinds of interpersonal relationships; specifically, friendship, love, family, and workplace relationships.

### Friendship

What is friendship? What are the types of friendship? What purposes does friendship serve? How does friendship differ in different cultures and between men and women?

- Friendship is an interpersonal relationship between two persons that is mutually productive and is characterized by mutual positive regard.

- The types of friendships are:
  - *Reciprocity,* characterized by loyalty, self-sacrifice, mutual affection, and generosity.
  - *Receptivity,* characterized by a comfortable and positive imbalance in the giving and receiving of rewards; each person's needs are satisfied by the exchange.
  - *Association,* a transitory relationship, more like a friendly relationship than a true friendship.
- Friendships serve a variety of needs and give us a variety of values, among which are the values of utility, affirmation, ego support, stimulation, and security.
- Friendship demands vary between collectivist and individualist cultures.

- Women share more and are more intimate with same-sex friends than are men. Men's friendships are often built around shared activities rather than shared intimacies.

## Love

What is love? What are the major kinds of love? What is the effect of love on communication? How does love vary in different cultures and between men and women?

- Love is a feeling that may be characterized by closeness and caring and by intimacy, passion, and commitment.
- Types of love:
  - *Eros love* focuses on beauty and sexuality, sometimes to the exclusion of other qualities.
  - *Ludus love* is seen as a game and focuses on entertainment and excitement.
  - *Storge love* is a kind of companionship, peaceful and slow.
  - *Pragma love* is practical and traditional.
  - *Mania love* is obsessive and possessive, characterized by elation and depression.
  - *Agape love* is compassionate and selfless, characterized as self-giving and altruistic.
- Verbal and nonverbal messages echo the intimacy of a love relationship. With increased intimacy, you share more, speak in a more personalized style, engage in prolonged eye contact, and touch each other more often.
- Members of individualist cultures are likely to place greater emphasis on romantic love than are members of collectivist cultures.
- Men generally score higher on erotic and ludic love, whereas women score higher on manic, pragmatic, and storgic love. Men generally score higher on romanticism than women.

## Family

What is a family? What are the types of families? How do families communicate?

- Characteristics of families:
  - *Defined roles.* Members understand the roles each of them serves.

- *Recognition of responsibilities.* Members realize that each person has certain responsibilities to the relationship.
  - *Shared history and future.* Members have an interactional past and an anticipated future together.
  - *Shared living space.* Generally, members live together.
  - *Established rules.* The relationship is rule governed, rather than random or unpredictable.
- Family types:
  - *Traditionals* see themselves as a blending of two people into a single couple.
  - *Independents* see themselves as primarily separate individuals, and see their individuality as more important than the relationship or the connection between the individuals.
  - *Separates* see their relationship as a matter of convenience rather than of mutual love or connection.
- Communication in families:
  - *Equality.* Each person shares equally in the communication transactions and decision making.
  - *Balanced split.* Each person has authority over different but relatively equal domains.
  - *Unbalanced split.* One person maintains authority and decision-making power over a wider range of issues than the other.
  - *Monopoly.* One person dominates and controls the relationship and the decisions made.

## Workplace Relationships

What types of relationships occur in the workplace, and what influence does the workplace have on such relationships?

- Romantic relationships in the workplace, although having a variety of benefits, are often frowned upon and often entail a variety of problems that would not arise in other contexts.
- Mentoring relationships help you learn the ropes of an organization through the experience and knowledge of someone who has gone through the processes you'll be going through.
- Networking enables you to expand your area of expertise and enables you to secure information bearing on a wide variety of problems you want to solve and questions you want to answer.

---

## Applying  Key Terms and Concepts in Friendship, Love, Family, and Workplace Relationships

1 When college students were asked to identify the features that characterize romantic love, the five qualities most frequently noted were trust, sexual attraction, acceptance and tolerance, spending time together, and sharing thoughts and secrets (Regan, Kocan, & Whitlock, 1998). How would you characterize love? Would men and women characterize love similarly? Would heterosexuals and homosexuals characterize love similarly?

2 Research generally shows that there are many similarities among the relationships of heterosexual, gay male, and lesbians couples (Spiers, 1998; Kurdek, 2004). Do you find that the media generally reflect the research in their depiction of these

relationships? In what ways do the media compare homosexual relationships compared to heterosexual relationships?

3 Psychotherapist Albert Ellis (1988) has argued that love and infatuation are actually the same emotion; he claims that we use the term "infatuation" to describe relationships that didn't work out and "love" to describe our current romantic relationships. How would you compare infatuation and love?

4 How would you describe your own family in terms of (1) the characteristics of primary relationships and families discussed in this chapter (defined roles, recognition of responsibilities, shared history and future, shared living space, and established rules); (2) the most often used communication pattern

(equality, balanced split, unbalanced split, or monopoly); and (3) the rules that are most important to them?

5 Although studies show there is no disadvantage in a child's growing up in a gay home (Goleman, 1992), the major argument made against granting adoption rights to gay men and lesbians is that the child will suffer. How do you account for this?

6 What are your feelings about romantic relationships in the workplace? Altercast—put yourself into both the position of the worker who sees great opportunities for relationships and the position of the manager who focuses on making sure the company makes money.

## Experiencing Key Terms and Concepts in Friendship, Love, Family, and Workplace Relationships

Go to www.ablongman.com/devito.

*These experiences look at a variety of interpersonal relationships and the communication that takes place within these interactions.*

❶ **Friendship Behaviors** stimulates you to look at friendship in terms of the responses friends are expected to have to a variety of situations. ❷ **How Can You Talk Cherishing?** examines a simple but powerful technique for increasing relationship satisfaction. ❸ **Mate Preferences: I Prefer Someone Who . . .** stimulates you to look at the kinds of qualities you look for in a mate. ❹ The **Television Relationship** provides a structured opportunity to look at relationships as presented in television sitcoms and dramas. ❺ The self-test **How Romantic Are You?** will enable you to measure your own degree of romanticism. ❻ To investigate your own preference for a mate, take the well-researched self-test **What Type of Relationship Do You Prefer?**

# Conflict in Interpersonal Relationships

⬆ *Million Dollar Baby* (2004)

*Million Dollar Baby* is on the surface a film about conflict in the boxing ring; on a deeper level, however, the film examines a wide variety of relationship conflicts and how conflicts develop and are resolved—topics we'll consider in this chapter.

> "The aim of an argument or discussion should not be victory, but progress." —Joseph Joubert

**Interpersonal conflict** is disagreement between or among connected individuals: close friends, lovers, family members, or coworkers. The word "connected" emphasizes the fact that each person's position and each person's actions affect the other person.

**Conflict** is a part of every interpersonal relationship, between parents and children, brothers and sisters, friends, lovers, coworkers. As Louis Nizer put it, "Where there is no difference, there is only indifference."

##  PRINCIPLES OF INTERPERSONAL CONFLICT

The importance and influence of conflict in all interpersonal relationships can be best appreciated if we understand some fundamental principles of this particular form of interaction. Here we look at (1) the inevitability of conflict, (2) conflict's positive and negative aspects, (3) conflict's focus on content and/or on relationships, (4) differing styles of conflict and their consequences, and (5) the influence of culture on conflict.

### Conflict Is Inevitable

As stated earlier, conflict is a part of every interpersonal relationship. One of the difficulties in dealing with interpersonal conflict, however, is that people often think that if they experience conflict in their friendships or romantic relationships, it means that something is wrong or that the relationship is in jeopardy or that the relationship will be damaged if these differences are brought up for discussion. These are myths that often get in the way of meaningful communication about differences and disagreements. As we'll see, conflict itself doesn't necessarily damage a relationship; more often, the crucial difference is in how the conflict is managed and resolved. If it's managed fairly and with respect for each person's opinion, the relationship is likely to prosper; if it's managed unfairly, the relationship is likely to suffer.

**Conflict Issues** To appreciate the inevitability of conflict, consider the broad range of topics on which relationship partners disagree (Canary, 2003). For example, a study on the issues argued about by gay, lesbian, and heterosexual couples, found that respondents identified six major issues that were virtually identical for all couples (Kurdek, 1994). These issues are arranged here in order, with the first being the most often mentioned. As you read this list, ask yourself how many of these issues you argue about.

- intimacy issues such as affection and sex
- power issues such as excessive demands or possessiveness, lack of equality in the relationship, friends, and leisure time
- personal flaws issues such as drinking or smoking, personal grooming, and driving style
- personal distance issues such as frequent absence and heavy school or job commitments

- social issues such as politics and social policies, parents, and personal values
- distrust issues such as previous lovers and lying

Another study found that any (or all) of four conditions generally led up to a couple's "first big fight": uncertainty over commitment, jealousy, violation of expectations, and/or personality differences (Siegert & Stamp, 1994). In workplace settings, the major sources of conflict among top managers revolved around the issue of executive responsibility and co-ordination. Other conflicts focused on differences in organizational objectives, on how resources were to be allocated, and on what constituted an appropriate management style (Morrill, 1992). In a study of same-sex and opposite sex friends, the four issues most often argued about were sharing living space or possessions, violating friendship rules, sharing activities, and disagreement about ideas (Samter & Cupach, 1998).

**SPEAKING**
>> **Interpersonal-E**

**E-Mail and Interpersonal Conflict.** In what ways do you find that e-mail can escalate interpersonal conflict? In what ways might it help resolve conflict?

**Online Conflicts**   The same conflicts you experience in face-to-face relationships can also arise in online communication. Here, however, let's look at a few conflict situations that are unique to online interactions. As you'll see, online conflict frequently results when people violate the rules of Internet courtesy discussed in Chapter 6.

Sending commercial messages to those who didn't request them often creates conflict. The receiver of junk e-mail often has to pay for the time it takes to read and delete these unwanted messages. And even if there is no financial cost, there is still a loss of time.

Sending a message to an entire listserv when it's relevant to only one member may annoy members who expect to receive messages relevant to the entire group and not personal exchanges between two people. This often occurs when someone sends out a general message seeking specific information, but then individual members reply not solely to the person seeking the information but to the entire listserv. Sometimes the reply is simply, "I can't help you with that question," a message relevant only to the person asking the question and not to the entire listserv.

Spamming often causes conflict. Spamming is sending someone unsolicited mail, repeatedly sending the same mail, or posting the same message in lots of newsgroups, even when the message is irrelevant to the focus of one or more groups. Like commercial messages, these unwanted messages absorb your valuable time and energy. Also, spamming clogs the system, slowing it down for everyone.

Flaming, especially common in newsgroups, is sending messages that personally attack another user. Frequently flaming leads to flame wars, in which everyone in the group gets into the act and attacks other members. Generally, flaming and flame wars prevent you from achieving your goals and are counterproductive.

Trolling—putting out purposely incorrect information or outrageous viewpoints to watch other people correct you or get emotionally upset by your message—can obviously lead to conflict, though some see it as fun.

Other potential causes of online conflict are ill-timed cell phone calls or text messaging. Often these messages interfere with more important matters and may generate resentment. And, of course, if you don't respond as the message sender thinks you should, conflict of a different sort can develop.

## Conflict Can Have Negative and Positive Effects

Because people are different and will necessarily see things differently, interpersonal conflict is inevitable. The way you deal with conflict, however, can have both negative and positive effects.

**Negative Effects**   Among the disadvantages of conflict is that it often leads to increased negative feelings. Many conflicts involve unfair fighting methods and focus largely on hurting the other person. If this happens, negative feelings are sure to increase. Conflict may also deplete energy better spent on other areas, especially when unproductive conflict strategies are used.

At times, conflict may lead you to close yourself off from the other individual. When you hide your feelings from your partner, you prevent meaningful communication and interaction; this, in turn, creates barriers to intimacy. Because the need for intimacy is so strong, one possible outcome is that one or both parties may seek intimacy elsewhere. This often leads to further conflict, mutual hurt, and resentment—all of which add heavily to the costs carried by the relationship. As the costs increase, the rewards may become more difficult to exchange. Here, then, is a situation in which costs increase and rewards decrease, a scenario that often results in relationship deterioration and eventual dissolution.

**Positive Effects**    Among the advantages of conflict is that it forces you to examine a problem and work toward a potential solution. If you use productive conflict strategies, your relationship is likely to become stronger, healthier, and more satisfying than it was before.

Conflict often prevents hostilities and resentments from festering. Say you're annoyed at your partner, who comes home from work and then talks on the phone with colleagues for two hours instead of giving that time to you. If you say nothing, your annoyance is likely to grow. Further, by saying nothing you implicitly approve of such behavior, so it's likely that the phone calls will continue. Through your conflict and its resolution, you each let your needs be known: Your partner needs to review the day's work to gain assurance that it's been properly completed, and you have a need for your partner's attention. If you both can appreciate the legitimacy of these needs, then you stand a good chance of finding workable solutions. Perhaps your partner can make the phone calls after your attention needs are met. Perhaps you can delay your need for attention until your partner gets closure about work. Perhaps you can learn to provide for your partner's closure needs and in doing so get your own attention needs met. Again, you have win–win solutions; each of your needs are met.

Consider, too, that when you try to resolve conflict within an interpersonal relationship, you're saying that the relationship is worth the effort; otherwise, you'd walk away. Although there may be exceptions—as when you confront conflict to save face or to gratify some ego need—confronting a conflict often indicates concern, commitment, and a desire to protect and preserve the relationship.

## Conflict Can Focus on Content and/or Relationship Issues

Using concepts developed earlier (Chapter 1), you can distinguish between content and relationship conflicts. *Content conflict* centers on objects, events, and persons in the world that are usually external to the people involved in the conflict. These include the millions of issues that you argue and fight about every day—the merits of a particular movie, what to watch on television, the fairness of the last examination, who should get promoted, the way to spend your savings.

*Relationship conflicts* are equally numerous and are concerned with the relationships between the individuals—with such issues as who's in charge, the equality or lack of it in the relationship, and who has the right to establish rules of behavior. Examples of relationship conflicts include those involving a younger brother who does not obey his older brother, two partners who each want an equal say in making vacation plans, or a mother and daughter who each want to have the final word concerning the daughter's lifestyle.

Relationship conflicts often are hidden and disguised as content conflicts. Thus, a conflict over where you should vacation may, on the content level, center on the advantages and disadvantages of Mexico versus Hawaii. On a relationship level, however, it may center on who has the greater right to select the place to vacation, who should win the argument, or who is the decision maker in the relationship.

## Conflict Styles Have Consequences

As mentioned earlier, the way in which you engage in conflict has consequences for the resolution of the conflict and for the relationship between the conflicting parties. Figure 13.1

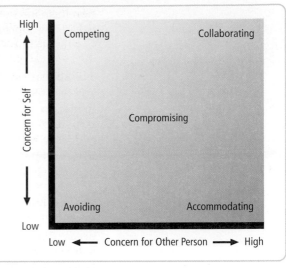

**→ FIGURE 13.1**

## Five Conflict Styles

This figure is adapted from Blake and Mouton's (1984) approach to managerial leadership and conflict and illustrates five styles of conflict. As you read about these styles, consider your own conflict style and the styles of those with whom you interact most frequently. Most important, consider how you can make your own conflict style more effective.

illustrates an approach to conflict that identifies five basic styles or ways of engaging in conflict and is especially relevant to an understanding of interpersonal conflicts (Blake & Mouton, 1984). The five styles, plotted along the dimensions of "concern for self" and "concern for the other person," provide insight into the ways people engage in conflict and into some of the advantages and disadvantages of each style. As you read through the following descriptions of these styles, try to identify your own often-used conflict style as well as the styles of those with whom you have close relationships.

**Competing—I Win, You Lose**  The competing style represents great concern for your own needs and desires and little for those of others. As long as your needs are met, the conflict has been dealt with successfully (for you). In conflict motivated by competitiveness, you'd be likely to be verbally aggressive while blaming the other person.

This style represents an *I win, you lose* philosophy. With this philosophy, you attempt to manage the conflict so that you win and the other person loses. As you can tell, this style might be appropriate in a courtroom or in buying a car, two situations in which one person benefits from the other person's losses. But in interpersonal situations this philosophy can easily lead to resentment in the person who lost, which in turn can easily morph into additional conflicts. Further, the fact that you win and the other person loses probably means that the conflict really hasn't been resolved, just concluded (for now).

**Avoiding—I Lose, You Lose**  Using the avoiding style suggests that you are relatively unconcerned with your own or with the other's needs or desires. The avoider shrinks from any real communication about the problem, changes the topic when the problem is brought up, and generally withdraws from the scene both psychologically and physically.

As you can appreciate, this style does little to resolve any conflicts and may be viewed as an *I lose, you lose* philosophy. Interpersonal problems rarely go away of their own accord; rather, if they exist, they need to be faced and dealt with effectively. The avoidance philosophy just allows the conflict to fester and probably to grow, only to resurface in another guise.

**Accommodating—I Lose, You Win**  In accommodating you sacrifice your own needs for the sake of the needs of the other person. Your major purpose is to maintain harmony and peace in the relationship or group. The accommodating style may help you attain the immediate goal of maintaining peace and perhaps satisfying the other person, but it does little to meet your own needs—which are unlikely to go away.

Accommodating represents an *I lose, you win* philosophy. And although this style may make your partner happy (at least on this occasion), it's not likely to prove a lasting resolu-

**Positiveness.** One study found that, generally at least, people are more positive in dealing with conflict in face-to-face situations than in computer-mediated communication (Zornoza, Ripoll, & Peiró, 2002). Do you notice this in your own interactions? If so, why do you think it's true?

tion to an interpersonal conflict. You'll eventually sense the unfairness and inequity inherent in this approach to conflict, and you may easily come to resent your partner and perhaps even yourself.

**Collaborating—I Win, You Win**   In collaborating your concern is with both your own and the other person's needs. Often considered the ideal, collaborating takes time and a willingness to communicate, and especially to listen to the perspectives and needs of the other person.

Ideally, collaborating will allow each person's needs to be being satisfied, an *I win, you win* situation. This is obviously the style that, ideally you would use in most of your interpersonal conflict. Collaborating promotes resolutions in which both people get something.

**Compromising—I Win and Lose, You Win and Lose**   The compromising style is in the middle; there's some concern for your own needs and some concern for the other's needs. Compromising is the kind of strategy you might refer to as "meeting each other halfway," "horse trading," or "give and take." This strategy is likely to result in maintaining peace, but there also will be dissatisfaction over the inevitable losses that have to be endured.

Compromising could be called an *I win and lose* and *you win and lose* strategy. There are lots of times when you can't both get exactly what you want. For example, you can't both get a new car if the available funds allow for only one. Still, you might each get a better car than what you now have—so you would win something, but not everything. You wouldn't get a new car, and the same would be true of your partner.

## Conflict Is Influenced by Culture

As is true with all communication processes, conflict is influenced by the culture of the participants—and especially by their beliefs and values about conflict. Culture influences the topics people fight about as well as what are considered appropriate and inappropriate ways of dealing with conflict. For example, cohabiting 18-year-olds are more likely to have conflict with their parents over their living style if they live in the United States than if they live in Sweden, where cohabitation is much more accepted. Similarly, male infidelity is more likely to cause conflict among American couples than among southern European couples. Students from the United States are more likely to pursue a conflict with another United States student than with someone from another culture. Chinese students, on the other hand, are more likely to pursue a conflict with a non-Chinese than with another Chinese student (Leung, 1988).

The topics of conflicts also will depend on whether the culture is high or low context (see Chapter 2). In high-context cultures, conflicts are more likely to center on violations of collective or group norms and values. Conversely, in low-context cultures, conflicts are more likely to come up when individual norms are violated (Ting-Toomey, 1985).

Cultures also differ in how they define what constitutes conflict. For example, in some cultures it's quite common for women to be referred to negatively and to be seen as less than equal. To most people in the United States, this would constitute a clear basis for conflict. To some Japanese women, however, this isn't uncommon and isn't perceived as abusive (*New York Times*, February 11, 1996, pp. 1, 12). Further, Americans and Japanese differ in their views of the aim or purpose of conflict. The Japanese see conflicts and their resolution in terms of compromise; Americans, on the other hand, see conflict in terms of winning (Gelfand, Nishii, Holcombe, Dyer, Ohbuchi, & Fukuno, 2001). African Americans and European Americans engage in conflict in very different ways (Kochman, 1981; Hecht, Jackson, & Ribeau, 2003). The issues that cause and aggravate conflict, the conflict strategies that are expected and accepted, and the attitude toward conflict vary from one group to the other.

Cultures vary widely in their responses to physical and verbal abuse. In some Asian and Hispanic cultures, for example, the fear of losing face or embarrassing the family is so great that people prefer not to report or reveal abuses. When looking over statistics, it may at first appear that little violence occurs in the families of certain cultures. Yet we know from

# Understanding Interpersonal Skills

## EQUALITY

In interpersonal communication the term **equality** refers to an attitude or approach that treats each person as an important and vital contributor to the interaction. In any situation, of course, there will be some inequality; one person will be higher in the organizational hierarchy, more knowledgeable, or more interpersonally effective. But despite this fact, an attitude of **superiority** is to be avoided. Interpersonal communication is generally more effective when it takes place in an atmosphere of equality.

**Communicating Equality.** Here are a few suggestions for communicating equality in all interactions, and especially in those involving conflict.

- Avoid "should" and "ought" statements (for example, "You really should call your mother more often" or "You should learn to speak up"). These statements put the listener in a one-down position.
- Make requests (especially courteous ones) and avoid demands (especially discourteous ones).
- Avoid interrupting; this signals an unequal relationship and implies that what you have to say is more important than what the other person is saying.
- Acknowledge the other person's contributions before expressing your own. Saying "I see," "I understand," or "That's right" lets the other person know you're listening and understanding.
- Recognize that different cultures treat equality very differently. In low-power-distance cultures there is greater equality than in high-power-distance cultures, in which status differences greatly influence interpersonal interactions.

research that wife beating is quite common in India, Taiwan, and Iran, for example (Counts, Brown, & Campbell, 1992; Hatfield & Rapson, 1996). In much of the United States, and in many other cultures as well, such abuse would not be tolerated no matter who was embarrassed or insulted.

Each culture seems to teach its members different views of conflict strategies (Tardiff, 2001). In one study, African American females were found to use more direct controlling strategies (for example, assuming control over the conflict and arguing persistently for their point of view) than did white females. White females, on the other hand, used more solution-oriented conflict styles than did African American females. African American and white men were similar in their conflict strategies; both avoided or withdrew from relationship conflict, preferring to keep quiet about their differences or make them seem insignificant (Ting-Toomey, 1986). Another example of this cultural influence on conflict is seen in the tendency of members of collectivist cultures to avoid conflict more, and to give greater importance to saving face, than members of individualist cultures (Dsilva & Whyte, 1998; Haar & Krabe, 1999; Cai & Fink, 2002; Oetzel & Ting-Toomey, 2003).

As in the wider culture, the cultural norms of organizations will influence the types of conflicts that occur and the ways in which they may be dealt with. In some work environments, for example, the expression of conflict with high-level management would not be tolerated; in others it might be welcomed. In individualist cultures there is greater tolerance for conflict within organizations, even when it may involve different levels of the hierarchy. In collectivist cultures there is less tolerance. And, not surprisingly, culture influences how conflicts will be resolved. For example, American managers (members of an individualistic culture) deal with workplace conflict by seeking to integrate the demands of the different sides; Chinese managers (members of a collectivist culture) are more likely to

# Understanding Interpersonal Theory and Research

## CONFLICT AND GENDER

Not surprisingly, research finds significant gender differences in interpersonal conflict. For example, men are more apt to withdraw from a conflict situation than are women. It's been argued that this may be due to the fact that men become more psychologically and physiologically aroused during conflict (and retain this heightened level of arousal much longer) than do women and so may try to distance themselves and withdraw from the conflict to prevent further arousal (Gottman & Carrere, 1994; Goleman, 1995b). Women, on the other hand, want to get closer to the conflict; they want to talk about it and resolve it. Even adolescents reveal these differences. In research on boys and girls aged 11 to 17, boys withdrew more than girls (Lindeman, Harakka, & Keltikangas-Jarvinen, 1997; Heasley, Babbitt, & Burbach, 1995).

Other research has found that women are more emotional and men are more logical when they argue. Another difference is that women are more apt to reveal their negative feelings than are men (Schaap, Buunk, & Kerkstra, 1988; Canary, Cupach, & Messman, 1995). Women have been defined as conflict "feelers" and men as conflict "thinkers" (Sorenson, Hawkins, & Sorenson, 1995).

Much research, however, fails to support these stereotypical gender differences in conflict style—the differences that cartoons, situation comedies, and films portray so readily and so clearly. For example, several studies dealing with both college students and men and women in business found no significant differences in the ways men and women engage in conflict (Wilkins & Andersen, 1991; Canary & Hause, 1993; Gottman & Levenson, 1999).

### Working with Theories and Research

New findings on gender differences continue to emerge, so update this discussion by logging on to Research Navigator (www.researchnavigator.com) or other databases and searching the communication, psychology, and sociology databases for current research on "gender" and "conflict." What can you add to the discussion presented here?

 **VIEWPOINT**

One of the most puzzling findings on violence is that many victims interpret it as a sign of love. For some reason, they see being beaten or verbally abused as a sign that their partner is fully in love with them. Also, many victims blame themselves for the violence instead of blaming their partners (Gelles & Cornell, 1985). Why do you think this is so? What part does force or violence play in conflicts in your own interpersonal relationships?

call on higher management to make decisions or to leave the conflict unresolved (Tinsley & Brett, 2001).

Another factor that influences conflict is your own position on the organizational hierarchy. For example, if you're a temporary worker in a large organization, you're not likely to have conflict with the CEO, because you'll probably never meet. But workplace conflicts with coworkers at your own level, or with those a level above or a level below, are much more likely to occur. When you experience conflict with, say, a supervisor, it's more likely to be job related—to focus on issues such as job satisfaction or organizational commitment. When you experience conflict with coworkers, it's more likely to be related to personal issues such as self-esteem or depression (Frone, 2000).

## CONFLICT MANAGEMENT STAGES

Before trying to manage or resolve a conflict, you need to prepare. Conflict resolution is an extremely important communication experience, and you don't want to enter it without adequate thought. Here are a few suggestions for preparing for resolving conflict.

Try to fight in private. When you air your conflicts in front of others, you create a variety of other problems. You may not be willing to be totally honest when third parties are present; you may feel you have to save face and therefore must win the fight at all costs. This may lead you to use strategies to win the argument rather than to resolve the conflict. You may become so absorbed by the image that others will have of you that you forget you have a relationship problem that needs to be resolved. Also, you run the risk of embarrassing your partner in front of others, and this embarrassment may create resentment and hostility.

Be sure you're each ready to fight. Although conflicts arise at the most inopportune times, you can choose the time to resolve them. Confronting your partner when she or he comes home after a hard day of work may not be the right time for resolving a conflict. Make sure you're both relatively free of other problems and ready to deal with the conflict at hand.

Know what you're fighting about. Sometimes people in a relationship become so hurt and angry that they lash out at the other person just to vent their own frustration. The problem at the center of the conflict (for example, the uncapped toothpaste tube) is merely an excuse to express anger. Any attempt to resolve this "problem" will be doomed to failure, because the problem addressed is not what is causing the conflict. Instead, the underlying hostility, anger, and frustration need to be addressed.

Fight about problems that can be solved. Fighting about past behaviors or about family members or situations over which you have no control solves nothing; instead, it creates additional difficulties. Any attempt at resolution will fail, because the problems are incapable of being solved. Often such conflicts are concealed attempts at expressing frustration or dissatisfaction.

Now that you're prepared for the conflict resolution interaction, refer to the model in Figure 13.2. It identifies the steps that will help you navigate through this process.

## Define the Conflict

Your first and most essential step is to define the conflict. Here are several techniques to keep in mind.

- *Define both content and relationship issues.* Define the obvious content issues (who should do the dishes, who should take the kids to school) as well as the underlying relationship issues (who has been avoiding household responsibilities, whose time is more valuable).

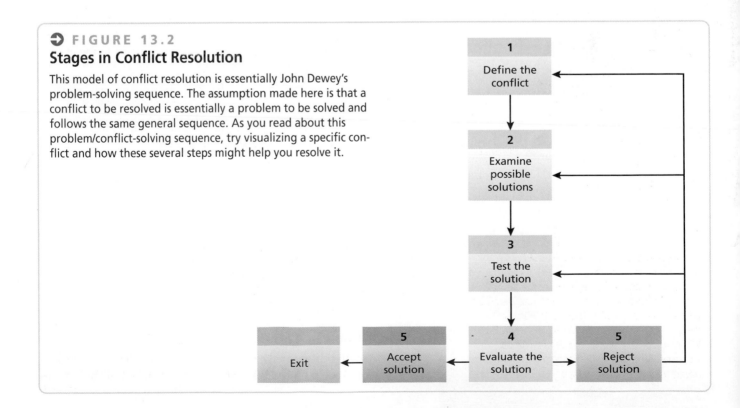

### ➜ FIGURE 13.2
### Stages in Conflict Resolution

This model of conflict resolution is essentially John Dewey's problem-solving sequence. The assumption made here is that a conflict to be resolved is essentially a problem to be solved and follows the same general sequence. As you read about this problem/conflict-solving sequence, try visualizing a specific conflict and how these several steps might help you resolve it.

1. Define the conflict
2. Examine possible solutions
3. Test the solution
4. Evaluate the solution
5. Accept solution → Exit
5. Reject solution

- *Define the problem in specific terms.* Conflict defined in the abstract is difficult to deal with and resolve. It's one thing for a husband to say that his wife is "cold and unfeeling" and quite another to say that she does not call him at the office, kiss him when he comes home, or hold his hand when they're at a party. These behaviors can be agreed on and dealt with, but the abstract "cold and unfeeling" remains elusive.
- *Focus on the present.* Avoid **gunnysacking** (a term derived from the large burlap bag called a gunnysack)—the practice of storing up grievances so they may be unloaded at another time. Often, when one person gunnysacks, the other person gunnysacks; for example, the birthdays you forgot and the times you arrived late for dinner are all thrown at you. The result is two people dumping their stored-up grievances on each other with no real attention to the present problem.
- *Empathize.* Try to understand the nature of the conflict from the other person's point of view. Why is your partner disturbed that you're not doing the dishes? Why is your neighbor complaining about taking the kids to school? Once you have empathically understood the other person's feelings, validate those feelings when appropriate. If your partner is hurt or angry and you believe such feelings are legitimate and justified, say so: "You have a right to be angry; I shouldn't have said what I did about your mother. I'm sorry. But I still don't want to go on vacation with her." In expressing validation, you're not necessarily expressing agreement; you're merely stating that your partner has feelings that you recognize as legitimate.
- *Avoid mind reading.* Don't try to read the other person's mind. Ask questions to make sure you understand the problem as the other person is experiencing it. Ask directly and simply: "Why are you insisting that I take the dog out now, when I have to call three clients before nine o'clock?"

The example in the next section will help us work through the remaining steps. This conflict revolves around Pat's not wanting to socialize with Chris's friends. Chris is devoted to these friends, but Pat actively dislikes them. Chris thinks they're wonderful and exciting; Pat thinks they're unpleasant and boring.

## Examine Possible Solutions

Most conflicts can probably be resolved through a variety of solutions. Here are a few suggestions. Brainstorm by yourself or with your partner. Try not to inhibit or censor yourself or your partner as you generate these potential solutions. Once you have proposed a variety of solutions, look especially for solutions that will enable each party to win—to get something he or she wants. Avoid win–lose solutions, in which one person wins and one loses. Such outcomes will cause difficulty for the relationship by engendering frustration and resentment.

Carefully weigh the costs and the rewards that each solution entails. Most solutions will involve costs to one or both parties. Seek solutions in which the costs and the rewards will be evenly shared. For example, among the solutions that Pat and Chris might identify are these:

1. Chris should not interact with these friends anymore.
2. Pat should interact with Chris's friends.
3. Chris should see these friends without Pat.

Clearly solutions 1 and 2 are win–lose solutions. In solution 1, Pat wins and Chris loses; in 2, Chris wins and Pat loses. Solution 3 has some possibilities. Both might win and neither must necessarily lose. This potential solution, then, needs to be looked at more closely.

## Test the Solution

First, test the solution mentally. How does it feel now? How will it feel tomorrow? Are you comfortable with it? In our example, will Pat be comfortable with Chris's socializing with these friends alone? Some of Chris's friends are attractive; will this cause difficulty for Pat and Chris's relationship? Will Chris give people too much to gossip about? Will Chris feel guilty? Will Chris enjoy these friends without Pat?

Second, test the solution in practice. Put the solution into operation. How does it work? If it doesn't work, then discard it and try another solution. Give each solution a fair chance, but don't hang on to a solution when it's clear that it won't resolve the conflict.

Perhaps Chris might go out without Pat once to test this solution. Afterward, the couple can evaluate the experiment. Did the friends think there was something wrong with Chris's relationship with Pat? Did Chris feel guilty? Did Chris enjoy this new experience? How did Pat feel? Did Pat feel jealous? Lonely? Abandoned?

## Evaluate the Solution

Did the solution help resolve the conflict? Is the situation better now than it was before the solution was tried? Share your feelings and evaluations of the solution.

Pat and Chris now need to share their perceptions of this possible solution. Would they be comfortable with this solution on a monthly basis? Is the solution worth the costs each will pay? Are the costs and rewards evenly distributed? Might other solutions be more effective?

Critical-thinking pioneer Edward deBono (1987) suggests that in analyzing problems, you use six "thinking hats" as a way of seeking different perspectives. With each hat you look at the problem from a different angle.

- *The fact hat* focuses attention on the facts and figures that bear on the problem. For example, how can Pat learn more about the rewards that Chris gets from the friends? How can Chris learn why Pat doesn't like these great friends?
- *The feeling hat* focuses attention on the emotional responses to the problem. How does Pat feel when Chris goes out with these friends? How does Chris feel when Pat refuses to meet them?
- *The negative argument hat* asks you to become the devil's advocate. How may this relationship deteriorate if Chris continues seeing these friends without Pat or if Pat resists interacting with Chris's friends?
- *The positive benefits hat* asks you to look at the upside. What are the opportunities that Chris's seeing friends without Pat might yield? What benefits might Pat and Chris get from this new arrangement?
- *The creative new idea hat* focuses on new ways of looking at the problem. In what other ways can Pat and Chris look at this problem? What other possible solutions might they consider?
- *The control of thinking hat* helps you analyze what you're doing; it asks you to reflect on your own thinking. Have Pat and Chris adequately defined the problem? Are they focusing too much on insignificant issues? Have they given enough attention to possible negative effects?

## Accept or Reject the Solution

If you accept the solution, you're ready to put it into more permanent operation. Let's say that Pat is actually quite happy with the solution. Pat was able to use the evening to visit college friends. The next time Chris goes out with the friends Pat doesn't like, Pat intends to go out with some friends from college. Chris feels pretty good about seeing friends without Pat. Chris explains that they have both decided to see their friends separately and both are comfortable with this decision. If, however, either Pat or Chris feels unhappy with this solution, they will have to try out another solution or perhaps go back and redefine the problem and seek other ways to resolve it.

Even after the conflict is resolved, there is still work to be done. Often, after one conflict is supposedly settled, another conflict will emerge—because, for example, one person feels that he or she has been harmed and needs to retali-

 **VIEWPOINT**

Take a good look at your own conflict behaviors. What changes would you make? What conflict skills and strategies would you seek to integrate into your own interpersonal and small group conflict resolution behavior?

ate and take revenge in order to restore a sense of self-worth (Kim & Smith, 1993). So it's especially important that the conflict be resolved and not be allowed to generate other, perhaps more significant conflicts.

Learn from the conflict and from the process you went through in trying to resolve it. For example, can you identify the fight strategies that merely aggravated the situation? Do you or your partner need a cooling-off period? Can you tell when minor issues are going to escalate into major arguments? Does avoidance make matters worse? What issues are particularly disturbing and likely to cause difficulties? Can they be avoided?

Keep the conflict in perspective. Be careful not to blow it out of proportion to the extent that you begin to define your relationship in terms of conflict. Avoid the tendency to see disagreement as inevitably leading to major blowups. Conflicts in most relationships actually occupy a very small percentage of the couple's time, and yet in recollection they often loom extremely large. Also, don't allow the conflict to undermine your own or your partner's self-esteem. Don't view yourself, your partner, or your relationship as a failure just because you had an argument or even lots of arguments.

Attack your negative feelings. Negative feelings frequently arise after an interpersonal conflict. Most often they arise because one or both parties used unfair fight strategies to undermine the other person—for example, personal rejection, manipulation, or force. Resolve to avoid such unfair tactics in the future, but at the same time let go of guilt and blame toward and yourself and your partner. If you think it would help, discuss these feelings with your partner or even a therapist. Apologize for anything you did wrong. Your partner should do likewise; after all, both parties are usually responsible for the conflict (Coleman, 2002).

Increase the exchange of rewards and cherishing behaviors to demonstrate your positive feelings and to show you're over the conflict and want the relationship to survive and flourish.

## CONFLICT MANAGEMENT STRATEGIES

In managing conflict you can choose from a variety of strategies, which we will explore below. First, however, realize that the strategies you choose will be influenced by a variety of factors such as (1) the goals to be achieved, (2) your emotional state, (3) your cognitive assessment of the situation, (4) your personality and communication competence, and (5) your family history (Koerner & Fitzpatrick, 2002). Understanding these factors may help you select strategies that are more appropriate and more effective. Research finds that using productive conflict strategies can have lots of beneficial effects, whereas using inappropriate strategies may be linked to poorer psychological health (Weitzman & Weitzman, 2000; Weitzman, 2001; Neff & Harter, 2002).

1. The *goals* (short-term and long-term) you wish to achieve will influence what strategies seem appropriate to you. If you just want to salvage this evening's date, you may want to simply "give in" and basically ignore the difficulty. On the other hand, if you want to build a long-term relationship, you may want to fully analyze the cause of the problem and to seek strategies that will enable both parties to win.

2. Your *emotional state* will influence your strategies. You're unlikely to select the same strategies when you're sad as when you're angry. You will choose different strategies when you're seeking to apologize than when you're looking for revenge.

3. Your *cognitive assessment* of the situation will exert powerful influence. For example, your attitudes and beliefs about what is fair and equitable will influence your readi-

ness to acknowledge the fairness in the other person's position. Your own assessment of who (if anyone) is the cause of the problem also will influence your conflict style. You may also assess the likely effects of your various options. For example, what do you risk if you fight with your boss by using blame or personal rejection? Do you risk alienating your teenager if you use force?

4. Your *personality and communication competence* will influence the way you engage in conflict. For example, if you're shy and unassertive, you may be more likely to try to avoid conflict than to fight actively. If you're extroverted and have a strong desire to state your position, then you may be more likely to fight actively and argue forcefully.

5. Your *family history* will influence the strategies you use, the topics you choose to fight about, and perhaps your tendencies to obsess or to forget about interpersonal conflicts.

A wide variety of conflict resolution skills already have been covered in earlier chapters. For example, active listening (Chapter 5) is a skill that has wide application in conflict situations. Similarly, using I-messages rather than accusatory you-messages (Chapter 5) will contribute to effective interpersonal conflict resolution (Noller & Fitzpatrick, 1993). Of course, the characteristics of interpersonal competence covered in the Understanding Interpersonal Skills boxes throughout the text are clear and effective, conflict resolution techniques. The following discussion identifies additional strategies detailing the unproductive strategies that should be avoided as well as their productive counterparts.

## Win–Lose and Win–Win Strategies

As indicated in the discussion of conflict styles, when you look at interpersonal conflict in terms of winning and losing, you get four basic types: (1) A wins, B loses; (2) A loses, B wins; (3) A loses, B loses; and (4) A wins, B wins.

Obviously, win–win solutions are the most desirable. Perhaps the most important reason is that win–win solutions lead to mutual satisfaction and prevent the resentment that win–lose solutions often engender. Looking for and developing win–win solutions makes the next conflict less unpleasant; it becomes easier to see the conflict as "solving a problem" rather than as a "fight." Still another benefit of win–win solutions is that they promote mutual face-saving; both parties can feel good about themselves. Finally, people are more likely to abide by the decisions reached in a win–win outcome than they are in win–lose or lose–lose resolutions.

In sum, you can look for solutions in which you or your side wins and the other person or side loses (win–lose solutions). Or you can look for solutions in which you and the other person both win (win–win solutions). Win–win solutions are always better. Too often, however, we fail even to consider the possibility of win–win solutions and what they might be.

Take an interpersonal example: Let's say that I want to spend our money on a new car (my old one is unreliable), but you want to spend it on a vacation (you're exhausted and feel the need for a rest). Through our conflict and its resolution, ideally, we learn what each really wants and may then be able to figure out a way for each of us to get what we want. I might accept a good used car, and you might accept a less expensive vacation. Or we might buy a used car and take an inexpensive road trip. Each of these win–win solutions will satisfy both of us; each of us wins, each of us gets what we wanted.

### ASK Yourself

#### Confronting a Problem

Your neighbor never puts out the garbage in time for pickup, so the garbage—often broken into by animals—remains until the next pickup. You're fed up with the rodents the garbage attracts, the smell, and the horrible appearance. Ask yourself: What might you say that could stop this problem and yet not make your next-door neighbor hate you?

## Avoidance and Active Fighting Strategies

**Avoidance** of conflict may involve actual physical flight; for example, leaving the scene of the conflict (walking out of the apartment or going to another part of the office), falling asleep, or blasting the stereo to drown out all conversation. It may also take the form of emotional or intellectual avoidance, whereby you leave the conflict psychologically by not dealing with the issues raised. Not surprisingly, as avoidance increases, relationship satisfaction decreases (Meeks, Hendrick, & Hendrick, 1998). This does not mean that taking time out to cool off is not a useful first strategy. Sometimes it is. When conflict is waged through e-mail, for example, this is an easy-to-use and often effective strategy. By delaying your response until you've had time to think things out more logically and calmly, you'll be better able to respond constructively and to address possible resolutions to the conflict and get the relationship back to a less hostile stage.

**Nonnegotiation** is a special type of avoidance. Here you refuse to discuss the conflict or to listen to the other person's argument. At times, nonnegotiation takes the form of hammering away at your own point of view until the other person gives in.

Another unproductive conflict strategy is the use of silencers. **Silencers** are conflict techniques that literally silence the other individual. Among the wide variety of silencers that exist, one frequently used technique is crying. When a person is unable to deal with a conflict or when winning seems unlikely, he or she may cry and thus silence the other person. Another silencer consists of feigning extreme emotionalism—yelling and screaming and pretending to be losing control. Still another is developing some physical reaction—headaches and shortness of breath are probably the most popular. One of the major problems with silencers is that you can never be certain whether they're strategies to win the argument or real physical reactions to which you should pay attention. Either way, however, the conflict remains unexamined and unresolved.

Instead of avoiding the issues or resorting to nonnegotiation or silencers, consider taking an active role in your interpersonal conflicts. If you wish to resolve conflicts, you need to confront them actively. Involve yourself on both sides of the communication exchange. Be an active participant as a speaker and as a listener; voice your own feelings and listen carefully to your partner's feelings.

An important part of active fighting involves taking responsibility for your thoughts and feelings. For example, when you disagree with your partner or find fault with her or his behavior, take responsibility for these feelings. Say, for example, "I disagree with . . ." or "I don't like it when you. . . ." Avoid statements that deny your responsibility, such as "Everybody thinks you're wrong about . . ." or "Chris thinks you shouldn't. . . ."

## Force and Talk Strategies

When confronted with conflict, many people prefer not to deal with the issues but rather to force their position on the other person. The **force** may be emotional or physical. In either case, however, the issues are avoided, and the person who "wins" is the one who exerts the most force. This is the technique of warring nations, children, and even some normally sensible adults. It seems also to be the technique of those who are dissatisfied with the power they perceive themselves to have in a relationship (Ronfeldt, Kimerling, & Arias, 1998).

In one study more than 50 percent of single and married couples reported that they had experienced physical violence in their relationship. If we add symbolic violence (for example, threatening to hit the other person or throwing something), the percentages are above 60 percent for singles and above 70 percent for marrieds (Marshall & Rose, 1987). In other research 47 percent of a sample of 410 college students reported some experience with violence in a dating relationship (Deal & Wampler, 1986). In most cases the violence was reciprocal—each person in the relationship used violence.

The only real alternative to force is talk. For example, the qualities of openness, positiveness, and empathy (discussed in the Understanding Interpersonal Skills boxes in Chapters 5, 10, and 11) are suitable starting points. In addition, be sure to listen actively and openly (Chapter 5). This may be especially difficult in conflict situations; tempers may run high,

# InterMedia

## VIOLENCE AND THE MEDIA

Does violence in the media lead to violent acts by viewers? Most of the research on media violence focuses on television (and to a lesser extent on films), but increasingly video and computer games and music are being examined for their violent content and potential influence on children (Dietz, 1998).

Generally research finds that media violence has the following effects (Rodman, 2001; Bok 1998):

- Media violence can teach young people how to be violent; it can teach the techniques of violence.
- It gives people (and children especially) role models to emulate. In many Indian films, for example, violence against women is eroticized; males are encouraged to identify with heroes who use violence to win women. In interviews Indian males revealed that they felt that the depiction of male–female relationships in films paralleled what they felt was the ideal male–female relationship (Derne, 1999).
- Media violence can desensitize people to the violence around them, which, often, is not as extreme as they regularly see on television and in the movies.
- It can make viewers afraid of becoming victims of violence.
- It can create a desire for greater depiction of increased violence, which may be the reason why films have become increasingly violent over the years.
- It can lead to bullying at school (Lee & Kim, 2004).

The extent to which media violence contributes directly to actual violence, however, has yet to be determined (Savage, 2004). Family and social factors, developmental and affective disorders, and substance abuse, for example, seem to interact with exposure to media violence to produce violent behavior (Withecomb, 1997).

### Follow Up

How do you feel about violence in the media? Has it influenced your own interpersonal relationships? Has it influenced the interpersonal relationships of those you know?

---

and you may find yourself being attacked or at least disagreed with. Here are some suggestions for talking and listening more effectively in the conflict situation.

- *Act the role of the listener.* Also, think as a listener. Turn off the television, stereo, or computer; face the other person. Devote your total attention to what the other person is saying. Make sure you understand what the person is saying and feeling. One way to make sure is obviously to ask questions. Another way is to paraphrase what the other person is saying and ask for confirmation: "You feel that if we pooled our money and didn't have separate savings accounts, the relationship would be more equitable. Is that the way you feel?"
- *Express your support or empathy* for what the other person is saying and feeling: "I can understand how you feel. I know I control the finances and that can create a feeling of inequality." If appropriate, indicate your agreement: "You're right to be disturbed."
- *State your thoughts and feelings* on the issue as objectively as you can; if you disagree with what the other person said, then say so: "My problem is that when we did have equal access to the finances, you ran up so many bills that we still haven't recovered. To be honest with you, I'm worried the same thing will happen again."

## Face-Detracting and Face-Enhancing Strategies

A face-detracting or face-attacking approach to interpersonal conflict involves treating the other person as incompetent or untrustworthy, as unable or bad (Donahue & Kolt, 1992). Such attacks can range from mildly embarrassing the other person to severely damaging

Persons with disabilities are often singled out for verbal abuse and physical violence and are often ignored when they complain (Roeher Institute, 1995). What factors do you think contribute to abuse against persons with disabilities? Are these the same factors that contribute to abuse against women, against newly arrived immigrants, and/or against gay men and lesbians?

his or her ego or reputation. So be especially careful to avoid "fighting words"—words that are sure to escalate the conflict rather than help to resolve it. Words like *stupid, liar,* and *bitch* as well as words like *always* and *never* (as in "You always . . ." or "You never . . .") invariably create additional problems. When such attacks become extreme, they may be similar to verbal aggression—a tactic explained in the next section.

One popular but destructive face-detracting strategy is **beltlining** (Bach & Wyden, 1968). Much like fighters in a ring, each of us has an emotional "beltline." When you hit below it, you can inflict serious injury. When you hit above the belt, however, the person is able to absorb the blow. With most interpersonal relationships, especially those of long standing, you know where the beltline is. You know, for example, that to hit Pat with the inability to have children is to hit below the belt. You know that to hit Chris with the failure to get a permanent job is to hit below the belt. This type of face-detracting strategy causes all persons involved added problems. Keep blows to areas your opponent can absorb and handle.

Face-enhancing techniques involve helping the other person to maintain a positive image, an image as competent and trustworthy, able and good. Even when you get what you want, say at bargaining, it's wise to help the other person retain positive face, because it makes it less likely that future conflicts will arise (Donahue & Kolt, 1992). Not surprisingly, people are more likely to make a greater effort to support the listener's "face" if they like the listener than if they don't (Meyer, 1994).

Generally, collectivist cultures place great emphasis on face, especially on maintaining a positive image in public. Face is generally less crucial in individualist cultures such as the United States. Consequently, collectivist peoples are less likely to use conflict strategies such as **blame** and personal rejection, as these are likely to result in a loss of face. Many collectivists are more likely to use strategies that preserve and enhance the opponent's public image. Those from individualist cultures that favor more open discussion of conflict may be more apt to use argumentativeness and to fight actively. If you're from a collective culture, you're more likely to prefer mediation and bargaining than would members of individualist cultures, who prefer a more adversarial and confrontational conflict style (Leung, 1987; Berry, Poortinga, Segall, & Dasen, 1992). But be careful not to think of all individualist or collectivist cultures as similar. For example, in one study Germans had more face concerns than Americans, although both are individualist cultures; and Chinese had more face concerns than Japanese, although both are collectivist cultures (Oetzel, Ting-Toomey, Masumoto, Yokochi, Pan, Takai, & Wilcox, 2001).

Confirming the other person's definition of self (Chapter 7), avoiding attack and blame, and using excuses and apologies as appropriate (Chapter 9) are some generally useful face-enhancing strategies.

## Verbal Aggressiveness and Argumentativeness Strategies

An especially interesting perspective on conflict has emerged from work on verbal aggressiveness and argumentativeness (Infante & Rancer, 1982; Infante & Wigley, 1986; Infante, 1988; Rancer, 1998). Understanding these concepts will help you understand some of the reasons things go wrong and some of the ways in which you can use conflict to actually improve your relationships.

**Verbal Aggressiveness**   **Verbal aggressiveness** is an unproductive coflict strategy in which one person tries to win an argument by inflicting psychological pain, by attacking the other person's self-concept. It's a type of disconfirmation (and the opposite of confirmation) in that it seeks to discredit the individual's view of self (see Chapter 7). To explore this tendency further, take the accompanying self-test on verbal aggressiveness.

Character attack, perhaps because it's extremely effective in inflicting psychological pain, is the most popular tactic of verbal aggressiveness. Other tactics include attacking the person's abilities, background, and physical appearance; cursing; teasing; ridiculing; threatening; swearing; and using various nonverbal emblems (Infante, Sabourin, Rudd, & Shannon, 1990).

Some researchers have argued that "unless aroused by verbal aggression, a hostile disposition remains latent in the form of unexpressed anger" (Infante, Chandler, & Rudd, 1989). There is some evidence to show that people in violent relationships are more often verbally aggressive than people in nonviolent relationships (Sutter & Martin, 1998).

Because verbal aggressiveness does not help to resolve conflicts, results in loss of credibility for the person using it, and actually increases the credibility of the target of the aggressiveness, you may wonder why people act aggressively (Infante, Hartley, Martin, Higgins, et al., 1992; Infante, Riddle, Horvath, & Tumlin, 1992; Schrodt, 2003).

**SPEAKING**

**>> Interpersonal-E**

**Online Aggressiveness.** As you read about verbal aggressiveness, consider how such aggressiveness is expressed in online communication. How is flaming— "the practice of posting messages that are deliberately hostile and insulting to a discussion board"— similar to and different from face-to-face verbal aggressiveness (cf. O'Sullivan & Flanagin, 2003)?

# TEST YOURSELF

## HOW VERBALLY AGGRESSIVE ARE YOU?

This scale is designed to measure how you try to obtain compliance from others. For each statement, indicate the extent to which you feel it's true for you in your attempts to influence others. Use the following scale: 1 = almost never true, 2 = rarely true, 3 = occasionally true, 4 = often true, and 5 = almost always true.

_____   1. I am extremely careful to avoid attacking individuals' intelligence when I attack their ideas.

_____   2. When individuals are very stubborn, I use insults to soften the stubbornness.

_____   3. I try very hard to avoid having other people feel bad about themselves when I try to influence them.

_____   4. When people refuse to do a task I know is important, without good reason, I tell them they are unreasonable.

_____   5. When others do things I regard as stupid, I try to be extremely gentle with them.

_____   6. If individuals I am trying to influence really deserve it, I attack their character.

_____   7. When people behave in ways that are in very poor taste, I insult them in order to shock them into proper behavior.

_____   8. I try to make people feel good about themselves even when their ideas are stupid.

_____   9. When people simply will not budge on a matter of importance, I lose my temper and say rather strong things to them.

_____  10. When people criticize my shortcomings, I take it in good humor and do not try to get back at them.

_____  11. When individuals insult me, I get a lot of pleasure out of really telling them off.

_____  12. When I dislike individuals greatly, I try not to show it in what I say or how I say it.

_____  13. I like poking fun at people who do things which are very stupid in order to stimulate their intelligence.

_____  14. When I attack a person's ideas, I try not to damage their self-concepts.

_____  15. When I try to influence people, I make a great effort not to offend them.

_____ 16. When people do things that are mean or cruel, I attack their character in order to help correct their behavior.

_____ 17. I refuse to participate in arguments when they involve personal attacks.

_____ 18. When nothing seems to work in trying to influence others, I yell and scream in order to get some movement from them.

_____ 19. When I am not able to refute others' positions, I try to make them feel defensive in order to weaken their positions.

_____ 20. When an argument shifts to personal attacks, I try very hard to change the subject.

**HOW DID YOU DO?** In order to compute your verbal aggressiveness score, follow these steps:

1. Add your scores on items 2, 4, 6, 7, 9, 11, 13, 16, 18, and 19.
2. Add your scores on items 1, 3, 5, 8, 10, 12, 14, 15, 17, and 20.
3. Subtract the sum obtained in step 2 from 60.
4. To compute your verbal aggressiveness score, add the total obtained in step 1 to the result obtained in step 3.

If you scored between 59 and 100, you're high in verbal aggressiveness; if you scored between 39 and 58, you're moderate in verbal aggressiveness; and if you scored between 20 and 38, you're low in verbal aggressiveness. In looking over your responses, make special note of the behaviors described in the 10 statements that indicate a tendency to act verbally aggressive. Note those inappropriate behaviors that you're especially prone to commit. High agreement (4s or 5s) with statements 2, 4, 6, 7, 9, 11, 13, 16, 18, and 19 and low agreement (1s and 2s) with statements 1, 3, 5, 8, 10, 12, 14, 15, 17, and 20 will help you highlight any significant verbal aggressiveness you might have.

**WHAT WILL YOU DO?** Because verbal aggressiveness is likely to seriously reduce interpersonal effectiveness, you probably want to reduce your tendencies to respond aggressively. Review the times when you acted verbally aggressive. What effect did such actions have on your subsequent interaction? What effect did they have on your relationship with the other person? What alternative ways of getting your point across might you have used? Might these have proved more effective? Perhaps the most general suggestion for reducing verbal aggressiveness is to increase your argumentativeness; as we'll see below.

_Source:_ From "Verbal Aggressiveness: An Interpersonal Model and Measure" by Dominic Infante and C. J. Wrigley. _Communication Monographs 53_, 1986, pp. 61–69. Reprinted by permission of the Speech Communication Association. Also see Levine et al. (2004).

Communicating with an affirming style (for example, with smiles, a pleasant facial expression, touching, physical closeness, eye contact, nodding, warm and sincere voice, vocal variety) leads others to perceive less verbal aggression in an interaction than communicating with a nonaffirming style. The assumption people seem to make is that if your actions are affirming, then your messages are also, and if your actions are nonaffirming, then your messages are also (Infante, Rancer, & Jordan, 1996).

**Argumentativeness** Contrary to popular usage, the term **argumentativeness** refers to a quality to be cultivated rather than avoided. Argumentativeness is your willingness to argue for a point of view, your tendency to speak your mind on significant issues. It's the preferred alternative to verbal aggressiveness (Infante & Rancer, 1996; Hample, 2004). Before reading about ways to increase your argumentativeness, take the self-test "How Argumentative Are You?"

At this point you may wish to examine your own behavior and ask yourself how argumentative you are. The following are sugges-

**Ask Yourself**
Talking Aggressively

Your relationship partner is becoming more and more verbally aggressive, and you're having trouble with this new communication pattern. You want your partner to realize that this way of communicating is not productive and may ultimately destroy the relationship. Ask yourself: What options do you have for trying to lessen or even eliminate this verbal aggressiveness?

# TEST YOURSELF

## HOW ARGUMENTATIVE ARE YOU?

This questionnaire contains statements about your approach to debating controversial issues. Indicate how often each statement is true for you personally according to the following scale: 1 = almost never true, 2 = rarely true, 3 = occasionally true, 4 = often true, and 5 = almost always true.

_____ 1. While in an argument, I worry that the person I am arguing with will form a negative impression of me.
_____ 2. Arguing over controversial issues improves my intelligence.
_____ 3. I enjoy avoiding arguments.
_____ 4. I am energetic and enthusiastic when I argue.
_____ 5. Once I finish an argument, I promise myself that I will not get into another.
_____ 6. Arguing with a person creates more problems for me than it solves.
_____ 7. I have a pleasant, good feeling when I win a point in an argument.
_____ 8. When I finish arguing with someone, I feel nervous and upset.
_____ 9. I enjoy a good argument over a controversial issue.
_____ 10. I get an unpleasant feeling when I realize I am about to get into an argument.
_____ 11. I enjoy defending my point of view on an issue.
_____ 12. I am happy when I keep an argument from happening.
_____ 13. I do not like to miss the opportunity to argue a controversial issue.
_____ 14 I prefer being with people who rarely disagree with me.
_____ 15. I consider an argument an exciting intellectual challenge.
_____ 16. I find myself unable to think of effective points during an argument.
_____ 17. I feel refreshed and satisfied after an argument on a controversial issue.
_____ 18. I have the ability to do well in an argument.
_____ 19. I try to avoid getting into arguments.
_____ 20. I feel excitement when I expect that a conversation I am in is leading to an argument.

### HOW DID YOU DO?  To compute your argumentativeness score, follow these steps:

1. Add your scores on items 2, 4, 7, 9, 11, 13, 15, 17, 18, and 20.
2. Add 60 to the sum obtained in step 1.
3. Add your scores on items 1, 3, 5, 6, 8, 10, 12, 14, 16, and 19.
4. To compute your argumentativeness score, subtract the total obtained in step 3 from the total obtained in step 2.

The following guidelines will help you interpret your score: Scores between 73 and 100 indicate high argumentativeness; scores between 56 and 72 indicate moderate argumentativeness; and scores between 20 and 55 indicate low argumentativeness.

Generally, those who score high in argumentativeness have a strong tendency to state their position on controversial issues and to argue against the positions of others. A high scorer sees arguing as exciting and intellectually challenging, and as an opportunity to win a kind of contest.

The person who scores low in argumentativeness tries to prevent arguments. This person experiences satisfaction not from arguing but from avoiding arguments. The low argumentative person sees arguing as unpleasant and unsatisfying. Not surprisingly, this person has little confidence in his or her ability to argue effectively.

Finally, the moderately argumentative person possesses some of the qualities of the high argumentative person and some of the qualities of the low argumentative person.

### WHAT WILL YOU DO?  The researchers who developed this test note that both high and low argumentatives may experience communication difficulties. The high argumentative, for example, may argue needlessly, too often, and too forcefully. The low argumentative, on the other hand, may avoid taking a stand even when it seems necessary. Persons scoring somewhere in the middle are probably the more interpersonally skilled and adaptable, arguing when it is necessary but avoiding arguments that are needless and repetitive. Does your experience support this observation? What specific actions might you take to improve your argumentativeness?

_Source:_ From Dominic Infante and Andrew Rancer, "A Conceptualization and Measure of Argumentativeness" _Journal of Personality Assessment 46_ (1982): 72–80. Copyright 1982 Lawrence Erlbaum Associates, Inc. Reprinted by permission of Lawrence Erlbaum Associates, Inc., and the authors.

# Ask the Researcher

## ARGUING ASSERTIVELY

 I'm very aggressive when I argue with friends, romantic partners, work colleagues, etc. After all, I want to win the argument. So what's so wrong with my being aggressive when I argue?

Scholars agree that all arguing is assertive and that assertiveness is a positive and constructive trait. Highly assertive individuals, then, would approach arguing controversial issues with enjoyment because argumentativeness is a constructive and positive trait. In fact, the challenge is in achieving individual goals. Yet two stumbling blocks to goal achievement hinge on relationship and situational factors. A competent communicator demonstrates flexibility and skill in adapting communicative behaviors in a wide variety of relationships and settings. For example, small group members high in argumentativeness are often perceived as stirring up conflict. Thus, it may be all right to always win arguments with friends and coworkers but not all right to always win arguments with a romantic partner or members of small groups. Trait researchers find that the situation and the relationship are key environmental factors warranting consideration. When training individuals to enhance assertiveness and argumentativeness abilities, trainers note the possible negative consequences of seeking to *always* win arguments, no matter what.

**For further information** see C. M. Anderson, P. R. Raptis, Y. Lin, and F. R. Clarke, "Motives as Predictors of Argumentativeness and Verbal Aggressiveness of Black and White Adolescents," *Communication Reports* 17 (2000): 115–126; C. M. Anderson and M. M. Martin, "The Relationship of Argumentativeness and Verbal Aggressiveness to Cohesion, Consensus, and Satisfaction in Small Groups," *Communication Research Reports* 12 (1999): 21–31; and D. A. Infante and A. S. Rancer, "Argumentativeness and Verbal Aggressiveness: A Review of Recent Theory and Research," in B. R. Burleson (ed.), *Communication Yearbook 19*, pp. 319–351. (Thousand Oaks, CA: Sage, 1996).

Carolyn M. Anderson (Ph.D., Kent State University) is a professor in the School of Communication of the University of Akron (canders@uakron.edu) and teaches graduate and undergraduate courses in small group, communication theory, leadership, and health communication. Dr. Anderson researches trait communication in interpersonal, group, organizational, family, and health settings. She serves the community as a consultant, public speaker, and organizational trainer.

tions for cultivating argumentativeness; ideally, most of these guidelines are already part of your communication behavior (Infante, 1988). If any are not a part of your conflict behavior, consider how you can adopt them.

① Treat disagreements as objectively as possible. Avoid assuming that because someone takes issue with your position or your interpretation, they're attacking you as a person.

② Avoid attacking the other person (rather than the person's arguments), even if this would give you a tactical advantage. Center your arguments on issues rather than personalities.

③ Reaffirm the other person's sense of competence. Compliment the other person as appropriate.

④ Avoid interrupting. Allow the other person to state her or his position fully before you respond.

⑤ Stress equality, and stress the similarities that you have with the other person (see the Understanding Interpersonal Skills box on p. 291). Stress your areas of agreement before attacking the disagreements.

⑥ Express interest in the other person's position, attitude, and point of view.

**SPEAKING**
**>> Interpersonal-E**

**Aggressiveness in Internet Communication.** In what ways might you express anger and aggressiveness in e-mail communication?

7. Avoid presenting your arguments too emotionally. Avoid using a loud voice or inter- jecting vulgar expressions, which will prove offensive and eventually ineffective.
8. Allow the other person to save face. Never humiliate the other person.

# Ethics in Interpersonal Communication

## ETHICAL FIGHTING

This chapter focuses on the dimension of effectiveness versus ineffectiveness in conflict strate- gies. But all communication strategies also have an ethical dimension, and it is important to look at the ethical implications of conflict resolution strategies. For example:

- Does conflict avoidance have an ethical dimension? For example, is it unethical for one relationship partner to refuse to discuss disagreements?
- Can the use of physical force to influence another person ever be ethical? Can you iden- tify a situation in which it would be appropriate for someone with greater physical strength to overpower another to compel the other to accept his or her point of view?
- Are face-detracting strategies inherently unethical, or might it be appropriate to use them in certain situations? Can you identify such situations?
- What are the ethical implications of verbal aggressiveness?

### What would you do?

At your high-powered and highly stressful job, you some- times smoke pot. This happens several times a month, but you don't use drugs at any other times. Your relationship part- ner—who you know hates drugs and despises people who use any recreational drug—asks you if you take drugs. Because it's such a limited use, and because you know that admitting this will cause a huge conflict in a re- lationship that's already having difficulties, you wonder if you can ethically lie about this.

# Reviewing Key Terms and Concepts in Interpersonal Conflict

This chapter examined principles of interpersonal conflict, con- flict management stages, and some of the popular productive and unproductive conflict strategies.

## Principles of Interpersonal Conflict

What is interpersonal conflict?

- Interpersonal conflict is a disagreement between connected individuals who each want something that is incompatible with what the other wants. Conflict is inevitable.
- Interpersonal conflict is neither good nor bad, but depend- ing on how the disagreements are resolved, the conflict can strengthen or weaken a relationship.

- Conflict can center on matters external to the relationship and on relationship issues such as who's the boss.
- Conflict may be pursued with different styles, each of which has different consequences.
- Conflict and the strategies used to resolve it are heavily influ- enced by culture.

## Conflict Management Stages

How do you go about managing a conflict or solving a problem?

- Before the conflict: Try to fight in private, fight when you're ready, know what you're fighting about, and fight about problems that can be solved.

- Define the conflict: Define the content and relationship issues in specific terms, avoiding gunnysacking and mind reading, and try to empathize with the other person.
- Examine the possible solutions: Try to identify as many solutions as possible, look for win–win solutions, and carefully weigh the costs and rewards of each solution.
- Test the solution mentally and in practice to see if it works.
- Evaluate the tested solution from a variety of perspectives.
- Accept the solution and integrate it into your behavior. Or reject the solution and begin again; for example, define the problem differently or look in other directions for possible solutions.
- After the conflict: Learn something from the conflict, keep the conflict in perspective, attack your negative feelings, and increase the exchange of rewards.

## Conflict Management Strategies

What are some of the strategies that people use that may help or hinder resolving a conflict?

- Become an active participant in the conflict; don't avoid the issues or the arguments of the other person.
- Use talk to discuss the issues rather than trying to force the other person to accept your position.
- Try to enhance the self-esteem, the face, of the person you're arguing with; avoid strategies that may cause the other person to lose face.
- Argue the issues, focusing as objectively as possible on the points of disagreement; avoid being verbally aggressive or attacking the other person.

## Applying Key Terms and Concepts in Interpersonal Conflict

1 Which characters from television frequently demonstrate verbal aggressiveness? Which characters frequently demonstrate argumentativeness? What distinguishes these types of characters?

2 Men generally score higher in argumentativeness (and in verbal aggressiveness) than women. Men are also more apt to be perceived (by both men and women) as more argumentative and verbally aggressive than women (Nicotera & Rancer, 1994). Why do you think this is so?

3 What changes would you like to see your relational partners (friends, family members, romantic partners) make in their own verbal aggressiveness and argumentativeness? What might you do to more effectively regulate your own verbal aggressiveness and argumentativeness?

4 What does your own culture teach about conflict and its management? What strategies does it prohibit? Are some conflict strategies prohibited with certain people (say, your parents) but not with others (say, your friends)? Does your culture prescribe certain ways of dealing with conflict? Does it have different expectations for men and for women? To what degree have you internalized these teachings? What effect do these teachings have on your actual conflict behaviors?

5 For each of the following conflict scenarios, try generating as many win–win solutions as you feel the individuals could reasonably accept. Give yourself two minutes for each case. If possible, share your win–win solutions with other individuals or groups. Also, consider ways in which you might incorporate win–win strategies into your own conflict management behavior.

- Pat and Chris won $4,500 in a state lottery. Pat wants to redecorate the living room, but Chris wants to save the money.
- Sara and Margaret want to go to Canada and get married, but both sets of parents are adamantly opposed to same-sex marriage and want Sara and Margaret to stop seeing each other and enter therapy.
- Pat is a fifth-grade teacher and is required to use a textbook on sex that contains a great many false and misleading statements. The principal demands that the textbook be followed without contradiction; Pat disagrees but needs the job.

6 Think about the major productive and unproductive conflict strategies discussed in this chapter as they might apply to the series of statements listed below. Assume that the statements are made by someone close to you. Try developing an unproductive response and an alternative productive response to any one or two of the statements.

- "You just spend too much money; we need to save something for emergencies. You're leading us into bankruptcy."
- "We need to move away from your parents; they're too possessive and intrude into every aspect of our lives. I can't stand it any more."
- "Again, this report is simply inadequate. The spelling, grammar, and logical development are horrendous. You're going to have to learn how to do this or you can find another job."

Go to www.ablongman.com/devito.

*These experiences focus on interpersonal conflict, especially on understanding the nature of conflict and how you can more effectively resolve and manage conflict.*

❶ **Analyzing a Conflict Episode** provides an opportunity to think critically about the messages used in a conflict interaction. ❷ **Dealing with Conflict Starters** looks at some of the messages that often begin conflicts. ❸ **Generating Win–Win Solutions** provides opportunities to experiment with strategies that can make conflict and its resolution more effective.

# Power in Interpersonal Relationships

⬆ *The Incredibles* (2004)

*The Incredibles* depicts a battle between a superhero and a giant killer ro-bot in a test of who is more powerful. This last chapter also focuses on power, but of a different type—the power of messages to influence and to help you accomplish what you want.

> "Communication is power. Those who have mastered its effective use can change their own experience of the world and the world's experience of them."
>
> —Anthony Robbins

This final chapter discusses perhaps the most important dimension of interpersonal communication, that of power. We'll examine key principles of power; the types of power you might wield; and the many ways in which you communicate power—in verbal and nonverbal messages, in your listening behaviors, in your use of compliance-gaining strategies, and in your ability to empower others.

##  PRINCIPLES OF POWER

Power influences what you do, when you do it, and with whom. It influences your choice of friends and your romantic and family relationships—and how successful you feel those relationships are. Interpersonal **power** is what enables one person to control the behavior of the other. Thus, if A has power over B, then A, by virtue of this power—through either its exercise or the threat of its being exercised—can control B's behaviors. Power in interpersonal relationships may best be introduced by a discussion of some of its most important principles. These principles explain how power operates interpersonally and offer insight on how you can more effectively manage power.

### Some People Are More Powerful Than Others

In the United States, all people are considered equal under the law and therefore equal in their entitlement to education, legal protection, and freedom of speech. But all people are not equal when it comes to just about everything else. Some are born into wealth, others into poverty. Some are born physically strong, good-looking, and healthy; others are born weak, less attractive, and with a variety of inherited illnesses.

Some people are born into power, and some of those who are not born powerful learn to become powerful. In short, some people control and others are controlled. Of course, the world is not quite that simple; some people exert power in certain areas of life, some in others. Some exert power in many areas, some in just a few.

Power bears a close relationship to interpersonal violence. For example, husbands who have less power in their relationship are more likely to be physically abusive toward their wives than husbands who have greater power (Babcock, Waltz, Jacobson, & Gottman, 1993). Further, in violent marriages the interpersonal power struggle is often characterized by unproductive and dysfunctional efforts at influence. For example, violent couples engage in greater blame and greater criticism of each other than do nonviolent couples (Rushe, 1996).

### Power Can Be Increased or Decreased

Although people differ greatly in the amount of power they wield at any time and in any specific area, everyone can increase their power in some ways. You can lift weights and increase your physical power. You can learn the techniques of negotiation and increase your power in group situations. You can learn the principles of communication and increase your persuasive power.

Power can also be decreased. Probably the most common way to lose power is by unsuccessfully trying to control another's behavior. For example, the person who threatens you with punishment and then fails to carry out the threat loses power. Another way to lose power is to allow others to control you; for example, to allow others to take unfair advantage of you. When you don't confront these power tactics of others, you lose power yourself.

## Power Follows the Principle of Less Interest

In any interpersonal relationship, the person who holds the power is the one less interested in and less dependent on the rewards and punishments controlled by the other person. If, for example, Pat can walk away from the rewards Chris controls or can suffer the punishments Chris can mete out, Pat controls the relationship. If, on the other hand, Pat needs the rewards Chris controls or is unable or unwilling to suffer the punishments Chris can administer, Chris maintains the power and controls the relationship. Put differently, Chris holds the relationship power to the degree that Chris is not dependent on the rewards and punishments under Pat's control.

The more a person needs a relationship, the less power that person has in it. The less a person needs a relationship, the greater that person's power. In a love relationship, for example, the person who maintains greater power is the one who would find it easier to break up the relationship. The person who is unwilling (or unable) to break up has little power, precisely because he or she is dependent on the relationship and the rewards provided by the other person.

Not surprisingly, if you perceive your partner as having greater power than you, you will probably be more likely to avoid confrontation and to be less expressive of criticism (Solomon & Samp, 1998).

## Power Has a Cultural Dimension

Recall the concept of power distance discussed in Chapter 2. There it was pointed out that cultures differ in the amount of power that exists between people and in the attitudes that people have about power, its legitimacy, and its desirability (Hofstede, 1983). In many Asian, African, and Arab cultures (as well as in many European cultures such as Italian and Greek), for example, there is a great power distance between men and women. Men have the greater power, and women are expected to recognize this and abide by its implications. Men, for example, make the important decisions and have the final word in any difference of opinion (Hatfield & Rapson, 1996).

In the United States the power distance between men and women is undergoing considerable changes. In many families men still have the greater power. Partly because they earn more money, they also make the more important decisions. As economic equality becomes more a reality than an ideal, however, this power difference may also change. In contrast, in Arab cultures the man makes the more important decisions not because he earns more money but because he is the man—and men are simply given greater power.

Some cultures perpetuate the power difference by granting men greater educational opportunities. For example, although

**⊕ VIEWPOINT**

In light of the principle that the person who has less interest in the relationship maintains the greater power and influence, would you find it advantageous to have your partner believe that you cared less about the relationship and had less need for the rewards provided by your partner than you actually do? Do you know people who do this? Do you find this ethical?

college education for women is taken for granted in most of the United States, it's the exception in many other cultures throughout the world.

In some Asian cultures persons in positions of authority—for example, teachers—have unquestioned power. Students do not contradict, criticize, or challenge teachers. This can easily create problems in the typical multicultural classroom. Students from cultures that teach that the teacher has unquestioned authority may have difficulty meeting the American teacher's expectation that students will interact critically with the material and develop interpretations of their own.

## Power Is Frequently Used Unfairly

Although it would be nice to believe that power was wielded for the good of all, it's often used selfishly and unfairly. Here are two examples: workplace sexual harassment and the use of power plays.

**Sexual Harassment**    One type of unfair use of power is workplace **sexual harassment,** a form of behavior that violates Title VII of the Civil Rights Act of 1964 and as amended by the Civil Rights Act of 1991 (http://www.eeoc.gov/laws/vii.html, last modified January 15, 1997, accessed May 4, 2002). Of course sexual harassment is not confined to the workplace; it takes place in social setting, and in educational settings, for example. Much of what is presented here is applicable to sexual harassment in general and not just to that which occurs in an organizational context.

**Defining Sexual Harassment**    There are two general categories of workplace sexual harassment: *quid pro quo* (a term borrowed from the Latin, which literally means "something for something") and the creation of a hostile environment.

In quid pro quo harassment, employment opportunities (as in hiring and promotion) are dependent on the granting of sexual favors. Conversely, quid pro quo harassment also involves situations in which reprisals and various negative consequences can result from

**SPEAKING**
**>> Interpersonal-E**

**Organizational Hierarchies.**
Some theorists believe that computer-mediated communication will eventually eliminate the hierarchical structure of organizations, largely because it "encourages wider participation, greater candor, and an emphasis on merit over status" (Kollock & Smith, 1996, p. 109). If valid, this theory also would suggest that high-power-distance cultures will gradually move in the direction of low power distance and become more democratic. What evidence can you find bearing on this issue?

# Understanding Interpersonal Theory and Research

## GROUP POWER

Recall (from Chapter 2) that high-power-distance cultures are those in which power is concentrated in the hands of a few and there's a great difference between the power held by these people and the power possessed by the ordinary citizen. In low-power-distance cultures power is more evenly distributed throughout the citizenry (Hofstede, 1997). Groups may also be viewed in terms of high and low power distances. In high-power-distance groups the leader is far more powerful than the members. In low-power-distance groups leaders and members differ much less in their power.

Of the groups in which you'll participate, some will be high-power-distance groups and others will be low. The skill is to recognize which is which, to follow the rules generally, and to break them only after you've thought through the consequences. For example, in low-power-distance groups and cultures, you're expected to confront a leader or supervisor assertively; acting assertively is in keeping with the general feeling of equality (Borden, 1991). In high-power-distance groups and cultures, direct confrontation and assertiveness toward the leader (or toward any person in authority, such as a teacher or doctor) may be viewed negatively (Westwood, Tang, & Kirkbride, 1992; also see Bochner & Hesketh, 1994).

### Working with Theories and Research

Visit Research Navigator (www.researchnavigator.com) or other databases and search the communication and sociology databases for "power." What types of questions engage the attention of researchers?

the failure to grant such sexual favors. Put more generally, quid pro quo harassment occurs when employment consequences (positive or negative) hinge on a person's response to sexual advances.

Hostile environment harassment is much broader and includes all sexual behaviors (verbal and nonverbal) that make a worker uncomfortable. For example, putting sexually explicit pictures on the bulletin board, using sexually explicit screen savers, telling sexual jokes and stories, and using sexual and demeaning language or gestures all constitute sexual harassment. "Sexual harassment," notes one team of researchers, "refers to conduct, typically experienced as offensive in nature, in which unwanted sexual advances are made in the context of a relationship of unequal power or authority. The victims are subjected to verbal comments of a sexual nature, unconsented touching and requests for sexual favors" (Friedman, Boumil, & Taylor, 1992). Attorneys note that under the law "sexual harassment is any unwelcome sexual advance or conduct on the job that creates an intimidating, hostile or offensive working environment" (Petrocelli & Repa, 1992).

The Equal Employment Opportunity Commission (EEOC) definition of workplace sexual harassment sums up these two basic types. In the definition numbers (1) and (2) refer to quid pro quo and number (3) refers to hostile environment.

> Unwelcome sexual advances, requests for sexual favors and other verbal or physical conduct of a sexual nature constitute sexual harassment when (1) submission to such conduct is made either explicitly or implicitly a term or condition of an individual's employment, (2) submission to or rejection of such conduct by an individual is used as the basis for employment decisions affecting such individual, or (3) such conduct has the purpose or effect of unreasonably interfering with an individual's work performance or creating an intimidating, hostile, or offensive working environment (Friedman, Boumil, & Taylor, 1992).

**Recognizing Sexual Harassment**   To determine whether behavior constitutes sexual harassment and to assess your own situation objectively rather than emotionally, ask yourself the following questions (VanHyning, 1993):

1. Is it real? Does this behavior have the meaning it seems to have?
2. Is it job related? Does this behavior have something to do with or will it influence the way you do your job?
3. Did you reject this behavior? Did you make your rejection of unwanted messages clear to the other person?
4. Have these types of messages persisted? Is there a pattern, a consistency to these messages?

If you answered yes to all four questions, then the behavior is likely to constitute sexual harassment (VanHyning, 1993).

Keep in mind three additional facts that are often misunderstood. First, members of either gender may sexually harass. Although most cases brought to public attention are committed by men against women, women may also harass men. Further, harassment may be committed by men against men and by women against women. Second, anyone in an organization can be guilty of sexual harassment. Although most cases of harassment involve harassment of subordinates by persons in authority, this is not a necessary condition. Coworkers, vendors, and even customers may be charged with sexual harassment. Third, sexual harassment is not limited to business organizations but can and does occur in schools; in hospitals; and in social, religious, and political organizations.

**Avoiding Sexual Harassment Behaviors**   Three suggestions will help you avoid committing workplace harassment (Bravo & Cassedy, 1992). First, begin with the assumption that coworkers are not interested in your sexual advances, sexual stories and jokes, or sexual gestures. Second, listen and watch for negative reactions to any sex-related discussion. Use the suggestions and techniques discussed throughout this book (for example, perception checking and critical listening) to become aware of such reactions. When in doubt, find out; ask questions, for example. Third, avoid saying or doing anything that you think your parent, partner, or child would find offensive in the behavior of someone with whom she or he worked.

**Responding to Sexual Harassment**    Should you encounter sexual harassment and feel the need to do something about it, consider these suggestions recommended by workers in the field (Petrocelli & Repa, 1992; Bravo & Cassedy, 1992; Rubenstein, 1993):

**A S K Yourself**
Harassing Behavior

You notice that your colleague at work is being sexually harassed by a supervisor but says nothing. You bristle inside each time you see this happen.    Ask yourself:  What are some of the things you can do (if you think you should do anything, that is) that might help end this harassment?

1. *Talk to the harasser.* Tell this person, assertively, that you do not welcome the behavior and that you find it offensive. Simply informing Fred that his sexual jokes aren't appreciated and are seen as offensive may be sufficient to make him stop this joke telling. In some instances, unfortunately, such criticism goes unheeded, and the offensive behavior continues.
2. *Collect evidence.* Perhaps seek corroboration from others who have experienced similar harassment at the hands of the same individual, or create a log of the offensive behaviors.
3. *Begin with appropriate channels within the organization.* Most organizations have established channels to deal with such grievances. This step will in most cases eliminate any further harassment. In the event that it doesn't, you may consider going farther.
4. *File a complaint with an organization or governmental agency or perhaps take legal action.*
5. *Don't blame yourself.* Like many who are abused, you may tend to blame yourself, feeling that you're responsible for being harassed. You aren't; however, you may need to secure emotional support from friends or perhaps from a trained professional.

**Power Plays**    **Power plays** are patterns (not isolated instances) of behavior that are used repeatedly by one person to take unfair advantage of another person (Steiner, 1981). Power plays aim to deny you the right to make your own choices and come in a variety of forms.

**Identifying Power Plays**    Power plays are not always easy to identify; often they seem to be only slight intrusions. But it's important to understand that their repeated use can prevent you from exercising your own rights. Let's look at a few of the major types to see how power plays are used and how they can be identified more easily.

One type is the "nobody upstairs" power play. In "nobody upstairs" the individual refuses to acknowledge your request, regardless of how or how many times you make it. One common form is the refusal to take no for an answer. Sometimes "nobody upstairs" takes the form of pleading ignorance of common socially accepted (but unspoken) rules, such as rules about knocking when you enter someone's room or refraining from opening another person's mail or wallet: "I didn't know you didn't want me to look in your wallet," or "Do you want me to knock the next time I come into your room?"

Another power play is "you owe me." Here others unilaterally do something for you and then demand something in return. They remind you of what they did for you and use this to get you to do what they want.

In "yougottobekidding," one person attacks the other by saying "You've got to be kidding" or some similar phrase, not out of surprise (which is fine) but out of a desire to put your ideas down: "You can't be serious." "You can't mean that." "You didn't say what I thought you said, did you?" The intention here is to express utter disbelief in the other's statement so as to make the statement and the person seem inadequate or stupid.

**Responding to Power Plays**    The power plays discussed above are examples; but there are, of course, many others that you have no doubt met on occasion. What do you do when you recognize a power play? One commonly employed response is to ignore the power play and allow the other person to take control. Another response is to treat the power play as an isolated instance (rather than as a pattern of behavior) and object to it. For example, you might say quite simply, "Please don't come into my room without knocking first," or "Please don't look in my wallet without permission."

A third response is a cooperative one (Steiner, 1981). In this response, you do the following:

■ *Express your feelings.* Tell the person that you're angry, annoyed, or disturbed by his or her behavior.
■ *Describe the behavior to which you object.* Tell the person—in language that describes rather than evaluates—the specific behavior you object to; for example, reading your mail, saying you owe the person for something, or responding to everything you say with disbelief.

■ *State a cooperative response you both can live with comfortably.* Tell the person—in a cooperative tone—what you want: For example: "I want you to knock before coming into my room," "I want you to stop telling me I owe you things," or "I want you to stop ridiculing my ideas."

A cooperative response to "nobody upstairs" might go something like this: "I'm angry (*expressing feelings*) that you persist in opening my mail. You have opened my mail four times this past week (*description of the behavior to which you object*). I want you to allow me to open my own mail. If there is anything in it that concerns you, I will let you know immediately" (*statement of cooperative response*).

# InterMedia

## REVERSING MEDIA'S INFLUENCE

Although you generally think of the media as exerting influence on you, you can also exert influence on the media—on radio, television, newspapers and magazines, film, and the Internet (Jamieson & Campbell, 1997; Postman & Powers, 1992). Here are some ways to accomplish this:

■ Register your complaints. Write letters or e-mails, or call a television station or an advertiser expressing your views. Write to a public forum, such as a newspaper or newsgroup, or to the Federal Communication Commission or to other regulatory agencies.
■ Exert group pressure. Join with others who think the same way you do. Bring group pressure to bear on television networks, newspapers, advertisers, and manufacturers.
■ Protest through an established organization. There's probably an organization already established for the issue with which you're concerned. Search the Internet for relevant newsgroups, professional organizations, and chat rooms that focus on your topic.
■ Protest by starting or joining a social movement, a technique used throughout history to gain civil rights. Forming a new movement or aligning yourself with an established movement can help you secure not only a large number of petitioners but also the media coverage that might enable you to communicate your message to a large audience.
■ Create legislative pressure. Exert influence on the state or federal level by influencing your local political representatives (through voting, calls, letters, and e-mails), who will in turn influence representatives at higher levels of the political hierarchy.

### Follow Up

Let's say that you're unhappy about the way in which the national and local media (television and newspapers) have treated the abortion controversy. How would you go about exerting pressure on the media to better reflect your own position in their coverage?

## TYPES OF POWER

Power is present in all relationships and in all communication interchanges. But the type of power varies greatly from one situation to another and from one person to another. Here we identify six types of power: referent, legitimate, expert, information or persuasion, reward, and coercive power (French & Raven, 1968; Raven, Centers, & Rodrigues, 1975; Raven, Schwarzwald, & Koslowsky, 1998). Differences in the amount and type of power influence who makes important decisions, who will prevail in an argument, and who will control the finances.

Before reading about these types of power, consider your own powers by responding to the following self-test, each item of which refers to a type of power discussed below.

---

## TEST YOURSELF
### HOW POWERFUL ARE YOU?

For each statement, respond using a scale of 1 to 5 on which 1 = true of 20 percent or less of the people you know; 2 = true of about 21 to 40 percent of the people you know; 3 = true of about 41 to 60 percent of the people you know; 4 = true of about 61 to 80 percent of the people you know; and 5 = true of 81 percent or more of the people you know.

_____ 1. People wish to be like you or to be identified with you. For example, high school football players may admire the former professional football player who is now their coach and may want to be like him.

_____ 2. Your position is such that you often have to tell others what to do. For example, a mother's position demands that she tell her children what to do, a manager's position demands that he or she tell employees what to do, and so on.

_____ 3. Other people realize that you have expertise in certain areas of knowledge. For example, a doctor has expertise in medicine, so others turn to the doctor to tell them what to do. Someone knowledgeable about computers similarly possesses expertise.

_____ 4. People realize that you possess the communication ability to present an argument logically and persuasively.

_____ 5. People see you as having the ability to give them what they want. For example, employers have the ability to give their employees increased pay, longer vacations, and improved working conditions.

_____ 6. People see you as having the ability to administer punishment or to withhold things they want. For example, employers have the ability to reduce voluntary overtime, to shorten vacation time, or to fail to improve working conditions.

**HOW DID YOU DO?**  These statements refer to the six major types of power. Low scores (1s and 2s) indicate your belief that you possess little of the types of power indicated; high scores (4s and 5s) indicate your belief that you possess a great deal of those types of power.

**WHAT WILL YOU DO?**  How satisfied are you with your level of power? If you're not satisfied, what might you do about it? A good starting place, of course, is to learn the skills of interpersonal communication discussed in this text. Consider the kinds of communication patterns that would help you communicate power in friendship, romantic, family, and workplace relationships.

---

## Referent Power

You have *referent power* (item 1 in the self-test) over others when they wish to be like you or to be identified with you. For example, an older brother may have power over a younger

brother because the younger brother wants to be like the older one. The assumption made by the younger brother is that he will be more like his older brother if he behaves and believes as his brother does. Once he decides to do so, it takes little effort for the older brother to exert influence or power over the younger. Referent power depends greatly on attractiveness and prestige; as they increase, so does identification and, consequently, power. When you are well liked and well respected, are of the same gender as the other person, and have the same attitudes and experiences as the other person, your referent power is especially great. One study found that in the United States supervisors who had referent power were especially effective in handling subordinates, but that in Bulgaria it was legitimate power (the type discussed next) that was associated with such effectiveness—a finding that underscores the cultural dimension of power (Rahim, Antonioni, Krumov, & Ilieva, 2000).

## Legitimate Power

You have *legitimate power* (item 2) over others when they believe you have the right, by virtue of your position, to influence or control their behavior. Legitimate power stems from our belief that certain people should have power over us, that they have a right to influence us because of who they are. Legitimate power usually derives from the roles people occupy. Teachers are often perceived to have legitimate power, and this is doubly true for religious teachers. Parents are seen as having legitimate power over their children. Employers, judges, managers, doctors, and police officers are others who hold legitimate power in different areas.

## Expert Power

You have *expert power* (item 3) over others when they see you as having expertise or knowledge. Your knowledge—as seen by others—gives you expert power. Usually expert power is subject specific. For example, when you're ill, you're influenced by the recommendation of someone with expert power related to your illness—say, a doctor. But you would not be influenced by the recommendation of someone to whom you don't attribute illness-related expert power—say, the mail carrier or a plumber. You give the lawyer expert power in matters of law and psychiatrists expert power in matters of the mind, but ideally you don't interchange them.

Your expert power increases when you're seen as unbiased and as having nothing to gain personally from influencing others. It decreases when you're seen as biased or as having something to gain from influencing others.

## Information or Persuasion Power

You have *information or persuasion power* (item 4) over others when they see you as having the ability to communicate logically and persuasively. If others believe that you have persuasive ability, then you have **persuasion** power—the power to influence others' attitudes and behavior. If you're seen as possessing significant information and the ability to use that information in presenting a well-reasoned argument, then you have information power.

## Reward and Coercive Powers

You have *reward power* (item 5) over others if you have the ability to reward them. Rewards may be material (money, corner office, jewelry) or social (love, friendship, respect). If you're able to grant others some kind of reward, you have control over them to the extent that they want what you can give them. The degree of power you have is directly related to the desirability of the reward as seen by others. Teachers have reward power over students because they control grades, letters of recommendation, social approval, and so on. Students, in turn, have reward power over teachers because they control social approval, student evaluations of faculty, and various other rewards. Parents control rewards for children—food, television privileges, rights to the car, curfew times, and the like—and thus possess reward power.

You have *coercive power* (item 6) over others when you have the ability to administer punishments or remove rewards if others fail to yield to your influence. Usually, if you have reward power, you also have coercive power. Teachers not only may reward with high grades, favorable letters of recommendation, and social approval but also may punish with low grades, unfavorable letters, and social disapproval. Parents may deny as well as grant privileges to their children, and hence they possess coercive as well as reward power.

The strength of coercive power depends on two factors: the magnitude of the punishment that can be administered and the likelihood that it will be administered as a result of noncompliance. When threatened by mild punishment or by punishment you think will not be administered, you're not as likely to do as directed as you would if the threatened punishment were severe and highly likely to be administered.

Reward and coercive power are opposite sides of a coin, and the consequences of using them are quite different. First, if you have reward power, you're likely to be seen as more attractive. People like those who have the power to reward them and who do in fact reward them. Coercive power, on the other hand, decreases attractiveness; people dislike those who have the power to punish them or who threaten them with punishment, whether they actually follow through or not.

Second, when you use rewards to exert power, you don't incur the same costs as when you use punishment. When you exert reward power, you're dealing with a contented and happy individual. When you use coercive punishments, however, you must be prepared to incur anger and hostility, which may well be turned against you in the future.

**VIEWPOINT**

Wielding coercive and legitimate powers has a negative impact when supervisors exercise these powers on subordinates in business settings (Richmond et al., 1984). Research also shows that students who see their teacher exercising coercive and legitimate power learn less effectively and have more negative attitudes toward the course, the course content, and the teacher. Further, students are less likely to take similar courses and are less likely to perform the behaviors taught in the course (Richmond & McCroskey, 1984; Kearney et al., 1984, 1985). On the basis of your own experience and in view of the research presented here, what suggestions would you make to your average college instructor?

Third, when you give a reward, it signals that you effectively exercised power and that you gained the compliance of the other person. You give the reward because the person did as you wanted. In the exercise of coercive power, however, the reverse is true. When you administer punishment, it shows that you have been ineffective in using the threat of coercive power and that there has been no compliance.

Fourth, when you exert coercive power, other bases of power frequently are diminished. There seems to be a boomerang effect in operation. People who exercise coercive power are seen as possessing less expert, legitimate, and referent power. Alternatively, when reward power is exerted, other bases of power increase.

People rarely utilize only one base of power to influence others; usually, multiple power bases are used in concert. For example, if you possess expert power, it's likely that you also possess information power and perhaps legitimate power as well. If you want to control the behavior of another person, you will probably use all three bases of power rather than relying on only one. As you can appreciate, certain individuals have numerous power bases at their disposal, whereas others seem to have few to none. This point brings us back to our first principle: Some people are more powerful than others.

Also, recognize that attempts to influence others may backfire. At times, negative power operates. Each of the six power bases may, at times, have this negative influence. For example, negative referent power is evident when a son rejects his father and wants to be his exact opposite. Negative coercive power may be seen when a child is warned against doing something under threat of punishment and then does exactly what he or she was told not to do; the threat of punishment may have made the forbidden behavior seem exciting or challenging.

##  COMMUNICATING POWER

You can communicate power much as you communicate any other message. Here we consider how you can communicate power through speaking, nonverbal communication, and listening; we'll also look at suggestions for gaining and resisting compliance and for empowering others.

### Speaking Power

The ways in which powerfulness and powerlessness are communicated through speech have received lots of research attention (Molloy, 1981; Kleinke, 1986; Johnson, 1987; Dillard & Marshall, 2003). Generally, research finds that men use more powerful language forms than do women (Lakoff, 1975; Timmerman, 2002). As you consider the major characteristics of powerful and powerless speech presented below, think of your own speech.

Do you avoid the following powerless forms of speech?

❶ Hesitations; for example, "I *er* want to say that *ah* this one is *er* the best, *you know?*" (Hesitations make you sound unprepared and uncertain.)
❷ Too many intensifiers; for example, *"Really,* this was *the greatest;* it was *truly phenomenal."* (Too many intensifiers make everything sound the same and don't allow you to intensify what should be emphasized.)
❸ Disqualifiers; for example, *"I didn't read the entire article,* but . . ." or *"I didn't actually see the accident,* but. . . ." (Disqualifiers signal a lack of competence and a feeling of uncertainty.)
❹ Tag questions; for example, "That was a great movie, *wasn't it?*" "She's brilliant, *don't you think?*" (Tag questions ask for another's agreement and therefore may signal your need for agreement and your own uncertainty.)
❺ Self-critical statements; for example, *"I'm not very good at this"* or *"This is my first public speech."* (Self-critical statements signal a lack of confidence and may make public your own inadequacies.)
❻ **Slang** and vulgar expressions; for example, "##!!!///****!" *"No problem!"* (Slang and vulgarity signal low social class and hence little power.)

### Nonverbal Power

Much nonverbal research has focused on the factors related to your ability to persuade and influence others (Burgoon, Buller, & Woodall, 1995). For example, clothing and other artifactual symbols of authority help people to influence others. Research shows you will be more easily influenced by someone in, for example, a respected uniform than in civilian clothes.

Affirmative nodding, facial expressions, and gestures help you express your concern for the other person and for the interaction and help you establish your charisma, an essential component of credibility. Self-manipulations (playing with your hair or touching your face, for example) and backward leaning will damage your persuasiveness.

Here are some popular suggestions for communicating power nonverbally in a business situation, most of which come from Lewis (1989). As you read this list, try to provide specific examples of these suggestions and how they might work in business, at home, or at school.

■ Be sure to respond in kind to another's eyebrow flash (raising the eyebrow as a way of acknowledging another person).
■ Avoid adaptors—self, other, and object—especially when you wish to communicate confidence and control.

- Use consistent packaging; be especially careful that your verbal and nonverbal messages don't contradict each other.
- When sitting, select chairs you can get in and out of easily; avoid deep plush chairs that you will sink into and will have trouble getting out of.
- To communicate confidence with your handshake, exert more pressure than usual and hold the grip a bit longer than normal.
- Other things being equal, dress relatively conservatively if you want to influence others; conservative clothing is usually associated with power and status. Trendy and fad clothing usually communicates a lack of power and status.
- Use facial expressions and gestures as appropriate; these help you express your concern for the other person as well as your comfort and control of the communication situation.
- Walk slowly and deliberately. To appear hurried is to appear as without power, as if you were rushing to meet the expectations of another person who had power over you.
- Maintain eye contact. People who maintain eye contact are judged to be more at ease and less afraid to engage in meaningful interaction than those who avoid eye contact. (Be aware, however, that in some contexts, if you use excessive or protracted direct eye contact, you may be seen as exercising coercive power; Aquinis & Henle, 2001.) When you break eye contact, direct your gaze downward; otherwise you'll communicate a lack of interest in the other person.
- Avoid vocalized pauses—the "ers" and "ahs" that frequently punctuate conversations when you're not quite sure of what to say next.

**A s k Yourself**
Gaining Recognition

In your weekly meetings at work, the supervisor who serves as group leader consistently ignores your cues that you want to say something; also, when you do manage to say something, no one seems to react or take special note of your comments. You're determined to change this situation. **Ask yourself:** What can you do to turn things around?

# Understanding Interpersonal Skills

## INTERACTION MANAGEMENT

The term **interaction management** refers to the techniques and strategies by which you regulate and carry on an interpersonal interaction. Effective interaction management results in an interaction that's satisfying to both parties. Neither person feels ignored or on stage; each contributes to, benefits from, and enjoys the interpersonal exchange.

**Managing Communication Interactions.** Of course, this entire text is devoted to the effective management of interpersonal interactions. Here, however, are a few specific suggestions.

- Maintain your role as speaker or listener and pass the opportunity to speak back and forth—through appropriate eye movements, vocal expressions, and body and facial gestures.
- Keep the conversation fluent, avoiding long and awkward **pauses.** For example, it's been found that patients are less satisfied with their interaction with their doctor when the silences between their comments and the doctor's responses are overly long (Rowland-Morin & Carroll, 1990).
- Communicate with verbal and nonverbal messages that are consistent and reinforce each other. Avoid sending **mixed messages** or contradictory signals—for example, a nonverbal message that contradicts the verbal message.

■ Maintain reasonably close distances between yourself and those with whom you interact. If the distance is too far, you may be seen as fearful or uninvolved. If the distance is too close, you may be seen as pushy or overly aggressive.

## Listening Power

Much as you can communicate power and authority through words and through nonverbal expression, you also communicate power through listening. Throughout your listening, you're communicating messages to others, and these messages comment in some way on your power.

Powerful listeners listen actively. They focus and concentrate (with no real effort) on what is being said, especially on what people say they want or need (Fisher, 1995). Listen to phrases such as "I want," "It would help if I had," or "I'm looking for." Too, respond to what others have said. For example, preface comments with "In light of what you said about," or "If you feel strongly about." Powerless listeners, on the other hand, listen passively, appear to be thinking about something else and only pretend to listen, and rarely refer to what the other person has said when they do respond.

Powerful listeners respond visibly but in moderation; an occasional nod of agreement or a facial expression that says "that's interesting" are usually sufficient. Responding with too little or too much reaction is likely to be perceived as powerless. Too little response says you aren't listening, and too much response says you aren't listening critically. Powerful listeners also use back-channeling cues—head nods and brief oral responses that say "I'm listening, I'm following you"—when appropriate. When no back-channeling cues are given, the speaker comes to wonder if the other person is really listening.

Powerful listeners maintain more focused eye contact than do those seen to have less power. In conversation, normal eye contact is intermittent—you glance at the speaker's face, then away, then back again, and so on. In a small group or public speaking situation, eye contact with the speaker is normally greater.

Adaptors—playing with your hair or a pencil—give the appearance of discomfort. Because of this, adaptors communicate a lack of power. These body movements show the listener to be more concerned with himself or herself than with the speaker. The absence of adaptors, on the other hand, makes the listener appear in control of the situation and comfortable in the role of listener.

Powerful listeners are more likely to maintain an open posture. When around a table or in an audience, they resist covering their abdomen or face with their hands. Persons who maintain a defensive posture with, for example, arms crossed may communicate a feeling of vulnerability and hence powerlessness.

Powerful listeners avoid interrupting the speaker in conversations or in small group situations. The reason is simple: Not interrupting is one of the rules of business communication that powerful people follow and powerless people don't. Completing the speaker's thoughts (or what the listener thinks is the speaker's thought) conveys a similar impression of powerlessness.

You also can signal power through visual dominance behavior (Exline, Ellyson, & Long, 1975), as mentioned in the discussion of eye communication in Chapter 8. For example, the average speaker maintains a high level of eye contact while listening and a lower level while speaking. When powerful individuals want to signal dominance, they may reverse this pattern. They may, for example, maintain a high level of eye contact while talking but a much lower level while listening.

## Compliance Gaining and Compliance Resisting

The use of compliance strategies clearly illustrates the way that power is exercised. **Compliance-gaining strategies** are tactics aimed at influencing others to do what you want them to do. **Compliance-resisting strategies** are tactics that enable you to say no and to resist another person's attempts to influence you.

## ACHIEVING POWER

**?** How can I become powerful at work without appearing power hungry? Are there more subtle ways to express and gain power in the workplace? Any suggestions?

Powerful people often never show it. Instead, they simply act powerful. How do they do that? First, sound confident. Not pushy, but confident. Talk using reasonably intense language, striking metaphors, and vivid details, with a voice that is neither meek nor boisterous. Second, "own" the room. Stroll into meetings and reach out to others, make suggestions without hesitation. Sit where everyone can see you. Enter meetings with something for people to react to. Even if they change your suggestions, you still have framed the meeting. Third, look powerful—dress a bit better than others. Fourth, be better prepared than others. Know what you want to say and marshal good support for what you communicate. Create the agenda. Fifth, influence informally. Persuade face-to-face and one-on-one. Be the master of the "presell." Get buy-in before any formal meeting. Sixth, seek out crises; they are where you get discovered. Seventh, build alliances—make ideas "our" ideas rather than "my" idea.

**For further information** see Dale Carnegie, *How to Win Friends and Influence People,* ed. Arthur R. Pell (New York: Simon & Schuster, 1936/1982); Robert Cialdini, *Influence: The Psychology of Persuasion* (New York: William Morrow, 1993); and Robert Cialdini, *Influence: Science and Practice,* 4th ed. (Boston: Allyn & Bacon, 2000).

John Daly (Ph.D., Purdue University) is the Liddell Professor of Communication & Management at the University of Texas. He teaches and studies interpersonal communication and advocacy and has worked with numerous corporations on topics related to influence.

**Compliance-Gaining Strategies**    Sixteen compliance-gaining strategies are presented in Table 14.1. In reviewing these strategies, keep in mind that compliance gaining, like all interpersonal processes, involves two people in a transaction. Reading down the list may give the impression that these strategies are one-way affairs, with one person using the strategy and the other person complying. Actually, compliance gaining is best viewed as a transactional, back-and-forth process. Conflict, compromise, renegotiation of the goal, rejection of the strategy, and a host of other responses—in addition to simple compliance—are possible.

**Compliance-Resisting Strategies**    Let's say that someone you know asks you to do something you don't want to do, such as lend your term paper so this person can copy it and turn it in to another teacher. Research with college students shows that there are four principal ways of responding (McLaughlin, Cody, & Robey, 1980; O'Hair, Cody, & O'Hair, 1991).

In *identity management,* you resist by trying to manipulate the image of the person making the request. You might do this negatively or positively. In negative identity management, you might portray the person as unreasonable or unfair and say, for example, "That's really unfair of you to ask me to compromise my ethics." Or you might tell the person that it hurts that he or she would even think you would do such a thing.

You might also use positive identity management. Here you resist complying by making the other person feel good about himself or herself. For example, you might say, "You know this material much better than I do; you can easily do a much better paper yourself."

> **A s k Yourself**
> **Asking for a Date**
>
> You decide to ask the most popular person on campus for a date; the worst that could happen, you figure, is that you'll be rejected. Ask yourself: What options do you have for asking for this date? Consider, for example, the types of dates you might propose, the channels for communicating your desire for a date, and the actual messages you'd use in asking for a date. What option would you be most likely to select?

## ⏷ TABLE 14.1
## Compliance-Gaining Strategies

As you read this table, realize that these strategies and the responses to them depend both on the personalities of the individuals and on their unique relationships. Which strategies you use, which strategies will work for you, and which strategies will backfire all depend on who you are, who the other person is, and the interpersonal relationship between you. These compliance-gaining strategies come from the research of Marwell and Schmitt (1967, 1990; also see Miller & Parks, 1982; Dillard, 1990; Dillard, Anderson, & Knobloch, 2002).

| Compliance Strategy | Example |
| --- | --- |
| **Pregiving.** Pat rewards Chris and then requests compliance. | **Pat:** I'm glad you enjoyed dinner. How about going back to my place for a nightcap and whatever? |
| **Liking.** Pat is friendly in order to get Chris in a good mood so that Chris will comply with Pat's request. | **Pat:** (After giving Chris a back rub) I'd really like to relax and bowl a few games with Terry. Okay? |
| **Promise.** Pat promises to reward Chris if Chris complies with Pat's request. | **Pat:** I'll give you anything you want if you will just give me a divorce; just give me my freedom. |
| **Threat.** Pat threatens to punish Chris for noncompliance. | **Pat:** If you don't give me a divorce, you'll never see the kids again. |
| **Aversive stimulation.** Pat punishes Chris, making cessation contingent on compliance. | **Pat:** (Screams and cries and stops only when Chris complies.) |
| **Positive expertise.** Pat promises rewards for compliance because of "the nature of things." | **Pat:** If you follow the doctor's advice, you'll be fine. |
| **Negative expertise.** Pat promises punishment for noncompliance because of "the nature of things." | **Pat:** If you don't listen to the doctor, you're going to wind up back in the hospital. |
| **Positive self-feelings.** Pat promises that Chris will feel better if Chris complies with Pat's request. | **Pat:** You'll see. You'll be a lot better off without me; you'll feel better after the divorce. |
| **Negative self-feelings.** Pat promises that Chris will feel worse if Chris does not comply with Pat's request. | **Pat:** You'll hate yourself if you don't give me this divorce. |
| **Positive altercasting.** Pat argues that Chris should comply because a good person would comply. | **Pat:** Any intelligent person would grant their partner a divorce when the relationship has died. |
| **Negative altercasting.** Pat argues that Chris should comply because only a bad person would not comply. | **Pat:** Only a cruel and selfish neurotic could stand in the way of another's happiness. |
| **Positive esteem.** Pat tells Chris that people will think more highly of Chris if Chris complies with Pat's request. | **Pat:** Everyone will respect your decision to place your parents in an assisted living community. |
| **Negative esteem.** Pat tells Chris that people will think poorly of Chris if Chris does not comply with Pat's request. | **Pat:** Everyone will think that you're paranoid if you don't join the club. |
| **Moral appeals.** Pat argues that Chris should comply because it's moral to comply and immoral not to comply. | **Pat:** Any ethical person would return the mistaken overpayment. |
| **Altruism.** Pat asks Chris to comply because Pat needs this compliance (relying on Chris's desire to help). | **Pat:** I would feel so disappointed if you quit college now. Don't hurt me by quitting. |
| **Debt.** Pat asks Chris to comply because of the past favors given to Chris. | **Pat:** Look at how we sacrificed to send you to college. |

Another way to resist compliance is to use *nonnegotiation,* a direct refusal to do as asked. You might simply say, "No, I don't lend my papers out."

In *negotiation,* you resist compliance by, for example, offering a compromise ("I'll let you read my paper but not copy it") or by offering to help the person in some other way ("If you write a first draft, I'll go over it and try to make some comments"). If the request is a romantic one—for example, a request to go away for a ski weekend—you might resist by discussing your feelings and proposing an alternative: For example, "Let's double date first."

# Ethics in Interpersonal Communication

## THE ETHICS OF COMPLIANCE-GAINING STRATEGIES

The list of compliance-gaining strategies in a Table 14.1 describes a variety of techniques that people often use in their efforts to influence others. But is it ethical to use these approaches? For example, is it ethical to threaten another person? Is it ethical to make the person feel guilty by recalling the past favors you did for him or her and implying that there is a debt owed you? Is it ethical to imply that the person's image or self-esteem will be adversely affected if he or she doesn't comply with your request? Review the selected strategies in Table 14.1 and indicate the ethical implications of each strategy.

### What would you do?

Because you've fallen behind schedule, you need your colleague's help to complete your current project on time. Would it be ethical to give your colleague an expensive watch she's been wanting a few days before you ask for her help? You figure that if she accepts the watch, she'll find it difficult to refuse your request to help with your project. What would you do in this situation?

---

Another way to resist compliance is through *justification*. Here you justify your refusal by citing possible consequences of compliance or noncompliance. For example, you might cite a negative consequence if you complied ("I'm afraid that I'd get caught, and then I'd fail the course"). Or you might cite a positive consequence of not complying ("You'll really enjoy writing this paper; it's a lot of fun").

Remember that compliance gaining and resisting—like all forms of interpersonal communication—are transactional processes in which all elements are interdependent; each element influences each other. Your attempts to gain compliance, for example, will be influenced by the responses of the person you wish to influence. These responses in turn will influence your responses, and so on. Also, just as your relationship (its type, length, and degree of intimacy, for example) will influence the strategies you use, so the strategies you use will influence your relationship. Inappropriate strategies will have negative effects, just as positive strategies will have positive effects.

## Empowering Others

Empowerment involves helping others (your relational partner, an employee, another student, a sibling) to gain increased control over themselves and their environment. Empowerment is not just an altruistic gesture on the part of one relationship partner or of management; for many, it is a basic philosophy. The reason empowerment is so much discussed and so much a part of modern business practices is that it provides lots of benefits. Empowered people are more likely to take a more personal interest in the job or in the relationship. Empowered people will be proactive; they will act and not just react. They're more likely to take on decision-making responsibilities, are willing to take risks, and are willing to take responsibility for their actions—all attributes that make relationships and business exciting. In an interpersonal relationship (though the same would apply to a multinational organization), two empowered partners are more likely to effectively meet the challenges and difficulties most relationships will encounter.

In empowering others, try to raise their self-esteem. Resist faultfinding: It doesn't really benefit the faultfinder and certainly doesn't benefit the other person. Faultfinding disempowers others. Any criticism that is offered should be constructive. Be willing to offer your perspective—to lend an ear to a first-try singing effort or to read a new poem. Also, avoid verbal aggressiveness and abusiveness. Resist the temptation to win an argument with unfair tactics, tactics that are going to hurt the other person.

Be open, positive, empathic, and supportive and treat the other person with an equality of respect. These, of course, are among the qualities of effectiveness that are identified in the Understanding Interpersonal Skills boxes throughout this book. Similarly, be attentive and listen actively. Attentiveness and active listening tell the other person that he or she is important. After all, what greater praise could you pay than to give another person your time and energy?

Share skills and share decision making. Be willing to relinquish control and allow the other person the freedom to make decisions. Encourage growth in all forms, academic and relational. Growth, like empowerment, is not something that a relationship has a limited supply of and that has to be parceled out. Both persons can grow and develop, and both persons can be empowered. The growth and empowerment of one person enhances the growth and power of the other.

Empowering others is especially important when you are talking with people who are shy or high in communication apprehension. Here are some suggestions based largely on the insights of shyness and apprehension researchers (Carducci & Zimbardo, 1995; Richmond & McCroskey, 1998).

- Don't overprotect the shy person, especially the shy child. If you constantly rush to a child's aid every time he or she experiences social anxiety, the child will never learn how to cope with it. Instead, be supportive (indirectly). Nudge, instead of push, the child (or the adult) to try out new communication situations. In this way you can help the shy person to interact in small doses and eventually to develop the self-confidence needed for more extended interaction.

- Demonstrate your understanding and empathy for shy individuals. Practice active listening, should you sense they wish to discuss their anxiety and shyness. Don't minimize their fear of communication situations as people with little apprehension often do.

- Avoid making shy people the center of attention. That is exactly what they don't want. And never make their shyness the topic of a group conversation. Saying, "Oh James; he's so bright, but he's so shy" only makes it more difficult for James even to open his mouth. At the same time, make sure that you give the shy person opportunities to speak and that you don't monopolize the conversation. For example, ask the person's opinion and, when appropriate, try to steer the conversation in the direction of the shy person's expertise and area of competence.

# Reviewing    Key Terms and Concepts of Power in Interpersonal Relationships

This chapter discussed the importance of power in interpersonal relationships, emphasizing the nature of power and its principles, its types, and the ways to communicate power.

## Principles of Power

What is power? What principles govern the operation of power in interpersonal relationships?

- Some people are more powerful than others; some are born to power, others learn it.
- Power can be increased or decreased; power is never static.
- Power follows the principle of less interest; generally, the less interest, the greater the power.

- Power has a cultural dimension; power is distributed differently in different cultures.
- Power is often used unfairly, as in sexual harassment and power plays.

## Types of Power

What types of power can one person have over another?

- *Referent:* B wants to be like A.
- *Legitimate:* B believes that A has a right to influence or control B's behavior.
- *Expert:* B regards A as having knowledge.

- *Information or persuasion:* B attributes to A the ability to communicate effectively.
- *Reward:* A has the ability to reward B.
- *Coercive:* A has the ability to punish B.

## Communicating Power

How can you communicate power?

- *Speaking power* includes, for example, avoiding hesitations, disqualifiers, and self-critical statements.
- *Nonverbal power* includes avoiding adaptors, using consistent packaging, and avoiding excessive movements.
- *Listening power* includes responding visibly, maintaining eye contact and an open posture, and avoiding interrupting.

- *Compliance-gaining and compliance-resisting tactics* enable you to influence others to do as you want or enable you to resist the influence attempts of others. Compliance-gaining tactics include expressing liking, making promises, and threatening. Compliance-resisting tactics include using identity management and negotiation.
- *Empowering* others enables them to gain power and control over themselves and over the environment. Empowering others has numerous advantages; for example, empowered people are more proactive and more responsible. Empowering others involves such strategies as being positive, avoiding verbal aggressiveness and abusiveness, and encouraging growth, and it is especially helpful and most often greatly appreciated in cases of shyness or high communication apprehension.

## Applying Key Terms and Concepts of Power in Interpersonal Relationships

**1** How satisfied are you with your command of each of the six bases of power? What might you do to increase those bases with which you're not satisfied?

**2** How would you evaluate your own speaking, nonverbal, and listening power? What might you do to increase your power in these areas?

**3** How would you use compliance-gaining strategies to influence someone to go on a date with you? How would you use compliance-resisting strategies to resist someone's persistent attempts to have you go on a date?

**4** How is interpersonal power illustrated on prime-time television? For example: (1) Do male and female characters wield the same types of power? (2) Do the story lines in sitcoms and dramas reward the exercise of some types of power and punish the exercise of other types? (3) How do these programs deal with the process of empowering others? Is it rewarded? Are men and women portrayed as empowering in the same way?

**5** Using a cooperative strategy in responding to the power plays of others is clearly the recommended strategy, at least usually. But are there situations in which it might be more useful to ignore the power play? In what types of interactions do you think ignoring might be used effectively? What reasons might you give for using such a strategy?

**6** In each of the following three dyads, there is a power difference. One person is significantly richer, of higher status, more educated, or more attractive than the other. How might the power differences create communication difficulties when the individuals are engaged (1) in informal conversation and (2) in romantic encounters?

- a young nurse and the chief of surgery at a prestigious hospital
- an uneducated parent and the high school principal
- two coworkers, one extremely attractive and one extremely unattractive

## Experiencing Key Terms and Concepts of Power in Interpersonal Relationships

Go to www.ablongman.com/devito.

*These experiences focus on interpersonal power, its nature, and how it can be dealt with.*

❶ **Dyadic Power** looks at selected dyads and asks you to identify the types of power that exist between them. ❷ **Empowering Others** offers scenarios in which you may effectively elect to empower other people. ❸ **Power Plays** presents situations in which power plays are used and provides the opportunity to develop and discuss strategies for dealing with them. ❹ Your beliefs about how easily other people can be manipulated are explored in the discussion and self-test of **Machiavellianism**. ❺ A discussion of the **Knowledge Gap** explores the relationship between knowledge and power.

# Glossaries

# Glossary of Interpersonal Communication Concepts

**acculturation.** The process by which your culture is modified or changed through contact with or exposure to another culture.

**active listening.** The process by which a listener expresses his or her understanding of the speaker's total message, including the verbal and nonverbal communication, the thoughts, and the feelings.

**adaptors.** Nonverbal behaviors that, when engaged in either in private or in public, serve some kind of need and occur in their entirety—for example, scratching your head until the itch is relieved.

**adjustment.** In verbal and nonverbal communications, the extent to which communicators share the same system of signals; this sharing makes effective communication possible.

**affect displays.** Movements of the facial area that convey emotional meaning such as anger, fear, or surprise.

**affinity-seeking strategies.** Behaviors designed to increase interpersonal attractiveness.

**affirmation.** The communication of support and approval.

**ageism.** Discrimination or prejudice based on age.

**aggression.** *See* **verbal aggression.**

**allness.** The illogical assumption that all can be known or said about a given person, issue, object, or event.

**alter-adaptors.** Body movements you make in response to your current interactions; for example, crossing your arms over your chest when someone unpleasant approaches or moving closer to someone you like.

**altercasting.** Placing the speaker in a specific role for a specific purpose and asking that he or she assume the perspective of this specific role; for example, "As a professor of communication, what would you say is . . . ?"

**ambiguity.** The condition in which a message may be interpreted as having more than one meaning.

**apprehension.** *See* **communication apprehension.**

**argumentativeness.** Willingness to argue for your point of view, to speak your mind. Distinguished from **verbal aggressiveness.**

**assertiveness.** A willingness to stand up for your rights but with respect for the rights of others.

**assimilation.** A process of message distortion in which messages are reworked to conform to your own attitudes, prejudices, needs, and values. *See also* **cultural assimilation.**

**attention.** The process of responding to a stimulus or stimuli; usually some consciousness of responding is implied.

**attitude.** A predisposition to respond for or against an object, person, or position.

**attraction.** The process by which one individual is emotionally drawn to another and finds that person satisfying to be with.

**attraction theory.** The theory that people develop relationships on the basis of attractiveness, proximity, and similarity.

**attractiveness.** Degree of physical appeal and/or pleasantness in personality.

**attribution.** The process of assigning causation or motivation to a person's behavior.

**attribution theory.** A theory concerned with the process of assigning causation or motivation to a person's behavior.

**avoidance.** An unproductive **interpersonal conflict** strategy in which a person takes mental or physical flight from the actual conflict.

**back-channeling cues.** Responses that a listener makes to a speaker while the speaker is speaking but which do not ask for the speaking role; for example, interjections such as "I understand" or "You said what?"

**barriers to intercultural communication.** Physical or psychological factors that prevent or hinder effective communication.

**behavioral synchrony.** Similarity in the behavior, usually nonverbal (such as postural stance or facial expressions), of two persons; generally taken as an indicator of liking.

**belief.** Confidence in the existence or truth of something; conviction.

**beltlining.** An unproductive **interpersonal conflict** strategy in which one person hits at a psychological or emotional level at which the other person cannot withstand the blow.

**blame.** An unproductive **interpersonal conflict** strategy in which we attribute the cause of the conflict to the other person or devote our energies to discovering who is the cause and avoid talking about the issues causing the conflict.

**boundary marker.** A **marker** that divides one person's territory from another's—for example, a fence.

**brainstorming.** An idea-generating group activity in which participants try to produce as many ideas as possible by following four basic rules: Strive for quantity, avoid negative evaluation, suggest ideas as wild as possible, and combine ideas that are generated.

**breadth.** In **social penetration theory,** the number of topics about which individuals in a relationship communicate.

**captology.** The study of the persuasive power of computer communication.

**censorship.** Restrictions imposed on people's right to produce, distribute, or receive various communications.

**central marker.** A **marker** or item that is placed in a territory to reserve it for a specific person—for example, a sweater thrown over a library chair to signal that the chair is taken.

**certainty.** An attitude of closed-mindedness that creates defensiveness among communicators. *Opposed to* **provisionalism.**

**channel.** The vehicle or medium through which signals are sent; for example, the vocal–auditory channel.

**cherishing behaviors.** Small behaviors we enjoy receiving from others, especially from our relational partner—for example, a kiss before the partner leaves for work.

**chronemics.** The study of the communicative nature of time, how a person's or culture's treatment of time reveals something about the person or culture; often divided into psychological and cultural time.

**civil inattention.** Polite ignoring of others (after a brief sign of awareness) so as not to invade their privacy.

**cliché.** An expression whose overuse calls attention to itself.

**closed-mindedness.** An unwillingness to receive certain communication messages.

**code.** A set of symbols used to translate a message from one form to another.

**collectivist culture.** A culture in which the group's goals rather than the individual's are given greater importance and in which, for example, benevolence, tradition, and conformity are given special emphasis. *Opposed to* **individualist culture.**

**color communication.** The use of color to communicate different meanings; each culture seems to define the meanings colors communicate somewhat differently.

**communication.** (1) The process or act of communicating; (2) the actual message or messages sent and received; (3) the study of the processes involved in the sending and receiving of messages.

**communication apprehension.** Fear or anxiety about communicating; usually identified as either trait apprehension (apprehensiveness in all communication situations) or state apprehension (apprehensiveness in specific communication situations).

**communicology.** The study of communication, particularly the subsection concerned with human communication.

**competence.** In **interpersonal communication,** knowledge about communication and the ability to engage in communication effectively. "Language competence" is a speaker's ability to use the language; it is a knowledge of the elements and rules of the language.

**complementarity.** A principle of **attraction** holding that you are attracted to people whose qualities you do not possess or you wish to possess, and to people who are opposite or different from yourself. *Opposed to* **similarity.**

**complementary relationship.** A relationship in which the behavior of one person serves as the stimulus for the complementary behavior of the other; in complementary relationships, behavioral differences are maximized.

**compliance-gaining strategies.** Behaviors designed to gain the agreement of others, to influence or persuade others to do as you wish.

**compliance-resisting strategies.** Behaviors directed at resisting the persuasive attempts of others.

**computer-mediated communication.** Communication between two or more people that takes place through a computer; for example, e-mail or instant messaging.

**confidence.** A quality of interpersonal effectiveness; a comfortable, at-ease feeling in interpersonal communication situations.

**confirmation.** A communication pattern that acknowledges another person's presence and indicates an acceptance of this person, this person's definition of self, and the relationship as defined or viewed by this person. *Opposed to* **rejection** and **disconfirmation.**

**conflict.** A disagreement or difference of opinion; a form of competition in which one person tries to bring a rival to surrender; a situation in which one person's behaviors are directed at preventing something or at interfering with or harming another individual. *See also* **interpersonal conflict.**

**congruence.** A condition in which both verbal and nonverbal behaviors reinforce each other.

**connotation.** The feeling or emotional aspect of meaning, generally viewed as consisting of the evaluative (for example, good–bad), potency (strong–weak), and activity (fast–slow) dimensions. *Opposed to* **denotation.**

**consistency.** A process that influences you to maintain balance in your perceptions of messages or people; a process that causes you to see what you expect to see and to be uncomfortable when your perceptions run contrary to expectations.

**contact.** The first stage in **relationship development;** consists of "perceptual contact" (you see or hear the person) and "interactional contact" (you talk with the person).

**content and relationship dimensions.** Two aspects to which messages may refer: the world external to both speaker and listener (content) and the connections existing between the individuals who are interacting (relationship).

**context.** The physical, psychological, social, and temporal environment in which communication takes place.

**conversation.** Two-person communication that usually follows five stages: opening, feedforward, business, feedback, and closing.

**conversational management.** The management of the way in which messages are exchanged in **conversation.**

**conversational maxims.** Principles that are followed in **conversation** to ensure that the goal of the conversation is achieved.

**conversational turns.** The process of passing the speaker and listener roles during conversation.

**cooperation.** An interpersonal process by which individuals work together for a common end; the pooling of efforts to produce a mutually desired outcome. In conversation, an implicit agreement between speaker and listener to work together for mutual comprehension.

**critical thinking.** The process of logically evaluating reasons and evidence and reaching a judgment on the basis of this analysis.

**cultural assimilation.** The process by which a person's culture is given up and he or she takes on the values and beliefs of another culture; as when, for example, an immigrant gives up his or her native culture to become a member of the new adopted culture.

**cultural display.** Signs that communicate a person's cultural identification, such as clothing or religious jewelry.

**cultural display rules.** Rules that identify what are and what are not appropriate forms of expression for members of the culture.

**cultural rules.** Standards and customs that are specific to a given culture.

**cultural time.** The meanings given to the ways time is treated in a particular culture.

**culture shock.** The reactions we experience at being in a culture very different from our own or from what we are used to.

**date.** An **extensional device** used to emphasize the notion of constant change and symbolized by a subscript: for example, John Smith$_{2000}$ is not John Smith$_{2006}$.

**decoder.** Something that takes a message in one form (for example, sound waves) and translates it into another form (for example, nerve impulses) from which meaning can be formulated. In human communication the decoder is the auditory mechanism; in electronic communication the decoder is, for example, the telephone earpiece. *Decoding* is the process of extracting a message from a code—for example, translating speech sounds into nerve impulses. *See also* **encoder.**

**defensiveness.** An attitude of an individual or an atmosphere in a group characterized by threats, fear, and domination; messages evidencing evaluation, control, strategy, neutrality, superiority, and certainty are thought to lead to defensiveness. *Opposed to* **supportiveness.**

**denial.** Process by which you ignore or refuse to acknowledge your emotions to yourself or to others; one of the obstacles to the expression of emotion.

**denotation.** The objective or descriptive meaning of a word; the meaning you'd find in a dictionary. *Opposed to* **connotation.**

**depenetration.** A condition in which the **breadth** and **depth** of a relationship decrease.

**depth.** In **social penetration theory,** the degree to which the inner personality—the inner core of an individual—is penetrated in interpersonal interaction.

**determinism.** The principle of verbal interaction that holds that all verbalizations are to some extent purposeful, that there is a reason for every verbalization.

**dialogue.** A form of **communication** in which each person is both speaker and listener; communication characterized by involvement, concern, and respect for the other person. *Opposed to* **monologue.**

**direct speech.** Speech in which the speaker's intentions are stated clearly and directly.

**disclaimer.** Statement that asks the listener to receive what you say without its reflecting negatively on you.

**disconfirmation.** Process by which a person ignores or denies the right of another individual even to define himself or herself. *Opposed to* **rejection** and **confirmation.**

**downward communication.** Communication from the higher levels of a hierarchy to the lower levels—for example, messages sent by managers to workers or from deans to faculty members.

**dyadic coalition.** A two-person group formed from some larger group to achieve a particular goal.

**dyadic communication.** Two-person communication.

**dyadic consciousness.** An awareness on the part of the participants that an interpersonal relationship or pairing exists between them; distinguished from situations in which two individuals are together but do not see themselves as a unit or twosome.

**dyadic effect.** The tendency for the behaviors of one person to stimulate similar behaviors in the other interactant; often used to refer to the tendency for one person's self-disclosures to prompt the other also to self-disclose.

**dyadic primacy.** The significance or centrality of the two-person group, even when there are many more people interacting.

**ear marker.** A **marker** that identifies an item as belonging to a specific person—for example, a nameplate on a desk or initials on an attaché case.

**effect.** The outcome or consequence of an action or behavior; communication is assumed always to have some effect.

**emblems.** Nonverbal behaviors that directly translate words or phrases—for example, the signs for "OK" and "peace."

**emotions.** The feelings we have—for example, our feelings of guilt, anger, or love.

**emotional communication.** The expression of feelings—for example, feelings of guilt, happiness, or sorrow.

**emotional contagion.** The idea that the emotions of one person are often transferred to another person, much as a contagious disease is transmitted from one person to another.

**empathy.** The ability to feel another person's feeling; feeling or perceiving something as does another person.

**encoder.** Something that takes a message in one form (for example, nerve impulses) and translates it into another form (for example, sound waves). In human communication the encoder is the speaking mechanism; in electronic communication the encoder is, for example, the telephone mouthpiece. *Encoding* is the process of putting a message into a code—for example, translating nerve impulses into speech sounds. *See also* **decoder.**

**enculturation.** The process by which culture is transmitted from one generation to another.

**E-prime.** A form of the language that omits the verb *to be* except when it is used as an auxiliary or in statements of existence.

**equality.** An attitude that recognizes that each individual in a communication interaction is equal, that no one is superior to any other; encourages supportiveness. *Opposed to* **superiority.**

**equilibrium theory.** A theory of **proxemics** holding that intimacy and physical closeness are positively related; as a relationship becomes more intimate, the individuals will maintain shorter distances between themselves.

**equity theory.** A theory claming that you experience relational satisfaction when there is an equal distribution of rewards and costs between the two persons in the relationship.

**etc.** An **extensional device** used to emphasize the notion of infinite complexity; because you can never know all about anything, any statement about the world or an event must end with an explicit or implicit "et cetera."

**ethics.** The branch of philosophy that deals with the rightness or wrongness of actions; the study of moral values; in communication, the morality of message behavior.

**ethnocentrism.** The tendency to see others and their behaviors through our own cultural filters, often as distortions of our own behaviors; the tendency to evaluate the values and beliefs of our own culture more positively than those of other cultures.

**euphemism.** A polite word or phrase used to substitute for some taboo or less polite term or phrase.

**evaluating.** Judging or placing a value on some person, object, or event.

**excuse.** An explanation designed to lessen the negative consequences of something done or said.

**expectancy violations theory.** A theory of **proxemics** holding that people have certain expectations about space relationships. When an expectation is violated (say, a person stands too close to you or a romantic partner maintains abnormally large distances from you), the relationship comes into clearer focus and you wonder why this "normal distance" is being violated.

**experiential limitation.** The limit on an individual's ability to communicate that is set by the nature and extent of that individual's experiences.

**expressiveness.** A quality of interpersonal effectiveness; genuine involvement in speaking and listening, conveyed verbally and nonverbally.

**extensional devices.** Linguistic devices proposed by Alfred Korzybski to make language a more accurate means for talking about the world. The extensional devices include **etc., date,** and **index.**

**extensional orientation.** A tendency to give primary consideration to the world of experience and only secondary consideration to labels. *Opposed to* **intensional orientation.**

**facial feedback hypothesis.** The hypothesis or theory that your facial expressions can produce physiological and emotional effects.

**facial management techniques.** Techniques used to mask certain emotions and to emphasize others; for example, intensifying your expression of happiness to make a friend feel good about a promotion.

**fact–inference confusion.** A misevaluation in which a person makes an inference, regards it as a fact, and acts on it as if it were a fact.

**factual statement.** A statement made by the observer after observation and limited to what is observed. *Opposed to* **inferential statement.**

**family.** A group of people who consider themselves related and connected to one another and among whom the actions of one member have consequences for others.

**feedback.** Information that is given back to the source. Feedback may come from the source's own messages (as when you hear what you're saying) or from the receiver(s) in forms such as applause, yawning, puzzled looks, questions, letters to the editor of a newspaper, increased or decreased subscriptions to a magazine. *See also* **negative feedback, positive feedback.**

**feedforward.** Information that is sent before a regular message, telling the listener something about what is to follow; a message that is prefatory to a more central message.

**feminine culture.** A culture in which both men and women are encouraged to be modest, oriented to maintaining the quality of life, and tender. Feminine cultures emphasize the quality of life and so socialize their people to be modest and to emphasize close interpersonal relationships. *Opposed to* **masculine culture.**

**flexibility.** The ability to adjust communication strategies and skills on the basis of the unique situation.

**force.** An unproductive **conflict** strategy in which you try to win an argument by physically or emotionally overpowering the other person, either by threat or by actual behavior.

**friendship.** An interpersonal relationship between two persons that is mutually productive, established and maintained through perceived mutual free choice, and characterized by mutual positive regard.

**fundamental attribution error.** In **attributions** of causality, the tendency to overvalue and give too much weight to the contribution of internal factors (the person's personality) and to undervalue and give too little weight to the contribution of external factors (the situation the person is in or the surrounding events).

**gender display rules.** Cultural rules that identify what are and what are not appropriate forms of expression for males and for females.

**General Semantics.** The study of the relationships among language, thought, and behavior.

**gossip.** Oral or written communication about someone not present, some third party, usually about matters that are private to this third party.

**grapevine messages.** Messages that do not follow any formal organizational structures; gossip related to a workplace or other community.

**gunnysacking.** An unproductive **conflict** strategy of storing up grievances—as if in a gunnysack—and holding them in readiness to dump on the opponent.

**halo effect.** The tendency to generalize a person's virtue or expertise from one area to other areas.

**haptics.** Technical term for the study of touch or **tactile communication.**

**heterosexist language.** Language that denigrates lesbians and gay men.

**high-context culture.** A culture in which much of the information in communication messages is left implied; it's "understood." Meaning is considered to be in the context or in the person rather than explicitly coded in the verbal messages. **Collectivist cultures** are generally high context. *Opposed to* **low-context culture.**

**home field advantage.** The increased power that comes from being in your own territory.

**home territories.** Territories for which individuals have a sense of intimacy and over which they exercise control—for example, a teacher's office.

**illustrators.** Nonverbal behaviors that accompany and literally illustrate verbal messages—for example, upward movements of the head and hand that accompany the verbal "It's up there."

**I-messages.** Messages in which you accept responsibility for your personal thoughts and behaviors; messages in which you state your point of view explicitly. *Opposed to* **you-messages.**

**immediacy.** A quality of interpersonal effectiveness; a sense of contact and togetherness; a feeling that the speaker has an interest in and a liking for the other person.

**implicit personality theory.** A theory of personality, complete with rules about what characteristics go with what other characteristics, that you maintain and through which you perceive others.

**inclusion.** Principle of verbal interaction holding that all members should be a part of (included in) the interaction.

**index.** An **extensional device** used to emphasize the assumption that no two things are the same and symbolized by a subscript—for example, even though two people may both be politicians, $politician1_{1[Smith]}$ is not $politician_{2[Jones]}$.

**indirect speech.** Speech that hides the speaker's true intentions; speech in which requests and observations are made indirectly.

**indiscrimination.** A misevaluation caused by categorizing people, events, or objects into a particular class and responding to them only as members of the class; a failure to recognize that each individual is unique.

**individualist culture.** A culture that gives greater importance to the individual's than to the group's goals and preferences. *Opposed to* **collectivist culture.**

**inevitability.** A principle of communication holding that communication cannot be avoided; all behavior in an interactional setting is communication.

**inferential statement.** A statement that can be made by anyone, is not limited to what is observed, and can be made at any time. *See also* **factual statement.**

**informal time terms.** Terms that express approximate rather than exact amounts of time; for example, "soon," "early," and "in a while."

**information overload.** A condition in which the amount or complexity of information is too great to be dealt with effectively by an individual, group, or organization.

**in-group talk.** Talk about a subject or in a vocabulary that some people present understand and others do not; has the effect of excluding those who don't understand.

**insulation.** A reaction to **territorial encroachment** in which you erect some sort of barrier between yourself and the would-be invaders; for example, a stone wall around your property, an unlisted phone number, or caller ID.

**intensional orientation.** A tendency to give primary consideration to the way things are labeled and only secondary consideration (if any) to the world of experience. *Opposed to* **extensional orientation.**

**interaction management.** A quality of interpersonal effectiveness in which the interaction is controlled and managed to the satisfaction of both parties; aspects of interaction management include effective management of conversational turns, fluency, and message consistency.

**intercultural communication.** Communication that takes place between persons of different cultures or between persons who have different cultural beliefs, values, or ways of behaving.

**interpersonal communication.** Communication between two persons or among a small group of persons, as distinguished from public or mass communication; communication of a personal nature, as distinguished from impersonal communication; communication between or among connected persons or those involved in a close relationship.

**interpersonal conflict.** A disagreement between two connected persons.

**interpersonal effectiveness.** The ability to accomplish interpersonal goals; interpersonal communication that is satisfying to both individuals.

**interpersonal perception.** The processes through which you become aware of, interpret, and evaluate people and their behavior.

**intimacy.** The closest interpersonal relationship; usually, the term denotes a close primary relationship.

**intimacy claims.** Obligations persons incur by virtue of being in a close and intimate relationship.

**intimate distance.** The closest distance in **proxemics**, ranging from touching to 18 inches.

**intrapersonal communication.** Communication with yourself.

**involvement.** The second stage in **relationship development,** in which you further advance the relationship, first testing each other and then intensifying your interaction.

**irreversibility.** A principle of communication holding that communication cannot be reversed; once something has been communicated, it cannot be uncommunicated.

**jargon.** The technical language of any specialized group, often a professional class, which is unintelligible to individuals not belonging to the group; shop talk. This glossary is an example of the jargon of a part of the communication field.

**Johari window.** A diagram of the four selves (open, blind, hidden, and unknown). The term *Johari* comes from the first names of Joseph Luft and Harry Ingham, who developed the model.

**kinesics.** The study of the communicative dimensions of facial and bodily movements.

**language.** The rules of syntax, semantics, and phonology by which sentences are created and understood; the name of any given language refers to the sentences that can be created in that language, such as English, Bantu, or Italian.

**language relativity.** See **linguistic relativity hypothesis.**

**lateral communication.** Communication between equals—manager to manager, worker to worker.

**leave-taking cues.** Verbal and nonverbal signals that indicate a person's desire to terminate a conversation.

**leveling.** A process of message distortion in which the number of details in a message is reduced as the message gets repeated from one person to another.

**linguistic relativity.** The theory or hypothesis that the language you speak influences your perceptions of the world and your behaviors and that therefore people speaking widely differing languages will perceive and behave differently as a result of the language differences.

**listening.** An active process of receiving aural stimuli consisting of five stages: receiving, understanding, remembering, evaluating, and responding.

**love.** An interpersonal relationship in which you feel closeness, caring, warmth, and excitement in relation to another person.

**low-context culture.** A culture in which most of the information in communication is explicitly stated in the verbal message rather than being left implied or assumed to be "understood." Low-context cultures are usually **individualist cultures.** *Opposed to* **high-context culture.**

**manner maxim.** A principle of **conversation** that holds that speakers cooperate by being clear and by organizing their thoughts into some meaningful and coherent pattern.

**markers.** Devices that signify that a certain territory belongs to a particular person. *See also* **boundary marker, central marker,** and **ear marker.**

**masculine culture.** A culture in which men are viewed as assertive, oriented to material success, and strong; women on the other hand are viewed as modest, focused on the quality of life, and tender. Masculine cultures emphasize success and so socialize their people to be assertive, ambitious, and competitive. *Opposed to* **feminine culture.**

**matching hypothesis.** The proposition that you date and mate people who are similar to yourself—who match you—in degree of physical attractiveness.

**meaningfulness.** A principle of **perception** that assumes that the behavior of people is sensible, stems from some logical antecedent, and is therefore meaningful rather than meaningless.

**mentoring relationship.** A relationship in which an experienced individual helps to train a less experienced person; for example, an accomplished teacher might mentor a younger teacher who has newly arrived or has never taught before.

**mere exposure hypothesis.** The theory that repeated or prolonged exposure to a stimulus may result in a change in attitude toward the stimulus object, generally in the direction of increased positiveness.

**message.** Any signal or combination of signals that serves as a **stimulus** for a receiver.

**metacommunication.** Communication about communication.

**metalanguage.** Language that refers to language.

**metamessage.** A message that makes reference to another message. For example, remarks such as "Did I make myself clear?" or "That's a lie" are metamessages, because they refer to other messages.

**mindfulness and mindlessness.** States of relative awareness. In a mindful state, you are aware of the logic and rationality of your behaviors and the logical connections existing among elements. In a mindless state, you're unaware of this logic and rationality.

**mixed message.** A message that communicates two different and often contradictory meanings; for example, a message that asks for two different (often incompatible) responses, such as "Leave me alone" combined with "Show me more attention." Often one meaning (usually the socially acceptable meaning) is communicated verbally and the other (usually the less socially acceptable meaning) nonverbally.

**model.** A representation of an object or process.

**monochronic time orientation.** A view of time in which things are done sequentially; one thing is scheduled at a time. *Opposed to* **polychronic time orientation.**

**monologue.** A form of **communication** in which one person speaks and the other listens; there's no real interaction among participants. *Opposed to* **dialogue.**

**negative feedback.** Feedback that serves a corrective function by informing the source that his or her message is not being received in the way intended. Looks of boredom, shouts of disagreement, letters critical of newspaper policy, and teachers' instructions on how better to approach a problem are examples of negative feedback that should (ideally) serve to redirect the speaker's behavior. *See also* **positive feedback.**

**networking.** Connecting with people who can help you accomplish a goal or help you find information related to your goal; for example, talking with many friends and other contacts when looking for a job.

**neutrality.** A response pattern lacking in personal involvement; encourages defensiveness. *Opposed to* **empathy.**

**noise.** Anything that interferes with your receiving a message as the source intended the message to be received. Noise is present in communication to the extent that the message received is not the message sent.

**nonallness.** The understanding that you can never know all about anything and that what you know, say, or hear is only a part of what there is to know, say, or hear.

**nonnegotiation.** An unproductive **conflict** strategy in which one individual refuses to discuss the conflict or to listen to the other person.

**nonverbal communication.** Communication without words; communication by means of space, gestures, facial expressions, touching, vocal variation, and silence, for example.

**nonverbal dominance.** Nonverbal behavior that allows one person to achieve psychological dominance over another.

**object-adaptors.** Movements that involve your manipulation of some object; for example, punching holes in a styrofoam coffee cup, clicking a ballpoint pen, or chewing on a pencil.

**object language.** Language used to communicate about objects, events, and relations in the world (rather than about words as in **metalanguage**).

**olfactory communication.** Communication by smell.

**openness.** A quality of interpersonal effectiveness encompassing (1) your willingness to interact openly with others, to self-disclose as appropriate; (2) your willingness to react honestly to incoming stimuli; and (3) your willingness to own your own feelings and thoughts.

**opinion.** A tentative conclusion concerning some object, person, or event.

**other-orientation.** A quality of interpersonal effectiveness involving attentiveness, interest, and concern for the other person.

**other-talk.** Talk about the listener or some third party. *Opposed to* **self-talk.**

**outing.** The process whereby a person's affectional orientation is made public by another person without the consent of the gay man or lesbian.

**overattribution.** The tendency to attribute a great deal or even everything a person does to one or two characteristics.

**owning feelings.** The process by which you take responsibility for your own feelings instead of attributing them to others.

**paralanguage.** The vocal but nonverbal aspect of speech. Paralanguage consists of voice qualities (for example, pitch range, resonance, tempo); vocal characterizers (laughing or crying, yelling or whispering); vocal qualifiers (intensity, pitch height); and vocal segregates ("uh-uh," meaning "no," or "sh" meaning "silence").

**passive listening.** **Listening** that may be attentive and supportive but that occurs without the listener's talking or directing the speaker in any nonverbal way; also (used negatively), inattentive and uninvolved listening.

**pauses.** Silent periods in the normally fluent stream of speech. Pauses are of two types: filled or vocalized pauses (interruptions in speech that are filled with such vocalizations as "er" or "um") and unfilled pauses (silences of unusually long duration).

**perception.** The process by which you become aware of objects, events, and people through your senses.

**perception checking.** The process of verifying your understanding of some message, situation, or feeling.

**perceptual accentuation.** A process that leads you to see what you expect or want to see—for example, the tendency to see people you like as better looking and smarter than people you don't like.

**personal distance.** The second closest distance in **proxemics,** ranging from 18 inches to 4 feet.

**personal rejection.** An unproductive **conflict** strategy in which one person withholds love and affection and seeks to win the argument by getting the other person to break down under this withdrawal.

**persuasion.** The process of influencing attitudes and behavior.

**phatic communication.** Communication that is primarily social; communication designed to open the channels of communication rather than to communicate something about the external world. "Hello" and "How are you?" in everyday interaction are examples.

**pitch.** The highness or lowness of the vocal tone.

**polarization.** A form of fallacious reasoning by which only two extremes are considered; also referred to as "black-or-white" and "either/or" thinking or as a two-valued orientation.

**politeness.** Behavior that most people in a given culture would consider to represent "good manners"; may include consideration, respect, modesty, etc.

**polychronic time orientation.** A view of time in which several things may be scheduled or engaged in at the same time. *Opposed to* **monochronic time orientation.**

**positive feedback.** Feedback that supports or reinforces the continuation of behavior along the same lines in which it is already proceeding, as when applause during a speech encourages the speaker to continue speaking this way. *See also* **negative feedback.**

**positiveness.** A characteristic of effective communication involving positive attitudes toward oneself, toward the interpersonal interaction, and toward expressing these attitudes to others (as in complimenting) along with acceptance and approval.

**power.** The ability to influence or control the behavior of another person; an inevitable part of interpersonal relationships.

**power play.** A consistent pattern of behavior in which one person tries to control the behavior of another.

**pragmatic implication.** An assumption that is logical (and therefore appears true) but is actually not necessarily true.

**pragmatics.** In interpersonal communication, an approach that focuses on communication behaviors and effects and on communication effectiveness.

**primacy–recency.** Phenomenon in interpersonal perception whereby we give more importance to that which occurs first (primacy) or to that which occurs last or most recently (recency).

**primary affect displays.** The communication of the six primary emotions: happiness, surprise, fear, anger, sadness, and disgust/contempt.

**primary relationship.** The relationship between two people that they consider their most (or one of their most) important; for example, the relationship between husband and wife or domestic partners.

**primary territory.** Areas that you consider your exclusive preserve—for example, your room or office.

**process.** Ongoing activity; communication is referred to as a process to emphasize that it's always changing, always in motion.

**projection.** A psychological process whereby you attribute characteristics or feelings of your own to others; often, the process whereby you attribute your faults to others.

**pronouncements.** Statements that are made to sound authoritative and that therefore imply that the speaker is in a position of authority and that the listener is in a childlike or learner role.

**protection theory.** A theory of **proxemics** holding that people establish a body buffer zone to protect themselves from unwanted closeness, touching, or attack.

**provisionalism.** An attitude of open-mindedness that leads to the development of a supportive relationship and atmosphere. *Opposed to* **certainty.**

**proxemics.** The study of the communicative function of space; the study of how people unconsciously structure spaces such as the distances between people in their interactions, the layouts of homes and offices, and even the design of cities.

**proximity.** Physical closeness—one of the qualities influencing interpersonal **attraction.** Also, as a principle of **perception,** the tendency to perceive people or events that are physically close as belonging together or representing some unit.

**psychological time.** Your emphasis on or orientation toward past, present, or future time.

**public distance.** The farthest distance in **proxemics,** ranging from 12 feet to more than 25 feet.

**public territory.** Areas that are open to all people—for example, restaurants or parks.

**punctuation.** The breaking up of continuous communication sequences into short sequences with identifiable beginnings and endings or stimuli and responses.

**pupil dilation.** The extent to which the pupil of the eye is expanded; generally, large pupils indicate positive emotional arousal.

**pupillometrics.** The study of communication through changes in the size of the pupils of the eyes.

**Pygmalion effect.** The condition in which you make a prediction of success, act as if the prediction were true, and thereby make it come true (for example, acting toward students as if they'll be successful influences them to become successful); a type of **self-fulfilling prophecy.**

**quality maxim.** A principle of **conversation** that holds that speakers cooperate by saying what they think is true and by not saying what they think is false.

**quantity maxim.** A principle of **conversation** that holds that speakers cooperate by being only as informative as necessary to communicate their intended meanings.

**racist language.** Language that denigrates, demeans, or is derogatory toward members of a particular race or ethnic group.

**rate.** The speed with which you speak, generally measured in words per minute.

**receiver.** Any person or thing that takes in messages. Receivers may be individuals listening to or reading a message, a group of persons hearing a speech, a scattered television audience, or machines that store information.

**reconciliation strategies.** Behaviors designed to repair a broken relationship.

**regulators.** Nonverbal behaviors that regulate, monitor, or control the communications of another person.

**rejection.** A response to an individual that acknowledges the other person but expresses disagreement. *Opposed to* **confirmation** and **disconfirmation.**

**relation maxim.** A principle of **cooperation** in **conversation** that holds that speakers communicate by talking about what is relevant and by not talking about what isn't.

**relationship communication.** Communication between or among intimates or those in close relationships; the term is used by some theorists as synonymous with interpersonal communication.

**relationship deterioration.** The stage of a relationship during which the connecting bonds between the partners weaken and the partners begin drifting apart.

**relationship development.** The progress of an interpersonal relationship, which takes place over a series of six stages.

**relationship dialectics theory.** A theory that describes relationships in terms of the tensions between pairs of opposite, competing desires or motivations, such as the desire for autonomy and the desire to belong to someone, desires for novelty and for predictability, and desires for closedness and for openness.

**relationship dissolution.** The termination or end of an interpersonal relationship.

**relationship maintenance.** Behaviors that help to continue and preserve a relationship; also, a stage of relationship stability in which the relationship does not progress or deteriorate significantly; a continuation as opposed to a dissolution (or an intensification) of a relationship.

**relationship messages.** Messages that comment on the relationship between the speakers rather than on matters external to them.

**relationship repair.** A relationship stage in which one or both parties seek to improve a deteriorating relationship.

**resemblance.** As a principle of **perception,** the tendency to perceive people or events that are similar in appearance as belonging together.

**response.** Any bit of overt or covert behavior.

**role.** The part an individual plays in a group; an individual's function or expected behavior.

**rules theory.** A theory that describes relationships as interactions governed by series of rules that couples agree to follow. When the rules are followed, a relationship is maintained; when they are broken, the relationship experiences difficulty.

**schemata** (singular: schema). Ways of organizing perceptions; mental templates or structures that help you organize the millions of items of information you come into contact with every day as well as those you already have in memory. Examples are general ideas about people (e.g., about Pat and Chris, Japanese, Baptists, or New Yorkers); about yourself (your qualities, abilities, and even liabilities); or about social roles (the characteristics of a police officer, professor, or multimillionaire CEO).

**script.** A type of **schema;** an organized body of information about some action, event, or procedure. A script is a general idea of how some event should play out or unfold, of the rules governing the events and their sequence.

**secondary territory.** Areas that do not belong to you but that you've occupied and which are therefore associated with you—for example, the seat you normally take in class.

**selective exposure.** Tendency of listeners to actively seek out information that supports their opinions and to actively avoid information that contradicts their existing opinions, beliefs, attitudes, and values.

**self-acceptance.** Being satisfied with yourself, your virtues and vices, your abilities and limitations.

**self-adaptors.** Movements that usually satisfy a physical need, generally serving to make you more comfortable; for example, scratching your head to relieve an itch, moistening your lips because they feel dry, or pushing your hair out of your eyes.

**self-attribution.** A process through which you seek to account for and understand the reasons and motivations for your own behaviors.

**self-awareness.** The degree to which you know yourself.

**self-concept.** Your self-image, the view you have of who you are.

**self-disclosure.** The process of revealing something about yourself to another—usually, revealing information that you'd normally keep hidden.

**self-esteem.** The value you place on yourself; your self-evaluation. Usually refers to the positive value people place on themselves.

**self-fulfilling prophecy.** Situation in which you make a prediction or prophecy and by making it cause it to come true. For example, expecting a person to be hostile, you act in a hostile manner toward this person and in so doing elicit hostile behavior in the person, thus confirming your prophecy.

**self-monitoring.** Manipulating the image you present to others in interpersonal interactions so as to give the most favorable impression of yourself.

**self-serving bias.** A bias that operates in the self-attribution process, leading people to take credit for the positive consequences and to deny responsibility for the negative consequences of their behaviors.

**self-talk.** Talk about yourself. *Opposed to* **other-talk.**

**semantics.** The area of language study concerned with meaning.

**sexist language.** Language derogatory to members of one gender, generally women.

**sexual harassment.** Unsolicited and unwanted verbal or nonverbal sexual messages.

**shyness.** Discomfort and uneasiness in interpersonal situations.

**signal-to-noise ratio.** A measure of what is meaningful (signal) versus what is interference (noise) relative to the participants and the context of an interaction.

**silence.** The absence of vocal communication; often misunderstood to refer to the absence of communication.

**silencers.** Unproductive **conflict** strategies (such as crying) that literally silence your opponent.

**similarity.** A principle of **attraction** holding that you're attracted to qualities similar to those you yourself possess and to people who are similar to yourself. *Opposed to* **complementarity.**

**slang.** Language used by special groups that the general society does not consider proper or standard.

**social comparison processes.** The processes by which you compare yourself (for example, your abilities, opinions, and values) with others and then assess and evaluate yourself on the basis of the comparison; one of the sources of **self-concept.**

**social distance.** The third farthest distance in **proxemics,** ranging from 4 feet to 12 feet; the distance at which business is usually conducted.

**social exchange theory.** A theory hypothesizing that you develop profitable relationships (those in which your rewards are greater than your costs) and that you avoid or terminate unprofitable relationships (those in which your costs exceed your rewards).

**social penetration theory.** A theory concerned with relationship development from the superficial to the intimate levels (**depth**) and from few to many areas of interpersonal interaction (**breadth**). *See also* **depenetration.**

**source.** Any person or thing that creates messages; for example, an individual speaking, writing, or gesturing or a computer solving a problem.

**speech.** Messages conveyed via a vocal–auditory channel.

**spontaneity.** The communication pattern in which you say what you're thinking without attempting to develop strategies for control; encourages **supportiveness.** *Opposed to* **strategy.**

**stability.** Principle of **perception** holding that your perceptions of things and of people tend to be relatively consistent with your previous conceptions.

**static evaluation.** An orientation that fails to recognize that the world is constantly changing; an attitude that sees people and events as fixed rather than as ever changing.

**status.** The relative level each person occupies in a hierarchy; status always involves a comparison, and thus one person's status is only relative to the status of another. In the United States occupation, financial position, age, and educational level are significant determinants of social status.

**stereotype.** In communication, a fixed impression of a group of people through which we then perceive specific individuals; stereotypes are most often negative ("Martians are stupid, uneducated, and dirty") but also may be positive ("Venusians are scientific, industrious, and helpful").

**stimulus.** Any external or internal change that impinges on or arouses an organism.

**stimulus–response models of communication.** Models of communication that assume that the process of communication is linear, beginning with a stimulus that then leads to a response.

**strategy.** The use of some plan for control of other members of a communication interaction; often encourages **defensiveness.** *Opposed to* **spontaneity.**

**subjectivity.** Principle of **perception** holding that your perceptions are not objective but are influenced by your wants and needs, your expectations and predictions.

**superiority.** A point of view or attitude that assumes that others are not equal to yourself; encourages **defensiveness.** *Opposed to* **equality.**

**supportiveness.** In communication, behavior that is descriptive rather than evaluative and provisional rather than certain; also, an attitude of an individual or an atmosphere in a group that is characterized by openness, absence of fear, and a genuine feeling of equality. *Opposed to* **defensiveness.**

**symmetrical relationship.** A relation between two or more persons in which one person's behavior serves as a stimulus for the same type of behavior in the other person(s); for example, a relationship in which anger in one person encourages anger in another person or in which a critical comment by one person leads the other person to respond in kind.

**taboo.** Forbidden; culturally censored. Taboo language is language that is frowned upon by polite society. Topics and specific words may be considered taboo—for example, death, sex, certain forms of illness, and various words denoting sexual activities and excretory functions.

**tactile communication.** Communication by touch; communication received by the skin.

**temporal communication.** The messages communicated by your time orientation and treatment of time.

**territorial encroachment.** The trespassing on, use of, or appropriation of one person's territory by another.

**territoriality.** A possessive or ownership reaction to an area of space or to particular objects.

**theory.** A general statement or principle applicable to various related phenomena.

**touch.** *See* **tactile communication.**

**touch avoidance.** The tendency to avoid touching and being touched by others.

**transactional perspective.** A point of view that sees communication as an ongoing process in which all elements are interdependent and influence one another.

**uncertainty reduction theory.** Applied to interpersonal relationships, theory holding that as relationships develop, uncertainty is reduced; relationship development is seen as a process through which individuals reduce their uncertainty about each other.

**universal of interpersonal communication.** A feature of communication common to all interpersonal communication acts.

**unproductive conflict strategies.** Ways of engaging in conflict that generally prove counterproductive, including **avoidance, force, blame, silencers, gunnysacking,** and **beltlining.**

**upward communication.** Communication sent from the lower levels of a hierarchy to the upper levels—for example, from line worker to manager or from faculty member to dean.

**value.** Relative worth of something; a quality that makes something desirable or undesirable; ideals or customs about which we have emotional responses, whether positive or negative.

**verbal aggressiveness.** An unproductive **conflict** strategy in which one person tries to win an argument by attacking the other person's **self-concept.**

**visual dominance.** The use of your eyes to maintain a superior or dominant position; for example, when making an especially important point, you might look intently at the other person.

**volume.** The relative loudness of the voice.

**you-messages.** Messages in which you deny responsibility for your own thoughts and behaviors; messages that attribute your **perception** to another person; messages of blame. *Opposed to* **I-messages.**

# Glossary of Interpersonal Communication Skills

**abstractions.** Use both abstract and specific terms when describing or explaining.

**accommodation.** Accommodate to the speaking style of your listeners in moderation. Too much mirroring of the other's style may appear manipulative.

**active and inactive listening.** Be an active listener: Paraphrase the speaker's meaning, express understanding of the speaker's feelings, and ask questions when necessary.

**active interpersonal conflict.** Engage in interpersonal conflict actively; be appropriately revealing, and listen to your partner.

**advantages and disadvantages of relationships.** In evaluating, entering, or dissolving relationships, consider both the advantages and the disadvantages.

**allness.** Avoid allness statements; they invariably misstate the reality and will often offend the other person.

**analyzing your perceptions.** Increase accuracy in interpersonal perception by identifying the influence of your physical and emotional states and making sure that you're not drawing conclusions from too little information.

**anger management.** Calm down as best you can; then consider your communication options and the relevant communication skills for expressing your feelings.

**appreciating cultural differences.** Look at cultural differences not as deviations or deficiencies but as the differences they are. Recognizing different ways of doing things, however, does not necessarily mean accepting them.

**appropriateness of self-disclosure.** When thinking of disclosing, consider the legitimacy of your motives, the appropriateness of the disclosure, the listener's responses (is the dyadic effect operating?), and the potential burdens such disclosures might impose.

**argumentativeness.** Avoid aggressiveness (attacking the other person's self-concept); instead, focus logically on the issues, emphasize finding solutions, and work to ensure that what is said will result in positive self-feelings for both individuals.

**artifactual communication.** Use artifacts (for example, color, clothing, body adornment, space decoration) to communicate desired messages.

**body movements.** Use body and hand gestures to reinforce your communication purposes.

**channel.** Assess your channel options (for example, face-to-face, e-mail, leaving a voice-mail message) before communicating important messages.

**checking perceptions.** Increase accuracy in perception by (1) describing what you see or hear and the meaning you assign to it and (2) asking the other person if your perceptions are accurate.

**communicating assertively.** Describe the problem, say how the problem affects you, propose solutions, confirm your understanding, and reflect on your own assertiveness.

**communicating power.** Avoid powerless message forms such as hesitations, excessive intensifiers, disqualifiers, tag questions, one-word answers, self-critical statements, overly polite statements, and vulgar and slang expressions.

**communication apprehension management.** To reduce anxiety acquire necessary communication skills and experiences, focus on prior successes, reduce unpredictability, and put apprehension in perspective.

**communication options.** In light of the inevitability, irreversibility, and unrepeatability of messages, assess your communication options before communicating.

**confirmation.** When you wish to be confirming, acknowledge (verbally and/or nonverbally) others in your group and their contributions.

**conflict styles.** Choose your conflict style carefully; each style has consequences. In relationship conflict, look for win–win solutions rather than solutions in which one person wins and the other loses.

**conflict, culture, and gender.** Approach conflict with an understanding of the cultural and gender differences in attitudes toward what constitutes conflict and toward how it should be pursued.

**connotative meanings.** Clarify your connotative meanings if you have any doubts that your listeners might misunderstand you; as a listener, ask questions if you have doubts about the speaker's connotations.

**content and relationship.** Listen to both the content and the relationship aspects of messages, distinguish between them, and respond to both.

**content and relationship conflicts.** Analyze conflict messages in terms of content and relationship dimensions, and respond to each accordingly.

**context adjustment.** Adjust your messages to the physical, cultural, social–psychological, and temporal context.

**conversational maxims.** Follow (generally) the basic maxims of conversation, such as the maxims of quantity, quality, relations, manner, and politeness.

**conversational rules.** Observe the general rules for conversation (for example, keeping speaking turns relatively short and avoiding interrupting), but break them when there seems logical reason to do so.

**conversational turns.** Maintain relatively short conversational turns; after taking your turn, pass the speaker's turn to another person nonverbally or verbally.

**cultural differences in listening.** Be especially flexible when listening in a multicultural setting, realizing that people from other cultures give different listening cues and may operate with different rules for listening.

**cultural identifiers.** Use cultural identifiers that are sensitive to the desires of others; when appropriate, make clear the cultural identifiers you prefer.

**cultural influences.** Communicate with an understanding that culture influences communication in all its forms.

**cultural influences on interpersonal relationships.** Be aware that culture exerts influences on all types of relationships, encouraging some and discouraging others.

**cultural sensitivity.** Increase your cultural sensitivity by learning about different cultures, recognizing and facing your fears, recognizing relevant differences, and becoming conscious of the cultural rules of other cultures.

**culture and perception.** Increase accuracy in perception by learning as much as you can about the cultures of those with whom you interact.

**dating statements.** Date your statements to avoid thinking of the world as static and unchanging. Reflect the inevitability of change in your messages.

**deciding to self-disclose.** Consider the potential benefits (for example, self-knowledge, increased communication effectiveness, and physiological health) as well as the potential personal, relationship, and professional risks.

**disclaimers.** Use disclaimers if you feel you might be misunderstood. But avoid them when they're not necessary; too many disclaimers can make you appear unprepared or unwilling to state an opinion.

**disconfirming language.** Avoid sexist, heterosexist, racist, and ageist language, which is disconfirming and insulting and invariably creates communication barriers.

**emotional communication.** Communicate emotions effectively: (1) Describe feelings, (2) identify the reasons for the feelings, (3) anchor feelings to the present, and (4) own your feelings and messages.

**emotional display.** Express emotions and interpret the emotions of others in light of the cultural rules dictating what is and what isn't "appropriate."

**emotionality in interpersonal communication.** Recognize the inevitable emotionality in your thoughts and feelings, and include emotion as appropriate in your verbal and nonverbal messages.

**emotional understanding.** Identify and describe emotions (both positive and negative) clearly and specifically. Learn the vocabulary of emotional expression.

**empathic and objective listening.** Punctuate the interaction from the speaker's point of view, engage in dialogue, and seek to understand the speaker's thoughts and feelings.

**empathic conflict.** Engage in conflict with empathy rather than blame. Also, express this empathy ("I can understand how you must have felt").

**empathy.** Communicate empathy when appropriate: Resist evaluating the person, focus on the person, express active involvement through facial expressions and gestures, reflect back the feelings you think are being expressed, self-disclose, and address mixed messages.

**ethnocentric thinking.** Recognize your own ethnocentric thinking and be aware of how it influences your verbal and nonverbal messages.

**evaluating.** Try first to understand fully what the speaker means and then look to identify any biases or self-interests that might lead the speaker to give an unfair presentation.

**expressiveness.** Communicate active involvement by using active listening, addressing mixed messages, using I-messages, and using appropriate variations in paralanguage and gestures.

**eye movements.** Use eye movements to seek feedback, exchange conversational turns, signal the nature of your relationship, or compensate for increased physical distance.

**face-saving strategies.** Use strategies that allow your opponents to save face; avoid beltlining, or hitting opponents with attacks that they will have difficulty absorbing and will resent.

**facial messages.** Use facial expressions to communicate involvement. In listening, look to the facial expressions of others as cues to their emotions and meaning.

**facts and inferences.** Distinguish facts (verifiably true past events) from inferences (guesses or hypotheses), and act on inferences with tentativeness.

**feedback.** Listen to both verbal and nonverbal feedback—from yourself and from others—and use these cues to help you adjust your messages.

**feedforward.** Use feedforward when you feel your listener needs background or when you want to ease into a particular topic, such as bad news.

**flexibility.** Because no two communication situations are identical, because everything is in a state of flux, and because everyone is different, cultivate flexibility and adjust your communication to the unique situation.

**friendships.** Establish friendships to help serve such needs as utility, ego support, stimulation, and security. At the same time, seek to serve your friends' similar needs.

**fundamental attribution error.** Avoid the fundamental attribution error, whereby you attribute someone's behavior solely to internal factors while minimizing or ignoring situational forces.

**gender differences in listening.** Understand that in general, women give more cues that they're listening and appear more supportive in their listening than men.

**giving space.** Give others the space they need. Look to the other person for any signs of spatial discomfort.

**high- and low-context cultures.** Adjust your messages and your listening in light of the differences between high- and low-context cultures.

**I-messages.** Use I-messages when communicating your feelings; take responsibility for your own feelings rather than attributing them to others.

**immediacy.** Maintain immediacy through close physical distances and eye contact and by smiling, using the other person's name, and focusing on the other's remarks.

**implicit personality theory.** Bring your implicit personality theory to your mindful state to subject your perceptions and conclusions to logical analysis.

**increasing assertiveness.** Increase assertiveness by analyzing the assertive messages of others, rehearsing assertive messages, and communicating assertively.

**indirect messages.** Use indirect messages when a more direct style might prove insulting or offensive, but be aware that they may create misunderstanding.

**indiscrimination.** Treat each situation and each person as unique (when possible) even when they're covered by the same label. Index key concepts.

**individualist and collectivist cultures.** Adjust your messages and your listening with an awareness of differences between individualist and collectivist cultures.

**initial impressions.** Guard against drawing impressions too quickly or from too little information and using initial impressions as filters; such filters can prevent you from forming more accurate perceptions on the basis of more information.

**intensional orientation.** Avoid intensional orientation. Look to people and things first and to labels second.

**interaction management.** Speak in relatively short conversational turns, avoid long and/or frequent pauses, and use verbal and nonverbal messages that are consistent.

**intercultural communication.** Become mindful of (1) differences between yourself and people who are culturally different, (2) differences within other cultural groups, and (3) cultural differences in meanings.

**listening to the feelings of others.** Empathize, focus on the other person, and encourage the person to explore his or her feelings.

**making excuses.** Repair conversational problems by offering excuses that demonstrate understanding, acknowledge your responsibility, acknowledge your regret, request forgiveness, and make clear that this will never happen again.

**managing relationship dissolution.** Break the loneliness–depression cycle, take time out, bolster self-esteem, seek support from nourishing others, and avoid repeating negative patterns.

**masculine and feminine cultures.** Adjust your messages and your listening to allow for differences in cultural masculinity and femininity.

**meanings depend on context.** Look at the context for cues as to how you should interpret the meanings of messages.

**meanings in people.** When deciphering meaning, the best source is the person; meanings are in people. When in doubt, find out—from the source.

**message overload.** Combat message overload by using and disposing of messages as they come to you, organizing, getting rid of extra copies, and distinguishing between messages to save and messages to throw away.

**metacommunication.** Metacommunicate when you want to clarify the way you're talking or what you're talking about by, for example, giving clear feedforward and paraphrasing your complex messages.

**mindfulness.** Increase your mindfulness by creating and recreating categories and being open to new information and points of view; also, beware of relying too heavily on first impressions.

**negatives and positives of conflict.** Approach conflict to minimize its negative aspects and to maximize the positive benefits of conflict and its resolution.

**networking.** Establish a network of relationships to provide insights into issues relevant to your personal and professional life, and be willing to lend your expertise to others.

**noise management.** Reduce physical, physiological, psychological, and semantic noise as best you can; use repetition and restatement and, when in doubt, ask if you're clear.

**nonjudgmental and critical listening.** Keep an open mind, avoid filtering out difficult messages, and recognize your own biases. When listening to make judgments, listen extra carefully, ask questions when in doubt, and check your perceptions before criticizing.

**nonverbal communication and culture.** Interpret the nonverbal cues of others with an awareness of the other person's cultural meanings (insofar as you can).

**open expression in conflict.** Try to express your feelings openly rather than resorting to silence or avoidance.

**openness.** Increase openness when appropriate by self-disclosing, responding spontaneously and honestly to those with whom you're interacting, and owning your own feelings and thoughts.

**other orientation.** Acknowledge the importance of the other person: use focused eye contact and appropriate facial expressions; smile, nod, and lean toward the other person.

**overattribution.** Avoid overattribution; rarely is any one factor an accurate explanation of complex human behavior.

**packaging.** Make your verbal and nonverbal messages consistent; inconsistencies often create uncertainty and misunderstanding.

**paralanguage.** Vary paralinguistic features to communicate nuances of meaning and to add interest and color to your messages.

**perceptual shortcuts.** Be mindful of your perceptual shortcuts so that they don't mislead you and result in inaccurate perceptions.

**polarization.** Avoid thinking and talking in extremes by using middle terms and qualifiers. But remember that too many qualifiers may make you appear unsure of yourself.

**positiveness.** Communicate positiveness by expressing your own satisfaction with the interaction and by complimenting others.

**power distance.** Adjust your messages and listening on the basis of the power-distance orientation of the culture in which you find yourself.

**power plays.** Respond to power plays with cooperative strategies: Express your feelings, describe the behavior to which you object, and state a cooperative response.

**present-focus conflict.** Focus your conflict resolution messages on the present; avoid gunnysacking, or dredging up and unloading old grievances.

**problem-solving conflicts.** Deal with interpersonal conflicts systematically as problems to be solved: Define the problem, examine possible solutions, test a solution, evaluate the solution, and accept or reject the solution.

**receiving.** Focus attention on both the verbal and the nonverbal messages; both communicate essential parts of the total meaning.

**reducing uncertainty.** Use passive, active, and interactive strategies to reduce uncertainty.

**relationship messages.** Formulate messages that are appropriate to the stage of the relationship. Also, listen to messages from relationship partners that may reveal differences in perceptions about your relationship stage.

**relationship repair.** Recognize the problem, engage in productive conflict resolution, pose possible solutions, affirm each other, integrate solutions into normal behavior, and take risks as appropriate.

**remembering.** Identify the central ideas, summarize the message in an easier-to-retain form, and repeat ideas (aloud or to yourself) to help you remember.

**responding.** Express support for the speaker using I-messages instead of you-messages.

**responding to others' disclosures.** Listen actively, support the discloser, and keep the disclosures confidential.

**romantic workplace relationships.** Before embarking on romantic relationships at work, be sure you have a clear understanding of the potential problems.

**self-awareness.** Increase self-awareness by listening to others, increasing your open self, and seeking out information to reduce blind spots.

**self-concept.** See yourself, as objectively as you can, through the eyes of others; compare yourself to similar (and admired) others; examine the influences of culture; and observe and evaluate your own message behaviors.

**self-esteem.** Raise your self-esteem: Challenge self-destructive beliefs, seek out nourishing people, work on projects that will result in success, and secure affirmation.

**self-fulfilling prophecy.** Take a second look at your perceptions when they correspond very closely to your initial expectations; the self-fulfilling prophecy may be at work.

**self-serving bias.** Become mindful of giving too much weight to internal factors (when explaining your positives) and too little weight to external factors (when explaining your negatives).

**sexual harassment management.** Talk to the harasser; if this doesn't stop the behavior, then consider collecting evidence, using appropriate channels within the organization, and filing a complaint.

**sexual harassment messages.** Avoid behaviors that are sexual in nature, that might be considered unreasonable, that are severe or pervasive, and that are unwelcome and offensive.

**silence.** Examine silence for meanings just as you would eye movements or body gestures.

**spatial and proxemic conversational distances.** Maintain distances that are comfortable and that are appropriate to the situation and to your relationship with the other person.

**stereotypes.** Focus on the individual rather than on the individual's membership in one group or another.

**supportive conflict.** Engage in conflict using a supportive approach, so as not to create defensiveness; avoid messages that evaluate or control, that are strategic or inappropriately neutral, or that express superiority or certainty.

**surface and depth listening.** Focus on both verbal and nonverbal messages, on both content and relationship messages, and on statements that refer back to the speaker. At the same time, do not avoid the surface or literal meaning.

**talk, not force.** Talk about problems rather than using physical or emotional force.

**time cues.** Be alert for time cues on the part of the person with whom you're interacting. Be especially sensitive to the person's leave-taking cues—remarks such as "It's getting late" or glances at his or her watch.

**touch and touch avoidance.** Respect the touch-avoidance tendencies of others; pay special attention to cultural and gender differences in touch preferences.

**turn-taking cues.** Respond to both the verbal and the nonverbal conversational turn-taking cues given you by others, and make your own cues clear to others.

**understanding.** Relate new information to what you already know, ask questions, and paraphrase what you think the speaker said to make sure you understand.

# Bibliography

# Bibliography

Acor, A. A. (2001). Employers' perceptions of persons with body art and an experimental test regarding eyebrow piercing. Ph.D. dissertation, Marquette University. *Dissertation Abstracts International: Second B: The Sciences and Engineering* 61, 3885.

Acuff, F. L. (1993). *How to negotiate anything with anyone anywhere around the world.* New York: American Management Association.

Adams-Price, C. E., Dalton, W. T., & Sumrall, R. (2004). Victim blaming in young, middle-aged, and older adults: Variations on the severity effect. *Journal of Adult Development* 11 (October), 289–295.

Adler, M. G., & Fagley, N. S. (2005). Appreciation: Individual differences in finding value and meaning as a unique predictor of subjective well-being. *Journal of Personality* 73 (February), 79–114.

Adrianson, L. (2001). Gender and computer-mediated communication: Group processes in problem solving. *Computers in Human Behavior* 17, 71–94.

Albada, K. F. (2002). Interaction appearance theory: Changing perceptions of physical attractiveness through social interaction. *Communication Theory* 12 (February), 8–40.

Alberti, R., & Emmons, M. (2001). *Your perfect right: Assertiveness and equality in your life and relationships,* 8th ed. Atascadero, CA: Impact.

Alberti, R. E., ed. (1977). *Assertiveness: Innovations, applications, issues.* San Luis Obispo, CA: Impact.

Alessandra, T. (1986). How to listen effectively. *Speaking of success* (Video Tape Series). San Diego, CA: Levitz Sommer Productions.

Allen, J. L., Long, K. M., O'Mara, J., & Judd, B. B. (2003). Verbal and nonverbal orientations toward communication and the development of intracultural and intercultural relationships. *Journal of Intercultural Communication Research* 32 (September–December), 129–160.

Allen, M., Bourhis, J., Emmers-Sommer, T., & Sahlstein, E. (1998). Reducing dating anxiety: A meta-analysis. *Communication Reports* 11, 49–55.

Almeida, E. P. (2004). A discourse analysis of student perceptions of their communication competence. *Communication Education* 53 (October), 357–364.

Alonzo, M., & Aiken, M. (2004). Flaming in electronic communication. *Decision Support Systems* 36 (January), 205–213.

Al-Simadi, F. A. (2000). Detection of deception behavior: A cross-cultural test. *Social Behavior & Personality* 28, 455–461.

Alsop, R. (2004). How to get hired: We asked recruiters what M.B.A. graduates are doing wrong. Ignore their advice at your peril. *Wall Street Journal* (September 22), R8.

Altman, I. (1975). *The environment and social behavior.* Monterey, CA: Brooks/Cole.

Altman, I., & Taylor, D. (1973). *Social penetration: The development of interpersonal relationships.* New York: Holt, Rinehart & Winston.

Amato, P. R. (1994). The impact of divorce on men and women in India and the United States. *Journal of Comparative Family Studies* 25, 207–221.

Anderson, I. (2004). Explaining negative rape victim perception: Homophobia and the male rape victim. *Current Research in Social Psychology* 10 (November), np.

Anderson, K. J. (1998). Meta-analysis of gender effects on conversational interruption: Who, what, when, where, and how. *Sex Roles* 39 (August), 225–252.

Andersen, P. A. (1991). Explaining intercultural differences in nonverbal communication. In *Intercultural communication: A reader,* 6th ed., L. A. Samovar & R. E. Porter (eds.). Belmont, CA: Wadsworth, pp. 286–296.

Andersen, P. A., & Leibowitz, K. (1978). The development and nature of the construct touch avoidance. *Environmental Psychology and Nonverbal Behavior* 3, 89–106. Reprinted in DeVito & Hecht (1990).

Angier, N. (1995a). Powerhouse of senses: Smell, at last, gets its due, *New York Times* (February 14), C1, C6.

Angier, N. (2003). Opposites attract? Not in real life. *New York Times* 152 (July 8), F1, 6.

Angier, N. (1995b). Scientists mull role of empathy in man and beast. *New York Times* (May 9), C1, C6.

Aquinis, H., & Henle, C. A. (2001). Effects of nonverbal behavior on perceptions of a female employee's power bases. *Journal of Social Psychology* 141 (August), 537–549.

Argyle, M. (1986). Rules for social relationships in four cultures. *Australian Journal of Psychology* 38, 309–318.

Argyle, M. (1988). *Bodily communication,* 2d ed. New York: Methuen.

Argyle, M., & Dean, J. (1965). Eye contact, distance and affiliation. *Sociometry* 28, 289–304.

Argyle, M., & Henderson, M. (1984). The rules of friendship. *Journal of Social and Personal Relationships* 1, 211–237.

Argyle, M., & Henderson, M. (1985). *The anatomy of relationships: And the rules and skills needed to manage them successfully.* London: Heinemann.

Argyle, M., Henderson, M., Bond, M., Iizuka, Y., et al. (1986). Cross-cultural variations in relationship rules. *International Journal of Psychology* 21, 287–315.

Argyle, M., & Ingham, R. (1972). Gaze, mutual gaze, and distance. *Semiotica* 1, 32–49.

Arliss, L. P. (1991). *Gender communication.* Englewood Cliffs, NJ: Prentice-Hall.

Armour, S. (2003). Cupid finds work as office romance no longer taboo. *USA Today* (February 11), Money Section, 1.

Aronson, E., Wilson, T. D., & Akert, R. M. (1999). *Social psychology,* 3d ed. Boston: Allyn & Bacon.

Aronson, J., Cohen, J., & Nail, P. (1998). Self-affirmation theory: An update and appraisal. In *Cognitive dissonance theory: Revival with revisions and controversies,* E. Harmon-Jones & J. S. Mills (eds.). Washington, DC: American Psychological Association.

Arrindell, W. A., Steptoe, A., & Wardle, J. (2003). Higher levels of state depression in masculine than in feminine nations. *Behaviour Research and Therapy* 41 (July), 809–817.

Asch, S. (1946). Forming impressions of personality. *Journal of Abnormal and Social Psychology* 41, 258–290.

Ashcraft, M. H. (1998). *Fundamentals of cognition.* New York: Longman.

Ashe, D. D., & McCutcheon, L. E. (2001). Shyness, loneliness, and attitude toward celebrities. *Current Research in Social Psychology* 6 (9).

Aspinwall, L. G., & Taylor, S. E. (1993). Effects of social comparison direction, threat, and self-esteem on affect, evaluation, and expected success. *Journal of Personality and Social Psychology* 64, 708–722.

Aune, R. K., & Kikuchi, T. (1993). Effects of language intensity similarity on perceptions of credibility, relational attributions, and persuasion. *Journal of Language and Social Psychology* 12, 224–238.

Authier, J., & Gustafson, K. (1982). Microtraining: Focusing on specific skills. In *Interpersonal helping skills: A guide to training methods, programs, and resources,* E. K. Marshall, P. D. Kurtz, and Associates (eds.). San Francisco: Jossey-Bass, pp. 93–130.

Axtell, R. E. (1990). *Do's and taboos of hosting international visitors.* New York: Wiley.

Axtell, R. E. (1994). *Do's and taboos around the world,* 3d ed. New York: Wiley.

Ayres, J. (1983). Strategies to maintain relationships: Their identification and perceived usage. *Communication Quarterly* 31, 62–67.

Ayres, J., Ayres, D. M., Grudzinskas, G., Hopf, T., Kelly, E., & Wilcox, A. K. (1995). A component analysis of performance visualization. *Communication Reports* 8, 185–192.

Ayres, J., & Hopf, T. (1993). *Coping with speech anxiety.* Norwood, NJ: Ablex.

Ayres, J., & Hopf, T. (1995). An assessment of the role of communication apprehension in communicating with the terminally ill. *Communication Research Reports* 12, 227–234.

Ayres, J., Hopf, T., & Ayres, D. M. (1994). An examination of whether imaging ability enhances the effectiveness of an intervention designed to reduce speech anxiety. *Communication Education* 43 (July), 252–258.

Babcock, J. C, Waltz, J., Jacobson, N. S., & Gottman, J. M. (1993). Power and violence: The relation between communication patterns, power discrepancies, and domestic violence. *Journal of Marriage and the Family* 60 (February), 70–78.

Bach, G. R., & Wyden, P. (1968). *The intimate enemy.* New York: Avon.

Bacon, B. (2004). *Meet me don't delete me: Internet dating: I've made all the mistakes so you don't have to.* Burbank, CA: Slapstick Publications.

Bailenson, J. N., Blascovich, J., Beall, A. C., & Loomis, J. M. (2001). Equilibrium theory revisited: Mutual gaze and personal space in virtual environments. *Presence: Teleoperators and Virtual Environments* 10 (December), 583–595.

Baker, A. (2002). What makes an online relationship successful? Clues from couples who met in cyberspace. *CyberPsychology and Behavior* 5 (August), 363–375.

Banerjee, N. (2005). Few but organized, Iraq veterans turn war critics. *New York Times,* (January 23), National Report, 16.

Banks, S. P., Altendorf, D. M., Greene, J. O., & Cody, M. J. (1987). An examination of relationship disengagement: Perceptions, breakup strategies, and outcomes. *Western Journal of Speech Communication* 51, 19–41.

Baringer, D. K., & McCroskey, J. C. (2000). Immediacy in the classroom: Student immediacy. *Communication Education* 49, 178–186.

Barker, L. L. (1990). *Communication,* 5th ed. Englewood Cliffs, NJ: Prentice-Hall.

Barker, L. L., Edwards, R., Gaines, C., Gladney, K., & Holley, F. (1980). An investigation of proportional time spent in various communication activities by college students. *Journal of Applied Communication Research* 8, 101–109.

Barna, L. M. (1997). Stumbling blocks in intercultural communication. In *Intercultural communication: A reader,* 7th ed., L. A. Samovar & R. E. Porter (eds.). Belmont, CA: Wadsworth, pp. 337–346.

Barnlund, D. C. (1975). Communicative styles in two cultures: Japan and the United States. In *Organization of behavior in face-to-face interaction,* R. Kendon, M. Harris, & M. R. Key (eds.). The Hague: Mouton.

Barnlund, D. C. (1989). *Communicative styles of Japanese and Americans: Images and realities*. Belmont, CA: Wadsworth.

Baron, R. (1990). Countering the effects of destructive criticism: The relative efficacy of four interventions. *Journal of Applied Psychology* 75 (3), 235–245.

Barrett, L., & Godfrey, T. (1988). Listening. *Person Centered Review* 3 (November), 410–425.

Barry, D. T. (2003). Cultural and demographic correlates of self-reported guardedness among East Asian immigrants in the U.S. *International Journal of Psychology* 38 (June), 150–159.

Bartholomew, K. (1990). Avoidance of intimacy: An attachment perspective. *Journal of Social and Personal Relationships* 7, 147–178.

Bassellier, G., & Benbasat, I. (2004). Business competence of information technology professionals: Conceptual development and influence on IT-business partnerships. *MIS Quarterly* 28 (December), 673–694.

Basso, K. H. (1972). To give up on words: Silence in Apache culture. In *Language and social context*, Pier Paolo Giglioli (ed.). New York: Penguin.

Bateson, G. (1972). *Steps to an ecology of mind*. New York: Ballantine.

Battaglia, D. M., Richard, F. D., Datteri, D. L., & Lord, C. G. (1998). Breaking up is (relatively) easy to do: A script for the dissolution of close relationships. *Journal of Social and Personal Relationships* 15, 829–845.

Bauer, T. N. (1995). How three factions rate job and applicant attributes. *Journal of Career Planning and Employment* 55 (January), 43–46.

Baumeister, R. F., Bushman, B. J., & Campbell, W. K. (2000). Self-esteem, narcissism, and aggression: Does violence result from low self-esteem or from threatened egotism? *Current Directions in Psychological Science* 9 (February), 26–29.

Baumeister, R. F., Zhang, L., & Vohs, K. D. (2004). Gossip as cultural learning. *Review of General Psychology* 8 (June), 111–121.

Bavelas, J. B. (1990). Can one not communicate? Behaving and communicating: A reply to Motley. *Western Journal of Speech Communication* 54, 593–602.

Baxter, L. A. (1983). Relationship disengagement: An examination of the reversal hypothesis. *Western Journal of Speech Communication* 47, 85–98.

Baxter, L. A. (1984). An investigation of compliance-gaining as politeness. *Human Communication Research* 10, 427–456.

Baxter, L. A. (1986). Gender differences in the heterosexual relationship rules embedded in break-up accounts. *Journal of Social and Personal Relationships* 3, 289–306.

Baxter, L. A. (1988). A dialectical perspective on communication strategies in relationship development. In *Handbook of personal relationships*, S. W. Duck (ed.). New York: Wiley.

Baxter, L. A. (1990). Dialectical contradictions in relationship development. *Journal of Social and Personal Relationships* 7, 69–88.

Baxter, L. A. (2004). Relationships as dialogues. *Personal Relationships* 11 (March), 1–22.

Baxter, L. A., & Bullis, C. (1986). Turning points in developing romantic relationships. *Human Communication Research* 12, 469–493.

Baxter, L. A., Dun, T., & Sahlstein, E. (2001). Rules for relating communicated among social network members. *Journal of Social and Personal Relationships* 18, 173–199.

Baxter, L. A., & Simon, E. P. (1993). Relationship maintenance strategies and dialectical contradictions in personal relationships. *Journal of Social and Personal Relationships* 10, 225–242.

Baxter, L. A., & Wilmot, W. W. (1984). Secret tests: Social strategies for acquiring information about the state of the relationship. *Human Communication Research* 11, 171–201.

Beach, W. A. (1990). On (not) observing behavior interactionally. *Western Journal of Speech Communication* 54, 603–612.

Beatty, M. (1988). Situational and predispositional correlates of public speaking anxiety. *Communication Education* 37, 28–39.

Beck, A. T. (1988). *Love is never enough*. New York: Harper & Row.

Bell, R. A., & Buerkel-Rothfuss, N. L. (1990). S(he) loves me, s(he) loves me not: Predictors of relational information-seeking in courtship and beyond. *Communication Quarterly* 38, 64–82.

Bell, R. A., & Daly, J. A. (1984). The affinity-seeking function of communication. *Communication Monographs* 51, 91–115.

Ben-Ze'ev, A. (2003). Primacy, emotional closeness, and openness in cyberspace. *Computers in Human Behavior* 19 (July), 451–467.

Bernard, M. (2004). Overcoming ageism, one student at a time. *Geriatrics* 59 (December), 11.

Bennett, M. (1990). Children's understanding of the mitigating function of disclaimers. *Journal of Social Psychology* 130, 29–37.

Berg, J. H., & Archer, R. L. (1983). The disclosure-liking relationship. *Human Communication Research* 10, 269–281.

Berger, C. R., & Bradac, J. J. (1982). *Language and social knowledge: Uncertainty in interpersonal relations*. London: Edward Arnold.

Berger, C. R., & Calabrese, R. J. (1975). Some explorations in initial interaction and beyond: Toward a theory of interpersonal communication. *Human Communication Research* 1, 99–112.

Berger, P. L., & Luckmann, T. (1980). *The social construction of reality*. New York: Irvington.

Berman, J. J., Murphy-Berman, V., & Singh, P. (1985). Cross-cultural similarities and differences in perceptions of fairness. *Journal of Cross-Cultural Psychology* 16, 55–67.

Bernstein, W. M., Stephan, W. G., & Davis, M. H. (1979). Explaining attributions for achievement: A path analytic approach. *Journal of Personality and Social Psychology* 37, 1810–1821.

Berry, J. N. III (2004). Can I quote you on that? *Library Journal* 129, 10.

Berry, J. W., Poortinga, Y. H., Segall, M. H., & Dasen, P. R. (1992). *Cross-cultural psychology: Research and applications.* Cambridge: Cambridge University Press.

Berscheid, E. (1985). Interpersonal attraction. In *Handbook of social psychology,* G. Lindzey & E. Aronson (eds.). New York: Random House, pp. 413–484.

Berscheid, E., & Reis, H. T. (1998). Attraction and close relationships. In *The handbook of social psychology,* 4th ed., Vol. 2, D. Gilbert, S. Fiske, & G. Lindzey (eds.). New York: W. H. Freeman, pp. 193–281.

Bierhoff, H. W., & Klein, R. (1991). Dimensionen der Liebe: Entwicklung einer Deutschsprachigen Skala zur Erfassung von Liebesstilen. *Zeitschrift for Differentielle und Diagnostische Psychologie* 12, 53–71.

Bippus, A., & Daly, J. A. (1999). What do people think causes stage fright? Naive attributions about the reasons for public speaking anxiety. *Communication Education* 48, 63–72.

Bishop, J. E. (1993). New research suggests that romance begins by falling nose over heels in love. *Wall Street Journal* (April 7), B1.

Black, H. K. (1999). A sense of the sacred: Altering or enhancing the self-portrait in older age? *Narrative Inquiry* 9, 327–345.

Blake, R. R., & Mouton, J. S. (1984). *The managerial grid III* (3d ed.). Houston, TX: Gulf Publishing.

Blieszner, R., & Adams, R. G. (1992). *Adult friendship.* Thousand Oaks, CA: Sage.

Bloch, J. (2002). Student/teacher interaction via email: The social context of Internet discourse. *Journal of Second Language Writing* 11 (May), 117–134.

Blood, R. O., Jr. (1973). Resolving family conflicts. In *Conflict resolution through communication,* F. E. Jandt (ed.). New York: Harper & Row, pp. 221–239.

Blumstein, P., & Schwartz, P. (1983). *American couples: Money, work, sex.* New York: Morrow.

Bochner, A. (1984). The functions of human communication in interpersonal bonding. In *Handbook of rhetorical and communication theory,* C. C. Arnold & J. W. Bowers (eds.). Boston: Allyn & Bacon, pp. 544–621.

Bochner, A., & Kelly, C. (1974). Interpersonal competence: Rationale, philosophy, and implementation of a conceptual framework. *Communication Education* 23, 279–301.

Bochner, S. (1994). Cross-cultural differences in the self-concept: A test of Hofstede's individualism/collectivism distinction. *Journal of Cross-Cultural Psychology* 25, 273–283.

Bochner, S., & Hesketh, B. (1994). Power distance, individualism/collectivism, and job-related attitudes in a culturally diverse work group. *Journal of Cross-Cultural Psychology* 25, 233–257.

Bodon, J., Powell, L., & Hickson III, M. (1999). Critiques of gatekeeping in scholarly journals: An analysis of perceptions and data. *Journal of the Association for Communication Administration* 28 (May), 60–70.

Bok, S. (1978). *Lying: Moral choice in public and private life.* New York: Pantheon.

Bok, S. (1983). *Secrets.* New York: Vintage.

Bok, S. (1998). *Mayhem: Violence as public entertainment.* Reading, MA: Perseus Books.

Bond, Jr., C. F., & Atoum, A. O. (2000). International deception. *Personality & Social Psychology Bulletin* 26 (March), 385–395.

Boneva, B., Kraut, R., & Frohlich, D. (2001). Using e-mail for personal relationships: The difference gender makes. *American Behavioral Scientist* 45, 530–549.

Booth-Butterfield, M. (1998). Measurement of communication flexibility: Working adults vs. college students. *Communication Research Reports* 15, 365–369.

Borden, G. A. (1991). *Cultural orientation: An approach to understanding intercultural communication.* Englewood Cliffs, NJ: Prentice-Hall.

Bosmajian, H. (1974). *The language of oppression.* Washington, DC: Public Affairs Press.

Bourland, D. D., Jr. (1965–66). A linguistic note: Writing in E-prime. *General Semantics Bulletin,* 32–33, 111–114.

Bourland, D. D., Jr. (2004). To be or not to be: E-prime as a tool for critical thinking. *ETC: A Review of General Semantics* 61 (December), 546–557.

Bowen, F., & Blackmon, K. (2003). Spirals of silence: The dynamic of diversity on organizational voice. *Journal of Management Studies* 40 (September), 1393–1417.

Bower, B. (2001). Self-illusions come back to bite students. *Science News* 159, 148.

Bower, S. A., & Bower, G. H. (2005). *Asserting yourself: A practical guide for positive change.* Cambridge, MA: DaCapo Press.

Bradac, J. J. (2001). Theory comparison: Uncertainty reduction, problematic integration, uncertainty management, and other curious constructs. *Journal of Communication* 51 (September), 456–476.

Brandes, P., Ravi, D., & Wheatley, K. (2004). Social exchanges within organizations and work outcomes: The importance of local and global relationships. *Group and Organization Management* 29 (June), 276–301.

Brandt, A. (2004). Does your online profile say something you wouldn't? *PC World* 22 (August), 1.

Bravo, E., & Cassedy, E. (1992). *The 9 to 5 guide to combating sexual harassment.* New York: Wiley.

Breidenstein-Cutspec, P., & Goering, E. (1989). Exploring cultural diversity: A network analysis of the communicative correlates of shyness within the black culture. *Communication Research Reports* 6, 37–46.

Bresnahan, M. I., & Cai, D. H. (1996). Gender and aggression in the recognition of interruption. *Discourse Processes* 21, 171–189.

Bridges, C. R. (1996). The characteristics of career achievement perceived by African American college administrators. *Journal of Black Studies* 26, 748–767.

Britnell, A. (2004). Culture shock-proofing. *Profit* 23 (November), 79–80.

Briton, N. J., & Hall, J. A. (1995). Beliefs about female and male nonverbal communication. *Sex Roles* 32, 79–90.

Briton, N. J., & Hall, J. A. (1995). Gender-based expectancies and observer judgments of smiling. *Journal of Nonverbal Behavior* 19, 49–65.

Brody, J. F. (1994). Notions of beauty transcend culture, new study suggests. *New York Times* (March 21), A14.

Brown, A., & Draper, P. (2003). Accommodative speech and terms of endearment: Elements of a language mode often experienced by older adults. *Journal of Advanced Nursing* 41 (January), 15–21.

Brown, C. T., & Keller, P. W. (1979). *Monologue to dialogue: An exploration of interpersonal communication,* 2nd ed. Englewood Cliffs, NJ: Prentice-Hall.

Brown, P. (1980). How and why are women more polite: Some evidence from a Mayan community. In *Women and language in literature and society,* S. McConnell-Ginet, R. Borker, & M. Furman (eds.). New York: Praeger, pp. 111–136.

Brown, P., & Levinson, S. C. (1988). *Politeness: Some universals of language usage.* Cambridge: Cambridge University Press.

Brownell, J. (1987). Listening: The toughest management skill. *Cornell Hotel and Restaurant Administration Quarterly* 27, 64–71.

Brownell, J. (2002). *Listening: Attitudes, principles, and skills,* 2d ed. Boston: Allyn & Bacon.

Buber, M. (1958). *I and thou,* 2nd ed. New York: Scribner's.

Bugental, J., & Zelen, S. (1950). Investigations into the "self-concept." I. The W-A-Y technique. *Journal of Personality* 18, 483–498.

Bull, R., & Rumsey, N. (1988). *The social psychology of facial appearance.* New York: Springer-Verlag.

Buller, D. B., LePoire, B. A., Aune, R. K., & Eloy, S. (1992). Social perceptions as mediators of the effect of speech rate similarity on compliance. *Human Communication Research* 19, 286–311.

Bumby, K. M., & Hansen, D. J. (1997). Intimacy deficits, fear of intimacy, and loneliness among sexual offenders. *Criminal Justice and Behavior* 24, 315–331.

Bunz, U., & Campbell, S. W. (2004). Politeness accommodation in electronic mail. *Communication Research Reports* 21 (winter), 11–25.

Burgoon, J. K. (1991). Relational message interpretations of touch, conversational distance, and posture. *Journal of Nonverbal Behavior* 15, 233–259.

Burgoon, J. K., & Bacue, A. E. (2003). Nonverbal communication skills. In *Handbook of communication and social interaction skills,* (pp. 179–220), J. O. Greene & B. R. Burleson (eds.). Mahwah, NJ: Lawrence Erlbaum.

Burgoon, J. K., Berger, C. R., & Waldron, V. R. (2000). Mindfulness and interpersonal communication. *Journal of Social Issues* 56, 105–127.

Burgoon, J. K., Buller, D. B., & Woodall, W. G. (1995). *Nonverbal communication: The unspoken dialogue,* 2d ed. New York: McGraw-Hill.

Burgoon, J. K., & Hale, J. L. (1988). Nonverbal expectancy violations: Model elaboration and application to immediacy behaviors. *Communication Monographs* 55, 58–79.

Burgoon, J. K., & Hoobler, G. D. (2002). Nonverbal signals. In *Handbook of Interpersonal Communication,* 3d ed. (pp. 240–299), M. L. Knapp & J. A. Daly (eds.). Thousand Oaks, CA: Sage.

Burgoon, M. (1971). The relationship between willingness to manipulate others and success in two different types of basic speech communication courses. *Communication Education* 20, 178–183.

Burnard, P. (2003). Ordinary chat and therapeutic conversation: Phatic communication and mental health nursing. *Journal of Psychiatric and Mental Health Nursing* 10 (December), 678–682.

Bushman, B. J., & Baumeister, R. F. (1998). Threatened egotism, narcissism, self-esteem, and direct and displaced aggression: Does self-love or self-hate lead to violence? *Journal of Personality and Social Psychology* 75, 219–229.

Buss, D. M., & Schmitt, D. P. (1993). Sexual strategies theory: An evolutionary perspective on human mating. *Psychological Review* 100, 204–232.

Butler, P. E. (1981). *Talking to yourself: Learning the language of self-support.* New York: Harper & Row.

Byers, E. S., & Demmons, S. (1999). Sexual satisfaction and sexual self-disclosure within dating relationships. *Journal of Sex Research* 36, 180–189.

Cabello, B., & Terrell, R. (1994). Making students feel like family: How teachers create warm and caring classroom climates. *Journal of Classroom Interaction* 29, 17–23.

Cai, D. A., & Fink, E. L. (2002). Conflict style differences between individualists and collectivists. *Communication Monographs* 69 (March), 67–87.

Camden, C., Motley, M. T., & Wilson, A. (1984). White lies in interpersonal communication: A taxonomy and preliminary investigation of social motivations. *Western Journal of Speech Communication* 48, 309–325.

Campbell, W. K., Foster, C. A., & Finkel, E. J. (2002). Does self-love lead to love for others? A story of narcissistic game playing. *Journal of Personality and Social Psychology* 83 (August), 340–354.

Canary, D. J. (2003). Managing interpersonal conflict: A model of events related to strategic choices. In *Handbook of communication and social interaction skills,* (pp. 515–550), J. O.

Greene & B. R. Burleson (eds.). Mahwah, NJ: Lawrence Erlbaum.

Canary, D. J., Cody, M. J., & Manusov, V. L. (2000). *Interpersonal communication: A goals-based approach*, (2d ed.). Boston: St. Bedford/St. Martins.

Canary, D.. J., Cupach, W. R., & Messman, S. J. (1995). *Relationship conflict: Conflict in parent-child, friendship, and romantic relationships.* Thousand Oaks, CA: Sage.

Canary, D. J., & Hause, K. S. (1993). Is there any reason to research sex differences in communication? *Communication Quarterly* 41, 129–144.

Canary, D. J., & Stafford, L. (1994). Maintaining relationships through strategic and routine interaction. In *Communication and relational maintenance*, D. J. Canary & L. Stafford (eds.). New York: Academic Press.

Canary, D. J., Stafford, L., Hause, K. S., & Wallace, L. A. (1993). An inductive analysis of relational maintenance strategies: Comparisons among lovers, relatives, friends, and others. *Communication Research Reports* 10, 5–14.

Cappella, J. N. (1993). The facial feedback hypothesis in human interaction: Review and speculation. *Journal of Language and Social Psychology* 12, 13–29.

Carducci, B. J., with Zimbardo, P. G. (1994). Are you shy? *Psychology Today* 28, 34–41, 64–70, 78–82.

Carey, B. (2005). Have you heard? Gossip turns out to serve a purpose. *New York Times* (August 16), F1, F6.

Carli, L. L. (1999). Gender, interpersonal power, and social influence. *Journal of Social Issues* 55 (spring), 81–99.

Carlock, C. J., ed. (1999). *Enhancing self-esteem,* 3d ed. Philadelphia, PA: Accelerated Development, Inc.

Carroll, D. W. (1994). *Psychology of language,* 2d ed. Pacific Grove, CA: Brooks/Cole.

Carson, J. W., Carson, K. M., Gil, K. M., & Baucom, D. H. (2004). Mindfulness-based relationship enhancement. *Behavior Therapy* 35 (summer), 471–494.

Cashdan, E. (2001). Ethnocentrism and xenophobia: A cross-cultural study. *Current Anthropology* 42, 760–765.

Castleberry, S. B., & Shepherd, C. D. (1993). Effective interpersonal listening and personal selling. *Journal of Personal Selling and Sales Management* 13, 35–49.

Cawthon, S. W. (2001). Teaching strategies in inclusive classrooms with deaf students. *Journal of Deaf Studies and Deaf Education* 6, 212–225.

Chadwick-Jones, J. K. (1976). *Social exchange theory: Its structure and influence in social psychology.* New York: Academic Press.

Chan, D., K., & Cheng, G. H. (2004). A comparison of offline and online friendship qualities at different stages of relationship development. *Journal of Social and Personal Relationships* 21 (June), 305–320.

Chaney, R. H., Givens, C. A., Aoki, M. F., & Gombiner, M. L. (1989). Pupillary responses in recognizing awareness in persons with profound mental retardation. *Perceptual and Motor Skills* 69, 523–528.

Chang, H., & Holt, G. R. (1996). The changing Chinese interpersonal world: Popular themes in interpersonal communication books in modern Taiwan. *Communication Quarterly* 44, 85–106.

Chanowitz, B., & Langer, E. (1981). Premature cognitive commitment. *Journal of Personality and Social Psychology* 41, 1051–1063.

Chapdelaine, R. F., & Alexitch, L. R. (2004). Social skills difficulty: Model of culture shock for international graduate students. *Journal of College Student Development* 45 (March–April), 167–184.

Charlton, S. G. (2004). Perceptual and attentional effects on drivers' speed selection at curves. *Accident Analysis and Prevention* 36 (September), 877–884.

Chen, G. (1992). Differences in self-disclosure patterns among Americans versus Chinese: A comparative study. Paper presented at the annual meeting of the Eastern Communication Association, Portland, ME.

Cheney, G., & Tompkins, P. K. (1987). Coming to terms with organizational identification and commitment. *Central States Speech Journal* 38, 1–15.

Chesebro, J. L., & McCroskey, J. C. (1998). The relationship of teacher clarity and teacher immediacy with students' experiences of state receiver apprehension. *Communication Quarterly* 46, 446–456.

Childress, H. (2004). Teenagers, territory and the appropriation of space. *Childhood: A Global Journal of Child Research* 11 (May), 195–205.

Cho, H. (2000). Asian in America: Cultural shyness can impede Asian Americans' success. *Northwest Asian Weekly* 19 (December 8), p. 6.

Christians, C. G. & Traber, M., eds. (1997). *Communication ethics and universal values.* Urbana, IL: University of Illinois Press.

Chun, K. M., Balls, O. P., & Marin, G. (2003). *Acculturation: Advances in theory, measurement, and applied research.* Washington, DC: American Psychological Association.

Chung, L. C., & Ting-Toomey, S. (1999). Ethnic identity and relational expectations among Asian Americans. *Communication Research Reports* 16 (spring), 157–166.

Chung, M. C., Farmer, S., Grant, K., Newton, R., Payne, S., Perry, M., Saunders, J., Smith, C., & Stone, N. (2002). Gender differences in love styles and post traumatic reactions following relationship dissolution. *European Journal of Psychiatry* 16 (October–December), 210–220.

Clark, R. A. (1991). *Studying interpersonal communication: The research experience.* Thousand Oaks, CA: Sage.

Clement, D. A., & Frandsen, K. D. (1976). On conceptual and empirical treatments of feedback in human communication. *Communication Monographs* 43, 11–28.

Cline, M. G. (1956). The influence of social context on the perception of faces. *Journal of Personality* 2, 142–185.

Coates, J., & Sutton-Spence, R. (2001). Turn-taking patterns in deaf conversation. *Journal of Sociolinguistics* 5 (November), 507–529.

Cody, M. J. (1982). A typology of disengagement strategies and an examination of the role intimacy, reactions to inequity, and relational problems play in strategy selection. *Communication Monographs* 49, 148–170.

Cohen, J. (2002). An e-mail affliction: The long goodbye. *New York Times* (May 9), G6.

Cohen, J. (2003). Parasocial breakups: Measuring individual differences in responses to the dissolution of parasocial relationships. *Mass Communication and Society* 6, 191–202.

Cohen, J. (2004). Parasocial break-up from favorite television characters: The role of attachment styles and relationship intensity. *Journal of Social and Personal Relationships* 21 (April), 187–202.

Cole, T., & Leets, L. (1999). Attachment styles and intimate television viewing: Insecurely forming relationships in a parasocial way. *Journal of Social and Personal Relationships* 16 (August), 495–511.

Coleman, P. (2002). *How to say it for couples: Communicating with tenderness, openness, and honesty.* Paramus, NJ: Prentice-Hall.

Colley, A., Todd, Z., Bland, M., Holmes, M., Khanom, N., & Pike, H. (2004). Style and content in e-mails and letters to male and female friends. *Journal of Language and Social Psychology* 23 (September), 369–378.

Collier, M. J. (1991). Conflict competence within African, Mexican, and Anglo American friendships. In *Cross-cultural interpersonal communication,* S. Ting-Toomey & F. Korzenny (eds.). Thousand Oaks, CA: Sage, pp. 132–154.

Collins, J. E., & Clark, L. F. (1989). Responsibility and rumination: The trouble with understanding the dissolution of a relationship. *Social Cognition* 7, 152–173.

Collins, N. L., & Miller, L. C. (1994). Self-disclosure and liking: A meta-analytic review. *Psychological Bulletin* 116 (November), 457–475.

Comer, L. B., & Drollinger, T. (1999). Active empathic listening and selling success: A conceptual framework. *Journal of Personal Selling and Sales Management,* 19, 15–29.

Conlin, M. (2002). Watch what you put in that office e-mail. *Business Week* (September 9), 114–115.

Constantine, M. G., Anderson, G. M., Berkel, L. A., Caldwell, L. D., & Utsey, S. O. (2005). Examining the cultural adjustment experiences of African international college students: A qualitative analysis. *Journal of Counseling Psychology* 52 (January), 57–66.

Cooley, C. H. (1922). *Human nature and the social order.* Rev. ed. New York: Scribner's.

Coon, C. A., & Schwanenflugel, P. J. (1996). Evaluation of interruption behavior by naive encoders. *Discourse Processes* 22, 1–24.

Cooper, A., & Sportolari, L. (1997). Romance in cyberspace: Understanding online attraction. *Journal of Sex Education and Therapy* 22, 7–14.

Coover, G. E., & Murphy, S. T. (2000). The communicated self: Exploring the interaction between self and social context. *Human Communication Research* 26, 125–147.

Coplin, B. (2004). For new graduates, "soft skills" are the secret weapon in job hunt. *USA Today* (June 10), 15A.

Cornwell, B., & Lundgren, D. C. (2001). Love on the Internet: Involvement and misrepresentation in romantic relationships in cyberspace vs. realspace. *Computers in Human Behavior* 17, 197–211.

Cottle, T. J. (2003). *A sense of self: The work of affirmation.* Amherst, MA: University of Massachusetts Press.

Counts, D. A., Brown, J. K., & Campbell, J. C. (1992). *Sanctions and sanctuary: Cultural perspectives on the beating of wives.* Boulder, CO: Westview Press.

Cramer, D. (2004). Emotional support, conflict, depression, and relationship satisfaction in a romantic partner. *Journal of Psychology: Interdisciplinary and Applied* 138 (November), 532–542.

Crampton, S. M., Hodge, J. W., & Mishra, J. M. (1998). The informal communication network: Factors influencing grapevine activity. *Public Personnel Management* 27 (winter), 569–584.

Crawford, D. W., Feng, D., Fischer, J. L., & Diana, L. K. (2003). The influence of love, equity, and alternatives on commitment in romantic relationships. *Family and Consumer Sciences Research Journal* 31 (March), 253–271.

Cristina, S. J. (2001). Gossip and social exclusion in females: Do they have positive or negative consequences for social behaviour? *Dissertation Abstracts International: Section B: The Sciences and Engineering* 62 (2-B). University of Ottawa, Canada (August), 1114.

Crohn, J. (1995). *Mixed matches: How to create successful interracial, interethnic, and interfaith relationships.* New York: Fawcett.

Cross, E. E., & Madson, L. (1997). Models of the self: Self-construals and gender. *Psychological Bulletin* 122, 5–37.

Crusco, A. H., & Wetzel, C. G. (1984). The Midas touch: The effects of interpersonal touch on restaurant tipping. *Personality and Social Psychology Bulletin* 10, 512–517.

Dahle, C. (2004). Choosing a mentor? Cast a wide net. *New York Times* (July 25), BU 9.

Dainton, M., & Stafford, L. (1993). Routine maintenance behaviors: A comparison of relationship type, partner similarity, and sex differences. *Journal of Social and Personal Relationships* 10, 255–272.

Davis, K. (1980). Management communication and the grapevine. In *Intercom: Readings in organizational communication,* (pp. 55–66), S. Ferguson & S. D. Ferguson (eds.). Rochelle Park, NJ: Hayden Books.

Davis, M. S. (1973). *Intimate relations.* New York: Free Press.

Davison, W. P. (1983). The third-person effect and the differential impact in negative political advertising. *Journalism Quarterly* 68, 680–688.

Davitz, J. R. (ed.). (1964). *The communication of emotional meaning.* New York: McGraw-Hill.

Deal, J. E., & Wampler, K. S. (1986). Dating violence: The primacy of previous experience. *Journal of Social and Personal Relationships* 3, 457–471.

Deaux, K., & LaFrance, M. (1998). Gender. In *The handbook of social psychology,* 4th ed., Vol. 1, D. Gilbert, S. Fiske, & G. Lindzey (eds.). New York: Freeman, pp. 788–828.

deBono, E. (1987). *The six thinking hats.* New York: Penguin.

DeCecco, J. (1988). Obligation versus aspiration. In *Gay relationships,* J. DeCecco (ed.). New York: Harrington Park Press.

DeFrancisco, V. (1991). The sound of silence: How men silence women in marital relations. *Discourse and Society* 2, 413–423.

Delia, J. G. (1977). Constructivism and the study of human communication. *Quarterly Journal of Speech* 63, 66–83.

Delia, J. G., O'Keefe, B. J., & O'Keefe, D. J. (1982). The constructivist approach to communication. In *Human communication theory: Comparative essays,* Frank E. X. Dance (ed.). New York: Harper & Row, pp. 147–191.

Dell, K. (2005). Just for dudes. *Time* (February, 14), B22.

Dereshiwsky, M. I., Moan, E. R., & Gahungu, A. (2002). Faculty perceptions regarding issues of civility in online instructional communication. *USDLA Journal* 16, No. 6 (June).

Derlega, V. J., Winstead, B. A., Wong, P. T. P., & Hunter, S. (1985). Gender effects in an initial encounter: A case where men exceed women in disclosure. *Journal of Social and Personal Relationships* 2, 25–44.

Derlega, V. J., Winstead, B. A., Greene, K., Serovich, J., & Elwood, W. N. (2004). Reasons for HIV disclosure/nondisclosure in close relationships: Testing a model of HIV-disclosure decision making. *Journal of Social and Clinical Psychology* 23 (December), 747–767.

Derlega, V. J., Winstead, B. A., Wong, P. T. P., & Greenspan, M. (1987). Self-disclosure and relationship development: An attributional analysis. In *Interpersonal processes: New directions in communication research,* M. E. Roloff, & G. R. Miller (eds.). Thousand Oaks, CA: Sage, pp. 172–187.

Derlega, V. J. (2004). Creating a "big picture" of personal relationships: Lessons we can learn from 1970s-era theories. *PsycCRITIQUES,* np.

Derne, S. (1999). Making sex violent: Love as force in recent Hindi films. *Violence Against Women* 5 (May), 548–575.

DeVito, J. A. (1989). *The nonverbal communication workbook.* Prospect Heights, IL: Waveland Press.

DeVito, J. A. (2003a). MEDUSA messages. *Etc: A Review of General Semantics* 60 (fall), 241–245.

DeVito, J. A. (2003b). SCREAM before you scream. *Etc: A Review of General Semantics* 60 (spring), 42–45.

DeVries, M. A. (1994). *Internationally yours: Writing and communicating successfully in today's global marketplace.* Boston: Houghton Mifflin.

DiBaise, R., & Gunnoe, J. (2004). Gender and culture differences in touching behavior. *Journal of Social Psychology* 144 (February), 49–62.

Dietz, T. L. (1998). An examination of violence and gender role portrayals in video games: Implications for gender socialization and aggressive behavior. *Sex Roles* 38 (March), 425–442.

Dillard, J. P., ed. (1990). *Seeking compliance: The production of interpersonal influence messages.* Scottsdale, AZ: Gorsuch Scarisbrick.

Dillard, J. P., Anderson, J. W., & Knobloch, L. K. (2002). Interpersonal influence. In *Handbook of interpersonal communication,* 3d ed. (pp. 425–474), M. L. Knapp & J. A. Daly (eds.). Thousand Oaks, CA: Sage.

Dillard, J. P., & Marshall, L. J. (2003). Persuasion as a social skill. In *Handbook of communication and social interaction skills,* (pp. 479–514), J. O. Greene & B. R. Burleson (eds.). Mahwah, NJ: Lawrence Erlbaum.

Dindia, K., & Baxter, L. A. (1987). Strategies for maintaining and repairing marital relationships. *Journal of Social and Personal Relationships* 4, 143–158.

Dindia, K., & Fitzpatrick, M. A. (1985). Marital communication: Three approaches compared. In *Understanding personal relationships: An interdisciplinary approach,* S. Duck & D. Perlman (eds.). Thousand Oaks, CA: Sage, pp. 137–158.

Dindia, K. & Timmerman, L. (2003). Accomplishing romantic relationships. In *Handbook of communication and social interaction skills* (pp. 685–721), J. O. Greene & B. R. Burleson (eds.). Mahwah, NJ: Erlbaum.

Dion, K., Berscheid, E., & Walster, E. (1972). What is beautiful is good. *Journal of Personality and Social Psychology* 24, 285–290.

Dion, K. K., & Dion, K. L. (1993a). Individualistic and collectivist perspectives on gender and the cultural context of love and intimacy. *Journal of Social Issues* 49, 53–69.

Dion, K. L., & Dion, K. K. (1993b). Gender and ethnocultural comparisons in styles of love. *Psychology of Women Quarterly* 17, 464–473.

Dion, K. K., & Dion, K. L. (1996). Cultural perspectives on romantic love. *Personal Relationships* 3, 5–17.

Dittman, D. A. (1997). Reexamining curriculum. *The Cornell Hotel and Restaurant Administration Quarterly* 38, 3.

Dolgin, K. G., Meyer, L., & Schwartz, J. (1991). Effects of gender, target's gender, topic, and self-esteem on disclosure to best and middling friends. *Sex Roles* 25, 311–329.

Dominick, J. R. (2006). *The dynamics of mass communication,* 8th ed. New York: McGraw-Hill.

Donahue, W. A., with Kolt, R. (1992). *Managing interpersonal conflict.* Thousand Oaks, CA: Sage.

Dorland, J. M., & Fisher, A. R. (2001). Gay, lesbian, and bisexual individuals' perception: An analogue study. *Counseling Psychologist* 29 (July), 532–547.

Dosey, M., & Meisels, M. (1976). Personal space and self-protection. *Journal of Personality and Social Psychology* 38, 959–965.

Douglas, W. (1994). The acquaintanceship process: An examination of uncertainty, information seeking, and social attraction during initial conversation. *Communication Research* 21, 154–176.

Dovidio, J. F., Gaertner, S. E., Kawakami, K., & Hodson, G. (2002). Why can't we just get along? Interpersonal biases and interracial distrust. *Cultural Diversity and Ethnic Minority Psychology* 8, 88–102.

Drass, K. A. (1986). The effect of gender identity on conversation. *Social Psychology Quarterly* 49, 294–301.

Dresser, N. (1996). *Multicultural manners: New rules of etiquette for a changing society.* New York: Wiley.

Drews, D. R., Allison, C. K., & Probst, J. R. (2000). Behavioral and self-concept differences in tattooed and nontattooed college students. *Psychological Reports* 86, 475–481.

Dreyfuss, H. (1971). *Symbol sourcebook.* New York: McGraw-Hill.

Drummond, K., & Hopper, R. (1993). Acknowledgment tokens in series. *Communication Reports* 6, 47–53.

Dsilva, M., & Whyte, L. O. (1998). Cultural differences in conflict styles: Vietnamese refugees and established residents. *The Howard Journal of Communication* 9, 57–68.

Duck, S. (1986). *Human relationships.* Thousand Oaks, CA: Sage.

Dunbar, R. I. M. (2004). Gossip in evolutionary perspective. *Review of General Psychology* 8 (June), 100–110.

Duncan, B. L., & Rock, J. W. (1991). *Overcoming relationship impasses: Ways to initiate change when your partner won't help.* New York: Plenum Press/Insight Books.

Duncan, S. D., Jr. (1972). Some signals and rules for taking speaking turns in conversation. *Journal of Personality and Social Psychology* 23, 283–292.

Dunn, D., & Cody, M. J. (2000). Account credibility and public image: Excuses, justifications, denials, and sexual harassment. *Communication Monographs* 67 (December), 372–391.

Duran, R. L., & Kelly, L. (1988). The influence of communicative competence on perceived task, social, and physical attraction. *Communication Quarterly* 36, 41–49.

Durst, U. (2003). Evidence for linguistic relativity. *Pragmatics and Cognition* 11, 379–386.

Eckstein, D., & Goldman, A. (2001). The couple's gender-based communication questionnaire (CGCQ). *Family Journal: Counseling and Therapy for Couples and Families* 9, 62–74.

Edelstein, A. S. (1993). Thinking about the criterion variable in agenda-setting research. *Journal of Communication* 43, 85–99.

Eden, D. (1992). Leadership and expectations: Pygmalion effects and other self-fulfilling prophecies in organizations. *Leadership Quarterly* 3 (winter), 271–305.

Eden, D. (1997). Leadership and expectations: Pygmalion effects and other self-fulfilling prophecies in organizations. In *Leadership: Understanding the dynamics of power and influence in organizations,* R. P. Vecchio (ed.). Notre Dame, IN: University of Notre Dame Press, pp. 177–193.

Eder, D., & Enke, J. L. (1991). The structure of gossip: Opportunities and constraints on collective expression among adolescents. *American Sociological Review* 56, 494–508.

Edstrom, A. (2004). Expression of disagreement by Venezuelans in conversation: Reconsidering the influence of culture. *Journal of Pragmatics* 36 (August), 1499–1508.

Edwards, R., & Bello, R. (2001). Interpretations of messages: The influence of equivocation, face-concerns, and ego-involvement. *Human Communication Research* 27, 597–631.

Ehrenhaus, P. (1988). Silence and symbolic expression. *Communication Monographs* 55, 41–57.

Einstein, E. (1995). Success or sabotage: Which self-fulfilling prophecy will the stepfamily create? In *Understanding stepfamilies: Implications for assessment and treatment,* D. K. Huntley (ed.). Alexandria, VA: American Counseling Association.

Eisenberger, N. I., Liberman, M. D., & Williams, K. D. (2003). Does rejection hurt? An fMRI study of social exclusion. *Science* 302 (October), 290–292.

Ekman, P. (1985). *Telling lies: Clues to deceit in the marketplace, politics, and marriage.* New York: Norton.

Ekman, P., & Friesen, W. V. (1969). The repertoire of nonverbal behavior: Categories, origins, usage, and coding. *Semiotica* 1, 49–98.

Ekman, P., Friesen, W. V., & Ellsworth, P. (1972). *Emotion in the human face: Guidelines for research and an integration of findings.* New York: Pergamon Press.

Elfenbein, H. A., & Ambady, N. (2002). Is there an in-group advantage in emotion recognition? *Psychological Bulletin* 128, 243–249.

Ellis, A. (1988). *How to stubbornly refuse to make yourself miserable about anything, yes anything.* Secaucus, NJ: Lyle Stuart.

Ellis, A., & Harper, R. A. (1975). *A new guide to rational living.* Hollywood, CA: Wilshire Books.

Ellis, K. (2004). The impact of perceived teacher confirmation on receiver apprehension, motivation, and learning. *Communication Education* 53 (January), 1–20.

Elmes, M. B., & Gemmill, G. (1990). The psychodynamics of mindlessness and dissent in small groups. *Small Group Research* 21, 28–44.

Epstein, R. (2005). The loose screw awards: Psychology's top 10 misguided ideas. *Psychology Today* (February), 55–62.

Epstein, R. M., & Hundert, E. M. (2002). Defining and assessing professional competence. *JAMA: Journal of the American Medical Association* 287, 226–235.

Exline, R. V., Ellyson, S. L., & Long, B. (1975). Visual behavior as an aspect of power role relationships. In *Nonverbal communication of aggression,* P. Pliner, L. Krames, & T. Alloway (eds.). New York: Plenum Press.

Fagan, J., & Barnett, M. (2003). The relationship between maternal gatekeeping, paternal competence, mothers' attitudes about the father role, and father involvement. *Journal of Family Issues* 24 (November), 1020–1043.

Feeley, T. H., & deTurck, M. A. (1995). Global cue usage in behavioral lie detection. *Communication Quarterly* 43, 420–430.

Fehr, B., & Broughton, R. (2001). Gender and personality differences in concepts of love: An interpersonal theory analysis. *Personal Relationships* 8, 115–136.

Fehr, B. (2004). Intimacy expectations in same-sex friendships: A prototype interaction-pattern model. *Journal of Personality and Social Psychology* 86 (February), 265–284.

Feng, J., Lazar, J., & Preece, J. (2004). Empathy and online interpersonal trust: A fragile relationship. *Behaviour and Information Technology* 23 (March–April), 97–106.

Fengler, A. P. (1974). Romantic love in courtship: Divergent paths of male and female students. *Journal of Comparative Family Studies* 5, 134–139.

Fernald, C. D. (1995). When in London . . . : Differences in disability language preferences among English-speaking countries. *Mental Retardation* 33, 99–103.

Fesko, S. L. (2001). Disclosure of HIV status in the workplace: Considerations and strategies. *Health and Social Work* 26 (November), 235–244.

Festinger, L., Schachter, S., & Back, K. W. (1950). *Social pressures in informal groups: A study of human factors in housing.* New York: Harper & Row.

Finn, J. (2004). A survey of online harassment at a university campus. *English* 19 (April), 468–483.

Fischer, C. S., & Oliker, S. J. (1983). A research note on friendship, gender, and the life cycle. *Social Forces* 62, 124–133.

Fisher, D. (1995). *People power: 12 power principles to enrich your business, career, and personal networks.* Austin, TX: Bard & Stephen.

Fisher, D. R. (1998). Rumoring theory and the Internet: A framework for analyzing the grass roots. *Social Science Computer Review* 16 (summer), 158–168.

Fitzpatrick, M. A. (1983). Predicting couples' communication from couples' self-reports. In *Communication yearbook 7*, R. N. Bostrom (ed.). Thousand Oaks, CA: Sage, pp. 49–82.

Fitzpatrick, M. A. (1988). *Between husbands and wives: Communication in marriage.* Thousand Oaks, CA: Sage.

Fitzpatrick, M. A. (1991). Sex differences in marital conflict: Social psychophysiological versus cognitive explanations. *Text* 11, 341–364.

Fitzpatrick, M. A., & Caughlin, J. P. (2002). Interpersonal communication in family relationships. In *Handbook of interpersonal communication,* (3d ed.), (pp. 726–777), M. L. Knapp & J. A. Daly. (eds.). Thousand Oaks, CA: Sage.

Floyd, J. J. (1985). *Listening: A practical approach.* Glenview, IL: Scott, Foresman.

Fodor, I. G., & Collier, J. C. (2001). Assertiveness and conflict resolution: An integrated Gestalt/cognitive behavioral model for working with urban adolescents. In *The heart of development: Vol. II: Adolescence: Gestalt approaches to working with children, adolescents and their worlds,* M. McConville & G. Wheeler (eds.), Cambridge, ME: Analytic Press, pp. 214–252.

Folkerts, J., & Lacy, S. (2004). *The media in your life: An introduction to mass communication,* 3d ed. Boston: Allyn & Bacon.

Forbes, G. B. (2001). College students with tattoos and piercings: Motives, family experiences, personality factors, and perception by others. *Psychological Reports* 89, 774–786.

Ford, S. (2003). "Dear Mr. Shawn": A lesson in e-mail pragmatics (netiquette). *TESOL Journal* 12 (spring), 39–40.

Foster, D. A. (2002). *Global etiquette guide to Mexico and Latin America.* New York: Wiley.

Foster, D. (2004). Standing on ceremony. *National Geographic Traveler* 21 (May–June), 97–99.

Franklin, C. W., & Mizell, C. A. (1995). Some factors influencing success among African-American men: A preliminary study. *Journal of Men's Studies* 3, 191–204.

Franklin, R. (2002). Office romances: Conduct unbecoming? *Business Week Online* (February 14), np.

Fraser, B. (1990). Perspectives on politeness. *Journal of Pragmatics* 14, 219–236.

Frazier, P. A., & Cook, S. W. (1993). Correlates of distress following heterosexual relationship dissolution. *Journal of Social and Personal Relationships* 10, 55–67.

Freedman, J. (1978). *Happy people: What happiness is, who has it, and why.* New York: Ballantine.

French, J. R. P., Jr., & Raven, B. (1968). The bases of social power. In *Group dynamics: Research and theory,* 3d ed., D. Cartwright & A. Zander (eds.). New York: Harper & Row, pp. 259–269.

Frentz, T. (1976). A general approach to episodic structure. Paper presented at the Western Speech Association Convention, San Francisco. Cited in Reardon (1987).

Fresko, S. L. (2001). Disclosure of HIV status in the workplace: Considerations and strategies. *Health & Social Work* 25, 235–244.

Friedman, J., Boumil, M. M., & Taylor, B. E. (1992). *Sexual harassment.* Deerfield Beach, FL: Health Communications, Inc.

Frone, M. R. (2000). Interpersonal conflict at work and psychological outcomes: Testing a model among young workers. *Journal of Occupational Health Psychology* 5, 246–255.

Fu, H., Watkins, D., & Hui, E. K. P. (2004). Personality correlates of the disposition towards interpersonal forgiveness: Chinese perspective. *International Journal of Psychology* 39 (August), 305–316.

Fuller, D. (2004). Electronic manners and netiquette. *Athletic Therapy Today* 9 (March), 40–41.

Furlow, F. B. (1996). The smell of love. *Psychology Today* 29, 38–45.

Furnham, A., & Bochner, S. (1986). *Culture shock: Psychological reactions to unfamiliar environments.* New York: Methuen.

Furnham, A. (2004). Foreign students: Education and culture shock. *Psychologist* 17 (January), 16–19.

Galliher, R. V., Rostosky, S. S., Welsh, D. P., & Kawaguchi, M. C. (1999). Power and psychological well-being in the late adolescent romantic relationships. *Sex Roles* 40 (May), 689–710.

Galvin, K. M., Bylund, C. L., & Brommel, B. J. (2004). *Family communication: Cohesion and change.* Boston: Allyn & Bacon.

Gamble, T. K., & Gamble, M. W. (2003). *The gender communication connection.* Boston: Houghton Mifflin.

Gamson, J. (1998). Publicity traps: Television talk shows and lesbian, gay, bisexual, and transgender visibility. *Sexualities* 1 (February), 11–41.

Gangestad, S., & Snyder, M. (1985). To carve nature at its joints: On the existence of discrete classes in personality. *Psychological Review* 92, 317–349.

Gao, G., & Gudykunst, W. B. (1995). Attributional confidence, perceived similarity, and network involvement in Chinese and American romantic relationships. *Communication Quarterly* 43, 431–445.

Gattis, K. S., Berns, S., Simpson, L. E., & Christensen, A. (2004). Birds of a feature or strange birds? Ties among personality dimensions, similarity, and marital quality. *Journal of Family Psychology* 18 (December), 564–574.

Gelfand, M. J., Nishii, L. H., Holcombe, K. M., Dyer, N., Ohbuchi, K., & Fukuno, M. (2001). Cultural influences on cognitive representations of conflict: Interpretations of conflict episodes in the United States and Japan. *Journal of Applied Psychology* 86, 1059–1074.

Gelles, R., & Cornell, C. (1985). *Intimate violence in families.* Thousand Oaks, CA: Sage.

Georgas, J., et al. (2001). Functional relationships in the nuclear and extended family: A 16-culture study. *International Journal of Psychology* 36, 289–300.

Gerbner, G., Gross, L. P., Morgan, M., & Signorielli, N. (1980). The 'Mainstreaming' of America: Violence profile No. 11. *Journal of Communication* 30, 10–29.

Gergen, K. J., Greenberg, M. S., and Willis, R. H. (1980). *Social exchange: Advances in theory and research.* New York: Plenum Press.

Gibb, J. (1961). Defensive communication. *Journal of Communication* 11, 141–148.

Gibbs, N. (2005). Parents behaving badly. *Time* (February 21), 40–49.

Giles, D. C. (2001). Parasocial interaction: A review of the literature and a model for future research. *Media Psychology* 4, 279–305.

Giles, D. C., & Maltby, J. (2004). The role of media figures in adolescent development: Relations between autonomy, at-tachment, and interest in celebrities. *Personality and Individual Differences* 36 (March), 813–822.

Giles, H., Mulac, A., Bradac, J. J., & Johnson, P. (1987). Speech accommodation theory: The first decade and beyond. In *Communication yearbook 10,* M. L. McLaughlin (ed.). Thousand Oaks, CA: Sage, pp. 13–48.

Gladstone, G. L., & Parker, G. B. (2002). When you're smiling, does the whole world smile with you? *Australasian Psychiatry* 10 (June), 144–146.

Glucksberg, S., & Danks, J. H. (1975). *Experimental psycholinguistics: An introduction.* Hillsdale, NJ: Erlbaum.

Goffman, E. (1967). *Interaction ritual: Essays on face-to-face behavior.* New York: Pantheon.

Goffman, E. (1971). *Relations in public: Microstudies of the public order.* New York: Harper Colophon.

Goldin-Meadow, S., Nusbaum, H., Kelly, S. D., & Wagner, S. (2001) Gesture—Psychological aspects. *Psychological Science* 12, 516–522.

Goldsmith, D. J., & Fulfs, P. A. (1999). "You just don't have the evidence": An analysis of claims and evidence. In *Communication yearbook,* 22 (pp. 1–49), M. E. Roloff (ed.). Thousand Oaks, CA: Sage.

Goleman, D. (1992). Studies find no disadvantage in growing up in a gay home. *New York Times* (December 2), C14.

Goleman, D. (1995a). *Emotional intelligence.* New York: Bantam.

Goleman, D. (1995b). For man and beast, language of love shares many traits. *New York Times* (February 14), C1, C9.

Gonzalez, A., & Zimbardo, P. G. (1985). Time in perspective. *Psychology Today* 19, 20–26. Reprinted in DeVito & Hecht (1990).

Gonzaga, G. C., Keltner, D., Lonhahl, E. A., & Smith, M. D. (2001). Love and the commitment problem in romantic relationships and friendships. *Journal of Personality and Social Psychology* 81 (August), 247–262.

Gonzenbach, W. J., King, C., & Jablonski, P. (1999). Homosexuals and the military: An analysis of the spiral of silence. *Howard Journal of Communication* 10 (October–December), 281–296.

Goodwin, R., & Findlay, C. (1997). "We were just fated together" . . . Chinese love and the concept of *yuan* in England and Hong Kong. *Personal Relationships* 4, 85–92.

Goodwin, R., & Gaines, S. O., Jr. (2004). Relationships beliefs and relationship quality across cultures: Country as a moderator of dysfunctional beliefs and relationship quality in three former Communist societies. *Personal Relationships* 11 (September), 267–279.

Goodwin, R., & Lee, I. (1994). Taboo topics among Chinese and English friends: A cross-cultural comparison. *Journal of Cross-Cultural Psychology* 25, 325–338.

Gordon, T. (1975). *P.E.T.: Parent effectiveness training.* New York: New American Library.

Gosling, S. D., Ko, S. J., Mannarelli, T., & Morris, M. E. (2002). A room with a cue: Personality judgments based on offices and bedrooms. *Journal of Personality and Social Psychology* 82 (March), 379–398.

Gottman, J. M. (1993). *What predicts divorce: The relationships between marital processes and marital outcomes.* Hillsdale, NJ: Erlbaum.

Gottman, J. M. (1994). *Why marriages succeed or fail.* New York: Simon and Schuster.

Gottman, J. M., & Carrere, S. (1994). Why can't men and women get along? Developmental roots and marital inequities. In D. J. Canary and L. Stafford (eds.). *Communication and relational maintenance,* San Diego, CA: Academic Press, pp. 203–229.

Gottman, J. M., Coan, J., Carrere, S., & Swanson, C. (1998). Predicting marital happiness and stability from newlywed interactions. *Journal of Marriage and the Family* 60, 5–22.

Gottman, J. M., & Levenson, R. W. (1999). Dysfunctional marital conflict: Women are being unfairly blamed. *Journal of Divorce and Remarriage* 31, 1–17.

Gould, S. J. (1995). No more "wretched refuse." *New York Times* (June 7), A27.

Grace, S. L., & Cramer, K. L. (2003). The elusive nature of self-measurement: The self-construal scale versus the twenty statements test. *Journal of Social Psychology* 143 (October), 649–668.

Graham, E. E. (1994). Interpersonal communication motives scale. In *Communication research measures: A sourcebook,* R. B. Rubin, P. Palmgreen, & H. E. Sypher (eds.). New York: Guilford, pp. 211–216.

Graham, E. E., Barbato, C. A., & Perse, E. M. (1993). The interpersonal communication motives model. *Communication Quarterly* 41, 172–186.

Graham, J. A., & Argyle, M. (1975). The effects of different patterns of gaze, combined with different facial expressions, on impression formation. *Journal of Movement Studies* 1, 178–182.

Graham, J. A., Bitti, P. R., & Argyle, M. (1975). A cross-cultural study of the communication of emotion by facial and gestural cues. *Journal of Human Movement Studies* 1, 68–77.

Greene, J. O. (2003). Models of adult communication skill acquisition: Practice and the course of performance improvement. In *Handbook of communication and social interaction skills,* J. O. Greene & B. R. Burleson (eds.). Mahwah, NJ: Erlbaum, pp. 51–92.

Greene, J. O., & Burleson, B. R. (eds.). (2003). *Handbook of communication and social interaction skills.* Mahwah, NJ: Erlbaum.

Greene, S. (2003). *The psychological development of girls and women: Rethinking change in time.* NY: Routledge.

Greengard, S. (2001). Gossip poisons business. HR can stop it. *Workforce* 80 (July), 24–28.

Greif, E. B. (1980). Sex differences in parent-child conversations. *Women's Studies International Quarterly* 3, 253–258.

Grice, H. P. (1975). Logic and conversation. In *Syntax and semantics,* Vol. 3, *Speech acts,* P. Cole & J. L. Morgan (eds.). New York: Seminar Press, pp. 41–58.

Griffin, E., & Sparks, G. G. (1990). Friends forever: A longitudinal exploration of intimacy in same-sex friends and platonic pairs. *Journal of Social and Personal Relationships* 7, 29–46.

Gross, L. (1991). The contested closet: The ethics and politics of outing. *Critical Studies in Mass Communication* 8, 352–388.

Gross, T., Turner, E., & Cederholm, L. (1987). Building teams for global operation, *Management Review* (June), 32–36.

Gu, Y. (1990). Polite phenomena in modern Chinese. *Journal of Pragmatics* 14, 237–257.

Gudykunst, W. B., ed. (1983). *Intercultural communication theory: Current perspectives.* Thousand Oaks, CA: Sage.

Gudykunst, W. B. (1989). Culture and the development of interpersonal relationships. In *Communication yearbook 12,* J. A. Anderson (ed.). Thousand Oaks, CA: Sage, pp. 315–354.

Gudykunst, W. B. (1991). *Bridging differences: Effective intergroup communication.* Newbury Park, CA: Sage.

Gudykunst, W. B. (1993). Toward a theory of effective interpersonal and intergroup communication: An anxiety/uncertainty management (AUM) perspective. In *Intercultural communication competence,* R. L. Wiseman (ed.). Thousand Oaks, CA: Sage.

Gudykunst, W. B. (1994). *Bridging differences: Effective intergroup communication,* 2d ed. Thousand Oaks, CA: Sage.

Gudykunst, W. B., & Kim, Y. W. (1992). *Communicating with strangers: An approach to intercultural communication,* 2d ed. New York: Random House.

Gudykunst, W. B., & Nishida, T. (1984). Individual and cultural influence on uncertainty reduction. *Communication Monographs* 51, 23–36.

Gudykunst, W. B., Nishida, T., & Chua, E. (1987). Perceptions of social penetration in Japanese-North American dyads. *International Journal of Intercultural Relations* 11, 171–189.

Gudykunst, W. B., & Ting-Toomey, S., with Chua, E. (1988). *Culture and interpersonal communication.* Thousand Oaks, CA: Sage.

Gudykunst, W. B., Yang, S., & Nishida, T. (1985). A cross-cultural test of uncertainty reduction theory: Comparisons of acquaintance, friend, and dating relationships in Japan, Korea, and the United States. *Human Communication Research* 11, 407–454.

Gueguen, N. (2003). Help on the Web: The effect of the same first name between the sender and the receptor in a request made by e-mail. *Psychological Record* 53 (summer), 459–466.

Guerin, B. (2003). Combating prejudice and racism: New interventions from a functional analysis of racist language. *Journal of Community and Applied Social Psychology* 13 (January), 29–45.

Guerrero, L. K. (1997). Nonverbal involvement across interactions with same-sex friends, opposite-sex friends, and romantic partners: Consistency or change? *Journal of Social and Personal Relationships* 14, 31–58.

Guerrero, L. K., & Andersen, P. A. (1991). The waxing and waning of relational intimacy: Touch as a function of relational stage, gender and touch avoidance. *Journal of Social and Personal Relationships* 8, 147–165.

Guerrero, L. K., & Andersen, P. A. (1994). Patterns of matching and initiation: Touch behavior and touch avoidance across romantic relationship stages. *Journal of Nonverbal Behavior* 18, 137–153.

Guerrero, L. K., Andersen, P. A., Jorgensen, P. F., Spitzberg, B. H., & Eloy, S. V. (1995). Coping with the green-eyed monster: Conceptualizing and measuring communicative response to romantic jealousy. *Western Journal of Communication* 59, 270–304.

Guerrero, L. K., DeVito, J. A., & Hecht, M. L., eds. (1999). *The nonverbal communication reader: Classic and contemporary readings.* Prospect Heights, IL: Waveland Press.

Guerrero, L. K., Eloy, S. V., & Wabnik, A. I. (1993). Linking maintenance strategies to relationship development and disengagement: A reconceptualization. *Journal of Social and Personal Relationships* 10, 273–282.

Gugerty, L, Rakauskas, M., & Brooks, J. (2004). Effects of remote and in-person verbal interactions on verbalization rates and attention to dynamic spatial scenes. *Accident Analysis and Prevention* 36 (November), 1029–1043.

Haar, B. F., & Krabe, B. (1999). Strategies for resolving interpersonal conflicts in adolescence: A German-Indonesian comparison. *Journal of Cross-Cultural Psychology* 30, 667–683.

Hafen, S. (2004). Organizational gossip: A revolving door of regulation and resistance. *Southern Communication Journal* 69, 223–240.

Haferkamp, C. J. (1991/1992). Orientations to conflict: Gender, attributes, resolution strategies, and self-monitoring. *Current Psychology: Research and Reviews* 10, 227–240.

Haidar-Yassine, H. (2002). Internet friendships: Can virtual be real? *Dissertation Abstracts International: Section B: The Sciences & Engineering* 63 (5-B), 2651.

Haga, Y. (1988). Traits de langage et caractere japonais. *Cahiers de Sociologie Economique et Culturelle* 9, 105–109.

Hall, E. T. (1959). *The silent language.* Garden City, NY: Doubleday.

Hall, E. T. (1963). System for the notation of proxemic behavior. *American Anthropologist* 65, 1003–1026.

Hall, E. T. (1966). *The hidden dimension.* Garden City, NY: Doubleday.

Hall, E. T. (1976). *Beyond culture.* Garden City, NY: Anchor Press.

Hall, E. T. (1983). *The dance of life: The other dimension of time.* New York: Anchor Books/Doubleday.

Hall, E. T., & Hall, M. R. (1987). *Hidden differences: Doing business with the Japanese.* New York: Anchor Books.

Hall, J. A. (1984). *Nonverbal sex differences.* Baltimore: Johns Hopkins University Press.

Hall, J. A. (1998). How big are nonverbal sex differences? The case of smiling and sensitivity to nonverbal cues. In *Sex differences and similarities in communication: Critical essays and empirical investigations of sex and gender in inter-*

action, (pp. 155–178), D. J. Canary, & K. Dindia (eds.). Mahawah, NJ: Lawrence Erlbaum.

Hall, J. K. (1993). Tengo una bomba: The paralinguistic and linguistic conventions of the oral practice Chismeando. *Research on Language and Social Interaction* 26, 55–83.

Hammer, M. R. (1986). The influence of ethnic and attitude similarity on initial social penetration. In *Interethnic communication: Current research,* Y. Y. Kim (ed.), *International and Intercultural Communication Annual* 10, 225–237.

Hample, D. (2004). Arguing skills. In *Handbook of communication and social interaction skills* (pp. 439–477), J. O. Greene & B. R. Burleson (eds.). Mahwah, NJ: Erlbaum.

Han, S., & Shavitt, S. (1994). Persuasion and culture: Advertising appeals in individualistic and collectivistic societies. *Journal of Experimental Social Psychology* 30, 326–350.

Hancock, J. T. (2004). Verbal irony use in face-to-face and computer-mediated conversations. *Journal of Language and Social Psychology* 23 (December), 447–463.

Haney, W. (1973). *Communication and organizational behavior: Text and cases,* 3d ed. Homewood, IL: Irwin.

Hardey, M. (2004). Mediated relationships. *Information Communication and Society* 7 (June), 207–222.

Harrell, W. A. (1990). Husband's masculinity, wife's power, and marital conflict. *Social Behavior and Personality* 18, 207–215.

Harris, M. (1993). *Culture, people, nature: An introduction to general anthropology,* 6th ed. Boston: Allyn & Bacon.

Hart, F. (1990). The construction of masculinity in men's friendships: Misogyny, heterosexism and homophobia. *Resources for Feminist Research* 19, 60–67.

Hart, R. P., & Burks, D. M. (1972). Rhetorical sensitivity and social interaction. *Communication Monographs* 39, 75–91.

Hart, R. P., Carlson, R. E., & Eadie, W. F. (1980). Attitudes toward communication and the assessment of rhetorical sensitivity. *Communication Monographs* 47, 1–22.

Harvey, J. H., Flanary, R., & Morgan, M. (1986). Vivid memories of vivid loves gone by. *Journal of Social and Personal Relationships* 3, 359–373.

Hasart, J. K., & Hutchinson, K. L. (1993). The effects of eyeglasses on perceptions of interpersonal attraction. *Journal of Social Behavior and Personality* 8, 521–528.

Hasegawa, T., & Gudykunst, W. B. (1998). Silence in Japan and the United States. *Journal of Cross-Cultural Psychology* 29, 668–684.

Hastings, S. O. (2000). "Egocasting" in the avoidance of disclosure: An intercultural perspective. In *Balancing the secrets of private disclosures.* (pp. 235–248), S. Petronio (ed.). Mahwah, NJ: Erlbaum.

Hatfield, E., & Rapson, R. L. (1992). Similarity and attraction in close relationships. *Communication Monographs* 59, 209–212.

Hatfield, E., & Rapson, R. L. (1996). *Love and sex: Cross-cultural perspectives.* Boston: Allyn & Bacon.

Haugh, M. (2004). Revisiting the conceptualization of politeness in English and Japanese. *Multilingua* 23, 85–109.

Hayakawa, S. I., & Hayakawa, A. R. (1989). *Language in thought and action,* 5th ed. New York: Harcourt Brace Jovanovich.

Hays, R. B. (1989). The day-to-day functioning of close versus casual friendships. *Journal of Social and Personal Relationships* 6, 21–37.

Heasley, J. B. S., Babbitt, C. E., & Burbach, H. J. (1995). The role of social context in students' anticipatory reaction to a "fighting word." *Sociological Focus* 27, 281–283.

Heath, W. P., Stone, J., Darley, J. M., & Grannemann, B. D. (2003). Yes, I did it, but don't blame me: Perceptions of excuse defenses. *Journal of Psychiatry and Law* 31(summer), 187–226.

Hecht, M. L., Jackson, R. L., & Ribeau, S. (2003). *African American communication: Exploring identity and culture,* 2d ed. Mahwah, NJ: Erlbaum.

Hellweg, S. A. (1992). Organizational grapevines. In *Readings in organizational communication,* (pp. 159–172), K. L. Hutchinson (ed.). Dubuque, IA: William. C. Brown.

Henderson, S., & Gilding, M. (2004). "I've never clicked this much with anyone in my life": Trust and hyperpersonal communication in online friendships. *New Media and Society* 6 (August), 487–506.

Hendrick, S. S. (2004). "All things being equal. . . ." *PsycCRITIQUES,* np.

Hendrick, C., & Hendrick, S. (1990). A relationship-specific version of the love attitudes scale. In *Handbook of replication research in the behavioral and social sciences* (special issue), J. W. Heulip (ed.), *Journal of Social Behavior and Personality* 5, 239–254.

Hendrick, C., Hendrick, S., Foote, F. H., & Slapion-Foote, M. J. (1984). Do men and women love differently? *Journal of Social and Personal Relationships* 1, 177–195.

Henley, N. M. (1977). *Body politics: Power, sex, and nonverbal communication.* Englewood Cliffs, NJ: Prentice-Hall.

Hensley, W. E. (1996). A theory of the valenced other: The intersection of the looking-glass-self and social penetration. *Social Behavior and Personality* 24, 293–308.

Hess, E. H. (1975). *The tell-tale eye.* New York: Van Nostrand Reinhold.

Hess, E. H., Seltzer, A. L., & Schlien, J. M. (1965). Pupil response of hetero- and homosexual males to pictures of men and women: A pilot study. *Journal of Abnormal Psychology* 70, 165–168.

Hess, U., Kappas, A., McHugo, G. J., Lanzetta, J. T., et al. (1992). The facilitative effect of facial expression on the self-generation of emotion. *International Journal of Psychophysiology* 12, 251–265.

Hewitt, J. P. (1998). *The myth of self-esteem: Finding happiness and solving problems in America.* New York: St. Martin's Press.

Hewitt, J. P., & Stokes, R. (1975). Disclaimers. *American Sociological Review* 40, 1–11.

Hian, L. B., Chuan, S. L., Trevor, T. M. K., & Detenber, B. H. (2004). Getting to know you: Exploring the development of relational intimacy in computer-mediated communication. *Journal of Computer Mediated Communication* 9 (3, April).

Hilton, L. (2000). They heard it through the grapevine. *South Florida Business Journal* 21 (August), 53.

Hirofumi, A. (2003). Closeness and interpersonal outcomes in same-sex friendships: An improvement of the investment model and explanation of closeness. *Japanese Journal of Experimental Social Psychology* 42 (March), 131–145.

Hoffmann, G. (2005). Rhetoric of Bush speeches: Purr words and snarl words. *Etc: A Review of General Semantics* 62 (April), 198–201.

Hoffner, C., et al. (2001). The third-person effect in perceptions of the influence of television violence. *Journal of Communication* 51 (June), 283–299.

Hofstede, G. (1983). National culture revisited. *Behavior Science Research* 18, 285–305.

Hofstede, G. (1997). *Cultures and organizations: Software of the mind.* New York: McGraw-Hill.

Hofstede, G. (2000). Masculine and feminine cultures. *Encyclopedia of psychology,* Vol. 5 (pp. 115–118), A. E. Kazdin (ed.). Washington, DC: American Psychological Association and Oxford University Press.

Hofstede, G., ed. (1998). *Masculinity and femininity: The taboo dimension of national cultures.* Thousand Oaks, CA: Sage.

Hoft, N. L. (1995). *International technical communication: How to export information about high technology.* New York: Wiley.

Holden, J. M. (1991). The most frequent personality priority pairings in marriage and marriage counseling. *Individual Psychology Journal of Adlerian Theory, Research, and Practice* 47, 392–398.

Holmes, J. (1986). Compliments and compliment responses in New Zealand English. *Anthropological Linguistics* 28, 485–508.

Holmes, J. (1995). *Women, men and politeness.* New York: Longman.

Honeycutt, J. (1986). A model of marital functioning based on an attraction paradigm and social penetration dimensions. *Journal of Marriage and the Family* 48, 51–59.

Hopper, R., Knapp, M. L., & Scott, L. (1981). Couples' personal idioms: Exploring intimate talk. *Journal of Communication* 31, 23–33.

Horenstein, V. D., & Downey, J. L. (2003). A cross-cultural investigation of self-disclosure. *North American Journal of Psychology* 5, 373–386.

Hornsey, J. J., Bath, M. T., & Gunthorpe, S. (2004). "You can criticize because you care": Identity attachment, constructiveness, and the intergroup sensitivity effect. *European Journal of Social Psychology* 34 (September–October), 499–518.

Horvath, L. S. (2004). Teasing: Functions and consequences in romantic relationships. *Dissertation Abstracts International: Section B: The Sciences and Engineering* 65 (2-B), 1030.

Hosman, L. A. (1989). The evaluative consequences of hedges, hesitations, and intensifiers: Powerful and powerless speech styles. *Human Communication Research* 15, 383–406.

How Americans Communicate (1999). http://www.natcom.org/Research/Roper/how_Americans_communicate.htm.

Howard, P. E. N., Rainie, L., & Jones, S. (2001). Days and nights on the Internet: The impact of a diffusing technology. *American Behavioral Scientist* 45, 383–404.

Hu, Y., Wood, J. F., Smith, V., & Westbrook, N. (2004). Friendships through IM: Examining the relationship between instant messaging and intimacy. *Journal of Computer-Mediated Communication* 10 (November), np.

Hunt, M. O. (2000). Status, religion, and the "belief in a just world": Comparing African Americans, Latinos, and whites. *Social Science Quarterly* 81 (March), 325–343.

Huston, M., & Schwartz, P. (1995). The relationships of lesbians and gay men. In *Under-studied relationships: Off the beaten track,* J. T. Wood, & S. Duck (eds.). Thousand Oaks, CA: Sage, pp. 89–121.

Imwalle, D. B., & Schillo, K. K. (2004). Masculinity and femininity: The taboo dimension of national cultures. *Archives of Sexual Behavior* 33 (April), 174–176.

Infante, D. A. (1988). *Arguing constructively.* Prospect Heights, IL: Waveland Press.

Infante, D. A., Chandler, T. A., & Rudd, J. E. (1989). Test of an argumentative skill deficiency model of interspousal violence. *Communication Monographs* 56, 163–177.

Infante, D. A., Hartley, K. C., Martin, M. M., Higgins, M. A., Bruning, S. D., & Hur, G. (1992). Initiating and reciprocating verbal aggression: Effects on credibility and credited valid arguments. *Communication Studies* 43, 182–190.

Infante, D. A., & Rancer, A. S. (1982). A conceptualization and measure of argumentativeness. *Journal of Personality Assessment* 46, 72–80.

Infante, D. A., & Rancer, A. S. (1996). Argumentativeness and verbal aggressiveness: A review of recent theory and research. In *Communication yearbook 19* (pp. 319–351), B. R. Burleson (ed.). Thousand Oaks, CA: Sage.

Infante, D. A., Rancer, A. S., & Jordan, F. F. (1996). Affirming and nonaffirming style, dyad sex, and the perception of argumentation and verbal aggression in an interpersonal dispute. *Human Communication Research* 22, 315–334.

Infante, D. A., Rancer, A. S., & Womack, D. F. (2003). *Building communication theory,* 4th ed. Prospect Heights, IL: Waveland Press.

Infante, D. A., Riddle, B. L., Horvath, C. L., & Tumlin, S. A. (1992). Verbal aggressiveness: Messages and reasons. *Communication Quarterly* 40, 116–126.

Infante, D. A., Sabourin, T. C., Rudd, J. E., & Shannon, E. A. (1990). Verbal aggression in violent and nonviolent marital disputes. *Communication Quarterly* 38, 361–371.

Infante, D. A., & Wigley, C. J. (1986). Verbal aggressiveness: An interpersonal model and measure. *Communication Monographs* 53, 61–69.

Ingram, M. P. B. (1998). A study of transformative aspects of career change experiences and implications for current models of career development, Ph.D. dissertation, Texas A&M University. *Dissertation Abstracts International Section A: Humanities and Social Sciences* 58, 4156.

Insel, P. M., & Jacobson, L. F., eds. (1975). *What do you expect? An inquiry into self-fulfilling prophecies.* Menlo Park, CA: Cummings.

Irizarry, C. A. (2004). Face and the female professional: A thematic analysis of face-threatening communication in the workplace. *Qualitative Research Reports in Communication* 5, 15–21.

Iverson, J. M., & Goldin-Meadow, S., eds. (1999). *The nature and functions of gesture in children's communication.* San Francisco: Jossey-Bass.

Ivy, D. K., & Backlund, P. (2000). *Exploring gender-speak: Personal effectiveness in gender communication,* 2d ed. New York: McGraw-Hill.

Jackson, L. A., & Ervin, K. S. (1992). Height stereotypes of women and men: The liabilities of shortness for both sexes. *Journal of Social Psychology* 132, 433–445.

Jacobson, D. (1999). Impression formation in cyberspace: Online expectations and offline experiences in text-based virtual communities. *Journal of Computer Mediated Communication* 5, np.

Jaksa, J. A., & Pritchard, M. S. (1994). *Communication ethics: Methods of analysis,* 2d ed. Belmont, CA: Wadsworth.

Jambor, E., & Elliott, M. (2005). Self-esteem and coping strategies among deaf students. *Journal of Deaf Studies and Deaf Education* 10 (winter), 63–81.

James, D. L. (1995). *The executive guide to Asia-Pacific communications.* New York: Kodansha International.

Jamieson, K. H., & Campbell, K. K. (2001). *The interplay of influence,* 5th ed. Belmont, CA: Wadsworth.

Jandt, F. E., & Nemnich, M. B. (1995). *Using the Internet in your job search.* Indianapolis, IN: Jist Works, Inc.

Jandt, F. E. (2004). *An introduction to intercultural communication: Identities in a global community,* 4th ed. Thousand Oaks, CA: Sage.

Janus, S. S., & Janus, C. L. (1993). *The Janus report on sexual behavior.* New York: Wiley.

Jaworski, A. (1993). *The power of silence: Social and pragmatic perspectives.* Thousand Oaks, CA: Sage.

Johannesen, R. L. (2001). *Ethics in human communication,* 5th ed. Prospect Heights, IL: Waveland Press.

Johansson, W., & Percy, W. A. (1994). *Outing: Shattering the conspiracy of silence.* New York: Harrington Park Press.

Johnson, A. J., Wittenberg, E., Villagran, M. M., Mazur, M., & Villagran, P. (2003). Relational progression as a dialectic: Examining turning points in communication among friends. *Communication Monographs* 70 (September), 230–249.

Johnson, C. E. (1987). An introduction to powerful and powerless talk in the classroom. *Communication Education* 36, 167–172.

Johnson, F. L., & Aries, E. J. (1983). The talk of women friends. *Women's Studies International Forum* 6, 353–361.

Johnson, M. P. (1973). Commitment: A conceptual structure and empirical application. *Sociological Quarterly* 14, 395–406.

Johnson, M. P. (1982). Social and cognitive features of the dissolution of commitment to relationships. In *Personal Relationships 4: Dissolving Personal Relationships,* (pp. 51–73), S. Duck, (ed.). New York: Academic Press.

Johnson, M. P. (1991). Commitment to personal relationships. In *Advances in personal relationships, Vol. 3* (pp. 117–143), W. H. Jones, & D. Perlman, (eds.). London: Jessica Kingsley.

Johnson, S. D., & Bechler, C. (1998). Examining the relationship between listening effectiveness and leadership emergence: Perceptions, behaviors, and recall. *Small Group Research* 29, 452–471.

Joinson, A. N. (2001). Self-disclosure in computer-mediated communication: The role of self-awareness and visual anonymity. *European Journal of Social Psychology* 31, 177–192.

Joinson, A. N. (2004). Self-esteem, interpersonal risk, and preference for e-mail to face-to-face communication. *CyberPsychology and Behavior* 7 (August), 472–478.

Jones, S. (1986). Sex differences in touch communication. *Western Journal of Speech Communication* 50, 227–241.

Jones, D. (2004). Cupid lurks in cubicles, so what's a worker to do? *USA Today* (April 2), Money Section, 5.

Jones, Q., Ravid, G., & Rafaeli, S. (2004). Information overload and the message dynamics of online interaction spaces: A theoretical model and empirical exploration. *Information Systems Research* 15 (June), 194–210.

Jones, S., & Yarbrough, A. E. (1985). A naturalistic study of the meanings of touch. *Communication Monographs* 52, 19–56. A version of this paper appears in DeVito & Hecht (1990).

Jörn, Rusen (2004). How to overcome ethnocentrism: Approaches to a culture of recognition by history in the twenty-first century. *History and Theory* 43 (December), 118–129.

Jourard, S. M. (1968). *Disclosing man to himself.* New York: Van Nostrand Reinhold.

Jourard, S. M. (1971a). *Self-disclosure.* New York: Wiley.

Jourard, S. M. (1971b). *The transparent self.* Rev. ed. New York: Van Nostrand Reinhold.

Joyner, R. (1993). An auto-interview on the need for E-prime. *Etc.: A Review of General Semantics,* 50 (Fall), 317–325.

Judge, T. A., & Cable, D. M. (2004). The effect of physical height on workplace success and income. *Journal of Applied Psychology* 89, 428–441.

Judson, O. (2005). Different but (probably) equal. *New York Times* (January 23), The Week in Review, 17.

Kallos, J. (2005). *Because netiquette matters! Your comprehensive reference guide to e-mail etiquette and proper technology use.* Philadelphia: Xlibris Corporation.

Kanemasa, Y., Taniguchi, J., Daibo, I., & Ishimori, M. (2004). Love styles and romantic love experiences in Japan. *Social Behavior and Personality: An International Journal* 32, 265–281.

Kanner, B. (1989). Color schemes. *New York Magazine* (April 3), 22–23.

Kapoor, S., Hughes, P. C., Baldwin, J. R., & Blue, J. (2003). The relationship of individualism–collectivism and self-construals to communication styles in India and the United States. *International Journal of Intercultural Relations* 27 (November), 683–700.

Kapoor, S., Wolfe, A., & Blue, J. (1995). Universal values structure and individualism–collectivism: A U.S. test. *Communication Research Reports* 12, 112–123.

Kassing, J. W. (1997). Development of the intercultural willingness to communicate scale. *Communication Research Reports* 14, 399–407.

Katz, E. M. (2004). *I can't believe I'm buying this book: A commonsense guide to successful Internet dating.* Berkeley, CA: Ten Speed Press.

Katz, S. (2003). *Down to earth sociology: Introductory readings,* 12th ed. (pp. 313–320), J. W. Henslin (ed.). New York: Free Press.

Kearney, P., Plax, T. G., Richmond, V. P., & McCroskey, J. C. (1984). Power in the classroom IV: Alternatives to discipline. In *Communication yearbook 8,* R. N. Bostrom (ed.). Thousand Oaks, CA: Sage, pp. 724–746.

Kearney, P., Plax, T. G., Richmond, V. P., & McCroskey, J. C. (1985). Power in the classroom III: Teacher communication techniques and messages. *Communication Education* 34, 19–28.

Keating, C. F., Mazur, A., & Segall, M. H. (1977). Facial gestures which influence the perception of status. *Sociometry* 40, 374–378.

Kennedy, C. W., & Camden, C. T. (1988). A new look at interruptions. *Western Journal of Speech Communication* 47, 45–58.

Kevin, M. C., Organista, P. B., & Marin, G. (eds.). (2003). *Acculturation: Advances in theory, measurement, and applied research.* Washington DC: American Psychological Association.

Keyes, K., Jr., & Keyes, P. (1987). *Gathering power through insight and love.* St. Mary, KY: Living Love.

Keyes, R. (1980). *The height of your life.* New York: Warner Books.

Kim, M., & Sharkey, W. F. (1995). Independent and interdependent construals of self: Explaining cultural patterns of interpersonal communication in multi-cultural organizational settings. *Communication Quarterly* 43, 20–38.

Kim, S. H., & Smith, R. H. (1993). Revenge and conflict escalation. *Negotiation Journal* 9, 37–43.

Kim, Y. Y. (1991). Intercultural communication competence. In *Cross-cultural interpersonal communication,* S. Ting-Toomey & F. Korzenny (eds.). Thousand Oaks, CA: Sage, pp. 259–275.

Kindred, J., & Roper, S. L. (2004). Making connections via instant messaging (IM): Student use of IM to maintain personal relationships. *Qualitative Research Reports in Communication* 5, 48–54.

Kirkpatrick, C., & Caplow, T. (1945). Courtship in a group of Minnesota students. *American Journal of Sociology* 51, 114–125.

Kirn, W. (2005). It's a glad, sad, mad world. *Time* (January 17), A65–A67.

Kivik, P. K. (1998). What silence says: Communicative style and identity. *Trames* 2 (1), 66–90.

Klein, J. (ed.). (1992). The E-prime controversy: A symposium [Special issue]. *Etc.: A Review of General Semantics,* 49(2).

Kleinfield, N. R. (1992). The smell of money. *New York Times* (October 25), 1, 8.

Kleinke, C. L. (1986). *Meeting and understanding people.* New York: W. H. Freeman.

Kleinke, D. L., & Dean, G. O. (1990). Evaluation of men and women receiving positive and negative responses with various acquaintance strategies. *Journal of Social Behavior and Personality* 5, 369–377.

Kline, S. L., & Stafford, L. (2004). A comparison of interaction rules and interaction frequency in relationship to marital quality. *Communication Reports* 17 (winter), 11–26.

Klineberg, O., & Hull, W. F. (1979). *At a foreign university: An international study of adaptation and coping.* New York: Praeger.

Kluger, J. (2005). The funny thing about laughter. *Time* (January 17), A25–A29.

Knapp, M. L. (1978). *Social intercourse: From greeting to goodbye.* Boston, MA: Allyn & Bacon.

Knapp, M. L., Ellis, D., & Williams, B. A. (1980). Perceptions of communication behavior associated with relationship terms. *Communication Monographs* 47, 262–278.

Knapp, M. L., & Hall, J. (2002). *Nonverbal behavior in human interaction,* 3d ed. New York: Holt, Rinehart & Winston.

Knapp, M. L., & Taylor, E. H. (1994). Commitment and its communication in romantic relationships. In *Perspectives on close relationships,* A. L. Weber & J. H. Harvey (eds.). Boston: Allyn & Bacon, pp. 153–175.

Knapp, M. L., & Vangelisti, A. (2005). *Interpersonal communication and human relationships,* 5th ed. Boston: Allyn & Bacon.

Knobloch, L. K., & Carpenter-Theune, K. E. (2004). Topic avoidance in developing romantic relationships. *Communication Research* (April), 173–205.

Knobloch, L. K., & Solomon, D. H. (1999). Measuring the sources and content of relational uncertainty. *Communication Studies* 50 (winter), 261–278.

Knox, D., Daniels, V., Sturdivant, L., & Zusman, M. E. (2001). College student use of the Internet for mate selection. *College Student Journal* 35, 158–160.

Kochman, T. (1981). *Black and white: Styles in conflict.* Chicago: University of Chicago Press.

Koerner, A. F., & Fitzpatrick, M. A. (2002). You never leave your family in a fight: The impact of family of origin on conflict behavior in romantic relationships. *Communication Studies* 53 (fall), 234–252.

Kollock, P., & Smith, M. (1996). Managing the virtual commons: Cooperation and conflict in computer communities. In *Computer-mediated communication: Linguistic, social, and cross-cultural perspectives* (pp. 109–128), S. Herring (ed.). Amsterdam: John Benjamins.

Komarovsky, M. (1964). *Blue collar marriage.* New York: Random House.

Korda, M. (1975). *Power! How to get it, how to use it.* New York: Ballantine.

Korzybski, A. (1933). *Science and sanity.* Lakeville, CT: The International Non-Aristotelian Library.

Kposowa, A. J. (2000). Marital status and suicide in the National Longitudinal Mortality Study. *Journal of Epidemiology and Community Health,* 54 (April), 254–261.

Kramer, R. (1997). Leading by listening: An empirical test of Carl Rogers's theory of human relationship using interpersonal assessments of leaders by followers. *Dissertation Abstracts, International Section A. Humanities and Social Sciences* 58, 514.

Kraut, R., et al. (1999). Internet paradox. *American Psychologist* 53, 1017–1031.

Krebs, G. L. (1989). *Organizational communication,* 2d ed. Boston: Allyn & Bacon.

Krivonos, P. D., & Knapp, M. L. (1975). Initiating communication: What do you say when you say hello? *Central States Speech Journal* 26, 115–125.

Krohn, F. B. (2004). A generational approach to using emoticons as nonverbal communication. *Journal of Technical Writing and Communication* 34, 321–328.

Kroløkke, C., & Sørensen, A. S. (2006). *Gender communication theories and analyses: From silence to performance.* Thousand Oaks, CA: Sage.

Kudo, E., & Numazaki, M. (2003). Explicit and direct self-serving bias in Japan: Reexamination of self-serving bias for success and failure. *Journal of Cross-Cultural Psychology* 34 (September), 511–521.

Kurdek, L. A. (1994). Areas of conflict for gay, lesbian, and heterosexual couples: What couples argue about influences relationship satisfaction. *Journal of Marriage and the Family* 56, 923–934.

Kurdek, L. A. (1995). Developmental changes in relationship quality in gay and lesbian cohabiting couples. *Developmental Psychology* 31, 86–93.

Kurdek, L. A. (2000). Attractions and constraints as determinants of relationship commitment: Longitudinal evidence from gay, lesbian, and heterosexual couples. *Personal Relationships* 7, 245–262.

Kurdek, L. A. (2004). Are gay and lesbian cohabiting couples really different from heterosexual married couples? *Journal of Marriage and Family* 66 (November), 880-900.

Lachnit, C. (2001). Giving up gossip. *Workforce* 80 (July), 8.

Laing, M. (1993). Gossip: Does it play a role in the socialization of nurses? *Journal of Nursing Scholarship* 25, 37–43.

Lakoff, R. (1975). *Language and women's place.* New York: Harper & Row.

Langer, E. J. (1989). *Mindfulness.* Reading, MA: Addison-Wesley.

Lansford, J. E., Antonucci, T. C., Akiyama, H., & Takahashi, K. (2005). A quantitative and qualitative approach to social relationships and well-being in the United States and Japan. *Journal of Comparative Family Studies* 36 (winter), 1–22.

Lantz, A. (2001). Meetings in a distributed group of experts: Comparing face-to-face, chat and collaborative virtual environments. *Behaviour and Information Technology* 20, 111–117.

Lanzetta, J. T., Cartwright-Smith, J., & Kleck, R. E. (1976). Effects of nonverbal dissimulations on emotional experience and autonomic arousal. *Journal of Personality and Social Psychology* 33, 354–370.

Laroche, C., & deGrace, G. R. (1997). Factors of satisfaction associated with happiness in adults. *Canadian Journal of Counseling* 31, 275–286.

Larsen, N. M. (2004). Marital satisfaction and equity in decision making. *Dissertation Abstracts International: Section B: The Sciences and Engineering* 65 (2-B), 1045.

Larsen, R. J., Kasimatis, M., & Frey, K. (1992). Facilitating the furrowed brow: An unobtrusive test of the facial feedback hypothesis applied to unpleasant affect. *Cognition and Emotion* 6, 321–338.

Lau, I., Chiu, C., & Hong, Y. (2001). I know what you know: Assumptions about others' knowledge and their effects on message construction. *Social Cognition* 19, 587–600.

Lauer, C. S. (2003). Listen to This. *Modern Healthcare* 33 (February 10), 34.

Lea, M., & Spears, R. (1995). Love at first byte? Building personal relationships over computer networks. In *Understudied relationships: Off the beaten track,* J. T. Wood & S. Duck (eds.). Thousand Oaks, CA: Sage, pp. 197–233.

Leaper, C., & Holliday, H. (1995). Gossip in same-gender and cross-gender friends' conversations. *Personal Relationships* 2, 237–246.

Leathers, D. G. (1997). *Successful nonverbal communication: Principles and applications,* 3d ed. New York: Macmillan.

Leavitt, H. J. (2005). *Top down: Why hierarchies are here to stay and how to manage them more effectively.* Cambridge, MA: Harvard Business School Publishing.

Lederer, W. J. (1984). *Creating a good relationship.* New York: Norton.

Lee, A. M., & Lee, E. B. (1972). *The fine art of propaganda.* San Francisco: International Society for General Semantics.

Lee, A. M., & Lee, E. B. (1995). The iconography of propaganda analysis. *ETC.: A Review of General Semantics* 52 (spring), 13–17.

Lee, E., & Kim, M. (2004). Exposure to media violence and bullying at school: Mediating influences of anger and contact with delinquent friends. *Psychological Reports* 95 (October), 659–672.

Lee, F. (1993). Being polite and keeping MUM: How bad news is communicated in organizational hierarchies. *Journal of Applied Social Psychology* 23, 1124–1149.

Lee, H. O., & Boster, F. J. (1992). Collectivism-individualism in perceptions of speech rate: A cross-cultural comparison. *Journal of Cross-Cultural Psychology* 23, 377–388.

Lee, J. (2005). Romance beckons (in case you missed it). *New York Times* (February 23), B4.

Lee, J. A. (1976). *The colors of love.* New York: Bantam.

Lee, K. (2000). Information overload threatens employee productivity. *Employee Benefit News* (November 1), p. 1.

Lee, R. M. (2005). Resilience against discrimination: Ethnic identity and other-group orientation as protective factors for Korean Americans. *Journal of Counseling Psychology* 52 (January), 36–44.

Lemieux, R., & Hale, J. L. (1999). Intimacy, passion, and commitment in young romantic relationships: Successfully measuring the triangular theory of love. *Psychological Reports* 85, 497–503.

Lemieux, R., & Hale, J. L. (2001). Intimacy, passion, and commitment among married individuals: Further testing of the triangular theory of love. *Psychological Reports* 89, 25–26.

Lemonick, M. D. (2005a). A smile doesn't always mean happy. *Time* (January 17), A29.

Lemonick, M. D. (2005b). Stealth attack on evaluation. *Time* (January 31), 53–54.

Leon, J. J., Philbrick, J. L., Parra, F., Escobedo, E., et al. (1994). Love styles among university students in Mexico. *Psychological Reports* 74, 307–310.

Leung, K. (1987). Some determinants of reactions to procedural models for conflict resolution: A cross-national study. *Journal of Personality and Social Psychology* 53, 898–908.

Leung, K. (1988). Some determinants of conflict avoidance. *Journal of Cross-Cultural Psychology* 19, 125–136.

Leung, S. A. (2001). Editor's introduction. *Asian Journal of Counseling* 8, 107–109.

Lever, J. (1995). The 1995 Advocate survey of sexuality and relationships: The women, lesbian sex survey. *The Advocate* 687/688, 22–30.

Levine, D. (2000). Virtual attraction: What rocks your boat. *CyberPsychology and Behavior* 3, 565–573.

Levine, M. (2004). Tell the doctor all your problems, but keep it to less than a minute. *New York Times* (June 1), F6.

Levine, T. R., Beatty, M. J., Limon, S., Hamilton, M. A., Buck, R., & Chory-Assad, R. M. (2004). The dimensionality of the verbal aggressiveness scale. *Communication Monographs* 71 (September), 245–268.

LeVine, R., Bartlett, K. (1984). Pace of life, punctuality, and coronary heart disease in six countries. *Journal of Cross-Cultural Psychology* 15, 233–255.

LeVine, R., Sato, S., Hashimoto, T., & Verma, J. (1994). Love and marriage in eleven cultures. Unpublished manuscript. California State University, Fresno, cited in Hatfield & Rapson (1996).

Lewin, K. (1947). *Human relations.* New York: Harper & Row.

Lewis, D. (1989). *The secret language of success.* New York: Carroll & Graf.

Lewis, P. H. (1995). The new Internet gatekeepers. *New York Times* (November 13), D1, D6.

Li, H. Z. (1999). Communicating information in conversations: A cross-cultural comparison. *International Journal of Intercultural Relations* 23 (May), 387–409.

Lin, Y., & Rancer, A. S. (2003a). Ethnocentrism, intercultural communication apprehension, intercultural willingness-to-communicate, and intentions to participate in an intercultural dialogue program: Testing a proposed model. *Communication Research Reports* 20 (spring), 189–190.

Lin, Y., & Rancer, A. S. (2003b). Sex differences in intercultural communication apprehension, ethnocentrism, and intercultural willingness to communicate. *Psychological Reports* 92 (February), 195–200.

Lindblom, K. (2001). Cooperating with Grice: A cross-disciplinary metaperspective on uses of Grice's cooperative principle. *Journal of Pragmatics* 33, 1601–1623.

Lindeman, M., Harakka, T., & Keltikangas-Jarvinen, L. (1997). Age and gender differences in adolescents' reactions to conflict situations: Aggression, prosociality, and withdrawal. *Journal of Youth and Adolescence* 26, 339–351.

Littlejohn, S. W. (1996). *Theories of human communication,* 6th ed. Belmont, CA: Wadsworth.

Lloyd, S. R. (2001). *Developing positive assertiveness,* 3d ed. Menlo Park, CA: Crisp Publications.

Lo, V. & Wei, R. (2002). Third-person effect, gender, and pornography on the Internet. *Journal of Broadcasting & Electronic Media* 46 (winter), 13–33.

Lu, L., & Shih, J. B. (1997). Sources of happiness: A qualitative approach. *Journal of Social Psychology* 137, 181–188.

Lubin, J. S. (2004). How to stop the snubs that demoralize you and your colleagues. *Wall Street Journal* (December 7), B1.

Luft, J. (1969). *Of human interaction.* Palo Alto, CA: Mayfield.

Luft, J. (1984). *Group processes: An introduction to group dynamics,* 3d ed. Palo Alto, CA: Mayfield.

Lujansky, H., & Mikula, G. (1983). Can equity theory explain the quality and stability of romantic relationships? *British Journal of Social Psychology* 22, 101–112.

Lukens, J. (1978). Ethnocentric speech. *Ethnic Groups* 2, 35–53.

Lurie, A. (1983). *The language of clothes.* New York: Vintage.

Lustig, M. W., & Koester, J. (2006). *Intercultural competence: Interpersonal communication across cultures,* 6th ed. Boston: Allyn & Bacon.

Lyons, A., & Kashima, Y. (2003). How are stereotypes maintained through communication? The influence of stereo-type sharedness. *Journal of Personality and Social Psychology* 85 (December), 989–1005.

Ma, K. (1996). *The modern Madame Butterfly: Fantasy and reality in Japanese cross-cultural relationships.* Rutland, VT: Charles E. Tuttle.

Ma, R. (1992). The role of unofficial intermediaries in interpersonal conflicts in the Chinese culture. *Communication Quarterly* 40, 269–278.

Maas, D. F. (2002). Make your paraphrasing plagiarism proof with a coat of E-prime. *ETC: A Review of General Semantics* 59 (summer), 196–205.

Mackey, R. A., Diemer, M. A., & O'Brien, B. A. (2000). Psychological intimacy in the lasting relationships of heterosexual and same-gender couples. *Sex Roles* 43, 201–227.

MacLachlan, J. (1979). What people really think of fast talkers. *Psychology Today* 13, 113–117.

Madon, S., Guyll, M., & Spoth, R. L. (2004). The self-fulfilling prophecy as an intrafamily dynamic. *Journal of Family Psychology* 18, 459–469.

Maggio, R. (1997). *Talking about people: A guide to fair and accurate language.* Phoenix, AZ: Oryx Press.

Mahaffey, A. L., Bryan, A., & Hutchison, K. E. (2005). Using startle eye blink to measure the affective component of antigay bias. *Basic and Applied Social Psychology* 27 (March), 37–45.

Main, F., & Oliver, R. (1988). Complementary, symmetrical, and parallel personality priorities as indicators of marital adjustment. *Individual Psychology Journal of Adlerian Theory, Research, and Practice* 44, 324–332.

Malandro, L. A., Barker, L. L., & Barker, D. A. (1989). *Nonverbal communication,* 2d ed. New York: Random House.

Malinowski, B. (1923). The problem of meaning in primitive languages. In *The Meaning of Meaning,* C. K. Ogden & I. A. Richards (eds.). New York: Harcourt Brace Jovanovich, pp. 296–336.

Mallen, M. J., Day, S. X., & Green, M. A. (2003). Online versus face-to-face conversation: An examination of relational and discourse variables. *Psychotherapy: Theory, Research, Practice, Training* 40, 155–163.

Manes, J., & Wolfson, N. (1981). The compliment formula. In *Conversational Routine,* Florian Coulmas (ed.). The Hague: Mouton, pp. 115–132.

Mao, L. R. (1994). Beyond politeness theory: "Face" revisited and renewed. *Journal of Pragmatics* 21, 451–486.

Marano, H. E. (2004). Unconventional wisdom. *Psychology Today* 37 (May–June), 10–11.

Markway, B. G., Carmin, C. N., Pollard, C. A., & Flynn, T. (1992). *Dying of embarrassment: Help for social anxiety and phobia.* Oakland, CA: New Harbinger Publications.

Marsh, P. (1988). *Eye to eye: How people interact.* Topside, MA: Salem House.

Marshall, E. (1983). *Eye language: Understanding the eloquent eye.* New York: New Trend.

Marshall, L. L., & Rose, P. (1987). Gender, stress, and violence in the adult relationships of a sample of college students. *Journal of Social and Personal Relationships* 4, 229–316.

Marston, P. J., Hecht, M. L., & Robers, T. (1987). True love ways: The subjective experience and communication of romantic love. *Journal of Personal and Social Relationships* 4, 387–407.

Martin, G. N. (1998). Human electroencephalographic (EEG) response to olfactory stimulation: Two experiments using the aroma of food. *International Journal of Psychophysiology* 30, 287–302.

Martin, M. M., & Anderson, C. M. (1995). Roommate similarity: Are roommates who are similar in their communication traits more satisfied? *Communication Research Reports* 12, 46–52.

Martin, M. M., & Anderson, C. M. (1998). The cognitive flexibility scale: Three validity studies. *Communication Reports* 11 (winter), 1–9.

Martin, M. M., & Rubin, R. B. (1994). A new measure of cognitive flexibility. *Psychological Reports* 76, 623–626.

Martin, M. M., & Rubin, R. B. (1998). Affinity-seeking in initial interactions. *Southern Communication Journal* 63, 131–143.

Marwell, G., & Schmitt, D. R. (1967). Dimensions of compliance-gaining behavior: An empirical analysis. *Sociometry* 39, 350–364.

Marwell, G., & Schmitt, D. R. (1990). An introduction. In *Seeking compliance: The production of interpersonal influence messages,* J. P. Dillard (ed.). Scottsdale, AZ.: Gorsuch Scarisbrick, pp. 3–5.

Masheter, C., & Harris, L. M. (1986). From divorce to friendship: A study of dialectic relationship development. *Journal of Social and Personal Relationships* 3, 177–189.

Maslow, A., & Mintz, N. L. (1956). Effects of esthetic surroundings: I. Initial effects of three esthetic conditions upon perceiving energy and well-being in faces. *Journal of Psychology* 41, 247–254.

Matsumoto, D. (1991). Cultural influences on facial expressions of emotion. *Southern Communication Journal* 56, 128–137.

Matsumoto, D. (1994). *People: Psychology from a cultural perspective.* Pacific Grove, CA: Brooks/Cole.

Matsumoto, D. (1996). *Culture and psychology.* Pacific Grove, CA: Brooks/Cole.

Matsumoto, D., & Kudoh, T. (1993). American-Japanese cultural differences in attributions of personality based on smiles. *Journal of Nonverbal Behavior* 17, 231–243.

May, R. A. B. (1999). Tavern culture and television viewing: The influence of local viewing culture on patron's reception of television programs. *Journal of Contemporary Ethnography* 28 (February), 69–99.

Maynard, H. E. (1963). How to become a better premise detective. *Public Relations Journal* 19, 20–22.

Mazulis, A., Abramsom, L. Y., Hyde, J. S., & Hankin, B. L. (2004). Is there a universal positivity bias in attributions? A meta-analytic review of individual, developmental, and cultural differences in the self-serving attributional bias. *Psychological Bulletin* 130 (September), 711–747.

McBroom, W. H., & Reed, F. W. (1992). Toward a reconceptualization of attitude-behavior consistency. Special Issue. Theoretical advances in social psychology. *Social Psychology Quarterly* 55, 205–216.

McCarthy, M. (2003). Talking back: Small interactional response tokens in everyday conversation. *Research on Language and Social Interaction* 36 (January), 33–63.

McCombs, M. E., Lopez-Escobar, E., & Llamas, J. P. (2000). Setting the agenda of attributes in the 1996 Spanish general election. *Journal of Communication* 50 (Spring), 77–92.

McCombs, M. E., & Shaw, D. L. (1972). The agenda-setting function of mass media. *Public Opinion Quarterly* 36, 176–185.

McCombs, M. E., & Shaw, D. L. (1993). The evolution of agenda-setting research: Twenty-five years in the marketplace of ideas. *Journal of Communication* 43, 58–67.

McCown, J. A., Fischer, D., Page, R., & Homant, M. (2001). Internet relationships: People who meet people. *CyberPsychology & Behavior* 4 (October), 593–596.

McCroskey, J. C. (2001). *Introduction to rhetorical communication,* 8th ed. Boston: Allyn & Bacon.

McCroskey, J. C., Booth-Butterfield, S., & Payne, S. K. (1989). The impact of communication apprehension on college student retention and success. *Communication Quarterly* 37, 100–107.

McCroskey, J. C., & Daly, J., eds. (1987). *Personality and interpersonal communication.* Thousand Oaks, CA: Sage.

McCroskey, J. C., & Richmond, V. P. (1990). Willingness to communicate: Differing cultural perspectives. *Southern Communication Journal* 56, 72–77.

McCroskey, J. C., & Wheeless, L. (1976). *Introduction to human communication.* Boston: Allyn & Bacon.

McDevitt, M., Kiousis, S., & Wahl-Jorgensen, K. (2003). Spiral of moderation: Opinion expression in computer-mediated discussion. *International Journal of Public Opinion Research* 15 (winter), 454–470.

McDonald, E. J., McCabe, K., Yeh, M., Lau, A., Garland, A., & Hough, R. L. (2005). Cultural affiliation and self-esteem as predictors of internalizing symptoms among Mexican American adolescents. *Journal of Clinical Child and Adolescent Psychology* 34 (February), 163–171.

McGill, M. E. (1985). *The McGill report on male intimacy.* New York: Harper & Row.

McLaughlin, M. L. (1984). *Conversation: How talk is organized.* Thousand Oaks, CA: Sage.

McLaughlin, M. L., Cody, M. L., & Robey, C. S. (1980). Situational influences on the selection of strategies to resist compliance-gaining attempts. *Human Communication Research* 1, 14–36.

McLoyd, V. C., & Wilson, L. (1992). Telling them like it is: The role of economic and environmental factors in single mothers' discussions with their children. *American Journal of Community Psychology* 20, 419–444.

McMillan, L. H. W., O'Driscoll, M. P., & Brady, E. C. (2004). The impact of workaholism on personal relationships. *British Journal of Guidance and Counseling* 32 (May), 171–186.

McNamee, S., & Gergen, K. J., eds. (1999). *Relational responsibility: Resources for sustainable dialogue.* Thousand Oaks, CA: Sage.

McNatt, D. B. (2001). Ancient Pygmalion joins contemporary management: A meta-analysis of the result. *Journal of Applied Psychology* 85, 314–322.

Medora, N. P., Larson, J. H., Hortascu, N., & Dave, P. (2002). Perceived attitudes towards romanticism: A cross-cultural study of American, Asian-Indian, and Turkish young adults. *Journal of Comparative Family Studies,* 33 (spring), 155–178.

Meeks, B. S., Hendrick, S. S., & Hendrick, C. (1998). Communication, love and relationship satisfaction. *Journal of Social and Personal Relationships* 15, 755–773.

Merton, R. K. (1957). *Social theory and social structure.* New York: Free Press.

Messick, R. M., & Cook, K. S., eds. (1983). *Equity theory: Psychological and sociological perspectives.* New York: Praeger.

Messmer, M. (1999). Skills for a new millennium: Accounting and financial professionals. *Strategic Finance Magazine* (August), 10ff.

Metts, S. (1989). An exploratory investigation of deception in close relationships. *Journal of Social and Personal Relationships* 6, 159–179.

Metts, S., & Planalp, S. (2002). Emotional communication. In *Handbook of Interpersonal Communication,* 3d ed., (pp. 339–373), M. L. Knapp & J. A. Daly (eds.). Thousand Oaks, CA: Sage.

Metz, M. E., Rosser, B. R., & Strapko, N. (1994). Differences in conflict resolution styles among heterosexual, gay, and lesbian couples. *Journal of Sex Research* 31, 293–308.

Meyer, J. R. (1994). Effect of situational features on the likelihood of addressing face needs in requests. *Southern Communication Journal* 59, 240–254.

Midooka, K. (1990). Characteristics of Japanese style communication. *Media, Culture and Society* 12, 477–489.

Miller, G. R., & Parks, M. R. (1982). Communication in dissolving relationships. In *Personal relationships 4. Dissolving personal relationships,* S. Duck (ed.). New York: Academic Press, pp. 127–154.

Miller, J. G. (1984). Culture and the development of everyday social explanation. *Journal of Personality and Social Psychology* 46, 961–978.

Miller, M. J., & Wilcox, C. T. (1986). Measuring perceived hassles and uplifts among the elderly. *Journal of Human Behavior and Learning* 3, 38–46.

Miller, S., & Weckert, J. (2000). Privacy, the workplace and the Internet. *Journal of Business Ethics* 28, 255–266.

Mintz, N. L. (1956). Effects of esthetic surroundings: II. Prolonged and repeated experience in a beautiful and ugly room. *Journal of Psychology* 41, 459–466.

Moen, P., Jim, J. E., & Hofmeister, H. (2001). Couples' work/retirement transitions, gender, and marital quality. *Social Psychology Quarterly* 64, 55–71.

Moghaddam, F. M., Taylor, D. M., & Wright, S. C. (1993). *Social psychology in cross-cultural perspective.* New York: W. H. Freeman.

Mole, J. (1990). *When in Rome . . . A business guide to cultures and customs in 12 European nations.* New York: American Management Association.

Mole, J. (1998). *Mind your manners: Managing business cultures in Europe.* London: Nicholas Brealey Publishing.

Molloy, J. (1981). *Molloy's live for success.* New York: Bantam.

Monin, B. (2003). The warm glow heuristic: When liking leads to familiarity. *Journal of Personality and Social Psychology* 85 (December), 1035–1048.

Monk, A., Fellas, E., & Ley, E. (2004). Hearing only one side of normal and mobile phone conversations. *Behaviour & Information Technology* 23 (September–October), 301–306.

Moon, D. G. (1966). Concepts of "culture": Implications for intercultural communication research. *Communication Quarterly* 44, 70–84.

Moon, Y. (2003). Don't blame the computer: When self-disclosure moderates the self-serving bias. *Journal of Consumer Psychology* 13, 125–137.

Moore, A., Masterson, J. T., Christophel, D. M., & Shea, K. A. (1996). College teacher immediacy and student ratings of instruction. *Communication Education* 45, 29–39.

Morahan-Martin, J., & Schumacher, P. (2003). Loneliness and social uses of the Internet. *Computers in Human Behavior* 19 (November), 659–671.

Moreland, R. L., & Beach, R. (1992). Exposure effects in the classroom: The development of affinity among students. *Journal of Experimental Social Psychology* 28, 255–276.

Morreale, S. P., Osborn, M. M., & Pearson, J. C. (2000). Why communication is important: A rationale for the centrality of the study of communication. *Journal of the Association for Communication Administration* 29 (January), 1–25.

Morrill, C. (1992). Vengeance among executives. *Virginia Review of Sociology* 1, 51–76.

Morris, D. (1977). *Manwatching: A field guide to human behavior.* New York: Abrams.

Morrison, E. W., Chen, Y., & Salgado, S. R. (2004). Cultural differences in newcomer feedback seeking: A comparison of the United States and Hong Kong. *Applied Psychology: An International Review* 53 (January), 1–22.

Morrison, R. (2004). Informal relationships in the workplace: Associations with job satisfaction, organizational commitment and turnover intentions. *New Zealand Journal of Psychology* 33, 114–128.

Morrow, G. D., Clark, E. M., & Brock, K. F. (1995). Individual and partner love styles: Implications for the quality of romantic involvements. *Journal of Social and Personal Relationships* 12, 363–387.

Motley, M. T. (1990a). On whether one can(not) not communicate: An examination via traditional communication postulates. *Western Journal of Speech Communication* 54, 1–20.

Motley, M. T. (1990b). Communication as interaction: A reply to Beach and Bavelas. *Western Journal of Speech Communication* 54, 613–623.

Mullany, L. (2004). Gender, politeness and institutional power roles: Humor as a tactic to gain compliance in workplace business meetings. *Multilingua* 23, 13–37.

Mullen, C. A. (2005). *Mentorship primer.* New York: Peter Lang.

Murray, C. (2005). Sex ed at Harvard. *New York Times* (January 23), The Week in Review, 17.

Murstein, B. I., Merighi, J. R., & Vyse, S. A. (1991). Love styles in the United States and France: A cross-cultural comparison. *Journal of Social and Clinical Psychology* 10, 37–46.

Myers, S. A., & Zhong, M. (2004). Perceived Chinese instructor use of affinity-seeking strategies and Chinese college student motivation. *Journal of Intercultural Communication Research* 33 (September–December), 119–130.

Nass, C. (2004). Etiquette equality: Exhibitions and expectations of computer politeness. *Communications of the ACM* 47 (April), 35–37.

Neff, K. D., & Harter, S. (2002). The authenticity of conflict resolutions among adult couples: Does women's other-oriented behavior reflect their true selves? *Sex Roles* 47 (November), 403–417.

Neimeyer, R. A., & Mitchell, K. A. (1988). Similarity and attraction: A longitudinal study. *Journal of Social and Personal Relationships* 5, 131–148.

Neimeyer, R. A., & Neimeyer, G. J. (1983). Structural similarity in the acquaintance process. *Journal of Social and Clinical Psychology* 1, 146–154.

Nelson, G. L., Al Batal, M., & El Bakary, W. (2002). Directness vs. indirectness: Egyptian Arabic and U.S. English communication style. *International Journal of Intercultural Relations* 26, 39–57.

Nelson, J. E., & Beggan, J. K. (2004). Self-serving judgments about winning the lottery. *Journal of Psychology: Interdisciplinary and Applied* 138 (May), 253–264.

Neugarten, B. (1979). Time, age, and the life cycle. *American Journal of Psychiatry* 136, 887–894.

Neuliep, J. W., Chaudoir, M., & McCroskey, J. C. (2001). A cross-cultural comparison of ethnocentrism among Japanese and United States college students. *Communication Research Reports* 18, 137–146.

Neuliep, J. W., & Grohskopf, E. L. (2000). Uncertainty reduction and communication satisfaction during initial interaction: An initial test and replication of a new axiom. *Communication Reports* 13 (summer), 67–77.

Neuliep, J. W., & McCroskey, J. C. (1997). The development of a U.S. and generalized ethnocentrism scale. *Communication Research Reports* 14, 385–398.

Ng, S. H., He, A., & Loong, C. (2004). Tri-generational family conversations: Communication accommodation and

brokering. *British Journal of Social Psychology* 43 (September), 449–464.

Nice, M. L., & Katzev, R. (1998). Internet romances: The frequency and nature of romantic online relationships. *CyberPsychology and Behavior* 1, 217–223.

Nicholas, C. L. (2004). Gaydar: Eye-gaze as identity recognition among gay men and lesbians. *Sexuality and Culture: An Interdisciplinary Quarterly* 8 (winter), 60–86.

Niemeier, S., & Dirven, R. (eds.). (2000). *Evidence for linguistic relativity.* Philadelphia: John Benjamins.

Nicotera, A. M., & Rancer, A. S. (1994). The influence of sex on self-perceptions and social stereotyping of aggressive communication predispositions. *Western Journal of Communication* 58, 283–307.

Noble, B. P. (1994, August 14). The gender wars: Talking peace. *New York Times,* p. 21.

Noelle-Neumann, E. (1973). Return to the concept of powerful mass media. In *Studies in broadcasting: An international annual of broadcasting science,* H. Eguchi & K. Sata (eds.). Tokyo: Nippon Hoso Kyokai, pp. 67–112.

Noelle-Neumann, E. (1980). Mass media and social change in developed societies. In *Mass communication review yearbook,* Vol. 1, G. C. Wilhoit & H. de Bock (eds.). Thousand Oaks, CA: Sage, pp. 657–678.

Noelle-Neumann, E. (1991). The theory of public opinion: The concept of the spiral of silence. *Communication yearbook/14,* J. A. Anderson (ed.). Thousand Oaks, CA: Sage, pp. 256–287.

Noller, P., & Fitzpatrick, M. A. (1993). *Communication in family relationships.* Englewood Cliffs, NJ: Prentice-Hall.

Nordhaus-Bike, A. M. (1999). Learning to lead. *Hospitals & Health Networks* 73, 28ff.

Norton, R., & Warnick, B. (1976). Assertiveness as a communication construct. *Human Communication Research* 3, 62–66.

Nowak, K. L. (2003). Sex categorization in computer mediated communication (CMC): Exploring the Utopian promise. *Media Psychology* 5, 83–103.

Ober, C., Weitkamp, L. R., Cox, N., Dytch, H., Kostyu, D., & Elias, S. (1997). *American Journal of Human Genetics* 61, 494–496.

Oberg, K. (1960). Cultural shock: Adjustment to new cultural environments. *Practical Anthropology* 7, 177–182.

Oetzel, J. G., & Ting-Toomey, S. (2003). Face concerns in interpersonal conflict: A cross-cultural empirical test of the face negotiation theory. *Communication Research* 30 (December), 599–624.

Oetzel, J., Ting-Toomey, S., Masumoto, T., Yokochi, Y., Pan, X., Takai, J., & Wilcox, R. (2001). Face and facework in conflict: A cross-cultural comparison of China, Germany, Japan, and the United States. *Communication Monographs* 68, 235–258.

O'Hair, D., Cody, M. J., Goss, B., & Krayer, K. J. (1988). The effect of gender, deceit orientation and communicator style on macro-assessments of honesty. *Communication Quarterly* 36, 77–93.

O'Hair, D., Cody, M. J., & McLaughlin, M. L. (1981). Prepared lies, spontaneous lies, Machiavellianism, and nonverbal communication. *Human Communication Research* 7, 325–339.

O'Hair, M. J., Cody, M. J., & O'Hair, D. (1991). The impact of situational dimensions on compliance-resisting strategies: A comparison of methods. *Communication Quarterly* 39, 226–240.

Okrent, D. (2005). Numbed by the numbers, when they just don't add up. *New York Times* (January 23), Section 4, 2.

Olaniran, B. A. (1994). Group performance in computer-mediated and face-to-face communication media. *Management Communication Quarterly* 7, 256–281.

Olson, E. (2002). Switzerland tells its men: Wash that pot! Mop that floor! *New York Times*, A14.

Onishi, N. (2005a). In Japan crash, time obsession may be culprit. *New York Times* (April 27), A1, A9.

Onishi, N. (2005b). In Japan's new texts, lessons in rising nationalism. *New York Times* (April 17), Wk 4.

Ono, H., & Zavodny, M. (2003). Gender and the Internet. *Social Science Quarterly* 84 (March), 111–121.

O'Sullivan, P. B., & Flanagin, A. J. (2003). Reconceptualizing "flaming" and other problematic messages. *New Media and Society* 5 (March), 69–94.

O'Sullivan, P. B., Hunt, S. K., & Lippert, L. R. (2004). Mediated immediacy: A language of affiliation in a technological age. *Journal of Language and Social Psychology* 23 (December), 464–490.

Oswald, D. L., Clark, E. M., & Kelly, C. M. (2004). Friendship maintenance: An analysis of individual and dyad behaviors. *Journal of Social and Clinical Psychology* 23 (June), 413–441.

Palmer, M. T. (1989). Controlling conversations: Turns, topics, and interpersonal control. *Communication Monographs* 56, 1–18.

Panyametheekul, S., & Herring, S. C. (2003). Gender and turn allocation in a Thai chat room. *Journal of Computer Mediated Communication* 9 (1, November).

Papa, M. J., & Natalle, E. J. (1989). Gender, strategy selection, and discussion satisfaction in interpersonal conflict. *Western Journal of Speech Communication* 53, 260–272.

Parker, J. G. (2004). Planning and communication crucial to preventing workplace violence. *Safety and Health* 170 (September), 58–61.

Parker, R. G., & Parrott, R. (1995). Patterns of self-disclosure across social support networks: Elderly, middle-aged, and young adults. *International Journal of Aging and Human Development* 41, 281–297.

Parks, J. B., & Roberton, M. A. (2004). Attitudes toward women mediate the gender effect on attitudes toward sexist language. *Psychology of Women Quarterly* 28 (September), 233–239.

Parks, M. R. (1995). Webs of influence in interpersonal relationships. In *Communication and social influence processes*, C. R. Berger & M. E. Burgoon (eds.). East Lansing: Michigan State University Press, pp. 155–178.

Parks, M. R., & Floyd, K. (1996). Making friends in cyberspace. *Journal of Communication* 46, 80–97.

Parks, M. R., & Roberts, L. D. (1998). "Making MOOsic": The development of personal relationships online and a comparison to their off-line counterparts. *Journal of Social and Personal Relationships* 15, 517–537.

Pasley, K., Kerpelman, J., & Guilbert, D. E. (2001). Gendered conflict, identity disruption, and marital instability: Expanding Gottman's model. *Journal of Personal and Social Relationships* 18, 5–27.

Patterson, C. (2000). Family relationships of lesbians and gay men. *Journal of Marriage and the Family* 62, 1052–1067.

Paul, A. M. (2001). Self-help: Shattering the myths. *Psychology Today* 34, 60ff.

Payne, K. E. (2001). *Different but equal: Communication between the sexes.* Westport, CT: Praeger.

Pearson, J. C. (1993). *Communication in the family*, 2d ed. Boston: Allyn & Bacon.

Pearson, J. C., & Spitzberg, B. H. (1990). *Interpersonal communication: Concepts, components, and contexts*, 2d ed. Dubuque, IA: William C. Brown.

Pearson, J. C., Turner, L. H., & Todd-Mancillas, W. (1991). *Gender and communication*, 2d ed. Dubuque, IA: William C. Brown.

Pearson, J. C., West, R., & Turner, L. H. (1995). *Gender and communication*, 3d ed. Dubuque, IA: William C. Brown.

Peltier, M. (2005). Etiquette lessons. *Time* (January 31), A4.

Penfield, J., ed. (1987). *Women and language in transition.* Albany: State University of New York Press.

Pennebacker, J. W. (1991). *Opening up: The healing power of confiding in others.* New York: Morrow.

Penton-Voak, I. S., Jacobson, A., & Trivers, R. (2004). Populational differences in attractiveness judgments of male and female faces: Comparing British and Jamaican samples. *Evolution and Human Behavior* 25 (November), 355–370.

Peplau, L. A. (1988). Research on homosexual couples: An overview. In *Gay relationships*, J. DeCecco (ed.). New York: Harrington Park Press, pp. 33–40.

Perez, A. (2005). Internalized oppression: How it affects members of the LGBT community. *Diversity Factor* 13 (winter), 25–29.

Perse, E. M., & Rubin, R. B. (1989). Attribution in social and parasocial relationships. *Communication Research* 16 (February), 59–77.

Peterson, C. C. (1996). The ticking of the social clock: Adults' beliefs about the timing of transition events. *International Journal of Aging and Human Development* 42, 189–203.

Petrocelli, W., & Repa, B. K. (1992). *Sexual harassment on the job.* Berkeley, CA: Nolo Press.

Pierce, C. A., & Aguinis, H. (2001). A framework for investigating the link between workplace romance and sexual harassment. *Group and Organization Management* 26, 206–229.

Pilkington, C. J., & Richardson, D. R. (1988). Perceptions of risk in intimacy. *Journal of Social and Personal Relationships* 5, 503–508.

Pilkington, C. J., & Woods, S. P. (1999). Risk in intimacy as a chronically accessible schema. *Journal of Social and Personal Relationships* 16, 249–263.

Pinker, S. (1994). *The language instinct: How the mind creates language.* New York: Morrow.

Piot, C. D. (1993). Secrecy, ambiguity, and the everyday in Kabre culture. *American Anthropologist* 95, 353–370.

Placencia, M. E. (2004). Rapport-building activities in corner shop interactions. *Journal of Sociolinguistics* 8 (May), 215–245.

Plaks, J. E., Grant, H., & Dweck, C. S. (2005). Violations of implicit theories and the sense of prediction and control: Implications for motivated person perception. *Journal of Personality and Social Psychology* 88 (February), 245–262.

Pollack, A. (1996). Happy in the East (^—^) or smiling (:—) in the West. *New York Times* (August 12), D5.

Pornpitakpan, C. (2003). The effect of personality traits and perceived cultural similarity on attraction. *Journal of International Consumer Marketing* 15, 5–30.

Porter, G. (1996). Organizational impact of workaholism: Suggestions for researching the negative outcomes of excessive work. *Journal of Occupational Health Psychology* 1 (January), 70–84.

Porter, R. H., & Moore, J. D. (1981). Human kin recognition by olfactory cues. *Physiology and Behavior* 27, 493–495.

Porter, S., Birt, A. R., Juille, J. C., & Lehman, D. R. (2000). Negotiating false memories: Interviewer and rememberer characteristics relate to memory distortion. *Psychological Science* 11 (November), 507–510.

Postman, N., & Powers, S. (1992). *How to watch TV news.* New York: Penguin.

Powers, W. G., & Love, D. E. (2000). Communication apprehension in the dating partner context. *Communication Research Reports* 17, 221–228.

Pratkanis, A., & Aronson, E. (1991). *Age of propaganda: The everyday use and abuse of persuasion.* New York: W. H. Freeman.

Prins, K. S., Buunk, B. P., & Van Yperen, N. W. (1994). Equity, normative disapproval, and extramarital sex. *Journal of Social and Personal Relationships* 10, 39–53.

Prosky, P. S. (1992). Complementary and symmetrical couples. *Family Therapy* 19, 215–221.

Prusank, D. T., Duran, R. L., & DeLillo, D. A. (1993). Interpersonal relationships in women's magazines: Dating and relating in the 1970s and 1980s. *Journal of Social and Personal Relationships* 10, 307–320.

Purcell, K. (2004). Making e-mentoring more effective. *American Journal of Health-System Pharmacy* 61, 284–286.

Purnell, R. B. (1982). Teaching them to curse: A study of certain types of inherent racial bias in language pedagogy and practices. *Phylon* 43, 231–241.

Rabinowitz, F. E. (1991). The male-to-male embrace: Breaking the touch taboo in a men's therapy group. *Journal of Counseling and Development* 69, 574–576.

Radford, M. H., Mann, L., Ohta, Y., & Nakane, Y. (1993). Differences between Australian and Japanese students in decisional self-esteem, decisional stress, and coping styles. *Journal of Cross-Cultural Psychology* 24, 284–297.

Rahim, M. A., Antonioni, D., Krumov, J., & Ilieva, S. (2000). Power, conflict, and effectiveness: A cross-cultural study in the United States and Bulgaria. *European Psychologist* 5, 28–33.

Rancer, A. S. (1998). Argumentativeness. In *Communication and Personality: Trait Perspectives,* J. C. McCroskey, J. A. Daly, M. M. Martin, & M. J. Beatty (eds.). Cresskill, NJ: Hampton Press, pp. 149–170.

Rancer, A. S., Kosberg, R. L., & Baukus, R. A. (1992). Beliefs about arguing as predictors of trait argumentativeness: Implications for training in argument and conflict management. *Communication Education* 41, 375–387.

Raney, R. F. (2000). Study finds Internet of social benefit to users. *New York Times* (May 11), G7.

Rankin, P. (1929). Listening ability. *Proceedings of the Ohio State Educational Conference's Ninth Annual Session.*

Rappaport, H., Enrich, K., & Wilson, A. (1985). Relation between ego identity and temporal perspective. *Journal of Personality and Social Psychology* 48, 1609–1620.

Rapsa, R., & Cusack, J. (1990). Psychiatric implications of tattoos. *American Family Physician* 41, 1481–1486.

Raven, B., Centers, C., & Rodrigues, A. (1975). The bases of conjugal power. In *Power in families,* R. E. Cromwell & D. H. Olson (eds.). New York: Halsted Press, pp. 217–234.

Raven, B. H., Schwarzwald, J., & Koslowsky, M. (1998). Conceptualizing and measuring a power/interaction model of interpersonal influence. *Journal of Applied Social Psychology* 28, 307–332.

Rawlins, W. K. (1983). Negotiating close friendship: The dialectic of conjunctive freedoms. *Human Communication Research* 9, 255–266.

Rawlins, W. K. (1989). A dialectical analysis of the tensions, functions, and strategic challenges of communication in young adult friendships. In *Communication yearbook 12,* (pp. 157–189), J. A. Andersen (ed.), Thousand Oaks, CA: Sage.

Rawlins, W. K. (1992). *Friendship matters: Communication, dialectics, and the life course.* Hawthorne, NY: Aldine DeGruyter.

Read, A. W. (2004). Language revision by deletion of absolutisms. *ETC: A Review of General Semantics* 61 (December), 456–462.

Reardon, K. K. (1987). *Where minds meet: Interpersonal communication.* Belmont, CA: Wadsworth.

Rector, M., & Neiva, E. (1996). Communication and personal relationships in Brazil. In *Communication in personal relationships across cultures,* W. B. Gudykunst, S. Ting-Toomey, & T. Nishida (eds.). Thousand Oaks, CA: Sage, pp. 156–173.

Regan, P. C., Kocan, E. R., & Whitlock, T. (1998). Ain't love grand! A prototype analysis of the concept of romantic love. *Journal of Social and Personal Relationships* 15, 411–420.

Reid, S. A., & Hogg, M. A. (2005). A self-categorization explanation for the third-person effect. *Human Communication Research* 31 (January), 129–161.

Reik, T. (1944). *A psychologist looks at love.* New York: Rinehart.

Reiner, D., & Blanton, K. (1997). *Person to person on the Internet.* Boston: AP Professional.

Reisman, J. (1979). *Anatomy of friendship.* Lexington, MA: Lewis.

Reisman, J. M. (1981). Adult friendships. In *Personal relationships. 2: Developing personal relationships,* S. Duck & R. Gilmour (eds.). New York: Academic Press, pp. 205–230.

Rezabeck, L. L., & Cochenour, J. J. (1995). Emoticons: Visual cues for computer-mediated communication. In *Imagery and Visual Literacy: Selected Readings from the Annual Conference of the International Visual Literacy Association* (Tempe, Arizona, October 12–16). Eric Document No. ED380096.

Rhee, K. Y., & Kim, W-B (2004). The adoption and use of the Internet in South Korea. *Journal of Computer Mediated Communication* 9 (4, July).

Rhee, S., Chang, J., & Rhee, J. (2003). Acculturation, communication patterns, and self-esteem among Asian and Caucasian American adolescents. *Adolescence* 38 (winter), 749–768.

Rich, A. L. (1974). *Interracial communication.* New York: Harper & Row.

Richards, I. A. (1951). Communication between men: The meaning of language. In *Cybernetics, Transactions of the Eighth Conference,* Heinz von Foerster (ed.).

Richmond, V. P., Davis, L. M., Saylor, K., & McCroskey, J. C. (1984). Power strategies in organizations: Communication techniques and messages. *Human Communication Research* 11, 85–108.

Richmond, V. P., & McCroskey, J. C. (1984). Power in the classroom II: Power and learning. *Communication Education* 33, 125–136.

Richmond, V. P., & McCroskey, J. C. (1998). *Communication: Apprehension, avoidance, and effectiveness,* 5th ed. Boston: Allyn & Bacon.

Riggio, R. E. (1987). *The charisma quotient.* New York: Dodd, Mead.

Rivlin, G. (2005). Hate Messages on Google Site Draw Concern. *New York Times* (February 7), C1, C7.

Robinson, W. P. (1993). Lying in the public domain. *American Behavioral Scientist* 36 (January), 359–382.

Rockwell, P., Buller, D. B., & Burgoon, J. K. (1997). The voice of deceit: Refining and expanding vocal cues to deception. *Communication Research Reports* 14, 451–459.

Rodman, G. (2001). *Making sense of media: An introduction to mass communication.* Boston: Allyn & Bacon.

Roeher Institute (1995). *Harm's way: The many faces of violence and abuse against persons with disabilities.* North York (Ontario): Roeher Institute.

Roger, D., & Nesshoever, W. (1987). Individual differences in dyadic conversational strategies: A further study. *British Journal of Social Psychology* 26, 247–255.

Rogers, C. (1970). *Carl Rogers on encounter groups.* New York: Harrow Books.

Rogers, C., & Farson, R. (1981). Active listening. In *Communication: Concepts and Processes,* 3d ed., J. DeVito (ed.). Englewood Cliffs, NJ: Prentice-Hall, pp. 137–147.

Rogers, E. M. (1995). *Diffusion of innovations,* 4th ed. New York: Free Press.

Rohlfing, M. E. (1995). "Doesn't anybody stay in one place anymore?" An exploration of the under-studied phenomenon of long-distance relationships. In *Under-studied relationships: Off the beaten track,* J. T. Wood & S. Duck (eds.). Thousand Oaks, CA: Sage, pp. 173–196.

Rokach, A. (1998). The relation of cultural background to the causes of loneliness. *Journal of Social and Clinical Psychology* 17, 75–88.

Rokach, A., & Brock, H. (1995). The effects of gender, marital status, and the chronicity and immediacy of loneliness. *Journal of Social Behavior and Personality* 19, 833–848.

Roloff, M. E., & Solomon, D. H. (2002). Conditions under which relational commitment leads to expressing or withholding relational complaints. *International Journal of Conflict Management* 13, 276–291.

Rollman, J. B., Krug, K., & Parente, F. (2000). The chat room phenomenon: Reciprocal communication in cyberspace. *CyberPsychology and Behavior* 3, 161–166.

Ronfeldt, H. M., Kimerling, R., & Arias, I. (1998). Satisfaction with relationship power and the perpetration of dating violence. *Journal of Marriage and the Family* 60 (February), 70–78.

Rosen, E. (1998). Think like a shrink. *Psychology Today* (October), 54–59.

Rosenbaum, M. E. (1986). The repulsion hypothesis. On the nondevelopment of relationships. *Journal of Personality and Social Psychology* 51, 1156–1166.

Rosenfeld, L. (1979). Self-disclosure avoidance: Why I am afraid to tell you who I am. *Communication Monographs* 46, 63–74.

Rosengren, A., et al. (1993). Stressful life events, social support, and mortality in men born in 1933. *British Medical Journal* (October 19). Cited in Goleman (1995a).

Rosenthal, R. (2002). The Pygmalion effect and its mediating mechanism. In *Improving academic achievement: Impact of psychological factors on education* (pp. 25–36), J. Aronson (ed.). San Diego, CA: Academic Press.

Rosenthal, R., & Jacobson, L. (1968). *Pygmalion in the class-room.* New York: Holt, Rinehart & Winston.

Rosnow, R. L. (1977). Gossip and marketplace psychology. *Journal of Communication* 27 (winter), 158–163.

Ross, H., Smith, J., Spielmacher, C., & Recchia, H. (2004). Shading the truth: Self-serving biases in children's reports of sibling conflicts. *Merrill-Palmer Quarterly* 50 (January), 61–85.

Rothblum, E. D., & Bond, L. A. (1996). *Preventing heterosexism and homophobia.* Thousand Oaks, CA: Sage.

Rowatt, W. C., Cunningham, M. R., & Druen, P. B. (1999). Lying to get a date: The effect of facial physical attractiveness on the willingness to deceive prospective dating partners. *Journal of Social and Personal Relationships* 16, 209–223.

Rowland-Morin, P. A., & Carroll, J. G. (1990). Verbal communication skills and patient satisfaction: A study of doctor-patient interviews. *Evaluation and the Health Professions* 13, 168–185.

Ruben, B. D. (1985). Human communication and cross-cultural effectiveness. In *Intercultural Communication: A Reader*, 4th ed., L. A. Samovar & R. E. Porter (eds.). Belmont, CA: Wadsworth, pp. 338–346.

Rubenstein, C. (1993). Fighting sexual harassment in schools. *New York Times* (June 10), C8.

Rubin, A., Perse, E., & Powell, R. (1985). Loneliness, parasocial interaction, and local television news viewing. *Human Communication Research* 12, 155–180.

Rubin, D. C., Groth, E., & Goldsmith, D. J. (1984). Olfactory cues of autobiographical memory. *American Journal of Psychology* 97, 493–507.

Rubin, R. B., Fernandez-Collado, C., & Hernandez-Sampieri, R. (1992). A cross-cultural examination of interpersonal communication motives in Mexico and the United States. *International Journal of Intercultural Relations* 16, 145–157.

Rubin, R. B., & Graham, E. E. (1988). Communication correlates of college success: An exploratory investigation. *Communication Education* 37, 14–27.

Rubin, R. B., & Martin, M. M. (1994). Development of a measure of interpersonal communication competence. *Communication Research Reports* 11, 33–44.

Rubin, R. B., & McHugh, M. (1987). Development of parasocial interaction relationships. *Journal of Broadcasting and Electronic Media* 31, 279–292.

Rubin, R. B., Perse, E. M., & Barbato, C. A. (1988). Conceptualization and measurement of interpersonal communication motives. *Human Communication Research* 14, 602–628.

Rubin, R. B., & Rubin, A. M. (1992). Antecedents of interpersonal communication motivation. *Communication Quarterly* 40, 315–317.

Rubin, Z. (1973). *Liking and loving: An invitation to social psychology.* New York: Holt, Rinehart & Winston.

Ruggiero, T. E. (2000). Uses and gratifications theory in the 21st century. *Mass Communication and Society* 3 (winter), 3–37.

Rundquist, S. (1992). Indirectness: A gender study of flouting Grice's maxims. *Journal of Pragmatics* 18, 431–449.

Rupley, S. (2004). Will Google read your e-mail? *PC Magazine* 23 (June 8), 21–22.

Rusbult, C. E., & Buunk, B. P. (1993). Commitment processes in close relationships: An interdependence analysis. *Journal of Social and Personal Relationships* 10, 175–204.

Ruscher, J. B. (2001). *Prejudiced communication: A social psychological perspective.* NE: Guilford Press.

Rushe, R. H. (1996). Tactics of power and influence in violent marriages. *Dissertation abstracts international: Section B: The Sciences and Engineering* (University of Washington), 57, 1453.

Rydell, R. J., McConnell, A. R., & Bringle, R. G. (2004). Jealousy and commitment: Perceived threat and the effect of relationship alternatives. *Personal Relationships* 11 (December), 451–468.

Sabatelli, R. M., & Pearce, J. (1986). Exploring marital expectations. *Journal of Social and Personal Relationships* 3, 307–321.

Sabath, A. M. (1999). *International business etiquette: Asia and the Pacific Rim.* Franklin Lakes, NJ: Career Press.

Sabath, A. M. (1999). *International business etiquette in Europe: What you need to know to conduct business abroad with charm and savvy.* New York: Career Press.

Sagula, D., & Rice, K. G. (2004). The effectiveness of mindfulness training on the grieving process and emotional well-being of chronic pain patients. *Journal of Clinical Psychology in Medical Settings* 11 (December), 333–342.

Sahlstein, E. M. (2004). Relating at a distance: Negotiating being together and being apart in long-distance relationships. *Journal of Social and Personal Relationships* 21 (October), 689–710.

Salminen, S., & Glad, T. (1992). The role of gender in helping behavior. *Journal of Social Psychology* 132, 131–133.

Samovar, L. A., & Porter, R. E., eds. (2003). *Communication between cultures,* 10th ed. Belmont, CA: Wadsworth.

Samter, W. (2004). Friendship interaction skills across the life span. In *Handbook of communication and social interaction skills,* (pp. 637–684), J. O. Greene & B. R. Burleson (eds.). Mahwah, NJ: Lawrence Erlbaum.

Samter, W., & Cupach, W. R. (1998). Friendly fire: Topics variations in conflict among same- and cross-sex friends. *Communication Studies* 49, 121–138.

Sanders, J. A., Wiseman, R. L., & Matz, S. I. (1991). Uncertainty reduction in acquaintance relationships in Ghana and the United States. In *Cross-cultural interpersonal communication,* S. Ting-Toomey & F. Korzenny (eds.). Thousand Oaks, CA: Sage, pp. 79–98.

Sapadin, L. A. (1988). Friendship and gender: Perspectives of professional men and women. *Journal of Social and Personal Relationships* 5, 387–403.

Sarquisse, V., Butler, J., & Pryor, B. (2003). A comparison of communication apprehension scores between Americans and Argentineans. *North American Journal of Psychology* 5, 223–227.

Sarwer, D. B., Kalichman, S. C., Johnson, J. R., Early, J., et al. (1993). Sexual aggression and love styles: An exploratory study. *Archives of Sexual Behavior* 22, 265–275.

Satir, V. (1983). *Conjoint Family Therapy,* 3d ed. Palo Alto, CA: Science and Behavior Books.

Savage, J. (2004). Does viewing violent media really cause criminal violence? A methodological review. *Aggression and Violent Behavior* 10 (November–December), 99–128.

Savin-Williams, R. C., & Ream, G. L. (2003). Sex variations in the disclosure to parents of same-sex attractions. *Journal of Family Psychology* 17 (September), 429–438.

Scandura, T. (1992). Mentorship and career mobility: An empirical investigation. *Journal of Organizational Behavior* 13, 169–174.

Scealy, M., Phillips, J. G., & Stevenson, R. (2002). Shyness and anxiety as predictors of patterns of Internet usage. *CyberPsychology & Behavior* 5 (December), 507–515.

Schaap, C., Buunk, B., & Kerkstra, A. (1988). Marital conflict resolution. In *Perspectives on marital interaction,* P. Noller & M. A. Fitzpatrick (eds.). Philadelphia: Multilingual Matters, pp. 203–244.

Schafer, R. B., & Keith, P. M. (1980). Equity and depression among married couples. *Social Psychology Quarterly* 43, 430–435.

Schcctz, L. P. (1995). *Recruiting trends 1995–1996. A study of 527 businesses, industries, and governmental agencies employing new college graduates.* East Lansing: Collegiate Employment Research Institute, Michigan State University.

Schegloff, E. (1982). Discourses as an interactional achievement: Some uses of "uh huh" and other things that come between sentences. In *Georgetown University roundtable on language and linguistics,* Deborah Tannen (ed.). Washington, DC: Georgetown University Press, pp. 71–93.

Scheufele, D. A., & Moy, P. (2000). Twenty-five years of the spiral of silence: A conceptual review and empirical outlook. *International Journal of Public Opinion Research* 12 (spring), 3–28.

Schmidt, T. O., & Cornelius, R. R. (1987). Self-disclosure in everyday life. *Journal of Social and Personal Relationships* 4, 365–373.

Schoeneman, T. J., & Rubanowitz, E. E. (1985). Attributions in the advice columns: Actors and observers, causes and reasons. *Personality and Social Psychology Bulletin* 11, 315–325.

Schott, G., & Selwyn, N. (2000). Examining the "male, anti-social" stereotype of high computer users. *Journal of Educational Computing Research* 23, 291–303.

Schramm, W., & Porter, W. E. (1982). *Men, women, messages and media: Understanding human communication.* New York: Harper & Row.

Schrodt, P. (2003). Students' appraisals of instructors as a function of students' perceptions of instructors' aggressive communication. *Communication Education* 52 (April), 106–121.

Schuter, R. (1990). The centrality of culture. *Southern Communication Journal* 55, 237–249.

Schutz, A. (1999). It was your fault! Self-serving biases in autobiographical accounts of conflicts in married couples. *Journal of Social and Personal Relationships* 16, 193–208.

Schwartz, E. (2005). Watch what you say. *InfoWorld* 27 (February 28), 8.

Schwartz, M., and the Task Force on Bias-Free Language of the Association of American University Presses (1995). *Guidelines for bias-free writing.* Bloomington: Indiana University Press.

Seiter, J. S., & Sandry, A. (2003). Pierced for success?: The effects of ear and nose piercing on perceptions of job candidates' credibility, attractiveness, and hirability. *Communication Research Reports* 20 (Fall), 287–298.

Sergios, P. A., & Cody, J. (1985). Physical attractiveness and social assertiveness skills in male homosexual dating behavior and partner selection. *Journal of Social Psychology* 125, 505–514.

Severin, W. J. & Tankard, J. W., Jr. (2001). *Communication theories: Origins, methods, and uses in the mass media.* Boston: Allyn & Bacon.

Shaffer, D. R., Pegalis, L. J., & Bazzini, D. G. (1996). When boy meets girl (revisited): Gender, gender role orientation, and prospect of future interaction as determinants of self-disclosure among same- and opposite-sex acquaintances. *Personality and Social Psychology Bulletin* 22, 495–506.

Shannon, J. (1987). Don't smile when you say that. *Executive Female* 10, 33, 43. Reprinted in DeVito & Hecht (1990), pp. 115–117.

Sharkey, W. F., & Stafford, L. (1990). Turn-taking resources employed by congenitally blind conversers. *Communication Studies* 41, 161–182.

Shaw, L. H., & Grant, L. M. (2002). Users divided? Exploring the gender gap in Internet use. *CyberPsychology & Behavior* 5 (December), 517–527.

Shechtman, Z., Hiradin, A., & Zina, S. (2003). The impact of culture on group behavior: A comparison of three ethnic groups. *Journal of Counseling and Development* 81 (spring), 208–216.

Sheppard, J. A., & Strathman, A. J. (1989). Attractiveness and height: The role of stature in dating preferences, frequency of dating, and perceptions of attractiveness. *Personality and Social Psychology* 15, 617–627.

Sheese, B. E., Brown, E. L, & Graziano, W. G. (2004). Emotional expression in cyberspace: Searching for moderators of the Pennebaker disclosure effect via e-mail. *Health Psychology* 23 (September), 457–464.

Shelton, J. N., & Richeson, J. A. (2005). Intergroup contact and pluralistic ignorance. *Journal of Personality and Social Psychology* 88 (January), 91–107.

Sherman, D. K., & Kim, H. S. (2005). Is there an "I" in "Team"? The role of the self in group-serving judgments. *Journal of Personality and Social Psychology* 88 (January), 108–120.

Shibazaki, K., & Brennan, K. A. (1998). When birds of different features flock together: A preliminary comparison of intra-ethnic and inter-ethnic dating relationships. *Journal of Social and Personal Relationships* 15, 248–256.

Shiu, E., & Lenhart, A. (2004). Pew Internet and American life project report: Instant Messaging. http://www.pewinternet.org/PPF/r/133/report_display.asp (accessed 7/29/05).

Short, J., Williams, E., & Christie, B. (1976). *The social psychology of telecommunication.* London: Wiley.

Shuper, P. A., Sorrentino, R. M., Otsubo, Y., & Walker, A. M. (2004). A theory of uncertainty orientation: Implications for the study of individual differences within and across cultures. *Journal of Cross-Cultural Psychology* 35 (July), 460–480.

Siavelis, R. L., & Lamke, L. K. (1992). Instrumentalness and expressiveness: Predictors of heterosexual relationship satisfaction. *Sex Roles* 26, 149–159.

Siegert, J. R., & Stamp, G. H. (1994). "Our first big fight" as a milestone in the development of close relationships. *Communication Monographs* 61, 345–360.

Silverman, T. (2001). Expanding community: The Internet and relational theory. *Community, Work and Family* 4, 231–237.

Silverstein, J., & Lasky, M. (2004). *Online dating for dummies.* Forest City, CA: IDG Books Worldwide.

Simpson, J. A. (1987). The dissolution of romantic relationships: Factors involved in relationship stability and emotional distress. *Journal of Personality and Social Psychology* 53, 683–692.

Singelis, T. M. (1994). The measurement of independent and interdependent self-construals. *Personality and Social Psychology Bulletin* 20, 580–591.

Singh, S., Wulf, D., Samara, R., & Cuca, Y. P. (2000). Gender differences in the timing of first intercourse: Data from 14 countries. *International Family Planning Perspectives* 26 (March), 21–30.

Sizemore, D. S. (2004). Ethnic inclusion and exclusion. *Journal of Contemporary Ethnography* 33 (October), 534–570.

Skinner, M. (2002). In search of feedback. *Executive Excellence* (June), 18.

Slade, M. (1995). We forgot to write a headline. But it's not our fault. *New York Times* (February 19), 5.

Slater, A., von der Schulengerg, C., Brown, E., Badenoch, M., Butterworth, G., Parsons, S., & Samuels, C. (1998). Newborn infants prefer attractive faces. *Infant Behavior and Development* 21, 345–354.

Smith, A., & Williams, K. D. (2004). R U There? Ostracism by cell phone text messages. *Group Dynamics* 8 (December), 291–301.

Smith, B. (1996). Care and feeding of the office grapevine. *Management Review* 85 (February), 6.

Smith, C. S. (2002). Beware of green hats in China and other cross-cultural faux pas. *New York Times* (April 30), C11.

Smith, C. S. (2005). Abduction, often violent, a Kyrgyz wedding rite. *New York Times* (April 30), A1, A7.

Smith, M. H. (2003). Body adornment: Know the limits. *Nursing Management* 34 (February), 22–23.

Smith, R. (2004). The teaching of communication skills may be misguided. *British Medical Journal* 328 (April 10), 1–2.

Smith, R. A., & Weber, A. L. (2005). Applying social psychology in everyday life. In *Applied social psychology: Understanding and addressing social and practical problems* (pp. 75–99), F. W. Schneider & J. A. Gruman (eds.). Thousand Oaks, CA: Sage.

Smith, S. M., & Shaffer, D. R. (1991). Celerity and cajolery: Rapid speech may promote or inhibit persuasion through its impact on message elaboration. *Personality and Social Psychology Bulletin* 17 (December), 663–669.

Smith, S. M., & Shaffer, D. R. (1995). Speed of speech and persuasion: Evidence for multiple effects. *Personality and Social Psychology Bulletin* 21 (October), 1051–1060.

Smoreda, Z., & Licoppe, C. (2000). Gender-specific use of the domestic telephone. *Social Psychology Quarterly* 63, 238–252.

Snyder, C. R. (1984). Excuses, excuses. *Psychology Today* 18, 50–55.

Snyder, C. R., Higgins, R. L., and Stucky, R. J. (1983). *Excuses: Masquerades in search of grace.* New York: Wiley.

Snyder, M. (1987). *Public appearances, private realities.* New York: W. H. Freeman.

Snyder, M. (1992). A gender-informed model of couple and family therapy: Relationship enhancement therapy. *Contemporary Family Therapy: An International Journal* 14 (February), 15–31.

Solomon, D. H., & Samp, J. A. (1998). Power and problem appraisal: Perceptual foundations of the chilling effect in dating relationships. *Journal of Social and Personal Relationships* 15, 191–209.

Solomon, G. B., Striegel, D. A., Eliot, J. F., Heon, S. N., et al. (1996). The self-fulfilling prophecy in college basketball: Implications for effective coaching. *Journal of Applied Sport Psychology* 8, 44–59.

Sommer, K. L., Williams, K. D., Ciarocco, N. J., & Baumeister, R. F. (2001). When silence speaks louder than words: Explorations into the intrapsychic and interpersonal consequences of social ostracism. *Basic and Applied Social Psychology* 23, 225–243.

Song, I., LaRose, R., Eastin, M. S., & Lin, C. A. (2004). Internet gratifications, Internet addiction: On the uses and abuses of new media. *CyberPsychology & Behavior* 7 (August), 384–394.

Sorenson, P. S., Hawkins, K., & Sorenson, R. L. (1995). Gender, psychological type and conflict style preference. *Management Communication Quarterly* 9, 115–126.

Spiers, C. J. (1998). Commitment and stability in lesbian relationships. *Dissertation Abstracts International Section B: The Sciences and Engineering* 59, 3076.

Spencer, T. (1993). A new approach to assessing self-disclosure in conversation. Paper presented at the Annual Convention of the Western Speech Communication Association, Albuquerque, New Mexico.

Spencer, T. (1994). Transforming relationships through everyday talk. In *The Dynamics of Relationships: Vol. 4. Understanding Relationships*, S. Duck (ed.). Thousand Oaks, CA: Sage.

Spitzberg, B. H. (1991). Intercultural communication competence. In *Intercultural communication: A reader*, L. A. Samovar & R. E. Porter (eds.). Belmont, CA: Wadsworth, pp. 353–365.

Spitzberg, B. H., & Cupach, W. R. (1984). *Interpersonal communication competence.* Thousand Oaks, CA: Sage.

Spitzberg, B. H., & Cupach, W. R. (1989). *Handbook of interpersonal competence research.* New York: Springer-Verlag.

Spitzberg, B. H., & Hecht, M. L. (1984). A component model of relational competence. *Human Communication Research* 10, 575–599.

Sprecher, S. (1987). The effects of self-disclosure given and received on affection for an intimate partner and stability of the relationship. *Journal of Social and Personal Relationships* 4, 115–127.

Sprecher, S. (2001). Equity and social exchange in dating couples: Associations with satisfaction, commitment, and stability. *Journal of Marriage and the Family* 63 (August), 599–613.

Sprecher, S., & Hendrick, S. S. (2004). Self-disclosure in intimate relationships: Associations with individual and relationship characteristics over time. *Journal of Social and Clinical Psychology* 23 (December), 857–877.

Sprecher, S., & Metts, S. (1989). Development of the "Romantic Beliefs Scale" and examination of the effects of gender and gender-role orientation. *Journal of Social and Personal Relationships* 6, 387–411.

Sprecher, S., & Schwartz, P. (1994). Equity and balance in the exchange of contributions in close relationships. In *Entitlement and the affectional bond: Justice in close relationships*, M. J. Lerner & G. Mikula (eds.). New York: Plenum, pp. 11–42.

Sprecher, S., & Toro-Morn, M. (2002). A study of men and women from different sides of earth to determine if men are from Mars and women are from Venus in their beliefs about love and romantic relationships. *Sex Roles* 46 (March), 131–147.

Stafford, L., Kline, S. L., & Dimmick, J. (1999). Home e-mail: Relational maintenance and gratification opportunities. *Journal of Broadcasting and Electronic Media* 43, 659–669.

Staines, G. L., Pottick, K. J., & Fudge, D. A. (1986). Wives' employment and husbands' attitudes toward work and life. *Journal of Applied Psychology* 71, 118–128.

Steil, L. K., Barker, L. L., & Watson, K. W. (1983). *Effective listening: Key to your success.* Reading, MA: Addison-Wesley.

Stein, M. M., & Bowen, M. (2003). Building a customer satisfaction system: Effective listening when the customer speaks. *Journal of Organizational Excellence* 22 (Summer), 23–34.

Steiner, C. (1981). *The other side of power.* New York: Grove.

Stephan, W. G., & Stephan, C. W. (1985). Intergroup anxiety. *Journal of Social Issues* 41, 157–175.

Stephen, R., & Zweigenhaft, R. L. (1986). The effect of tipping of a waitress touching male and female customers. *Journal of Social Psychology* 126 (February), 141–142.

Stephens, G. K., & Greer, C. R. (1995). Doing business in Mexico: Understanding cultural differences. *Organizational Dynamics* 24, 39–55.

Sternberg, R. J. (1986). A triangular theory of love. *Psychological Review* 93, 119–135.

Sternberg, R. J. (1988). *The triangle of love: Intimacy, passion, commitment.* New York: Basic Books.

Sternglanz, R. W., & DePaulo, B. (2004). Reading nonverbal cues to emotions: The advantages and liabilities of relationship closeness. *Journal of Nonverbal Behavior* 28 (winter), 245–266.

Stewart, L. P., Cooper, P. J., Stewart, A. D., with Friedley, S. A. (2003). *Communication and gender*, 4th ed. Boston: Allyn & Bacon.

Strassberg, D. S., & Holty, S. (2003). An experimental study of women's Internet personal ads. *Archives of Sexual Behavior* 32 (June), 253–260.

Strecker, I. (1993). Cultural variations in the concept of "face." *Multilingua* 12, 119–141.

Stritzke, W. G. K., Nguyen, A., & Durkin, K. (2004). Shyness and computer-mediated communication: A self-presentational theory perspective. *Media Psychology* 6, 1–22.

Stromer-Galley, J. (2003). Diversity of political conversation on the Internet: Users' perspectives. *Journal of Computer Mediated Communication* 8 (3 April).

Suler, J. (2004). The online disinhibition effect. *CyberPsychology and Behavior* 7 (June), 321–326.

Sunnafrank, M., & Ramirez, A. (2004). At first sight: Persistent relational effects of get-acquainted conversations. *Journal of Social and Personal Relationships* 21 (June), 361–379.

Sutcliffe, K., Lewton, E., & Rosenthal, M. M. (2004). Communication failures: An insidious contributor to medical mishaps. *Academic Medicine* 79 (February), 186–194.

Sutter, D. L., & Martin, M. M. (1998). Verbal aggression during disengagement of dating relationships. *Communication Research Reports* 15, 318–326.

Swim, J. K., Mallett, R., & Stangor, C. (2004). Understanding subtle sexism: Detection and use of sexist language. *Sex Roles* 51, 117–128.

Szapocznik, J. (1995). Research on disclosure of HIV status: Cultural evolution finds an ally in science. *Health Psychology* 14, 4–5.

Tannen, D. (1990). *You just don't understand: Women and men in conversation.* New York: Morrow.

Tannen, D. (1994a). *Gender and discourse.* New York: Oxford University Press.

Tannen, D. (1994b). *Talking from 9 to 5.* New York: Morrow.

Taraban, C. B., & Hendrick, C. (1995). Personality perceptions associated with six styles of love. *Journal of Social and Personal Relationships* 12, 453–461.

Tardiff, T. (2001). Learning to say "no" in Chinese. *Early Education and Development* 12, 303–323.

Taris, T. W., Van Horn, J. E., & Schaufeli, W. B. (2004). Inequity, burnout and psychological withdrawal among teachers: A dynamic exchange model. *Stress and Coping: An International Journal* 17 (March), 103–122.

Tata, J. (2000). Toward a theoretical framework of intercultural account-giving and account evaluation. *International Journal of Organizational Analysis* 8, 155–178.

Taveggia, T. C., & Santos, N. G. (2001). Cross cultural adjustment: A test of "uncertainty reduction principle." *International Journal of Cross Cultural Management* 1 (August), 153–171.

Taylor, D. M., & Jaggi, V. (1974). Ethnocentrism and causal attribution in a South Indian context. *Journal of Cross-Cultural Psychology* 5, 162–171.

Thelen, M. H., Sherman, M. D., & Borst, T. S. (1998). Fear of intimacy and attachment among rape survivors. *Behavior Modification* 22, 108–116.

Thibaut, J. W., & Kelley, H. H. (1959). *The social psychology of groups.* New York: Wiley. Reissued (1986). New Brunswick, NJ: Transaction Books.

Thomlison, D. (1982). *Toward interpersonal dialogue.* New York: Longman.

Thompson, C. A., & Klopf, D. W. (1991). An analysis of social style among disparate cultures. *Communication Research Reports* 8, 65–72.

Thompson, C. A., Klopf, D. W., & Ishii, S. (1991). A comparison of social style between Japanese and Americans. *Communication Research Reports* 8, 165–172.

Thorne, B., Kramarae, C., & Henley, N. (Eds.). (1983). *Language, gender and society.* Rowley, MA: Newbury House.

Tidwell, L. C., & Walther, J. B. (2002). Computer-mediated communication effects on disclosure, impressions, and interpersonal evaluations: Getting to know one another a bit at a time. *Human Communication Research* 28 (July), 317–348.

Tierney, P., & Farmer, S. M. (2004). The Pygmalion process and employee creativity. *Journal of Management* 30 (June), 413–432.

Timmerman, L. J. (2002). Comparing the production of power in language on the basis of sex. In *Interpersonal communication research: Advances through meta-analysis,* M. Allen & R. W. Preiss (eds.). Mahwah, NJ: Erlbaum, pp. 73–88.

Ting-Toomey, S. (1981). Ethnic identity and close friendship in Chinese-American college students. *International Journal of Intercultural Relations* 5, 383–406.

Ting-Toomey, S. (1985). Toward a theory of conflict and culture. *International and Intercultural Communication Annual* 9, 71–86.

Ting-Toomey, S. (1986). Conflict communication styles in black and white subjective cultures. In *Interethnic communication: Current research,* Y. Y. Kim (ed.). Thousand Oaks, CA: Sage, pp. 75–88.

Tinsley, C. H., & Brett, J. M. (2001). Managing workplace conflict in the United States and Hong Kong. *Organizational Behavior and Human Decision Processes* 85, 360–381.

Titlow, K. I., Rackoff, J. E., & Emanuel, E. J. (1999). What will it take to restore patient trust? *Business & Health* 17 (6A), 61–64.

*TMA Journal* 19 (July/Aug 1999), p. 53.

Tolhuizen, J. H. (1986). Perceiving communication indicators of evolutionary changes in friendship. *Southern Speech Communication Journal* 52, 69–91.

Tolhuizen, J. H. (1989). Communication strategies for intensifying dating relationships: Identification, use, and structure. *Journal of Social and Personal Relationships* 6, 413–434.

Trager, G. L. (1958). Paralanguage: A first approximation. *Studies in Linguistics* 13, 1–12.

Trager, G. L. (1961). The typology of paralanguage. *Anthropological Linguistics* 3, 17–21.

Traub, J. (2005). Lawrence Summers, provocateur. *New York Times* (January 23), The Week in Review, 4.

Traxler, A. J. (1980). *Let's get gerontologized: Developing a sensitivity to aging.* Springfield, IL: Illinois Department of Aging.

Trower, P. (1981). Social skill disorder. In *Personal Relationships* 3, S. Duck & R. Gilmour (eds.). New York: Academic Press, pp. 97–110.

Tsiantar, D. (2005). The cost of incivility. *Time* (February 14), B5.

Turner, J. H. (2002). *Face to face: Toward a sociological theory of interpersonal behavior.* Riverside, CA: Stanford University Press.

Turner, M. M., Mazur, M. A., Wendel, N., & Winslow, R. (2003). Relational ruin or social glue? The joint effect of relationship type and gossip valence on liking, trust, and expertise. *Communication Monographs* 70 (June), 129–141.

Ueleke, W., et al. (1983). Inequity resolving behavior as a response to inequity in a hypothetical marital relationship. *A Quarterly Journal of Human Behavior* 20, 4–8.

Unger, F. L. (2001). Speech directed at able-bodied adults, disabled adults, and disabled adults with speech impairments. *Dissertation Abstracts International: Second B: The Sciences and Engineering,* 62, 1146.

Urbaniak, G. C., & Kilmann, P. R. (2003). Physical attractiveness and the "nice guy paradox": Do nice guys really finish last? *Sex Roles* 49 (November), 413–426.

Uris, A. (1986). *101 of the greatest ideas in management.* New York: Wiley.

VanHyning, M. (1993). *Crossed signals: How to say no to sexual harassment.* Los Angeles: Infotrends Press.

Vainiomaki, T. (2004). Silence as a cultural sign. *Semiotica* 150, 347–361.

Varonis, E. M., & Gass, S. M. (1985). Miscommunication in native/nonnative conversation. *Language in Society* 14, 327–343.

Veenendall, T. L., & Feinstein, M. C. (1995). *Let's talk about relationships: Cases in study.* Prospect Heights, IL: Waveland Press.

Velting, D. M. (1999). Personality and negative expectations: Trait structure of the Beck Hopelessness Scale. *Personality and Individual Differences* 26, 913–921.

Victor, D. (1992). *International business communication.* New York: HarperCollins.

Von Hassell, M. (1993). Issei women: Silences and fields of power. *Feminist Studies* 19, 549–569.

von Tetzchner, S., & Jensen, K. (1999). Interacting with people who have severe communication problems: Ethical considerations. *International Journal of Disability, Development and Education* 46 (December), 453–462.

Vrij, A., & Mann, S. (2001). Telling and detecting lies in a high-stake situation: The case of a convicted murderer. *Applied Cognitive Psychology*, 15 (March–April), 187–203.

Waddington, K. (2004). Psst—spread the word—gossiping is good for you. *Practice Nurse* 27, 7–10.

Wade, N. (2002). Scent of a man is linked to a woman's selection. *New York Times* (January 22), F2.

Wallis, C. (2005). The new science of happiness. *Time* (January 17), A1–A9.

Walster, E., Walster, G. W., & Berscheid, E. (1978). *Equity: Theory and research.* Boston: Allyn & Bacon.

Walster, E., Walster, G. W., & Traupmann, J. (1978). Equity and premarital sex. *Journal of Personality and Social Psychology* 36, 82–92.

Walther, J. B., & Parks, M. R. (2002). Cues filtered out, cues filtered in: Computer-mediated communication and relationships. In *Handbook of interpersonal communication,* (pp. 529–563), M. L. Knapp and J. A. Daly (eds.). Thousand Oaks, CA: Sage.

Walther, J. D. (1992). Interpersonal effects in computer-mediated interaction: a relational perspective. *Communication Research* 19, 52–90.

Wan, C. (2004). The psychology of culture shock. *Asian Journal of Social Psychology* 7 (August), 233–234.

Ward, C., Bochner, S., & Furnham, A. (eds.). (2001). *The psychology of culture shock.* Hove, UK: Routledge.

Ward, S. F. (2003). Lawyers in love. *ABA Journal* 89 (September), 37.

Watzlawick, P. (1977). *How real is real? Confusion, disinformation, communication: An anecdotal introduction to communications theory.* New York: Vintage.

Watzlawick, P. (1978). *The language of change: Elements of therapeutic communication.* New York: Basic Books.

Watzlawick, P., Beavin, J. H., & Jackson, D. D. (1967). *Pragmatics of human communication: A study of interactional patterns, pathologies, and paradoxes.* New York: Norton.

Weathers, M. D., Frank, E. M., & Spell, L. A. (2002). Differences in the communication of affect: Members of the same race versus members of a different race. *Journal of Black Psychology* 28, 66–77.

Weigel, D. J., & Ballard-Reisch, D. S. (1999). Using paired data to test models of relational maintenance and marital quality. *Journal of Social and Personal Relationships* 16, 175–191.

Weinberg, H. L. (1959). *Levels of knowing and existence.* New York: Harper & Row.

Weiner, B., Amirkhan, J., Folkes, V. S., & Verette, J. A. (1987). An attributional analysis of excuse giving: Studies of a naive theory of emotion. *Journal of Personality and Social Psychology* 52, 316–324.

Weinstein, E. A., & Deutschberger, P. (1963). Some dimensions of altercasting. *Sociometry* 26, 454–466.

Weitzman, P. F. (2001). Young adult women resolving interpersonal conflicts. *Journal of Adult Development* 8, 61–67.

Weitzman, P. F., & Weitzman, E. A. (2000). Interpersonal negotiation strategies in a sample of older women. *Journal of Clinical Geropsychology* 6, 41–51.

Werner, E. K. (1975). *A study of communication time.* M.A. Thesis, University of Maryland, College Park. Cited in Wolvin & Coakley (1982).

Wert, S. R., & Salovey, P. (2004). A social comparison account of gossip. *Review of General Psychology* 8 (June), 122–137.

Wertz, D. C., Sorenson, J. R., & Heeren, T. C. (1988). Can't get no (dis)satisfaction: Professional satisfaction with professional-client encounters. *Work and Occupations* 15, 36–54.

West, C., & Zimmerman, D. H. (1977). Women's place in everyday talk: Reflections on parent-child interaction. *Social Problems* 24, 521–529.

Westefeld, J. S., & Liddell, D. (1982). Coping with long-distance relationships. *Journal of College Student Personnel* 23, 550–551.

Westwood, R. I., Tang, F. F., & Kirkbride, P. S. (1992). Chinese conflict behavior: Cultural antecedents and behavioral consequences. *Organizational Development Journal* 10, 13–19.

Wetzel, P. J. (1988). Are "powerless" communication strategies the Japanese norm? *Language in Society* 17, 555–564.

Wheeless, L. R., & Grotz, J. (1977). The measurement of trust and its relationship to self-disclosure. *Human Communication Research* 3, 250–257.

Whitty, M. T. (2003a). Cyber-flirting: Playing at love on the Internet. *Theory and Psychology* 13 (June), 339–357.

Whitty, M. T. (2003b). Logging onto love: An examination of men's and women's flirting behaviour both offline and on the Internet. *Australian Journal of Psychology* 55, 68–72.

Whitty, M. T., & Carr, A. (2003). Cyberspace as potential space: Considering the web as a playground to cyber-flirt. *Human Relations* 56 (July), 869–891.

Whitty, M., & Gavin, J. (2001). Age/sex/location: Uncovering the social cues in the development of online relationships. *CyberPsychology and Behavior* 4, 623–630.

Wiederman, M. W., & Hurd, C. (1999). Extradyadic involvement during dating. *Journal of Social and Personal Relationships* 16, 265–274.

Wiemann, J. M. (1977). Explication and test of a model of communicative competence. *Human Communication Research* 3, 195–213.

Wilkins, B. M., & Andersen, P. A. (1991). Gender differences and similarities in management communication: A meta-analysis. *Management Communication Quarterly* 5, 6–35.

Williams, A. (2004). E-dating bubble springs a leak. *New York Times* (December 12), Sunday Styles, 1, 6.

Williamson, K., Wright, S., Schauder, D., & Bow, A. (2001). The Internet for the blind and visually impaired. *Journal of Computer Mediated Communication* 7 (1), October.

Wilmot, W. W. (1999). *Relational communication.* New York: McGraw-Hill.

Wilson, J. H., & Taylor, K. W. (2001). Professor immediacy as behaviors associated with liking students. *Teaching of Psychology* 28, 136–138.

Wilson, R. A. (1989). Toward understanding E-prime. *Etc.: A review of General Semantics* 46, 316–319.

Wilson, S. R., & Sabee, C. M. (2003). Explicating communicative competence as a theoretical term. In *Handbook of communication and social interaction skills* (pp. 3–50), J. O. Greene & B. R. Burleson (eds.). Mahwah, NJ: Erlbaum.

Windy, D., Constantinou, D. (2005). *Assertiveness step by step.* London: Sheldon Press.

Winquist, L. A., Mohr, C. D., Kenny, D. A. (1998). The female positivity effect in the perception of others. *Journal of Research in Personality* 32, 370–388.

Withecomb, J. (1997). Causes of violence in children. *Journal of Mental Health* 6 (October), 433–442.

Witt, P. L., & Wheeless, L. R. (2001). An experimental study of teachers' verbal and nonverbal immediacy and students' affective and cognitive learning. *Communication Education* 50, 327–342.

Wolak, J., Mitchell, K. J., & Finkelhor, D. (2003). Escaping or connecting? Characteristics of youth who form close online relationships. *Journal of Adolescence* 26 (February), 105–119.

Wolfson, N. (1988). The bulge: A theory of speech behaviour and social distance. In *Second language discourse: A textbook of current research,* J. Fine (ed.). Norwood, NJ: Ablex.

Wolpe, J. (1958). *Psychotherapy by reciprocal inhibition.* Stanford, CA: Stanford University Press.

Wolvin, A. D., & Coakley, C. G. (1996). *Listening.* Dubuque, IA: William C. Brown.

Won-Doornink, M. J. (1985). Self-disclosure and reciprocity in conversation: A cross-national study. *Social Psychology Quarterly* 48, 97–107.

Won-Doornink, M. J. (1991). Self-disclosure and reciprocity in South Korean and U.S. male dyads. In *Cross-cultural interpersonal communication,* S. Ting-Toomey & F. Korzenny (eds.). Thousand Oaks, CA: Sage, pp. 116–131.

Wood, A. F., & Smith, M. J. (2005). *Online communication: Linking technology, identity, and culture.* Mahwah, NJ: Lawrence Erlbaum.

Wood, J. T. (1994). *Gendered lives: Communication, gender, and culture.* Belmont, CA: Wadsworth.

Wright, J., & Chung, M. C. (2001). Mastery or mystery? Therapeutic writing: A review of the literature. *British Journal of Guidance and Counseling* 29 (August), 277–291.

Wright, J. W., & Hosman, L. A. (1983). Language style and sex bias in the courtroom: The effects of male and female use of hedges and intensifiers on impression formation. *Southern Speech Communication Journal* 48, 137–152.

Wright, P. H. (1978). Toward a theory of friendship based on a conception of self. *Human Communication Research* 4, 196–207.

Wright, P. H. (1984). Self-referent motivation and the intrinsic quality of friendship. *Journal of Social and Personal Relationships* 1, 115–130.

Wright, P. H. (1988). Interpreting research on gender differences in friendship: A case for moderation and a plea for caution. *Journal of Social and Personal Relationships* 5, 367–373.

Yau-fair Ho, D., Chan, S. F., Peng, S., & Ng, A. K. (2001). The dialogical self: Converging East-West constructions. *Culture and Psychology* 7, 393–408.

Yela, C. (2000). Predictors of and factors related to loving and sexual satisfaction for men and women. *European Review of Applied Psychology* 50, 235–243.

Young, K. S., Griffin-Shelley, E., Cooper, A., O'Mara, J., & Buchanan, J. (2000). Online infidelity: A new dimension in couple relationships with implications for evaluation and treatment. *Sexual Addiction and Compulsivity* 7, 59–74.

Yun, H. (1976). The Korean personality and treatment considerations. *Social Casework* 57, 173–178.

Zajonc, R. B. (1968). Attitudinal effects of mere exposure. *Journal of Personality and Social Psychology Monograph* Suppl. 9, no. 2, pt. 2.

Zemanek, J. E. (1995). How salespersons' use of a power base can affect customers' satisfaction in a social system: An empirical examination. *Psychological Reports* 76 (February), 211–218.

Zimbardo, P. A. (1977). *Shyness: What it is and what to do about it.* Reading, MA: Addison-Wesley.

Zimmer, T. A. (1986). Premarital anxieties. *Journal of Social and Personal Relationships* 3, 149–159.

Zimmerman, D. H., & West, C. (1975). Sex roles, interruptions and silences in conversations. In *Language and sex:*

# Index

# Index

*Note:* Italicized letters *f, t,* and *b* following page numbers indicate figures, tables, and boxes, respectively.

functions of, 182–183
and power, 318
CMC. *See* Computer-mediated communication
Coalitions, dyadic, 5–6
Code, 11
Coercive power, 317, 317*b*
Cognitive disclaimer, 209
Cognitive restructuring
    for increasing self-esteem, 62
    for managing apprehension, 76
Collectivist culture
    characteristics of, 42–43, 44*t*
    conflict in, 291–292, 300
    family in, 275–276
    friendship in, 264
    high-context culture as, 44
    romantic relationships in, 270–271
    self-awareness in, 60
College. *See* Higher education
Color, 182, 187, 188*t*
Commission, lie by, 126*b*
Commitment, in relationships, 241*b*
Communication. *See also* Conversation; Speech(es)
    about communication, 122*b*
    ambiguity of, 22–24
    areas of, 11*t*
    axioms of, 21–29
    channels of. *See* Channels of communication
    characteristics of, 5–6
    competence in, 12*f*, 18–21, 20*t*, 36
    computer-mediated. *See* Computer-mediated
        communication
    content dimensions of, 25–26
    context of, 12*f*, 17–18, 19*t*
    culture in. *See* Culture
    definition of, 5
    dyadic approach to, 5–6
    effectiveness of, self-disclosure and, 68–69
    elements of, 9–21, 12*f*, 19*t*–20*t*, 21–22, 22*f*
    encoding-decoding in, 11
    in family, 277–278
    fear or anxiety about. *See* Apprehension
    in friendships, 262–264
    importance of, 2–5, 3*b*
    inevitability of, 27–28
    irreversibility of, 28–29
    messages in. *See* Messages
    nature of, 5–9
    nonverbal. *See* Nonverbal communication
    perception in. *See* Perception
    phatic, 14, 195
    of power, 318–324
    purposes of, 7–9, 10*f*
    in relationships, 25–26, 243–245, 251*f*, 262–264, 269–270
    as series of punctuated events, 26–27, 27*f*

source-receiver in, 10, 12*f*, 19*t*
theories of, 21*b*
as transactional process, 21–22, 22*f*
universals of, 1–30, 12*f*, 119–138
unrepeatability of, 29
Communication accommodation theory, 50–51
Communication tips
    for blind and sighted people, 15, 16*t*
    for deaf and hearing people, 105*t*
    for people with and without disabilities, 52*t*
    for people with speech and language disorders, 195*t*
Comparison level in relationships, 239
Competence, 12*f*, 18–21, 20*t*, 36
Complaining, 250*b*
Complementarity, 237
Complementary relationships, 24
Compliance-gaining strategies, 320, 321, 322*t*, 323*b*
Compliance-resisting strategies, 320, 321–323
Compliments, 120, 147, 224*b*
Computer games, violent, 88*b*
Computer-mediated communication (CMC). *See also*
        Internet; Online relationships
    adjusting screen in, 175*b*
    apprehension in, 74*b*
    attribution in, 92*b*
    blogging as, 10*b*, 26*b*, 144*b*, 164*b*
    captology in, 9
    compressing files in, 176*b*
    contact stage in, 220
    conversation style of, 208*b*
    definition of, 5*b*
    directness of messages in, 132*b*
    elements of, 19*t*–20*t*
    ethics of, 20*t*, 203*b*
    flirting, 9*b*, 220*b*
    forms of, 6–7. *See also specific forms*
    gender and, 7*b*, 9, 203*b*, 206*b*, 208*b*, 240
    information overload in, 14–15
    irony in, 123*b*
    irreversibility of, 28–29
    by lonely people, 41*b*
    monitoring, 158*b*
    nonverbal messages in, 120–121, 121*b*, 123*b*
    ostracism in, 57*b*
    politeness of, 127–129
    political, 49*b*
    and power, 311*b*
    primacy–recency in, 89*b*
    in relationship maintenance, 240, 240*b*, 243–244
    religious, 50*b*
    self-disclosure in, 65, 67, 68, 68*b*
    self-esteem and use of, 62*b*
    social presence theory of, 64*b*
    stereotyping in, 49
    storage space in, 115*b*

# Credits

## ADDITIONAL TEXT CREDITS

Page 3: Reprinted by permission of Sherwyn P. Morreale.

Page 33: Reprinted from *International Journal of Intercultural Relations, 5,* Stella Ting-Toomey, "Ethnic Identity and Close Friendship in Chinese-American College Students," pp. 383–406. Copyright © 1981 with permission from Elsevier.

Page 38: Reprinted by permission of Molefi Asante.

Page 63: Reprinted by permission of Linda Costigan Lederman.

Page 74: From "Communication Apprehension in the Dating Partner Context," by W. G. Powers and D. E. Love, *Communication Research Reports, 17,* pp. 221–228. Copyright © 2000. Used by permission of Eastern Communication Association.

Page 88: Reprinted by permission of Elizabeth M. Perse.

Page 116: Reprinted by permission of Deborah Borisoff.

Page 124: Reprinted by permission of Teresa L. Thompson, Ph.D. Copyright © 2005.

Page 152: Reprinted by permission of Lance Strate.

Page 174: Reprinted by permission of Kelly A. Rocca.

Page 208: Reprinted by permission of Susan B. Barnes.

Page 227: Reprinted by permission of Barbara M. Montgomery.

Page 255: Reprinted by permission of Prof. Shirlee A. Levin, College of Southern Maryland.

Page 274: Reprinted by permission of Anita Vangelisti.

Page 304: Reprinted by permission of Carolyn M. Anderson, Professor, School of Communication, University of Akron, Akron, OH 44325.

Page 321: Reprinted by permission of John Daly.

## PHOTO CREDITS

Page 1: © Miramax/courtesy Everett Collection; 13: Ariel Skelley/CORBIS; 14: Imagebroker/Alamy; 15: PhotoDisc/Getty Images; 18: Helen Norman/CORBIS; 24: Superstock; 28: Alan Schein Photography/CORBIS; 31: © United Artists/courtesy Everett Collection; 38: Dee Snider/The Image Works; 41: Rubberball Productions/Getty Images; 43: AP/Wide World Photos; 47: Digital Vision/SuperStock; 51: Digital Vision/SuperStock; 55: © Fox Searchlight Pictures/20th Century Fox/The Kobal Collection; 60: Tetra Images/Alamy; 62: Masterfile Royalty-Free/Masterfile; 66: ImageSource Royalty-Free/PictureQuest; 76: AP/Wide World Photos; 80: © Lucasfilm/20th Century Fox/The Kobal Collection; 83: Michael Newman/PhotoEdit; 84: Royalty-Free/CORBIS; 87: CHIP EAST/Reuters/CORBIS; 95: © HBO/Courtesy Everett Collection; 101: © New Line/courtesy Everett Collection; 103: Brand X Pictures/PictureQuest; 106: The Everett Collection; 107: PhotoDisc/Getty Images; 111: Myrleen Ferguson Cate/PhotoEdit; 115: